PROFESSIONAL APPLICATION LIFECYCLE MANAGEMENT WITH VISUAL STUDIO 2012

PROFESSIONAL

Application Lifecycle Management with Visual Studio® 2012

Mickey Gousset
Brian Keller
Martin Woodward

WILEY

John Wiley & Sons, Inc.

Professional Application Lifecycle Management with Visual Studio® 2012

Published by
John Wiley & Sons, Inc.
10475 Crosspoint Boulevard
Indianapolis, IN 46256
www.wiley.com

Copyright © 2012 by John Wiley & Sons, Inc., Indianapolis, Indiana

Published simultaneously in Canada

ISBN: 978-1-118-31408-1

ISBN: 978-1-118-43937-1 (ebk)

ISBN: 978-1-118-33209-2 (ebk)

ISBN: 978-1-118-33533-8 (ebk)

Manufactured in the United States of America

10 9 8 7 6 5 4 3 2 1

For general information on our other products and services please contact our Customer Care Department within the United States at (877) 762-2974, outside the United States at (317) 572-3993 or fax (317) 572-4002.

Wiley publishes in a variety of print and electronic formats and by print-on-demand. Some material included with standard print versions of this book may not be included in e-books or in print-on-demand. If this book refers to media such as a CD or DVD that is not included in the version you purchased, you may download this material at http://booksupport.wiley.com. For more information about Wiley products, visit www.wiley.com.

Library of Congress Control Number: 2012944683

CREDITS

EXECUTIVE EDITOR
Robert Elliott

PROJECT EDITOR
Tom Dinse

TECHNICAL EDITORS
Steve St. Jean
Ed Blankenship

PRODUCTION EDITOR
Kathleen Wisor

COPY EDITOR
Charlotte Kughen, Wordsmithery LLC

EDITORIAL MANAGER
Mary Beth Wakefield

FREELANCER EDITORIAL MANAGER
Rosemarie Graham

ASSOCIATE DIRECTOR OF MARKETING
David Mayhew

MARKETING MANAGER
Ashley Zurcher

BUSINESS MANAGER
Amy Knies

PRODUCTION MANAGER
Tim Tate

VICE PRESIDENT AND EXECUTIVE GROUP PUBLISHER
Richard Swadley

VICE PRESIDENT AND EXECUTIVE PUBLISHER
Neil Edde

ASSOCIATE PUBLISHER
Jim Minatel

PROJECT COORDINATOR, COVER
Katie Crocker

PROOFREADERS
James Saturino, Word One
Louise Watson, Word One

INDEXER
Jack Lewis

COVER DESIGNER
Ryan Sneed

COVER IMAGE
© Ben Blankenburg/istockphoto.com

ABOUT THE AUTHORS

 MICKEY GOUSSET is a Principal Consultant for Infront Consulting Group, a consulting company focused on the Microsoft System Center family of products. He has been a Microsoft Application Lifecycle Management MVP seven years running, and he is co-author of the books *Professional Team Foundation Server* (Wiley, 2006) and *Professional Application Lifecycle Management with Visual Studio 2010* (Wiley, 2010). Gousset runs ALM Rocks! (www.almrocks.com), where he writes about Visual Studio, TFS, and ALM in general. He is also a co-host of the popular Team Foundation Server podcast, Radio TFS (www.radiotfs.com). He has spoken around the world on ALM and System Center topics. When not writing or working with computers, Mickey enjoys a range of hobbies, from playing on Xbox Live (Gamer Tag: HereBDragons) to participating in local community theater. Nothing beats his favorite pastime though — sitting on his couch with his lovely wife Amye, and their two Chihuahuas, Lucy and Linus.

 BRIAN KELLER is a Senior Technical Evangelist for Microsoft, specializing in Visual Studio and application lifecycle management. He has been with Microsoft since 2002 and has presented at conferences all over the world, including TechEd, Professional Developers Conference (PDC), Build, and MIX. This is his third book for Wiley. He is also a regular personality on MSDN's Channel 9 website and is co-host of the popular show, *This Week on Channel 9*. Outside of work, you can usually find him enjoying the great outdoors while either rock climbing, backpacking, surfing or spending time with the love of his life, Elisa.

 MARTIN WOODWARD is a Senior Program Manager for Microsoft Visual Studio Team Foundation Server specializing in the Eclipse and Cross-Platform Tooling. Before joining Microsoft, Martin was awarded MVP of the Year for Visual Studio Application Lifecycle Management, and he has spoken about Team Foundation Server at international events. Not only does Martin bring a unique insight into the inner workings of the product, but he has many years of experience at companies large and small that he is always happy to share. When not working or speaking, you can find Martin at his blog www.woodwardweb.com or on the podcast http://radiotfs.com.

ACKNOWLEDGMENTS

First off, I want to thank Brian and Martin for taking this journey with me once again. You have been incredible people to work with, and this book couldn't have been created without you. I'll write with y'all any day. I'd like to thank everyone at Wiley and Wrox, specifically Bob Elliot and Tom Dinse, our editors. This book could not have happened without their help and constant attention to detail. Ed Blankenship and Steven St. Jean, thank you for the excellent technical editing job. You kept me sane. Mr. Gene, thank you for keeping my lawn from looking like a jungle, and Mrs. Kathy, those fudge brownies were just the thing for those all-night writing sessions. Mom, thank you for all your support and help during this process. Finally, a big thank you to Amye, Emma, and Meg for your understanding, love, and support during the late nights and long weekends when I disappeared into my office to write.

—Mickey Gousset

First and foremost, thanks once again to Elisa for believing in me and inspiring me to be the best person I can be. You make every day brighter, I am so lucky to have you in my life! Thanks to the Developer Division at Microsoft for building such a wonderful set of products and technologies for me to write about and evangelize — you make my job easy. Thanks to Ed Blankenship, Steven St. Jean, and Ravi Shanker for your expert guidance on this book. And of course to Mickey, Martin, and the great team at Wiley — I still can't believe you talked me into writing another book, but it's been worth it.

—Brian Keller

First, I would like to thank my co-authors, Brian and Mickey, for allowing me to help them in putting this book together — you will struggle to meet two nicer people, and I am lucky to count you both as my friends.

I would like to acknowledge the help, advice and assistance from the people both inside and outside the Visual Studio team at Microsoft. Special thanks go to Jamie Cool, Buck Hodges, Grant Holliday, Matthew Mitrik, Ed Holloway, Peter Provost, and William Bartholomew — without whom my contributions to this book would not have been possible. Thanks also to Rob Caron, Jeff Beehler, Corey Steffen, Jamie Cool, and Brian Harry for encouraging my involvement in the Visual Studio and Eclipse communities over the past eight years.

Finally, I would also like to thank my wife, Catherine, for her encouragement, her support and for sacrificing the countless evenings and weekends to enable me to take part in this book. For such an otherwise intelligent and rational woman, I've yet to figure out why she agreed to marry me in the first place. But ten years on she is still as caring and beautiful as the girl I fell in love with in our first year at university, and she is still way, way out of my league. Luckily she doesn't read anything I write, so hopefully she'll never find out.

— Martin Woodward

CONTENTS

CONTENTS

INTRODUCTION

OVER THE LAST FIFTEEN YEARS, Microsoft's software development tooling has matured to address not only the needs of a lone programmer, but the needs of an entire software development team. This includes business analysts, project managers, architects, testers, programmers, managers, stakeholders, and even operations personnel who will deploy and maintain applications. This book was written to help teams understand and adopt these tools with the end goal of making them more cohesive, productive, and ultimately to produce higher-quality software on time and on budget.

Whether you already own Visual Studio 2012, or are considering purchasing it, this book will help you evaluate and adopt the right tools for your project. This book considers all of the roles which make up a modern software development project. The tools and technologies which are relevant to each role are examined in detail, including walkthroughs which will help you learn and apply each tool within your team.

WHO IS THIS BOOK FOR

This book primarily targets teams of professionals in the field of commercial or enterprise software development — in other words, intermediate to advanced users. You are likely to find the book useful if you are any of the following:

➤ A developer, tester, or architect who wants to learn how the Visual Studio 2012 family of products can help you perform your job

➤ A project manager who must manage a software development project

This book is not designed for the absolute beginner. The focus is on practical application of the tools, code samples, and hands-on scenarios. The book's organization makes it easy to use as both a step-by-step guide and a reference for modeling, designing, testing, and coordinating enterprise solutions at every level.

Visual Studio 2012 is designed for software teams of all sizes. So, whether you have a team of 5 or 2,000 members, this book includes useful information for you related to Visual Studio 2012 and application lifecycle management. Unlike most Wrox books, this book targets all roles in the software development organization — architects, developers, testers, project leads, and management — not just developers.

WHAT DOES THIS BOOK COVER

This book includes a complete overview of the application lifecycle management capabilities of Visual Studio 2012. The book is divided into six main parts, based around the different aspects of application lifecycle management:

- ➤ Part I: Team Foundation Server
- ➤ Part II: Building the Right Software
- ➤ Part III: Project Management
- ➤ Part IV: Architecture
- ➤ Part V: Software Development
- ➤ Part VI: Testing

Part I: Team Foundation Server

Because Team Foundation Server is at the heart of Microsoft's application lifecycle management solution, this book starts with an examination of its capabilities. It discusses the architecture of Team Foundation Server 2012, and then delves into the version control system and some best practices surrounding branching and merging using Team Foundation Server. Finally, there is an in-depth look at the automated build process — Team Foundation Build — followed by some examples of common customizations you can make to Team Foundation Server.

Part II: Building the Right Software

Microsoft's application lifecycle management offerings in this release of Visual Studio 2012 have expanded to recognize the role that stakeholders play in the software development process. Stakeholders could be future end users of an application, the decision makers who are authorizing payment for an application, lawyers who need to approve applications for regulatory requirements, or any number of people external to the development team who have a vested interest in the outcome of a particular development project. In this section of the book, you find out about new tooling available to engage with stakeholders early and often throughout the development process. These tools can lead to higher-quality software that is more likely to meet expectations and deliver continuous value while minimizing the amount of rework required.

Part III: Project Management

This section of the book deals with the project and process management functionality of Visual Studio 2012 and Team Foundation Server 2012. This section examines the process templates that ship with the product, and it covers the new web-based Agile planning and tracking capabilities. Part III also discusses the reports that ship with Team Foundation Server. Whether you are practicing a lightweight development methodology such as Scrum, or a more formal, rigorous development process, you will discover that Team Foundation Server will provide you with the tooling you need to manage your projects.

Part IV: Architecture

This section of the book examines the tools available in Visual Studio 2012 for defining and analyzing application architecture. After a brief introduction to architecture concepts, the discussion dives into all the new UML tools available, including use case diagrams, activity diagrams, sequence diagrams, class diagrams, and component diagrams. You then learn about the Architecture Explorer and how you can use it to understand the architecture of your application. Finally, this section wraps up with a discussion of layer diagrams.

Part V: Software Development

This section of the book covers topics of most interest to a software developer using Visual Studio 2012. The topics selected for this section of the book are those that pertain most to building either complex applications or working with teams. For example, the section explains how unit testing, static code analysis, profiling, code coverage, and the new code clone analysis feature are ways to improve your application's overall quality and maintainability. Part V introduces the new built-in code review capability and how you can use it to collaborate with other developers. You find out how the ability to suspend and resume work in progress makes it easier to deal with interruptions. Finally, the section provides in-depth coverage of debugging applications with IntelliTrace, including a new way of using IntelliTrace for debugging applications in a production environment.

Part VI: Testing

Visual Studio 2012 has numerous tools available for testers to use. The examination starts with a look at the manual testing functionality available in Microsoft Test Manager, as well as the ability to automate user interface tests with coded user interface (UI) tests. Web performance testing and load testing enable you to create tests that can help you ensure that users of your website will experience the best possible performance, even under heavy load. The section concludes with a look the improved lab management capabilities of Visual Studio 2012, which enable you to make use of physical or virtual environments that you can use to automate build-deploy-test workflows.

TEAM FOUNDATION SERVER ADMINISTRATORS

If you are the person on your team who is responsible for administering your Team Foundation Server deployment, you should consider purchasing this book as well as its sister book — *Professional Team Foundation Server 2012* (Wrox, 2012. ISBN 978-1-118-31409-8) — which dives deeper into setup, configuration, and administration of Team Foundation Server 2012. You find out more about the possible deployment topologies you can choose from, how to make changes to process templates, advanced security settings, considerations for disaster recovery and geographically distributed teams, and much more.

CONVENTIONS

To help you get the most from the text and keep track of what's happening, we've used a number of conventions throughout the book.

> **WARNING** *Boxes like this one hold important, not-to-be forgotten information that is directly relevant to the surrounding text.*

> **NOTE** *Notes, tips, hints, and tricks are offset and placed in italic like this.*

> **SIDEBAR**
>
> Asides to the current discussion are offset like this.

As for styles in the text:

➤ We *highlight* new terms and important words when we introduce them.

➤ We show keyboard strokes like this: Ctrl+A.

➤ We show filenames, URLs, and code within the text like so: `persistence.properties`.

➤ We present code in two different ways:

```
We use a monofont type with no highlighting for most code examples.
We use boldface to emphasize code that is particularly important in the
present context.
```

SOURCE CODE

As you work through the examples in this book, you may choose either to type in all the code manually, or to use the source code files that accompany the book. All the source code used in this book is available for download at `www.wrox.com`. When you're at the site, simply locate the book's title (either by using the Search box, or by using one of the title lists) and click the Download Code link on the book's detail page to obtain all the source code for the book.

> **NOTE** *Because many books have similar titles, you may find it easiest to search by ISBN; this book's ISBN is 978-1-118-31408-1.*

After you download the code, just decompress it with your favorite compression tool. Alternatively, you can go to the main Wrox code download page at www.wrox.com/dynamic/books/download .aspx to see the code available for this book and all other Wrox books.

ERRATA

We make every effort to ensure that there are no errors in the text or in the code. However, no one is perfect, and mistakes do occur. If you find an error in one of our books, such as a spelling mistake or a faulty piece of code, we would be very grateful for your feedback. By sending in errata, you may save another reader hours of frustration, and you will be helping us provide even higher quality information.

To find the errata page for this book, go to www.wrox.com and locate the title using the Search box or one of the title lists. Then, on the book details page, click the Book Errata link. On this page, you can view all errata that has been submitted for this book and posted by Wrox editors. A complete book list, including links to each book's errata, is also available at www.wrox.com/misc-pages/ booklist.shtml.

> **NOTE** *A complete book list including links to errata is also available at* www.wrox.com/misc-pages/booklist.shtml.

If you don't spot "your" error on the Book Errata page, go to www.wrox.com/contact/ techsupport.shtml and complete the form to alert us to the error you have found. We'll check the information and, if appropriate, post a message to the book's errata page and fix the problem in subsequent editions of the book.

P2P.WROX.COM

For author and peer discussion, join the P2P forums at http://p2p.wrox.com. The forums are a web-based system for you to post messages relating to Wrox books and related technologies, and to interact with other readers and technology users. The forums offer a subscription feature to e-mail you topics of interest of your choosing when new posts are made to the forums. Wrox authors, editors, other industry experts, and your fellow readers are present on these forums.

At http://p2p.wrox.com, you can find several different forums that will help you not only as you read the book, but also as you develop your own applications. To join the forums, just follow these steps:

1. Go to http://p2p.wrox.com and click the Register link.
2. Read the terms of use and click Agree.

3. Complete the required information to join, as well as any optional information you want to provide, and click Submit.

4. You will receive an e-mail message with information describing how to verify you account and complete the joining process.

You can read messages in the forums without joining P2P, but in order to post your own messages, you must join.

After you join, you can post new messages and respond to messages other users post. You can read messages at any time on the Web. If you would like to have new messages from a particular forum emailed to you, click the Subscribe to this Forum icon by the forum name in the forum listing.

For more information about how to use the Wrox P2P, be sure to read the P2P FAQs for answers to questions about how the forum software works, as well as many common questions specific to P2P and Wrox books. To read the FAQs, click the FAQ link on any P2P page.

1

Introduction to Application Lifecycle Management with Visual Studio 2012

WHAT'S IN THIS CHAPTER?

➤ Defining application lifecycle management

➤ Learning about the Visual Studio 2012 product family

➤ Understanding the structure of this book

In June of 1999, Microsoft started to re-evaluate how Visual Studio was being used as part of the software development process. Microsoft was continuing to serve the needs of an individual programmer through the highly productive "code-focused rapid-application-development" features of Visual Studio, but wasn't doing much to help programmers work together as a team. And what about software architects—how should they be working with the programming team? And testers? Project managers?

Many teams had begun to set up their own solutions using a mixture of third-party, in-house, and vendor-provided tools to address such challenges as version control, bug tracking, and team communications. But this mishmash of tools can be tricky to set up and maintain, and even more difficult to integrate. Microsoft sought to address this challenge by providing an integrated set of tools designed to address the needs of the entire software development team. Thus, Visual Studio Team System was born, and was first released with the Visual Studio 2005 product line.

At the heart of Team System, *Team Foundation Server* was created to provide a hub for all members of the development team to collaborate. Team Foundation Server is uniquely positioned from its predecessors across the industry by being the first tool of its kind built from the ground up to provide an integrated solution for many capabilities which had historically been offered as standalone tools. Team Foundation Server provides a unified solution for storing source code (along with a history of changes), work item tracking (which can include bugs, requirements, and so on), and automated builds. By providing a single solution with all of these capabilities, Microsoft delivered the ability to link all these artifacts for end-to-end traceability, reporting, process enforcement, and project management.

Team System also included "client" functionality, which surfaced in the various editions of Visual Studio development tools. Visual Studio seamlessly integrated with Team Foundation Server, but much of this tooling could also be used independently or with third-party source control solutions. Visual Studio Team System also introduced role-specific tooling that lived outside of the core Visual Studio development environment by recognizing that team members such as project managers are oftentimes more comfortable using tools such as Excel or Project, both of which could be used to manage and track work that lived in Team Foundation Server.

Team System was built from a foundation of tools and technologies that Microsoft had been using internally for many years to build some of the most complex software projects ever undertaken. Team System appealed not only to programmers, but to all members of the development team— architects, application developers, database developers, and project managers.

Three years later, Visual Studio 2008 Team System evolved from the previous version to include even more tools and functionality for all members of the project team to use. Two years after that, Visual Studio 2010 added even more functionality, including an entirely new set of tools for general- ist testers (also referred to as manual testers), bringing a new audience of prospective users into the same set of tooling used by the rest of the team.

APPLICATION LIFECYCLE MANAGEMENT

Along with the release of Visual Studio 2010, Microsoft also stopped using the sub-brand "Team System" to describe these capabilities. Instead, Microsoft started referring to these tools as the *application lifecycle management* capabilities of Visual Studio. Application lifecycle management is a term that has gained momentum in the development industry to describe the way an application is managed from its conception, through its creation and deployment, to its eventual retirement.

It is important to note that application lifecycle management is a more comprehensive concept than its more popular predecessor, *software development lifecycle* (SDLC). SDLC is primarily focused on the core coding activities that comprise the creation of an application's life, beginning with a requirement for an application and ending when that application is built and delivered. Application lifecycle management recognizes that requirements aren't simply born out of thin air. They evolve based on business needs, or ideas for new opportunities, and stakeholders who are considered external to the development team may still play a role during the development of an application in helping to refine requirements and provide feedback on implementations. Application lifecycle management also recognizes that a development team's job isn't done the moment they hand off a "finished" application. The development team will likely be called upon to help troubleshoot the application when things go wrong in the production environment, or to create subsequent ver- sions of the application based on feedback from users or analytics from the operations team. Visual Studio itself has matured over time to grow from being a tool targeted squarely at programmers during the software development lifecycle to becoming a true solution for end-to-end application lifecycle management.

VISUAL STUDIO 2012 PRODUCT LINEUP

Table 1-1 outlines the product lineup for Visual Studio 2012.

TABLE 1-1: Visual Studio 2012 Product Lineup

PRODUCT NAME	DESCRIPTION
Microsoft Visual Studio Ultimate 2012 with MSDN	The comprehensive suite of application lifecycle management tools for software teams to help ensure quality results from design to deployment.
Microsoft Visual Studio Premium 2012 with MSDN	A complete toolset to help developers deliver scalable, high-quality applications.
Microsoft Visual Studio Professional 2012 with MSDN	The essential tool for basic development tasks to assist developers in implementing their ideas easily.
Microsoft Visual Studio Test Professional 2012 with MSDN	The primary tool for manual and generalist testers who need to define and manage test cases, execute test runs, and file bugs.
Microsoft Visual Studio Team Foundation Server 2012	The server component for team development, version control, work item tracking, build automation, project management, lab management, and reporting.
Microsoft Visual Studio Team Foundation Server Express 2012	A free edition of Team Foundation Server that provides most of the same capabilities (including version control, work item tracking, and build automation) for a team of up to five users.

Visual Studio Premium contains all the functionality of Visual Studio Professional, and Visual Studio Ultimate contains all the functionality of Visual Studio Premium. Visual Studio Premium and Ultimate also include all of the functionality available in Visual Studio Test Professional.

There are a few additional standalone tools and technologies that comprise the Visual Studio 2012 family that are not listed. For example, in Chapter 9 you learn about the new Microsoft Feedback Client, which stakeholders use to provide rich feedback about an application that is stored in Team Foundation Server. In Chapter 2, you learn about Team Explorer Everywhere, which Eclipse developers use to work with Team Foundation Server. You learn about these additional tools throughout this book, but Table 1-1 showcases the primary products that Microsoft markets as part of the Visual Studio 2012 product family.

For a detailed breakdown of the functionality available in each product, a comparison chart is available at www.microsoft.com/VisualStudio.

> **NOTE** *Software licensing is potentially a complex topic. It is important to ensure that the members of your team are adequately licensed to use Visual Studio and the related technologies that make up your development and testing environments. The Visual Studio Licensing Whitepaper attempts to synthesize all of the licensing requirements for Visual Studio, Team Foundation Server, and related technologies into an easy-to-read format. You can find the latest version of the Visual Studio Licensing Whitepaper at* http://www.microsoft.com/visualstudio/licensing.

APPLICATION LIFECYCLE MANAGEMENT CHALLENGES

Software developers share common challenges, regardless of the size of their teams. Businesses require a high degree of accountability—software must be developed in the least amount of time, and there is no room for failure.

Some of these challenges include the following:

➤ *Tool integration problems*—Most tools commonly used by software development teams come from third-party vendors. Integrating with those tools can pose a major challenge—in many cases, it requires duplicating or copying data into multiple systems. Each application has a learning curve, and transmitting information from one application to another (incompatible) application can be frustrating and time consuming.

➤ *Geographically distributed teams*—Many development and management tools don't scale for geographically distributed teams. Getting accurate reporting can be difficult, and there is often poor support for communication and collaborative tools. As a result, requirements and specifications might be captured incorrectly, causing delays and introducing errors. Global teams require solid design, process, and software configuration management to be integrated into one package. There aren't many software packages that can deliver all these features, and those that do exist tend to be incredibly expensive.

➤ *Segmentation of roles*—Specialization can be a huge problem on a team. Experts can assume that other departments are aware of information that doesn't end up in the status reports but that may greatly affect the project as a whole. Interdepartmental communication is a huge and prevalent challenge. These barriers exist between developers and testers, developers and stakeholders, developers and operations, and even developers and others developers.

➤ *Bad reporting*—This is an offshoot of the segmentation problem. In most cases, reports must be generated manually by each team, which results in a lack of productivity. There aren't any effective tools that can aggregate all the data from multiple sources. As a result, the project lead lacks the essential data to make effective decisions.

➤ *Lack of process guidance*—Ad hoc programming styles simply don't scale. If you introduce an off-cycle change to the code, it can cascade into a serious problem requiring hours and days of work. Today's software has a high level of dependencies. Unfortunately, most tools don't incorporate or enforce process guidance. This can result in an impedance mismatch between tools and process.

➤ *Testing as a second-class citizen*—Shorter cycles and lack of testing can introduce code defects late in the process. Additionally, poor collaboration between developers and testers often results in wasted back-and-forth effort and software defects.

➤ *Communication problems*—Most companies use a variety of communication methods (such as e-mail, instant messaging, memos, and sticky notes) to send information to team members. You can easily lose a piece of paper, or delete an important e-mail message, if you are not careful. There aren't many centralized systems for managing team communications. Frequent and time-consuming status meetings are required to keep the team on track, and many manual processes are introduced (such as sending e-mail, as well as cutting and pasting reports).

Companies introduce methodologies and practices to simplify and organize the software design process, but these methodologies must be balanced. The goal is to make the process predictable because, in a predictable environment, methodologies keep projects on track. It is often said that predictability reduces complexity. Conversely, methodologies add tasks to the process (such as generating reports). If your developers spend too much time doing these tasks, they'll be less productive, and your company won't be able to react competitively.

ENTER VISUAL STUDIO 2012

There are three founding principles behind the application lifecycle management capabilities of Visual Studio 2012: *productivity*, *integration*, and *extensibility*.

Productivity is increased in the following ways:

➤ *Collaboration*—Team Foundation Server centralizes all team collaboration. Bugs, requirements, tasks, test cases, feedback, code reviews, source code, and builds are all managed via Team Foundation Server 2012. All reporting is also centralized, which makes it easy for project leads to track the overall progress of the project, regardless of where the metrics are coming from.

➤ *Manage complexity*—Software development projects are more complex than ever, and getting more complex year by year. Team Foundation Server helps to manage this complexity by centrally tracking your entire software development process, ensuring that the entire team can see the state and workflow of the project at any given time.

Integration is improved in the following ways:

➤ *Integrated tools*—These facilitate communication between departments. More importantly, they remove information gaps. With the Visual Studio 2012 family of products, integration isn't an afterthought—it's a core design consideration for the toolset.

➤ *Role-specific tools*—Instead of asking every member of an extended development team to conform to using the same tool, such as Visual Studio, Microsoft recognizes that many members of a team already have a preferred tool that they use every day. Correspondingly, Microsoft has integrated into those tools directly to provide comfortable interfaces back to Team Foundation Server—whether it's Visual Studio, Eclipse, Excel, Project, Project Server, or simply a web browser.

➤ *Visibility*—Visual Studio and Team Foundation Server increase the visibility of a project. Project leads can easily view metrics related to the project and can proactively address problems by identifying patterns and trends.

Extensibility is provided in the following ways:

➤ *Team Foundation Core Services API*—Most of the platform is exposed to the developer, providing many opportunities for extensibility and the creation of custom tools that integrate with Team Foundation Server.

➤ *IDE*—The Visual Studio integrated development environment (IDE) itself is extensible, allowing third parties and end users to add everything from additional tool capabilities to new language compilers to the development environment.

APPLICATION LIFECYCLE MANAGEMENT IN ACTION

To best demonstrate how Visual Studio 2012 can help in the process of application lifecycle management, let's run through a typical scenario with a fictional software development company called eMockSoft. eMockSoft has recently signed a partnership with a distributor to release its catalog of products. The distributor has requested a secure website to manage inventory and pricing information for internal and external partner organizations.

Let's look at the scenario as it applies to application lifecycle management and the Visual Studio 2012 tools.

Requirements

The business analyst meets with the project sponsor and other stakeholders to obtain requirements for the project. During this discussion, the business analyst and an application designer use the new PowerPoint Storyboarding capabilities of Visual Studio 2012 to build a storyboard that visually models the application they believe their stakeholders are asking for. They share this storyboard with the stakeholders to review the proposed user interface, workflows, and transitions. The stakeholders provide valuable feedback that helps to refine the design, even before a single line of code is written.

The storyboard then becomes the basis of new requirements that inform the development team about what the project sponsor expects the software to deliver. The project manager uses the new web-based Agile planning tools to store these requirements in Team Foundation Server. She then works with the development team to decompose these requirements into tasks that the team will implement on an iterative basis. She also uses Microsoft Project to create a more detailed project schedule based on this work by importing work items.

The infrastructure architect can now begin the system design.

System Design and Modeling

Based on the client specifications, the infrastructure architect can use the UML tools in Visual Studio 2012 to define the architecture for the website. These designs help to inform the programming team about what to implement. As the architecture evolves, the infrastructure architect will use the dependency graph generation tools to analyze the application's architecture and propose architectural changes that can improve code maintainability and quality.

Code Generation

The developer receives work assignments and reviews the UML diagrams that were designed by the architect. The developer writes the necessary code, and does some preliminary testing, using the static code analysis and unit testing tools built into Visual Studio. Throughout the day, the developer checks the code and tests into Team Foundation Server 2012. As work is completed, the developer uses the new web-based task board provided with Team Foundation Server to track the progress of his work and keep the rest of the team updated about his status.

When necessary, the developer uses the built-in code review tooling to invite senior developers to view and comment on the code he is writing. This entire conversation is preserved within Team Foundation Server, making it possible to later conduct audits to discover why certain decisions were made about implementation choices.

Testing

The tester checks the progress of the development team by monitoring the nightly builds and automated tests. Using the lab management capabilities of Team Foundation Server 2012, each nightly build triggers the automatic creation of a virtual environment that is ready each morning for the tester to begin testing with. The tester uses Visual Studio Test Professional to author, manage, and execute a suite of manual test cases each day to surface potential bugs for the development team. The tester files bugs in Team Foundation Server that are assigned to development team to fix.

All bug reports are stored in Team Foundation Server, and provide team members and project sponsors with full visibility into the progress of the project. The bugs automatically contain a rich set of information for the developer, including a video of the test case being run by the tester, screenshots, an event log from the time the test was being run, and a pointer to a snapshot of the virtual environment where it was uncovered. The developer uses all this information to quickly diagnose and fix the bug.

Feedback

When the development team has finished an initial version of the website, they decide to ask the original stakeholders to review their progress to ensure that they are on the right track. The business analyst uses Team Foundation Server 2012 to request feedback from the appropriate stakeholders on the areas of the application that are ready for review. Each stakeholder receives an e-mail along with an invitation to provide feedback. The stakeholders use the new Microsoft Feedback Client to capture their feedback as they are using the new application. The Feedback Client enables each stakeholder to capture a video recording the application as they are using it, along with notes, screenshots, and audio annotations describing what they like and what they would like to see changed in the application. This feedback is rich and timely, helping the development team refine their implementation before the iteration is finished.

Operations

After the application has been built and signed off by the testing team, it's ready to be deployed in the on-premises datacenter. eMockSoft uses System Center 2012 to monitor the production servers, so the testing team is quickly alerted in the event that the application breaks or begins performing slowly. Using System Center Operations Manager, an operations engineer can choose to assign the issue to engineering, which automatically creates a bug in Team Foundation Server, including rich diagnostics from Operations Manager's application performance monitoring capabilities. If a developer needs even more information to diagnose an issue, he can ask the operations team to capture an IntelliTrace file from the running application, which he can use to review everything that happened during the application's execution and look for clues about how to resolve such an issue. By using these types of tools, the company can ensure better collaboration between the development and operations team than had been achieved in the past.

Putting It into Context

This is a simple example that examines just a few of the ways in which Visual Studio 2012 can assist with application lifecycle management. Throughout this book, you discover other examples that can help your team become a more cohesive unit and ship better software.

SUMMARY

In this chapter you learned about the overall Visual Studio 2012 product family and how it has been designed to help you address the entire application lifecycle management of your development projects. The rest of this book will dive more deeply into how you can apply these tools to your own team.

PART 1
Team Foundation Server

2

Introduction to Team Foundation Server

WHAT'S IN THIS CHAPTER?

- ➤ What is Team Foundation Server
- ➤ Core concepts central to Team Foundation Server
- ➤ Getting access to Team Foundation Server and connecting to it for the first time
- ➤ What's new in Team Foundation Server 2012
- ➤ Planning your Team Foundation Server adoption

Because Team Foundation Server is so fundamental to the Application Lifecycle Management offering from Microsoft, later chapters go into more depth about utilizing different aspects of the product, such as how to use it to plan your work, how to use version control when developing software, and how to make use of the build automation capabilities. In each case, the use of Team Foundation Server is explained within the context of the task you are doing — but before we can do that you need to know what Team Foundation Server is, what it provides, and how to get it.

Although a full treatment of Team Foundation Server is therefore necessary in a book about Microsoft's Application Lifecycle Management solution, this book deliberately focuses on how to *use* Team Foundation Server to develop software and effectively organize your teams. Team Foundation Server is highly customizable and extensible by an administrator. The book *Professional Team Foundation Server 2012* (Wrox, 2011) is targeted at administrators of Team Foundation Server and individuals who wish to customize their instance heavily, though Chapter 6 of this book will give you a taste of the customizations that are possible and provide a starting point to learn more.

WHAT IS TEAM FOUNDATION SERVER?

Developing software is difficult, a fact that is repeatedly proven by how many projects fail. Developing software is a creative endeavor, not a manufacturing process. Consequently, an essential factor in the success of any software development team is how well the members of the team communicate with each other and with the people who wanted the software developed in the first place.

Microsoft Visual Studio Team Foundation Server 2012 provides the core collaboration functionality for your software development teams in a very tightly integrated product. The functionality provided by Team Foundation Server includes the following:

➤ Project management and planning

➤ Work item tracking (WIT)

➤ Version control

➤ Test case management

➤ Build automation

➤ Reporting

➤ Virtual lab management

Team Foundation Server is a server product separate from Visual Studio. Logically, Team Foundation Server is made up of the following two tiers, which can be physically deployed across one or many machines:

➤ *Application tier* — The *application tier* primarily consists of a set of web services with which the client machines communicate by using a highly optimized web service–based protocol.

➤ *Data tier* — The *data tier* is made up of a SQL Server database containing the database logic of the Team Foundation Server application, along with the data for your Team Foundation Server instance. The data stored in the database is used by Team Foundation Server's reporting functionality. All the data stored in Team Foundation Server is stored in this SQL Server database, thus making it easy to back up.

Team Foundation Server was designed with extensibility in mind. There are comprehensive APIs in .NET and Java for integrating with Team Foundation Server, and a set of events that enables outside tools to integrate with Team Foundation Server as first-class citizens. The same APIs and event system are used by Microsoft itself in the construction of Team Foundation Server, as well as the client integrations into Visual Studio, Microsoft Office, and Eclipse.

Team Foundation Server has competitors, including other enterprise Application Lifecycle Management suites and purpose-specific solutions (such as source control, a build server, or a work tracking system). As discussed in Chapter 1, the main benefit of having all these capabilities in one product is the tight integration that Microsoft has been able to achieve between the tools that you use to develop software and the tools that you use to communicate with your team and your stakeholders.

ACQUIRING TEAM FOUNDATION SERVER

Team Foundation Server is a server-side product that must be acquired, installed, and configured. There are several options available for purchasing access to a server for your team. To begin with you should to decide if you want to run the Team Foundation Server inside your own firewall or if you want to explore a hosted Team Foundation Server offering.

Hosted Team Foundation Server

The easiest way to acquire Team Foundation Server is to rent it from a provider and access it over the Internet. Trial options are available, which means you can get started with no cost, and there is no need to wait for hardware to be purchased. When it comes to hosted options, there are two main routes: hosting from Microsoft or hosting from a third-party provider.

However, hosting is not suitable for everyone. Some organizations have a legal obligation to keep the data that they would store inside Team Foundation Server inside the firewall; others may require the tight user identity integration provided by Team Foundation Server's Active Directory integration. Others are just not comfortable making their source code, work items, and build accessible from any machine over the Internet. For these types of people a hosted solution probably isn't the answer.

Hosting from Microsoft

Microsoft makes available a massive cloud-hosted instance of Team Foundation Server, which, at the time of writing, was in preview form at `http://tfspreview.com`. Eventually this will become a full, commercial service available for customers who want to purchase Team Foundation services for their team at a low, predictable cost. At the time of writing access to the service is available for free, but Microsoft has stated that when the service becomes fully available there will be a commercially competitive charge for use of the service. However, despite the fact that the service is currently in preview mode, Microsoft still allows you to use this instance for hosting of live project data, which makes it an enticing option for people new to Team Foundation Server who want to try it out.

Tfspreview.com is hosted on Windows Azure and makes use of all the services provided by Microsoft's cloud operating system to ensure high availability, resiliency, and a full backup of your data. However, because the system is scaled to support the thousands of users who access it over the Internet — and because it is just the basic core Team Foundation services that are available, tfspreview.com comes with some limitations compared with a full on-premise installation. For example, there is no integration with SharePoint for a project portal and document library. There are also limited reporting features currently available and restrictions to the amount of customization that you can do to the server instance.

However, tfspreview.com provides all the version control, work item tracking, build automation, and project management capabilities of Team Foundation Server. Being available over the Internet makes it very easy to use when your team is distributed globally, and it is easy to get started on using the service. All you need to do is visit tfspreview.com, create an account, and your team can be up and running before you have finished reading this chapter. Access to tfspreview.com is controlled by federated Internet-based credentials; at the time of writing you need to have a Live Id from Microsoft to authenticate with the service.

As tfspreview.com is maintained by the Team Foundation Server team at Microsoft, it is always running the very latest version of the server software during their development process. Therefore new features will show up on tfspreview.com before they are made available in the standard retail installation of Team Foundation Server via an update or a new major release. For this reason you may notice some differences between some of the screens displayed in the figures of this book and the appearance of tfspreview.com at the time of reading.

> **NOTE** *This cloud-hosted version of Team Foundation Server from Microsoft is the same in many ways as the Team Foundation Server available elsewhere and installed on your own servers, but there are some ways in which it operates differently (such as with regard to authentication). Throughout the rest of the book, we distinguish between the "Hosted Service" behavior and the regular (that is, "On-Premises") behavior when it is important to do so — however, the majority of this book describes the behavior of Team Foundation Server in general regardless of where it is installed.*

Third-Party Hosted Team Foundation Server Providers

Many commercial companies can host your Team Foundation Server for you over the Internet for a small charge. They have the advantage that they have all the Team Foundation Server administrative knowledge in house and have a great deal of experience running their servers for many customers. As these companies are dealing on a different scale than that of Microsoft's hosted service, they can often be much more flexible in the capabilities they provide (at a cost). Depending on the hosting provider, you may also be able to purchase SharePoint portal capabilities, along with a full reporting instance, and get the same capabilities as if you were running Team Foundation Server in house without having to go through the up-front costs of acquiring the hardware to run Team Foundation Server or purchasing the software licenses in full before use.

The version of Team Foundation Server used by the third-party hosted providers is exactly the same as the version you would get if you installed it on premises. The only difference is that Team Foundation Server is running in their data centers or private clouds and your team accesses it over the Internet. In this book, behavior categorized as *On-Premises* refers to the behavior you would expect to see from your third party–hosted Team Foundation Server provider as opposed to the *Hosted Service* behavior provided by Microsoft's hosted offering (tfspreview.com).

> **NOTE** *Microsoft provides a list of companies offering commercial hosting services for Team Foundation Server at* `http://aka.ms/tfshosting`.

As mentioned previously, in some organizations, using a third party to host such important data as your company's source code is not acceptable, and some other companies may actually be required by law to keep such data within the bounds of the corporate firewall. In those instances an on-premises option is the only one available.

On-Premises Installation

The way that the vast majority of customers enjoy the features of Team Foundation Server is by locally installing a version of the software inside the firewall. Trial versions of Team Foundation Server are available for you to download and install locally so you can get up and running quickly. You can also download a prebuilt virtual machine from Microsoft with all the software necessary to help you evaluate the product.

> **NOTE** *You can find the latest version of the virtual machine at* `http://aka.ms/VS11ALMVM` *or you can download an Express or a Trial version of Team Foundation Server to install locally at* `http://aka.ms/tfs2012.`

To purchase Team Foundation Server to run locally, you can acquire the software in retail or via a MSDN Subscription, a Volume Licensing purchase, or through a Microsoft Partnership agreement.

Also available for the first time in the 2012 release is a new version called Team Foundation Server Express. This includes the code developer features such as version control, work item tracking, build automation, all of which is available free of charge for individuals and teams of up to five users. The Express edition comes with a few limitations, namely: no support for SharePoint integration, limited to five named users, supports only SQL Express (so no reporting and a maximum database size of 10GB), and no sprint/backlog planning or feedback management.

You can upgrade from a Trial or Express edition of Team Foundation Server to a full edition at any time without losing any data. In addition you can purchase additional Client Access Licenses (CALs) if you require more than the five named users that come with the Express edition.

> **NOTE** *For more information about installing or administrating a Team Foundation Server instance, see* Professional Team Foundation Server 2012 *(Wrox, 2012).*

TEAM FOUNDATION SERVER CORE CONCEPTS

Let's take a look at some of the core concepts that are critical to understanding Team Foundation Server. If you have been using previous versions of Team Foundation Server for a while (especially the previous Team Foundation Server 2010 release) then you might want to skip to the "What's New in Team Foundation Server 2012" section later in this chapter.

Figure 2-1 provides an overview of the Team Foundation Server components, which are explained in the following sections.

In addition to the components shown in Figure 2-1, the concepts of teams and team builds are necessary to a complete understanding of Team Foundation Server. Those concepts are also covered in the following sections.

Team Foundation Server

A Team Foundation Server instance can be physically split into many different machines. The *application tier* refers to the running web application that is handling all requests for data from client machines running Visual Studio. The data in a Team Foundation Server instance is stored in a *data tier*, which is essentially a SQL Server installation being accessed by the application tier. Although the application tier and the data tier are logically separate, you can have both installed on a single physical machine. As the application tier is the level at which you access a Team Foundation Server instance, the application tier machine name is often referred to as simply the Team Foundation Server. You refer to your Team

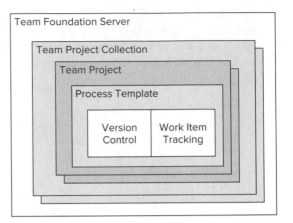

FIGURE 2-1

Foundation Server by name or URL (that is, `tfsserver` or `http://tfsserver:8080/tfs`) when Team Foundation Server is installed in the default virtual directory in IIS on the default port. When talking to a Team Foundation Server hosted over the Internet, you most often use the full URL, such as `https://proalm.tfspreview.com`.

Team Foundation Server can scale to support a very large number of active users, depending on the hardware supporting it. Therefore, for most organizations, Team Foundation Server instances tend to be scoped according to who pays for the installation and operation of the instance, not by scaling limitations of the server.

Team Project Collection

The *team project collection* concept was first introduced in Team Foundation Server 2010. This is a container for team projects. Each server has one or many team project collections, and a project collection can have zero or more team projects.

The team project collection is the main level of isolation between instances on a server. In a hosted Team Foundation Server, the collection is what is provided as your *account*. Global security groups take effect at the project collection level. The identifiers for work items and for changesets in version control are all numbered with sequential IDs that are unique at the project collection level.

A team project collection has a one-to-one relationship with a database instance in SQL Server. Therefore, you can back up and restore at the project collection level. You can move project collections between Team Foundation Servers, and you can split the project collection to break up the distribution of team projects between the resulting collections. Using this process, you can move a team project into a new collection by cloning the existing project collection and then deleting the appropriate team projects from each of the cloned project collections.

Each Team Foundation Server instance has a default project collection, usually called `DefaultCollection`. As project collections were not introduced until the 2010 release, older clients that were created for Team Foundation Server 2008 will only be able to see this default collection.

Team Project

A *team project* is a collection of work items, code, tests, or builds that encompass all the separate tools that are used in the lifecycle of a software development project. A team project can contain any number of Visual Studio solutions or projects, or, indeed, projects from other development environments. A team project is usually a fairly long-running thing with multiple areas and iterations of work.

You need at least one team project to start working with Team Foundation Server. When the team project is created, the following are also created by default:

➤ Path in version control

➤ Default work item queries

➤ Default areas and iterations

➤ Default team

If using a Team Foundation Server instance that is also attached to a SharePoint and SQL Server Reporting Services instance, then the following are also created:

➤ Team project website

➤ Document library

➤ Stock reports

> **WARNING** *It is not possible to rename a team project after it's been created. Also, the number of team projects in the team project collection has a performance effect on the system, so you do not want to have more than around 250 per project collection. Therefore, you want to think carefully before creating a new team project.*
>
> *It is often useful to experiment with Team Foundation Server features in a sandboxed test instance of Team Foundation Server. Many people download the Team Foundation Server Trial Virtual PC image from Microsoft for this purpose or get a trial account for a Microsoft-hosted Team Foundation Service instance at* http://tfspreview.com, *but some organizations have enterprise-wide test instances of Team Foundation Server for people to experiment in.*

The granularity that you choose for your team project has important implications for how you structure your work and when you move from one team project to another.

Team projects are intended to represent the largest unit of work in your organization. For example, in Microsoft Developer Division, the whole of a Visual Studio release lives in a single team project with Team Foundation Server as an area of that project.

A team project has a single process template, and changes made to the process template of a running team project affect that team project only. The default reports and work item queries are all scoped by team project, making it easy to track and find work for that team project as an entity.

The following are also linked to the team project that they belong to and, in general, are difficult to move between team projects:

➤ *Work Items* — Each *work item* is attached to the team project and uses the process template assigned to it. For this reason, it is not possible to move a work item from one team project to another, although you may copy the work item between projects in the same project collection and include a link to the source work item for reference.

➤ *Document Libraries* — The team project optionally refers to a project website based on Windows SharePoint Services (WSS). The *document libraries* in this website are linked to this project, and all the documents, projects plans, process guidance, or other non-deliverable assets contained in the document library therefore correspond to the team project.

➤ *Reports* — All the *reports* created as part of one of the stock process templates are scoped to the team project level, making it easy to determine the progress of work inside that team project.

➤ *Builds* — Each build definition is tied to a team project, as are the build controllers and build agents performing the *builds*.

➤ *Version Control* — All items stored in *version control* must be stored under a team project node in the repository. All settings for version control (such as check-in policies, check-in notes, and multiple check-out support) are controlled at the team project level.

➤ *Classifications* — A team project is typically broken up into areas and iterations. An *area* is typically a functional area of the code that may have a subset of the whole team typically working on it. For example, a particular application may be broken into tiers: the web tier, application tier, and database tier. It is common that a feature or requirement may affect all tiers of the application, but a task or bug may just affect a small area of the code. Therefore, areas are organized hierarchically so that a feature could be assigned to the whole application in the team project, but an ASP.NET form development task may be assigned to a child area. *Iterations* are similarly organized. For Version 1 of the application, you may split development into several phases and, in each phase, have several short iterations (or *sprints*). These can be organized hierarchically in the iterations section.

SCOPE OF A TEAM PROJECT

In general, a team project is "bigger than you think." A good way of thinking about what needs to be grouped into a single team project is to think about the effect of a typical requirement for your software development project. If the requirement would affect the ASP.NET front end, Java middleware, and SQL database repository, then all these projects and teams of developers probably want to be working in the same team project.

Following are three general areas that are used when scoping a team project, but every organization is different, and yours might need to combine these aspects when deciding on your approach:

➤ Application

➤ Release

➤ Team

For some organizations, it makes sense to only have a single team project in a single project collection. Others may have more than 100.

Team Project per Application

The Team Project per Application model is a common approach, as generally requirements are addressed by the entire application, and a group of people are assigned to work on it. The applications typically have a long lifecycle, going from the inception phase, through active development and support, and finally to the end-of-life phase. However, a common mistake is for a single team responsible for several applications to have those applications split into team projects. This makes it difficult to manage the priorities of work across those projects. The Team Project per Application model is more suited to large applications that have a dedicated team or teams working on the application throughout the application's lifecycle.

Team Project per Release

This is the methodology adopted by Microsoft Developer Division as they develop Visual Studio. It is useful for very large teams working on long-running projects. After every major release (such as Visual Studio 2010), you create a new team project. At this point in time, you can carry out changes that might have come about from your post-release review. You might take the opportunity to reorganize your version control tree, improve process templates, and copy over work items from the previous release that didn't make it.

This methodology tends to be suited to large independent software vendors (ISVs) working with products with a very long lifetime. In these cases, it is generally safer to start as a Team Project per Application and then move to a Team Project per Release if required to make reporting easier. It is very rare that this type of team project model is applicable to everyday business development. For that, Team Project per Team is usually more common.

Team Project per Team

For smaller teams (fewer than 50 people) where the size and responsibilities of the team tend to stay fairly consistent but the applications they work on are in a constant state of flux, the Team Project per Team approach is often the most suitable. If your team members are often working on more than one application at a time, the same team or a subset of the team works together on those projects over time, or the project lifecycle is measured in months rather than years, then you should consider this approach as a starting point.

Team

In Team Foundation Server 2012, teams are modeled as a core concept within Team Foundation Server. When you create a new team project, a new team is created for you by default with the name of that project. For example, if you create a team project called AdventureWorks, then a team called

AdventureWorks Team is automatically created. The team initially contains just one member (who is also an Administrator), the person who created the team project, but you can easily add members to the team using their domain credentials in an on-premise install or by e-mail address for the hosted service.

As well as membership and administrators, a team has the following items associated with it:

➤ Description of the team, for example what they are responsible for

➤ Security permissions in Team Foundation Server given to members of the Team

➤ Areas that the team are responsible for

➤ Iterations that the team will be taking part in. The iterations have a start date (in the past) and end date (in the future) that control which iteration is the "current" one.

➤ A backlog of work associated to that team (that is, work items in that team's Area)

➤ A board of backlog items, showing for each product backlog item or story what associated tasks there are for that work item. Team members can easily drag and drop them into other states such as In Progress or Done.

➤ Alert events, for example sending an email notification when a build fails or a work item is associated to a team member

➤ Favorites, such as work item queries, source control paths, or build definitions that may be important to that team

For many smaller team projects the concepts of *team* and *team project* merge. But for larger team projects, you may want to create additional teams, which is why it is important to call out what belongs to the team and what belongs to the team project.

Any areas, iterations, work items, work item queries, builds, and most actual Team Foundation Server artifacts that you create are created at the team project level. By default, other teams can see them and interact with them. You can think of the team as a filter on the team project data to show which information is most relevant to that team, and therefore to you as a member of one or more teams.

Under the covers in Team Foundation Server, a team is actually just a Team Foundation Server security group with some additional properties and metadata associated with it.

Process Templates

An important fact about software development projects is that there is no single process that is suitable for delivering all types of solutions to all types of businesses with all types of teams. Therefore, Team Foundation Server was designed from the ground up to be flexible in how you want your teams to work.

The *process template* is a set of XML files that provide the details of how you would like your process to work. Microsoft provides the following three process templates with the default installation of Team Foundation Server:

➤ *Microsoft Visual Studio Scrum* — Previously available as an optional add-on, in Team Foundation Server 2012 the Scrum process template is not only installed by default but is the default process template used when creating new projects. It is a template designed for teams that want to base their software development on the highly popular Scrum methodology (at the time of writing the most popular of the formal Agile development methodologies). Users' needs are tracked by *Product Backlog Item* work items, which are broken down into Task work items. There are also work items for Bugs, Impediments, and Test Cases. The work items' states follow those recommended by the Scrum software development practice.

> **NOTE** *For more information on the Scrum software development process in general, visit* `http://scrum.org`.

➤ *Microsoft Solutions Framework (MSF) for Agile Software Development* — This is a lightweight template designed for teams following a delivery process based on general Agile software development practices. User needs are tracked by *User Story* work items, as well as types for Bugs, Issues, Tasks, and Test Cases. In general, the work items have a simple state progression from active to resolved to closed. It is also an excellent starting point for people who want to customize a process to fit with their development organization.

➤ *MSF for Capability Maturity Model Integration (CMMI) Process Improvement* — This is a more detailed template designed for teams with more traditional process requirements — that is, those that typically have longer lifecycles and possible governance requirements that the process template would help fulfill. Note that if your organization is striving for CMMI compliance you should not consider this template as your only choice; you should still evaluate the possibilities offered by the MSF for the Agile Software Development template, among others.

In addition to the templates installed by default, many more are available to download online. If you have an existing process in your organization, it is possible to create a custom process template to match the process.

> **NOTE** *To obtain information about additional process templates available from Microsoft and its partners, see* `http://go.microsoft.com/fwlink/?LinkId=80608`.

After you have created a team project with a process template, it is possible to modify all aspects of it while the project is in flight, including work item types, fields, states, and so on. This was another critical design decision taken by Microsoft in designing Team Foundation Server because Microsoft recognized that the best teams are those that continually improve and adapt their processes, and that, as the project continues, more is learned about the domain, as well as the strengths and weaknesses of the team.

Work Item Tracking

Work items in Team Foundation Server are things such as requirements, bugs, issues, and test cases. In other words, these are the items of work that your organization needs to track to manage the delivery of a software development project.

The work item tracking system is highly extensible. You can control which fields are presented to the user, which fields are rolled up into the reporting data warehouse, how the work item looks, what states the work item can be in, and how to transition from one state to the next.

All work items share certain common fields such as ID, State, and Title, as shown in Figure 2-2. They have a full history of changes recorded to every field in the work item and by whom. You can also link work items, files, web pages, or other elements in Team Foundation Server.

The work item type definitions are all configurable at the team project level. The work item types are created from the process template definition during project creation, but they can be modified as the team project is in flight. Changing the work item types for one team project in flight does not affect those in another team project, even if they were created using the same original process template.

All data about the work item is stored in the Team Foundation Server database. Any file attachments are also stored in the database.

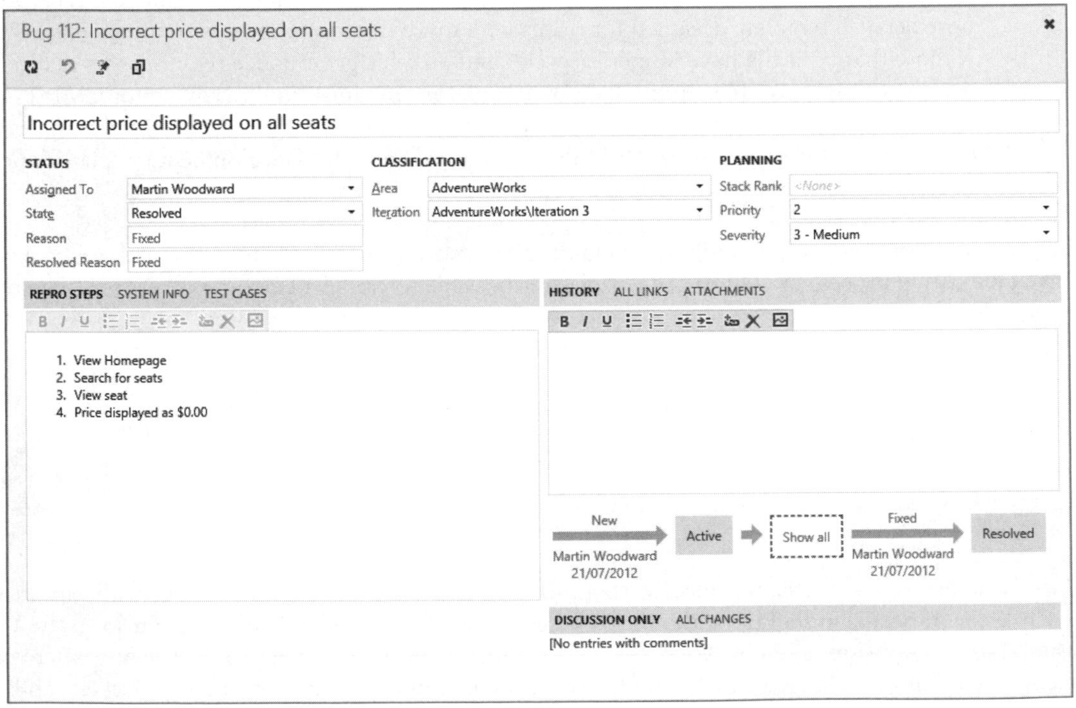

FIGURE 2-2

> **NOTE** *You learn more about work items in Chapters 22 through 26, all of which are included in Part VI of this book.*

Version Control

Team Foundation Server includes a full enterprise-class, centralized version control system that has been designed from the ground up to work well in environments that are spread across a wide geographical area over high-latency, low-bandwidth connections.

TEAM FOUNDATION SERVER AND VSS

There's an important misconception to get out of the way: Although Team Foundation Server provides version control capabilities, it is in no way related to Microsoft's previous version control system, Visual SourceSafe (VSS). In terms of core concepts, it actually shares more in common with the version control system that was previously used internally in Microsoft, a product with the code name "Source Depot." Team Foundation Server is actually based on an entirely new code base and contains features not found in either product.

The basic model of version control in Team Foundation Server will feel very familiar if you have used Visual SourceSafe (VSS), Polytron Version Control System (PVCS), Perforce, or Subversion, but is different from Distributed Version Control Systems, such as Git or Mercurial. There have been very significant improvements in Team Foundation Server 2012 in the version control system (read more details about them in Chapter 3). There are now two modes of operation for version control; one is used with Server Workspaces, which will be familiar to users of older versions of Team Foundation Server. With a Server Workspace, all files are read-only in the local file system until you check out a file to edit it.

The new mode of operation (and the default for new installations) is Local Workspaces, which will be much more familiar to users of tools such as Subversion or CVS. With Local Workspaces, files are read-write–enabled locally, and no check-out is required before you can edit the file. This makes working offline and working outside of Visual Studio significantly easier. However, the cost of this convenience is that you have to check which files have been changed before updating those files (or "checking them in") to the server. Also, as no server call is made before a file is updated, you receive no warning if another team member is working on a file at the same time as you until you go to perform a check-in. However, for most teams with a regular-sized code base (that is, fewer than 100,000 files) the reduction in friction in editing the files outside of Visual Studio or when offline from Team Foundation Server means that Local Workspaces are a sensible default starting point.

As is common with centralized version control systems, all check-in operations are performed against the server; you cannot check in locally.

The project collection administrator can configure which modes of operation are available and can, for example, force Server Workspaces if a more controlled environment is preferred.

In either mode, by default, Team Foundation Server allows multiple people to edit the same text-based files at the same time. This is particularly useful for .sln, .vbproj, and .csproj files in a Visual Studio project. When you go to check the file in to the server, if the latest version of that file is newer than the one you checked out, then you are prompted to merge your changes with the changes made by your colleagues.

> **NOTE** *Chapter 3 provides more in-depth information about version control.*

Team Foundation Server version control contains the following features:

➤ *Atomic check-ins* — Changes you make to the files are batched up into a *changeset*. When you check in the files in a changeset, they are taken as a single atomic transaction. If a single file cannot be checked in (for example, because of a merge conflict) then the whole changeset is not committed. Only after the whole changeset has been successfully applied do any of the files become the latest version. This way, you can ensure the consistency of your code base.

➤ *Associate check-ins with work items* — When you perform a check-in, you may associate that changeset with one or more work items. In this way, you are able to get full traceability of requirements from the initial feature desired by the user, to the tasks required to create it, to the check-ins into version control that were required to implement the feature. This information is surfaced in the work item that you linked to, as well as being shown in the build report and also passed into the reporting system in Team Foundation Server.

➤ *Branching and merging* — Team Foundation Server supports a full path space branching model. If you desire parallel development on a code base, then you can create a branch of the code in two separate places in the version control repository, and then merge changes that have been applied to one branch into the other.

> **NOTE** *Chapter 4 provides more information about branching and merging in Team Foundation Server.*

➤ *Shelving* — This includes the capability to store files on the server without committing them to the main version control repository. This is useful in a couple of different scenarios. You may want to back up changes made on your local machine to the server if you are going to be working on the files for more than a few hours or if you need to work on a different task temporarily and resume later. Another scenario is when you want to copy changes from one machine to another without checking them in (for example, a shelveset is used during a code review, to have a colleague verify your changes).

> **NOTE** *Chapter 3 provides more information on performing a code review with Visual Studio 2012.*

➤ *Labeling* — In Team Foundation Server, you can tag a set of files at a particular version with a textual label. This is useful for indicating which files were included in a certain build or which files are ready to move to your quality assurance (QA) process. Note that in Team Foundation Server, labels are always editable. Provided you have permission, you may add or remove files from that label at any time.

➤ *Concurrent check-outs* — Also known as the Edit-Merge-Commit model, by default, multiple people may edit a file at the same time. If a file were modified while you were working on it, then you would be prompted to merge the changes with the latest version of the file.

➤ *Follow history* — If you rename or branch a file then you are able to view the history of that file before it was renamed or branched. You can also follow the history of a file from before it was branched or merged.

➤ *Check-in policies* — When performing a check-in, Team Foundation Server provides the capability for the client to run code to validate that the check-in should be allowed. This includes performing actions such as checking that the change is associated with a work item, checking that the code passes static code analysis rules, and so on. Check-in policies are also an extension point in Team Foundation Server so that you can create your own, should you wish to do so.

➤ *Check-in notes* — In some organizations, it is necessary to capture metadata about a check-in (such as the code reviewer, or a reference to a third-party system). In other version control systems, this is frequently accomplished by requiring that the check-in comment follow certain unenforced conventions. Team Foundation Server provides check-in note functionality to capture this metadata. A team project administrator may add or remove check-in notes at the team project level, as well as make a particular check-in note mandatory.

➤ *Team Foundation Server proxy* — Frequently, organizations have regional development centers separated from the main development offices or the data center hosting the Team Foundation Server environment. When a "Get" is performed from version control, files are downloaded to the client machine. In the remote office environment, this often means that the same files are downloaded over the wide-area network (WAN) to every client machine involved in the development. Team Foundation Server provides an optional proxy server that may be installed in these remote offices. In those scenarios, the clients may be configured to perform the download via the proxy so that the proxy may cache the downloaded files at the remote location. In that way, the majority of the developers in the remote office will be downloading files from the proxy server local to them, thus removing traffic from the WAN and improving performance.

Team Build

Team Foundation Server provides a fully featured build automation server to enable you to standardize the build infrastructure for your team. Team builds are set up in the system as a *build definition*. You provide the build definition with information as to *what* you want build — that is, the folders or files in Team Foundation Server version control that contain the sources to be built, and the projects or solutions in those folders to build. You also specify *when* to perform the build using a trigger, such as building on every single check-in (*Continuous Integration*), building on a schedule, or validating that your changes pass the build process before check-in (known as a *Gated Check-in*).

> **NOTE** *Chapter 5 provides more information on the build automation capabilities.*

ACCESSING TEAM FOUNDATION SERVER

There are many ways for a team member to interact with the core services in Team Foundation Server, including the following:

- ➤ Web browser
- ➤ Visual Studio
- ➤ Eclipse-based development environments
- ➤ Microsoft Test Manager
- ➤ Team Foundation Server Administration Console
- ➤ Microsoft Excel
- ➤ Microsoft Project
- ➤ Command-line tools
- ➤ Third-party integrations

The following sections examine each of these, including the functionality they provide and basic usage.

TEAM FOUNDATION SERVER LICENSING

You must ensure that you are licensed to connect to an on-premise Team Foundation Server. In general, for Team Foundation Server, this means that you need to have a Client Access License (CAL), which is typically included with the MSDN subscription. People without MSDN can purchase it separately. It is your responsibility to ensure that you have the correct licenses required to cover your on-premises usage of Team Foundation Server. If you're in doubt, contact your Team Foundation Server administrator. If your organization needs help understanding its licensing needs then contact your local Microsoft representative for licensing assistance.

Accessing Team Foundation Server from Visual Studio

Team Foundation Server functionality is installed as a standard part of the install of a Visual Studio edition (including the Express editions).

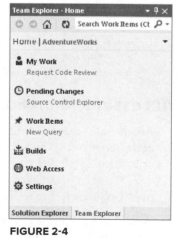

Assuming that you have an account, connect to your Team Foundation Server by clicking on the Connect to Team Foundation Server link on the Visual Studio Start Page or in Team Explorer (View, Team Explorer).

If your desired server is not available in the Servers drop-down, click the Servers button and then click the Add button to connect to your Team Foundation Server. As shown in Figure 2-3, you can enter the

FIGURE 2-3

server name or provide the full URL given to you by your Team Foundation Server administrator.

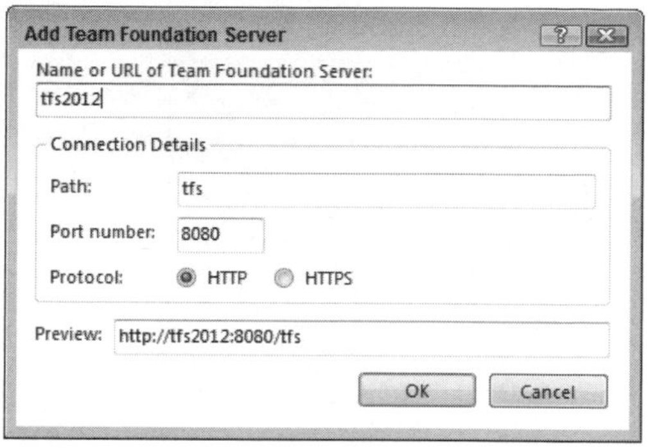

After you have added the server, select the project collection that contains your team projects and select the team project or projects that you want to work on.

Your selected team project displays in the Team Explorer window. The Team Explorer window will come as the first big surprise for users used to an older version of Visual Studio. In Visual Studio 2012 the Team Explorer experience has been completely revised to remove clutter and have a more focused experience. The home page that displays when you first connect to a team project is shown in Figure 2-4.

The sections that appear in the page depend on the version of Visual Studio that you have installed and the capabilities installed in your Team Foundation Server. For example, the My Work section is only displayed in Premium and Ultimate versions of Visual Studio. The Documents section displays when the team project is connected to a SharePoint portal, and the Reports section displays when the project has an associated reporting service site. However, all versions of Team Explorer display the Pending Changes section along with Work Items, Builds, and Settings. Clicking each section takes you to that page, which contains other sections. For example, clicking on Work Items takes you to a page that contains your favorite work item queries and a tree of the available work item queries on the server (see Figure 2-5).

FIGURE 2-4

To change pages or projects or to connect to a different project, click the page header and a drop-down menu displays that enables you to change pages or connect to a different team or project (see Figure 2-6).

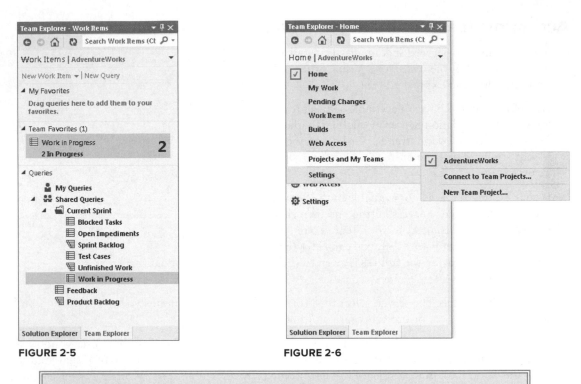

FIGURE 2-5   **FIGURE 2-6**

> **NOTE** *If you have additional sections for each team project then you probably have the Team Foundation Server power tools installed on your machine. This excellent set of tools is provided by the team at Microsoft to further enhance your Team Foundation Server experience. The Team Explorer, like most parts of Team Foundation Server, is extensible, so you can install extensions, or create your own, that take advantage of this.*

Accessing Team Foundation Server through a Web Browser

Another area that has undergone major changes in Team Foundation Server 2012 is the web-based view of the server (often called *Web Access*). You can view your server by navigating to its URL in a browser or by clicking the Web Access link in the Team Explorer. For example, if your server internally is called `tfs2012`, then by default you would navigate to `http://tfs2012:8080/tfs`. If your machine is accessed over the Internet, then a URL such as `proalm.tfspreview.com` is probably used.

Web Access (Figure 2-7) is ideal for users who do not want to install a dedicated Team Foundation Server client on their machines. At a high level, "when fully licensed," it offers the following functionality from the browser:

➤ Backlog and iteration planning

➤ Task board

➤ Create and edit work items and work item queries

➤ Manage areas and iterations

➤ Administer permissions and team membership

➤ Read-only access to version control

➤ Queue and manage build definitions

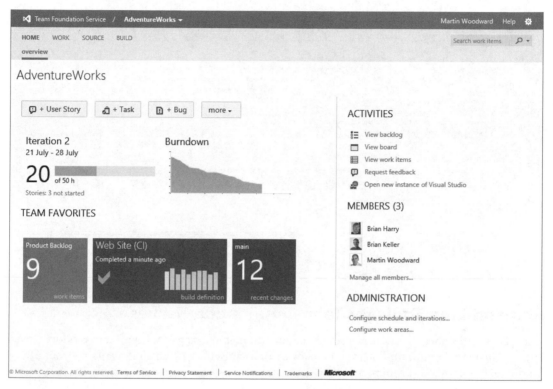

FIGURE 2-7

Using Team Foundation Server in Microsoft Excel

As part of the Visual Studio Team Explorer installation, integration into Microsoft Excel is provided by default and a Team tab is available on the ribbon in Excel. This allows the capability to add and edit work items directly from Excel spreadsheets, as shown in Figure 2-8, as well as the creation of Excel-based reports using data directly from Team Foundation Server.

Using Team Foundation Server in Microsoft Project

Integration into Microsoft Project is also provided as part of the Team Explorer installation. This provides the capability to add and edit work items directly from Microsoft Project and to view data about the progress of these work items.

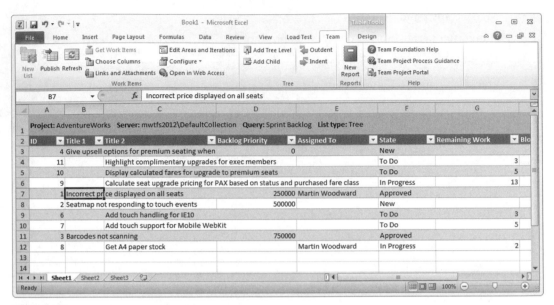

FIGURE 2-8

> **NOTE** *Chapter 10 describes this integration in more detail.*

Command-Line Tools for Team Foundation Server

Team Foundation Server includes a set of command-line tools as part of the Team Explorer installation. The main command-line tool to be aware of as a user is tf, which is available from a Visual
Studio 2012 command prompt. You can also install it separately on non-Windows–based systems
such as Mac OS X, Linux, and many other Unix flavors.

The tf command provides full access to Team Foundation Server version control functionality, including features in Team Foundation Server version control that are not exposed via the graphical clients.

> **NOTE** *For more information and full reference information on the com-
> mand-line tools available for Team Foundation Server, see* http://aka.ms/
> tfsCommands.

Accessing Team Foundation Server from Eclipse

For members of the team who are using Eclipse-based IDEs (including IBM Rational Application
Developer or one of the many other Eclipse-based environments), full access to the Team
Foundation Server capabilities are available from Microsoft using the TFS Plug-in for Eclipse as part
of Team Explorer Everywhere.

As you can see in Figure 2-9, at a high level, the Eclipse integration provides all the same functionality that a developer inside Visual Studio would utilize, including the following:

➤ Full version control integration (check-out, check-in, history, branch, merge, label, synchronize, and so on)

➤ Full work item tracking (create, edit work items, and work item queries)

➤ Full team build integration (create, edit, and manage builds and build definitions)

➤ Access to team reports and documents

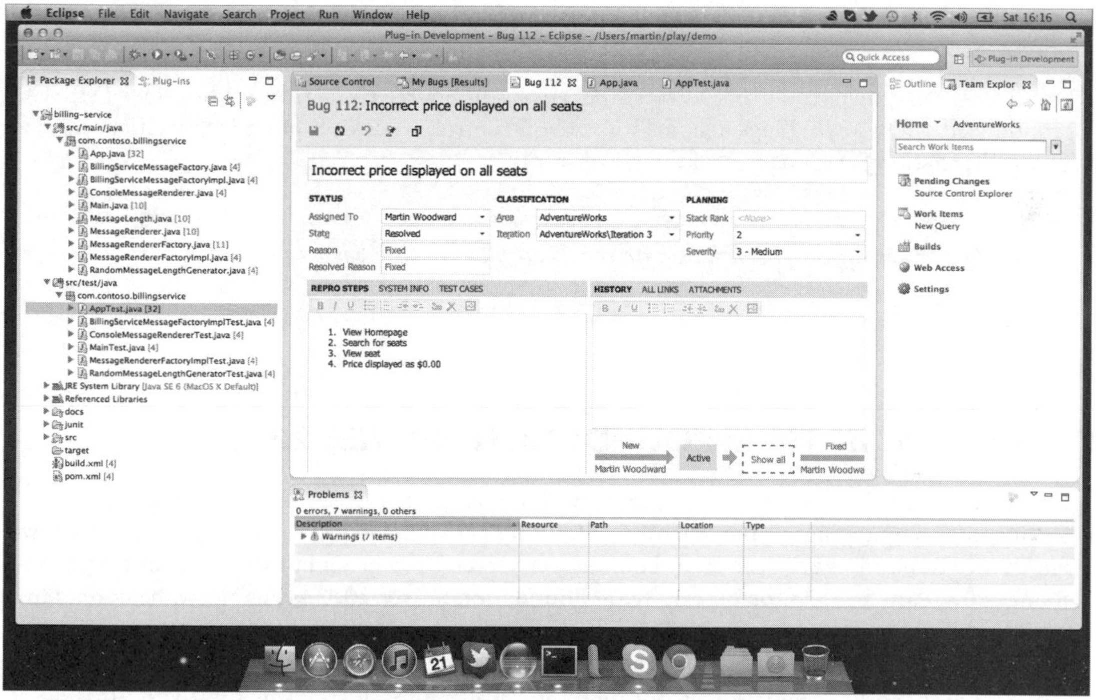

FIGURE 2-9

> **NOTE** *Check-in policies for the cross-platform and Eclipse clients must be separately configured inside that client. Also, the Java build extensions power tool available at* http://aka.ms/tfpt *is required on the build server to integrate with the Ant or Maven build processes that are common in Java environments.*

Windows Explorer Integration with Team Foundation Server

As part of the Team Foundation Server power tools available at http://aka.ms/tfpt, a Windows Explorer shell extension is available as an optional installation. This provides access to the basic version control functionality of Team Foundation Server from a standard Windows Explorer window and is most useful when working with Team Foundation Server version control outside of Visual Studio or Eclipse.

Access to Team Foundation Server via Other Third-Party Integrations

Team Foundation Server supports a rich and vibrant third-party ecosystem. As discussed previously, the same .NET and Java object models used by Microsoft to talk to Team Foundation Server are also available for developers in third-party companies to integrate with. Integrations are available into other parts of the Microsoft Office suite (such as Word and Outlook). In addition, many development tools now integrate with Team Foundation Server using the extensibility hooks provided by Microsoft.

For older development tools that support the Microsoft Source Code Control Interface (MSSCCI, pronounced "miss-key") plug-in model for version control, Microsoft has a MSSCCI provider for Team Foundation Server as part of the power tools.

> **NOTE** *For more information on the Team Foundation Server power tools visit* `http://aka.ms/tfpt`.

WHAT'S NEW IN TEAM FOUNDATION SERVER 2012

There have been three major changes in Team Foundation Server 2012: improving developer productivity, enhancing support for Agile planning best practices, and moving to the cloud with the Team Foundation Service. Team Foundation Server 2010 brought in significant architectural changes to Team Foundation Server. Team Foundation Server 2012 keeps the same core architectural building blocks as the 2010 release, but a whole new set of features has been built on top of it. Although many of these features are explained throughout this book, if you have used a previous version of Team Foundation Server then the features described in the following sections will be new to you.

Version Control

Team Foundation Server 2012 has brought in the biggest fundamental change to Team Foundation Version Control since the original release in 2005 with a feature called *Local Workspaces*, which is explained in detail in Chapter 3. In previous versions of Team Foundation Server, all state information about the files from version control that you had on your machine was stored in a *Workspace* on the server (or what is called a *Server Workspace* in Team Foundation Server 2012). Similar to Microsoft's earlier version control system, Visual SourceSafe, files were read-only locally until you explicitly checked out the file from version control, letting the server (and potentially everyone else connected to your team project) know that you were working on it. When getting files from version control, the server was already aware of the state of your local machine through the Server Workspace, and so it could quickly send you only the files that had changed since your last Get. When checking files in to version control, only the files you had checked out needed to be sent to the server. This had great advantages in terms of scalability (as the server thought it knew everything about your file system and so had to send you only the items that had changed) and in terms of collaboration (as the server could warn other team members when someone was working on the same file as they were). However, this meant frequent calls to the server every time you wanted to work on a file, which made it harder to work when you needed to be offline from the server.

In Team Foundation Server 2012, a Local Workspace stores all this workspace state locally, meaning fewer calls to the server during editing of files and a better offline experience. There's also another important advantage. Files in a local workspace are read/write when a Get is first performed against the server. This makes it a great deal easier to work with files in Team Foundation Version Control when working outside of the IDE integration built into Visual Studio or Eclipse. There is no longer an explicit check-out operation involving communication with the server, and, even better, the last version downloaded from the server is kept locally, which means it is very easy to compare your local changes with the version you had downloaded from the server without requiring any server calls.

These benefits come at the cost of features that Server Workspaces have — namely that when a check-in is performed, a scan of the files in the local workspace has to be conducted to see which have changed since they were downloaded from the server. When a Get is performed, the server has to query the client to ask which versions of all the files it has, so that it can send you the files that have changed since the last time you did a Get. Finally, because you are not telling the server when you are editing a file, other team members are not made aware of this, and so it is easier to find two team members working on the same file at the same time.

Despite these disadvantages, it was found that the improved offline functionality and the reduced friction in editing files outside of Visual Studio makes Local Workspaces a more attractive proposition for the majority of development teams, and Local Workspaces are now the default in Visual Studio 2012. However, for teams that have very large code bases or that prefer the increased communication to tell who is working on which files, the option exists to set the default workspace type to the traditional Server Workspace.

The changes to version control in 2012 go way beyond Local and Server Workspaces. A user's full name (the Display Name in Active Directory) is now used in all views instead of the logon ID, which in some organizations could be very obscure. Functionality has been added to the server to allow the transparent handling of the execute bit found on many non-Windows file systems. Merge capabilities have been enhanced, with more changes automerged than in previous versions. In general, lots of small usability improvements have been made to make working with Team Foundation Server Version Control a lot easier for the average developer.

Web Access

The most visible change to Team Foundation Server 2012 is the completely rewritten web interface. Not only does the web interface use the Metro design language common in many new Microsoft products, but it is much more responsive and scales to support many more concurrent users than before. The interface has also been rebuilt from the ground up to take advantage of modern browser technologies; therefore, it does a lot of the work of saving data to the server in an asynchronous fashion, which further improves the user experience. With the addition of supporting things like keyboard navigation and limited support for touch-based technologies, the web interface is now a more-than-credible, full-featured client for people who want to work with Team Foundation Server but who do not want the overhead of installing client software. In fact, in the areas of managing security or alerts or performing project planning, the web interface is the only interface. The only time a user would absolutely need to install the client software is when he wants to use version control or wants integration with other applications on the client machine (such as Excel or Microsoft Project).

Several new features have been added into the completely revised web interface: product backlog management, sprint planning, and task board experience (detailed in Chapter 11). All security and permissions management is done through the web interface. In addition, a powerful new alerts subscription experience has been added via the web interface.

Team Explorer

The old tree-based Team Explorer originally seen in Team Foundation Server 2005 has been replaced in Team Foundation Server 2012 with a new version based on a hierarchy of pages. The idea is to be task-focused in Visual Studio and Eclipse, be more user friendly, and give more pertinent data to the user while requiring less screen real estate to do so. The new Team Explorer is still the on-ramp into the majority of Team Foundation Server functionalities in the clients, but it is now also team-focused.

Teams

As mentioned earlier in the chapter, Team Foundation Server 2012 finally promotes the notion of a team as a first-class concept. When you create a team project, a default team is created and you pick which team you are working on in Team Explorer. Visual Studio takes data about your team to help set default areas and iterations in the work item–tracking experience. In Web Access, the entire experience is team-aware, showing you data about your team's current iteration.

Work Item Tracking

The improvements to the work item–tracking experience do not stop at the web interface. Visual Studio's work item–tracking experience has been enhanced with a new, more simplified look and feel, as well as several more low-level features.

The Cloud

By making available a hosted Team Foundation Service in the cloud at `http://tfspreview.com`, Microsoft has removed the barrier of entry for teams that want to use the Application Lifecycle Management features of Visual Studio but do not want to run their own Team Foundation Server. The effect of making Team Foundation Server available over the Internet has also brought about changes to many aspects of the system — for example, you are now able to authenticate with this hosted Team Foundation Service using a browser-based federated authentication mechanism rather than being forced to use a Windows-based login. The Team Foundation Build service now uses a polling-based model to detect when a new build is requested rather than the old push model, which makes using a build server in a different domain or outside the firewall much easier for on-premise installations of Team Foundation Server as well.

ADOPTING TEAM FOUNDATION SERVER

The value of Team Foundation Server is realized when it is utilized in a team. Therefore, ensuring a successful Team Foundation Server adoption requires cooperation from many people in your organization. This section should help you avoid some common pitfalls and provide you with some suggestions on where to start with what may seem like a large and daunting product.

When introducing any new tooling into a large organization, it is important that you address the key pain points first. For many companies, traceability of work through the development lifecycle is often an area that is being poorly addressed by existing tooling. For others, the version control system being used may be out of date and performing poorly. It is, therefore, usually the work item–tracking or version control components that people first start using when adopting Team Foundation Server.

Luckily, Team Foundation Server is flexible enough that you can still get value from the product when only using one or two components of the system. When you have adopted both version control and work item tracking, the next area to tackle to gain the most benefit is likely to be Team Foundation Build. By automating your build system and increasing the frequency of integrations, you reduce the amount of pain that always occurs when integrating components to form a product.

The key is to gradually remove the unknown and unpredictable elements from the software delivery process, all the time looking for wasted effort that can be cut out.

Automating the builds not only means that the build and packaging process becomes less error prone, it also means that the feedback loop of requirements traceability is completed. You are now able to track work from the time that it is captured, all the way through to a change to the source code of the product, and into the build that contains those changes.

After a period of time, you will have built up a repository of historical data in your Team Foundation Server data warehouse, and you can start to make use of the reporting features to predict if you will be finished when you expect (that is, if the amount of estimated work remaining on the system is reducing at the required rate). You will also be able to drill into areas that you might want to improve — for example, which parts of the code are causing the most bugs.

It is after a period of getting used to the tooling that you want to look at your process templates and ensure that all the necessary data is being captured — but, equally, that all the work item types and transitions are required. If there are unnecessary steps, then consider removing them. If you notice problems because of a particular issue, consider modifying the process to add a safety net.

It is important to adjust the process not only to fit the team and organization, but also to ensure that you only adjust your processes when you need to, and not just because you can.

Check-in policies represent a key area where Team Foundation Server administrators have a temptation to go overboard at first. Check-in policies prevent checking in of code that doesn't meet the requirements programmatically defined in the check-in policy. However, each policy has a performance penalty for the whole team, not only in running the policy on each check-in, but also in ensuring that the policy will pass before checking in the code.

A problem with developers who are not checking in code in small iterative changes cannot be easily remedied by introducing a check-in policy — the policy alone will provide some discouragement for checking in. Therefore, check-in policies should be introduced over time and when the need is identified by the whole team.

SUMMARY

This chapter introduced Team Foundation Server and discussed its role in bringing the team together when developing an application. You learned about some of the core concepts at the heart of Team Foundation Server, different ways to access the data in your organization's server, and what is new in the 2012 release of the product. Finally, you learned about some points that you should bear in mind when planning your Team Foundation Server deployment.

Chapter 3 looks in detail at using the version control features of Team Foundation Server and discusses the important new changes brought about in this latest release.

3

Team Foundation Version Control

If you are a developer you live in a world of source code. When you have more than one person working on a project, versioning becomes an issue. If two developers work on the same assembly, how do you merge their code? How do you prevent accidentally overwriting files? Incredibly, although the practice is rapidly declining, many organizations still just use file shares to store source code. If you are unfamiliar with version control, you can think of it as a filesystem with an extra dimension—time. You are able to share the current state of any file or folder with your team members, but you can go back in time to see what other versions have existed and what the source code looked like at any point in the history of the source code repository.

One of the key reasons you are likely to have chosen Visual Studio Team Foundation Server 2012 is its version control management system. It offers a number of features, including the capability to branch, merge, and shelve your source code, atomic check-ins, policies, security—all the features you expect from an enterprise version control solution. The core engine for this tool is Microsoft SQL Server so you can rely on the resilience of this proven database engine for the integrity of the data stored in it, the procedures and processes to back it up, and the scalability solutions that it provides.

> **NOTE** *Notice that the title of the chapter is, "Team Foundation Version Control." However, when you start using the feature, a lot of the tools and windows say "source control," such as in "Source Control Explorer." The version control title is there to indicate that the product can handle much more than source code. You can upload images, test data, work products, build files—anything you want, really.*

As well as the built-in integration to Team Foundation Server provided as part of the Visual Studio 2012 installation experience, the Team Foundation Server command line (tf) is also installed to enable you to perform version control operations from a command line if you prefer. There is a Windows Explorer shell extension available as a Team Foundation Server Power Tool. You can also access Team Foundation Server from Eclipse using the free Team Explorer Everywhere plug-in. Team Explorer Everywhere is also where you look to find a version of the Team Foundation Server command-line client for non-Windows systems such as Mac OS X, Linux, Solaris, and other flavors of Unix.

Team Foundation Server provides a centralized version control system—that is, there is a single master repository on which you back up, manage, maintain, and control permission. The server has a highly flexible path-based permission system, with access protected by the same Active Directory login used to authenticate with Windows.

Team Foundation Server 2012 introduced a new mode of working—a concept known as *Local Workspaces*. In previous versions of TFS Server Workspaces (where the state about which files are checked out and so on is stored on the server) were the only option, but the introduction of Local Workspaces stores the state of the files in the workspace on the local filesystem, meaning that you do not have to be connected to TFS to edit a file. Local Workspaces are the default workspace type in Team Foundation Server 2012, so this chapter begins with the assumption that you are working with a Local workspace. Later on in the chapter we discuss both Local and Server workspaces, the differences between them, and which type is suitable for which method of working. In Team Foundation Server 2012 there have been many other improvements in version control as part of the most recent release to make the version control experience more transparent for developers and to reduce friction for developers doing everyday work. The user experience for version control has also been dramatically changed from previous versions—making use of the new unified Team Explorer view for the majority of common version control operations.

In this chapter, you find out about the main features of Team Foundation Version Control, such as checking in and checking out code, setting check-in policies, and temporarily shelving your code for easy access at a later date. The Team Foundation version control system also supports a number of other features, such as atomic check-ins, workspaces, and changesets, all of which are covered in this chapter.

> **NOTE** *One of the common misconceptions about Team Foundation version control is that it is a new version of Microsoft Visual SourceSafe (VSS). This is completely untrue—Team Foundation version control was written from scratch. And, unlike SourceSafe, it has been designed to scale well to a large number of developers (more than 2,000). The two are completely different products.*

TEAM FOUNDATION VERSION CONTROL AND VISUAL SOURCESAFE (VSS) 2005

Visual SourceSafe (VSS) 2005 reached the end of mainstream support in 2011 and extended support will end in 2016. No new versions of the product will be released. With the 2012 release of Team Foundation Server, Microsoft has made several changes to both the product and its licensing to make it suitable for all sizes of development teams.

Team Foundation version control is part of a greater Software Configuration Management (SCM) solution. Unlike VSS, Team Foundation version control is designed to scale to large development teams and can support distributed and outsourced teams in remote locations. Plus, you can avoid problems such as the occasional corruption of your source code files (because the data is written to a real database, rather than flat files).

Like VSS before it, Team Foundation Server is now available in all MSDN subscriptions including Visual Studio. Team Foundation Server is available for significantly less cost than VSS ever was, yet it is a much more modern, full-featured product with a healthy community and significant on-going investment from Microsoft. Therefore, it is now time to move away from any existing VSS databases toward Team Foundation Server. Fortunately, Microsoft has made it even easier to upgrade a VSS repository into Team Foundation Server by providing a new wizard based solution for performing a VSS migration (with history if required). For more information on using the new Visual SourceSafe upgrade wizard with Team Foundation Server 2012 see `http://aka.ms/vssUpgrade`.

SETTING UP VERSION CONTROL

Assuming that you've never used a version control system, where do you start? Even if you have used other version control systems, all version control systems work in slightly different ways and have a different model for working with files, so how do you effectively set up and use Team Foundation version control? Let's walk you through the process step-by-step.

After you have connected to your Team Foundation Server project collection, you can create a new team project by clicking File ➪ New ➪ New Team Project. This is typically done by your Team Foundation Server administrator, but at this point you are offered a series of options. You get two version control options to set up a new parent folder, as shown in Figure 3-1.

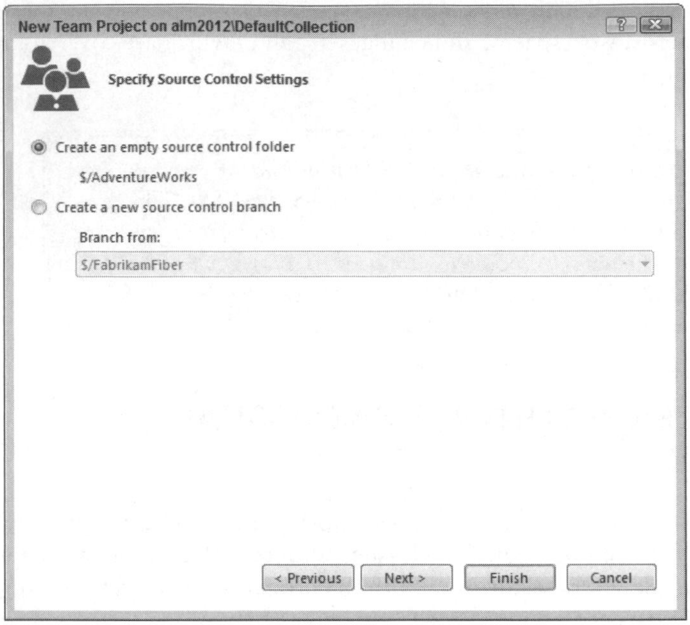

FIGURE 3-1

In this window, you have the following two options:

➤ You can create a brand-new parent version control folder (based on the name of your project). For most occasions, choose this option.

➤ You can create a branch based on a pre-existing project. This option is especially compelling if you want to create another version of an existing application or implement a new process to develop an existing application. However, unless you really know that you want to do this, you can safely go with the first option.

USING THE SOURCE CONTROL EXPLORER

The Source Control Explorer is similar to other explorers in Visual Studio. It enables you to browse and manage the entire version control repository, as well as view projects, branches, and individual folders. You can add and delete files; check in, check out, and view any of your pending changes; and view the status of your local code compared to the code in Team Foundation version control. Think of it as your master control area for all tasks related to source code management. Following are some of the important tasks it enables you to do:

➤ Map folders

➤ Add files

➤ Get files

➤ Check in changes

➤ Create shelvesets

➤ View historical data

➤ Branch and merge

➤ Compare files and folders

➤ Label your files and folders

➤ Change security settings for files and folders

> **NOTE** *As you learn later in this chapter, a shelveset is a collection of changes stored in a "shelf," or area, to temporarily store your source code without committing it to the repository.*

Many of these topics are examined later in this chapter. To access the Source Code Explorer, simply click View ➪ Other Windows ➪ Source Control Explorer. Alternatively there is a shortcut link to the Source Control Explorer on the Team Explorer Home page.

Another way you can open a solution from version control in Visual Studio is by clicking File ➪ Source Control ➪ Open from Source Control. Visual Studio prompts you to connect to the Team Foundation Server and select the source code repository of your choice if you are not connected.

Figure 3-2 shows the Source Control Explorer interface. It is divided into three main areas: the source tree view on the left (which enables you to navigate and select source folders from your project), the details view on the right, and the source location bar and version control toolbar at the top.

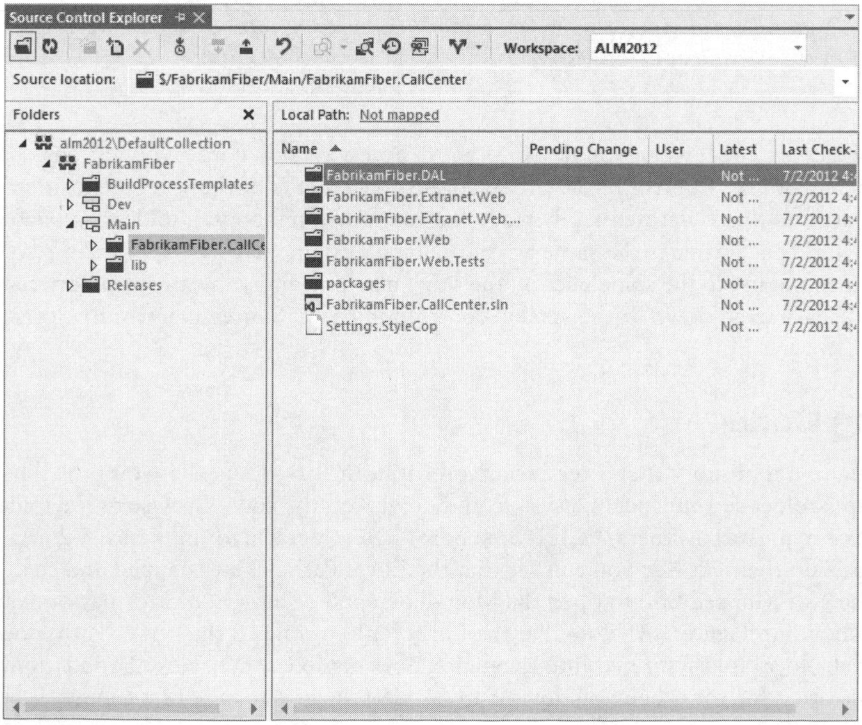

FIGURE 3-2

The Source location shows the server path of the currently selected folder in the Source Control Explorer. In Team Foundation Server version control, server paths are given in the format `$/TeamProjectName/FolderPath/File.txt` where the path separators are a forward slash (/) and the root of the repository is represented by the dollar symbol ($).

Setting Up Your Workspace

Your workspace represents the local working copy of files on your filesystem. You can think of a *workspace* as your personal sandbox to work on source code; it is the bridge between code on the server and your client machine. A workspace has one or many folders mapped in Team Foundation version control with your local filesystem. Whenever you get files, they are downloaded from the repository in Team Foundation Server and placed into your workspace for you to work on them. To get your changes back into the server repository you *check in* (commit) the changes. Workspaces provide isolation; they enable you to work on your code to make up your application without affecting any changes the rest of your team might be making.

The workspace itself is bound to a machine and owner. If you move to a different machine you have to create a new workspace. Files that you have edited in your workspace live on the associated machine only. This is an important difference to keep in mind with some other version control systems.

> **NOTE** *Working folder mappings provide a wealth of features that you can use to perform sophisticated operations and mappings locally. However, to begin with, stick to one local folder mapped to a single folder (usually the branch you are working on in the version control system).*

In Team Foundation Server 2012, when you first attempt to access version control operations on the server (such as using Source Control Explorer to browse the contents of the server repository), a Local workspace is created that is automatically ready for you to begin mapping folders and getting files. By default the workspace name is the same as your computer name. However, you can have multiple workspaces belonging to the same user on the same machine and you can swap between them using the Workspace drop-down in the version control toolbar in Source Control Explorer (refer to Figure 3-2).

Getting Existing Code

If you are connecting to a repository that already has code in it, the first thing that you probably want to do is to map a folder to your local filesystem and download the code. Browse to the folder that you would like to map (such as the `$/FabrikamFiber/Main` folder shown in Figure 3-2). At the top of the details pane on the right side you can see that the Local Path is Not Mapped and that is underlined. Click the Not Mapped link to open the Map dialog and point it at a directory on your local filesystem, as shown in Figure 3-3. Note that the Local Path (or indeed the Server Path) does not need to exist. If the local folder entered into the dialog does not exist then Team Foundation Server attempts to create it for you when you download (or Get) the files for the first time.

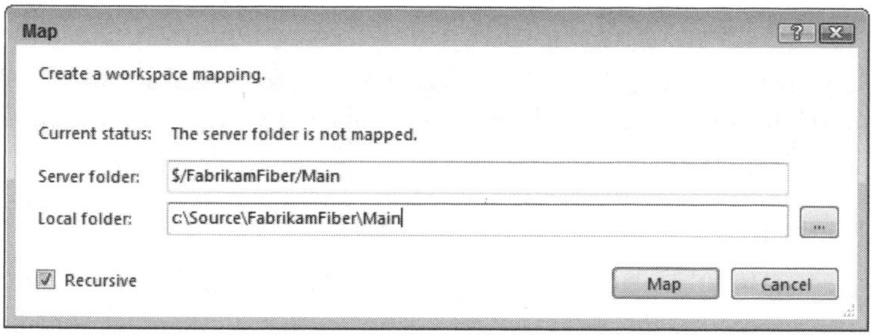

FIGURE 3-3

Whenever you create or change your working folder mappings, Team Foundation Server prompts you if you would like to perform a Get so that the files on the server are downloaded locally as shown in Figure 3-4. Select Yes in the dialog, and the latest version of the Main folder is downloaded into the directory specified.

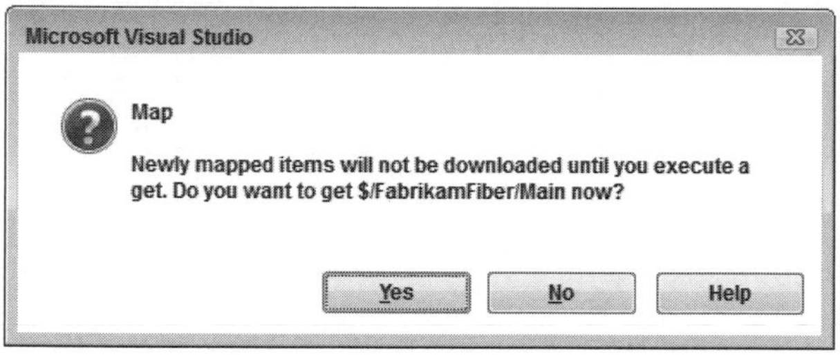

FIGURE 3-4

The Local Path in the details pane of Source Control Explorer now shows the path that you are currently viewing, and clicking on the path link opens that directory in the local filesystem. The files in Source Control Explorer are also now in black text rather than gray to show that you have a local copy and the Latest column says Yes.

> ## LOCAL FOLDER MAPPINGS AND THE 260-CHARACTER PATH LIMIT
>
> Note that on Windows-based systems, certain APIs only support a path length of 260 characters. Therefore, .NET imposes a path length restriction to local paths of 260 characters. This path limitation is carried into Team Foundation Server. When mapping files into your Local workspace you should generally try to map to a folder that is fairly close to the root of your drive or filesystem to give you a lot of spare characters to grow into. This is particularly important when programming in languages such as Java. On Windows, Visual Studio by default uses the C:\ Users\Username\Documents\Visual Studio 2012\Projects folder to store new projects, and it is tempting to map your Team Foundation Server projects in there. However, using a folder such as C:\Source at the root of your drive gives you another 40 or so characters from the 260-character path limit and also enables you to keep your working folder mappings simple.

Sharing Projects in Version Control

If you are sharing new code with your team using Team Foundation Server for the first time then you can import the associated source files into the repository in a number of ways. The process of sharing code in Team Foundation Server is called *checking in*.

Sharing a Solution in Visual Studio

To share a solution in Visual Studio, right-click the solution in Solution Explorer and select Add Solution to Source Control. If you are not already connected to a Team Foundation Server project collection you select the server and project collection that you want to connect to. Then you select the location in the central version control repository that you want to use for sharing your source code.

If you are sharing code into a new Team Project then a good practice is to create a folder called Main under your Team Project and share the solution into it as shown in Figure 3-5.

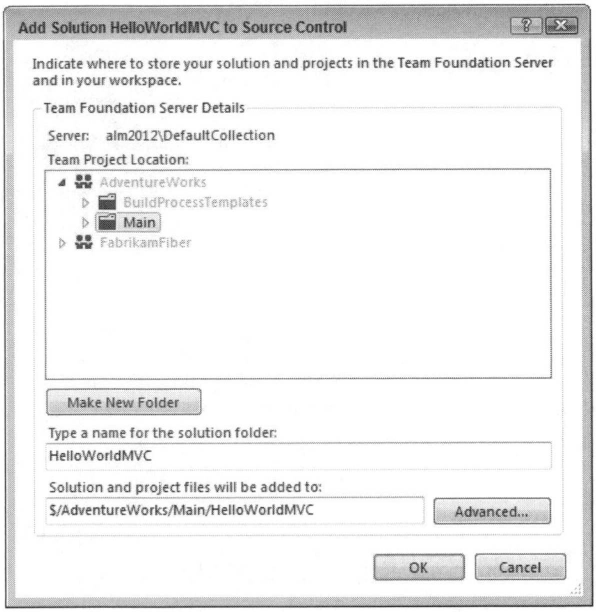

FIGURE 3-5

After you have set the location you want to use for sharing your files, click the OK button on the Add Solution to Source Control dialog window. The solution displays in Solution Explorer with a plus symbol to the left of it (see Figure 3-6). The plus sign indicates that the file is pending addition into version control.

This solution is not yet shared with Team Foundation Server. TFS Version Control works using a two-phased process. You first build up a list of changes that you want to make in version control and then you commit the changes in a single transaction called a *changeset*.

To check the files into version control, go to the Pending Changes page in Team Explorer by right-clicking on the solution in Solution Explorer and selecting Check In. Alternatively you can go to the Team Explorer view and then select the Pending Changes page. A third alternative is to go to View ⇨ Other Windows ⇨ Pending Changes.

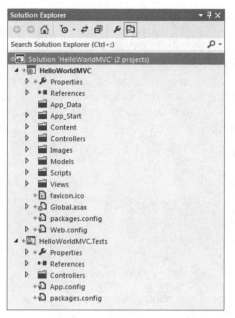

FIGURE 3-6

The next section reviews the pending changes page. You commit your changes from there.

Sharing a Project in Eclipse

Microsoft provides an Eclipse plug-in as part of Team Explorer Everywhere. After you have the TFS Plug-in for Eclipse installed, you may share a project in Eclipse easily. Right-click the project in Package Explorer and select Team ⇨ Share Project. The Share Project Wizard shows the installed team providers in your Eclipse instance (see Figure 3-7).

FIGURE 3-7

Select Team Foundation Server and then choose the project collection that you want to connect to (if you have not already connected) and then select the desired TFS workspace. (You can also press Next to select the default TFS workspace, which is usually correct.) The Share Location page of the Share Project Wizard displays as shown in Figure 3-8. From here you select a path in version control to share the files. As previously discussed you want to add your files into a folder called `Main`, so you simply enter the full server path into the Project folder path text box that you want to share at. As mentioned earlier in the chapter, it does not matter that the `Main` folder does not exist yet; it is automatically created on the server when you perform the check-in.

FIGURE 3-8

Pressing Finish creates pending ads for all the files in the project into version control. The file icons are annotated in the Package Explorer with a small check mark to indicate that they are pending adds to version control (see Figure 3-9). Note, just as with Visual Studio, these files are not yet stored on the server; you must first check them in. To get the pending changes view in Eclipse, go to Windows ⇨ Show View ⇨ Other Windows ⇨ Team Foundation Server ⇨ Team Explorer and click the Pending Changes page.

In the next section, you find out how to work with the pending changes view to check in code to the source repository. You also find out about changesets and how to configure team check-in policies.

FIGURE 3-9

CHECK-IN PENDING CHANGES

Frequent check-ins and gets are an essential part of a developer's workflow. You need to check-in the code so that it is shared with the rest of your team, and you need to frequently *Get Latest* so that you are developing and testing against the very latest version of the source code that makes up your application.

When making changes in your Local workspaces, Team Foundation Server maintains a list of the files that are being changed and their change types (that is, add, edit, rename, delete) in the pending changes window.

This is one area where the experience in Team Foundation Server 2012 is very different from previous versions. Rather than have another view active in Visual Studio or Eclipse, Microsoft moved the pending changes experience into Team Explorer (see Figure 3-10) to allow more space in the development environment for the code editing window. The pending changes experience was also changed from a horizontal view to a vertical one as part of the move to the new Team Explorer. This was reflective of the fact that most developers now use monitors with a widescreen aspect ratio, so space to the sides of the code being edited is usually available.

Checking In an Item

A *changeset* contains all of the information related to a check-in, such as work item links, file revisions, notes, policies, and owner and date/time details. Team Foundation version control bundles all the information into this logical container. A changeset is created after you check code into the repository, and, as a container, it reflects only the changes you checked in. You can also view it as the state of the repository at a particular moment in time of the repository. The usefulness of a changeset comes from the fact that you can, on a very atomic level, return to any moment of change and troubleshoot your code.

> **NOTE** *Team Foundation Server contains four main types of artifacts related to source code: work items, changesets, source code files, and builds. For example, you can associate a work item to a source code file. You can also link builds to work items if you want. This is a really powerful concept. Imagine that you are having trouble with a build. You can automatically call up the changeset with the problem code. You can also generate a work item to get a developer to fix the problem. The integration possibilities are endless.*

The Pending Changes page, shown in Figure 3-10, enables you to view all of the files in your workspace that Team Foundation Server considers changed from the latest version that you copied into your workspace from the server. You can access this list at any time via Team Explorer or via the View ➪ Other Windows ➪ Pending Changes menu option.

The pending changes view shown in Figure 3-10 highlights most of the key areas. In addition to the areas shown, there is also a notification area at the top of the page that is used to inform you when you have successfully checked in changes, so that you know that they are stored on the server. It also gives you a quick reference to the changeset ID that was created.

At the top of the page you see any policy warnings that are currently being given. Check-in policies are covered later in this chapter, but in simple terms you can think of them as code that runs on the client to validate whether a check-in is valid.

Next there is an area to provide a comment. Best practice is that you should provide a short but meaningful comment with every check-in, ideally explaining why you made the changes you are making—not what you changed. To see what you changed, any authorized user can simply look at those changeset details and compare (or "diff" as it is sometimes called) the files inside the changeset. However, a changeset comment explaining why you changed those files is very useful to help others understand why things happened the way they did.

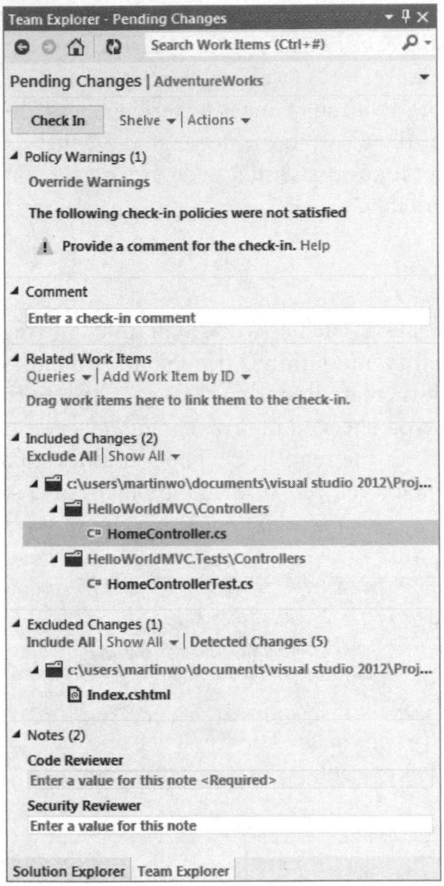

FIGURE 3-10

Files listed in the Included Changes section are the files that you want to make up your next changeset. These are the files that you are modifying, creating, or deleting as part of the change. For users of older versions of Team Foundation Server, this is equivalent to having a check in the box next to the file in the old Pending Changes view except that the inclusion or exclusion of a file in the pending changes list is now persisted so you no longer accidentally include a file that you thought you had excluded.

Files that are in the Excluded Changes section are those that you have positively modified as part of your changes but you have told Team Foundation Server that you do not want to check them in. Perhaps you have modified a `web.config` file to enable local debugging or you are still working on some changes and you do not want to check them in yet. If you find that you are frequently having files in the excluded changes window just because you haven't finished working with them then you should consider making use of the Shelvesets feature of Team Foundation Server, which is discussed in the "Shelving" section later in this chapter.

Finally, the Notes section lists the check-in notes that have been configured for the Team Project. Check-in notes are covered in the "Shelving" section later in this chapter. In simple terms check-in notes are additional string-based metadata that you can configure in your repository. The check-in notes can also optionally be specified with one or more of them to be mandatory (such as the Code Review example in Figure 3-10).

In the next section you find out how to associate work items with a particular check-in, which many teams find a good practice to ensure that every change is associated with a particular work item (either a bug or a task). As a result you can have end-to-end requirements traceability (from the initial story, requirement, or product backlog item through to the task to implement it, through to the check-in that provided that feature, and finally to the build in which the feature was included).

Candidate Changes

Before moving from the Pending Changes view, it is worth discussing Candidate Changes, which are a new feature unique to a Local Workspace in Team Foundation Server 2012.

Inside the Excluded Changes section there is a Detected Changes link. Clicking it shows any *Candidate Changes* that Team Foundation Server has detected (see Figure 3-11). If you have made changes in the filesystem, such as adding or deleting a file outside of Visual Studio, then these changes are not automatically pended by Team Foundation Server. They are flagged as changes that you might want to add into your pending changeset. The example shown in Figure 3-11 shows five candidate changes.

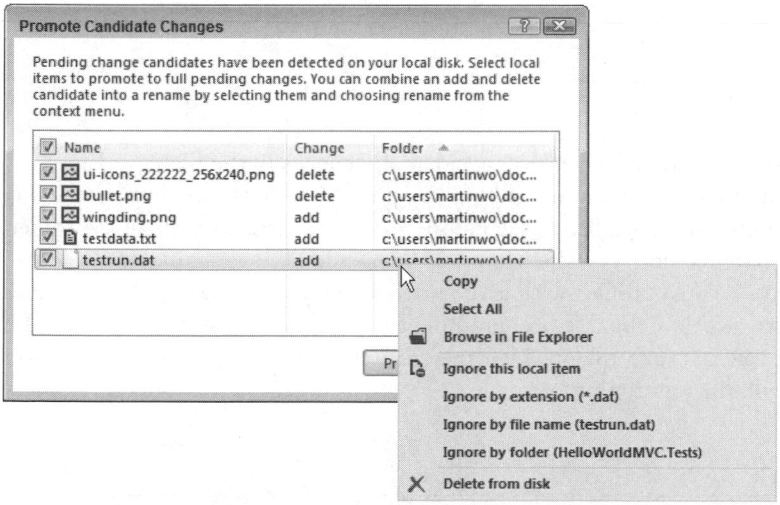

FIGURE 3-11

In this case, the `ui-icons` image file was deleted by the developer from Windows Explorer as she realized that the file was no longer needed in the website. The developer renamed `bullet.png` to `wingding.png` while she had no network connection to Team Foundation Server and was working offline. The developer added `testdata.txt` in Windows Explorer as a data file to be used during testing, but she did not specifically add it to the solution, which is why Visual Studio did not explicitly pend an add against it. And finally `testrun.dat` was automatically created in the source tree as part of a unit test run, and the developer wants to make sure that she and her colleagues never accidentally check in this file.

As the developer renamed the `bullet.png` file inside Windows Explorer, Team Foundation Server has no way to automatically detect that this was a rename operation. It sees the changes as an add and a delete. If the change had been made inside of Visual Studio from Source Control Explorer or Solution Explorer then the rename would have been automatically detected and pended as such, which would have preserved the history on the file under the new name. The developer would like to preserve that this was a rename operation and selects both `bullet.png` and `wingding.png` (by holding down Ctrl while making the selection) and then selects the Promote as Rename option as shown in Figure 3-12. This creates a new pending change on `wingding.png` specifying that it was renamed from `bullet.png`.

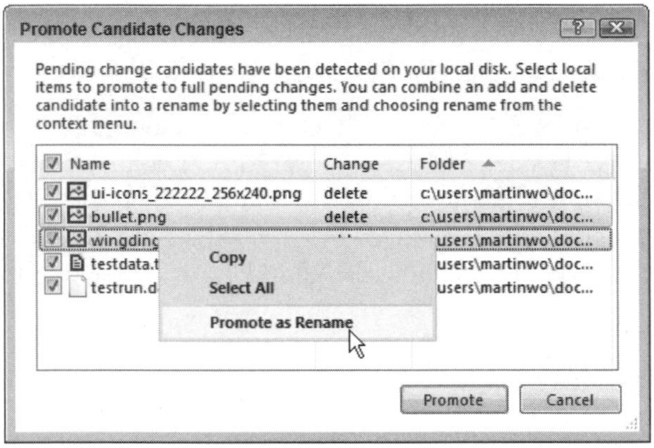

FIGURE 3-12

Next the developer wants to ensure that no one ever accidentally checks in the file `testrun.dat` as this is generated as part of a unit test run and doesn't make up the code of the application. She right-clicks the file and selects Ignore This Local Item (see Figure 3.11). This creates a file in the folder called `.tfIgnore` that tells TFS to ignore this file from ever being added to version control. Note that the developer could have ignored all files with a `.dat` extension, or files called `testrun.dat` regardless of where they appear below the folder containing the `.tfIgnore` file. She even could have ignored the whole `HellWorldMVC.Tests` folder. After the `.tfIgnore` file is checked in to version control, other developers will also ignore that file.

.TFIGNORE SYNTAX

The `.tfIgnore` file has a rich syntax of patterns that can be supported when ignoring files from version control. When a `.tfIgnore` file is created by Team Foundation Server it is created with a set of comments detailing the syntax. Wildcards (such as `*` and `?`) are supported. For example a line containing `Test*.txt` would exclude any files in that directory or children of that directory matching the pattern. In addition prefixing a line with a "`!`" means that you are specifically including that pattern. For example `!\libs\*.dll` would positively include DLL files in the libs folder (perhaps because they are binary dependencies for your project) when DLL files are typically excluded from being added to version control.

The developer is left with two candidate changes (see Figure 3-13) that are both checked. She clicks the Promote button as she wants to make sure that those candidate changes are included in her next changeset.

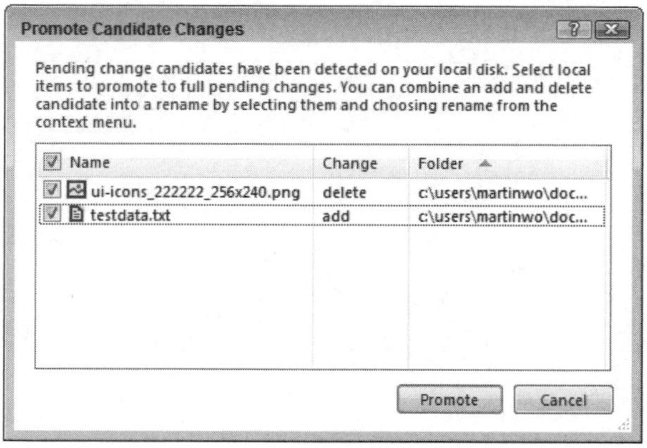

FIGURE 3-13

Performing the Check-in

Figure 3-14 shows that you now have the changes and how you want them recorded. There is a changeset comment, and a work item associated with the check-in will be marked as resolved when you perform the check-in. Click the Check In button and the changes are committed to TFS in a single atomic transaction and given a changeset ID.

Note that if TFS could not have performed the check-in for some reason (perhaps another developer had checked in a conflicting change to the `HomeController.cs` file while you were editing your version) then none of the changes would have been checked in. You would have been notified about the conflict and given options to resolve the conflict before you were allowed to complete the check-in. Only when all the files included in the changeset can be committed to the repository is the changeset created and given the next incremented changeset ID for that project collection.

Note that as well as checking in from the Pending Changes view, there are a number of other actions on the drop-down menus next to the Check In button. You can shelve or unshelve code, resolve conflicts, undo changes that have in the pending changeset with the version that you last got from the server, manage your version control workspaces, and, if you have an appropriate version of Visual Studio, you can request a code review.

> **NOTE** *For more information on Code Review see Chapter 17. For more information on managing conflicts see Chapter 4, which discusses conflict resolution in detail during the discussion on branching and merging.*

Creating and Administering Check-In Policies

Check-in policies provide a way for the team and individuals to effectively manage quality and workflow to the source management process used by the team. They are implemented as code that is run on the client before each check-in to validate if it is able to occur or not. Because the code is run on the client, check-in policies are configured separately for the .NET-based clients (such as Visual Studio, the Windows Shell Extensions, or the Team Foundation command line on Windows) and the Java-based clients provided by Team Explorer Everywhere (such as the TFS Plug-in for Eclipse or the cross-platform command-line client).

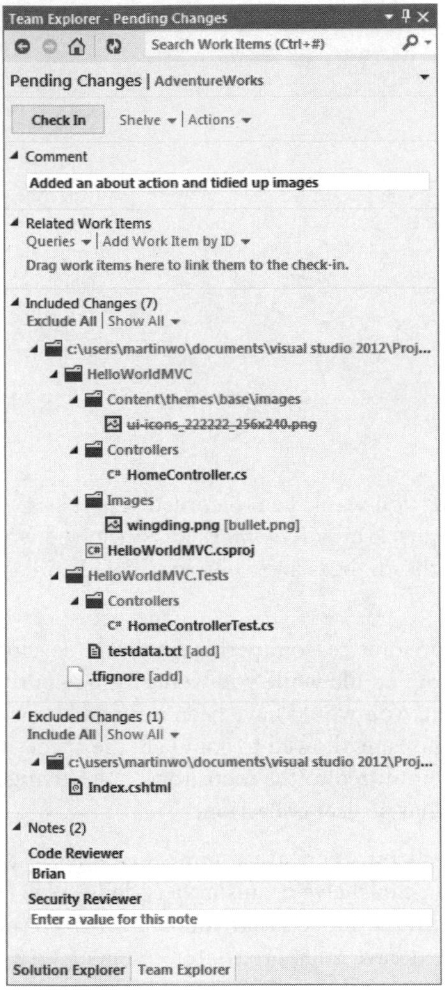

FIGURE 3-14

As a team project administrator, to configure the check-in policies for Visual Studio users, right-click your Team Foundation project and select Team Project Settings ➪ Source Control. Under the Check-in Policy tab (see Figure 3-15), you find several options for modifying the check-in policies.

If you click the Add button in the Source Control Settings dialog box (see Figure 3-15), you are prompted to select a check-in policy type. The list shown in Figure 3-15 are those provided out of the box in Visual Studio 2012 (note that the Changesets Comments policy is now in the box, but the Testing Policy is no longer shipped by default). More check-in policies are provided by the Team

Foundation Server power tools, and your administrator may have installed further custom check-in policies for your organization. Selecting each of the check-in policies provides more information about it.

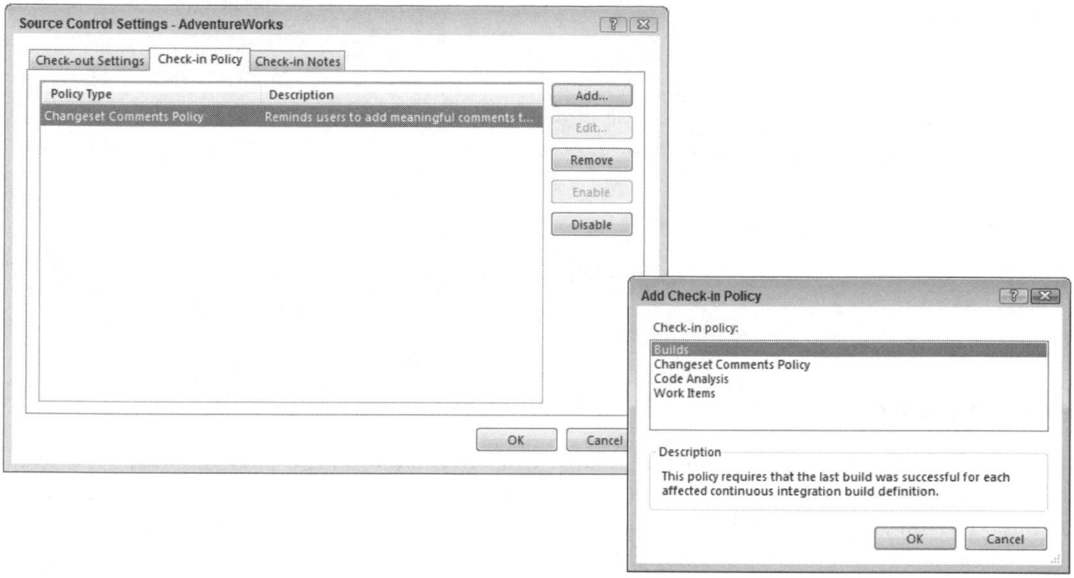

FIGURE 3-15

After the check-in policy has been created, try checking in code without complying with the new policies. The policy failure warning is displayed in the pending changes view as shown in Figure 3-10. Note that for a check-in policy failure warning you have the ability to override it and perform the check-in anyway.

> **NOTE** *You should override the check-in policy only when absolutely necessary; otherwise, it starts to negate the reason for introducing the policy in the first place. The check-in policy-overrides are reported into the data warehouse so that these can be acted on by the team; you can also configure alerts so that an email is sent out every time a check-in is performed with a policy override. If it is found that a particular check-in policy is frequently overridden then you might want to question why it is enabled in the first place. If a particular individual or group of individuals is found to be frequently overriding a check-in policy, then you may want to consult with them to help them understand the reason that the policy is in place.*

To set the check-in policies for your Team Explorer Everywhere users, a team project administrator should connect to the team project in Eclipse, view the Settings page in Team Explorer, select Check-In Policies, and then enable the desired check-in policies as provided by Team Explorer Everywhere, shown in Figure 3-16.

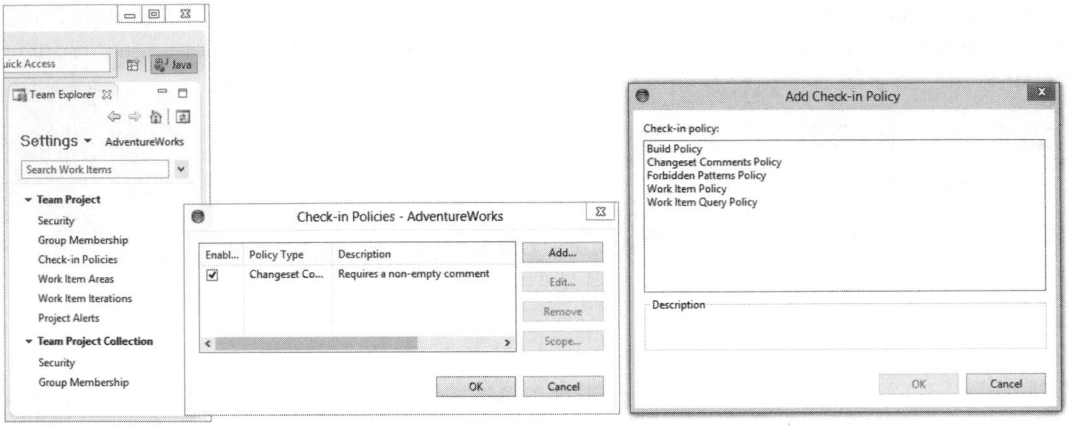

FIGURE 3-16

Viewing History

To view the history of a file or folder, in Source Control Explorer, right-click the file or folder and select View History from the context menu. The View History menu option is usually available via a context menu from many other places where the file is shown, such as when you right-click the file itself in the code editor, from Solution Explorer, in the Pending Changes view, and more. Viewing history on a file opens a new document tab, as shown in Figure 3-17.

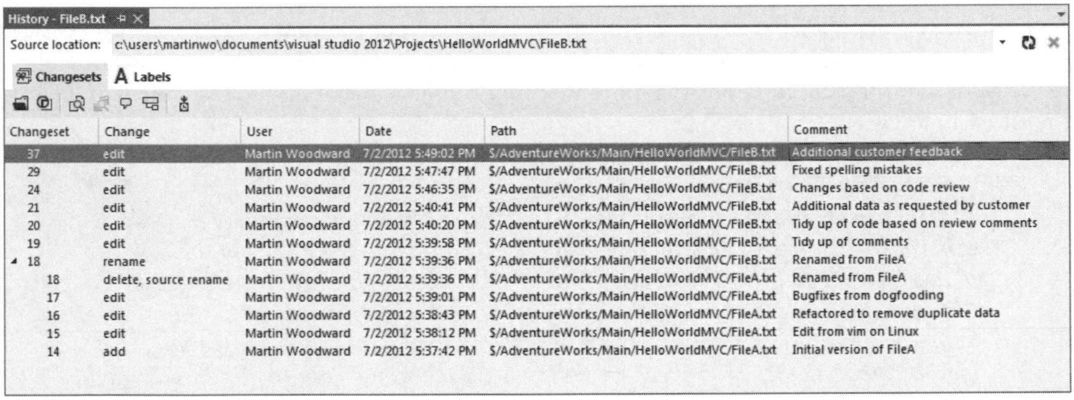

FIGURE 3-17

The History window is now a tabbed document window in Visual Studio and Eclipse. This enables you to open multiple History windows for research. Notice that the window in Visual Studio has two sub-tabs: Changesets and Labels. The History window now gives you a view of both the changesets associated with the file or folder, as well as any labels. Notice that the changeset ID's for a file are not sequential. The changeset ID's are incremented globally to represent a point in time of the entire repository for the project collection. The changeset IDs for the file show the changesets in which that file was modified. This is a different versioning mechanism to systems such as VSS in which individual files have version numbers; in Team Foundation Server the only version number that matters is the changeset ID.

You have several options from the Changeset sub-tab. You can select a changeset and click the View button to view the file version for that particular changeset. You can click the Changeset Details button to view the details for a particular changeset, including all the files that make up the changeset and any associated work items. You can compare two different versions of a file or folder to see the differences. Clicking the Annotate button enables you to see, line by line, who made what changes to a particular file. Selecting Rollback reverts all the changes made in that particular changeset. You are able to track the changeset across branches to see if those changes have made it into the other trees of your source code, you can also request a code review if you have an appropriate version of Visual Studio.

> **NOTE** *For more information on Code Review see Chapter 17. For more information on tracking changesets across branches see Chapter 4.*

Finally, you can select a changeset and click the Get This Version button. This replaces the current version of this file in your workspace with the selected version, enabling you to easily return to an earlier version of a file.

When viewing the history of a single file, the History window also enables you to expand the history of that file prior to a rename or a merge from another branch.

Labeling Files

A *label* is a marker or a tag that can be attached to files and folders in Team Foundation version control. This marker allows all the files and folders labeled together to be retrieved as one collective unit. Although labels are often generated by things like an automated build, in Team Foundation Server labels are editable by users with the appropriate security permissions. They are not designed to provide auditable points of reference, for that you should make note of the changeset ID as that represents an exact point in time of the source code repository.

To create a new label, in Source Control Explorer, right-click the file or folder you want to label, and select Apply Label from the context menu. The New Label window displays.

In this window, you can enter the label name and a comment. You can also select the version that you want to label. You can choose to label by Changeset, Date, Label, Latest Version, or Workspace Version. Click the Create button to create the label.

Notice next that the Create button is a drop-down arrow. Clicking the arrow provides you with two options. You can create the label as is, or you can create the label and then edit it. If you select Create and Edit, the label is created, and you are presented a new tab, as shown in Figure 3-18.

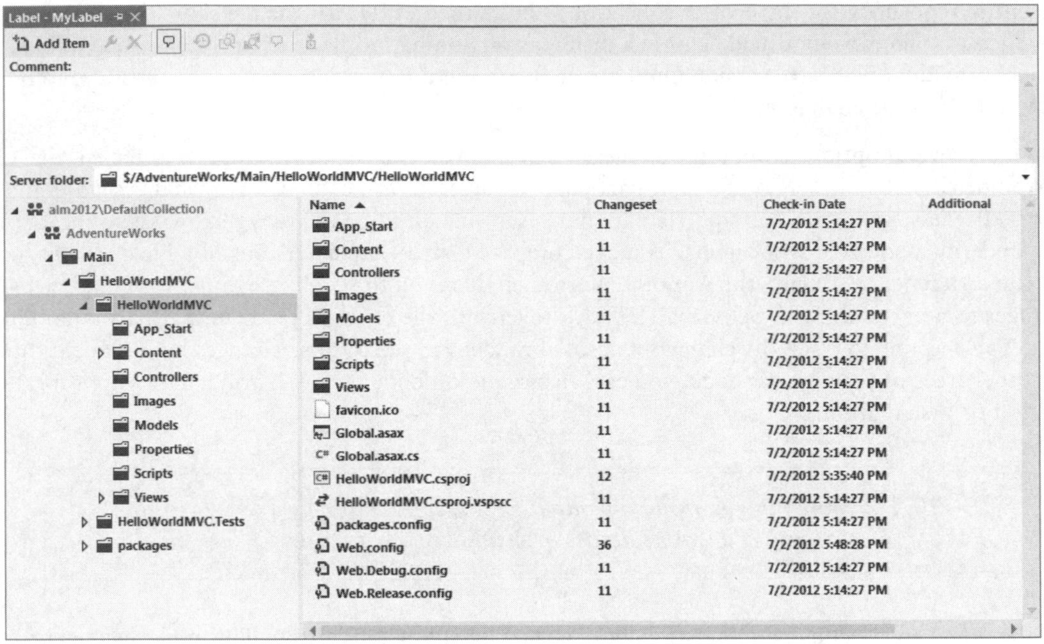

FIGURE 3-18

This tab enables you to make multiple changes to the label. You can add new files to the label. You can change the version of a file that the label is currently applied to. And you can remove files from the label. All of this is made easily accessible by using the Tree View control.

SHELVING

There are times when you won't be ready to commit your source code into the core repository. For example, maybe you need to go home for the evening but haven't been able to check-in and you want to make sure you have a back-up of your work. Or say that you are working on solving a bug and you want to share the changes you have made with a colleague to get his assistance on a particular issue. *Shelving* enables you to quickly and easily store files and code aside on the server without committing them to the main code base. The collections of stored pending changes that haven't been committed are called *shelvesets*.

> **WARNING** *The security settings for a shelveset are determined by the item permissions. You must have read- and pending change permission for the item changes you want to unshelve.*

The process of creating a shelveset is fast and easy. From the Pending Changes page in Team Explorer, click the Shelve link. Enter a name for your shelveset in the box that displays (see Figure 3-19) and the options to preserve the pending changes locally as well as to evaluate the check-in policies and check-in notes before shelving.

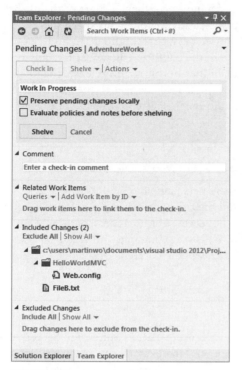

FIGURE 3-19

Shelvesets contain the same level of information as a changeset, including associated work items, comments, and check-in notes. Team Foundation Server is able to store other metadata alongside a shelveset as properties, which are used by the Code Review functionality detailed in Chapter 17. Keep in mind that, unlike with a changeset, the changes are not versioned. Shelvesets can be permanently deleted (which is something you can't do with changesets). You can't link directly to a shelveset from a work item and you can override the data stored in a shelveset at any time by creating a new one with the same name as one created previously by that user.

Unshelving source files is as easy as shelving them. First, bring up the Pending Changes page of Team Explorer and then from the Actions drop-down select Find Shelvesets. By default your own shelvesets are shown as in Figure 3-20, however you can also search for the shelvesets of a team member by entering her username or display name and pressing Enter.

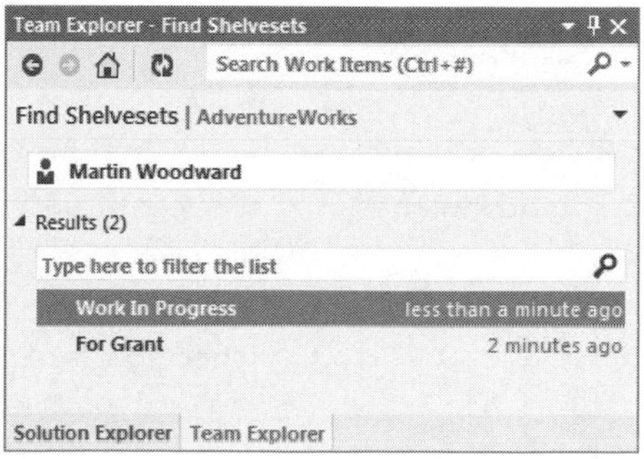

From the shelveset results you have the option to view the shelveset details, unshelve those changes into your

FIGURE 3-20

workspace, delete the shelveset completely from the server, or, in certain versions of Visual Studio, request a code review on the contents of the shelveset.

A new feature in Team Foundation Server 2012 detects and handles conflicts as part of the unshelve process. In previous versions if you had a conflicting change already in your workspace then you would not be able to unshelve the contents of the shelveset. In Visual Studio 2012 and Team Explorer Everywhere 2012, unshelving conflicts are shown in the conflicts editor just like any other merge conflict. In addition, due to the new automerge capabilities in this recent release, the likelihood of getting a conflict on unshelve is much lower (for example two changes to the same file in different places would be automatically merged when you did the unshelve and would not result in a conflict).

> **KEEP YOUR SHELVE(SET)S TIDY**
>
> Although it is easy to filter shelvesets in the Find Shelvesets page, having lots of old and out-of-date shelvesets can make it harder to find the code you are looking for. They also take up a small amount of resources on the server (as the server has to store a copy of every file in the shelveset). Therefore, it is good practice to delete a shelveset when you no longer need it, just as you tidy away the contents of shelves at home from time to time.

Workspaces

As discussed earlier, the majority of this chapter has dealt with using Team Foundation Server version control via a Local Workspace, which is the default option. However, this is a new a different workspace type than was available previously with Team Foundation Server. Table 3-1 describes the two workspace types, how they differ, how your usage of TFS version control changes, and when you would select one workspace type over another.

TABLE 3-1: Local and Server Workspaces Compared

TYPE	LOCAL	SERVER
Description	Files are read-write locally on Get, no explicit check-out operation required, workspace data stored on the local machine in a `$tf` folder at the root of the workspace.	Files are read-only locally on Get, explicit check-out operation is required, workspace data stored on the server.
Advantages	Easier to work with files outside of Visual Studio or Eclipse. Offline working much improved as no explicit check-out is required and developers can work with files without needing a connection to server.	Scales to huge (multi-gigabyte) workspace sizes.

continues

TABLE 3-1 *(continued)*

TYPE	LOCAL	SERVER
Advantages	Only files that are different from the original workspace version are shown in the Pending Changes view. More familiar to users of version control systems such as Subversion.	Optionally allows the ability to specify exclusive check-outs (i.e. only one person can work on a file at the same time). Enables optionally setting Visual Studio to automatically get the latest version of a file before a check-out is performed. Notifications presented if you begin editing a file that is currently checked out by another user. More familiar to users of version control systems such as VSS.
Disadvantages	Performance of local workspaces degrades the more files in the workspace and the speed of the hard drive also has an important influence. Not recommended for workspaces > 100,000 files on a regular 7200rpm hard drive.	Requires the server to be informed of all changes to the local filesystem including deletes, edits, and so on.

Note that a Team Project Collection administrator can define which workspace type is the default for projects within that collection by using Team ⇨ Team Project Collection Settings ⇨ Source Control and selecting the Workspace Settings tab as shown in Figure 3-21. In addition the server administrator is able to enable asynchronous checkouts for Server workspaces where an explicit check-out operation is required. Checking the option enables Visual Studio to check out the file automatically in the background without blocking the user because enabling that feature disables features that may prevent that check-out from succeeding.

A user can convert his Local workspace to a Server workspace or vice-versa simply from the Manage Workspaces dialog by going to File ⇨ Source Control ⇨ Workspaces. Select the workspace and press Edit to get to the Edit Workspace dialog and press the >> Advanced button to see all the properties as shown in Figure 3-22.

To convert between a Local and a Server workspace, change the drop-down for the Location property.

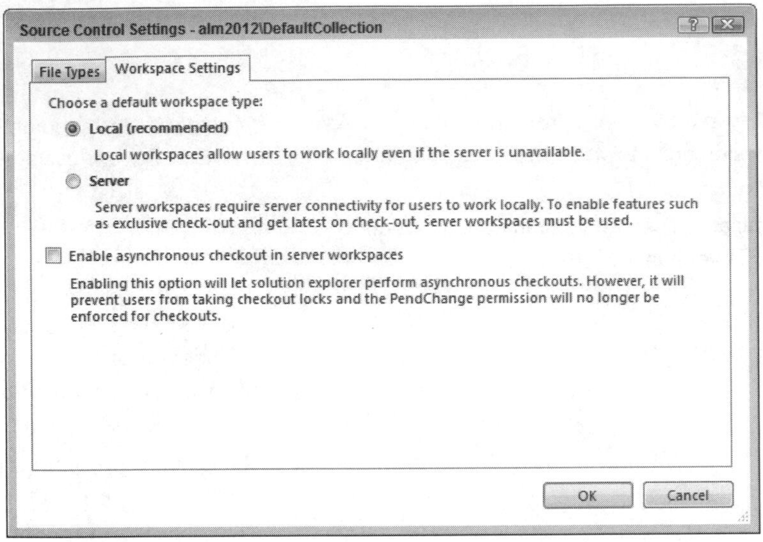

FIGURE 3-21

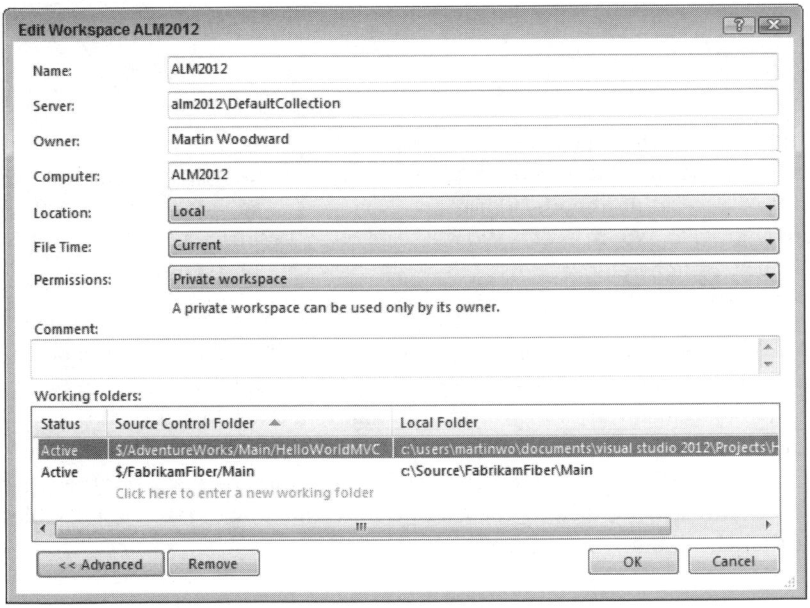

FIGURE 3-22

There are other advanced options worth noting at this point. As introduced in Team Foundation Server 2010, a user can adjust the permissions on the workspace. Table 3-2 shows the different permission features available.

TABLE 3-2: Table 3-2: Permission Features

PERMISSION	DESCRIPTION
Private workspace	A private workspace can be used only by its owner.
Public workspace (limited)	A limited public workspace can be used by any valid user, but only the workspace owner can check in or administer the workspace.
Public workspace	A fully public workspace can be used, checked in, and administered by any valid user.

Public workspaces make it easier for teams to collaborate when sharing a single machine. One specific example would be merging bug fixes into a mainline branch. By utilizing a public workspace, multiple team members can work together on a common machine to resolve merge conflicts, thereby making the merge process run faster and smoother.

A new setting in Team Foundation Server 2012, however, is the File Time setting. In previous versions of TFS the timestamp of the file in the local filesystem is the time at which that file was downloaded to the local machine (that is, the last time a get was performed on it that involved a modification to the file). If desired, you can set the File Time option to Check In, which means that the timestamp of the file in the local filesystem is that at which the file was originally checked in to Team Foundation Server. This makes it easier to work with certain legacy tools or build/deployment processes that rely on the file modification date to determine if an action should be performed on it.

Server Workspaces

In a Server Workspace, when a Get is performed to download the file to the local filesystem the server tracks which version of the file is on the local machine and the file is set to read-only. This way the server is aware of exactly which file versions you have locally. Consequently, when you tell the server you would like to Get Latest, the server can simply send you the latest versions of all the files that you don't have yet because it is aware of exactly what you have. When you want to edit the file you must perform an explicit check-out operation (however, this is frequently automated for you by the IDE integration in Visual Studio or Eclipse). If you are able to check out the file (that is, nobody has an exclusive lock of the file) then the file is set to read-write in the local filesystem, and you may perform edits.

Files are listed in your Pending Changes view the moment that they are checked out. For example, if you start to edit a file in Visual Studio, undo your changes, and save the file again then it is still shown with an edit pending. However, if you check in a file that has not been modified then the server removes it from the changeset before it is committed.

Because an explicit check-out operation is performed, the server can notify users (via the console window) if they are editing a file that another user has also checked out. This allows for early collaboration between developers when they discover they are working on the same file.

However, the user must inform the server about any operation they are performing to their local files. If the server is not aware that a local file has been modified or deleted (for example if that was done outside of Visual Studio) then it does not know to re-send that file when a Get Latest is performed. This is the most frequent source of the complaint with older versions of Team Foundation Server, that sometimes "get didn't get" when the user was expecting it to. The requirement to force a check-out before edit also made it harder for the user to work with tools outside of the source code management environment.

In addition, as the server needs to be informed explicitly before a file is edited, a Server workspace works best when there is a permanent online connection to the server. The offline behavior of server workspaces has been improved with each version of TFS and has been improved further still in the latest release. (For example, many of the tool windows now work asynchronously so that they do not lock up the user experience. If they suddenly find that they are waiting a long time for a server call to return when unknown to the UI, it is because the network connection to the server has been terminated.) However, server workspaces, by design, work best when an online connection is available so the experience for frequently disconnected users is not good.

Local Workspaces

With a Local workspace, the metadata about the versions of files in the workspace are stored in a hidden folder at the root of the workspace called $tf on Windows filesystems or .tf on Unix filesystems. This allows for edit, add, rename, delete, undo, and some compare operations to be carried out locally without any communication with a server. The $tf folder contains a copy of the last version of the file that was downloaded into the workspace along with some additional metadata. This allows for edits to be performed on the local filesystem without requiring an explicit check-out operation to the server, meaning that the files in the Local workspace can be read/write on Get.

Making the files read/write on Get dramatically reduces the friction when editing with other tools outside the source code management environment (such as Notepad on Windows or Xcode on the Mac). The lack of an explicit check-out operation also means that working offline is much improved.

Another advantage of Local workspaces is that as changes are detected by the disk scanner, it is easy to determine when you have deleted files on disk and so performing a get on those files allows them to be downloaded again. In addition, a file is only shown as pending edit (that is, checked out) when the contents of it are different than the last version downloaded from the server. Therefore, if you edit a file, save it, and then undo the changes and save it, the file does not show in the Pending Changes list as there are no changes to submit.

However, to enable all these great features, the workspace contents have to be scanned and compared with the last copy downloaded into the workspace. Therefore, the larger the number of files in the workspace, the slower this disk-scan operation can become. That said, modern computers and hard disks are very fast, and users with fewer than 100,000 files in their workspaces should not notice much of a slowdown. Even when they do, it is a linear reduction in performance. The number of files in the Local workspace before a slowdown becomes a problem is increased using faster 10K hard drives or is improved even more when using SSD devices and so on.

Because of the reduced friction to developers in using Local workspaces, they are the default option out the box with Team Foundation Server 2012. However, some organizations, especially those requiring a high degree of control, may value the features provided by Server workspaces, in which case the default can be defined as the default using the dialog shown in Figure 3-21.

COMMAND-LINE TOOLS

You can manipulate any part of the version control system using the Team Foundation command-line tool. The tool itself is called `tf.exe` (short for Team Foundation) and is installed with Visual Studio. For Unix-based systems (such as Mac OS X, Linux, Solaris, and so on) a cross-platform command-line client (simply `tf`) is available as part of Team Explorer Everywhere, which is a free download.

For example, to create a new workspace, simply type the following command:

```
> tf workspace -new MobileExplorerProject -collection:http://tfsServer:8080/tfs/
    YourProjectCollection
```

In the preceding example, a new workspace is created, called `MobileExplorerProject`. You can exercise a great deal of control over the version control system using the tool. For example, you can manipulate workspaces, add working folders, set permissions, view changesets, labels, and much more. The command-line tool has the most functionality available of all the version control clients for Team Foundation Server. Features are exposed via the command line that are not available from the user interface (UI) in Visual Studio or Eclipse.

You can also use the command-line tool to view the changes in your workspace by simply typing the following inside the workspace:

```
> tf status
```

To view a list of all possible commands using the command-line tool, run the following command:

```
> tf help
```

To get more help on a particular command, such as `checkin` simply type:

```
> tf help checkin
```

This provides a list of all options, along with some additional help information. You can also refer to the MSDN online documentation for more information.

SUMMARY

In this chapter, you examined the core features of Team Foundation version control and how to use it for day-to-day development.

You found out how to use the Source Control Explorer and how to check in code, showing you the concepts of workspaces, changesets, and shelvesets. You learned how to view the history of files and apply labels. The chapter also covered advanced concepts, such as workspaces and the differences between Local and Server workspaces.

Version control is the most important tool you can use to help you manage your development process by providing an effective way of organizing your source code. In Chapter 4, you learn some branching and merging, some best practices, and how to configure Team Foundation Server to implement those strategies. Part IV of this book talks more about software development in general and provides guidance about how to make sure the code that you are checking in is good code.

4

Branching and Merging

WHAT'S IN THIS CHAPTER?

➤ Understanding branching terminology and concepts

➤ Getting to know common branching strategies

➤ Using the branching and merging tools

The use of branching in version control can open up a whole world of possibilities for improving development productivity through parallelization. Yet, for many developers, branching and merging is slightly scary and full of uncertainty. Because of a lack of good tooling in the past, many developers still shy away from making use of branching and merging despite the good support in Team Foundation Server. At the other extreme, some people — who see the great branch and merge functionality now available — can go a little crazy with their newly found power. Overuse of branches can affect developer productivity and reduce the maintainability of their repository as a result.

No matter which side of the spectrum you find yourself on, this chapter explains the fundamental principles behind the important branching and merging strategies and provides some key guiding principles to help you apply them to your organization's needs. This chapter highlights the branching and merging tooling available with Team Foundation Server 2012, and then concludes by walking you through the application of this tooling with some example scenarios.

BRANCHING DEMYSTIFIED

There are lots of terms and concepts peculiar to the world of branching and merging. The following sections provide some definitions and context for those basic terms and concepts.

Branch

A *branch* is a copy of a set of files in a different part of the repository that allows two or more teams of people to work on the same part of a project in parallel. In Team Foundation Server 2012 branching is a lightweight server-side operation; when you perform the branch, it doesn't actually create new copies of all those files on the server. It just creates a record pointing to them and does not take up any significant extra storage — one of the reasons why creating a new branch containing thousands or even millions of files can be done quickly.

Merge

A *merge* is the process of taking code in two branches and combining it back into one codebase. For example, if you have two teams of developers working on two branches, and you want to bring the changes together, then you merge them. If the changes consist simply of edits to different files in the branches, then the merge is simple — but it can get more complicated, depending on what was edited in both branches.

For example, if the same line of the same file has been edited in both branches, the person performing the merge must make a decision as to which change should take precedence. In some circumstances, this results in a *hybrid merge*, where the combination of the *intent* behind the two changes requires a different result than simply the *text* in those versions being combined. When you branch, Team Foundation Server keeps track of the relationship between branches, as shown in Figure 4-1.

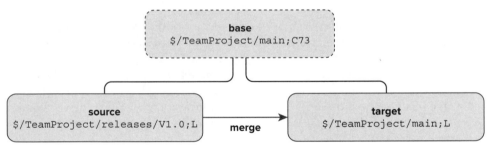

FIGURE 4-1

The branch containing the changes that you want to merge is called the *source branch*. The branch that you want to push the changes into is the *target branch*. The common ancestor, that is to say the changeset which indicates the version from which these branches are derived, is called the *base version*. When you merge, you can select a range of changes in the source branch to merge into the target branch.

Conflict

If the same file has been edited in both the source and target branches, Team Foundation Server will flag this as a *conflict*. For certain changes (such as a file that was edited in two different places), Team Foundation Server can make a good guess about what should happen (that is, you want to see a file containing the changes from both places). This is called an *automerge*. In Team Foundation

Server 2012 there have been significant improvements to the abilities of the automerge capabilities and the occasions in which they are available. A best practice is to let the tool perform an automerge, but you should then validate the merge results afterward to ensure the correct intent of the two changes has occurred. For example, if two different bugs were fixed, you probably want both changes. However, if the two changes were just fixing the same bug in two different ways, perhaps a different solution is in order. In most cases, where the development team has good communication, the changes are a result of different changes being made to the file. Automerge usually does a great job of merging them together, making it easy for the developer to simply validate the changes.

There can also be many cases where the actual outcome is unclear, so automerging is not available. For example, if you deleted the file in one branch and edited it in another, do you want to keep the file with the changes or have it removed? The person performing the merge is responsible for deciding the correct *conflict resolution* based on an understanding of the code, and communicating with the team members who made the conflicting changes to understand their intent.

As with life in general, conflict is never good in version control. Making the decision about the correct conflict resolution in version control can be a complex and time-consuming process. Therefore, it is best to adopt a branching strategy that minimizes the likelihood of conflicts occurring. However, conflicts will occur, and Team Foundation Server provides the tooling to deal with them, so conflicts should not be feared.

Branch Relationships

When you branch a folder, the relationships between those branches form a standard hierarchical relationship. The source of the branch is the *parent*, and the target of the branch is the *child*, as shown in Figure 4-2. Children who have the same parent are called *sibling branches*.

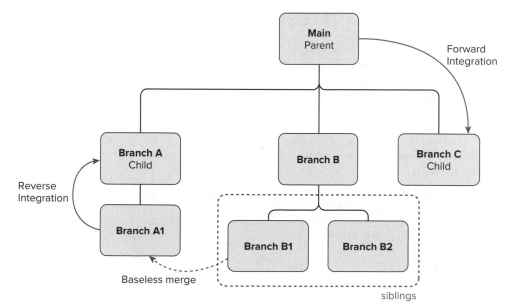

FIGURE 4-2

Baseless Merge

A *baseless merge* is a merging of two arbitrary branches in version control without reference to a base version. This is sometimes necessary if the source code was originally imported in a flat structure without the branch relationship being in place, or if you want to merge between one branch and another branch that is not a direct parent or child (for example, `Branch A1` and `Branch B1` in Figure 4-2).

Because no base version is being used to compare against, the probability of the server detecting conflicts occurring between the two branches is much higher. For example, if a file is renamed in one branch and edited in the other, it shows up as a file delete conflicting with the file edit, and then a file add that gives no hint as to which file it is related to, or that there is an edit intended for this file in the other branch. For this reason, baseless merges are discouraged and your branching model should attempt to constrain most merges between parent and child branches to minimize the amount of baseless merging required.

Forward/Reverse Integration

Forward integration (FI) occurs when you merge code from a parent branch to the child branch. *Reverse integration* (RI) occurs when you merge code from a child branch up to the parent branch. The terms FI and RI can often shoot around quite freely during a branching debate, so it is important to understand what they mean. If you are doing feature development in branches, it is common to use FI at various points during the feature development cycle, and then to use RI at the end. See the "Feature Branching" section later in this chapter for more information.

COMMON BRANCHING STRATEGIES

Depending on the organization of your team, and the software that you need to develop, there are numerous branching strategies that you can adopt, all with various pros and cons. However, just as every strategy in chess is made up of simple moves, every branching strategy uses one or more combinations of some basic techniques. This section details some of the basic techniques, how they are used, and why.

When developing your own branching strategy, you should take into account the needs of your organization. In all likelihood, you may adopt a strategy that combines one or many of the basic techniques described here.

When looking at any strategy for branching and merging, you should keep in mind the following important rules:

> ➤ Prefer simplicity over control.

> ➤ Only branch when you really need to. (You can branch after the fact if you find you need to.)

> ➤ If you ever want to merge two branches together, keep the time between merges to a minimum.

> ➤ Ensure that your branch hierarchy matches the path you intend your merges to follow.

> **NOTE** *For additional guidance on branching and merging with Team Foundation Server, see the "Visual Studio TFS Branching Guide" project on CodePlex at* `http://tfsbranchingguideiii.codeplex.com/`. *This guidance is created by a community of Visual Studio ALM Rangers, and combines the knowledge of Microsoft people with Microsoft Most Valued Professionals (MVPs) and other technical specialists in the community. The guidance also includes hands-on labs, along with a set of diagrams that can be a useful starting point when creating your own branching plan.*

No Branching

mwtfs2012\DefaultCollection
AdventureWorks
BuildProcessTemplates
Main

FIGURE 4-3

It may be counterintuitive, but the simplest branching technique is to not branch at all. This should always be your default position. Do not branch unless you know you need to. Remember that you are using a version control tool that tracks changes over time. You can branch at any point in the future from any point in the past. This gives you the luxury of not having to create a branch "just in case" — only create branches when you know you need them.

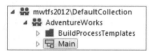

However, there are things you can do to prepare yourself to make branching easier in the future if you decide you need a branch.

Figure 4-3 illustrates the most important thing that you should do if you think you might possibly need to branch in the future. When you first create your team project in Team Foundation Server, create a folder called `Main` and check it in. Then, right-click the folder in Source Control Explorer and select Branching and Merging ➪ Convert to Branch to get to the screen shown in Figure 4-4.

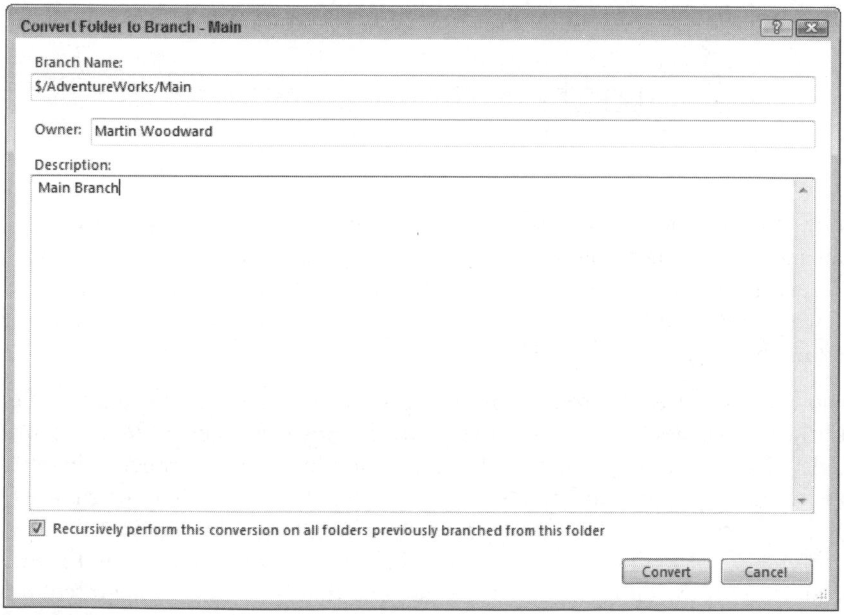

Convert Folder to Branch - Main
Branch Name:
$/AdventureWorks/Main
Owner:
Martin Woodward
Description:
Main Branch
Recursively perform this conversion on all folders previously branched from this folder
Convert
Cancel

FIGURE 4-4

With no branching, you only have one branch of code to work in for all teams. This technique works great when you have small teams working on the same codebase, developing features for the same version of the application, and only supporting one version of the application at a time. At some point, no matter how complex your branching strategy evolves to support your business needs, you need at least one stable area that is your *main* (or *mainline*) code. This is a stable version of the code that will be used for the build that you will create, test, and deploy.

However, during stabilization and test periods, while you are getting ready to release, it may be necessary for the team to not check in any new code into the codebase (that is, undergo a *code freeze*). With smaller teams working on a single version, this does not affect productivity because the people who would be checking in code are busy testing to ensure that the application works, as well as getting ready for deployment.

With this technique there is no way to start work on something new before the final build of the current version has been performed. The code freeze period can, therefore, be very disruptive because there is no way to start work on the next version until the current one has shipped. It's these times when other strategies become useful for teams of any size, even a team of one.

Branch per Release

After no branching, the second most common branching technique is *branch per release*. With this technique, the branches contain the code for a particular release version, as shown in Figure 4-5.

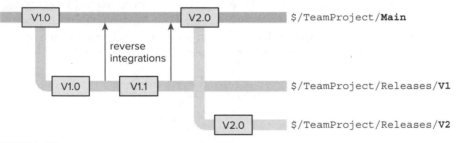

FIGURE 4-5

Development starts in the Main branch. After a period of time, when the software is considered ready, a branch is made to the V1 branch, and the final builds are performed from it. It is then released into production (with the code in the final production build getting a label to indicate which versions of which files were in that version). Meanwhile, development of new features for version 2 (V2) continues on the Main branch.

Let's say that some bugs are discovered in production that must be addressed, and a small change is necessary to reflect how the business needs something to work. However, the development group does not want to include all the work for V2 that has been going on in the Main branch. Therefore, these changes are made in the V1 branch, and builds are taken from it. Any bug fixes or changes that must also be included in the next version (to ensure the bug is still fixed in that next release) are merged back (that is, reverse-integrated) into the Main branch. If a bug fix was already in the Main branch, but needed to go into V1, then it might simply be merged (that is, forward-integrated) into it. At a certain point, the build is determined to be good, and a new V1.1 build is performed from the V1 branch and deployed to production.

During this time, development on the next version can continue uninterrupted without the risk of features being added into the code accidentally and making their way into the V1.X set of releases. At a certain point, let's say that it is decided that V2.0 is ready to go out the door, the mainline of code is branched again to the V2 branch, and the V2.0 build is created from it. Work can continue on the next release on the Main branch, but it is now easy to support and release new builds to customers running on any version that you want to keep supporting.

Branch per release is very easy to understand and allows many versions to be supported at a time. It can be extended to multiple supported releases very easily, and makes it trivial to view and compare the code that was included in a particular version of the application. Branch per release is well-suited to organizations that must support multiple versions of the code in parallel — such as a typical software vendor.

However, for a particular release, there is still no more parallelism of development than in a standard "no branching" strategy. Also, if the organization must only support two or three versions at a time (that is, the latest version, the previous version, and, perhaps, the version currently being tested by the business) then this model can lead to a number of stale branches. Although having lots of old, stale branches doesn't affect the performance of Team Foundation Server, or even cause any significant additional storage requirements, it can clutter the repository and make it difficult to find the versions you are interested in — especially if the organization releases new versions frequently. If this is the case, you may want to move old branches into an Archive folder, and only have the active branches (that is, the versions that the development team are currently supporting) in the Releases folder.

Code-Promotion Branching

An alternative to the branch per release technique is *code-promotion branching* (or *promotion-level branching*). This technique involves splitting the branches into different promotion levels, as shown in Figure 4-6.

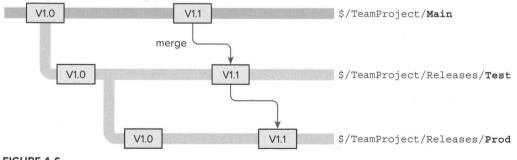

FIGURE 4-6

As before, development starts with just the Main branch. When the development team is ready to test the application with the business, it pushes the code to the Test branch (also often called the QA branch). While the code is being tested, work on the next development version is carried out in the Main branch. If any fixes are required during testing, they can be developed on the Test branch and merged back into the Main branch for inclusion in the next release. When the code is ready to release, it is branched again from Test to Prod. When the next release cycle comes along, the same is done again. Changes are merged from Main to Test and then Test to Prod.

Code-promotion branching works well in environments that have a single version running in production, but have long test-validation cycles that do not involve all of the development team. This allows development to continue on the next version in Main while test and stabilization of the build occurs in the Test branch. It also makes it trivial for the development team to look at the code currently on each system. Finally, the branch structure makes it easy to create an automated build and deployment system using Team Foundation Build that can automatically update the QA/Test environment as code is pushed to the QA branch.

> **NOTE** *For more information on the build capabilities of Team Foundation Server, see Chapter 5.*

Feature Branching

The previous branching strategies involve a single team working on the system in its entirety as they work toward a release. All features for that release are developed in parallel, and the build can only be deployed when all features in flight have been completed and tested. However, in large systems, or systems that require very frequent deployment (such as a large commercial website), *feature branching* (or *branch per feature*), as shown in Figure 4-7, can be useful.

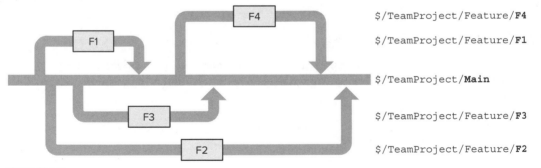

FIGURE 4-7

Feature branching is used when a project requires multiple teams to be working on the same codebase in parallel. In Figure 4-7, you see four feature teams working in separate branches (F1, F2, F3, and F4). Note that in a real branching structure, the feature branches themselves would likely have meaningful names such as FlightSelling, InsuranceExcess, or whatever shorthand is used by the project to refer to the feature under development. The Main branch is considered "gold code," which means that no active development goes on directly in this branch. However, a feature must be reverse-integrated into this branch for it to appear in the final release build and for other teams to pick it up.

Initially, F1 is started with a branch from Main. But, while F1 is being developed, second and third teams start F2 and F3, respectively. At the end of development of the feature, F1 is merged back into the Main branch, and the F1 branch is deleted. Then that team starts on feature F4. The next feature to finish is F3, followed by F2. At each point, after the feature is merged into the Main branch, a new version of the software is released to the public website, but only one version is ever supported at any time.

Feature branching allows for a large amount of parallel development. However, this comes at the cost of delaying the pain of integrating each team's changes together until the feature is complete and you are merging the feature branch back into Main branch. For example, in Figure 4-7, when merging the F2 branch, all changes and inevitable conflicts introduced by features F1, F2, F3, and F4 must be analyzed and resolved.

The longer a period of time that code is separated into branches, the more independent changes occur, and, therefore, the greater the likelihood of merge conflicts. To minimize conflicts, and to reduce the amount of *integration debt* building up, you should do the following:

➤ *Keep the life of a feature short* — The time taken to develop features should be as short as possible, and should be merged back into the Main branch as soon as possible.

➤ *Take integrations from the* Main *branch regularly* — In the example shown in Figure 4-7, when F1 is merged back into Main, the feature teams still working on their features should merge those changes into their feature branches at the earliest possible convenient point.

➤ *Organize features into discrete areas in the codebase* — Having the code related to a particular feature in one area will reduce the amount of common code that is being edited in multiple branches, and, therefore, reduce the risk of making conflicting changes during feature development. Often, the number of teams that can be working in parallel is defined by the number of discrete areas of code in the repository.

When using feature branching, the whole team doesn't necessarily have to be involved. For example, one or two developers might split off from the rest of the team to go work on a well-isolated feature when there is a risk of the move not being possible (that is, they are working on a proof of concept), or when it is decided that the current release should not wait for that particular feature to be implemented.

IMPLEMENTING BRANCHING STRATEGIES

So far, this chapter has covered a lot of the theory behind branching. This section puts that theory into action as it walks you through implementing a branching strategy using the branch tools available with Team Foundation Server 2012.

The Scenario

For this example, let's look at a fictional organization called Tailspin Toys that has installed Team Foundation Server and is using the version control functionality. Let's say that you are a member of the internal IT team which supports an order-fulfillment intranet site critical to the operation of the business. The team has only one version of the site in production at any one time. However, because of the criticality of the software, the IT team has lengthy test cycles involving a series of expert (but non-technical) users who come in from the business to ensure that the software is working as required.

The IT team has a single team project called IT and a single ASP.NET web application checked into the team project root folder at $/IT/Orders. They also have an automated build set up in Team Foundation Server.

The team has some issues when it comes to managing source. The development process is plagued by problems and inefficiencies. There are significant periods when developers are forbidden from checking in to the repository while getting ready for a release. The delays cause the developers to end up creating large shelvesets filled with changes that become unmanageable.

Occasionally, urgent bugs are required to be fixed in the production codebase. This is done by the developer getting the label that represents the production codebase, adding the fix, building it on a local machine, and manually pushing the modified files out to production. Ensuring that the correct files are pushed to production and that the source code fix is added back into version control is a manual process that has caused some problems. There have been instances where fixes to production were missing when the next version rolled out, and those fixes had to be repeated.

But, luckily, there are some people in the development organization who recognize the problems and want to come up with a branching plan to alleviate some of them. You have been selected to roll out this plan.

The Plan

After some careful consideration, the team decides that a code-promotion strategy fits their organization quite well. Figure 4-8 shows the plan that the organization has decided to adopt.

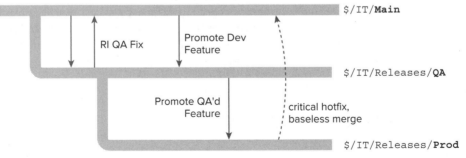

FIGURE 4-8

The code will consist of the following three branches, as suggested by the code-promotion branching strategy:

➤   Main — This is where the main development effort is conducted. This is the branch from which the regular continuous integration build is performed, and where new features are developed.

➤   QA — This is where the code will live while it is being tested by the business. Because these test periods can be very lengthy, new code development will carry on in the Main branch.

Any fixes or modifications to the version under test will be performed directly on the QA branch and reverse-integrated back into Main. An automated build will be created that will run early in the morning during the week. The results of that build will be pushed to the QA web server daily for testing by the business the following day.

➤ Prod — This represents the code that is currently running in production. Code normally goes from Main to QA and then into Prod. A build is also created for this branch so that urgent hotfixes can be checked in and repeatedly built. Urgent hotfixes like this are very much the exception, though. If an urgent hotfix is performed, a baseless merge is performed to push that fix back into Main. Note that the results of the Prod build are first deployed to a test environment to ensure that they work as expected before manually running a script that pushes the code to production.

Implementation

Figure 4-9 shows the current codebase.

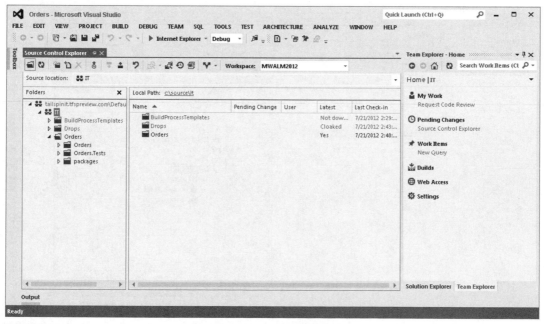

FIGURE 4-9

The first thing you want to do is to move the code currently at the root of the team project in version control into a Main branch. This is the most disruptive of the changes, because it requires the build to be reconfigured, and team members must re-sync their workspaces. So, you decide to do this late one night, a few weeks before the IT team is due to push a release to the test team.

To move the code into a branch, you right-click the `Orders` folder that contains the solution and select Move. Then you manually enter a path of **$/IT/Main/Orders** in the Move dialog shown in Figure 4-10. Note that the `Main` folder does not have to exist at this point. Check in the move by going to Pending Changes in Team Explorer and pressing Check In. This will then create the Main folder for the rest of the team and the Orders solution will be inside it.

FIGURE 4-10

As soon as this is done, you edit the build definition's workspace so that it only looks at the `Orders` Source Control Explorer folder under the `Main` folder, as shown in Figure 4-11.

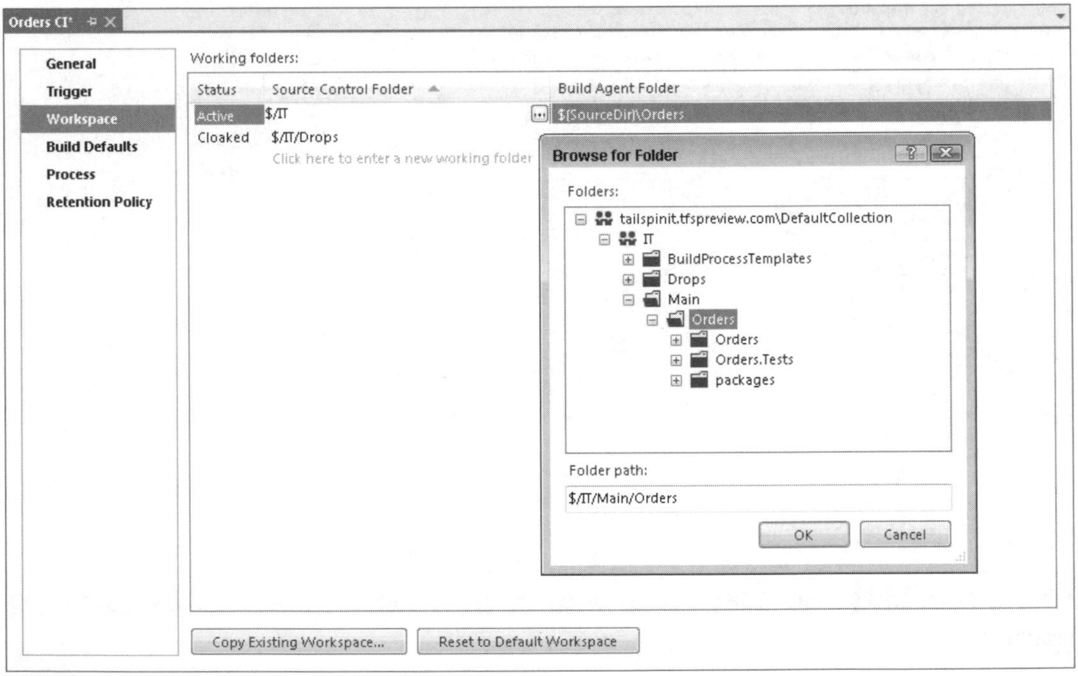

FIGURE 4-11

In this example, the build definition is set to copy build outputs to source control, and the build definition is set to point at the Team Project root (`$/IT`). Therefore, Visual Studio had automatically added the `Drops` folder as cloaked in the build workspace. This is so that file binary build outputs are not copied across to the build machine for each build. However, as you are now changing the build definition to be more specific by referencing a folder inside `Main`, you no longer need to have the `Drop` folder cloaked. You delete the mapping for it by right-clicking the `$/Drops` line shown in Figure 4-11 and selecting Delete.

> **NOTE** *The ability to drop files to version control is a new feature only available in the hosted Team Foundation Service and is discussed in more detail in Chapter 5. However, storing build drops in version control has some important implications to your branching behavior which we discuss in this chapter.*

As you are going to have multiple builds defined for the different branches, and you also want these results to be placed in version control, you edit the Staging Location in the Build Defaults to be `$/IT/Drops/Main` (see Figure 4-12). Then you move the existing build drops from the `$/IT/Drops/Orders CI` folder to the `$/IT/Drops/Main/Orders CI` folder in the same way that you performed the move in Figure 4-10. Note that you do not place the `Orders CI` build results directly into the `Main` folder that you moved the source code into but create a new folder called `Main` under `Drops`. This is because you do not want your build results included in the branches; they are kept separately at the root of the Team Project. See Figure 4-15 for the eventual folder layout that you are aiming for.

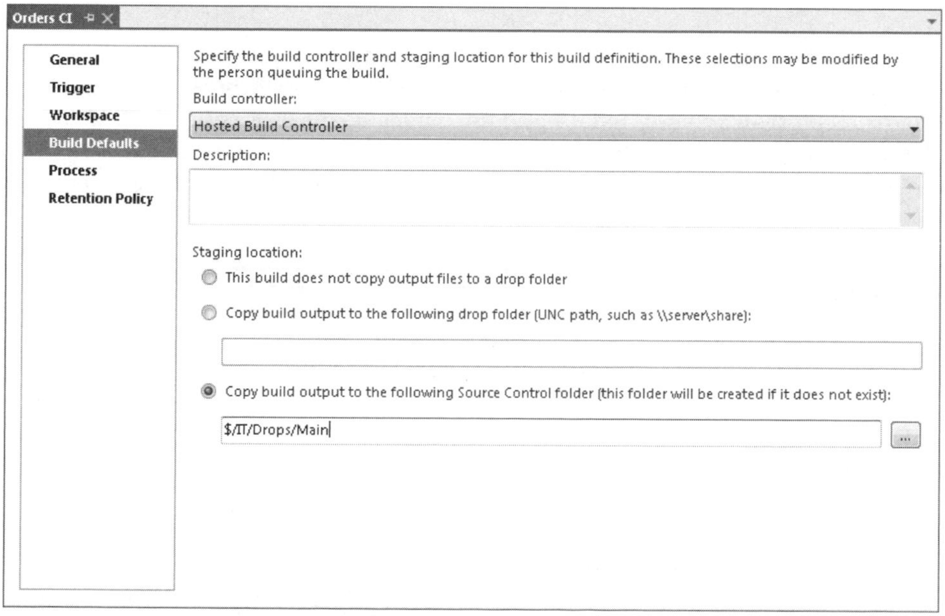

FIGURE 4-12

You also modify the process for the build to remove the solution file from the old location, and add it in again at the new location, as shown in Figure 4-13. You then manually queue a new build to ensure that everything is working well. Everything works, so you send an e-mail notifying the team of the change to version control, and you go home for the evening.

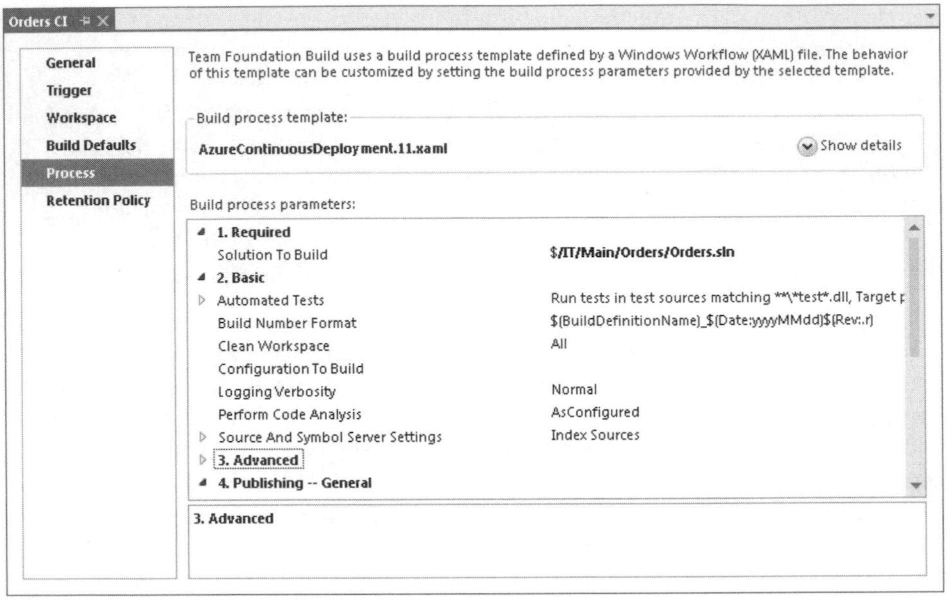

FIGURE 4-13

Now, as an aside, note that the source is in the correct path, but the `Main` folder is not yet a branch. In Team Foundation Server, branches are a first-class entity in version control. They are represented by a different icon than a folder, and have additional metadata such as Owner, Description, and Branch Relationships. To convert a folder to a branch, right-click the folder in Source Control Explorer and select Branching and Merging ⇨ Convert to Branch. This displays the Convert Folder to Branch dialog shown in Figure 4-14.

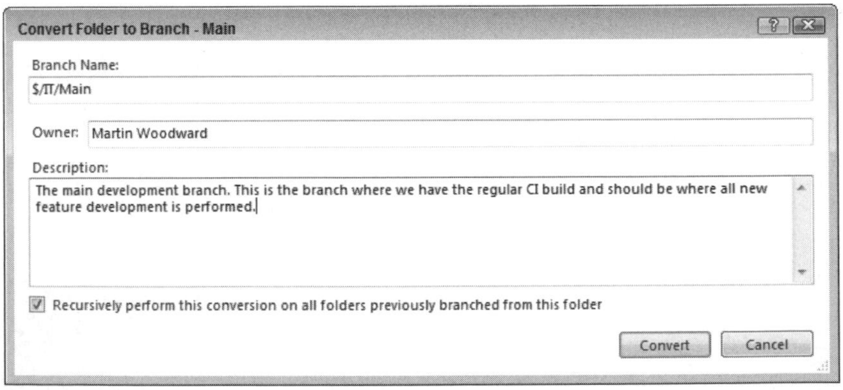

FIGURE 4-14

Note that to convert a folder to a branch, you must have the Manage Branch permission in Team Foundation Server. Also, after you have converted a folder to a branch, no folders above or below it may be a branch.

In the future if you need to convert a branch back to a regular folder, go to Visual Studio and select File ⇨ Source Control ⇨ Branching and Merging ⇨ Convert to Folder.

Now, let's get back to the example implementation. You come in the next morning and start to get the branches set up. You perform the Convert to Branch operation on Main as described previously, and the source tree is now as shown in Figure 4-15.

When the build is ready to be released to the QA team, instead of invoking the code freeze period that used to be enforced, you take the latest version of code and branch it to create the QA branch. You do this by right-clicking the Main branch and selecting Branching and Merging ⇨ Branch, which displays the Branch dialog for a branch (Figure 4-16).

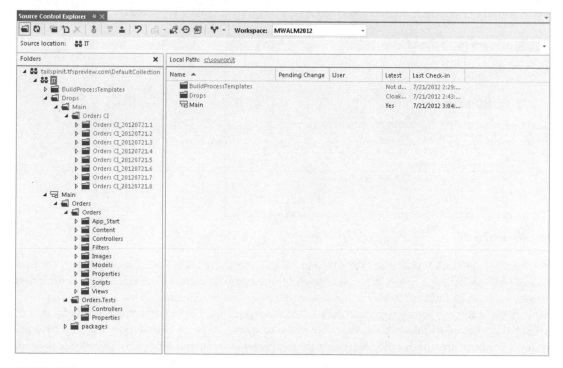

FIGURE 4-15

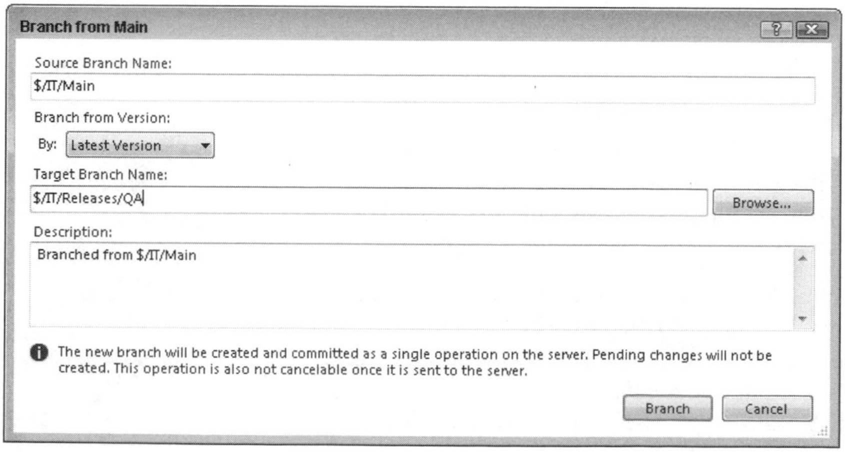

FIGURE 4-16

In this dialog, you enter the full path that you would like to create, which, in this example scenario, is **$/IT/Releases/QA**. If the `Releases` folder does not already exist, it is created automatically as part of this operation. When you press the Branch button there is a warning that the change will be committed to the repository as part of a single transaction; click Yes to continue.

This behavior is slightly different from that experienced when branching a folder or file. When you branch a folder or file in the Visual Studio or Eclipse clients, it is assumed that you are making a copy of the file in your local workspace as well. Figure 4-17 shows an example of the branch dialog when a folder is selected.

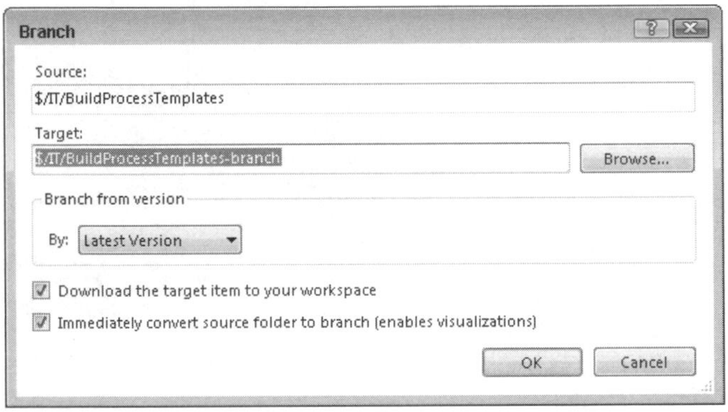

![Branch dialog showing Source: $/IT/BuildProcessTemplates, Target: $/IT/BuildProcessTemplates-branch with Browse button, Branch from version By: Latest Version dropdown, checkboxes for "Download the target item to your workspace" and "Immediately convert source folder to branch (enables visualizations)", and OK/Cancel buttons]

FIGURE 4-17

You also get the option to convert the folders to a full branch in Team Foundation Server — but you do not have to. This is a subtle point. Although branches are first-class objects in Team Foundation Server, you can branch any folder or file to another place in the repository. This is a great way to copy areas of the repository to a different part of the repository, but make the history of changes that occurred in the old location easily accessible in the new one. In Team Foundation Server, a rename is actually implemented under the covers as a simultaneous branch, and a delete of the source location.

In the instance of branching a file or folder, this is done as a two-phase operation. The branch changes are made in your workspace, and then you check these in.

However, in the vast majority of instances, you want to branch an entire branch in version control. Usually, you will not be making changes to the files or performing validation before check-in.

Performing these in a single atomic transaction is a much more efficient use of server resources. (This is functionally equivalent to the `tf branch` command line with the `/checkin` option supplied.) So, you have performed the branch as indicated in Figure 4-16 and the source tree is now as shown in Figure 4-18.

A new build definition (called `Orders QA`) is created for the `QA` branch, with a scheduled trigger of 6 a.m. Monday to Friday. That way, a fresh build is ready and waiting for the test team each morning if changes have been made to the `QA` branch during the day. The drop folder is set to be `$/Drops/QA`. A new QA build is triggered to make sure you have set everything up correctly.

FIGURE 4-18

> **NOTE** *Chapter 5 provides more information on creating build definitions, however there is also a* `tfpt builddefinition /clone` *command available in the power tools to help you create copies of a build definition after taking a branch in version control. See* `http://aka.ms/tfpt` *for more information*

Dealing with Changesets

During initial testing, someone notices that there is a small bug with the stylesheet on Internet Explorer 6 on Windows XP. None of the development team is running this configuration, but it is still used inside the company's network, so the team decides to create a fix for it.

The modification is made to the `Site.css` file in the `QA` branch and checked in as changeset `48`. The next scheduled build (`Orders QA_20120721.2`) picks up this change and adds it to the code running in the test environment. When the fix has been verified, the fix must be merged into the `Main` branch.

For merges like this, it is best if the merge is performed as soon as possible by the developer that made the change. That way, it is fresh in his or her mind, so the fix isn't misunderstood or forgotten about. The testing team has set a policy that the related bug cannot move to the Closed state until an urgent fix has been merged into the `Main` branch — which is a sensible policy.

To merge that code, the developer right-clicks the source branch in Source Control Explorer (in this case, the `QA` branch) and selects Branching and Merging ➪ Merge. The Merge Wizard dialog displays, as shown in Figure 4-19.

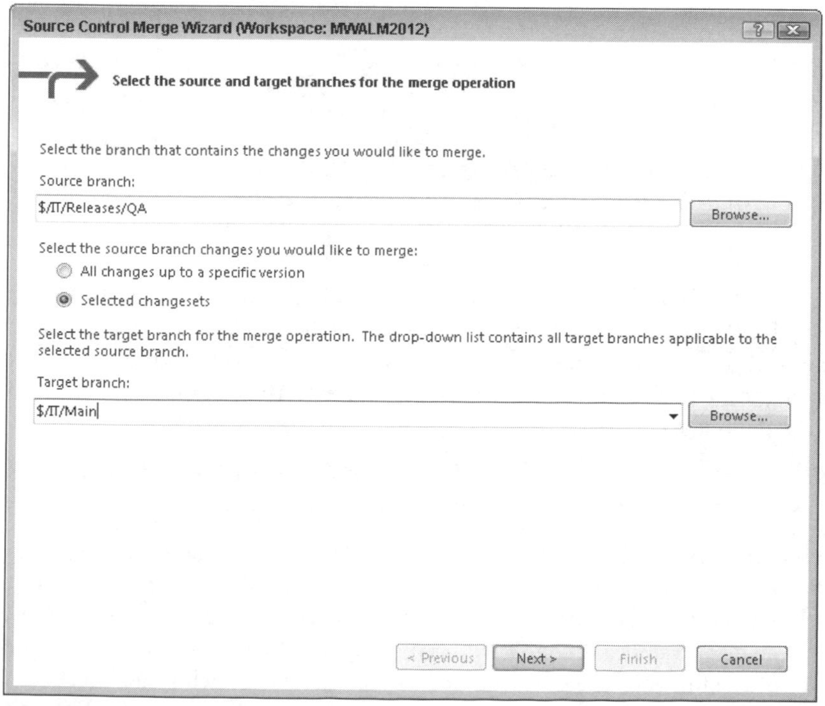

FIGURE 4-19

The developer opts to merge selected changesets to ensure that only the change the developer is aware of is picked up. The developer checks that the target branch has been identified as `Main` and then clicks Next. This displays the changesets selection page.

On this page, the developer can select a single changeset or a continuous range of changesets that need to be merged. In the case of the example testing team, they just have the one changeset that they are interested in (79), as shown in Figure 4-20, so the developer selects that and clicks Next. This provides a final confirmation page and, when the developer clicks Finish, the merge is performed in the user's workspace.

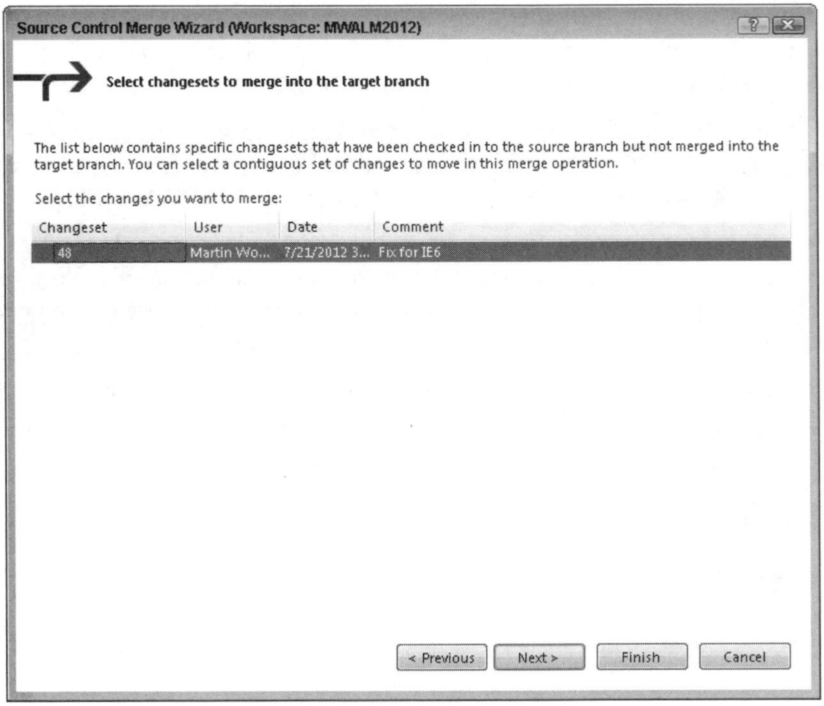

FIGURE 4-20

Note that the stylesheet file in the Main branch currently has a pending merge on it. At this point, it is good practice to compare the current version of the file with the latest version to ensure that the change you are making is still the correct one. In this case, it is, so the developer compiles and tests to make sure everything is good and then associates the changeset with the original bug, checks in the merge, and then marks the bug as Closed.

At this point, if you right-click the file in Source Control Explorer and select View History, you see the History for the file, as shown in Figure 4-21 (after the tree nodes have been expanded).

In Figure 4-21, you can see the merge of the changes back into `Main` at changeset 84. By expanding the node, you can see the changes made to that file in the source branch (in this case, the edit of the file in the `QA` branch in changeset 79). Then, further back in history, you can see the rename (move) of the file when the code was moved under the `Main` folder. Finally, if you expand that rename node, you can see all the history of the file before it was renamed in the current branch structure.

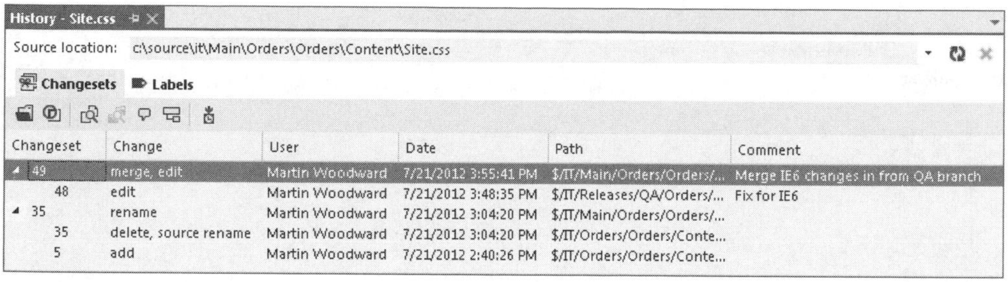

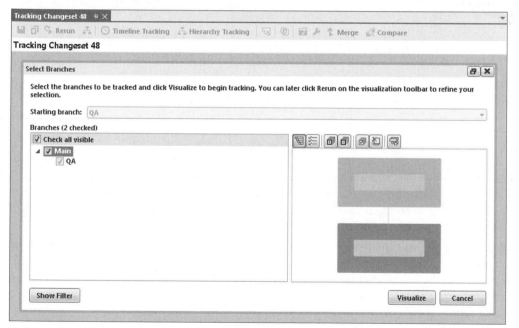

FIGURE 4-21

Another way to visualize this change and see that it made it into the correct branches is to right-click changeset 48 in the History view and select Tracking Changeset. This displays the Select Branches dialog inside the Tracking Changeset editor tab (Figure 4-22) that allows you to select which branches you would like to view.

FIGURE 4-22

For this example scenario, the developer selects the Check All Visible check box and clicks the Visualize button. Initially, this sequence shows a hierarchical view of branches, which are colored according to which branches the changes in changeset 48 made it into. If you were to look at Figure 4-23 in color, you would see the result for this scenario was that everything showed up colored green to indicate that everything was good.

An alternative visualization is available by clicking the Timeline Tracking button, as shown in Figure 4-23. This displays the changes in a familiar timeline style view, as shown in Figure 4-24. Again, if this were in color, you would see that all the branches are green, which means that the code made it to all branches.

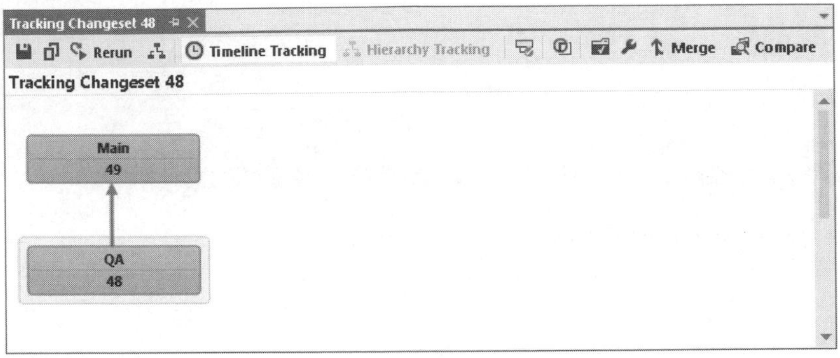

FIGURE 4-23

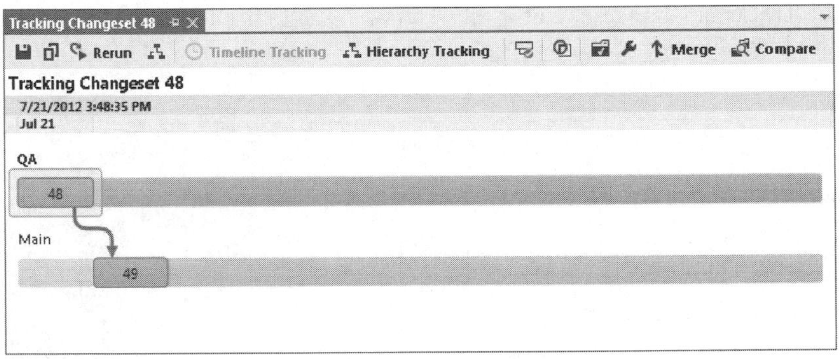

FIGURE 4-24

Back at Tailspin Toys, the IT product has undergone a bunch more testing on the QA branch, and development continues in the Main branch. At the end of the testing period, it is decided that the application is good, and so the build that was created with the stylesheet fix in changeset 48 (build Orders QA_20120721.2) is deployed to production.

However, all is not well. Once deployment to production, the Chief Information Officer (CIO) of the company notices an incorrect footer file at the bottom of the main page. The page footer still contains text from the initial template that reads, My ASP.NET MVC Application. Although this doesn't affect functionality in anyway, the CIO would like the issue fixed ASAP because she is about to demo the application to the board of directors.

It's a small, low-risk fix. In days gone by, this would be exactly the sort of thing for which one of the IT team would jump into the production environment and just fix it. However, it's exactly the sort of change that can be forgotten about in the development branch. So, to ensure that the change is not overlooked, the team decides to do it in version control using the new branch plan.

First, they must create the Prod branch. There are two ways to do this. One is to create the branch from the label that was applied as part of the build process. Another is to branch by the changeset that included the required fix. Let's take a brief look at both methods and see which is more appropriate for this example scenario.

Branch from Label

As previously discussed, it is possible to create branches after the fact by right-clicking the QA branch in Source Control Explorer and selecting Branching and Merging ⇨ Branch as well as from the `tf branch` command line. From the Branch from QA dialog, select Label from the Branch from Version dropdown as shown in Figure 4-25 and then click the ellipsis (...) button to find the label created by the build process (each build by default labels the files included in that build with the build number). Enter the target branch name of `$/IT/Releases/Prod` and click Branch.

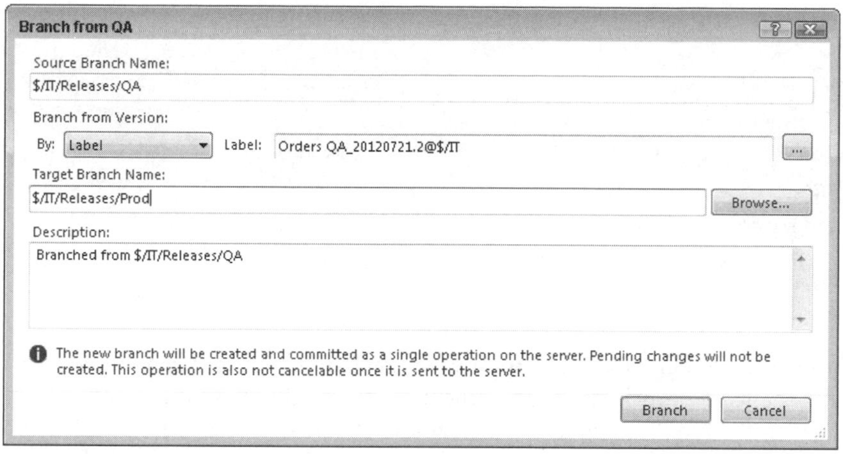

Branch from QA

Source Branch Name:

$/IT/Releases/QA

Branch from Version:

By: Label   Label: Orders QA_20120721.2@$/IT   [...]

Target Branch Name:

$/IT/Releases/Prod   Browse...

Description:

Branched from $/IT/Releases/QA

ⓘ The new branch will be created and committed as a single operation on the server. Pending changes will not be created. This operation is also not cancelable once it is sent to the server.

Branch   Cancel

FIGURE 4-25

The advantage of branching by label is that it branches only the files that were included in the specified label, and that label was created automatically by the build process to only include the files that were in the workspace definition of the build at the time the build was performed.

The major downside is that, as stated in Chapter 3, labels in Team Foundation Server are editable. Someone with appropriate permissions could have edited the label, and removed or included certain key files after the label was created by the build process. This is unlikely in the example Tailspin Toys environment, but it is possible.

Branch from Changeset

From the build report shown in Figure 4-26, you can see the build associated with changeset `48` was successful. As discussed in Chapter 3, the changeset represents a unique (immutable) point in time in the version control repository. Therefore, if you were to branch from changeset `48`, this would include the files at the exact state that they were in when the build was performed.

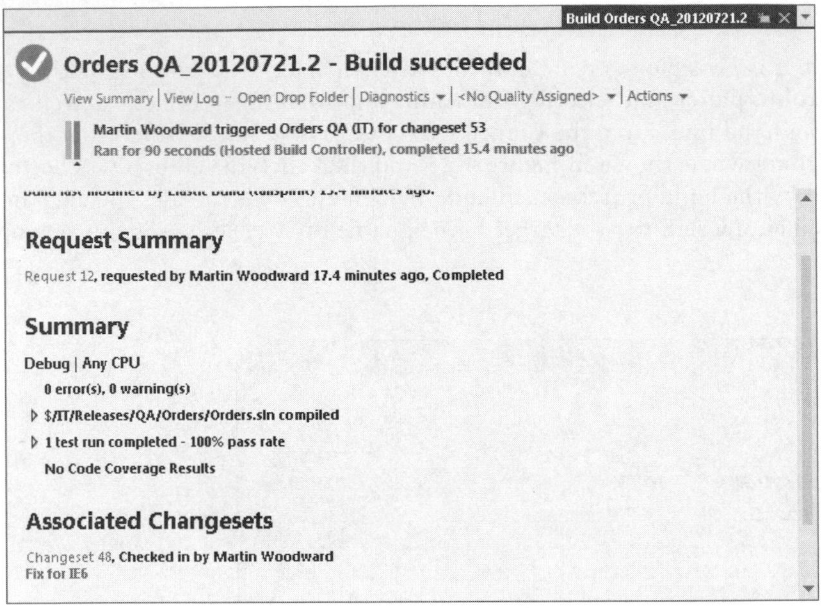

FIGURE 4-26

The team decides to branch by changeset 48 so as to include all changes up until changeset 48 in the QA branch when creating the Prod branch. To do this, the developer right-clicks on the QA branch in Source Control Explorer, and selects Branching and Merging ⇨ Branch. The developer then changes the Branch from Version to changeset 48, and sets the Target Branch Name to be $/IT/Releases/Prod.

After the branch is created, the version control repository looks like Figure 4-27.

FIGURE 4-27

If you were to right-click the Main branch and select Branching and Merging ⇨ View Hierarchy, you could see a visualization of the current branch structure, as shown in Figure 4-28. If you hover over each branch with the mouse, you see a tooltip with the additional metadata about that branch, including any description that you have entered.

At this point, the developer can now create a fix in the Prod branch. The developer simply edits the offending cshtml file and checks it in as changeset 59. The developer then creates a build and deploys this to production. Now you must ensure that the fix is in the appropriate branches so that it also gets included in the future releases.

To do this you right-click on the Prod branch and select View History. Then you right-click on the changeset just created (59) and select Track Changeset. As before, you select the Check All Visible check box and click Visualize. The change shows in green in the Prod branch only, as represented by the bottom box in Figure 4-29.

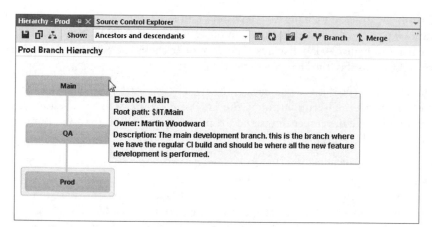

FIGURE 4-28

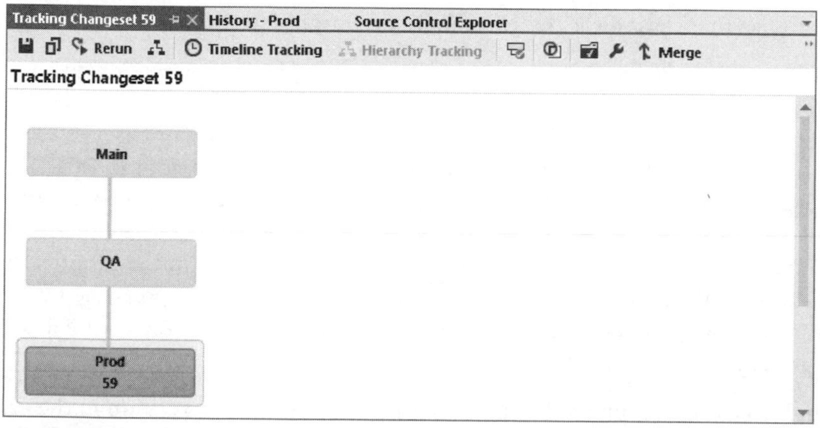

FIGURE 4-29

To merge this change into Main, the developer now has two choices: a ladder merge or a baseless merge. If you find that during your branch process you frequently must perform baseless merges or merges through other branches (that is, ladder merges), this is a good indication that the model is no longer optimized for the typical circumstances encountered in your environment, and you may want to revise it.

However, in the Tailspin Toys scenario, making ad hoc changes to production is very much an exception case, so the IT team wants to optimize the branch plan for the usual case of a change starting in Main, getting promoted on to QA, and then to Prod. So, the developer must use a ladder merge or a baseless merge to go from Prod to Main.

Ladder Merge

As shown in Figure 4-29, the team has a change in Prod. To get that fix into Main using standard merges, the developer must first merge it into the QA branch, and then, from there, into Main. This is because in Team Foundation Server, a standard merge can flow from parent to child, or vice versa.

To merge the changes, from the Tracking Changeset view shown in 4-29, the developer simply drags and drops the `Prod` branch up to the `QA` branch using the mouse. The standard Source Control Merge Wizard (shown earlier in Figure 4-19) displays. The developer clicks the Selected Changesets radio button and clicks Next to display the changeset selection page.

On this page, the developer selects the desired changeset (`59`) and clicks Finish. The developer then checks in the merged file and clicks the Rerun button in the Tracking Changeset view to show the change in the `QA` branch. Finally, the developer drags and drops the `QA` branch to the `Main` branch, and repeats the process through the Merge Wizard.

In this particular example, because of when the change occurred in production, it actually would have been possible to get the change into `Main` in this way. However, if the change had been required when there was a different (newer) version of the software in the `QA` branch, you may have not wanted to merge the changes in this way. Instead, you could have opted to do a baseless merge directly into `Main`, and then the change would make it back up to the `QA` branch with the next release to the test team.

Let's take a look at how to use that option for the Tailspin Toys example scenario.

Baseless Merge

A simple drag-and-drop operation is not supported for a baseless merge. The use of baseless merges are discouraged due to the increased likelihood of hard-to-resolve conflicts. Instead, the Tailspin Toys IT developer must right-click the `Prod` branch and select Merge. The Source Control Merge Wizard (refer to Figure 4-19) displays with the available target paths shown in the dropdown. Only paths that the source branch has a direct branch relationship with are displayed in the dropdown (in the example `$/IT/Releases/QA` is the only option). To perform a baseless merge, press the Browse button and then select the `Main` branch. The merge dialog then shows a warning (see Figure 4-30) that a baseless merge is going to be performed.

In this example scenario, because development has been ongoing by the rest of the team in the `Main` branch, it is highly likely that a conflict will occur during the baseless merge. In Team Foundation Server 2012 there have been a lot of improvements to the automerge logic. For example, if a file was edited by one developer and checked in, and in the meantime another developer was editing a different part of that same file, then when the second developer goes to check in those changes are merged automatically. The same is true in edits that have occurred in different places in the same file across branches which then have a baseless merge. However, in the example scenario someone has renamed the `_Layout.cshtml` file in the `Main` branch to `_MainLayout.cshtml`. If you had done a ladder merge, Team Foundation Server would have been able to use the common base version to be able to detect the rename operation and so merge the changes into the file with the new filename (`_MainLayout.cshtml`). However, with a baseless merge, there is no common base version, and Team Foundation Server can only use the current state of the two branches when working out the automatic merges. It is impossible for Team Foundation Server to detect that the rename that occurred on `_Layout.cshtml` in `Main` was after the branch to `Prod` was taken, and so Team Foundation server can't suggest that you want to merge changes into the `_MainLayout.cshtml` file. Instead, it thinks that you want to add `_Layout.cshtml` back into `Main`, but as it knows that a file used to exist by that name it is not sure that this is what you want to do. The user receives notification of a conflict as shown in Figure 4-31.

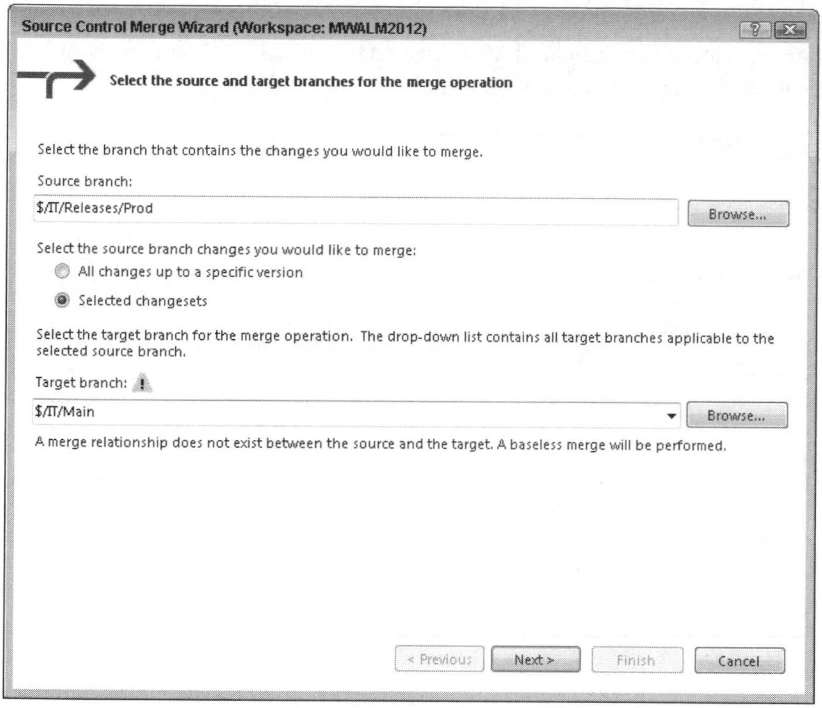

FIGURE 4-30

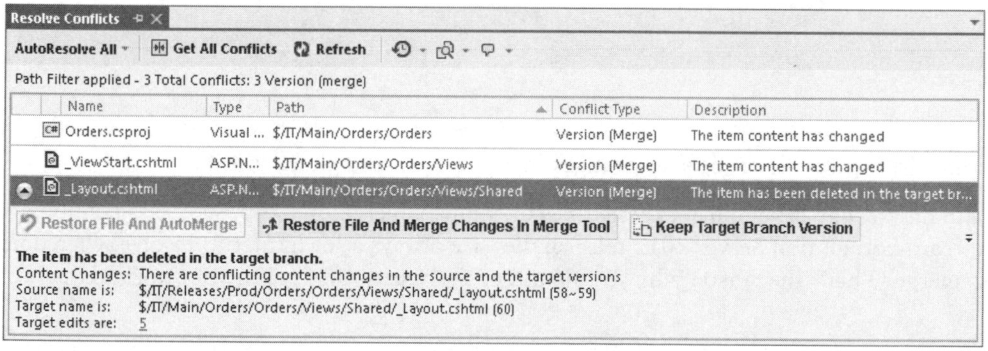

FIGURE 4-31

In this particular instance, you can see that something is wrong. If you look at the history of _Layout.cshtml in Main you see it was renamed to _MainLayout.cshtml after the branch was taken. None of the options Team Foundation Server presented to resolve the conflict are what you want as they all involve either getting rid of the changes to _Layout.cshtml from Prod or adding the _Layout.cshtml file back into Main. Therefore you should choose Take Source Branch Version to keep the _MainLayout.cshtml file unchanged. However, by doing this you haven't pushed up the changes from _Layout.cshtml in Prod. To do that, what you want to do is merge the changes from _Layout.cshtml in Prod into _MainLayout.cshtml in Main by first undoing the pending merge change on _Layout.cshtml in Main. Then from Source Control Explorer you right-click the _Layout.cshtml file in Prod, select Branching and Merging ⇨ Merge and then perform a baseless merge of that single file with _MainLayout.cshtml in Main as shown in Figure 4-32.

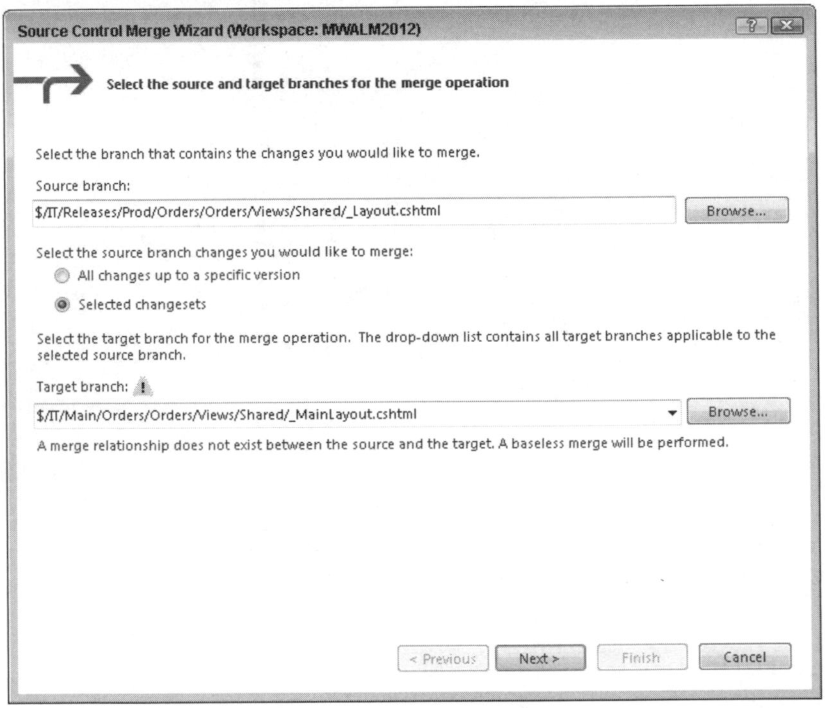

FIGURE 4-32

Validate that the file has all the correct changes that you want and check it in.

Although in day-to-day development these types of complex merge operations are less common with the latest Team Foundation Server 2012 release, they are always a lot harder to resolve when doing a baseless merge. That's the reason why you should avoid baseless merges in your normal operating procedure.

Now, when the developer clicks the Rerun button for tracking changeset 59, the visualization shows a dotted line between Prod and Main as shown in Figure 4-33, indicating a baseless merge.

You can also switch to the Timeline tracking view. In the example shown in Figure 4-34, the baseless merge was actually done by two different developers who were responsible for different areas of the codebase. As you can see, the first merge is highlighted in a different color with cross-hatching (yellow, when viewing the actual screen), and the changeset number has an asterisk after it (65*). This is because only some of the changes have been merged into the branch in the initial baseless merge. After the second developer completes the merge in the second changeset (70), the branch goes to a solid color (green when viewing the actual screen), indicating that all the changes in changeset 59 have now been merged.

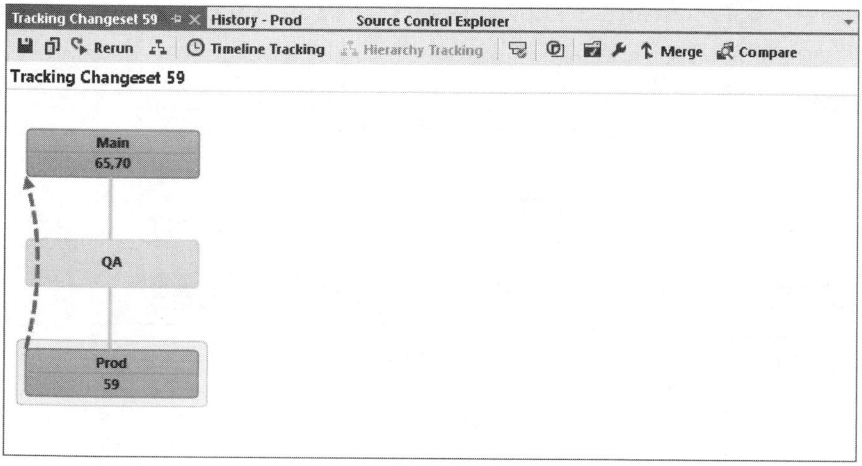

FIGURE 4-33

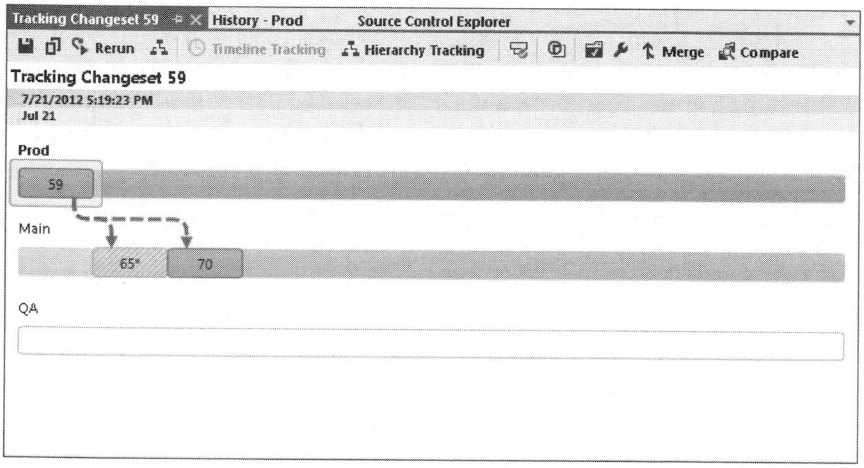

FIGURE 4-34

Tracking Change through Branches

As you have seen thus far, the branch visualization tooling in Visual Studio 2012 provides some powerful capabilities for viewing your branch hierarchy and tracking the progress of changes through it. Using the View Hierarchy functionality, you can immediately see the relationships of the branches in your source tree and navigate to their locations in the repository. By selecting

Track Changeset for a changeset in the History view, you see into which branches that change has been made, and even merge the change into other branches by dragging and dropping between branches.

The Tracking Changeset visualization has some additional features that are not always displayed in simple examples such as the ones presented so far. Figure 4-35 shows an example from a more complex branch hierarchy.

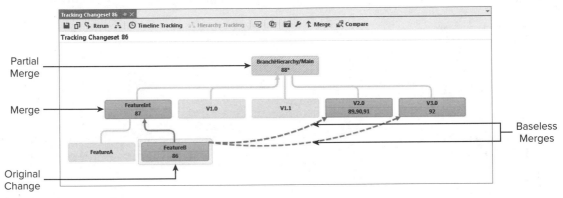

FIGURE 4-35

In the example shown in Figure 4-35, the original change occurred in the FeatureB branch as changeset 86. This was reverse-integrated into the FeatureInt branch as a standard merge in changeset 87. That change was then merged into Main. But not all files were copied over as part of the merge as the cross-hatching and the asterisk next to changeset 88 indicate. This should instantly be an area to query to investigate which files were checked in and why this was a partial merge. Double-clicking on the branch shows the changeset details to begin the investigation.

Then, rather than a standard merge back down from Main into the V2.0 branch, you can see that three baseless merges have occurred to get all the changes into that branch (changesets 89, 90 and 91). Finally, a single baseless merge took the code into V3.0. Figure 4-35 shows that the changes have yet to make it into the FeatureA branch or into the V1.0 and V1.1 branches. Clicking the Timeline Tracking button displays the timeline view for changeset 86, as shown Figure 4-36.

The timeline tracking view does not show the relationships between branches (that is, the hierarchy) but instead shows the merges as they happened. The sequence of events around the partial merges into Main and V2.0, and the subsequent full merge into V2.0 are therefore much more clearly represented. Hovering over each branch provides additional metadata, including its owner and description.

SUMMARY

As you can tell from this chapter, the branch and merge capabilities of Team Foundation Server not only allow for some complex software configuration management scenarios, but they also provide the tooling to help understand what is happening with changes in your version control repository. There have also been significant improvements in Team Foundation Server 2012 by supporting baseless merging from Visual Studio as well as improved auto-merge functionality, which reduces, but cannot completely eliminate, merge conflicts.

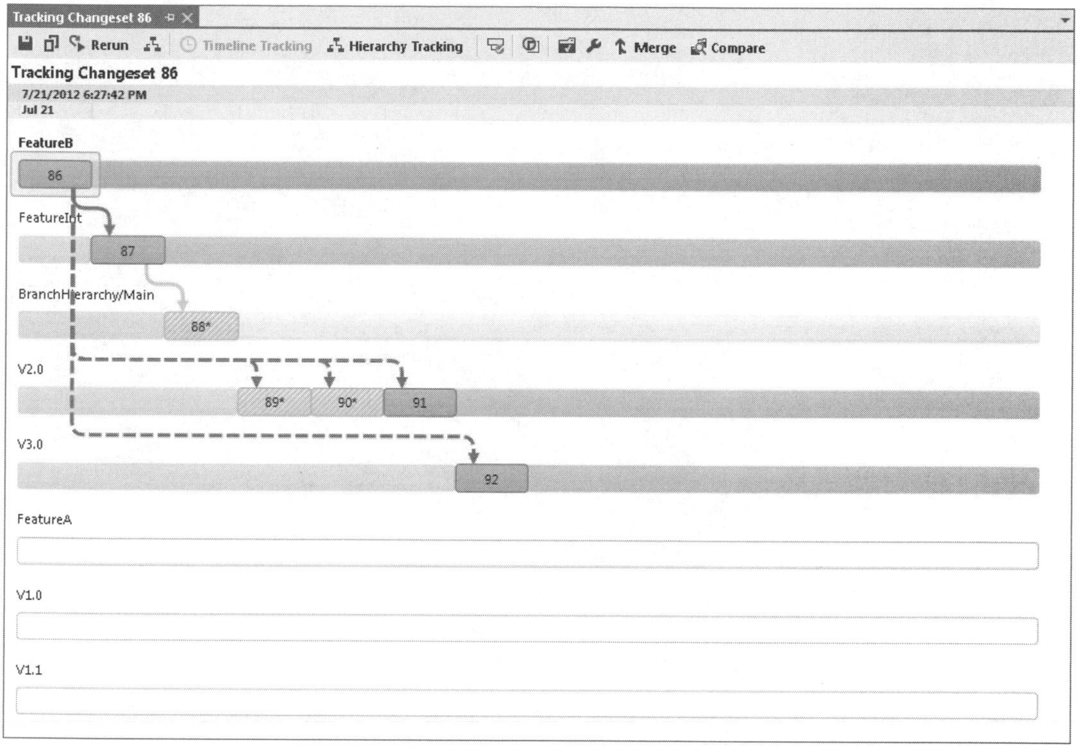

FIGURE 4-36

The chapter began by looking at the terminology used in branching, discussed some common branching techniques, and then provided a detailed walkthrough of implementing a basic branching strategy in an organization using the tools provided in Visual Studio 2012. Finally, this chapter looked at the changeset tracking functionality available to determine to which branches a particular change has propagated.

This chapter briefly mentioned Build Definitions and how to change their properties when setting up a branching strategy. Chapter 5 covers using the build automation capabilities in Team Foundation Server, why build automation is a very important method to improve software quality, how to create a build definition in Team Foundation Server, and where you should start when customizing the build process.

5
Team Foundation Build

This chapter examines the build automation capabilities of Team Foundation Server—what is provided out-of-the-box, how to use it, and how to customize it to suit your organizational requirements. But first, let's take a quick look at build automation in general.

After version control, automating the build is the second most important thing you can do to improve the quality of your software.

Only after the parts of your application come together can you tell if your application works and does what it is supposed to. Assembling the parts of an application is often a complex, time-consuming, and error-prone process. There are so many parts to building the application that without an automated build, the activity usually falls to one or two individuals on the team who know the secret. Without an automated build, even they sometimes get it wrong, with show-stopping consequences that are often discovered very late, making any mistakes expensive to fix.

Imagine having to recall an entire manufacturing run of a DVD because you missed an important file. Worse still, imagine accidentally including the source code for your application in a web distribution, or leaving embarrassing test data in the application when it was deployed to production. All these things make headlines when they happen to organizations that build software, yet they can easily be avoided.

Integration of software components is the difficult part. Teams work on their features in isolation, making various assumptions about how other parts of the system function. Only after the parts are assembled are the assumptions tested. If you integrate early and often, the integrations are tested as soon as possible in the development process—therefore reducing the cost of fixing the inevitable issues.

It should be trivial for everyone involved in the project to run a copy of the latest build. Only then can you tell if your software works and does what it is supposed to. Only then can you tell if you are going to have your product ready on time. A regular, automated build is the heartbeat of your team.

In Visual Studio 2012, a developer is usually able to run his or her application by pressing the infamous F5 key to run the code in debug mode. This assembles the code on the local workstation and executes it. This makes it trivial for the developer to test his or part of the code base. But what it doesn't do is ensure that the code works with all the latest changes committed by other members of the team. In addition, pressing the F5 key simply compiles the code that's ready for manual testing. As part of an automated build, you can also run full a suite of automated tests, giving you a high degree of confidence that no changes that have been introduced have broken something elsewhere.

Pressing the F5 key is easy for a developer. You want your automated build to make it just as easy to run your application—if not easier.

TEAM FOUNDATION BUILD

Build automation is so important to the quality of the software development process that Team Foundation Server 2012 provides build services as part of the core platform.

> **NOTE** *Chapter 2 provides more information on the other services offered by Team Foundation Server (including version control, work item tracking, and reporting).*

The build services provided by Team Foundation Server offer an enterprise-class, distributed build platform. Utilization of the build services is done inside the development environment in which the code is being created (either in Visual Studio or Eclipse). Information on the build services is tightly integrated with the version control, work item tracking, and the testing features provided by Team Foundation Server.

In addition, data obtained from the build system is fed into the Team Foundation Server data warehouse, thus allowing for the analysis of historical reports and trends. The build services provide notifications on build events using the standard Team Foundation Server eventing mechanisms, which means that e-mail alerts can easily be sent to the team regarding build status. As part of the standard installation in Visual Studio 2012, the Build Notifications tool is installed alongside Visual Studio, which can provide the capability for additional build notifications via the application that runs in the system notification area.

Team Foundation Server provides a number of ways to trigger the build. Builds may be started by a manual request, automatically triggered by a check-in to Team Foundation Server version control, or run on a specified schedule. Team Foundation Server also has a concept called *gated check-ins*.

A gated check-in means that a developer's changes must successfully build on the build server when merged with the latest code from version control before the code is then checked in on behalf of the user, thus preventing "broken" code from ever being checked in.

Team Foundation Build also has a full API in .NET or Java. These are the same APIs used by the Visual Studio and Eclipse integrations as well as the build notification tool. They provide you with deep integration into the build services. Combined with the build events, there is a highly extensible platform to integrate any additional systems that you can imagine.

BRIAN THE BUILD BUNNY

Some integrations with Team Foundation Server are more imaginative than others. A popular way of encouraging the team to pay attention to the current state of the build is to create creative and eye-catching build status notification mechanisms. Although wall displays, lava lamps, or even integrations with Microsoft Kinect are a popular way of communicating this information to the team, one of the authors of this book has even gone so far as to connect a talking, moving robot rabbit into Team Foundation Server. For more information on this project (including a prize-winning YouTube video and full source code), see `http://aka.ms/BuildBunny`.

WHAT'S NEW IN TEAM FOUNDATION BUILD 2012

The build services offered by Team Foundation Server have been changed significantly since the initial version in Team Foundation Server 2005.

In the first version, Team Foundation Build was based heavily on MSBuild, along with a build server machine called the *build agent*. All configuration of the build was done by editing files stored in version control.

In the 2008 release, build management was greatly improved with the capability to trigger builds automatically, queue builds, and manage builds. This second version introduced the Build Definition as a Team Foundation Server entity in its own right that contained various configuration data about the build (such as the build name, workspace definition, default build agent, drop location, and build trigger). The file describing how to do the build (the TFSBuild.proj file) was still based on MSBuild.

The 2010 release continued much of the work done in 2008, with some notable changes that include the following:

- ➤ Windows Workflow 4.0
- ➤ Gated check-ins
- ➤ Private builds
- ➤ Build notifications
- ➤ Build controller

➤ Properties exposed for common customizations

➤ Integration with symbol and source server

➤ Enhanced build deletion options

By the 2010 release Team Build capabilities matured significantly since the original release, therefore this most recent 2012 release was more evolutionary than revolutionary. However, there are a few significant changes worth noting:

➤ Hosted build services

➤ Drop to version control

➤ Batched gated check-in

➤ Changes to the Build Service protocol

➤ Updated build report

Hosted Build Services

The hosted Team Foundation Service (`http://tfspreview.com`) not only provides a hosted Team Foundation Server instance for version control and work item tracking but also provides virtualized hosted build infrastructure. By default, every project collection in the hosted service also has a Hosted Build Controller available that you can use for your builds as shown in Figure 5-1. When a build is queued, the hosted service creates a new virtual machine, attaches it to your project collection, executes the build, and then returns the machine into the pool ready for the next account that wants to perform a build. Because the build virtual machines are created from a fresh image for each invocation, incremental builds are not currently supported. In addition, if your build requires any dependencies are not pre-installed in the standard hosted image then you need to have those checked in to version control and configure those as part of the build.

Drop to Version Control

When building against the hosted service, network shares are not easily accessible over the Internet. Therefore, a new option was created that is only enabled for hosted builds to enable results of the build to be copied to version control as shown in Figure 5-1. Note that when builds are deleted (either by the retention policy settings or by manually deleting the build) and deletion of build drops has been requested, the results of the builds are not only deleted from version control but destroyed. This means that they no longer occupy space within the version control system in Team Foundation Server thereby reducing the amount of space consumed by your project collection.

Batched Gated Check-in

Team Foundation Server 2010 introduced the gated check-in feature. As previously discussed, having a frequent automated build is one of the most important things you can do to improve your software development process. The key is to ensure that the latest code in your repository always compiles and runs and that it passes any associated automated tests. After you have your working build, the team must ensure that it stays good.

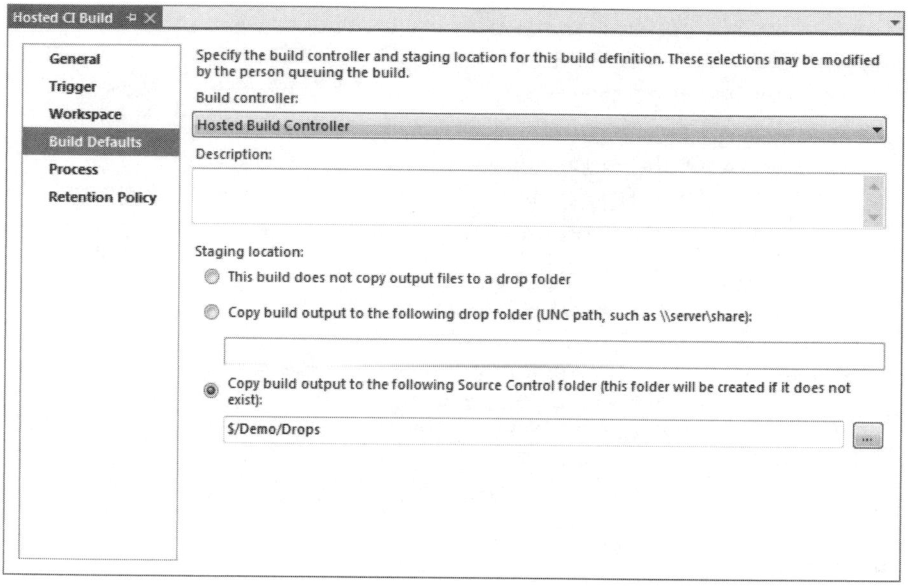

FIGURE 5-1

For very large teams, keeping your builds clean can be an issue. Imagine that a good developer might check in something that breaks the build once a year. If you have 500 people working on code bases, you quickly get into a situation where the build is breaking twice a day, every day. In these circumstances, configuring a build as a gated check-in may help.

A *gated check-in* means that the code is submitted as a shelveset rather than it being checked in to version control. The build server then takes the latest code, merges that with the changes contained in your shelveset, and performs the build. If the build is successful, the changes in your shelveset are checked in automatically on your behalf by the build server.

Gated check-ins have proven to be a very popular feature of Team Foundation Server. However, a limitation of them is that to prevent conflicts, only one gated check-in may be executing at a time and large teams who check in frequently may end up with a large queue of builds awaiting validation. The longer a developer needs to wait between submitting a check-in for validation and the check-in being committed into the repository, the less valuable the automated build process is. If this becomes an issue for your team then in Team Foundation Server 2012 you may choose to Merge and build a number of submissions in the queue—specifying a maximum number of build requests to be included in each gated build as shown in Figure 5-2.

When gated builds are batched together, the maximum specified number of check-ins are merged and validated in one build. If there is no backlog of builds then the gated check-in performs just as the feature did in Team Foundation Server 2010. However, if several check-ins are built together and a failure is detected, then the build is requeued with just the individual check-ins to allow the invalid check-in request to be detected. In practice, as the majority of check-ins pass validation, this can be an effective mechanism to avoid a gated check-in backlog.

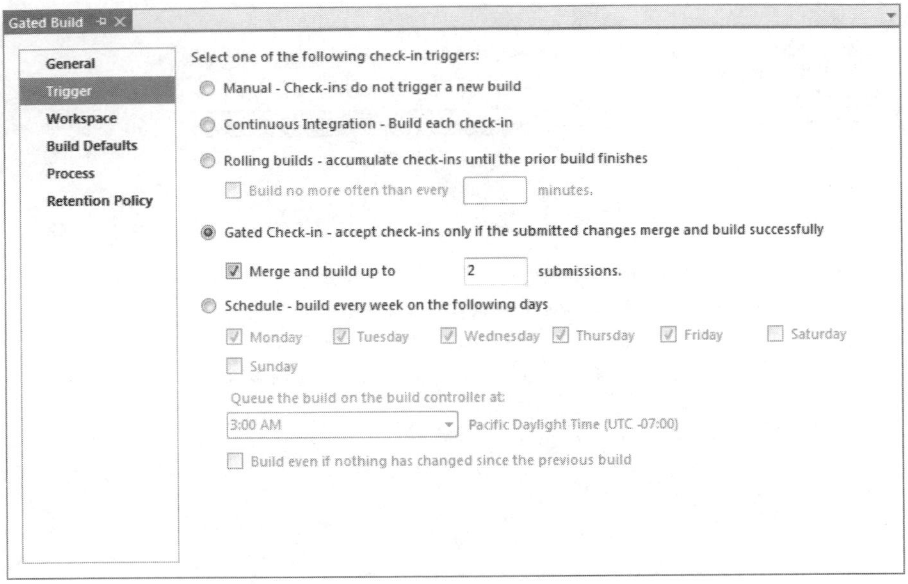

FIGURE 5-2

Changes to the Build Service Protocol

In previous versions of Team Foundation Server, the build agent and controller have been notified by the build agent initiating a TCP connection to the machine hosting the build service and a SOAP notification sent over TCP/IP. This is better than the traditional polling mechanisms used by many third-party build solutions, and it means the minimum load is placed on the network and on the Team Foundation Server Application Tier (AT). The problem with this approach is that there must be an open outbound port rule enabled in the firewalls between the AT and the build machine. In addition, because the build machine must be able to confirm the authorization of the build agent to access it, the build machine and the AT effectively had to be on the same domain or have an appropriate domain trust relationship established.

To work around these issues—and also to allow a build agent to more easily be configured against an AT that is accessed over the Internet—the build service protocol has been reversed. In Team Foundation Server 2012, the build service hosting the build controller and build agent processes establishes an outbound connection to the AT (usually using the standard HTTPS port 443 for an externally hosted instance or HTTP port 8080 for on-premises installations of TFS). The protocol is designed to place minimal network load in a similar mechanism to how so-called "push notification" e-mail delivery to cellular devices is achieved. That is, the build service does not constantly poll version control. Instead, it notifies the AT about the open connection and then sends minimal heartbeat traffic to keep the channel open, which allows inbound responses from the AT to notify the Build Service when it has a build request needing action. The build service maintains the open channel to the AT and has the suitable retry logic to re-establish the connection should it be severed for some reason.

Updated Build Report

The Build report was updated in Team Foundation Server 2012 to provide additional diagnostic capabilities and to more clearly display the relevant build information. The build report also now updates during the build process in the web browser and in Eclipse, just as it always did in Visual Studio 2010.

TEAM FOUNDATION BUILD ARCHITECTURE

As shown in Figure 5-3, several logical components are used as part of the Team Foundation Build services.

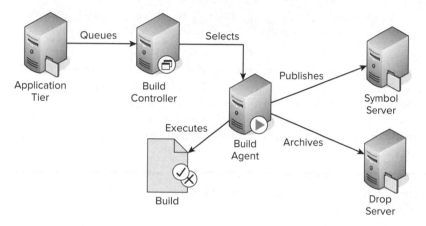

FIGURE 5-3

When a build is triggered, the Application tier sends a notification to a server called the *build controller* using a communication channel established by the build service and queues the build. The controller then downloads the build's Windows Workflow–based process and executes it. By default, this is then allocated to the next available build agent in the controller's pool of agents.

The *build agent* is the machine that actually executes the main portion of the build process as coded in the build's workflow—including calling MSBuild to perform the actual compilation step. It then archives the build results (that is, your executable binaries or your website) to a Windows file share provided as the *drop location*, and publishes symbols to the symbol server (if configured). Note that if you're utilizing the hosted build service on http://tfspreview.com then the build drop location may be in version control and the symbol server capabilities will not be available.

For an on-premises installation, the build controller and the build agent services are provided by the Visual Studio Team Foundation Build service host installed from the Team Foundation Server installation media. The build controller and build agent are configured using the Team Foundation Server Administration Tool.

> **NOTE** *For information on how to install and configure the Team Foundation Server Build service, see the Team Foundation Server Installation Guide. The guide is included in the install media for Team Foundation Server. However, the latest version is published at* `http://aka.ms/tfsInstallGuide`*. Microsoft continues to update the guide download to include extra guidance or any new issues that surface. Therefore, it is always worth working from the latest downloaded version.*
>
> *After you download the installation guide, you cannot view its contents unless you right-click the* `.chm` *file, click Properties, and then click Unblock. As an alternative, you can double-click the* `.chm` *file to open the Open File-Security Warning dialog box, clear the Always Ask Before Opening This File check box and then click Open.*

The build controller and build agent may live on the same machine as the Team Foundation Server Application tier. However, because a build is typically very CPU and disk I/O intensive, the build agent should at least be located on a separate server to avoid affecting the performance of the main Team Foundation Server application. If you run the build agent on the same machine as Team Foundation Server, this may cause some performance issues if certain intensive diagnostics data collectors are used as part of the build.

The actual details of the build (such as the build name, what to build, when to build it, how to build it, and what to do with the results) are all configured in the *build definition*. The results of individual builds are called the *build details*.

WORKING WITH BUILDS

This section examines working with team builds in Visual Studio. Figure 5-4 shows the key windows that you need to use:

➤ Team Explorer

➤ Build Explorer

➤ Build Details

Team Explorer

You should already be familiar with the Team Explorer view (accessed in Visual Studio through View ⇨ Team Explorer). Team Explorer contains a Builds page that provides you with access to all the functionality you need to interact with the build services in Team Foundation Server. The New Build Definition link at the top of the page enables you to create a build definition. There is also an Actions link that provides you with additional functionality such as being able to manage the Build Controller settings, set Build Qualities, and configure security permissions.

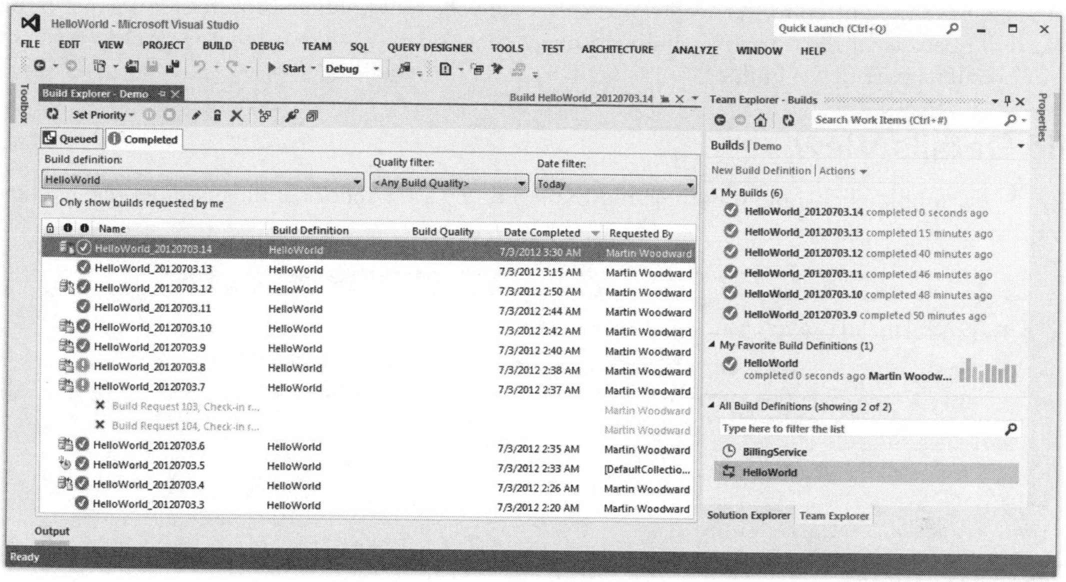

FIGURE 5-4

Under My Builds you find your most recently executed builds (that is to say builds that you have triggered either manually or by checking into a version control folder that is being monitored by a continuous integration, rolling, or gated trigger. My Favorite Build Definitions displays a summary of the build definitions that you have marked as a personal favorite in Visual Studio, Web Access, or Eclipse. Finally, under All Build Definitions you find all the defined builds for that team project and a search box that enables you to quickly find a particular build definition from that list. Double-clicking one of these or clicking the build in the Favorites opens the Build Explorer for that build definition.

Build Explorer

The Build Explorer view enables you to see all the builds that are currently executing (or awaiting execution) in the Queued tab, and those that have run on the system in the Completed tab.

Queued Builds

From the Queued tab of the Build Explorer, you can pause or change the priority of builds that are currently awaiting execution. You can also cancel paused builds or stop builds that are currently executing.

Completed Builds

From the Completed tab of the Build Explorer, you can view the build details, delete the build details, or set the quality of the build.

The *build quality* is a text string allocated to particular builds to denote the quality of that particular build (that is, "Released," "Ready for Test," and so on). In addition, you may mark the build with Retain Indefinitely to exclude it from any automatic retention policies on the build definition.

You also have the option to Reconcile Workspace with the build, which is useful for a gated or private build because it removes any pending changes that you may still have that were checked in on your behalf as part of the build.

Build Details View

When you double-click a build in the Build Explorer, you see a report of the build details, as shown in Figure 5-5.

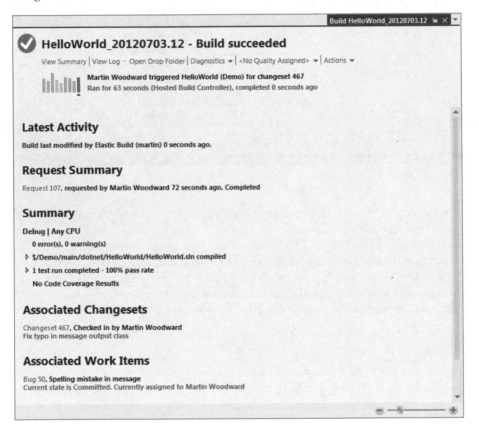

FIGURE 5-5

While the build is queuing, details are given about the build's position in the queue and the mean time that builds have been queued. After the build is executing, summary data about the execution time compared to previous builds is displayed. Clicking the Build Details link shows you more information about the build in progress and is automatically refreshed to show you the current build log data. A small bar chart in the top-left corner displays the currently executing build time against previous builds, which can give you an indication of how long the build might run.

When the build has completed, you see the build summary view showing all the projects, compilations, and tests runs, as well as any unit test results, code coverage, or test impact data. You also see information regarding the changesets included in the build since the last successful build of that build definition, along with any work items associated with those changesets when they were checked in.

In this way, you can start to see how full requirements traceability is obtained in Team Foundation Server, from the requirement being logged as a work item through to the development task to implement the requirement, to the change in source code to implement that task, and then, finally, the build of the software that includes that check-in. All the data is passed into the Team Foundation Server data warehouse to allow historical trend analysis and reporting.

From the build details view, you are able to open the drop folder in Windows Explorer to access the outputs of your build. You may modify the build quality assigned to that build, mark it to be retained indefinitely, or delete the build and associated results. You may also view the logs in the drop location (either in the drop network share or in version control) and perform many other additional activities from under the Actions link.

Creating a Build Definition

A build definition describes how, what, when, and where to perform your build. You create a new team build definition by right-clicking the New Build Definition link at the top of the Builds page in Team Explorer. Alternatively, from Visual Studio you may go to Build ⇨ New Build Definition.

You see a new build definition form inside Visual Studio. The form is split into two parts—a set of areas on the left side that basically function like tabs, and the main area for that section on the right side. You may notice that, when you first open the dialog, a number of the sections on the left side have warnings associated with them; this is completely normal. The purpose of these warnings is to highlight areas that need information before the definition can be saved.

You can save the definition by using the usual mechanisms (File ⇨ Save, or Ctrl+S, etc.) When saved, the definition is stored in Team Foundation Server and appears in the Builds page for all team members. You may mark your build definition as a personal favorite to make it easier to find later by right-clicking the created build definition and selecting Add to Favorites.

General Section

On the Builds page in Build Explorer, click General in the left-hand pane to bring up the General section. Then you must give the build definition a name, and, optionally, a description, as shown in Figure 5-6.

As you can easily search by name in the Builds page in Team Explorer, it may be useful to develop a naming convention for your builds to make them easier to find when filtering. A convention such as "Team: Project (Trigger)" is useful for large team projects. For example, the BizApps team might have two build definitions defined for their Framework, one that is a CI build triggered on every check-in to give quick feedback on the state of the build, and another scheduled build that not only does a full build but packages up the latest version and generate documentation, making it easy to consume by other teams. They might call these builds "BizApps: Framework (CI)" and BizApps: Framework (Nightly)".

For the description of your project, you should provide a short, one-line summary of what the build is for, and contact details for the owner or "build master" for the build. The first three lines of the build description are displayed in other dialogs in Team Foundation Server before scrolling is required. Therefore, this important information should be placed at the top so that people working with the builds can see what the build is for and who to contact for questions.

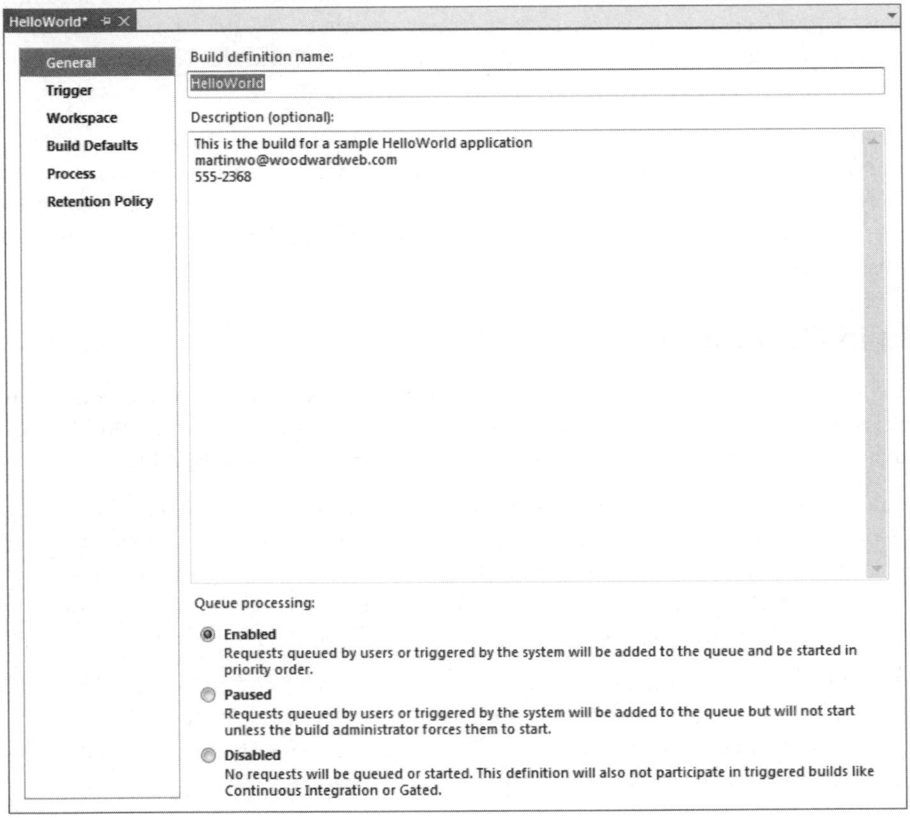

FIGURE 5-6

When creating a new build definition the Queue Processing should be set to Enabled as this allows builds to be triggered as soon as the build definition is saved. However, it may be useful to adjust the Queue Processing when performing maintenance to the build definition or build controllers. For example, if you are customizing the build process you can mark the build as Paused. New builds are queued if they get triggered as a continuous integration build or a gated build. However, they do not run until the build is enabled or a build administrator forces the build by right-clicking the queued build request in Build Explorer and selecting Start Now. This enables you to safely test that your changes to the build customization are working before re-enabling the build definition for use by the team. After the build is re-enabled, queued jobs are processed according to priority level and the order that they were submitted.

Trigger Section

Located in the Trigger section, the build trigger tells Team Foundation Server *when* to perform a build. As shown in Figure 5-7, there are a number of triggers available, including the following:

➤ Manual

➤ Continuous Integration

➤ Rolling Builds

➤ Gated Check-in

➤ Schedule

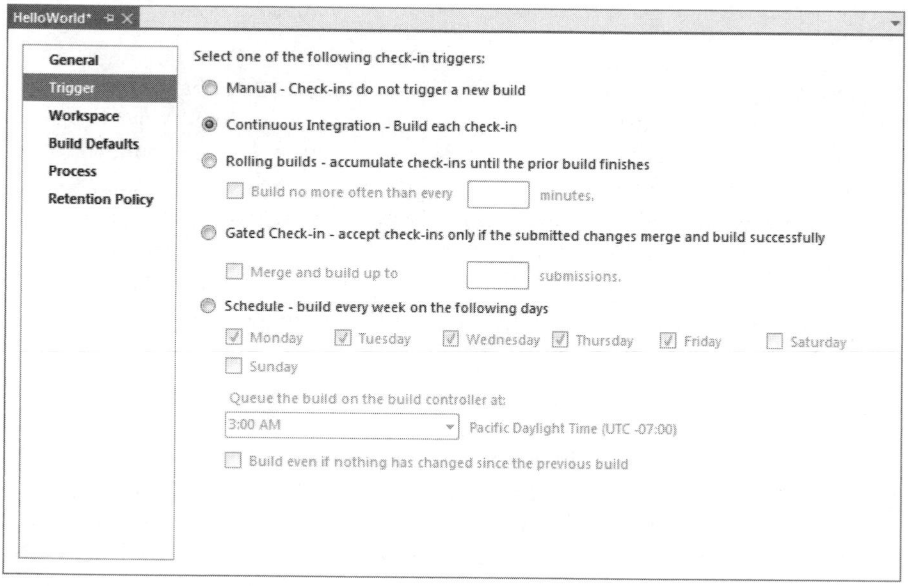

FIGURE 5-7

Manual

When you configure a build for a Manual trigger, the build only runs when explicitly queued, by using the user interface, by using the command line (that is, tfsbuild.exe), by using the Team Foundation Server .NET object model or the TFS SDK for Java.

Continuous Integration

In Team Foundation Server, the Continuous Integration trigger is one that queues a build for every check-in performed on the areas of code that you define as related to your build. (The "Workspace" section, later in this chapter, provides more information on defining those areas.)

Check-ins to Team Foundation Server are a discrete, atomic transaction represented by a changeset. By rebuilding the system for every changeset, you can easily determine which change broke the build (as well as who checked in that change). The downside to this is that there are, obviously, a lot of builds performed. Therefore, it is essential that build times are kept short to ensure rapid and frequent feedback to the development team as to the status of the current code base.

MARTIN FOWLER ON CONTINUOUS INTEGRATION

The term *continuous integration* (CI) emerged from agile software development methodologies such as Extreme Programming (XP) at the turn of the millennium. Martin Fowler's paper on continuous integration from 2000 is still worth reading today at `http://www.martinfowler.com/articles/continuousIntegration .html`.

Note that, as originally described, the term refers to increasing the speed and quality of software delivery by decreasing the integration times, and not simply the practice of performing a build for every check-in. Many of the practices expounded by Fowler's paper are supported by tooling in Team Foundation Server — not simply this one small feature of the build services. However, the term "continuous integration" has come to be synonymous with building after a check-in has occurred and is, therefore, used by Team Foundation Server as the name for this type of trigger.

Rolling Builds

Rolling Builds are similar to the Continuous Integration trigger in that a check-in will trigger a build. However, rather than building on every check-in, rolling builds batch several check-ins together to ensure that the build server never becomes backlogged—and optionally setting a minimum time interval between which a new build may be triggered. This is the type of trigger that may be familiar to those who have experience with build servers that support multiple version control tools such as CruiseControl, CruiseControl.NET, or Hudson/Jenkins.

Performing rolling builds has the advantage of reducing the number of builds performed, which helps to reduce the number of builds queued at peak times (and, therefore, the time before the results of an individual developer's check-ins are known). However, it has the disadvantage of grouping changes together, therefore making it more difficult to determine the check-in responsible for the build failure. For this reason, many people stick with the Continuous Integration trigger and instead focus efforts on increasing the speed of the build or the number of build agents available to perform the build.

Gated Check-in

A Gated Check-in trigger means that check-ins to the areas of version control covered by the build are not allowed by the server until a build has been performed and passed successfully. When a user attempts to check in a file, they are presented with the dialog shown in Figure 5-8.

The changes are stored as a shelveset in version control. The build server takes the shelved changes and merges those changes with the latest version of code from version control before performing the build. In the event of a successful build, the changes are then checked into the build server, and the user is notified via the build notification tool in the system notification area. At this point, the user may "reconcile" his or her workspace to remove the pending changes that were committed as part of the build from the current pending changes list.

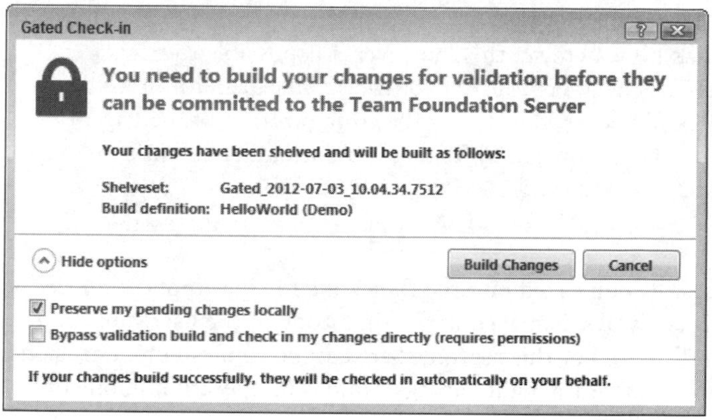

FIGURE 5-8

Because of the automatic merge process that is performed by the build server, it is important to realize that the actual code committed by the gated check-in may differ from the code submitted as part of the shelveset.

If you have two build definitions with overlapping workspace mappings that both have Gated Check-in triggers, the user will get to pick which one gets built to verify his or her changes at the time of check-in. In addition, even though Team Foundation Server 2012 has build agent pooling features, only one build of a gated check-in may be executed at a time to prevent conflicting merges from being submitted.

As discussed earlier in the chapter, due to the fact that only one gated build can be executed at a time, a backlog of queued builds can form when a large team is doing frequent gated check-ins. Therefore, as shown in Figure 5-2, Team Foundation Server 2012 has the ability to merge a number of queued gated check-ins working on the assumption that the build is likely to be successful. This helps reduce check-in validation times. If the build fails for some reason, then the build requests are requeued individually to allow the problem build to be identified and rejected. This is shown in Figure 5-4 where two check-ins have been merged into `HelloWorld_20120703.7` which failed, so `HelloWorld_20120703.8` and `HelloWorld_20120703.9` were queued up, each containing the individual check-ins. In that case it turned out that the check-in included in `HelloWorld_20120703.8` was bad so that is rejected and the user notified, but the check-in included in `HelloWorld_20120703.9` was good and so that was checked in on that user's behalf.

Schedule

Builds may be triggered by a particular schedule—that is, a daily or nightly build. Note that a single time may be specified for each build definition for the chosen days of the week—repeated weekly. Also note that, in the case of a nightly build, the build time should be set outside of any backup or other regular maintenance jobs.

SCHEDULING BUILDS MORE FREQUENTLY

Sometimes, the standard scheduling triggers provided by Team Foundation Server are not sufficient — perhaps you want to automatically build twice a day, or maybe every three weeks.

The Build Definition trigger has no way to set this, however it is possible to trigger a build as a scheduled task (see `http://aka.ms/scheduledTaskBuilds` for more information on how to do this). However, this makes the configuration of the trigger happen outside the user interface provided by Team Foundation Server, so it should be used only if absolutely necessary.

The time for a scheduled build is actually converted into the time zone for the Application tier when the build definition is saved. But this is always displayed in the time zone of the user's machine when editing the build definition in Visual Studio. For this reason, there can be some slight confusion as to the actual build time during periods where Daylight Savings Time is in operation in one of the time zones and not the other.

Workspace

The Workspace section enables you to define the working folder mappings that should be used for your build. These working folder mappings not only determine where on disk the files should be located but also which files on the server are considered relevant to the build.

The default working folder mapping for a new build definition is given as mapping the root of the team project (for example, `$/Demo`) to the sources directory represented by the environment variable (`$(SourceDir)`). This is almost always too broad for your build, and includes too many files, which not only slows down the build (because more files must be downloaded from version control), but also means that some check-ins to the project risk triggering a build even though they do not affect the results of the build.

Therefore, you should always modify the server path of the build to only include the files you need, as shown in Figure 5-9. You may also make use of cloaked working folder mappings to exclude certain subfolders or files from a working folder mapping that do not affect the build (such as a folder containing the source PSD image files used in a website).

NOTE *Chapter 3 provides more information on working with folder mappings in Team Foundation Server version control.*

Build Defaults

On the Build Defaults section shown in Figure 5-10, you specify which build controller you would like to use for the definition and where to copy the outputs from your build.

FIGURE 5-9

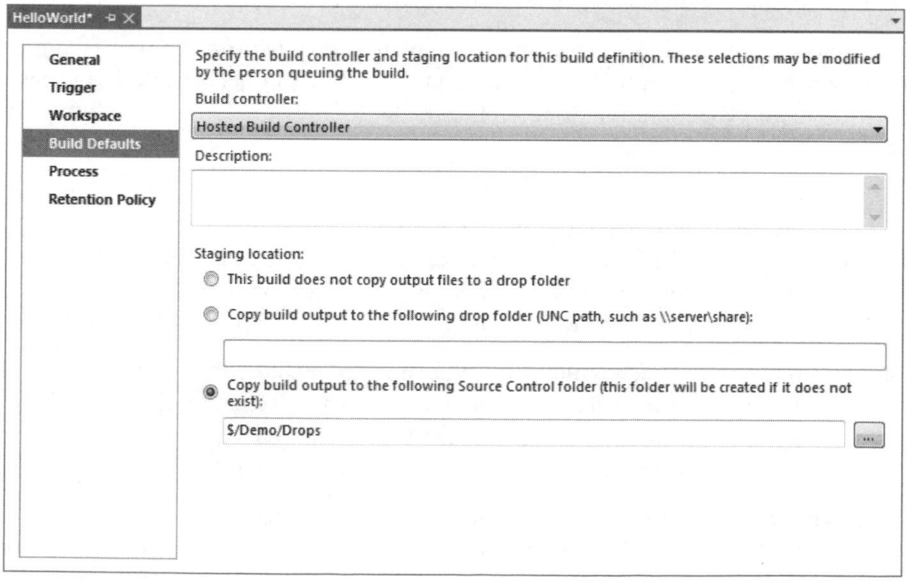

FIGURE 5-10

In Team Foundation Server 2012, build controllers and build agents are responsible for notifying the Team Foundation Server application tier of their existence as they are installed. If you have no build controllers available in the controller dropdown, then your Team Foundation Server administrator must install a build controller (and build agent) using the Team Foundation Server Setup media and configure it to point to your project collection. The description field displays the description given to the build controller, and it is not editable from this dialog. Note that when using the hosted Team Foundation Service at `tfspreview.com`, a Hosted Build Controller is present for every project collection that allows builds to be performed using a build controller in the cloud.

For regular builds, the drop folder location must be a Windows file share on the network to which the user running the build agent services has access. There is a limit (inherited from the .NET base class libraries) of 260 characters for the full path of all files copied to the drop folder location, so you should ensure that your server and share names are as short as possible, leaving you with the maximum space for your output. That being said, you should put your builds in directories corresponding to the build definition inside your drop folder location to help keep them organized. When talking to the hosted service you also have the option to store files in version control. Note that the build definition name is appended to the path specified so there is no need to specify it in the dialog.

Process

When talking to a Team Foundation Server 2012 server, you are required to select which process should be used to perform the build, as shown in Figure 5-11. These processes are Windows Workflow 4.0-based processes. The initial list of processes are defined by the process template used, and can then be added to from the Process section. Each process has a number of easily customizable properties that are designed to be used to alter the behavior of that process. Processes with mandatory inputs are marked with a warning triangle when the build definition is created.

From this section, you may edit and customize the build process parameters. (For more information on this, see the section "Team Build Process," later in this chapter.)

For the creation of a basic team build using the DefaultTemplate, the only property that you must initially configure is which solution or project to build. Simply click the Projects to Build property and click the ... button to add your solution or project to the list.

Retention Policy

After you start automating builds, you quickly end up with a lot of build results in your archive. Finding the build that you are looking for can get complicated—not to mention the large amount of disk space required to store all the build results. Team Foundation Server has automatic retention policies to help with this, as displayed in the Retention Policy section shown in Figure 5-12.

The retention policies determine, for each build result type, how many of those results you would like to keep by default. Note that, at any time, you can mark a build with the Retain Indefinitely Retention Policy from the build details context menu in the Build Explorer view. Marking a build as Retain Indefinitely means that it will be excluded from these automatic retention policies.

There are separate retention policies to control the team builds that are triggered or manually queued from the private builds of individual developers. Changing the private build retention policy affects all the developers performing private builds on that build definition—not just the developer editing the setting.

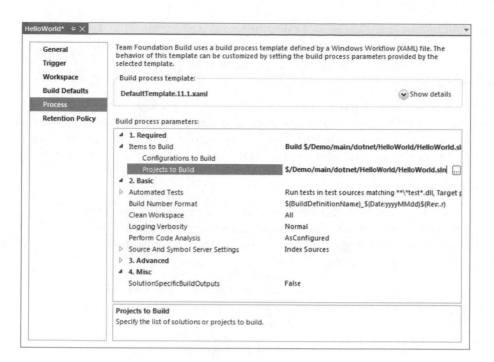

FIGURE 5-11

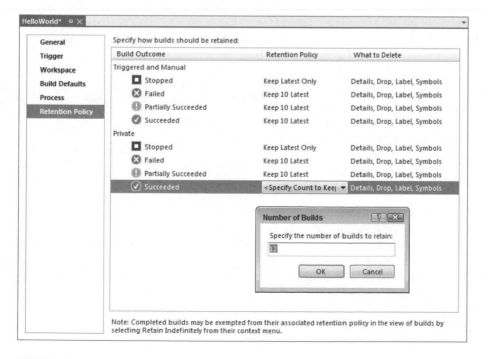

FIGURE 5-12

If you're storing build drops in version control using the hosted service, when the build binaries are deleted they are destroyed in version control to allow the disk space to be recovered.

Queuing a Build

Whenever you create a new build definition or make significant changes to it, you should manually queue the build the first time to ensure that it is working as desired. The first successful build for a build definition also acts as the baseline for that build. Every build from that point on records the changesets included since the last successful build for that definition. This information is stored in the build detail for each build, and reports into the Team Foundation Server data warehouse, thus allowing for historical trends over time.

A build can be manually invoked from the Builds node in Team Explorer by using the TFSBuild .exe command-line tool, or by using the Team Foundation Server API. Alternatively, the build might be triggered using one of the triggers defined earlier in this chapter (such as on a check-in into version control or on a specified schedule).

> **NOTE** *Microsoft Team Explorer installs a number of command-line tools, one of which is the* TFSBuild *command. The* TFSBuild *command can be used to perform a limited number of Team Foundation Build tasks and is also useful in scripting scenarios where full access to the Team Foundation Sever API is not required. For more information on the* TFSBuild *command, open a Developer Command Prompt and type* **TFSBuild help***, or visit* http://aka.ms/tfsBuildexe.

To manually queue a build in Visual Studio, right-click the build definition in Team Explorer and select Queue New Build. You are presented with the Queue Build dialog, as shown in Figure 5-13. The build definition is preselected in the build definition dropdown at the top of the dialog, and its description is displayed underneath.

When you manually queue a build, you have options of selecting an alternative build controller (if one is available), adjusting the priority of the build, and modifying the drop folder location to be different from the default. Based on the selected queue priority, you are also given an indication of the current position in the queue that your build would get if it were submitted.

On the Parameters tab you find all the customizable properties defined for the process, so you can alter the value of that property for this single invocation of the build.

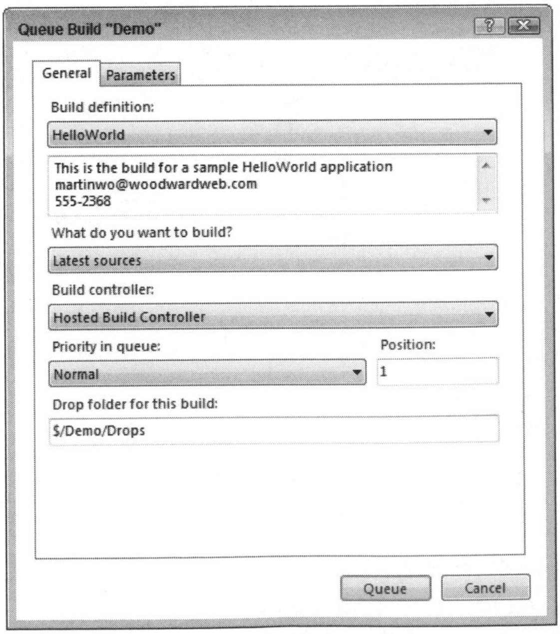

FIGURE 5-13

Private Builds

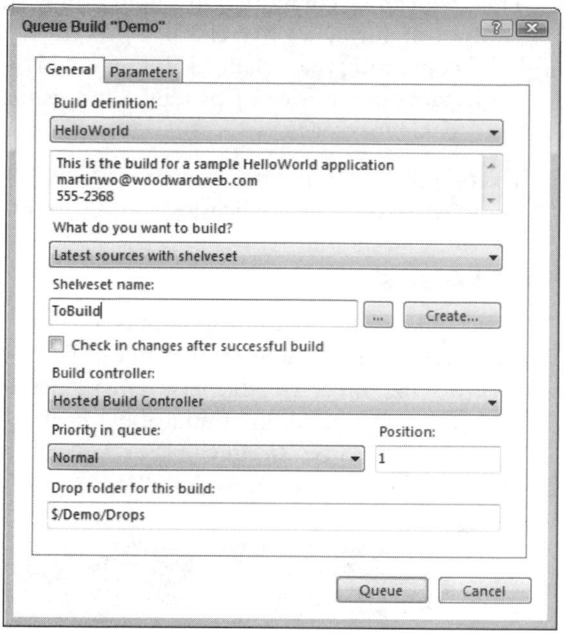

You can adjust what you want to build from the General tab in the Queue Build dialog (Figure 5-14). You can either build from the latest version in source control at the time that the build is submitted to the queue, or you can take the latest version and apply a specified shelveset to the build before it is performed.

If you decide to perform a build that includes a shelveset of your changes not yet checked in to version control, this is called a *private build*, which can sometimes be referred to as a *buddy build*.

Private builds are useful when you want to check that you are including all the changes necessary to successfully perform the build on a different machine before you commit your changes to version control. Another use for them is when you may not have all the dependencies to perform that particular build definition on your local machine (such as a code signing certificate installed), but you want to test that your code functions correctly when built with those dependencies.

FIGURE 5-14

In many ways, a private build is similar to a gated check-in, apart from the fact that your changes are not automatically checked in to version control after a successful build, but you can choose to have them checked in if you want.

Private builds do not follow the same build numbering mechanism defined for the regular team builds, and have separate retention policies. The build results for a private build are displayed to the developer who is invoking the private build, not to the whole team.

Build Notifications

Team Foundation Server exposes a powerful eventing model and both .NET- and Java-based APIs that allow for custom integrations of any imaginable application or device for notification of build results—from standard e-mail alerts to lava lamps, confetti-filled leaf blowers, and even talking robot rabbits. However, two main notification systems are exposed to the developer out of the box—the build notification tool and e-mail alerts.

Build Notification Tool

The build notification tool is a separate application installed with Visual Studio. As shown in Figure 5-15, it is a small application that runs in the system notification area of Windows and notifies the end user of build events via an Outlook-style pop-up message in the bottom-right corner of the screen.

FIGURE 5-15

This tool can be configured to automatically start when you log in to Windows. However, it is always run during a gated check-in process so that the developers are aware of the status of the build containing their changes. If the build is a success, the developers can easily reconcile their workspaces to remove any pending changes that were included in the gated check-in shelveset from their local workspace.

To configure the build notification tool, while the tool is running right-click the icon and select Options. To quit the application entirely, right-click the icon and select Exit.

E-mail Alerts

Basic and custom e-mail alerts can be configured from the web. To quickly view the appropriate web page from Visual Studio, go to the Team ⇨ Project Alerts menu. Using the interface shown in Figure 5-16, you can enable basic e-mail alerts when a build quality changes, when any build completes, or when builds are initiated by the developer. For a more powerful alerts editor, click the Custom Alerts link. (In previous versions of Team Foundation Server, this level of control over alerts required use of power tools or the command line.)

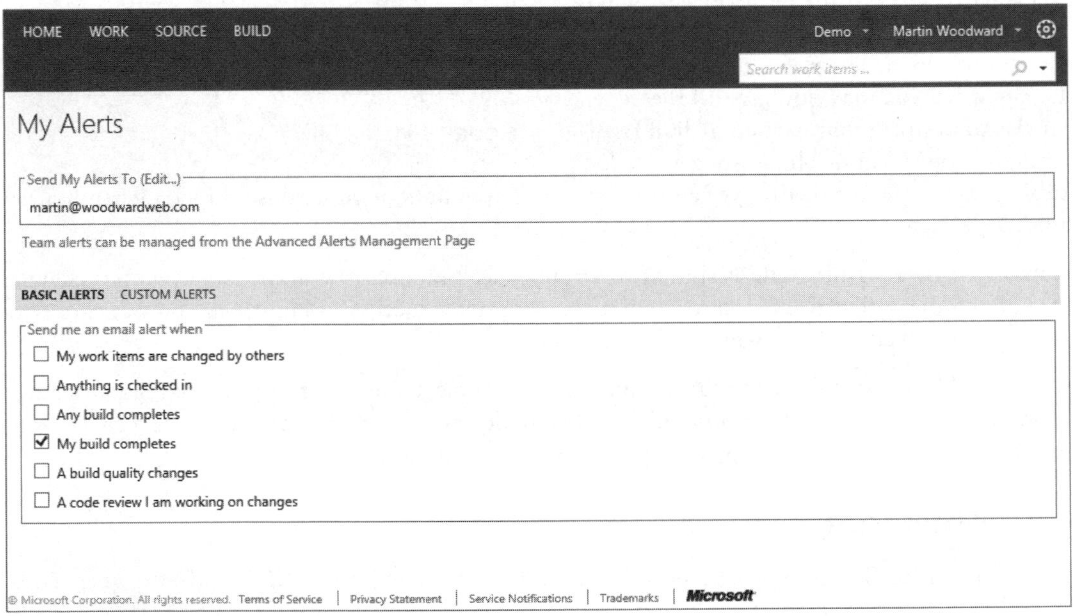

FIGURE 5-16

As shown in Figure 5-16, a link is also provided on the My Alerts page to configure advanced alerts that are applicable to the whole team. Clicking the link takes you into the administrative configuration web portal for your team project.

E-mails can be sent to any e-mail address, including team aliases, provided the Team Foundation Server Application tier is configured with the correct SMTP server details to send the messages.

On the Team Foundation Server Application tier machine, the `BisSubscribe.exe` command is available in the `Team Foundation Server\Tools` folder, and can be used to script the creation of project alerts.

TEAM BUILD PROCESS

The process controlling the end-to-end build process in Team Foundation Server is described in a Windows Workflow 4.0 XAML file. The build process templates are created as part of the project creation process and are defined in the process template.

In the Scrum, MSF Agile, and MSF CMMI processes, the following build processes are included:

➤ *DefaultTemplate*—This is the default template to be used for most new builds created for Team Foundation Server. This is the template that is the primary focus of discussion in the remainder of this chapter.

➤ *UpgradeTemplate*—This is the default template for builds upgraded from Team Foundation Server 2008, or newer builds that make heavy use of MSBuild rather than Windows Workflow. Basically, it performs some housekeeping, and then just wraps the call to the `TFSBuild.proj` file for an MSBuild-based build configuration. Java builds created by Team Explorer Everywhere make use of the UpgradeTemplate to provide a thin wrapper around Ant or Maven. This allows all the configuration files to be edited by a simple text editor and does not require knowledge of Windows Workflow—but it pushes the majority of the build logic down into the Ant or Maven build script that is invoked.

In addition, the LabDefaultTemplate build process template is also installed for the Lab Management functionality by the Lab section of the MSF processes.

> **NOTE** *Chapter 26 provides more information on Lab Management functionality in Visual Studio 2012.*

All the build process templates are stored as files in version control, allowing for quick and easy auditing of any changes to the process used to perform the build. By default, these are stored in a folder called BuildProcessTemplates at the root of the team project in version control, but may be located inside your team project branch structure, if that's more convenient.

The majority of the remainder of this chapter focuses on the DefaultTemplate—how it works, how to use it, and how to modify it.

DefaultTemplate Process

The DefaultTemplate is used for most new, un-customized build definitions. The process is outlined at a high level in Figure 5-17, but you can explore it in detail by opening the `DefaultTemplate.xaml` file from version control inside Visual Studio.

```
┌─────────────────────────────────────────────────┐
│ DefaultTemplate Process                           │
│  ╭─────────────────────────────────────────────╮ │
│  │ Get the Build Definition                      │ │
│  ╰─────────────────────────────────────────────╯ │
│  ╭─────────────────────────────────────────────╮ │
│  │ Update Build Number                           │ │
│  ╰─────────────────────────────────────────────╯ │
│  ╭─────────────────────────────────────────────╮ │
│  │ Create Drop Folder                            │ │
│  ╰─────────────────────────────────────────────╯ │
│  ╭─────────────────────────────────────────────╮ │
│  │ Get Build Agent                               │ │
│  ╰─────────────────────────────────────────────╯ │
│  ┌─────────────────────────────────────────────┐ │
│  │ Run On Agent                                  │ │
│  │  ╭───────────────────────────────────────╮   │ │
│  │  │ Get Build Directory                     │   │ │
│  │  ╰───────────────────────────────────────╯   │ │
│  │  ╭───────────────────────────────────────╮   │ │
│  │  │ Initialize Workspace                    │   │ │
│  │  ╰───────────────────────────────────────╯   │ │
│  │  ╭───────────────────────────────────────╮   │ │
│  │  │ Get Source                              │   │ │
│  │  ╰───────────────────────────────────────╯   │ │
│  │  ╭───────────────────────────────────────╮   │ │
│  │  │ Create Label                            │   │ │
│  │  ╰───────────────────────────────────────╯   │ │
│  │  ╭───────────────────────────────────────╮   │ │
│  │  │ Compile                                 │   │ │
│  │  ╰───────────────────────────────────────╯   │ │
│  │  ╭───────────────────────────────────────╮   │ │
│  │  │ Test                                    │   │ │
│  │  ╰───────────────────────────────────────╯   │ │
│  │  ╭───────────────────────────────────────╮   │ │
│  │  │ Associate Work Items                    │   │ │
│  │  ╰───────────────────────────────────────╯   │ │
│  │  ╭───────────────────────────────────────╮   │ │
│  │  │ Calculate Impacted Tests                │   │ │
│  │  ╰───────────────────────────────────────╯   │ │
│  │  ╭───────────────────────────────────────╮   │ │
│  │  │ Index Sources                           │   │ │
│  │  ╰───────────────────────────────────────╯   │ │
│  │  ╭───────────────────────────────────────╮   │ │
│  │  │ Publish Symbols                         │   │ │
│  │  ╰───────────────────────────────────────╯   │ │
│  │  ╭───────────────────────────────────────╮   │ │
│  │  │ Copy Build Outputs to Drop Folder       │   │ │
│  │  ╰───────────────────────────────────────╯   │ │
│  └─────────────────────────────────────────────┘ │
│  ╭─────────────────────────────────────────────╮ │
│  │ Check-in Gated Changes for CheckInShelveset   │ │
│  │ Builds                                        │ │
│  ╰─────────────────────────────────────────────╯ │
└─────────────────────────────────────────────────┘
```

FIGURE 5-17

On the build controller, the build number is calculated and the drop location for the build is created. Then the build agent is determined, and the majority of the rest of the process is performed on the selected agent from the controllers build agent pool.

The working directory for the build is calculated by using the build agent working directory setting as defined in the Build Agent Properties dialog. Then the workspace is created (if required), and source is downloaded from version control. The version that is downloaded is usually the changeset that represented the latest version in the project collection at the time the build was triggered. If a subsequent change has been made while the build was queued, this change is not included. The files that were downloaded are then labeled in version control with the build number.

Next, the process calls MSBuild to perform the actual compilation of the desired project files for the configuration, and then any specified automated tests are executed. The build agent then looks at the changesets included since the last successful build of the build definition, and records any work items that were associated with those check-ins. For work items that were marked as resolved during check-in, the Fixed-In Build field for the work item is updated with the current build number.

From the files changed since the last successful build, the build agent then calculates which tests have been affected, and records them. The source code is then indexed and linked with the symbols that are published to the symbol server (if provided). Finally, on the build agent, the output from the build is copied over to the drop folder location previously created by the controller.

The process then moves back to the controller for the final step, which, for a build with a Gated Check-in trigger, is to check in the shelveset that contained the modified files included in the build.

Build Process Parameters

The build process templates are configured to make a number of parameters visible in the user interface in either the Build Definition editor or the Queue Build dialog (or both). These parameters (Figure 5-18) are provided to control the behavior of the selected build process.

When you create the build definition, you set one of these parameters, Items to Build, to be the solution file that you want to build. However, there are many other parameters provided for you to adjust the behavior of the template. If you select one of the parameters, additional information is displayed about the parameter in the comments box at the bottom of the process parameter table.

In the default process templates, these parameters are broken down into four categories: Required, Basic, Advanced, and Misc. Some of these parameters are worth calling out in this chapter, and are examined in the following discussions. However, it is worth familiarizing yourself with all the parameters and what they do.

Configurations to Build

The default Visual Studio build configuration to use is the default build configuration for your solution. To modify the configuration, use the Configurations dialog that is available when you press the ... button in the Configurations to Build parameter under Required, Items to Build.

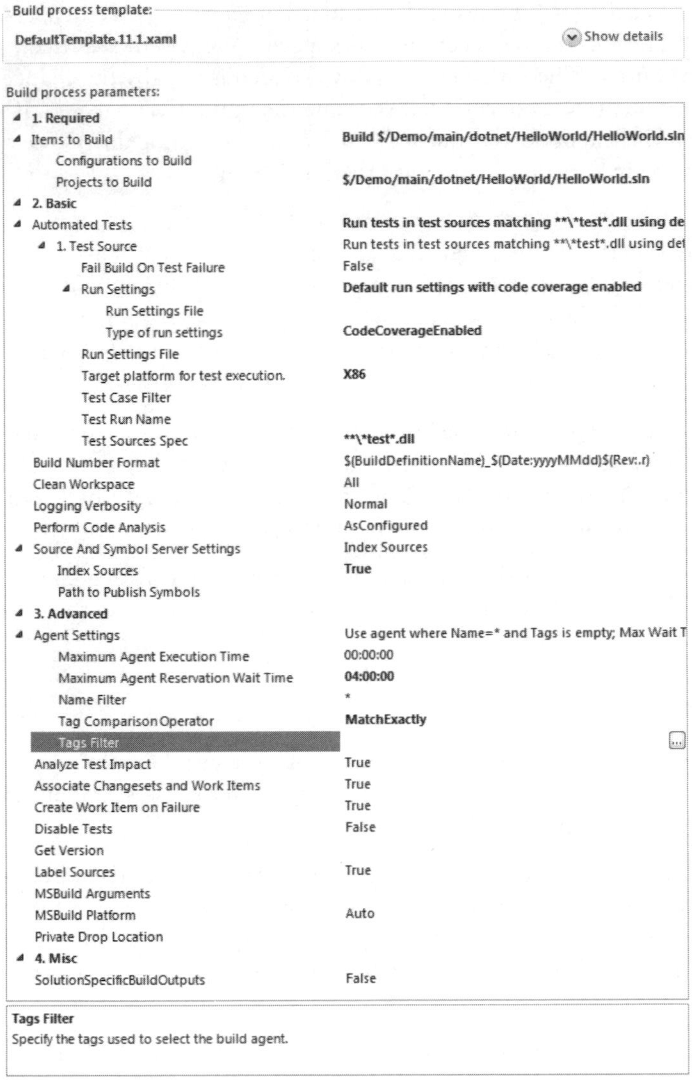

Build process template:

DefaultTemplate.11.1.xaml   ⌄ Show details

Build process parameters:

▲ 1. Required	
▲ Items to Build	Build $/Demo/main/dotnet/HelloWorld/HelloWorld.sln
Configurations to Build	
Projects to Build	$/Demo/main/dotnet/HelloWorld/HelloWorld.sln
▲ 2. Basic	
▲ Automated Tests	Run tests in test sources matching ***test*.dll using de
▲ 1. Test Source	Run tests in test sources matching ***test*.dll using def
Fail Build On Test Failure	False
▲ Run Settings	Default run settings with code coverage enabled
Run Settings File	
Type of run settings	CodeCoverageEnabled
Run Settings File	
Target platform for test execution.	X86
Test Case Filter	
Test Run Name	
Test Sources Spec	***test*.dll
Build Number Format	$(BuildDefinitionName)_$(Date:yyyyMMdd)$(Rev:.r)
Clean Workspace	All
Logging Verbosity	Normal
Perform Code Analysis	AsConfigured
▲ Source And Symbol Server Settings	Index Sources
Index Sources	True
Path to Publish Symbols	
▲ 3. Advanced	
▲ Agent Settings	Use agent where Name=* and Tags is empty; Max Wait T
Maximum Agent Execution Time	00:00:00
Maximum Agent Reservation Wait Time	04:00:00
Name Filter	*
Tag Comparison Operator	MatchExactly
Tags Filter	...
Analyze Test Impact	True
Associate Changesets and Work Items	True
Create Work Item on Failure	True
Disable Tests	False
Get Version	
Label Sources	True
MSBuild Arguments	
MSBuild Platform	Auto
Private Drop Location	
▲ 4. Misc	
SolutionSpecificBuildOutputs	False

Tags Filter
Specify the tags used to select the build agent.

FIGURE 5-18

SOLUTION CONFIGURATIONS

Team Foundation Build typically deals with *solution configurations*. These enable you to specify a named collection of project-level platforms and configurations that should be built. For more information on solution configurations, see the blog post from Aaron Hallberg of the Team Foundation Build team at Microsoft, available at http://aka.ms/slnConfigs.

Logging Verbosity

By default, only messages above normal priority get included in the build log. However, you can adjust the logging priority to change the level of detail recorded. The more detailed the log, the slower the build will be performed, and the longer it will take to download build data to Visual Studio.

When diagnosing build problems, it is often useful to manually queue a build with this property set to Diagnostic. In that way, the log priority is only set for a single run of the build, rather than for all builds from that definition. The logging verbosity parameter can be found in the Basic category.

Agent Settings

Agent Settings can be found in the Advanced category of parameters. As well as limits for how long a build can run or wait for an available build agent, the Agent Settings group of process parameters includes both the Name Filter and Tags Filter. Together, these are used to determine on which build agent the build will be executed. If multiple build agents match the agent requirements, then the agent with the least number of builds running executes the build.

Specifying the Name of a build agent enables you to force it to run on a particular machine. You can also adopt a naming convention for your build agents, and then use wildcards in the Name Filter to assign builds to a pool containing a subset of all the build agents for the project collection (for example, "ProjectX*" for all build agents assigned to "ProjectX").

A more flexible way you can limit which build agents are used for a build is to make use of the tagging feature for build agents. From the build agent properties dialog, you can assign *tags* (which are a set of text strings) to an agent to denote certain features. For example, you could use "CodeSign" if you have the project's code signing certificate installed on the machine, "Datacenter1" if it is located in your main data center, or "Ireland" if the build server is located in your remote office in Ireland. You can then filter on which tags are required for your build agent by using the Tags Filter in the Agent Requirements; only agents with that tag will be used.

To edit the tags applied to a particular agent, you can use the Team Foundation Server Administration Console on the build agent machine itself, or you can select the Actions ⇨ Manage Build Controllers... menu item in the Builds page in Team Explorer. You then select your build agent and click the Properties button. You are presented with the Build Agent Properties dialog, and, provided you have sufficient permissions, you are able to edit the assigned tags.

Clean Workspace

By default, the Clean Workspace parameter is set to All, meaning that all existing build outputs and sources for that build definition are deleted for every build. Although this is the safest option, it is also the slowest, because all the files must be downloaded from version control, and everything is rebuilt for every build, regardless of what has changed.

If you have a lot of source files (or some very large files in your source), then you could set the value of this parameter to Outputs. This simply deletes the build outputs every time the build is performed, and only gets the files that have changed between builds from version control.

If you set the value of the parameter to None, then neither the sources nor the build outputs are deleted at the start of a build. Only the files that have changed in version control are downloaded each time, and only the things that have changed are recompiled as part of the build. Because not a lot of things usually change between builds, this normally gives your builds a significant performance boost by taking much less time to complete. It is also often useful for things such as ASP.NET-based websites, where you might want to subsequently only publish the items that have changed to your public website to minimize the upgrade effect for new versions.

However, if you have customized your build process and you make any of the source files writable for some reason (for example, to modify the `AssemblyInfo` files to contain your version number), or if your customized build process assumes a clean output directory, then you may run into issues with altering the default value of the Clean Workspace. So, use with caution.

Note that on the hosted service at `http://tfspreview.com`, all build agents are created from a fresh image each time a build is executed so there is no persistence of the workspace in between builds. Therefore, altering this setting has no affect when using a hosted build agent.

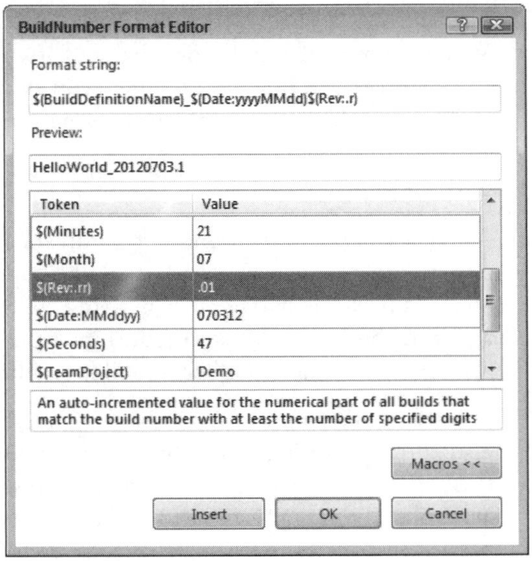

FIGURE 5-19

Build Number Format

By default, Team Foundation Server numbers the builds in the format `$(BuildDefinitionName) _$(Date:yyyyMMdd)$(Rev:.r)`. For example, in `HelloWorld_20090927.5`, the 5 is the fifth build executed for that build definition on that day. Build numbers must be unique across a team project, and this format serves as a good default. However, it is often not the format that people want.

Thankfully, starting in Team Foundation Server 2010, editing the build number is very easy using the Build Number Format parameter. When you edit the Build Number Format parameter, you are presented with a dialog, similar to Figure 5-18, that gives you the format string, a preview of what a build number of that format will look like when generated, and a set of macro strings that can be used in the format. Clicking each macro gives you more information about its behavior in the command section at the bottom of the dialog.

A common number format to use is `$(BuildDefinitionName)_V1.0.0$(Rev:.r)`, where you are currently working on version 1.0.0 of the product, and the `$(Rev:.r)` macro translates to an incrementing number that makes the build number unique.

Path to Publish Symbols

The DefaultTemplate in Team Foundation Server includes a step to index source code and publish symbols to a symbol server in the organization. As mentioned earlier in this chapter, a symbol server is simply a file share that is used to store the symbols for your executable binaries. Visual Studio can then be configured with details of this server. From then on, when debugging code live, or using the advanced historical debugging features, Visual Studio is able to take you directly to the version of the source code from which the binary was generated, regardless of which version of the code that you have on your local system at that time.

The configuration of the symbol server is performed by adding the UNC file path of the share to be used as the symbol sever in the "Path to Publish Symbols" process parameter under "Basic, Source and Symbol Server Settings."

Automated Tests

In the basic category of process parameters, you are able to configure automated tests that should run as part of the build using the Automated Tests parameter. By default, a new build runs all unit tests in assemblies matching the pattern `*test*.dll`. This means that, if you have created some unit tests in a companion test project called `HelloWorldTests`, for example, then they will be run automatically.

Pressing the ... button opens the Automated Tests dialog shown in Figure 5-20, where you can add additional tests to run, or you can edit the test configuration.

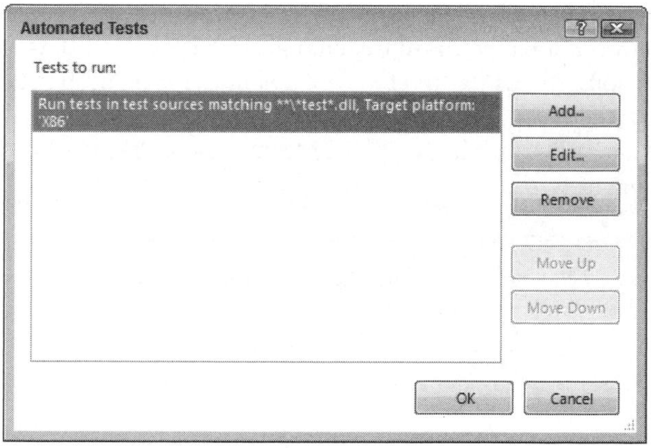

FIGURE 5-20

If you select the existing test configuration and click Edit, the Add/Edit Test dialog shown in Figure 5-21 is displayed, enabling you to edit aspects of your test run. For example, you can configure it to fail the build on test failure, modify the test case filter criteria, specify the test runner, or enable code coverage data collection.

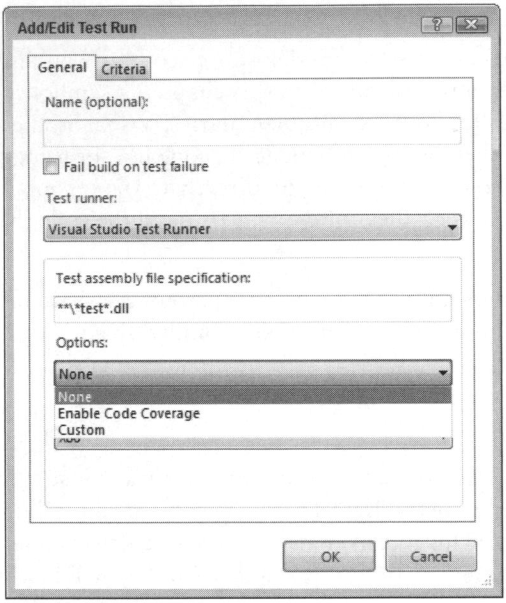

FIGURE 5-21

Get Version

Builds are usually performed with the latest sources from version control. However, occasionally you may want to perform a build of the source at a particular date, changeset, or label. In those circumstances, you can modify the Get Version process parameter which is in the Advanced section. This is usually done as you queue the build by clicking the Parameters tab. The value provided should be a valid version specification such as C1234 for changeset 1234, D2008-04-22T17:37 for a date/time, or LmyLabel for a label called myLabel.

> **NOTE** *For more information on the TFS version specification formats to use when specifying changesets, labels, or dates to use as the Get Version see the* VersionSpecs *section in MSDN* http://aka.ms/tfsVersionSpecs.

SUMMARY

In this chapter, you examined the build services provided by Team Foundation Server 2012 and how they have been enhanced from previous versions.

You learned how to create build definitions, trigger builds, and view and manage build results. You also learned how the new Windows Workflow–based build process works and how to perform common customizations by editing the process parameters.

In Chapter 6, you learn about common Team Foundation Server customizations, including how to edit the process template used by your builds to include new logic and parameters that do not ship in the default build processes.

6

Common Team Foundation Server Customizations

WHAT'S IN THIS CHAPTER?

➤ Examining the Team Foundation Server Object Model

➤ Customizing Team Foundation Build

➤ Customizing Team Foundation Version Control

➤ Customizing Work Item Tracking

➤ Customizing the TFS Eventing Model

One of Microsoft's goals when Team Foundation Server (TFS) 2005 was first released was to make the platform extensible. Although Microsoft's intention was to provide a set of tools and guidance for conducting application lifecycle management using TFS, the company also knew that people and organizations already have their own methodologies. And although people may want to use TFS for their tooling, they still want to follow their own software development process.

So Microsoft provided several extensibility points within TFS to extend different aspects of the system as needed. It also provided an API that developers can use for creating custom applications to access and utilize different systems in TFS, such as work item tracking and version control.

As you've seen in previous chapters, TFS itself is made up of a variety of web services, so you might think that you could just write custom applications to utilize those web services. And you could, but that would not be considered best practice. Instead, you should make use of the APIs (which interact with the web services). This ensures that any customizations or extensions you create should be forward compatible with future versions of TFS.

This chapter is about some of the common ways you can customize Team Foundation Server. It's designed to be a high-level overview—to whet your appetite for the types of things you can do. As such, there are not many step-by-step examples of the customizations.

> **NOTE** *For more detailed information on customizing and extending Team Foundation Server, read* Professional Team Foundation Server 2012 *by Ed Blankenship, Martin Woodward, Grant Holliday, and Brian Keller (Wrox, 2012)*

OBJECT MODELS

To start off this talk on customization and extensibility, let's look at the available object models in Team Foundation Server. Although TFS is composed of several different web services, in general, you do not want to interact with the web services directly when building customizations to TFS. Instead, you want to use the different object models (that is, APIs) that are available to you to provide a level of abstraction between yourself and the TFS Web Services, as shown in Figure 6-1.

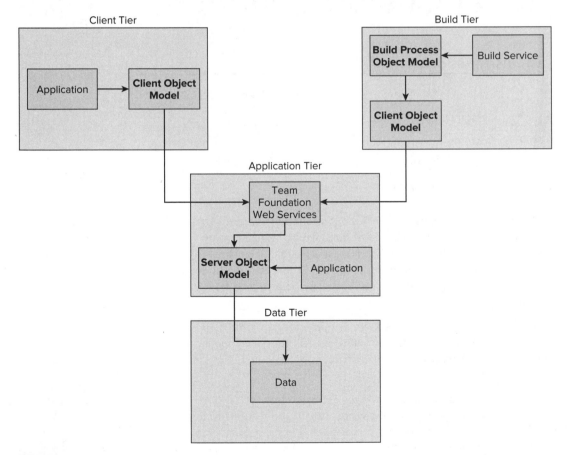

FIGURE 6-1

This ensures that as the web services in future versions of TFS are updated, any code you've written should continue to function as expected.

There are three main object models: client, server, and build process.

Client Object Model

You use the client object model for developing custom applications or extensions that will mostly run from a client-side perspective—for example, creating a custom work item control for the work item tracking system, or creating a custom application for accessing the version control system.

Some of the things you can do with the client object model include accessing Team Foundation Server and viewing team project and project collection information. You can also access all the different TFS subsystems, such as work item tracking, version control, and build. You can also use this object model to extend team projects, adding new functionality and extending Team Explorer.

Server Object Model

You use the server object model to develop applications that must run on the application tier. Typically this is used to integrate other tools or data from other applications with Team Foundation Server.

For example, you can use the server object model to create a custom data warehouse adapter, to store custom data in the TFS data warehouse. Or you can use the server object model to customize the eventing service in Team Foundation Server (more on this in the section "Team Foundation Server Event Service" later in this chapter).

Build Process Object Model

You use the build process object model to customize the Team Foundation build process. In most cases you use this object model to help build custom build workflow activities. You learn more about build customization later in this chapter.

Simple Object Model Example

This section demonstrates a simple example of connecting to Team Foundation Server and listing the project collection information it contains. This example shows you the basics of using the client object model, and you can use it as a basis for future customizations.

In Visual Studio, create a new C# console application, and name it `Chapter6Example`. First, you need to add a reference to the `Microsoft.TeamFoundation.Common` and `Microsoft.TeamFoundation.Client` assemblies. In Solution Explorer, right-click on the References folder and select Add Reference. Click the `Browse` button, and navigate to `%ProgramFiles%\Microsoft Visual Studio 11.0\Common7\IDE\ReferenceAssemblies\v2.0`. Select the two assemblies listed above and click `Add`. Click `OK` to close the Reference Assembly window.

Add the following `using` statements to `Program.cs`:

```
using System.Collections.ObjectModel;
using Microsoft.TeamFoundation.Client;
using Microsoft.TeamFoundation.Framework.Common;
using Microsoft.TeamFoundation.Framework.Client;
```

Next, add the following code snippet into the `Main` method:

```
// Connect to Team Foundation Server
Uri tfsUri = new Uri("http://VSALM:8080/tfs");

TfsConfigurationServer tfsServer =
            TfsConfigurationServerFactory.GetConfigurationServer(tfsUri);

// Get team project collections
ReadOnlyCollection<CatalogNode> tpCollections = tfsServer.CatalogNode.QueryChildren(
            new[] { CatalogResourceTypes.ProjectCollection },
            false, CatalogQueryOptions.None);

// write out the team project collections
foreach (CatalogNode node in tpCollections)
{

    Guid nodeId = new Guid(node.Resource.Properties["InstanceId"]);
    TfsTeamProjectCollection tpCollection =
     tfsServer.GetTeamProjectCollection(nodeId);

Console.WriteLine("");
Console.Writeline("TFS: " + tfsURI);
Console.Writeline("");
Console.WriteLine("Collection: " + tpCollection.Name);
}
```

Build and run this console application and you should see output similar to Figure 6-2. You will be able to build off the preceding code to create your own extensions and customizations.

FIGURE 6-2

> **NOTE** *To make this code run, you need to change* `http://VSALM:8080/tfs` *to be the URL for your TFS installation.*

Java SDK for TFS

From its beginnings with Team Foundation Server 2005, TFS was designed with extensibility in mind. As such, Microsoft provided a .NET library (please see the previous section for more details) for interacting with and extending TFS.

Microsoft has extended this into the Java space, with the addition of the Team Foundation Server SDK for Java. This SDK enables you to extend TFS using Java just as easily as you can using .NET. One of the nice features of this is that it enables users of Team Explorer Everywhere to fully customize their development environments, either in or out of Eclipse. This enables you to create the same TFS extensions for both the .NET and Java developers in your organization.

The TFS Java SDK includes the following information:

➤ A redistributable JAR file containing the TFS APIs and the native code libraries used by the TFS API.

➤ Full API documentation in Javadoc format

➤ Code samples

From a licensing perspective, you can use the SDK in your own applications, redistributing the files at no charge. And you can create applications that run on any of the operating systems supported by the API.

> **NOTE** *You can find more information on the Team Foundation Server SDK for Java at* `http://aka.ms/TFSJavaSDK`.

CUSTOMIZING TEAM FOUNDATION BUILD

In Chapter 5 you learned about Team Foundation Build, the build process, and build process templates. The "out of the box" options for Team Foundation Build probably work for most people, at least initially. At some point though, you are going to want to modify the build process. This section discusses a couple of common ways for customizing Team Foundation Build.

Creating Custom Build Process Templates

In Chapter 5 you learned about the DefaultTemplate build process template, and how its preconfigured properties enable you to perform common build scenarios. However, to perform more complex build activities, such as being able to parallelize parts of the build across multiple build agents, or create MSI installers, you are going to have to customize the build process. To do this, you need to create a custom build process template.

To create a new build process template, start by editing the build definition. In the Process section of the dialog, click the New button near the top of the screen. This opens the New Build Process Template dialog, shown in Figure 6-3.

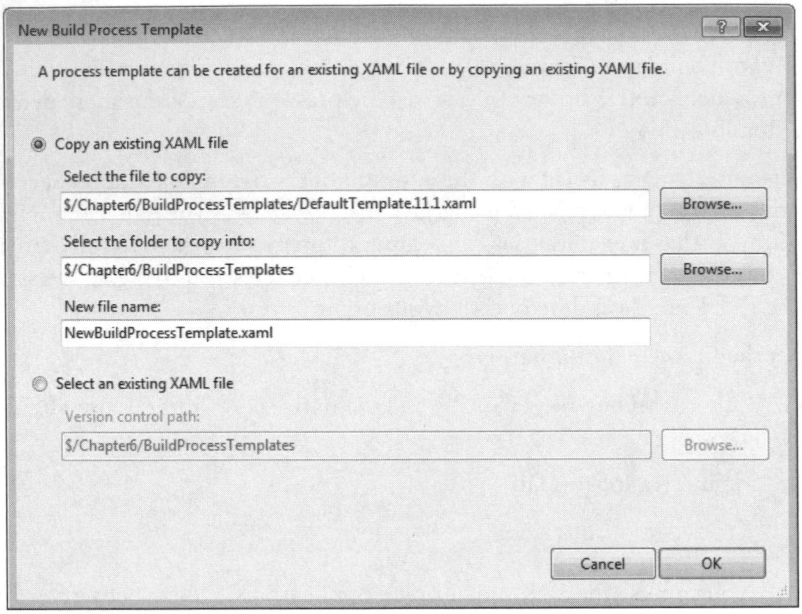

FIGURE 6-3

In the dialog, select Copy an Existing XAML File and point it to `DefaultTemplate.xaml`. Select the folder in which to create the new process template and enter the new filename—in this case, let's use `NewBuildProcessTemplate.xaml`.

This creates the file in version control. You can now start using this template when creating build definitions. You can also double-click the file from within Source Control Explorer to open it for editing (see Figure 6-4).

Team Foundation Server ships with a set of additional workflow activities related to the build process in the assembly `Microsoft.TeamFoundation.Build.Workflow`. This includes all the build-related activities called by the build process templates that ship with the product, along with several other activities that are useful when performing common build customizations.

If you look in Figure 6-4, you can see that a `WriteBuildMessage` activity has been added to the top of the build. You can see the properties for this activity in the properties window at the bottom right. The `Display Name` has been set to Log Welcome Message, and a message has been included to write to the build log.

> **NOTE** *For more information on creating custom build process templates, see* `http://aka.ms/CustomBuildProcessTemplates`.

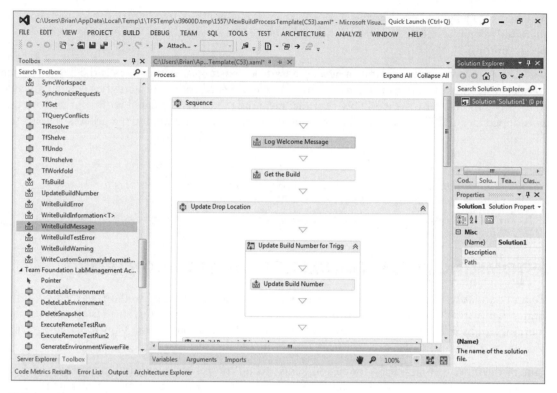

FIGURE 6-4

Creating Custom Build Workflow Activities

As you saw in the previous section, it is possible to edit the build process template to build increased functionality. Sometimes, however, you may want to collect common workflow activities in a custom, re-usable Workflow Activity Library. Also, sometimes you might not want to simply build activities out of other activities, but also execute your own .NET code.

Team Foundation Build allows for this, enabling you to create your own Windows Workflow activity libraries in .NET 4.0, build them as a compiled assembly containing your activities, and then use them in your build process. The Team Build workflow activities are provided in this way.

There are four main ways to author a new activity:

➤ Write a new `CodeActivity`

➤ Write a new `NativeActivity`

➤ Compose your custom activity in XAML

➤ Compose your custom activity in code

The first two ways involve creating code using the Windows Workflow libraries. Although not incredibly complicated, it does require some exposure and knowledge of Windows Workflow programming.

The last two ways involve creating a new activity from existing activities. This is the best approach to take, when possible, for a few reasons. It re-uses well-tested code. The activities created are automatically cancelable by the workflow runtime, meaning that a build created with your activity can be stopped cleanly. They can be easily tracked as they execute. And finally, the process is comparably easy.

> **NOTE** *For more information on building custom workflow activities for Team Foundation Build, see* `http://aka.ms/CustomWorkflowActivities`.

CUSTOMIZING TEAM FOUNDATION VERSION CONTROL

Team Foundation Version Control is very powerful tool that works very well out of the box. It integrates well with Visual Studio and provides some enterprise-level features, such as branching and merging, and shelvesets. In addition to accessing Team Foundation Version Control from within Visual Studio, you can also access it from the command line, using the `tf.exe` tool.

One of the more common ways for customizing version control includes building custom check-in policies. You can also use the client object model to create your own custom applications for accessing the version control system.

> **NOTE** *For more information on using the client object model with Team Foundation version control, see* `http://aka.ms/ExtendingVersionControl`.

Custom Check-in Policies

As you learned in Chapter 3, check-in policies provide a way for the team and individuals to effectively manage quality and workflow to the source management process used by the team. Check-in policies run on the actual client, and are configured at the team project level in Team Foundation Server.

You get several check-in policies out of the box with Team Foundation Server, and more can be added by installing the Team Foundation Power Tools. You also have the capability to create your own custom policy, using the client object model.

First, you have to build a custom policy class that derives from the `PolicyBase` base class in the `Microsoft.TeamFoundation.VersionControl.Client` namespace. When the policy is created, it needs to be installed on any machine that will be checking in code that will be affected by the check-in policy. Remember, check-in policies execute on the client side; as such, they must be present on the machine trying to execute the policy, or code cannot be checked in without overriding the policy.

Finally, after the policy has been deployed, it needs to be added to the team project. This ensures that the policy is evaluated each time a developer checks in a file to this team project.

> **NOTE** *For more information on building custom check-in policies, see* `http://aka.ms/CustomCheckinPolicies`.

TEAM FOUNDATION SERVER EVENT SERVICE

The `EventService` service in Team Foundation Server exposes a set of events that, when fired by TFS, can trigger other actions, such as sending an e-mail, or making a web service call to another application. The following events are registered by default for publishing within the service:

- ➤ `Build Completion Event`
- ➤ `Build Status Changed Event`
- ➤ `BranchMovedEvent`
- ➤ `NodeCreatedEvent`
- ➤ `NodePropertiesChangedEvent`
- ➤ `NodeRenamedEvent`
- ➤ `NodesDeletedEvent`
- ➤ `ProjectCreatedEvent`
- ➤ `ProjectDeletedEvent`
- ➤ `CheckinEvent`
- ➤ `WorkItemChanged`

You can make use of the `BisSubscribe.exe`, a TFS command-line tool, to subscribe to the events in the preceding list. When you subscribe to an event, you can either trigger a web service or send an e-mail. This enables you to receive notifications when certain events occur, or trigger other functionality to execute based off the event. The `BisSubscribe.exe` tool has filtering options available, which enables you to control exactly what types of events trigger what functionality.

You can also make use of the `EventService` service to create your own custom events that can be subscribed to. To do this, you need to create a class library that contains a class that represents the new event. After this class library has been built, you need to create an `.xsd` file that represents the event class. This is an XML schema file representing the event class that can be generated from the class library. This `.xsd` file will be placed on TFS, which then enables users to subscribe to the new event.

> **NOTE** *You can find more information on how to use and customize the Team Foundation Server Event Service at* `http://aka.ms/TFSEventService`.

CUSTOMIZING WORK ITEM TRACKING

You find out about the work item tracking system in Chapter 10. This system is used to help plan and track your software development projects. Out of all the areas in TFS, it is probably the one that is the most heavily customized; it helps to control the process and workflows you will use to develop your applications. You can do things such as make fields required or read-only, or change the workflow from moving from one state to the next.

The two main ways for customizing the work item tracking system are modifying the work item type definitions to follow your custom process, and creating custom work item controls for use on the work item form.

Modifying Work Item Type Definitions

A work item type definition is simply an XML file. This XML file is stored in Team Foundation Server as part of a process template, and defines the fields, workflows, and form layout for a particular type of work item, such as a Task or a Bug. There will be times when you want to customize a work item type, such as the Task work item, to contain custom fields, or to follow a workflow other than the default workflow.

There are two main tools you can use for modifying work item type definitions: the `witadmin` command-line tool and the Team Foundation Power Tools Process Template Editor.

You can use the `witadmin` command-line tool to export a work item type definition from Team Foundation Server into an XML text file. You can then open this XML file using your favorite XML/text editor of choice and make your customizations. Keep in mind this is an XML file, so if you mistype something or violate the XML schema, the changes will not load back into TFS. After you have finished your changes, you can use the `witadmin` tool to load the new work item type back into TFS, where it takes effect.

For those who want a more graphical interface for working with work item type definitions, you can use the Process Template Editor that is available with the Team Foundation Power Tools. The Process Template editor provides a complete GUI for working with all aspects of a process template, including work item type definitions.

> **NOTE** *The Team Foundation Power Tools are utilities released by the TFS team outside of the product release cycle/timeframe. For more information see* `http://aka.ms/TFPowerTools`.
>
> *For more information on work item type customizations, see* `http://aka.ms/WITCustomizations`.

Creating Custom Work Item Controls

You can also extend the work item tracking system to allow for custom user controls. These controls enable you to enhance the user interface and extend the workflow capabilities. You can bind custom controls to fields within a work item type, which enables users to view and edit data as needed. The controls can also read and write from external data sources, enabling you to query databases or web services for data to pull back and provide in the form.

Some examples of custom controls include a timesheet control for tracking time on a work item, or a web browser control for hosting a web page or passing values to that web page.

Custom controls act like any other control on a work item form. You can place them on the form, using the default design layout constraints, and you can use their values as part of a state change workflow.

There are some restrictions to be aware of when dealing with custom controls:

➤ Multiple value fields are not directly supported.

➤ You can't extend existing work item controls.

➤ The binaries for each custom control must be installed on the client computer.

➤ Custom controls not configured correctly or not installed must not cause the client to crash when accessing a work item type that uses that control.

One of the most important things to remember is that the custom controls must be deployed to individual client machines. Remember, the work item type definition is stored in Team Foundation Server. However, when you open a work item type that contains a custom user control, it tries to access the control assembly information on the local client machine. As such, the assembly that defines the custom user control must exist on the client machine.

For detailed information on building custom work item tracking controls, see the post "Work Item Tracking Custom Controls" by Gregg Boer at `http://aka.ms/WITCustomControls`.

> **NOTE** *For some prebuilt custom work item controls, as well as the source code associated with them, see the Custom Controls for TFS Work Item Tracking project at codeplex.com:* `http://witcustomcontrols.codeplex.com/`.

SUMMARY

In this chapter, you gained a high-level understanding of the different ways that Team Foundation Server can be extended and customized.

You learned about the different object models available within Team Foundation Server, and when to use them. You also saw a step-by-step example of using the client object model to connect to Team Foundation Server and list the project collections contained within.

You learned how to customize Team Foundation build, including the creation of custom build process templates, and custom build workflow activities. And you learned how to customize the version control process using custom check-in policies.

Finally, you saw how the eventing service in TFS works, and how you can customize it, as well as how you can modify the work item tracking system by using custom work item type definitions and custom work item controls.

In Chapter 7, you learn about the importance of engaging early and frequently with your software development project's stakeholders. You also learn about the tools that Microsoft and its partners have built to facilitate requirements management and collaboration among project stakeholders.

PART II
Building the Right Software

7

Introduction to Building the Right Software

WHAT'S IN THIS CHAPTER?

➤ Understanding the importance of engaging stakeholders throughout the software development process

➤ Learning how Microsoft is extending its ALM toolset in this release to incorporate stakeholders

➤ Discovering other ways of integrating stakeholder feedback with Team Foundation Server 2012

Every software development project begins with requirements. These requirements may be stated explicitly, such as the need for a payroll system to initiate direct deposits twice each month so that employees can get paid, taking into account the salary rate for each employee, minus any deductions for taxes and other withholdings. Or requirements may be more implicit, even abstract, such as the need for a video game to be fun and enjoyable.

In some software development projects, requirements are stated up front, before any code is written. In these software development projects, coding can only begin after the requirements have been finalized. This is traditionally referred to as a *waterfall* approach to building software. With a waterfall approach, the outputs from one phase of the development lifecycle flow into the inputs for the next phase (requirements flow into architectural design which flows into coding which flows into testing and so on).

With *agile* software development projects, there is an explicit recognition that requirements will likely change and evolve over time, even during the lifespan of a single software development project. Business opportunities present themselves, competition forces innovation, new regulations and compliance policies are introduced, and even the introduction of new technologies makes some requirements obsolete while enabling other solutions. Requirements can even evolve as your software users start to use early builds of your software; this may cause them to change their opinions about their original requirements, or could inspire entirely new requirements.

The Agile Manifesto (`http://www.agilemanifesto.org`) says this about software requirements:

> *Welcome changing requirements, even late in development. Agile processes harness change for the customer's competitive advantage.*

Regardless of the software development approach you take, it is vital to understand the requirements you are attempting to fulfill with your software. Arguably, the only software mistake more expensive than a bug is that of building the wrong software in the first place. At least bugs can be fixed whereas building the wrong software may cause you to need to scrap the effort entirely. This is such a serious problem in the software industry that we have invented a unique term for it: *shelfware*. Software that is either too hard to implement or doesn't meet the necessary requirements is doomed to sit on the shelf unused.

So how do we ensure that we adequately understand the requirements our software must fulfill? How do we account for changes to those requirements over time? How should we prioritize the requirements that we work on? A big part of the answer is to engage early and often with your software development project's *stakeholders*.

> **NOTE** *Neither this book, nor Microsoft's toolset, endorses one particular process — waterfall or agile — as the universal solution for software development projects. Every software development project is different. A waterfall approach may be well suited for building the software for a lunar lander or a back-end banking system because requirements can be expressed explicitly up front. But a waterfall approach is typically ill suited for managing the development of a social media website because the ever-changing preferences of your users and fierce competition can drive rapid changes to requirements. An agile approach is typically better suited for this type of software development project.*
>
> *Many projects even employ an approach that blends waterfall and agile techniques. Dave West of Forrester commonly refers to this as* waterscrumfall. *Microsoft built Team Foundation Server and the accompanying ALM tools with this flexibility in mind, which enables teams to customize the tools even if that means blending seemingly competing processes.*

STAKEHOLDERS

A stakeholder can be anybody outside of the development team who has a vested interest in the outcome of a software development project. For example, end-user of the software is certainly a stakeholder and is perhaps the first person who comes to mind when we think of stakeholders. Another stakeholder may be the person who is funding a particular project. After all, end users may *want* an application to have a key piece of functionality, but if the person paying for the project believes that it is too expensive to implement then that's important for the software development team to know before they start writing code. A lawyer may also be a stakeholder because some applications may need to undergo scrutiny to ensure that certain compliance and regulatory requirements are met. If you are in the business of selling software then your product's marketing team will likely have a seat at the table. You can probably think of other stakeholders for your software as well.

Whoever the stakeholders are for your project, they are a vital part of your extended development team. Stakeholders can play a role in some or all of the following activities:

➤ *Requirements elicitation* — This is the process of gathering requirements from stakeholders through brainstorming, focus groups, role playing, prototyping, and other techniques designed to capture what a stakeholder may need your software to do today and in the future.

➤ *Requirements analysis* — During the analysis phase, the software development team determines which, if any, requirements need additional detail from stakeholders. This is also the time to resolve any conflicting requirements that may have been introduced by different stakeholders.

➤ *Requirements validation* — As the software development team begins to capture and analyze requirements, they often turn these requirements into written specifications, use case models, visual storyboards, or other such artifacts which attempt to capture what they heard from stakeholders during the requirements elicitation and analysis phases. This is an important point in time for stakeholders to provide feedback about the intended implementation.

➤ *Requirements prioritization* — As requirements are defined, they need to be prioritized. This phase is less important for waterfall-based projects. But if your project's stakeholders are expecting incremental deliveries of software, such as in an agile project, then it is important to determine in which order requirements should be implemented.

➤ *Feedback* — As working code begins to take shape, it may be possible to further refine requirements by asking stakeholders to use interim builds of your software and provide feedback. When this step is implemented early enough, it can help uncover disconnects between the stakeholder's expectations and the development team's implementation in time to affect that upcoming release milestone.

The phases described in the preceding list are typically referred to collectively as *requirements management*. Like other aspects of software development, requirements management is both an art and science, and it has been covered extensively by other books (both Dean Leffingwell and Karl Weigers have written great books on software requirements). For the purposes of this book, we are focusing on the tooling that is provided as part of Visual Studio for working with requirements. In this section, you learn about the new PowerPoint Storyboarding add-in, as well as the new Microsoft Feedback Client. In this chapter you also learn about a few of Microsoft's partners who offer complementary products in the requirements management space. In Chapter 11, you learn how Team Foundation Server enables teams to prioritize the order in which your team will implement requirements.

> **NOTE** *Henry Ford is quoted as having said that if he would have asked customers what they wanted they would have replied, "A faster horse." Instead, Ford invented the Model T, which ushered in the automobile era, rendering even the fastest horses obsolete. The implication is that customers don't always know what they want, so it's sometimes up to us as developers to deliver what they need before they realize they need it. But be careful not to be lured into a false conclusion that you no longer need to learn about your customers' wants and needs. The reality is that you may need to get to know your customers even better than they know themselves in order to map observed needs to solutions you can deliver.*

STORYBOARDING

Storyboarding is a technique that was pioneered by the cartoon and film industry to help visualize sequences before the expensive process of filming or animating had begun. Because storyboards are composed of simple sketches, they are quick to create and easy to re-create if needed based on feedback, filming constraints, script changes, and so on. After the director is satisfied with the overall flow represented by the storyboard, the expensive processes of designing sets, configuring shots, filming, editing, and so on can begin.

Storyboards have since found their way into software user interface design. A series of storyboard panels could show the way in which a user interacts with a website when researching and ordering a new coffee table. The storyboard can then be shared with prospective users, market researchers, information architects, and other stakeholders and experts whose opinions help to shape the storyboard into the best possible design for the software development team to implement. The storyboard then becomes an artifact that the software development team can use to help plan their implementation.

With Visual Studio 2012, Microsoft has released a new tool for creating and sharing storyboards. This tool is known as the PowerPoint Storyboarding add-in, and, as the name implies, it is based on Microsoft PowerPoint. In Chapter 8 you learn about the capabilities of this tool and how to use it to quickly and cheaply iterate on user interface design with your project's stakeholders prior to writing a single line of code.

CAPTURING STAKEHOLDER FEEDBACK

Wouldn't it be great if we could talk to our stakeholders about what they want our software to do, go off for a few weeks to build it, and then give it to our stakeholders and smile while they congratulate us on building *exactly* what they wanted? Unfortunately this rarely happens in the software development world. The very nature of software development is highly complex. There are technical challenges to overcome; complex business rules and other requirements must be captured and implemented precisely; and different machine environments must be considered, such as which web browser the users prefer, what languages they speak, what accessibility constraints they have, and so on. And if all that isn't challenging enough, we have to account for the users' taste and style preferences. We have all been in this situation: You are demonstrating your software; it works flawlessly; everything is going well; and then somebody complains that they *hate* the font you chose for the user interface. It makes you wonder if Leonardo da Vinci ever received complaints about the frames his masterpieces went into.

But "the customer is always right," and it is up to us as the software development team to listen to their feedback and respond to the best of our ability to create the best possible deliverables. The Agile Manifesto pays credence to this idea throughout, such as in the first principle:

> *Our highest priority is to satisfy the customer through early and continuous delivery of valuable software.*

Many agile teams even go so far as to treat the customer as an integral part of the software development team. An end user or other stakeholder may attend weekly progress reviews or even participate in discussions about possible implementations. When this type of face-to-face interaction is possible, it can be invaluable for ensuring that the vision of the software development team is closely aligned with that of the stakeholders. But how can you achieve this type of cooperation when your stakeholders are geographically disbursed, time shifted, or too numerous to practically incorporate into the regular cadence of development team meetings?

> **NOTE** *The term* customer *from the Agile Manifesto is synonymous with the earlier discussion of the term* stakeholder. *Stakeholder is sometimes preferred to* customer *because the latter implies an exchange of goods or services for money, whereas the former recognizes that money isn't always an underlying consideration when defining a person's interest or involvement in a project's outcome.*

Microsoft has introduced another new tool with Visual Studio 2012 designed to facilitate this type of interaction. The Microsoft Feedback Client captures rich data about the interactions of a stakeholder with your software, as well as their reactions. The development team can start by initiating a request for a stakeholder to provide feedback about a user story or requirement that has been implemented. The stakeholder can then run the Microsoft Feedback Client while they are using the interim build of your software. Along the way, that stakeholder can choose to capture video and audio recordings, notes, and screenshots that reflect things that they like or dislike about your software. All of this data is centrally stored in Team Foundation Server so that the development team can analyze and react to it. You learn how to use the Microsoft Feedback Client in Chapter 9.

WORK ITEM ONLY VIEW

Another way of collecting input from your stakeholders is by allowing them to file bugs or enhancement requests directly to Team Foundation Server. This centralizes feedback in one repository that the development team can then react to and track over time. Microsoft does this for a wide range of

Microsoft products via their Microsoft Connect website (`http://connect.microsoft.com`). Product groups at Microsoft synchronize data from Connect directly into their own Team Foundation Server work item databases, and any responses about the customer's request are returned to the user via the public website.

You can use Team Foundation Server for this purpose as well. But for most organizations, obtaining a Team Foundation Server client access license (CAL) for every possible stakeholder can be cost prohibitive. In recognition of this, Microsoft created a licensing exemption for stakeholders who may file bugs or enhancement requests. From the Visual Studio licensing whitepaper:

> *A user does not need a CAL or External Connector License to create new work items or to update work items that that same user has created. This exception applies only to work items related to defect filing or enhancement requests. However, a CAL is required when a user views or modifies a work item created by another user or interacts with Team Foundation Server in any other way.*

> **NOTE** *The latest version of the Visual Studio Licensing Whitepaper can be found at* `http://www.microsoft.com/visualstudio/licensing`. *This whitepaper attempts to synthesize all of the licensing requirements for Visual Studio, Team Foundation Server, and related technologies into an easy-to-read format.*

Because stakeholders are not likely to have Visual Studio installed, the most common way of asking stakeholders to provide feedback in this manner is via Team Web Access, which is covered in Chapter 2. Stakeholders who don't already have access to Team Foundation Server can be added to the Work Item Only View License Group in Team Foundation Server. Users who are a member of this group are only permitted to create and update work items they create, per the terms of the aforementioned licensing clause. If a stakeholder requires more comprehensive access to Team Foundation Server they need to be licensed and permissioned appropriately.

> **NOTE** *Detailed steps for adding users to the Work Item Only View License Group can be found at* `http://aka.ms/WIOV`.

THIRD-PARTY REQUIREMENTS MANAGEMENT SOLUTIONS

There are a number of approaches and solutions to requirements management and stakeholder engagement employed by software development teams. Although Microsoft has made forays into requirements management with the Visual Studio 2012 release by introducing the aforementioned tools, it continues to rely on tis broad ecosystem of partners to provide complementary requirements management solutions that integrate with Team Foundation Server. Three popular examples of these partner solutions are covered next. For information on other third-party requirements management solutions that integrate with Team Foundation Server, please visit `http://aka.ms/` `TFSRequirementsPartners.`

TeamSpec

One of the most widely used requirements management "tools" on the planet is Microsoft Word. Microsoft Word is popular, easy to use, and facilitates sharing and collaboration via tracked changes and comments. It's no wonder then that many software requirements live their lives as specifications in Word documents. TeamSolutions, a Microsoft partner, recognized the popularity of Microsoft Word in the requirements management space and saw an opportunity to keep requirements documents relevant by integrating Word and Team Foundation Server. They created a solution called TeamSpec to bring Microsoft Word–based requirements into a company's ALM process, and it has become popular among teams who use Team Foundation Server.

TeamSpec, shown in Figure 7-1, maintains a link between requirements in your document and pertinent work items in Team Foundation Server. One feature enables teams to compose requirements using customizable templates in Microsoft Word. The templates define fields that represent the elements of the requirement that will be mapped to Team Foundation Server. For example, the template for a user story may define fields for a title, a description, and the person on the development team responsible for that user story. The requirement document in Word can then be shared with project stakeholders for validation. The stakeholders can make proposed edits or comments to send it back to the development team just like they would with any other Word document. Then after the stakeholders have signed off on a requirement document it can be synchronized with Team Foundation Server as a work item or group of work items. TeamSpec is responsible for providing this synchronization by examining the contents of each field in the document template and pushing it into a corresponding work item field.

Another capability of TeamSpec is that it can be used in the other direction to generate Word documents from work items in Team Foundation Server. This feature is especially useful when the software development team has made changes to a requirement that must be communicated to the stakeholders. In this way, TeamSpec recognizes that requirements often evolve over time and that keeping the requirements in-sync, for all stakeholders, is imperative. You can learn more about TeamSpec at `http://www.teamsystemsolutions.com/`.

TeamLook

Another popular stakeholder collaboration tool, also from TeamSolutions, is TeamLook. TeamLook, shown in Figure 7-2, integrates work items from Team Foundation Server directly into Microsoft Outlook. TeamLook makes it easy to turn e-mails into work items, such as e-mails from a customer who may e-mail a bug or enhancement request that you want to capture in Team Foundation Server for the development team to triage and react to. Conversely, you can use TeamLook to generate e-mails from work items in Team Foundation Server — such as to provide the latest status of an enhancement-request work item to an important customer.

TeamSolutions also produces a related free tool called TeamBox, which is an automated e-mail service that converts any e-mail it receives into Team Foundation Server work items. Hence, you could configure `Bugs@Fabrikam.com` to automatically create bug work items for the development team to triage. You can learn more about TeamLook and TeamBox at `http://www.teamsystemsolutions.com/`.

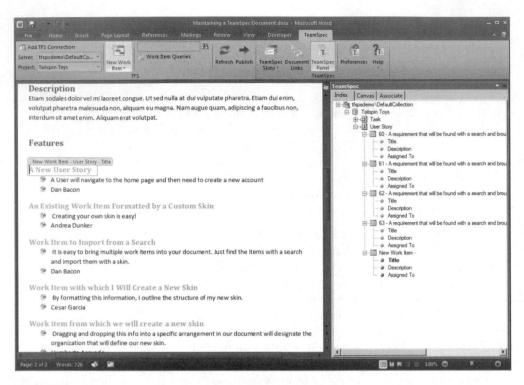

FIGURE 7-1

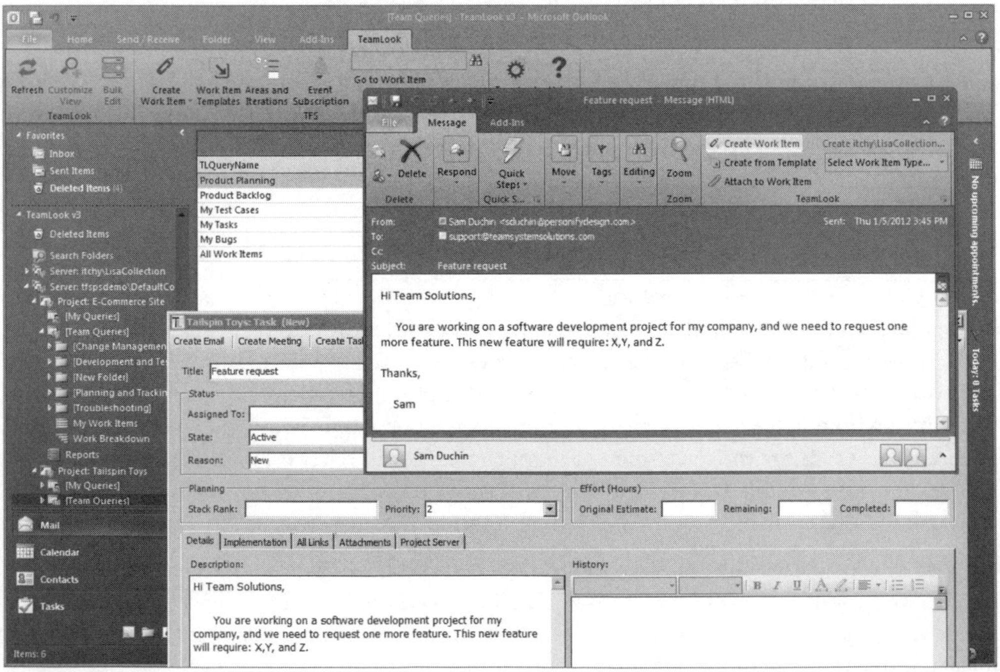

FIGURE 7-2

inteGREAT

inteGREAT, by eDevTECH (http://www.edevtech.com) is a requirements lifecycle management platform that integrates bidirectionally with Team Foundation Server 2012, with Team Foundation Server providing the centralized application and database store for inteGREAT.

inteGREAT, shown in Figure 7-3, enables users to elicit, analyze, validate, review, and manage requirements. inteGREAT also offers bidirectional integration with Microsoft Excel and Word, allowing business users to author requirements in tools that are familiar to them. It embeds Visio controls within the tool to facilitate the creation of many types of diagrams. It also integrates with Microsoft Project, publishes documents and an HTML knowledgebase to SharePoint and produces XAML code from its screen mock-up functionality. It even integrates third-party solutions such as CA ERwin and HP Quality Center.

If you are seeking a requirements definition and management solution that allows you to baseline projects and provides a more formal and comprehensive approach than that currently offered by Microsoft or Team Solutions, then you should consider evaluating inteGREAT.

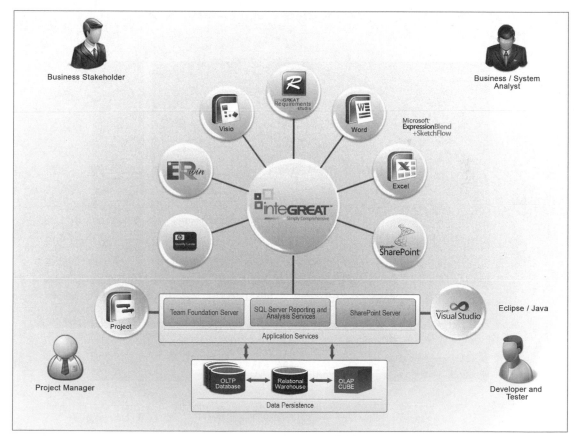

FIGURE 7-3

SUMMARY

In this chapter, you learned about the importance of engaging early and frequently with your software development project's stakeholders. During this process you capture, analyze, and validate the requirements your software needs to implement before you begin coding. Then, as your software evolves, you learned about getting additional feedback from stakeholders, which can influence the ongoing implementation to ensure that the development team is building the right software. Microsoft and its partners have built several tools to facilitate requirements management and collaboration with your project's stakeholders. These tools integrate with Team Foundation Server alongside the rest of your software development project's artifacts.

In Chapter 8 you learn more about the PowerPoint Storyboarding add-in that Microsoft has introduced with Visual Studio 2012.

8
Storyboarding

WHAT'S IN THIS CHAPTER?

➤ Using the PowerPoint Storyboarding add-in to create storyboards

➤ Using layouts, custom shapes, and animations to create and maintain storyboards to capture requirements from your stakeholders

➤ Linking storyboards with Team Foundation Server work items

In Chapter 7 you discovered that, with Visual Studio 2012, Microsoft is extending its application lifecycle management tooling to better address the needs and feedback of project stakeholders throughout the lifecycle. In this chapter, you learn more about one of these new tools, PowerPoint Storyboarding, which adds a form of lightweight requirements elicitation to Microsoft's offerings. After reading this chapter you will have a better understanding of how to use these new tools to create user interface designs and workflows that you can socialize with your project stakeholders to collect feedback and signoff early in the process.

WHY STORYBOARDING?

Chapter 7 explained that *storyboarding* is a technique that has its roots in the cartoon and film industry. Disney is credited with inventing and refining the technique in the early twentieth century for animation, and the technique quickly found its way into film and eventually software development. Figure 8-1 shows an example of a storyboard used for a film. A storyboard for a film is created and refined by a team of creative professionals, including writers, directors, and storyboard artists. During this process, storyboards typically undergo several iterative changes before filming begins. The finished storyboard then becomes a design artifact that helps to inform set designers, camera crews, actors, editors, and others who are responsible for ultimately converting the creative and artistic direction into a finished film.

By Sam Garland, used with permission.

FIGURE 8-1

Creating a storyboard is similar to sketching an idea on a whiteboard or the back of a napkin, and these activities all share a collection of common benefits that make them popular:

➤ Storyboards are visual, and humans are visual creatures. The saying "a picture is worth a thousand words" is especially true when you consider the additional level of detail that can be quickly conveyed through a picture or a series of pictures that might otherwise be incredibly time consuming or error-prone to communicate over, say, a telephone discussion or e-mail exchange. In this way, you can say that a good storyboard is worth a thousand-page spec.

➤ Storyboards are cheap to create. "Pixel-perfect" precision is rarely expected during the storyboarding phase, and anybody with a pencil and paper can create a storyboard.

➤ Storyboards convey motion. By sequencing together multiple panels of a storyboard you can convey the flow expected as you move from one state to the next. In film, this can convey action or plot; in software, you might use this to represent a workflow, such as an accountant interacting with tax filing software to calculate an income tax return.

➤ More importantly, storyboards are quick and easy to iterate on. Chapter 7 covers the importance of being able to respond quickly to stakeholder feedback in order to best ensure that your team delivers great software. Unfortunately, software is relatively slow to change, and it only gets slower and more expensive to change the more complex it becomes. Consequently, any time you can spend up front proposing a storyboard design, listening to your stakeholders give you feedback, and reacting to that feedback *before* you start writing code is ultimately going to help you create better software with less time and effort.

It's clear that a storyboard can help immensely with the task of creating a great user interface for a software project. Just as a storyboard for a film can help inform the set designer and camera crew, a storyboard for a software project can help graphic designers and user interface programmers collaborate to turn ideas into reality. Software testers can use them to begin to author test cases to validate what a piece of software should (and shouldn't) do. Documentation teams can begin to outline their help topics. Even the marketing team can use storyboards to convey to a set of prospective customers what your software will do when finished, even before the team has written a single line of code.

Microsoft's new PowerPoint Storyboarding tool was built to make it easy for software development teams to quickly create and iterate on storyboard designs. Whiteboards and napkins may work well for simple designs that need to be collaborated on by team members who are all in the same location. But with project stakeholders often located around the world in different time zones, and software becoming increasingly more complicated with branching workflows, the art of storyboarding has needed to evolve beyond whiteboards and napkins.

There are other storyboarding tools on the market already, such as Balsamiq. Microsoft even has two other tools that many teams already use for storyboarding: Microsoft Visio and Microsoft Expression SketchFlow. So why do we need yet another storyboarding solution? As the name indicates, PowerPoint Storyboarding is based on Microsoft PowerPoint. In their research for Visual Studio 2012, Microsoft observed that an overwhelming number of software developers and the stakeholders they serve already own PowerPoint and know how to use it for creating at least basic presentations. As it turns out, many of the features needed to create storyboards are already included in PowerPoint (such as 2-D graphics, animations, layouts, linking, and collaboration features such as notes and review comments). Hence, Microsoft concluded that a storyboarding tool built on PowerPoint would be comfortable and familiar to the set of users who care most about storyboarding. In the rest of this chapter you learn how to use PowerPoint Storyboarding to create rich storyboards.

POWERPOINT STORYBOARDING

To work with PowerPoint Storyboarding you need to first install Visual Studio Test Professional 2012, Visual Studio Premium 2012, or Visual Studio Ultimate 2012. PowerPoint Storyboarding is compatible with Microsoft PowerPoint 2007 and 2010 and is expected to remain compatible with future versions of PowerPoint as well. Screenshots and instructions in this chapter are based on PowerPoint 2010 but are similar in other versions.

> **NOTE** *You can share PowerPoint Storyboards with stakeholders who have an appropriate version of PowerPoint or the free PowerPoint Viewer installed, even if they don't own a Visual Studio license. Those users won't, however, get access to the unique capabilities provided by the PowerPoint Storyboarding add-in, which you learn about in this chapter.*

Launch PowerPoint Storyboarding by clicking Start ⇨ All Programs ⇨ Visual Studio 2012 ⇨ PowerPoint Storyboarding. You can also launch PowerPoint from the Office menu or by opening an existing PowerPoint file. Because PowerPoint Storyboarding is just an add-in for PowerPoint, you can work with this functionality any time you are using PowerPoint.

The PowerPoint Storyboarding add-in introduces a new tab to your PowerPoint ribbon (see Figure 8-2). Several of the buttons exposed on this tab are existing capabilities you may already be familiar with in PowerPoint, such as the Align button that enables you to easily align shapes. These capabilities are generally useful when working with storyboards, and as such are surfaced on the Storyboarding ribbon tab for convenience. Some other capabilities, such as the Storyboard Shapes and Storyboard Links buttons, are new with the add-in and you learn about them in this chapter.

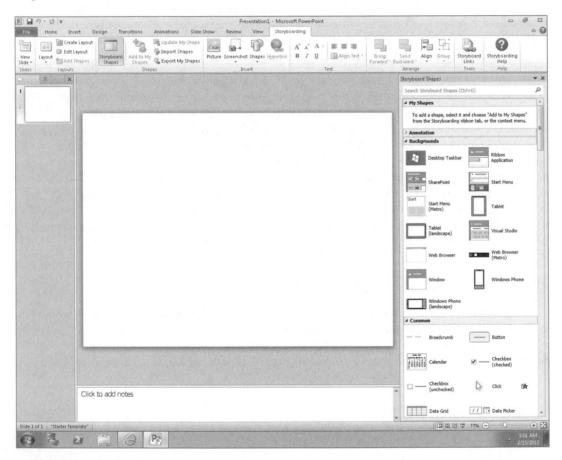

FIGURE 8-2

Storyboard Shapes

Much of the value in the PowerPoint Storyboarding add-in is found in the rich set of shapes available for easily modeling Windows applications, web applications, and even phone and tablet applications. The Storyboard Shapes pane pictured in Figure 8-3 shows just a few of these shapes. If Storyboard Shapes is not open, you can click the Storyboard Shapes button from the Storyboarding ribbon tab. Spend a few minutes exploring the shapes you can work with.

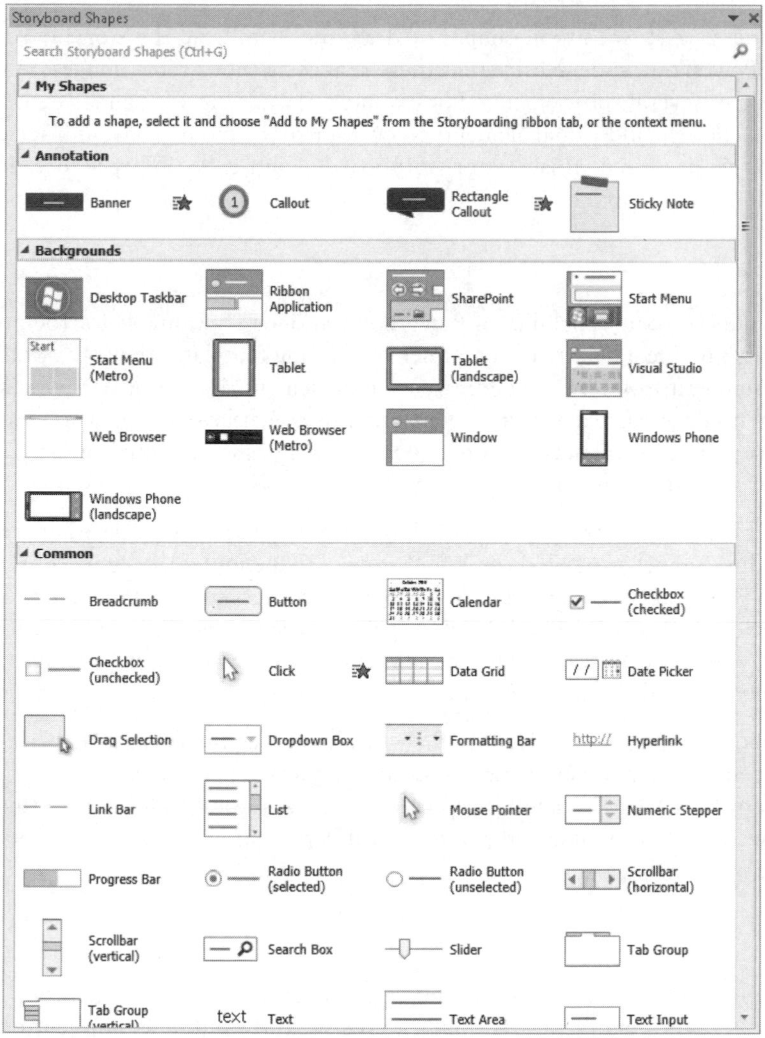

FIGURE 8-3

Notice that there are backgrounds that provide templates for representing the class of application you are developing, such as tablet, web, phone, traditional desktop apps, SharePoint applications, and so on. Annotations such as sticky notes and callouts give you the ability to convey additional meaning about a storyboard to stakeholders. The Storyboarding add-in also includes a large collection of icons and all of the standard controls you expect for applications, such as buttons, lists, dropdowns, dialogs, media controls, and so on.

Some shapes, such as the Click shape, are even animated by default, but you can add animations to any shape. The Search box can be helpful for quickly finding a shape you are looking for. Finally, the My Shapes category is a place for you to store your own custom shapes. You learn how to work with in the My Shapes section later in this chapter.

Spend some time familiarizing yourself with some shapes by dragging them from the Storyboard Shapes pane onto an empty PowerPoint slide. Notice that these shapes are not simply images; many are complex shapes consisting of several sub-elements. For example, try adding a Calendar control to your storyboard. You can click the individual elements to customize the month, day, and selected date. Most of the time you won't need to do this in your storyboards, but the flexibility is there if you need it.

Layouts

The ability to work with layouts is a core capability of PowerPoint and is very valuable for the practice of storyboarding. Layouts provide a hierarchical manner of defining templates that each of the slides in your storyboard can inherit from. By embedding common elements in your layout, you save yourself time later when you need to create a new storyboard that uses that layout. You also save time in maintaining your storyboard if you need to update core elements, such as your company's logo in the header or a copyright date in the footer.

If you added shapes to your blank slide in the previous section, clean up that slide by deleting those shapes. From the Storyboarding Shapes pane, find the Web Browser shape under the Backgrounds category and drop that onto your empty slide. Position it so that the corners of the shape match the corners of your slide. In the address box of the Web Browser shape, type the base URL for your web application, such as `http://www.fabrikam.com`. This is the template that you will use for multiple slides in your storyboard, so you should turn it into a layout.

From the Storyboarding ribbon tab click Create Layout. Provide a name for this layout, such as Fabrikam Fiber Intranet. Open the Slide Master view, pictured in Figure 8-4, by clicking on Edit Layout. Your new layout, Fabrikam Fiber Intranet, is represented as the second child node in this hierarchy. The first child node is an empty slide and can be useful if you need to create a storyboarding slide that should not use your new layout.

Screenshots

Many applications use common elements across multiple pages or screens in the application, such as a common masthead, footer, and menus. If this is a greenfield (brand new) application, you can use the Storyboard Shapes and other graphical tools (such as Photoshop) to create a look and feel for your application. But often, you might be creating a storyboard to represent new functionality that you want to add to an existing application. The Screenshot capability of PowerPoint makes it easy to import these existing visual elements into your storyboard.

In a web browser, open an existing web application that you want to import design elements from. This can be any web application for now, such as Microsoft.com. Maximize the window for your web browser and position it so that you can see the visual elements that you want to import. Now switch back to PowerPoint and click the Storyboarding ribbon tab. Click the Screenshot button.

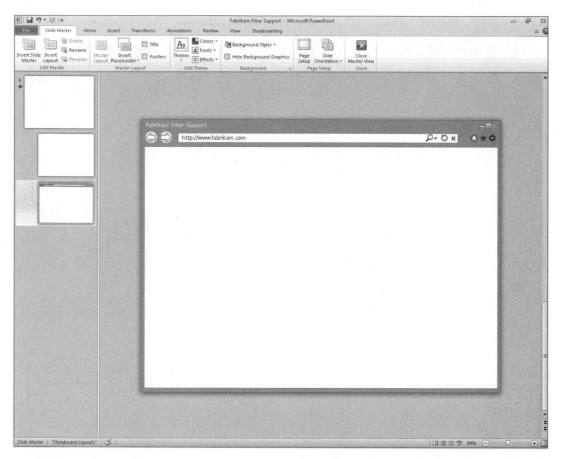

FIGURE 8-4

The Screenshot button expands to display thumbnails that represent the other windows you have open, including the web browser you just opened. You can import the entire window, but doing so also includes the chrome from the browser (menus, address bar, and so on). Instead, you can click Screen Clipping to briefly minimize PowerPoint and click and drag a rectangle that captures the section of the web application that you want to import. Figure 8-5 shows the screen clipping capability being used to select the masthead from the existing Fabrikam Fiber web application.

> **NOTE** *When using the Screen Clipping capability, it is necessary to ensure that the last window you had open prior to switching back into PowerPoint is the window that you want to capture a screen clipping from. If you try to switch to a new window by clicking the running application on the task bar, the screen clipping capability instead assumes that you are trying to capture a screen clipping from the task bar.*

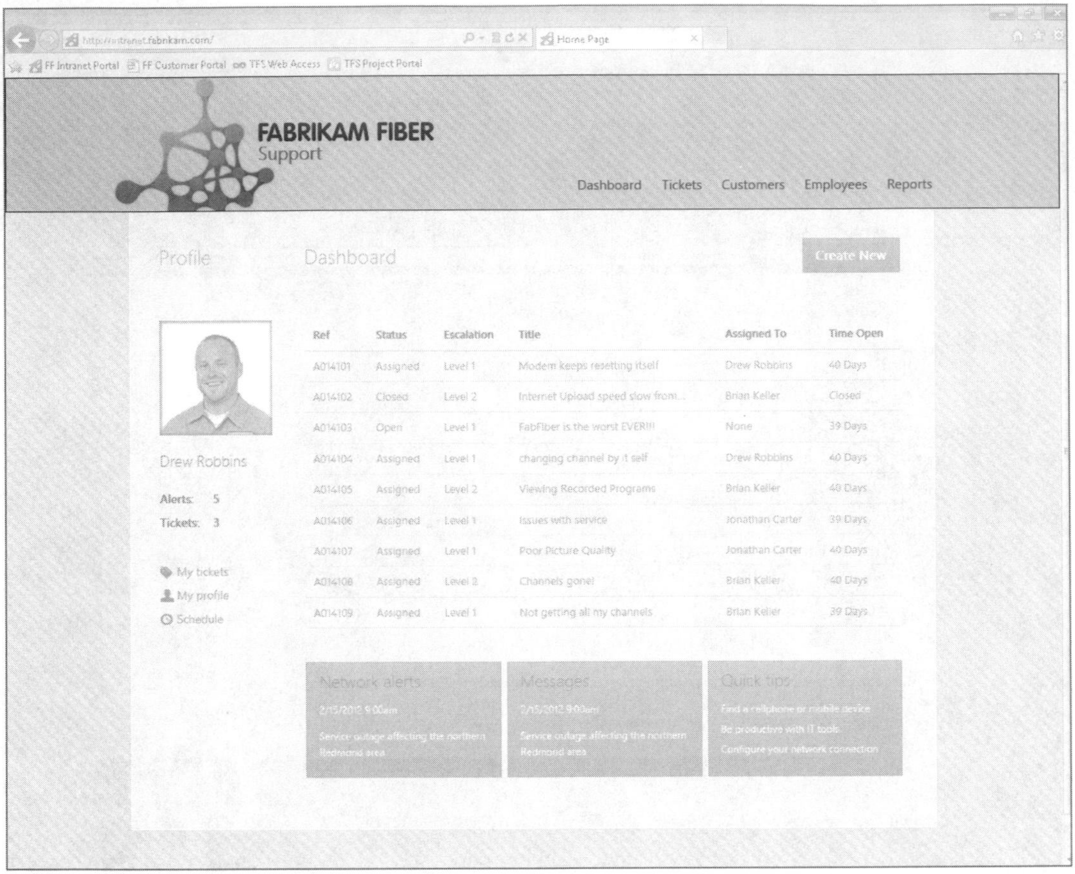

FIGURE 8-5

After you've imported an image, you can select it and use the Format ribbon tab to crop it or make other adjustments. For example, you may want to use the Color button to set the saturation to 0%. This makes the shape plain grayscale, which is sometimes a useful technique for getting stakeholders to focus on providing feedback on the functionality of an application, instead of focusing on design elements such as color selection. You can always revisit the Color button later to restore the image to its original saturation.

You can now add any other common elements, such as sidebars or footers. When you are finished building your layout, click the Slide Master ribbon tab and click Close Master View. You have just created your first layout, which you can apply to any slide in your storyboard as shown in Figure 8-6. To select a layout for a slide, you can right-click that slide and select the Layouts fly-out menu, or use the Layout pull-down menu from the Storyboarding ribbon tab. You can repeat this process to create as many layouts as you wish.

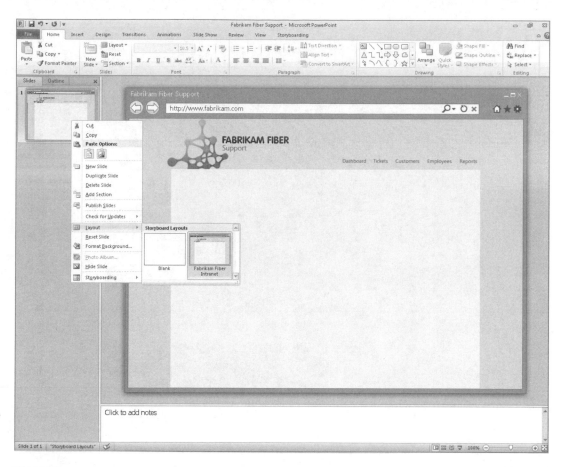

FIGURE 8-6

Note that outside of the Slide Master view you cannot edit any of the shapes you added to this layout, so if you need to edit them again you need to visit the Storyboarding ribbon tab and click Edit Layout to return to the Slide Master. Be thoughtful about what you put in your layouts. When used correctly they can save you a lot of time. For example, if a logo changes you can easily update it in the layout and the change is automatically inherited by all slides that use that layout.

You can now use a combination of Storyboard Shapes, screen clippings, and other sources available from the Insert ribbon tab to construct the first web page you want to model in your storyboard. Figure 8-7 shows an example of a finished page that you might want to present to your users. In this way you can continue to create new slides for each page or dialog in your application that you want to storyboard.

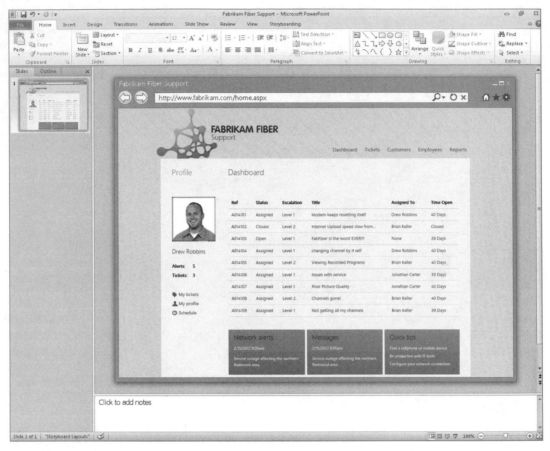

FIGURE 8-7

> **NOTE** *You might notice in Figure 8-7 that the URL in the address bar is* `http://www.fabrikam.com/home.aspx`, *but if you try to manipulate the address field of a slide that inherits the address field from a layout you aren't able to edit it. This effect was achieved by simply adding a new textbox (Insert ➪ Textbox) immediately after the existing URL and typing* `/home.aspx` *into the textbox. This attention to detail can help your stakeholders understand where they are within your application.*

My Shapes

The My Shapes category of the Storyboard Shapes pane makes it possible to create your own private library of shapes that you might want to reuse. An illustration of how My Shapes works can be achieved by creating a stylized button. Add a button from the Storyboard Shapes pane to your storyboard slide. Right-click this button and click Format Shape to access advanced properties that enable you to adjust the visual style of this button. Try changing the fill color and adding a shadow. Click OK when finished. Change the default text for the button and set a custom color for the text using the Font Color button in the Storyboarding ribbon tab (the Font Color selector is represented by the icon of the letter A with a colored bar underneath it).

The exact customizations you make to this button are not important. The point is that sometimes you may invest in styling shapes to meet requirements you have for the look and feel of your application, but individually making these customizations from scratch takes time. Instead, you can use the My Shapes category to store your customized shapes for future reuse. Select your finished shape and click Add to My Shapes from the Storyboarding ribbon tab. This adds your shape to the My Shapes category of the Storyboard Shapes pane as shown in Figure 8-8. You can give your shape a meaningful name, such as the Fabrikam Button in this example. Now, when you drag this shape back onto the slide you have a copy of the button that already includes your custom style applied to it.

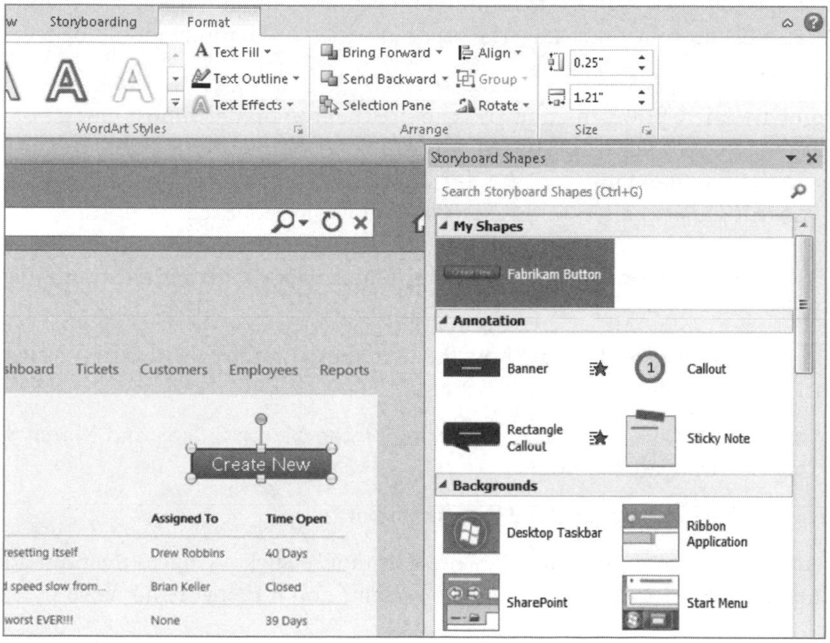

FIGURE 8-8

This was a simple example, but you can apply the same technique to advanced composite shapes you might create, such as a menu bar or a panel consisting of multiple controls. Just select the group of shapes you want to include in your custom shape and then click Add to My Shapes.

Finally, you can share your custom shapes with others by using the Import Shapes and Export My Shapes buttons on the Storyboarding ribbon tab.

Animations

The ability to program animations in PowerPoint is another capability which is incredibly useful when working with storyboards. You can use animations to make your storyboard come to life for a stakeholder by illustrating the way that a user is expected to interact with an application.

Two of the most useful animations you can add to a storyboard are to show mouse movement and text entry. To see how this works, start by adding a Click shape from the Storyboard Shapes pane. The Click shape is programmed with a custom animation. You can press F5 (or Shift – F5 to start on the current slide) to start presentation mode and see this animation in action. Press the space bar or click your mouse button to trigger the animation. When you are finished, press the Escape key to return to the PowerPoint editor.

To understand how this default animation was programmed for the Click shape, click the Animations ribbon tab and enable the Animation Pane. From here you can see that this is a Custom Path animation triggered to start with a mouse click (which means that the animation starts whenever the presenter clicks the mouse or by pressing most keys on the keyboard, such as the space bar). You can change the timing to be faster or slower, or you can simply click the endpoints of the animation path to change the start and end locations.

You can select another shape and click Add Animation to apply a new animation for that shape. Notice that in the Animation Pane you can change the order in which animations should be triggered, timed, and so on.

Animations in PowerPoint are fairly powerful, and you can use them to model almost any set of user interactions you can imagine for your storyboard. For full details on working with animations please consult the PowerPoint documentation. Figure 8-9 shows a bit of what is possible by using animations with a storyboard. This example animates in the following sequence:

1. The text in each of the text boxes appears via a Wipe animation, simulating the user typing text into these fields.

2. Next, the mouse cursor moves to illustrate how the user clicks on the calendar icon to open the full calendar.

3. The mouse moves to illustrate how the user is clicking on the March 8 date, and March 8 then displays in the Service Date textbox.

4. The mouse moves to show the user clicking the Create button.

5. After this animation sequence is finished, a key press or mouse click advances the presentation to the next slide in the storyboard or ends the presentation if there are no more slides.

In this manner you can easily string together multiple slides and animation sequences to represent a full end-to-end interaction that a user might have with your application.

Hyperlinks

You might decide that you want to allow your stakeholders to click through your storyboard in a non-linear fashion to access various pieces of functionality you are designing. Hyperlinks provide a way for you to do this. For example, in Figure 8-9 you might want to allow the stakeholder who is viewing this storyboard to click the Reports link in the menu to see the storyboard for your reporting capabilities. To program this, simply select a shape and use the Hyperlink button. You can then select another slide by clicking Place In This Document, or you can hyperlink to external resources, such as a detailed spec or a working prototype on a staging server.

Another use for hyperlinks is to create a table of contents slide at the beginning of the presentation, to allow somebody viewing the presentation to select individual requirements he wants to view. For example, the User Story that describes how a user signs up for a new account might be represented by slides 5 through 8, whereas the section of your storyboard that describes how a user pays with a credit card is represented on slides 28 through 34. Hyperlinks enable you to make it easy for stakeholders to jump directly to the section of the storyboard document they are most interested in reviewing. At the end of each section you can then direct the user back to the original table of contents.

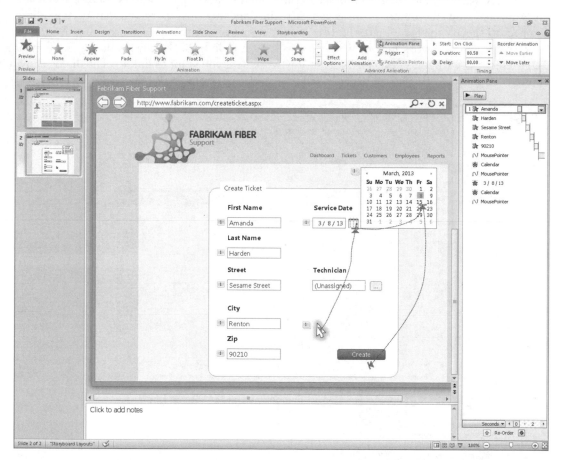

FIGURE 8-9

Storyboard Links

None of the capabilities mentioned in this chapter to this point require Team Foundation Server. You can create and share storyboards with stakeholders by using traditional mechanisms such as e-mail, SharePoint, or file shares. But if you are using Team Foundation Server to manage your application development, you might want to link the storyboard artifacts you are creating to a work item in Team Foundation Server that represents the functionality being storyboarded.

To achieve this, you first need to save your storyboard file on either a network share (such as \\MyTeamServer\Fabrikam\Storyboards) or a SharePoint document library. This should be a location that is accessible by the stakeholders whom you plan to interact with as you create and get feedback on this storyboard. Ideally, this location is also backed up on a regular basis so that you don't accidentally lose your work.

After you have saved the document to one of these valid locations, select Storyboard Links from the Storyboarding ribbon tab. If this is your first time opening this dialog you may need to click Connect to specify the location of the Team Foundation Server instance you are using. Next, click Link To and find the work item or work items you want to link to. Usually this is a User Story or a Requirement work item, but it can really be any work item you want to link to. The dialog shown in Figure 8-10 shows a storyboard being linked to a work item from the Product Backlog query.

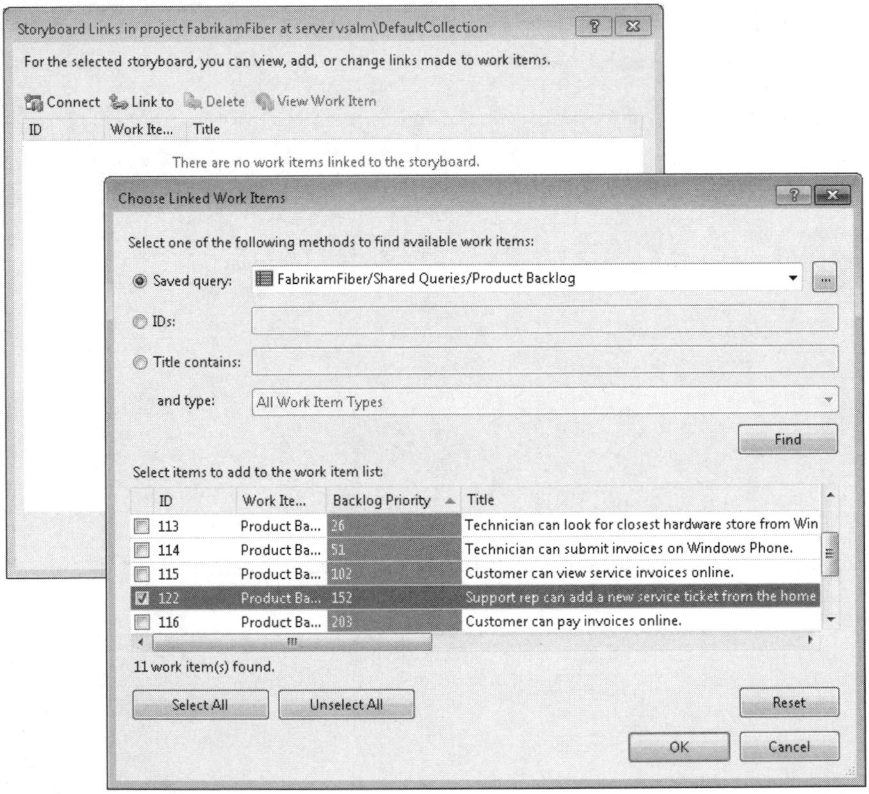

FIGURE 8-10

After it is linked it can be opened from the work item as shown in Figure 8-11. This helps to ensure that you get full end-to-end traceability across all of the artifacts that go into defining, developing, and testing your software.

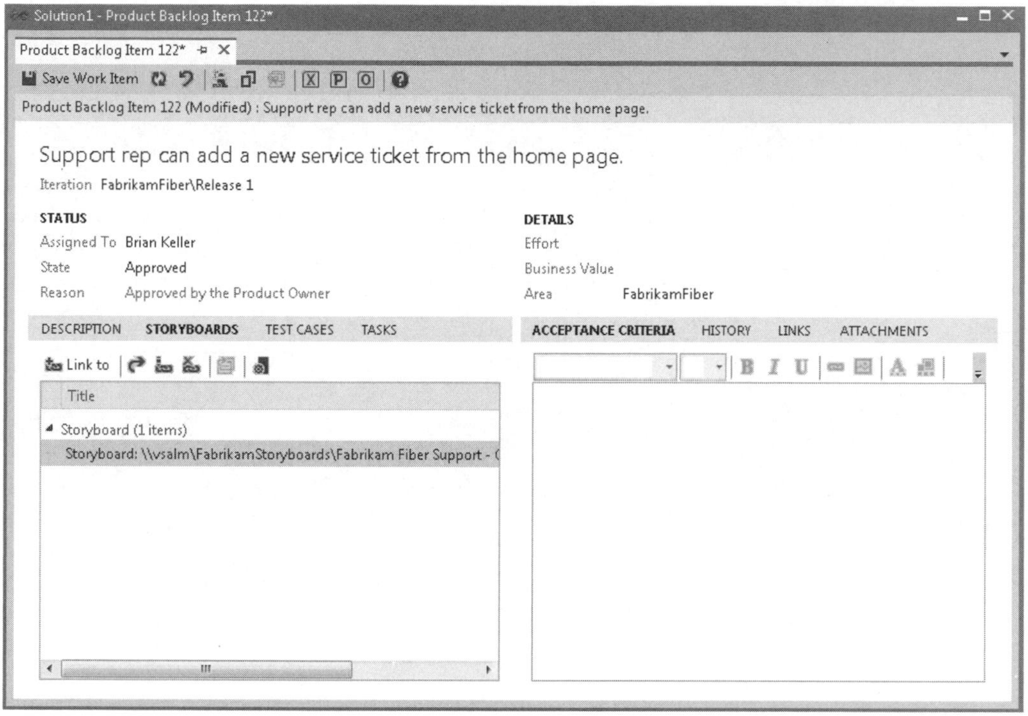

FIGURE 8-11

NOTE *Certain work items, such as Product Backlog Items in the Scrum process template or User Stories in the MSF for Agile process template, have a Storyboards tab on the work item that lists all linked storyboards. If you decide to link to another work-item type that doesn't have the Storyboarding tab, such as a bug, you can always find linked storyboards from the Links tab.*

SUMMARY

In this chapter, you learned about how storyboarding can be a valuable part of the requirements elicitation phase of your software project's lifecycle. You learned about the new PowerPoint Storyboarding add-in from Microsoft that enables you to quickly create storyboards, seek feedback, and iterate on them before turning them over to the designers and programmers who make them into working software.

The next chapter covers how the new Microsoft Feedback Client enables development teams to continue to get feedback from stakeholders about the working software being developed. By continuously seeking stakeholder feedback throughout the development process, you can again ensure that the stakeholders' wants and needs are adequately represented in the high-quality software you are delivering.

9

Capturing Stakeholder Feedback

WHAT'S IN THIS CHAPTER?

➤ Discovering how the development team can request feedback from stakeholders on specific features or requirements

➤ Learning how project stakeholders can use the Microsoft Feedback Client to provide rich feedback about your software

So far in this section you have learned about the importance of engaging with your software development project's stakeholders to ensure that you have a clear understanding of what your stakeholders want you to build before you start implementing it. But regardless of how much time you spend up front during this requirements elicitation phase, the first iteration of software you create is rarely going to meet all of their expectations.

There are a variety of reasons for this. Technical challenges might get in the way of the originally planned implementation; business requirements may evolve from the time when you first capture them to the time that you implement the first working code; the opinions of users can be fickle, and may even be influenced by seeing the software in action for the first time; you may not have truly understood what your stakeholders were asking for when you were capturing their requirements; or you may not have had time to implement all the requirements in the initial release.

These possibilities will be anticipated by any Agile software development team who embraces the fact that software development is something of an art form, requiring iterative cycles of requirements gathering, implementation, and feedback, which in turn informs an additional round of requirements and changes that must be implemented. But the challenge for any team is finding a way to effectively capture feedback from their stakeholders in a manner that can be analyzed, synthesized, and acted upon. This problem is made harder when stakeholders are time-shifted or geography-shifted away from the software development team. But even if the development team shares a common location with their stakeholders, finding a systematic way of gathering feedback from all of their stakeholders on a recurring basis can be a burdensome task.

In this release of Visual Studio 2012, Microsoft has integrated the process of collecting stakeholder feedback directly into their application lifecycle management tooling capabilities. In this chapter you find out how to use this tool to solicit and capture feedback from your stakeholders in a rich, actionable way.

REQUESTING FEEDBACK

The first step toward getting great feedback from your stakeholders about your software is to properly frame the question of what you are asking for feedback on. The question of whether or not your software provides the right level of *functionality* is a very different question from whether or not your software is *designed* properly. Functionally, a tractor can get me from my house to my office in the morning, but it's not what I feel comfortable being seen in as I pull into the parking lot at work. But early on in a software development iteration, the team may be focused squarely on strictly implementing the required functionality with the understanding that they can make it look nice later on. Unless you properly scope your request to the stakeholders when you ask for feedback, you may get a lot of feedback on things that you haven't yet started to address in the software.

With Team Foundation Server 2012 you can request specific feedback from your stakeholders by visiting the Team Web Access home page for your project. See Chapter 2 for more information about accessing Team Foundation Server via Team Web Access. In the list of Activities, click Request Feedback. You are presented with the dialog shown in Figure 9-1, which allows you to specify what you are requesting feedback on and from whom.

> **NOTE** *If you don't see Request Feedback under the list of Activities, this indicates that your Team Foundation Server instance has not been configured to use an SMTP email server. Contact your Team Foundation Server administrator. You will also need to ensure that your user account has appropriate licensing rights to request feedback. Only users with Visual Studio Test Professional 2012, Visual Studio Premium 2012, or Visual Studio Ultimate 2012 are permitted to request feedback using this capability.*

Follow the steps in the dialog to request feedback from your stakeholders:

1. Specify the names of the users you want to request feedback from. These users need to be recognized as users who have access to your team project.

2. Specify how users should access the functionality you are asking them to test. For a web application users might need to access a staging server that contains a recent build. For other applications users might need to remote into another machine, or install an interim build. Use this space to give the users any specific instructions they need in order to get started with your software.

3. Specify up to five aspects of your software that you want feedback on.

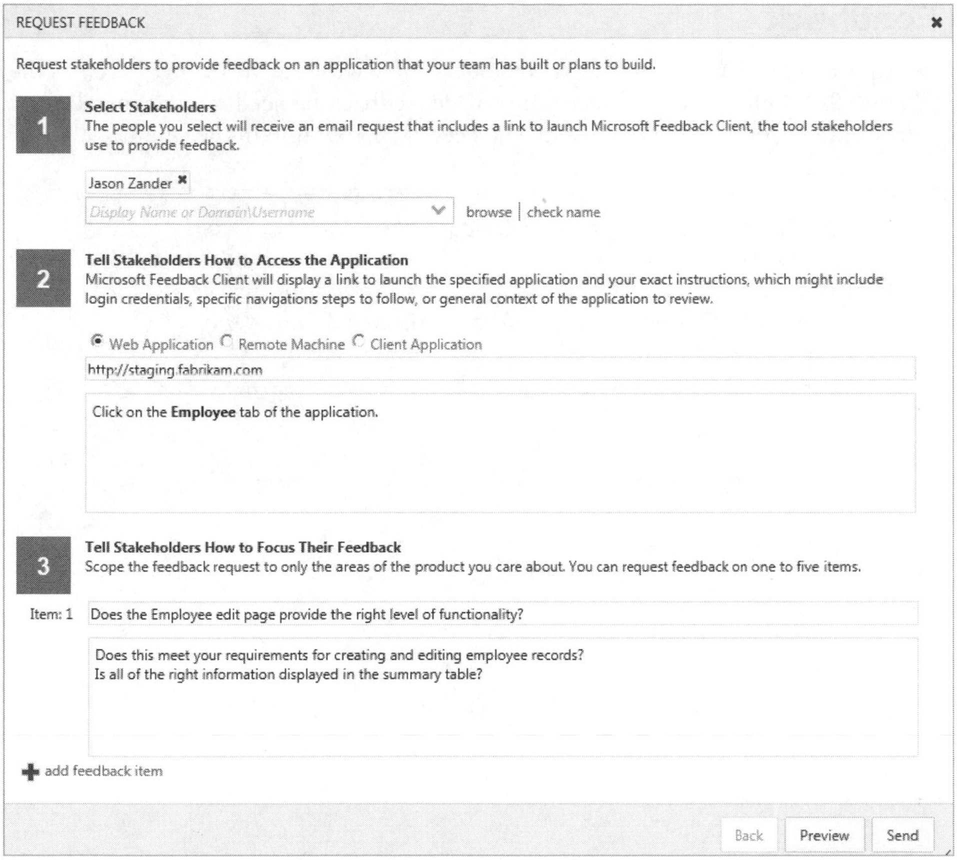

FIGURE 9-1

When specifying what you want to collect feedback on, be as specific as possible. You can also use the area below each feedback title to provide additional instructions that might help your stakeholders access certain features or scope their feedback to what you care most about. When applicable, you might want to also specify the things that you do *not* want feedback on. For example, if you know that the staging server you are using is very slow and doesn't reflect the performance of your production environment, then you might want to mention this to the users so that they don't waste time giving you a lot of feedback on the performance of the application. If the user interface hasn't yet received attention from a designer (affectionately known as "programmer art"), be sure to specify this as well so that users don't spend time critiquing anything other than the application's functionality.

After you have told your users how to access your software and what you are looking for feedback on, click Preview to see the email that your stakeholders will receive. Click Send to deliver an email to the stakeholders you specified earlier, and also create Feedback Request work items (up to five, one for each item you added in step 3 above) for you to track this request in Team Foundation Server.

Providing Feedback

After you have requested feedback from your stakeholders, they will receive an email such as the one shown in Figure 9-2. Before a stakeholder can provide feedback he needs to first install the Microsoft Feedback Client by clicking the Install The Feedback Tool link in the email.

> **NOTE** *The Feedback Client is freely downloadable from Microsoft and does not require a Team Foundation Server client access license. Users will, however, need to have appropriate permissions to your Team Foundation Server instance. At a minimum, users will need to be a member of the Work Item Only View Licensing Group. See* `http://aka.ms/WIOV` *for details.*

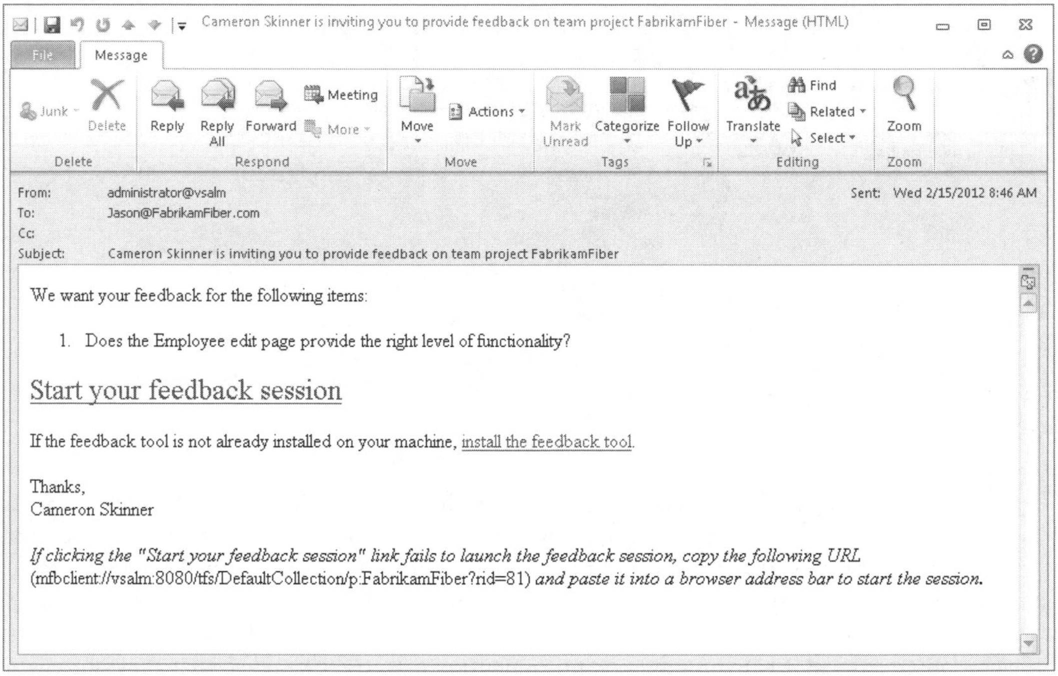

FIGURE 9-2

After the feedback tool is installed and a stakeholder is ready to give feedback, he can click the Start Your Feedback Session link in the email to open the Feedback Client shown on the left side of Figure 9-3. The menu at the top enables the stakeholder to dock the Feedback Client on either side of the monitor or to float the window to another monitor. The instructions provided on this first page are from the feedback request that you created earlier. After the stakeholder has installed or otherwise launched the application for which he is providing feedback, he can click the Next button to start giving feedback.

Figure 9-4 shows a stakeholder in the middle of providing feedback on this web application. The top half of the Feedback Client scopes the specific questions the stakeholder has been asked to address. In this case, we asked if the right information is displayed in the summary table. The stakeholder responded by asking if an Employee ID column can be added to this table. He then used the Screenshot button to capture a snippet of the table, and double-clicked on that snippet so that he could annotate it with a red rectangle showing where he would like the Employee ID column to go.

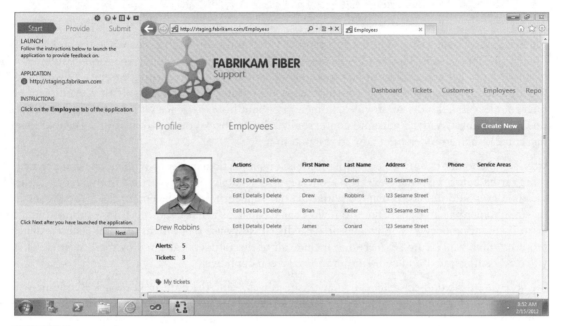

FIGURE 9-3

FIGURE 9-4

> **NOTE** *By default, Microsoft Paint is used to edit a screen clipping any time the user double-clicks within the Feedback Client. You can configure the Feedback Client to use your own favorite image-editing tool by clicking on the gear icon at the top of the window.*

The Feedback Client can also be used to capture video and audio recordings while the stakeholder is using the application. This can be the next best thing to actually being in the room watching over the shoulder of the stakeholder as he uses the application. A video recording can be a powerful way of truly understanding the way in which a user tends to interact with your software. Audio annotations enable a stakeholder to provide commentary about his experience without having to take the time to type notes. Video and audio contextualize the feedback you get from your stakeholders so that you can better understand how to respond to it.

After a stakeholder is finished providing feedback on a particular feedback item, she can provide a star rating before clicking Next. If there were other feedback items specified in this request, the stakeholder would now be prompted with each one sequentially. At the end of the feedback session the stakeholder has an opportunity to review the feedback she has captured before submitting it to Team Foundation Server. This creates new Feedback Response work items (one for each Feedback Request which was created earlier) that include all of the artifacts captured by the Feedback Client (video recordings, text and audio annotations, screen clippings).

The software development team can view this feedback using the built-in Feedback Requests work item query (see Figure 9-5). If a piece of feedback results in a new bug or new requirement, the team can use the New Linked Work Item button to create a new work item linked to this specific Feedback Response work item. By linking the feedback directly from the stakeholders into the new work item, you can provide additional context and traceability for the developer who is assigned to implement the fix or new requirement specified in that work item.

After feedback has been reviewed and any necessary actions have been taken (such as fixing bugs or implementing requirements), you can transition the State field of each Feedback Response to Closed.

Voluntary Feedback

Stakeholders can also provide unsolicited or voluntary feedback at any time by launching the Feedback Client directly (Start ➪ Microsoft Visual Studio 2012 ➪ Microsoft Feedback Client) instead of from a feedback request email. They are first prompted to connect to the appropriate Team Foundation Server instance and team project where they want to provide feedback. After doing so, they can file feedback using video, audio, text, and screen clippings as they did previously. The one thing to be careful of here is that Feedback Response work items created when using a voluntary feedback method do not show up in the default Feedback Requests work item query. Instead, you should write a custom query to search for all work items of type Feedback Response. Feedback that is generated by the Feedback Client in an unsolicited manner will by default have a title that starts with `Voluntary`.

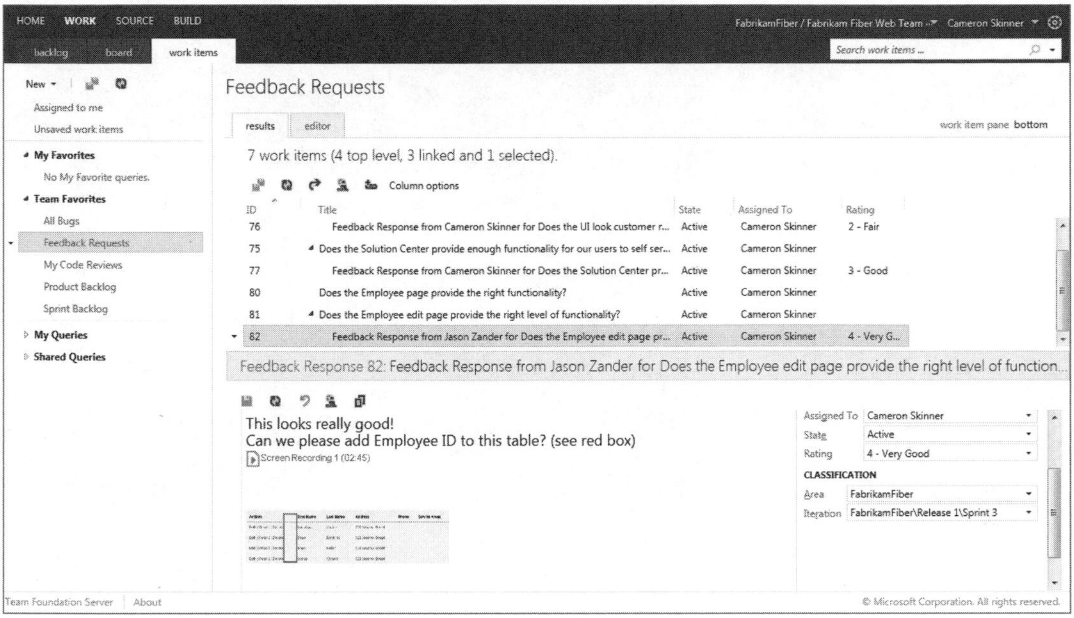

FIGURE 9-5

SUMMARY

In this chapter, you learned how you can request scoped feedback from your stakeholders to get actionable data that can help you refine your application development. You learned about the new Feedback Client that can capture rich information — including video recordings, text and audio annotations, and screen clippings — from your users as they give feedback about your applications. Finally, you learned how you can use this feedback to create actionable bugs or new requirements that your team can use to ensure that you are continuing to build the right software to please your stakeholders.

In the next chapter you begin to learn about the project management capabilities of Team Foundation Server 2012.

PART III
Project Management

10

Introduction to Project Management

WHAT'S IN THIS CHAPTER?

➤ Getting to know the additions and enhancements to project management capabilities in Team Foundation Server 2012

➤ Understanding work items and process templates

➤ Managing and querying work items with Visual Studio, Excel, Project, and Team Web Access

In Part I, you learned about the support that Team Foundation Server 2012 has for source control. In Part II, you learned about the importance of engaging with your project's stakeholders early and often during the development cycle to ensure that you are building the right software. In Part III, you learn about how Team Foundation Server 2012 helps you plan and track your software development projects in an agile manner.

Project management can involve many aspects of developing software, such as tracking remaining work and open bugs, determining how much work you can commit to with your available resources, and even helping to enforce a standard process of interaction between your team members. You will see that Team Foundation Server 2012 provides capabilities to help you achieve all of these things, and more.

This chapter starts with the enhancements to project management available in this release. It also provides an overview of work item tracking, including some ways to manage and query work items from Visual Studio, Excel, Project, and other clients. You find out about the importance of process templates, including an overview of the process templates provided by Microsoft for use with Team Foundation Server 2012.

In Chapter 11, you take a deeper look at the agile project management tools, which you can use to manage your backlog, plan your iterations, and track your work. Chapter 12 examines using reporting and SharePoint dashboards to get real-time insights into how your software development project is going. You might also want to consider obtaining a copy of *Professional Team Foundation Server 2012* (Wrox, 2012. ISBN 978-1-118-31409-8), to find out how you can extend and customize the process templates in Team Foundation Server 2012 to meet the unique needs of your team.

PROJECT MANAGEMENT ENHANCEMENTS IN TEAM FOUNDATION SERVER 2012

Team Foundation Server 2012 continues to build upon the project management enhancements made to Team Foundation Server 2010, which was a substantial upgrade to the project management capabilities available in prior releases. This section highlights some of the most significant improvements and additions in this release, and recaps some of the enhancements first available in Team Foundation Server 2010. If you are brand new to Team Foundation Server, concepts such as work items are explained in greater detail later in this chapter.

Rich Work Item Relationships

Rich work item relationships were introduced in Team Foundation Server 2010, but this capability is worth covering here in case you are upgrading from an older release. According to Microsoft, the top-requested project management feature by users of Team Foundation Server releases prior to 2010 was representing rich relationships between work items. In releases of Team Foundation Server prior to 2010, it was only possible to relate work items with one another via a simple linking mechanism. But these links didn't provide any explicit meaning, directionality, or cardinality.

For example, a common project management use case for many software development projects is to be able to model parent/child relationships between work items, such as for modeling a feature catalog or for detailing the tasks required to implement a particular requirement. You could link these work items using releases of Team Foundation Server prior to 2010, but the links didn't carry enough meaning to convey proper parent/child relationships. Without directionality, it's not easy to discern which work item is the parent and which work item is the child in this representation. Furthermore, without cardinality, there isn't a mechanism for restricting that each child work item could only have (at most) one parent work item.

With Team Foundation Server 2010, Microsoft introduced rich relational linking between work items, allowing for rich relationships between work items using a variety of link types. These link types can also include directionality and cardinality. The most commonly used link types available in Team Foundation Server are the following:

> *Parent/child* — This is a useful link type for representing hierarchies such as feature catalogs, or for detailing task work items (children) that are used to implement a requirement or user story (parent). Any work item can have zero or more child work items, and zero or one parent work item.

➤ *Tests/tested by* — This link type is primarily intended to model the relationships between test case work items and the requirements or user stories that they test. This makes it easier to determine the quality of a given requirement or user story by examining the recent results for its related test cases. A work item can test zero or more work items.

➤ *Successor/predecessor* — The successor/predecessor link type is used to indicate work items that have a dependency relationship with one another. For example, designing the user interface for a web page is generally a predecessor to writing the code and markup that provides the implementation of that web page. A work item can have zero or more successor and/or predecessor links to other work items.

➤ *Related* — The related link type is the same as the legacy linking system found in previous releases of Team Foundation Server. These link types are not directional, and they provide no additional context about the type of relationship. If you had linked work items in a project that was upgraded to Team Foundation Server 2010 or Team Foundation Server 2012, those relationships are represented by the related link type.

You will discover that rich work item relationships provide the basis for other features and enhancements across the project management capabilities of Team Foundation Server, such as enhanced querying and reporting. It is also possible to define your own link types if you want, although for most teams, the provided link types are sufficient. You can find more information on creating custom link types at http://aka.ms/WICustomLinks.

> **NOTE** *Team Foundation Server does not have a mechanism for ensuring that your links are semantically correct. For example, it's possible to create circular chains of successor/predecessor links, or tests/tested by relationships between two work items that don't involve a test case. If you notice that you have invalid link types in your project, you can easily delete them at any time.*

Agile Planning Tools

A new set of web-based tools in Team Foundation Server 2012 provides an agile way of planning and tracking your software development project. This tooling is immediately familiar to any development team that practices Scrum, because it includes tools for managing your product backlog, tracking velocity, planning iterations (or sprints), and viewing a burndown of hours remaining for a given iteration. It even includes a modern-day incarnation of sticky notes on a whiteboard for tracking your project, as shown in Figure 10-1, which you can use to track work through to completion.

It is important to point out, however, that you can use this tooling regardless of whether or not you are practicing a Scrum development methodology. All of the process templates included with Team Foundation Server 2012 work out-of-the-box with the agile planning and tracking tools, and you can adapt your own custom or third-party process templates to utilize this tooling as well. The process of customizing and adapting your own process templates to use this tooling is covered in depth in *Professional Team Foundation Server 2012*.

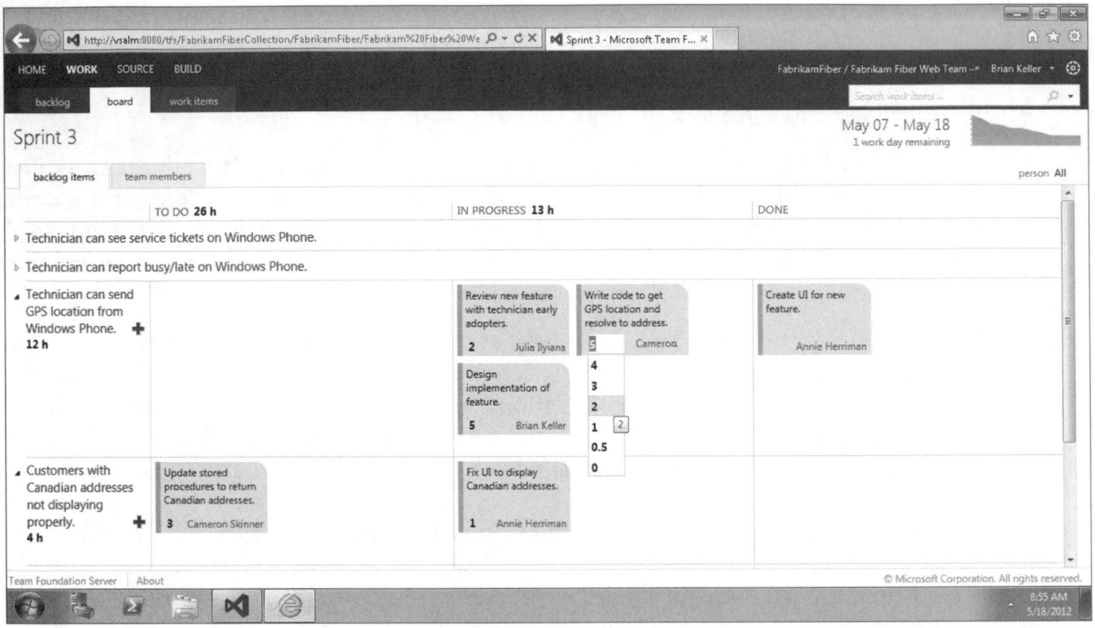

FIGURE 10-1

> **NOTE** *You learn more about using the web-based Agile Planning Tools in Chapter 11.*

> **NOTE** *If you used Team Foundation Server 2010, you may have used the Agile Planning Workbooks that came with the Microsoft Solutions Framework (MSF) for Agile Software Development process template. The Agile Planning Workbooks were a set of Excel-bound workbooks available to help you manage your backlog, iterations, and resources. These workbooks are no longer included with Team Foundation Server 2012 because the functionality they provided has been replaced by the Agile Planning Tools you learn about in Chapter 11.*

Test Case Management

Test cases began to be represented as work items in Team Foundation Server 2010. This made it possible to create rich relationships between the code you are implementing and the results of your quality assurance (QA) efforts.

For example, test case work items can be linked (via a tests/tested by link type) to requirements work items. As tests are run, results can be reported on by querying a given requirement work item, traversing to the related test cases, and viewing the results of recent test runs. Many of the new default reports make use of this information to expose new perspectives on software quality.

> **NOTE** *You learn more about software testing and test case management in Part VI.*

Feedback Management

Chapter 9 covered how feedback can be requested and stored in Team Foundation Server 2012. Two work item types were added to Team Foundation Server 2012 to support this: Feedback Request and Feedback Response.

By storing feedback as work items in Team Foundation Server, you are able to link it to other work items. For example, you might receive a Feedback Response from a stakeholder asking you to add a new piece of functionality. This may in turn get linked to a new User Story that your team plans to implement. This way when the development team wants to understand more details about the original request, including who asked for it, they can view the original Feedback Response to learn more.

You can also query feedback work items just like you would query any other work items in Team Foundation Server. For example, you might query for Feedback Requests which have fewer than five Feedback Response child work items to determine if there are areas of your application that have not yet been adequately reviewed by stakeholders.

Enhanced Reporting

One of the primary reasons Microsoft originally designed Team Foundation Server as an integrated solution (including source control, project management, build automation, and so on) is to enable multidimensional views into software development projects. Effectively managing a software project is not unlike managing other complex projects. Making smart decisions requires you to have a rich set of information resources available, usually in real time, which can help to inform resource allocations, prioritizations, cuts, schedule changes, and other important evaluations.

The rich work item relationships that were added since Team Foundation Server 2010 have enabled Microsoft to significantly enhance the types of reports available. As just one example, parent/child relationships between user stories and tasks can produce a report showing the amount of work required in order to finish implementing any given user story. By further analyzing the tests/tested by links, you can get a view into software quality for those same user stories based on the results of your test cases. There are countless other examples.

Along with the improvements made to Team Foundation Server 2010, Microsoft also made it much easier to customize existing reports, or create new ones, using Microsoft Excel to create reports based on work item queries.

> **NOTE** *You learn more about reporting with Team Foundation Server 2012 in Chapter 12.*

SharePoint Server Dashboards

Most software development projects involve many stakeholders. In addition to the core programming team, a team may include project managers, business analysts, testers, architects, and so on. There may also be external stakeholders — such as end users or executive management — who have a vested interest in monitoring the progress of your project. Most of these people don't use Visual Studio; so how do you effectively communicate project status to everyone?

Microsoft has integrated Team Foundation Server with SharePoint for this reason. Whenever you create a team project with Team Foundation Server, you can optionally create a new SharePoint site (or use an existing one). You can use this site as a dashboard to provide everybody on your extended team with a view into your project. Your SharePoint site provides a web-based view of reports from your team project, along with a document repository where you can store artifacts such as specifications and storyboards.

> **NOTE** *In Chapter 12, you learn about how you can use these SharePoint dashboards and customize them for your team.*

WORK ITEMS

If you're brand new to Team Foundation Server, you may be wondering what exactly a work item is. A *work item* is the basic building block of the project management capabilities in Team Foundation Server. Microsoft defines a work item as "… a database record that Team Foundation uses to track the assignment and progress of work."

Work Item Types

There are many kinds of work items, known as *work item types*. An instance of a work item type is a work item, in much the same way that, in object-oriented programming (OOP), an instance of a class is an object. A work item can represent explicit work that needs to be completed (or has been completed), such as with a *Task* work item type. Work items can capture details of the software you are building, such as with a *Requirement* or *User Story* work item types. You can use work items to capture problems, such as the *Bug* work item type (which indicates a problem with your software) or the *Issue* work item type (which might describe a problem with tooling, processes, or people that may be slowing down your project, or even preventing work from happening). Team Foundation Server includes other default work item types as well, and you can customize these or even create your own.

> **NOTE** *You can learn more about work item type customization in Professional Team Foundation Server 2012.*

Work items include a handful of key elements, as shown in Table 10-1.

TABLE 10-1 Work Item Elements

ELEMENT	DESCRIPTION
Field	*Fields* contain the information that can be captured as part of a work item. There are some fields that are shared by all work item types (called *system fields*). Examples of system fields include Title (a one-line description of your work item), ID (a number that is globally unique across your team project collection), and Assigned to (which can be a user, such as a developer, who is working on a fix for a bug work item). Other fields might be specific to a given work item type, such as the Steps to reproduce field, which is found in the Bug work item type and describes how a bug was discovered.
Rule	*Rules* can dictate which values are allowed for given fields. For example, you might decide that the Priority field for bugs should be assigned a value of 0, 1, or 2 and cannot be left blank.
Form	A *form* describes the way work items are displayed by work item clients such as Visual Studio. (You learn more about some of the ways to view and interact with work items later in this chapter.)
State	*States* indicate where in your project workflow a work item is. For example, a Bug work item type in the MSF for Agile Software Development process template starts out in an Active state when it is first created. After a developer declares that the code has been written or modified to fix a bug, the developer changes the state of the Bug work item to Resolved. If a tester can verify that the bug can no longer be reproduced, the tester changes the bug work item state to Closed. But if a tester can still reproduce the bug, the work item needs to be reactivated (that is, the tester changes the state of the bug back to Active). This signals to the developers that they still have work to do.
Transition	*Transitions* are similar to rules, but they define how a work item moves from one state to another. In the previous example, a bug work item must begin in an Active state, and then it can move into a Resolved or Closed state. But, from a Resolved state, it is also possible to move back to an Active state. This is all defined by the transition model as part of the work item type. Additionally, transitions can dictate that certain fields should be required in order to move from one state to another. For example, to move a bug from an Active to a Resolved state, a developer must assign a Reason (such as Fixed, As Designed, Cannot Reproduce, and so on).
Link	Work items can include *links* to other work items, using any of the link types you read about in the preceding section.
History	Work items also contain a full *history* that includes information about all changes to fields and transitions.

Figure 10-2 shows an example of a bug work item form that has been resolved by the developer. This screenshot is taken from a bug that was created with the MSF for Agile Software Development process template. You learn more about process templates later in this chapter.

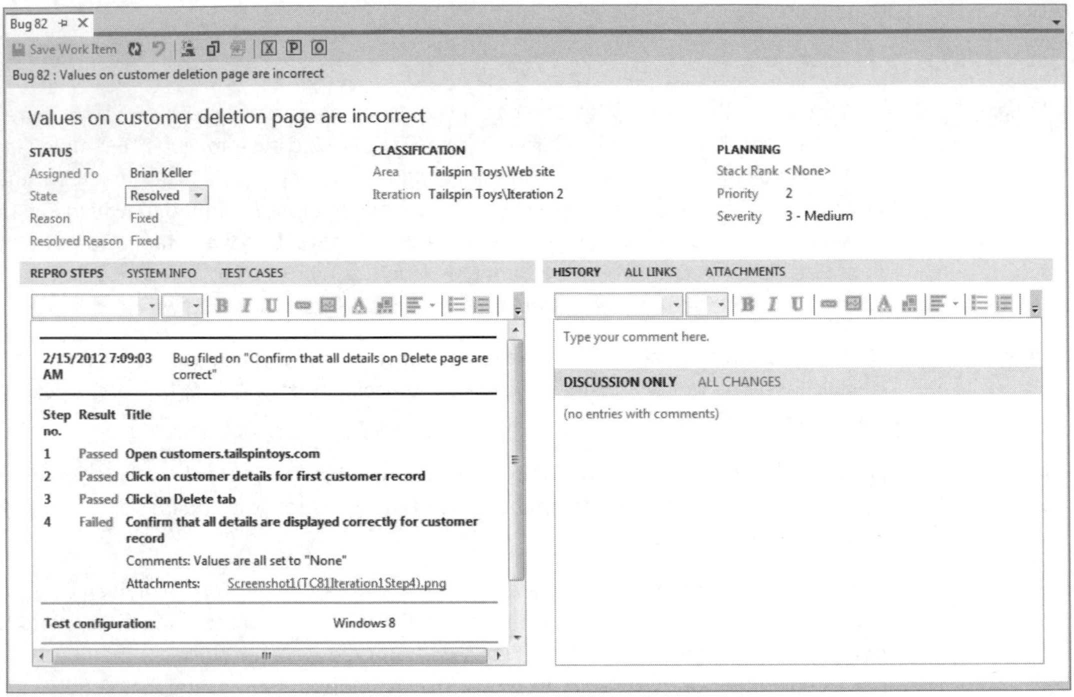

FIGURE 10-2

Figure 10-3 is a state diagram showing the transitions for the default Bug work item type included with the MSF for Agile Software Development process template. State diagrams for each work item type are included with the documentation for the process templates provided by Microsoft. They are useful for understanding how a work item behaves.

Areas and Iterations

Most of the system fields available for work items (such as Title and ID) are fairly self-explanatory. But there are two important fields — Area and Iteration — that warrant further discussion.

The *Area field* is a versatile field that you can use to create logical categories for your work items. There are many ways to use areas, but a common approach is to define an area for each logical part of your application.

For example, in Figure 10-2, this bug is assigned to the Tailspin Toys\Web site area to indicate that it is part of the web application being developed for the Tailspin Toys team project. The complete string that is used for this designation is referred to as an area path. Other area paths might include Tailspin Toys\Database, Tailspin Toys\Mobile Application, and paths can be several levels deep, such as Tailspin Toys\Web site\Shopping cart\Update controller.

The *Iteration field* is useful for project planning and can indicate a time frame for when you plan to address a work item. In Figure 10-2, this work item is assigned to Tailspin Toys\Iteration 2, where

Tailspin Toys is the name of the team project, and Iteration 2 is the specific iteration this work item is assigned to.

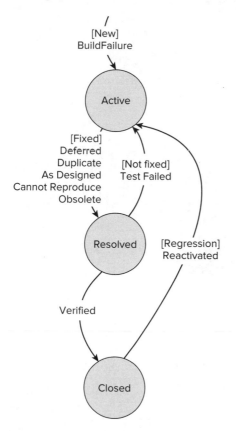

FIGURE 10-3

You can name your iterations whatever you'd like; some teams choose sequential iterations (such as Iteration 1, Iteration 2, and so on), whereas others choose to map them to milestone releases (such as Beta 1, Beta 2, and so on). You can also create trees of iterations and employ a blend of naming strategies, such as Tailspin Toys\Version 2.0\Beta 1\Iteration 2.

You are not required to use iterations and areas to categorize your work items, but they can be very useful for querying, managing, and reporting your work items as your team project grows. When used effectively, areas and iterations can enable you to employ a single team project for dozens or even hundreds of applications across many years of iterative releases.

A team project administrator can manage the list of valid areas and iterations by opening Visual Studio ⇨ Team Explorer ⇨ Settings and then clicking on either Work Item Areas or Work Item Iterations. Figure 10-4 and Figure 10-5 show the dialogs for editing areas and iterations, respectively. You can also access these menus directly from Team Web Access by clicking on the administrative icon in the upper-right corner.

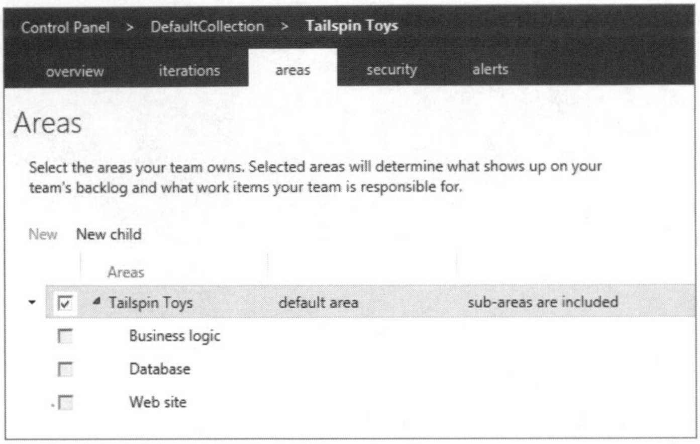

FIGURE 10-4

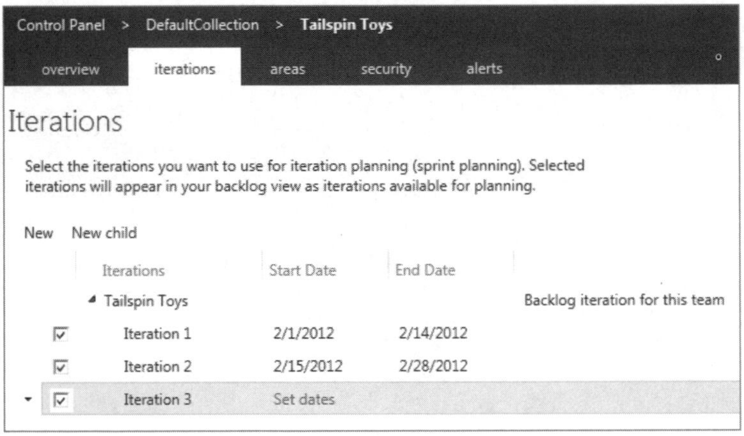

FIGURE 10-5

A nice feature of area and iteration administration is that you can define granular permissions for indicating who is allowed to modify or even read work items in each part of your team project. For example, maybe you work for a government security contractor and there are bugs of a sensitive nature that should only be viewed by team members with a certain security clearance. Or, maybe you are building a prototype of the next version of your application and want to restrict access to minimize the potential for leaks that your competitors could get access to. These sorts of restrictions are possible by using iteration and area security settings. To access the permissions menu, highlight an area path or iteration path then click the small down arrow on the left side of the row.

At any time, you can return to the area and iteration settings dialogs to add, rename, move, or delete areas and iterations. You can move nodes to be children of other nodes by simply dragging and dropping them on top of one another. If you rename or move areas or iterations for which there are existing work items, those work items are automatically reassigned by Team Foundation Server using the new name or location you choose. If you delete an area or iteration for which there are existing work items, you are prompted for the value that Team Foundation Server should use to replace the iteration or area value in affected work items.

Starting with Team Foundation Server 2012, you can also use the iteration settings dialog to assign start and end dates to iterations. This information is used by the Agile Planning Tools you can read about in Chapter 11 to determine which iteration is currently active. Iteration dates are also used to help Team Foundation Server render certain reports, such as the burndown report, which shows the amount of work remaining for an iteration and how remaining work is trending over time.

You will discover that work items are used throughout Team Foundation Server. You can use them to help you manage your product backlog and plan your iterations, which is covered in Chapter 11. Work items form the basis of many of the reports you read about in Chapter 12. You can link them to changesets (which you read about in Part I) to provide more information about what changes were made to a set of files and why. Project managers and team leaders can also use work items for project planning and to help control which work team members should be focused on, and how they should interact with other team members.

Work items, work item types, and all of the activities involving work items (editing, querying, reporting, and so on) are usually referred to collectively as the *work item tracking* capability of Team Foundation Server. Now that you understand the basics of work items, you are ready to learn about process templates, which include the definitions for work item types.

PROCESS TEMPLATES

A *process template* defines the default characteristics of any new team project. Process templates are a powerful concept in Team Foundation Server. A process template includes the default work item types, reports, documents, process guidance, and other associated artifacts that provide you with everything you need to get started with your software project.

Choosing the right process template is an important step in creating a new team project. You should carefully choose the best process template for your team's preferred work style and the type of project you are working on. This section helps you understand the types of process templates available. While you are reading this section, you should be thinking about the following types of questions:

➤ How does your team work today?

➤ Are there ways your team works today that you'd like to change?

➤ Do you need a formal process, or do you work better as a more ad-hoc team?

➤ Are there areas of your process where you prefer to be more agile, but other areas where you need to be more formal? (For example, maybe you want to manage your team's iterations in an agile manner, but decisions about requirements require formal negotiations with your customer.)

➤ Do you have resources to invest in and maintain your own custom process template, or would one provided by Microsoft or a reputable third party be a better solution?

➤ What other stakeholders should be involved in the decision-making process for answering these questions?

If answering these questions proves difficult for you or your team, you may want to start with a small pilot project first and see how your team performs when using one of the existing process templates. You can then use the findings from that pilot to determine which process template to start with, and what changes (if any) you need to make to that process template before using it for subsequent projects. Process template customization is covered in *Professional Team Foundation Server 2012*.

Embracing the *right* process template can have a transformational effect on an organization by providing everybody on the team with a predictable and repeatable process for capturing and communicating information, making decisions, and ensuring that you are delivering on customer expectations. This, in turn, can drive up software quality and development velocity, which ultimately delivers more value to your customers.

MSF for Agile Software Development

The MSF for Agile Software Development v6.0 process template included with Team Foundation Server 2012 is designed for teams who are practicing agile methodologies, such as Scrum or eXtreme Programming (XP). These methodologies have their roots in the now-famous Agile Manifesto (www.agilemanifesto.org).

If you are practicing Scrum as a development methodology, you may prefer the relatively newer Visual Studio Scrum process template described later in this section. Visual Studio Scrum uses terminology which will immediately be familiar to any team practicing Scrum. In practice, teams that practice Scrum can use both of these process templates, but the MSF for Agile Software Development process template provides a bit more rigor and structure than the Visual Studio Scrum process template.

> **NOTE** *MSF version 1 was introduced by Microsoft in 1993, and version 4 was first codified as a set of process templates with the release of Team Foundation Server 2005. MSF provides guidelines, role definitions, and other materials to help organizations deliver IT solutions, including software development projects. Many of the guiding principles of MSF align closely with those of the Agile Manifesto.*

A key tenet of agile methodologies is that requirements will evolve over time, both as business needs change and as customers begin to use interim releases of your software. For this reason, the MSF for Agile Software Development process template assumes that teams will be frequently refining requirements and reprioritizing work by maintaining a common backlog of requirements (which are captured as user stories in this template). Periods of work are time-boxed into short lengths of time (iterations). Prior to each iteration, the development team works with the customer to prioritize the backlog, and the top user stories on the backlog are then addressed in that iteration.

Another important aspect of agile methodologies is, as the Agile Manifesto describes it, valuing "individuals and interactions over processes and tools." This doesn't mean that processes and tools shouldn't be used at all, but instead that they sometimes can get in the way of empowering people to communicate and work together in order to make smart decisions. This principle is also reflected in the MSF for Agile Software Development process template, which defines a relatively small number of states, fields, transitions, and work item types as compared with other process templates such as the MSF for Capability Maturity Model Integration (CMMI) Process Improvement process template. By keeping the process simple, the goal is to prevent any unnecessary burdens from getting in the way of people making the right decisions.

Following are the work item types available in the MSF for Agile Software Development process template:

➤ Bug

➤ Issue

➤ Task

➤ Test Case

➤ User Story

> **NOTE** *There are a few additional work item types present in all of the Microsoft-supplied process templates (and available to be added to custom and third-party process templates) which cannot be created directly, but are instead created during special situations. Code Review Request and Code Review Response work items are used to provide the code review functionality which you read about in Chapter 3. Feedback Request and Feedback Response work item types are created during the process of requesting feedback and providing feedback from stakeholders, as you read about in Part II. Finally, the Shared Steps work item type is essentially a special instance of a Test Case. You learn more about Shared Steps and Test Cases in Part VI. Most team members won't interact with Shared Steps directly, so they are excluded from the preceding list.*

> **NOTE** *You can explore the MSF for Agile Software Development v6.0 process template in depth, including more detail on each of the included work item types, at* http://aka.ms/MSFAgile6.

MSF for CMMI Process Improvement

The MSF for CMMI Process Improvement v6.0 process template is designed for teams who want to, or may have to, take a more formal approach toward developing software. This process template is based on the Capability Maturity Model Integration (CMMI) for Development, which was developed by the Software Engineering Institute, a part of Carnegie Mellon University. CMMI defines not only a framework for developing software, but also prescribes ways for an organization to constantly improve their processes in an objective and repeatable way. An organization can even become certified by an outside appraiser who can verify whether or not it is performing at one of five CMMI maturity levels.

CMMI is a popular model for developing software by such organizations as systems integrators (SIs) and software factories. There is very little subjectivity in the model, so it allows an organization to represent its services using a standard that is well understood globally, and can be appraised and certified by a neutral third-party organization. CMMI is also used for developing many mission-critical systems, such as by NASA or defense contractors. In fact, the Software Engineering Institute at Carnegie Mellon was originally funded by the United States Department of Defense to help them find better ways of managing their projects.

As you might expect, the MSF for CMMI Process Improvement process template is more complex than its Agile counterpart. The CMMI template includes the following work item types:

➤ Bug

➤ Change Request

➤ Issue

➤ Requirement

➤ Review

➤ Risk

➤ Task

➤ Test Case

> **NOTE** *The Feedback, Code Review, and Shared Steps work item types are also omitted from this list for the same reason as mentioned previously in the discussion of the MSF for Agile Software Development process template.*

In addition to including three additional work item types, the work item types themselves are also more complex in the CMMI process template than in the Agile process template. Compare the screenshot of a bug work item form from the Agile process template, shown earlier in Figure 10-2, with a bug work item form from the CMMI process template, shown in Figure 10-6. Take note of the additional fields, such as Severity, Triage, and Blocked, which were not in the bug work item from the Agile process template. There are also additional tabs across the lower half of the bug work item from the CMMI process template.

The states and transitions of work item types from the CMMI process template are also more complex than in the Agile process template. Now, compare the state diagram of the bug work item type from the Agile process template, shown in Figure 10-3, with the state diagram of the bug work item type from the CMMI process template, shown in Figure 10-7.

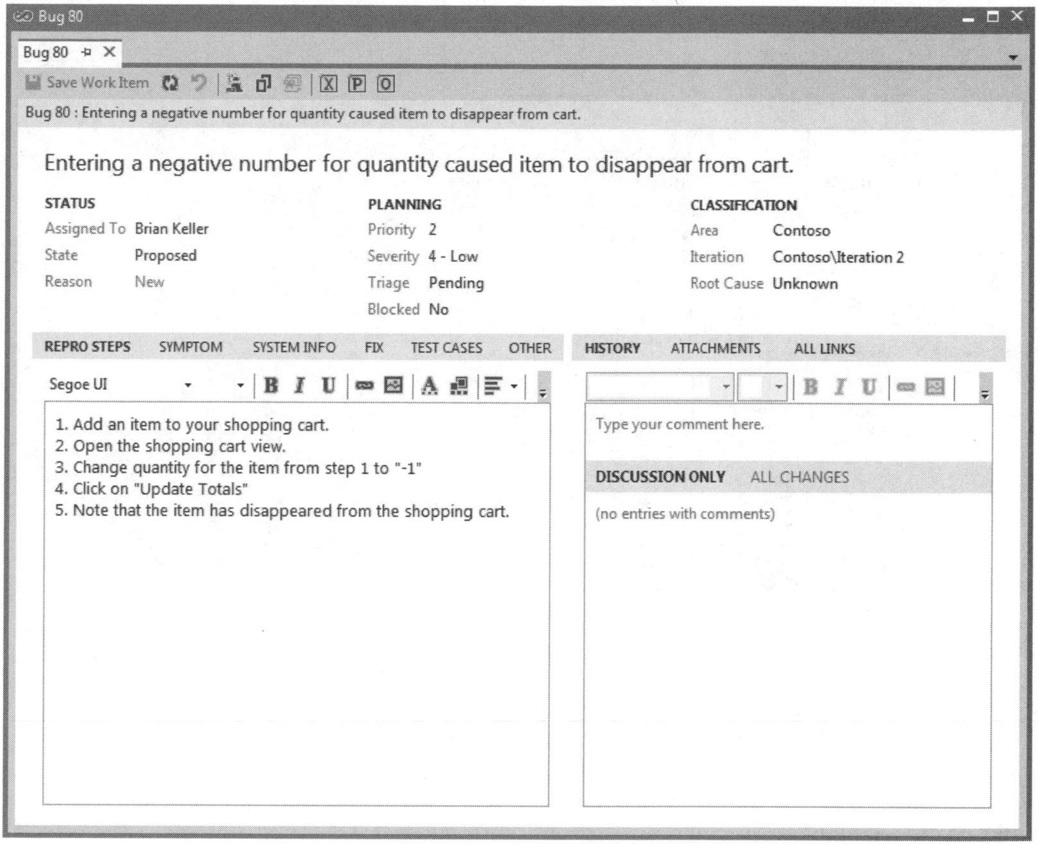

FIGURE 10-6

The key difference you should notice between these two state diagrams is that the CMMI process template introduces an additional state — *Proposed*. This explicit decision stage is required in the CMMI process template before a developer is ever assigned to work on a bug. This should cause the team to ask such questions as, "Is this really a bug, or does this represent a request to change the way certain functionality was designed? Will fixing this bug have unintended side effects on other parts of the software? If we choose to work on this bug, how should it be prioritized against our other work?"

This shouldn't imply that those aren't important questions to be asking even if you are using the Agile process template, and a seasoned team practicing an agile methodology will likely already be mentally following this checklist as they triage bugs. But the CMMI process template makes this step explicit, which helps to ensure that this step takes place for every bug, regardless of the experience level of the development team.

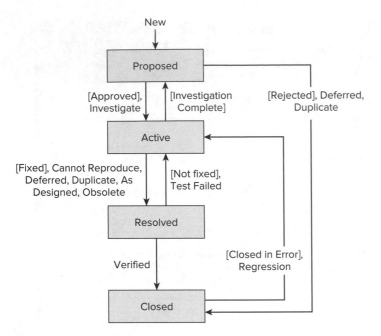

FIGURE 10-7

Another way of thinking of CMMI is to realize that by following the model, NASA isn't guaranteed that it will never again develop a rocket that fails because of a software defect. But if NASA is following CMMI correctly, then it can guarantee that an agreed-upon process was used to make decisions leading up to that defect. And conversely, in the event of a defect, it can audit the process that was used, examine the assumptions that went into the decision-making process, and learn from those mistakes in the interest of refining its process and helping to ensure that the same mistake never happens again.

It is also important to point out that using the MSF for CMMI Process Improvement process template alone does not ensure that an organization can successfully pass a CMMI certification audit. This is akin to the fact that simply having a smoke alarm and a fire extinguisher on hand won't keep a family safe if they don't know how to properly use and maintain this equipment.

But Team Foundation Server, along with the MSF for CMMI Process Improvement process template, can be very useful for helping an organization that wants to adopt CMMI as its model of development. Team Foundation Server features such as end-to-end traceability, multidimensional reporting, rich linking (between work items, and with other artifacts such as builds and changesets), and preservation of history are all incredibly useful capabilities that can help an organization to prepare for and pass a CMMI audit.

> **NOTE** *You can explore the MSF for CMMI Process Improvement v6.0 process template in depth, including more detail on each of the included work item types, at* http://aka.ms/MSFCMMI6.

CMMI DEVELOPMENT METHODOLOGY

There is a common misconception that CMMI dictates a waterfall, or "Big Design Up Front," development methodology. Although there is certainly a strong correlation between teams practicing waterfall methodologies and those following a CMMI model, CMMI actually does not define a development methodology. You can choose to use an agile development methodology along with the MSF for CMMI Process Improvement process template if you want to, although you might have a hard time selling agile diehards from your team on the value of the additional rigor imposed by its processes.

As a compromise solution, another approach is to pick the aspects of the CMMI process template that are most interesting to you and incorporate those into the Agile process template as a custom process template. For example, maybe you like the explicit decision point created by having your bugs begin in a Proposed state before being activated, but you don't see a need for the additional work item types in the CMMI template. In this example, you could start with the Agile process template and import the Bug work item type from the CMMI process template.

Visual Studio Scrum

Although there are many development methodologies that make up the agile movement, Scrum has established itself as the most popular. Scrum defines clear roles, responsibilities, and activities that team members practicing Scrum must follow.

A team practicing Scrum uses a standard vocabulary to define what they are doing. Teams hold daily *stand-ups* (meetings where team members talk about what they did yesterday, what they will do today, and anything that might be blocking them — called an *impediment*). Instead of a project manager, a team practicing Scrum is usually led by a *ScrumMaster*. There are other terms as well, which you can learn about in any of the dozens of books about Scrum, or from the hundreds of Scrum user groups or trainers around the world.

The Visual Studio Scrum process template was introduced specifically to help teams who want to practice Scrum and use Team Foundation Server. It was made available as a download a few months after Team Foundation Server 2010 first shipped, and it is now included as a built-in process template with Team Foundation Server 2012.

So, you might now be wondering what purpose the Visual Studio Scrum process template has if the MSF for Agile Software Development process template is designed to support any of the agile development methodologies — including Scrum. The Visual Studio Scrum process template was created to provide teams practicing Scrum with the *specific* artifacts and terminology used universally by teams who have adopted Scrum.

Instead of User Stories or Requirements, Visual Studio Scrum uses *Product Backlog Item work item types*. Instead of Issues or Risks, Visual Studio Scrum uses *Impediment work item types*. In short, if you practice Scrum or are considering practicing Scrum, the Visual Studio Scrum process template is designed to help you do so while making the most of Team Foundation Server.

If you used the Visual Studio Scrum 1.0 process template that shipped as an add-on to Team Foundation Server 2010, you will notice that Visual Studio Scrum 2.0 in Team Foundation Server 2012 no longer includes the *Sprint work item type*. The Sprint work item type was used by Visual Studio Scrum 1.0 to enable teams to define start and end dates for their iterations, and it was somewhat of a hack. The need for representing this information in a work item has disappeared now that Team Foundation Server 2012 enables you to define start and end dates for your iterations, as you discovered earlier in this chapter.

> **NOTE** *You can explore the Visual Studio Scrum 2.0 process template in depth, including more detail on each of the included work item types, at* `http://aka .ms/Scrum2`.

COMPROMISING WITH SCRUM

If you want to practice Scrum, the Visual Studio Scrum process template provides a great option for doing so. But you shouldn't feel locked into this process template if there are other process templates you like better, such as the MSF for Agile Software Development process template.

For example, you may prefer some of the additional reports that are included with the Agile process template. You can still use the Agile process template and practice Scrum, but you need to make some mental translations between the terminology you use as a Scrum team and the way the Agile process template expects you to enter information (such as referring to Product Backlog Items as User Stories). As you discover in Chapter 11, you can still take advantage of the Agile Planning Tools for managing your product backlog, planning your iterations, and tracking your progress in a very Scrum-like manner regardless of which process template you use. These tools are even available for teams who choose the MSF for CMMI process template.

Third-Party Process Templates

Several third parties provide process templates for use with Team Foundation Server. A list of some of these third-party process templates can be found at `http://aka.ms/ProcessTemplates`. Process templates from third parties are usually licensed for free use, and sometimes additional services such as consulting or complementary products are available for purchase from the organizations building those process templates.

There are several great third-party process templates available, but you should carefully consider the support and road map implications of adopting a third-party process template. For example, when the next version of Team Foundation Server is released, will the process template be upgraded to take advantage of new or improved features? If so, what is the upgrade path for migrating existing projects to the new version of the process template?

If you aren't prepared to take over the maintenance of the process template in the event that the third party chooses to stop investing in it, then you might want to consider one of the aforementioned process templates that are built and supported by Microsoft.

Custom Process Templates

Finally, you might decide that none of the process templates provided by Microsoft or third parties fit the needs of your team or your development project. Although you could certainly create your own process template from scratch, a far more common approach is to start with an existing process template and customize it to suit your needs. You can learn about customizing process templates in the companion to this book, *Professional Team Foundation Server 2012*.

Now that you understand your options for choosing a process template, the next section introduces you to some of the different ways you can manage your work items.

MANAGING WORK ITEMS

There are many ways of accessing your work items within Team Foundation Server 2012. Because work items are used by many stakeholders across your team (including programmers, testers, project managers, and so on), and some of these roles don't use Visual Studio as their primary tool, Microsoft provides many client options for managing work items.

In this section you are introduced to using Visual Studio, Excel, Project, and Team Web Access to access your work items. This chapter doesn't cover every aspect of accessing work items from each of these clients, but it gives you a better idea of the ways each client can be used, as well as the relative benefits of each, and provides you with pointers to detailed documentation for each client.

The list of clients in this section isn't exhaustive. There are also dozens of third-party clients. Testers might use Microsoft Test Manager (discussed in Part VI). Eclipse users can utilize Team Explorer Everywhere. You can even write your own clients using the Team Foundation Server object model if you want to, and partner solutions are plentiful, such as TeamLook which integrates work items directly into Microsoft Outlook.

Using Visual Studio

In Chapter 2, you learned about using Team Explorer to access Team Foundation Server from within Visual Studio. Team Explorer not only provides access for Visual Studio users wanting to connect to Team Foundation Server, but it also installs the add-ins required to work with Excel and Project. So, even if you don't plan to use Visual Studio, if you want to use Excel or Project with Team Foundation Server, you should install Team Explorer. Team Explorer itself is a free download from Microsoft, but you need to be properly licensed with a client access license before you are permitted to access Team Foundation Server.

Creating Work Items

Work items are easy to create using Visual Studio. Open the Team Explorer window of Visual Studio 2012 (click View ➪ Team Explorer if this window is not visible) and click the Work Items link. (If you don't see the Work Items link, try first clicking the Home icon at the top of the Team Explorer pane.) Now, click the New Work Item link. The fly-out menu reveals the work item types that are available in your team project. Click the work item type that you want to create an instance of. An empty work item form displays, similar to that shown in Figure 10-2.

The new work item form varies in appearance based on the work item type you chose to create. For the most part, filling out the work item form is self-explanatory, but there are a few things to notice when creating and editing work items.

The first is that your work item won't have an ID until it has been successfully saved for the first time. The ID is a number that is globally unique across your team project collection, numbered sequentially, starting with 1. This means that the first work item you save within a new team project won't have an ID of 1 if there are existing team projects in your team project collection that also contain work items.

> **NOTE** *Occasionally, you may encounter work item types that you can't edit completely within a particular work item client. The Steps tab of the Test Case and Shared Steps work item types exhibit this behavior; this tab cannot be edited within Team Explorer. The Steps tab is implemented as a custom control, and is designed to be edited by testers with Microsoft Test Manager. (Microsoft Test Manager is discussed in greater detail in Part VI.)*

For now, your work item probably says something like "New Bug 1" at the top of the form. The number 1 isn't your work item's ID; it's just a temporary number used by Visual Studio to track unsaved work items. In fact, until it is saved, Team Foundation Server won't know about your work item.

Before you can successfully save this work item, you need to provide a Title for it at a minimum. There may be other required fields as well, depending on the work item type you selected. An error message at the top of the form will indicate any remaining fields that you must complete. Some required fields may appear on other tabs.

Another thing to notice about work items is that you can't skip states. A work item must be saved in one state prior to moving to the next state. For example, if you refer to Figure 10-3, notice that a bug from the MSF for Agile Software Development process template generally moves from Active to Resolved to Closed.

But you can't immediately create a new bug and save it in the Resolved state, even if you already fixed the bug that you found, and you're just creating the bug work item as a record of what you did. You must first save it in an Active state, change the state to Resolved and save it again.

This may seem cumbersome at first, but the reason for this requirement is that the work item type may define rules that must be satisfied as a work item transition from one state to another. Additionally, the meaning of some fields changes during a work item's lifecycle, so each time you save in a new state, the available choices for a field may change. For example, when you create a new bug using the Agile process template, the Reason field helps to indicate how a bug was discovered. When you are transitioning the same bug from Active to Resolved, the Reason state indicates why you are doing so (the bug was fixed, or couldn't be reproduced, or was a duplicate, and so on).

The interface for creating and editing work items with Visual Studio is very straightforward. What can be difficult to master is an understanding of all of the fields found throughout the work item types, their transitions, when to use them, and so on.

For the process templates provided by Microsoft, the documentation is very thorough, and is recommended reading to help you decide how to best adopt these process templates within your team. But wholesale adoption of these templates isn't for every team. You should feel empowered as a team to decide which fields are more or less important than others. You may even decide to add to or simplify the work item types to better meet your needs.

DELETING WORK ITEMS

A common complaint by people who are new to using work items with Team Foundation Server is that work items can't (easily) be deleted. This was a design decision by Microsoft. Organizations do not want bugs, requirements, or other important work items in a project to be accidentally (or maliciously) deleted, so there isn't an option within Visual Studio or the other clients in this chapter for deleting work items.

But deletion of a work item is possible from a command prompt. Open a command prompt, navigate to `\Program Files\Microsoft Visual Studio 11.0\Common7\IDE`, and type `witadmin destroywi /?` for the command-line syntax help. This action is not reversible, so take care when using it.

Microsoft's recommended approach is to transition work items as appropriate instead of deleting them. For example, if you examine the state diagram in Figure 10-3, notice that valid reasons for resolving a Bug work item using the MSF for Agile process template include indicating that the bug can't be reproduced, it's obsolete (maybe it refers to a feature or functionality that has been removed or changed), or it's a duplicate of a bug that already exists. The Visual Studio Scrum process template defines a Removed state for this purpose.

Although it might be tempting to just want to delete these work items instead of resolving them using one of these reasons, the resolution data might prove useful later. For example, a QA lead could discover that a tester isn't doing his or her job effectively when filing erroneous bugs. It's easy to generate a report later on showing, for example, all of the bugs created by a tester that were later discovered to be duplicates of existing bugs. But if those same work items are deleted, they won't show up in such a report.

Work Item Queries

Now that you know how to create work items, the next task you should learn about is how to find them. You can always search for work items by typing the work item ID or some other text into the

Search Work Items textbox at the top of Team Explorer. But this assumes that you know the ID or some text for the work items you are looking for. Chances are you'll want to use queries most of the time.

The process template you are using probably includes some useful built-in queries already. Open Team Explorer ⇨ Work Items to reveal the My Queries and Shared Queries folders. The Shared Queries folder is visible to everybody on the team, whereas My Queries provides a location to save your own personal queries, which may only be useful to you. By keeping specialized queries in My Queries, you can avoid creating too much clutter for your fellow team members. You can also use subfolders in both of these categories to further organize your queries.

> **NOTE** *You should consider using permissions to lock down queries within the Shared Queries node to prevent someone from accidentally overwriting a shared query with their own, which might cause unexpected results for others. An administrator can set security on a query or query folder within Shared Queries by right-clicking it and selecting Security.*

If you have an existing query, you can simply double-click it to run it. Your results will vary based on the type of query you run, and the number of matching work items in your team project, but it should look something like the query results shown in Figure 10-8.

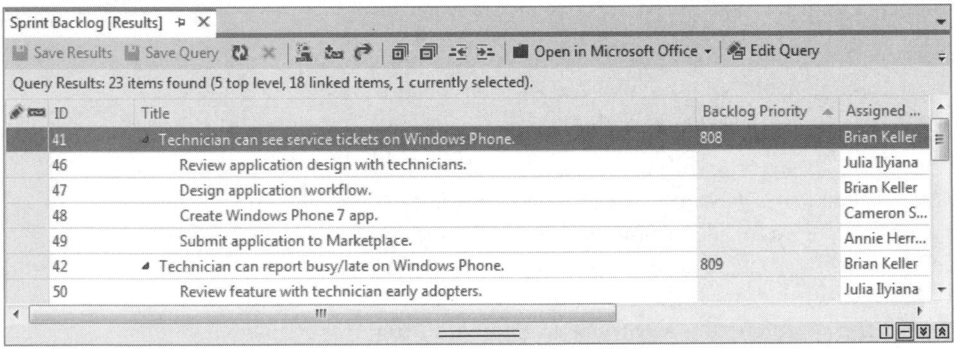
Sprint Backlog [Results]
Save Results
Save Query
Open in Microsoft Office
Edit Query
Query Results: 23 items found (5 top level, 18 linked items, 1 currently selected).
ID
Title
Backlog Priority
Assigned ...
41 Technician can see service tickets on Windows Phone. 808 Brian Keller
46 Review application design with technicians. Julia Ilyiana
47 Design application workflow. Brian Keller
48 Create Windows Phone 7 app. Cameron S...
49 Submit application to Marketplace. Annie Herr...
42 Technician can report busy/late on Windows Phone. 809 Brian Keller
50 Review feature with technician early adopters. Julia Ilyiana

FIGURE 10-8

The query results shown in Figure 10-8 are from a Tree of Work Items query. This figure shows a Sprint Backlog query from a team project that was created using the Visual Studio Scrum process template, but other tree queries look similar. Tree queries return a list of work items matching your query, and groups them according to their parent/child relationships. In this example, there are top-level Product Backlog Item work items that are linked to child Task work items.

Another type of query is Work Items and Direct Links. This type of query is similar to the Tree of Work Items query, except that you are not limited to parent/child links. For example, you can specify that you want to see all user stories and their test cases as represented by a tested by link type. You can even construct a query that shows all of your user stories that *do not* have linked test cases; this is useful for spotting potential holes in your test plan.

Finally, the Flat List query type does not show any link types and is the same type of query found in versions of Team Foundation Server prior to 2010.

From within the query results window, you can open a work item simply by double-clicking it. You also have several options available to you from the toolbar located at the top of the query results window. You can place your mouse over these toolbar icons to learn more about them. The available options vary slightly between query types, but all of them enable you to create new work items (linked to any work items you have highlighted), to open your query results in Microsoft Project or Excel (more on this later), to change which columns are displayed in your query results (and in which order), and to edit the query you are working with.

The query editor shown in Figure 10-9 is the result of having opened the query from Figure 10-8 and clicking Edit Query.

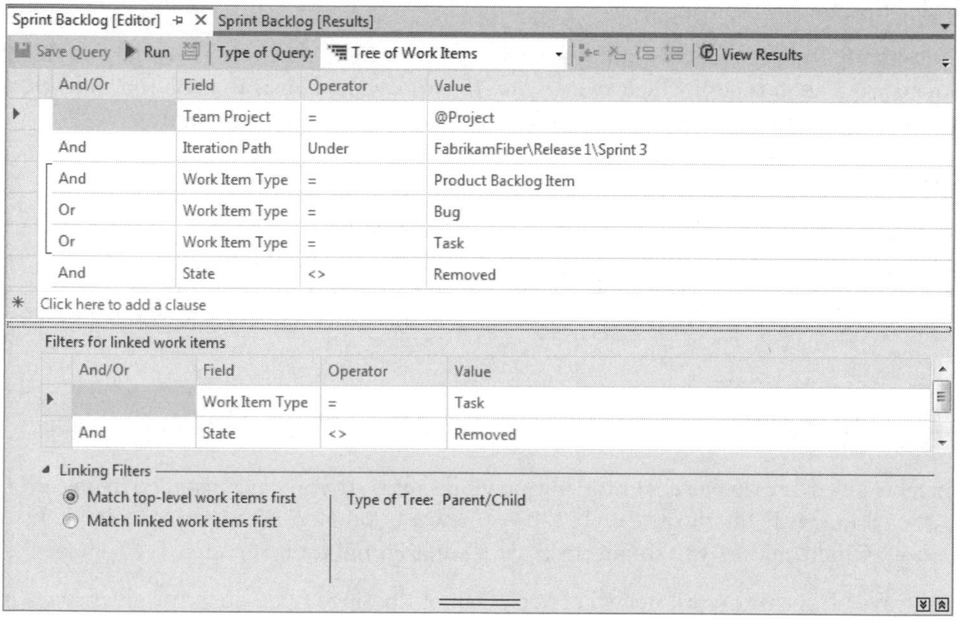

FIGURE 10-9

Even if you've never used queries with Team Foundation Server before, this query should be fairly straightforward to reverse-engineer to learn what it does.

The first row (Team Project = @Project) means that your query results should be scoped to the team project where the project is saved. If you delete this row, your results may return work items from the entire team project collection. @Project is a query variable. Query variables are converted into their respective values when the query is executed. So, for this project, @Project resolves to FabrikamFiber. By using query variables, you can write more flexible queries. The two other query variables available to you are @Me (which is converted into the username of the person running a query) and @Today (which is converted into today's date).

The next row of the query (AND Iteration Path Under FabrikamFiber\Release 1\Sprint 3) defines the specific iteration this query should look for work items in. You could change this clause to look for work items from Sprint 4 by changing the 3 to a 4, or from the entire Release 1 path by simply removing "\Sprint 3" from the end of this clause.

Clauses three, four, and five are grouped (as shown by the vertical bracket on the far-left side of the query). This means that they should be interpreted together in much the same way that math operations within parentheses or brackets are interpreted together. These clauses, when interpreted together, mean *Only return work items with a work item type of Product Backlog Item OR a work item type of Task OR a work item of type Bug.*

The last clause indicates that work items with a State of Removed should not be returned. In the "Deleting Work Items" note earlier you learned that Removed is a state that is available in the Visual Studio Scrum process template to enable you to easily remove work from your backlog without formally deleting the work item.

Finally, because the query type for this query is a Tree of Work Items, there is a second grid (labeled Filters for linked work item types), which enables you to specify any constraints on the child work items that are returned. In this example, only task work items are returned as children.

> **NOTE** *Work item queries can be very powerful, and the options for creating queries are endless. You can find a full guide for understanding how to use queries at* `http://aka.ms/TFSQueries`.

Using Microsoft Excel

Microsoft Excel is another popular client for editing work items. If you have installed Team Explorer on a machine with Microsoft Excel (2007 or newer), you have a Team tab available from the Office ribbon, which enables you to interface with Team Foundation Server.

There are two ways of opening work items in Excel. One option is to open query results from within Team Explorer and then, from the query results toolbar, click Open in Microsoft Office ➪ Open in Microsoft Excel. The other approach is to start in Excel, open the Team tab from the Office ribbon, and then click New List. You are prompted to select your Team Foundation Server and team project, along with the query for the work items you want to manage. Or, instead of a query, you can start with an empty list. This enables you to enter new work items or to select individual work items to add to your list by clicking Get Work Items.

Managing work items in Excel is a fairly rich experience. You can create new work items, make edits to existing work items, and even manage Trees of Work Items. Figure 10-10 shows the results of the same query you saw earlier. Note that parent/child relationships are represented here as well. Parent work items have their titles listed in the Title 1 column, and their children have their titles listed in the Title 2 column. If you add a third level to the tree, grandchild work items are listed in a column named Title 3, and so on.

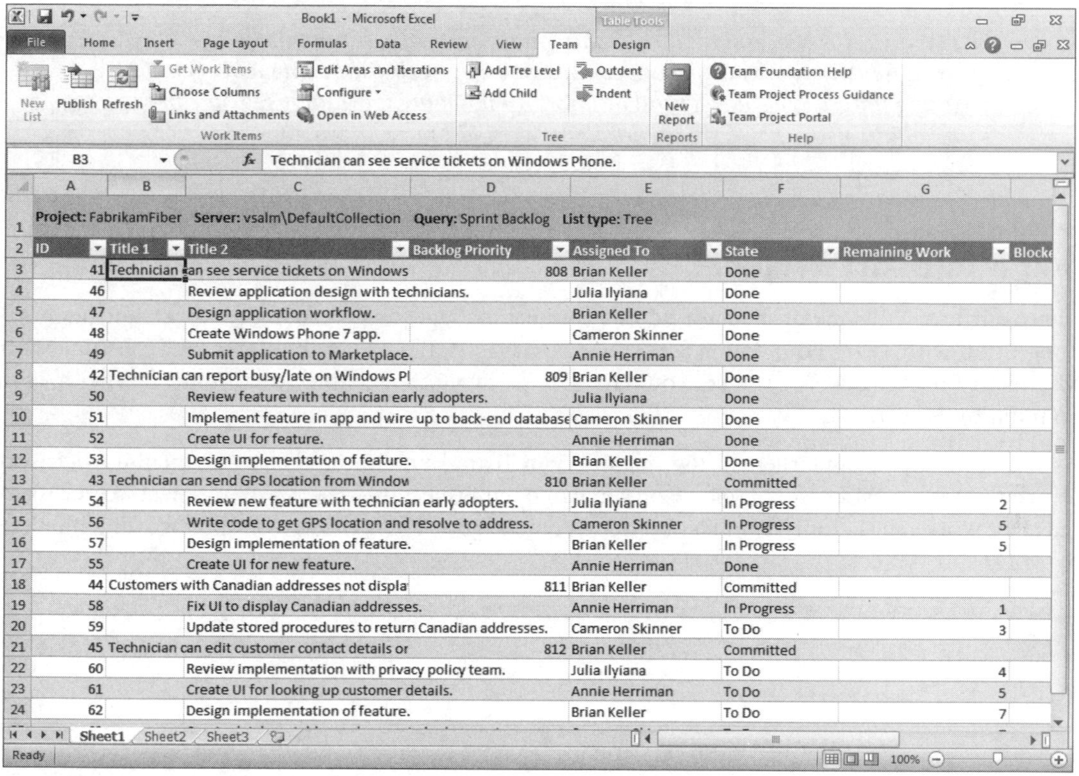

FIGURE 10-10

You can make any changes you want to within your Excel grid. You can add new work items for a Tree of Work Items query by clicking an existing work item and clicking Add Child from the Team tab of the ribbon. For queries of type Flat List or Work Items and Direct Links (which is also compressed to a flat list view in Excel), you can simply place your cursor on a new row at the bottom of your grid, and start typing to begin creating a new work item.

Note, however, that none of your work is persisted to Team Foundation Server until you click Publish from the Team tab of the ribbon. Even if you save the Excel workbook file, your work items aren't synchronized to Team Foundation Server until you publish them.

> **NOTE** *In order to access the Publish button from the Team tab, your cursor needs to be within a cell that is a part of your work item grid. Otherwise, the Publish button is disabled.*

You receive an error message if the values you entered for work items in Excel do not conform to the validation rules or state transition workflow for the work item type. At this point, you can even view the offending work items using the same form view you are familiar with from Visual Studio.

> **NOTE** *Excel is a useful tool for making bulk edits of work items, for quickly copying several work items between team projects, or for people who just prefer working with Excel over Visual Studio for managing work items. You can read more about using Excel as a work item client at* `http://aka.ms/TFSExcel`*.*

Using Microsoft Project

Microsoft Project is one of the most popular project management tools in the world, and supports integration with Team Foundation Server. If you have installed Team Explorer on a machine with Microsoft Project (2007 or newer), you have a Team menu that enables you to interface with Team Foundation Server.

As with Excel, you can either start with a query in Team Explorer (and choose Open in Microsoft Office ⇨ Open in Microsoft Project), or you can open Project and use the Team menu to access a query of work items from Team Foundation Server. Figure 10-11 shows work items being managed by Microsoft Project.

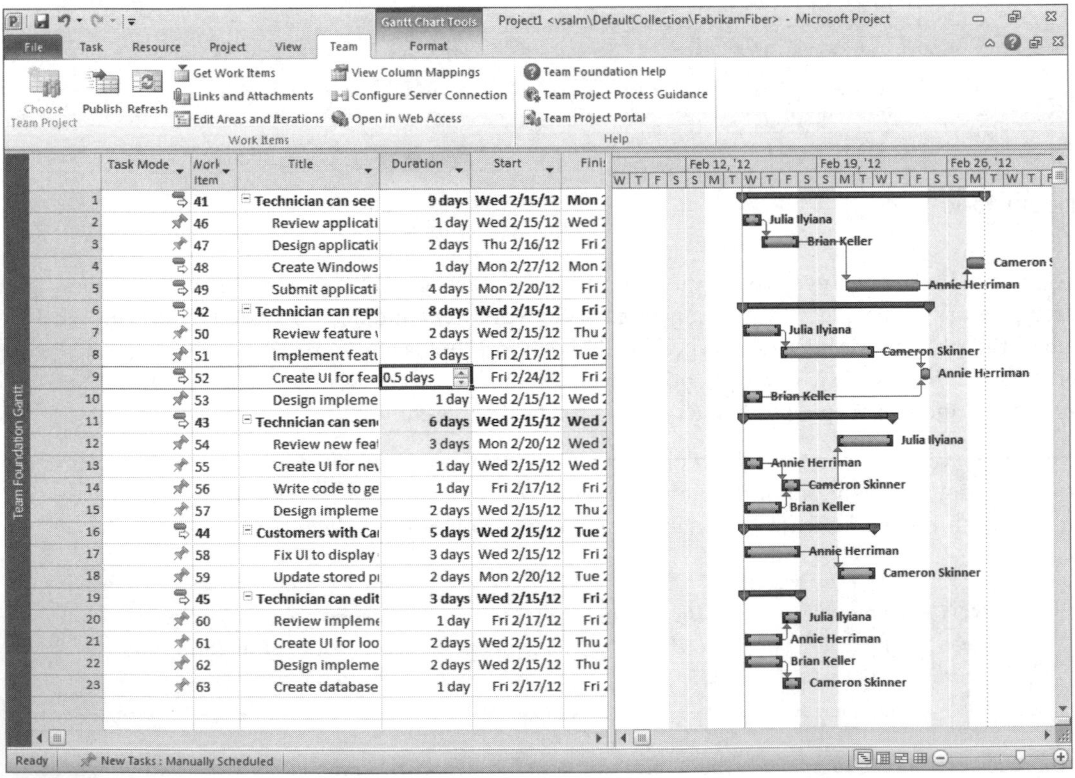

FIGURE 10-11

Project also displays work items according to their parent/child relationships. A major benefit of using Project to view your work items is that it's easy to visualize dependency relationships (successor/predecessor) using the built-in Gantt chart visualization that Project is popular for. In Figure 10-11, it's easy to see that some work items have dependencies on others, which can be helpful for teams deciding how to prioritize their work.

Like Excel, changes to work items that you make within Project are not synchronized to Team Foundation Server until you click Publish from the Team menu.

> **NOTE** *You can learn more about using Project for managing work items at* `http://aka.ms/TFSProject`.

Using Team Web Access

Team Web Access provides yet another way of managing your work items. You learned about how to connect to Team Web Access in Chapter 2. Team Web Access provides a rich, web-based way of accessing Team Foundation Server. An obvious benefit of Team Web Access is that users do not need to have any software other than a web browser. Figure 10-12 shows Team Web Access being used to manage work items.

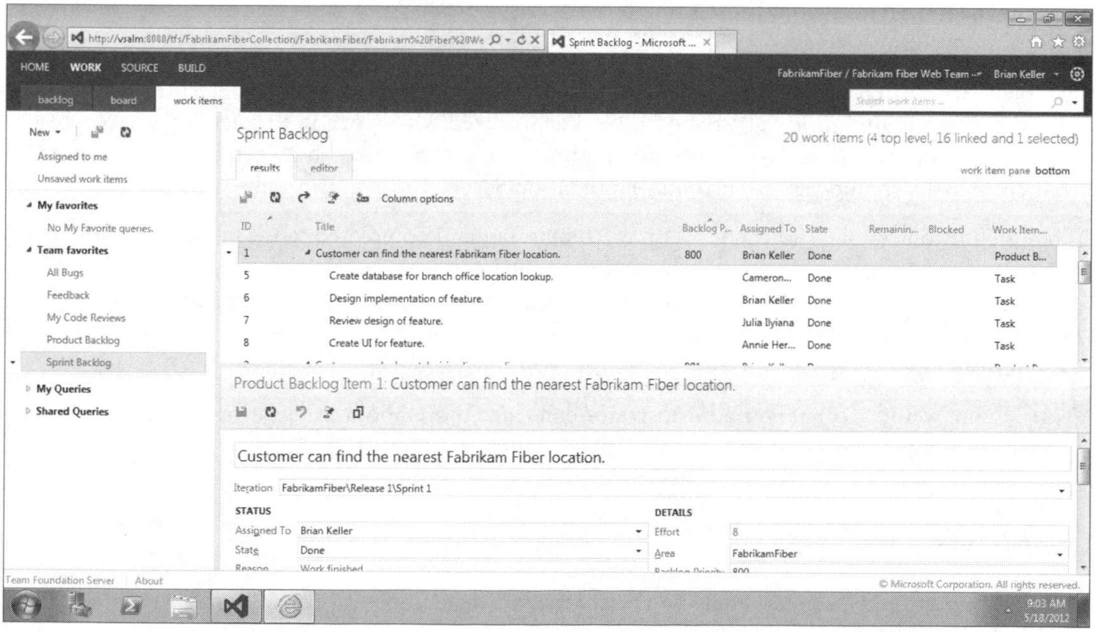

FIGURE 10-12

Team Web Access provides a surprising number of features for a web-based client. Team Web Access makes an ideal work item client for users who don't have Team Explorer installed. Some organizations even encourage end users to file bugs and enhancement requests about their software using Team Web Access. And as you see in the next chapter, Team Web Access provides new Agile Planning Tools to help you manage your plan and track your work.

> **NOTE** *You can read more about using Team Web Access as a work item client at* `http://aka.ms/TFSWebAccess`.

PROJECT SERVER INTEGRATION

Earlier in this chapter, you learned how you can use Microsoft Project to create project plans with your work items in Team Foundation Server. But organizations that utilize Project Server may also be interested in the capability of Team Foundation Server to integrate with their Project Server (2007 or newer) deployments.

This integration allows planning and status information from your development team, using Team Foundation Server, to flow through to your project management office, using Project Server. This enables the software development team to use a single tool — Team Foundation Server — for managing their work, while enabling Project Server users to easily report on and participate in project management activities from those same projects.

In order to enable this integration, you must configure Team Foundation Server to integrate with a Project Server deployment. As part of this configuration process, you can determine which work items in Team Foundation Server should be synchronized with work in Project Server. You can even decide, for example, that parent user stories should be synchronized between the two systems, but that child tasks should remain in Team Foundation Server.

The integration service can then roll up the remaining and completed work being recorded against those tasks and synchronize that information to the User Story work item when it is updated in Project Server. This provides near real-time information to the project management office without overwhelming them with implementation details about your development project that they may not be interested in.

Your Team Foundation Server administrator can learn more about integrating Team Foundation Server and Project Server in *Professional Team Foundation Server 2012*.

SUMMARY

In this chapter, you learned about the project management capabilities of Team Foundation Server 2012, with a focus on work item tracking.

You first learned about some of the new enhancements related to project management that have been introduced in this release and the preceding Team Foundation Server 2010 release. You were introduced to work items, including the key components that make up work item types. You discovered the importance of process templates, which include predefined work item types, and you read overviews of the three process templates included by Microsoft for use with Team Foundation Server 2012. Finally, you were introduced to a variety of ways that you can manage your work items with Team Foundation Server 2012, including from within Visual Studio, Excel, Project, via a web browser, and through integration with Project Server.

In Chapter 11, you learn about the new Agile Planning Tools that you can use to help you plan and track your software development projects.

11

Agile Planning and Tracking

WHAT'S IN THIS CHAPTER?

➤   Defining and managing your product backlog

➤   Planning an iteration while balancing resource capacity

➤   Tracking your work using task boards

➤   Understanding options for customizing the agile planning and tracking tools

The Agile Manifesto defines several guiding principles that have implications on the ways in which teams manage projects. Instead of attempting to define an entire project schedule up front, as with a waterfall methodology, an agile team allows the plan to evolve over time. Work is broken down into multiple successive *iterations*, each of which might last between one and four weeks.

Teams practicing an agile development methodology tend to embark upon a journey of mutual discovery with their customers to determine new work dynamically, based on changing business priorities or on feedback from work done in previous iterations. The customer, or at least a proxy for the customer, is considered a virtual member of the team and participates in defining and prioritizing (and often re-prioritizing) work over time.

The pursuit to embrace agile development, with dynamic schedules and evolving requirements, has meant that many of the tools and techniques used for traditional project management are no longer sufficient. Agile practitioners have needed to look for different ways of capturing work, balancing resource capacity, tracking status, and so on.

Scrum, which is by far the most popular agile development methodology in use today, defines such tools, terminology, and methodology. Future work is captured and prioritized on a *product backlog*, which can then be committed into specific iterations, called *sprints*. Each sprint has its own *sprint backlog* in which work is further decomposed into smaller units of work. This work is tracked to completion on a *task board*, which usually takes the form of sticky notes on a whiteboard.

Team Foundation Server 2012 has embraced these concepts by providing a set of web-based tooling for managing your product backlog, decomposing your work into iterations, and tracking your work using a digital task board. Anyone familiar with or practicing Scrum should feel immediately at home with this set of tooling, although it cannot be understated that this same set of tooling can be adopted by any team who wants to use it, even if they aren't practicing Scrum per-se. One of the design principles of Team Foundation Server has always been that teams can use any process they want to, and Team Foundation Server provides the right level of flexibility and customization to support such a process.

In this chapter you find out about the new web-based tooling available within Team Foundation Server 2012 to support agile project management and tracking. This book is not a true primer on how to run a project using a Scrum (or any other) development methodology, but there are several great books to choose from which cover this topic.

DEFINING A TEAM

Team Foundation Server 2012 has introduced the notion of a *team*, which you can use to organize people who are working together. This should not be confused with the concept of a *team project* within Team Foundation Server, which is a large container of work, consisting of source control and work items that all share a common process template. A team project can contain multiple teams, and each team can have its own product backlog, iterations, and task board. A single person might also participate in more than one team. For instance, a graphic designer might be a shared resource responsible for contributing artwork to different teams.

To create a team, follow these steps:

1. Open a browser and visit the Team Web Access home page for your team project. You can access this by clicking the Web Access link in Team Explorer. The address takes the format of `http://<server>:<port>/tfs/<collection-name>/<team-project-name>`.

2. Now open the administrative context by clicking the gear icon in the upper-right corner. If you do not have administrative privileges for your team project, you need to contact your team project administrator to perform these steps. On this screen you should see a list of any teams that are already configured for your team project.

3. Click New Team to display the Create New Team dialog as shown in Figure 11-1. You can provide a name and description for your team, and specify what default permissions new team members should inherit. From the Settings tab you can also declare any users who should be team administrators, and you can opt to create a new area for this team.

   You were introduced to the concept of areas in Chapter 10. Areas provide a way for you to categorize your work within a team project. You can choose to create areas for each of your teams, so that (for example) bugs that are filed against the `\Fabrikam Fiber Web Site` area path are automatically routed to the Fabrikam Fiber Web Team.

4. Click Create Team when you are finished to create your team and return to the list of teams on your team project. Click your team in this list to display the team administrative dialog shown in Figure 11-2. From here you can easily add new team members or team administrators. You can also change the name of your team, the description, or even choose an image to represent your team.

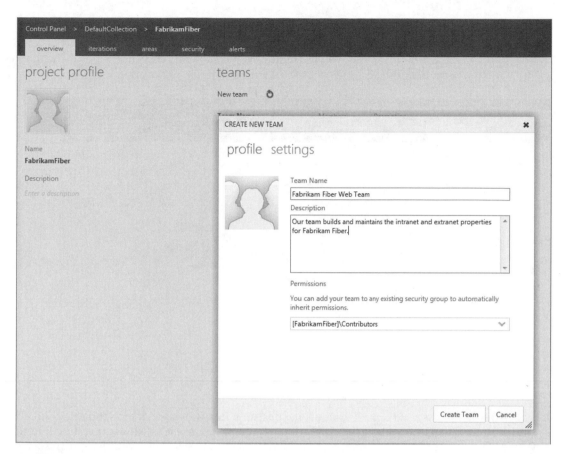

FIGURE 11-1

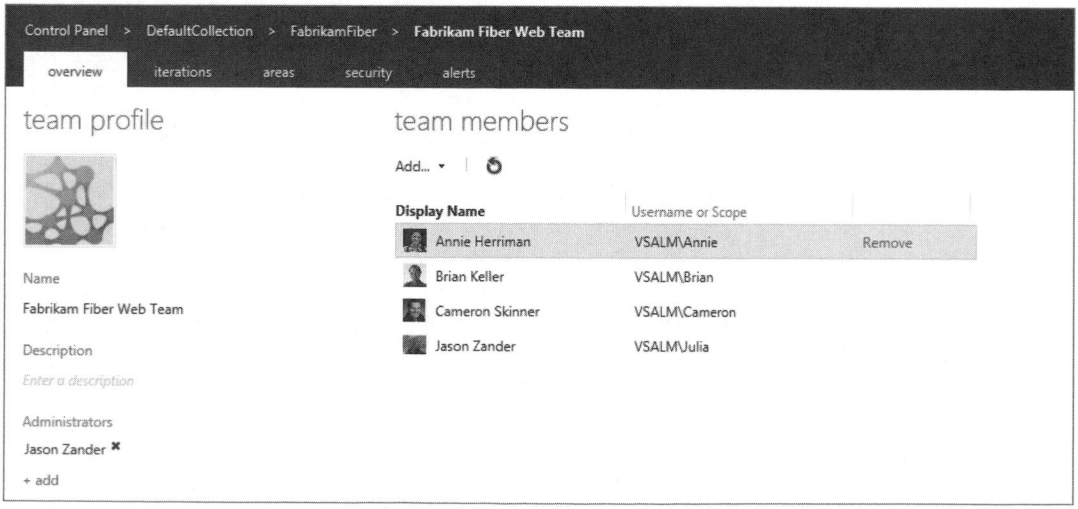

FIGURE 11-2

5. Click the Iterations tab to select the iterations your team is participating in, as shown in Figure 11-3. In Chapter 10 you learned how to manage iterations and assign start and end dates to them. On this screen, you are indicating which iterations your team is using to structure its work. You should ensure that the iteration dates do not overlap.

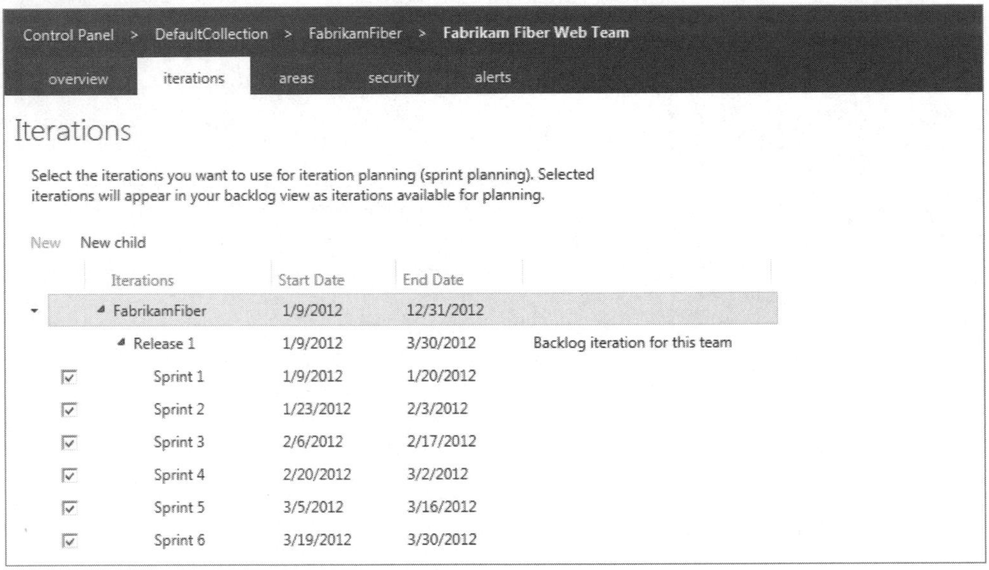

Control Panel > DefaultCollection > FabrikamFiber > **Fabrikam Fiber Web Team**

overview   iterations   areas   security   alerts

Iterations

Select the iterations you want to use for iteration planning (sprint planning). Selected iterations will appear in your backlog view as iterations available for planning.

New   New child

	Iterations	Start Date	End Date	
	⁴ FabrikamFiber	1/9/2012	12/31/2012	
	⁴ Release 1	1/9/2012	3/30/2012	Backlog iteration for this team
☑	Sprint 1	1/9/2012	1/20/2012	
☑	Sprint 2	1/23/2012	2/3/2012	
☑	Sprint 3	2/6/2012	2/17/2012	
☑	Sprint 4	2/20/2012	3/2/2012	
☑	Sprint 5	3/5/2012	3/16/2012	
☑	Sprint 6	3/19/2012	3/30/2012	

FIGURE 11-3

Your iterations need to be hierarchical, consisting of at least one parent and one child. This is required so that your backlog iteration (representing unscheduled work) can exist at the root or parent node, and specific iterations (representing scheduled work) are represented by child nodes. In Figure 11-3, `Release 1` is the parent node representing the backlog iteration. You can select a new backlog iteration by highlighting that iteration, clicking the small dropdown arrow to the left of the iteration name, and then selecting Set as Team's Backlog Iteration. But you need to first ensure that your desired backlog iteration has at least one child iteration.

> **NOTE** *It may be necessary to create different iteration structures for each team within your team project. For example, if your Web Team is using the term "Sprint 3" to define an iteration that begins on March 1, but your Database Team thinks of Sprint 3 as beginning on April 15, then each team should have its own iteration structure. You can use any naming convention you want for this, such as WebTeam\Sprint3 and DataTeam\Sprint3. This way each node can have its own start and end date independently.*

Similarly, click Areas to configure which area paths your team is using to manage its work as shown in Figure 11-4. You can select multiple areas, or the root area path, although if you have many people using your team project you might want to use areas to more carefully segregate work.

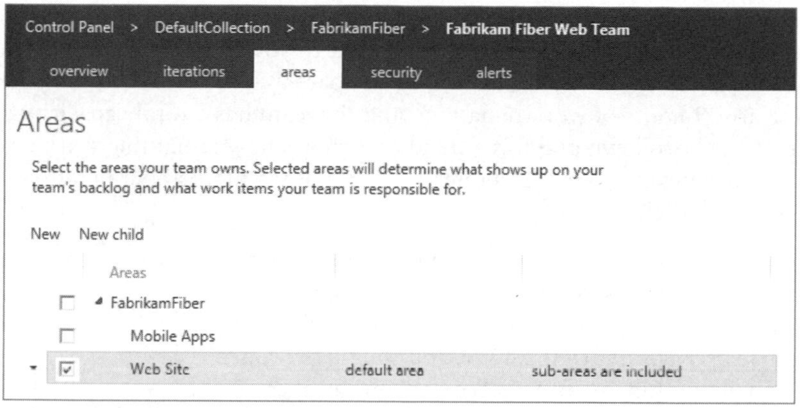

FIGURE 11-4

You can use the Security tab to configure permissions for your team. Finally, you can use the Alerts tab to configure e-mail notifications for your team. For example, you might want to automatically send an e-mail to any team member if a work item that is assigned to that person changes. Or you can e-mail the entire team if a daily build fails.

6. Close the administrative context when you are finished, and return to Team Web Access. You can now access the team home page for any team you are a member of by clicking the dropdown list in the upper-right of the Team Web Access view and selecting the appropriate team. For example, Figure 11-5 shows the home page for the Fabrikam Fiber Web Team.

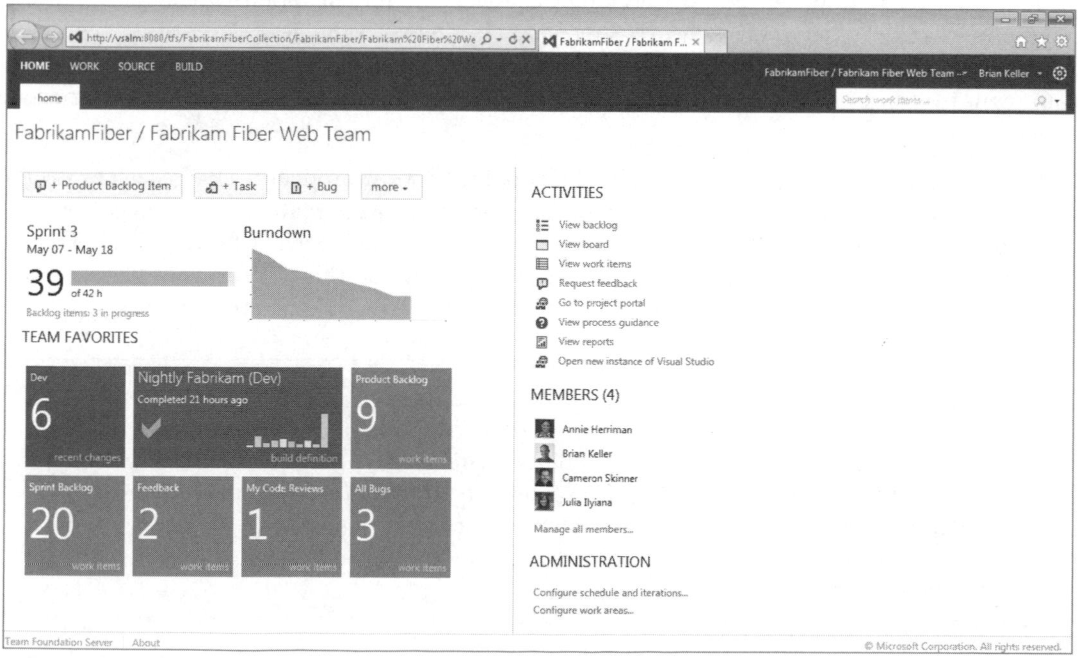

FIGURE 11-5

If you just created a brand-new team then your home page won't yet look as rich as the one shown in Figure 11-5. The top half of this view shows information relevant to your current iteration. The status bar on the left shows the amount of work remaining as compared with the capacity of your team (in this example, there are 39 hours of work remaining and the team has a total capacity of achieving 42 hours of work). The burndown graph is a trend that shows how remaining work has decreased (or increased) over time during your current iteration. You learn more about iteration capacity and burndowns later in this chapter.

The bottom half of this view shows any Team Favorites you have configured. These can represent queries—such as open bugs, or in-progress tasks. They can also display graphs of recent builds, or even recent changesets that have been checked into a particular branch. To add Team Favorites to this view, you should first open a relevant query, branch, or build within Team Web Access. You can then click the small dropdown arrow located to the left of the object and select Add to Team Favorites, as shown in Figure 11-6. This adds a new tile to your team's home page, which can make it easy for the entire team to see the metrics you believe are most important to track.

Next, you see how to define and manage your team's product backlog.

MAINTAINING PRODUCT BACKLOGS

FIGURE 11-6

A *product backlog* is essentially just a list of work that your team has identified but hasn't yet scheduled for implementation. The product backlog is a useful tool for collaborating with customers or other project stakeholders. As new work is requested by your stakeholders, you can track it in a central location on the product backlog. You can also estimate and prioritize this work can, usually with input from your customer or stakeholders, to help determine which items are most important to deliver first.

From your team's home page, click View Backlog to display your product backlog, such as the one shown in Figure 11-7. The "quick add" panel at the top of this page enables you to quickly enter new work as it is identified. You can select the type of work to add (such as Product Backlog Item or Bug), provide a title, and press Enter (or click Add) to quickly add this work to your backlog. When you do this, you automatically create a new work item within Team Foundation Server.

> **NOTE** *The screenshots in this chapter reflect a team project that was created with the Visual Studio Scrum 2.0 process template included with Team Foundation Server 2012. The terminology varies slightly if you are using either the MSF for Agile or MSF for CMMI process templates, but you can still take advantage of the same tooling. You can even customize this tooling for use with your own custom or third-party process templates. Customization options are discussed later in this chapter.*

If you highlight a row within your backlog, any new work you add from the "quick add" panel is inserted above this highlighted row. The exception to this rule is if you have highlighted the last row in your backlog; new work is added at the end of your backlog.

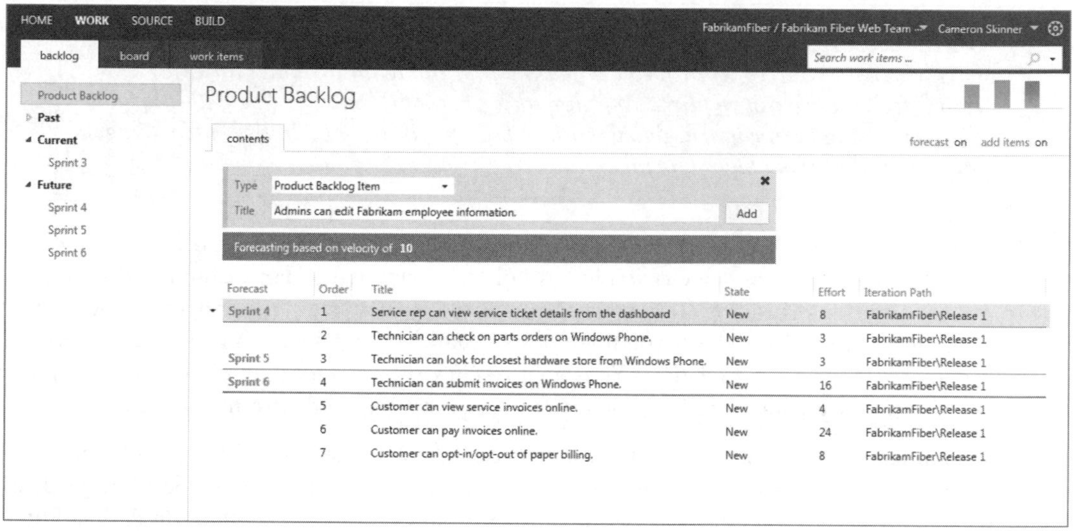

FIGURE 11-7

You can easily reprioritize work by simply dragging and dropping it on the backlog. Changes you make here are saved to Team Foundation Server in the background. You can also double-click an item in this view to open the work item editor to provide additional detail or make changes.

> **NOTE** *If you have used previous versions of Team Foundation Server then you are used to changing priority by hand-editing a field within each work item. But notice that the Priority field is no longer visible within Team Web Access or Visual Studio when viewing work items. Backlog Priority is now a hidden field by default. The recommended way of setting this value is to use the Team Web Access view to drag items up and down the backlog. Behind the scenes, Team Web Access uses large integers to assign Backlog Priority values. The use of large integer values here makes it possible to insert a work item between two items on a backlog without needing to make updates to each of the surrounding items.*

Teams practicing Scrum will be familiar with a concept known as *velocity*. Velocity is a metric used to calculate the amount of work that a team is able to deliver for a given iteration. It is usually measured in *story points* on Scrum teams. Other teams may prefer to do their estimations in hours, or days, or ideal days, and so on. Regardless of the estimation technique used by your team, you can use the product backlog view to get a sense for when you will be able to deliver items on your backlog. The only requirement is that you should be consistent with your estimation techniques. For example, when some people on the team are estimating in days and other people are estimating in story points, it's difficult to create consistent plans.

Toggle *forecast lines* on or off by clicking on the "on/off" link in the upper-right of this page labeled "forecast." Forecast lines display, as shown in Figure 11-7, to indicate when work is estimated to be delivered based on your current team's velocity. This approach requires that you have estimated your backlog items by providing a value for effort. Do this by double-clicking each item in your backlog to provide this additional level of detail.

> **NOTE** *Most teams practicing Scrum also transition the state of an item on the backlog from New to Approved at the time that the team provides an Effort estimate. You are not required to follow this protocol, but it can be helpful for differentiating between truly new work (which might only be in the "idea" stage) and work that your team has taken time to estimate.*

The Forecasting Based on Velocity Of textbox enables you to experiment with different values to see the effect that given values for velocity might have on delivering work. For example, you might be able to ask for additional funding from your customer to hire new team members and speed up the rate at which items are delivered. Or you might know that there are several upcoming holidays that will affect your team's ability to deliver. You can also click the velocity graph in the upper-right corner of this screen to see your historical velocity for the preceding (and current) iterations.

The forecast lines are purely estimates. In order to actually schedule work for a given iteration, you can drag and drop it onto either the current or future iterations listed on the left-hand side of this view. When you drag and drop work onto an iteration the value in the Iteration Path column is updated to reflect the assigned iteration, and the Iteration field is updated within the work item in Team Foundation Server.

> **NOTE** *Even though you have assigned work to a particular iteration, it continues to show up in your product backlog until you have transitioned the work item to a state that represents it is in progress. For the Scrum process template, work is considered to be in progress when it reaches the Committed state. By convention, most teams typically wait until they have broken work down into child tasks before they transition it to a Committed state. In the following section you find out how to break work down.*

PLANNING ITERATIONS

After you have identified the work that you want to deliver for a given iteration, you can click an iteration from the list on the left-hand side of the product backlog view to open the iteration planning view shown in Figure 11-8. This figure shows an iteration that is mid-sprint, meaning that the team has already completed some work and is preparing to finish this iteration.

When you first add items to an iteration (such as a product backlog item, or a bug) you are only declaring your intention to deliver this functionality. The next phase of planning this work is to actually break it down into the individual tasks that people on your team need to complete in order to perform the work. Click the plus (+) sign next to an item in your iteration contents to display the dialog shown in Figure 11-9, which enables you to add a new task work item as a child to the parent you clicked on.

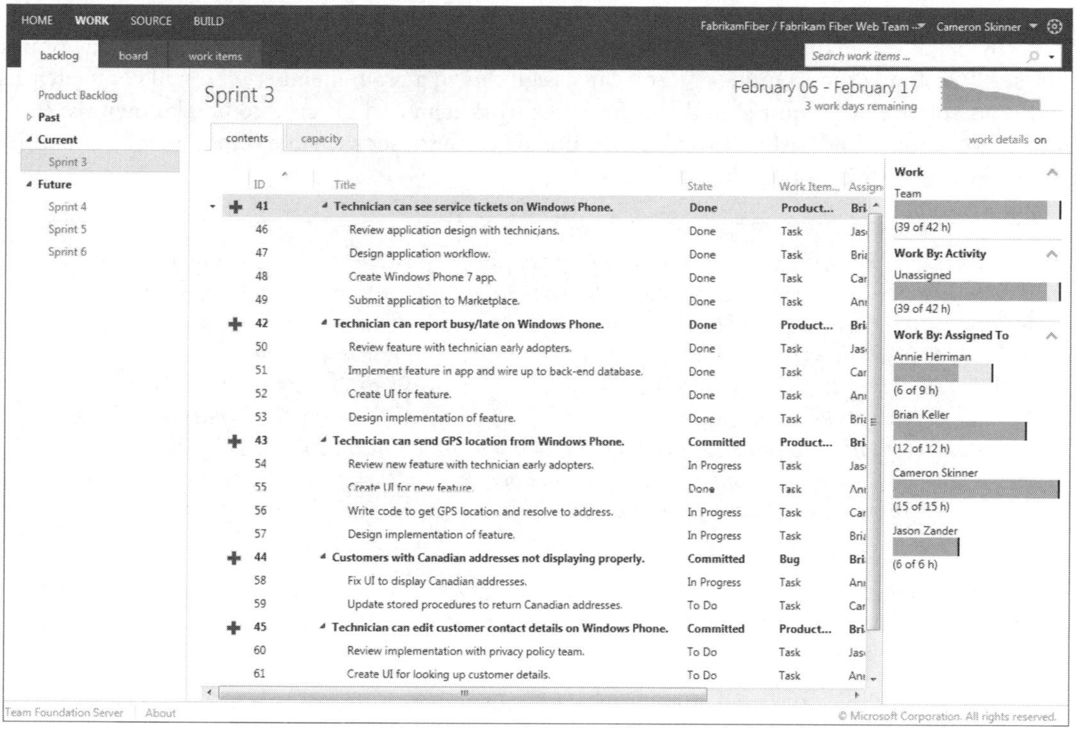

FIGURE 11-8

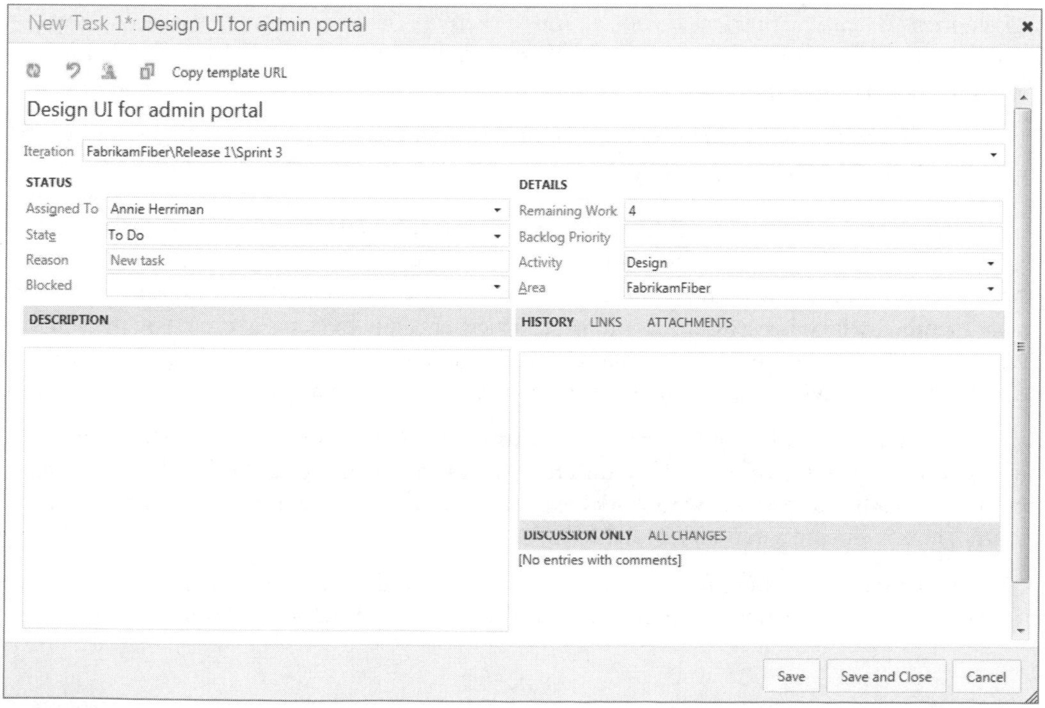

FIGURE 11-9

You should provide a title for this task and, if possible, an estimate for the amount of remaining work. By default, remaining work is assumed to be provided in hours, but you can also customize this (see "Customization Options"). You can assign this to a team member who will complete this work, but you are not required to do so. Save this work item and proceed to break down the rest of your work into child tasks. If you haven't already done so, set the state of parent work items to Committed as each item is broken down.

> **NOTE** *A common question that many people have is about the relationship between effort, provided earlier when defining an item for the backlog, and remaining work, provided for tasks. Effort is typically a rough estimate used to provide a quick indication about the size of work in relation to other items on the backlog. Remaining work values in your iteration should be much more precise, and represent the additional level of planning and estimation analysis that has been given to considering how a given feature or user story will be implemented. As a team gains experience they become better at providing more realistic estimates while the product backlog is being defined.*

As you begin to create tasks with values for remaining work, you will notice that the capacity graphs on the right-hand side of this screen begin to render. These graphs are broken into three areas:

➤ *Work* — shows the total amount of work remaining for this iteration, calculated as the sum of the remaining work across all task work items.

➤ *Work By:Activity* — enables you to categorize the amount of remaining work into categories. When creating tasks, you can use the activity field to categorize tasks, such as Documentation, or Design, and so on. If you don't provide a value for activity, work simply shows up as Unassigned.

➤ *Work By:Assigned To* — shows the amount of remaining work that is assigned to each person on your team.

Click the Capacity tab to assign the capacity for each of the members of your team as shown in Figure 11-10. The Capacity Per Day column enables you to specify the average number of hours per day that a given resource is working on tasks. The Activity column enables you to specify the discipline of a team member, which is necessary if you want to view capacity by activity type. Finally, you can use Days Off to define days that a team member is sick or on holiday, and you can use Team Days Off to define days that the whole team will be unavailable, such as during a holiday or company retreat.

The values you enter for this table are specific to this team and this iteration. So a shared resource who works on multiple teams might have different values for Capacity Per Day or Days Off depending on the team. Also, a resource who works five hours per day on one iteration might only work two hours per day during a subsequent iteration.

After you assign capacity values for your team, the capacity indicators on the right change to either green, if a resource is at or under capacity, or red, if there is too much work given the planned capacity. The iteration plan is designed to be viewed on a regular basis so that you can make adjustments to the plan as needed. For example, if a team member is sick, you might need to reschedule work that was originally planned for this iteration. You can drag and drop parent items from this list onto other iterations on the left-hand side of the page.

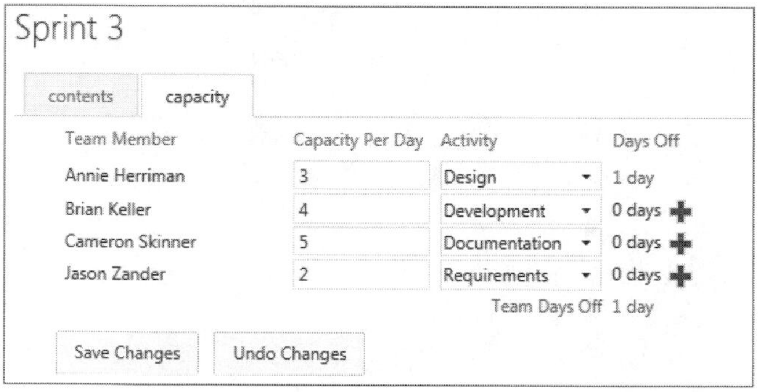

Sprint 3

| contents | capacity |

Team Member	Capacity Per Day	Activity		Days Off
Annie Herriman	3	Design	▾	1 day
Brian Keller	4	Development	▾	0 days
Cameron Skinner	5	Documentation	▾	0 days
Jason Zander	2	Requirements	▾	0 days
		Team Days Off		1 day

| Save Changes | Undo Changes |

FIGURE 11-10

TRACKING WORK

When you are satisfied with the iteration plan, it's time to start writing code, authoring documentation, designing user interfaces, and doing all the other work that's required to develop great software. During the course of this activity, it can be helpful to have a single location to easily determine the status of the work that everybody is doing.

Scrum teams typically use a *task board* for this purpose. In its simplest form, a task board takes the form of a whiteboard with sticky notes on it that you move from the left side of the board (work that is not yet started) to the middle (work that is in progress) to the right (completed work). This technique works very well for teams that are co-located, especially if they share a team room, because anybody can quickly look up at the white board to determine the state of the team's work. Of course, this approach has its challenges for teams who work in different locations or have individual offices.

Team Foundation Server 2012 provides a digital task board that overcomes the limitations imposed by traditional physical task boards. Click Board at the top of Team Web Access to access the task board shown in Figure 11-11.

Each row on this task board represents a parent backlog item from your current iteration. The tiles on this task board represent the individual child tasks that you created. Each task begins in the To Do column. When a team member is ready to begin a task, he can drag and drop it onto the In Progress column. As he makes progress against a given task, he can click the number on the task to update the remaining work. Or if he has finished as task, he drags it into the Done column to automatically set the amount of remaining work to 0. Clicking the name of the team member for a given task opens a dropdown menu that enables you to quickly reassign work.

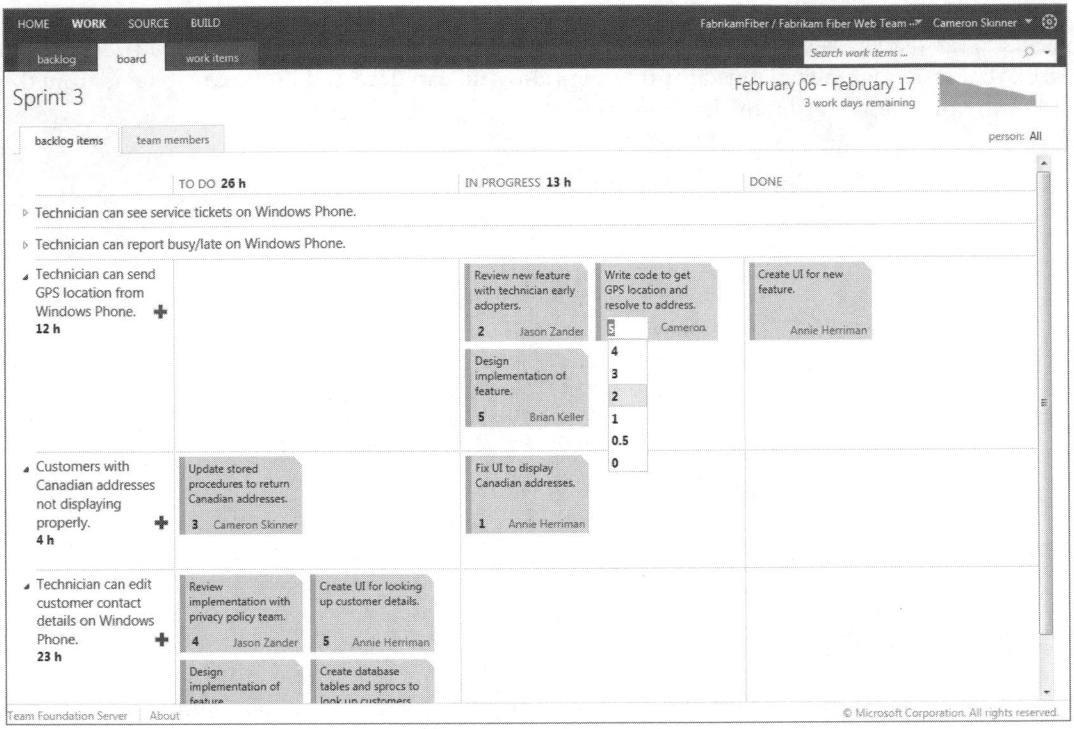

FIGURE 11-11

Double-click a task to open it in a full editor, such as the one in Figure 11-9. This is often helpful if you realize that a task is going to take more time than originally estimated, and you need to increase the amount of remaining work.

> **NOTE** *The task board understands the rules and limitations of the underlying process template your team project is based upon. For example, consider a scenario where you have prematurely moved a task from In Progress to Done — perhaps by mistake, or perhaps you realized there is additional work that needs to be finished. If you try to move work from the Done column back to the In Progress column, you receive an error message indicating that work that is In Progress cannot have a value of 0 for remaining work. To fix this, double-click the task to open the full editor and assign a new value for remaining work.*

The entire interface is touch-friendly. If you have a touch screen monitor, such as in a shared team room, you can configure it to display your task board and make it easy for team members to update the status of their work whenever they walk by it. And because everything is stored in Team Foundation Server, remote workers can access the same view in any modern web browser to see what their colleagues are working on and provide their own statuses.

If you find yourself constrained for space in this view, you can collapse finished backlog items by clicking the arrow to the left of the parent work item title. You can also use your browser's zoom functionality (usually Ctrl + - and Ctrl + +) to fit more work on a single screen.

You can generate a personalized view of this screen by clicking the Person: All link and selecting the name of any team member. This highlights the work that is assigned to that team member, making it easier to differentiate from the rest of the team's work.

You can also click the Team Members tab to display a view in which tasks are organized by the team member they are assigned to, instead of by their parent work item. This is a helpful view for team meetings, where team members might be expected to tell their peers what they worked on yesterday and what they are planning on working on today. This view is also helpful for seeing whether there are any team members with too much work remaining, and whether other team members might have capacity for picking up some of that work.

As work is finished, the team can transition parent backlog items to a state of Done. Open a parent backlog item by clicking the title of the item on the left-hand side of the screen. This state transition is not done automatically when all of the tasks are finished because there may be additional checkpoints or quality gates in place before work is considered to be truly finished. For example, you might want to request feedback from your project's stakeholders to ensure that everybody is satisfied with the work as it has been implemented.

The burndown graph in the upper-right corner of this screen displays a trend of the remaining work over time for your iteration. This graph is updated in real time as your team completes work (or identifies new work) during the course of an iteration. You can display the burndown graph in full screen by clicking it, as shown in Figure 11-12.

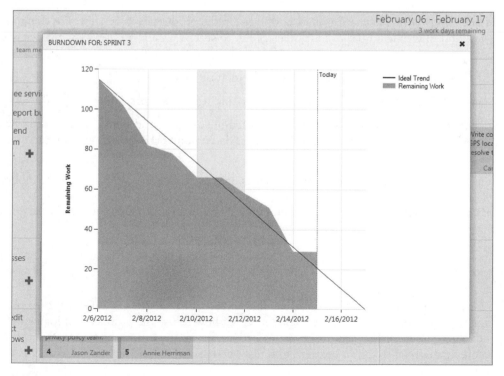

FIGURE 11-12

CUSTOMIZATION OPTIONS

As mentioned previously, the examples in this chapter follow the default experience you get by using the Visual Studio Scrum 2.0 process template for a team project. If you are practicing Scrum today, then you are likely already familiar with the types of tools available in this chapter. But even if you aren't practicing Scrum or using the Scrum process template, you can still benefit from these tools.

Depending on the process template you choose, the default terminology and views might vary. For example, a team using the MSF for CMMI process template tracks Requirements instead of Product Backlog Items as the parent work item type to be planned. An MSF for CMMI task board contains four columns (Proposed, Active, Resolved, and Closed) instead of the three shown earlier for a Scrum project (To Do, In Progress, and Done).

If you are using a team project that was created using one of the process templates provided by Microsoft with Team Foundation Server 2012 (Scrum 2.0, MSF for Agile 6.0, or MSF for CMMI Process Improvement 6.0) then this tooling is preconfigured automatically to work with your team projects. If you are upgrading an existing team project from an earlier release of Team Foundation Server then you need to perform some additional steps in order to begin using the agile planning and tracking tools mentioned in this chapter. These steps are outlined at `http://aka.ms/TeamProjectUpgrade`.

There are also several ways you can customize these tools to change their appearance and behavior. For example:

➤   Add or remove fields from the "quick add" pane in the product backlog view. For example, in addition to setting a title, you might also want to specify an effort estimate with each new item.

➤   Add or remove columns from the backlog and iteration views.

➤   Change the list of activities that task work items and team members can be assigned to.

➤   Change the working days to be used when calculating capacity and rendering the burndown graph. By default, Saturday and Sunday are considered nonworking days, but you can modify the days.

➤   Configure the types of work items to be used as parents and children throughout the tooling.

All of these customizations and more can be configured by following the steps outlined in the documentation at `http://aka.ms/CustomizingProcess`.

SUMMARY

In this chapter, you discovered the new tools available with Team Foundation Server 2012 for planning and tracking work in an agile manner. You found out how to use the product backlog view for defining and managing items that your team may schedule and implement in the future. You then saw how to break down work for an iteration into tasks and examined the remaining work for these tasks against the capacity of your team.

Finally, you learned about using the task board to track work during the course of an iteration so that everybody on the team can easily understand what their colleagues are working on and how much work is left to deliver in an iteration.

In Chapter 12 you find out how you can use the rich sets of reports and SharePoint dashboards to provide even more information that can be used to better manage your software development projects.

12

Using Reports, Portals, and Dashboards

WHAT'S IN THIS CHAPTER?

➤   Understanding Team Foundation Server data stores

➤   Understanding the reporting tools available

➤   Creating and customizing reports using Excel

➤   Creating Report Definition Language (RDL) reports with Report Designer and Business Intelligence Development Studio (BIDS)

Capturing information throughout the project is critical not only to project managers but to all team members. Equally important is the capability to analyze the information that was captured and understand it. With Visual Studio Team Foundation Server 2012, the mundane tasks associated with capturing is mostly automated, and gives crucial time back to the team to focus on building software rather than capturing information associated with building it.

The agile planning tooling discussed in Chapter 11 shows ways in which you can use the real-time data from work items to help track work and plan sprints, but Team Foundation Server also provides powerful features used to analyze the data and understand it. All types of data are captured about the software development process, not just work progress but data about version control, build, test and feedback. Tracking a project and monitoring it throughout its lifecycle is made easy with Team Foundation Server Reporting and the dashboards.

This chapter examines the reporting capabilities of Team Foundation Server, working with reports, customizing reports, and the reviewing of reports shipped out-of-the box. Dashboards serve the purpose of providing useful information in an easy-to-consume form to all stake-holders, even to those outside the core software development team. This chapter also shows how to customize the team project portal as a way to keep everyone up to date with the status of the project and the team.

Let's start with the reporting capabilities of Visual Studio Team Foundation Server 2012.

TEAM FOUNDATION SERVER REPORTING

Reporting is one of the most powerful features of Team Foundation Server. Right from the first release of Team Foundation Server (that is, Team Foundation Server 2005), the central repository and the reports have been cornerstones for software development teams and the management team alike. You can view any data stored in the Team Foundation Server repository as a report, which enables you to view and organize project metrics very easily. This includes work item tracking, build reports, version control stats, test results, quality indicators (performance and code coverage), and overall project health reports. Team Foundation Server ships with a set of reports out-of-the-box (more on that later), but you can also create custom reports.

The reporting tools are not only useful for project managers, but also for team members in every role. For example, a developer can look at test results and hone in on specific bugs. Testers can look at a report to identify the work complete for testing, and so on.

Before looking into the details of reports, how to create custom reports, or the tools available to create reports, let's first look at how Team Foundation Server stores data. As you see in Figure 12-1, there are essentially three different data stores that Team Foundation Server uses:

➤ Team Foundation Server operational store

➤ Team Foundation Server data warehouse

➤ Team Foundation Server OLAP cube

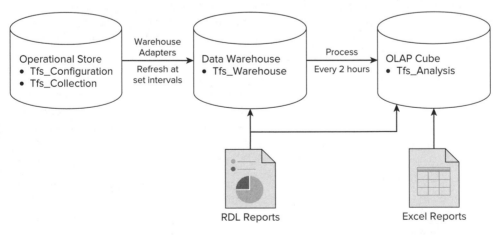

FIGURE 12-1

Team Foundation Server Operational Store

The Team Foundation Server operational store is the set of databases that store all the data to run the Team Foundation Server application, including source control, build reports, test results, work item tracking, and so on. These are the relational databases that handle all live data. Hence, they are optimized for speed and performance. Multiple databases serve as the operational store, including the `Tfs_Configuration` database and the various databases for each team project collection. Typically, you don't have to deal with (or understand) the structure of this set of databases. You should never modify the data in this store directly as you can very easily corrupt your TFS installation in doing so. You will not go against this store to do reporting, due to the performance impact that you could very easily have on the running Team Foundation Server application. In addition, the schema of the operation store frequently changes in-between releases of Team Foundation Server (even in-between service pack releases) making any reports against the operation store fragile.

Team Foundation Server Data Warehouse

Team Foundation Server data warehouse is specifically designed for querying and reporting, unlike the operational store that is designed for transactions. The schema of the warehouse is much easier to understand, it has a star schema and includes all historical data in a manner designed to be used for analysis. Despite the fact that the schema of the operational store changes significantly between releases (and so changes greatly between the 2010 and 2012 release), the relational schema in the warehouse remains pretty much unchanged since the Team Foundation Server 2010 release. This is by design as it allows reports to be written against the data warehouse to have much greater resilience when the server is upgraded. The only schema changes in the 2012 release to the relation warehouse are the addition of start and end dates to iterations and the removal of some fields in 2010 that were used for configuration only.

Team Foundation Server data warehouse gets the data from the operational stores on regularly set intervals. There are adapters for each of the databases in the operational store that take care of pushing the data into the warehouse. In Team Foundation Server 2012 the update from the operational store to the warehouse is based on various events. When an event fires up, the corresponding adapter is scheduled to execute and refresh the data in the warehouse. The interval for this execution is configurable.

In Team Foundation Server 2012, you use the warehouse control service to change the refresh interval. Go to `http://<TFS Server Name:port>>/tfs/TeamFoundation/Administration/v3.0/WarehouseControlService.asmx`. You must have the permission to update the warehouse setting to access this service. The `WarehouseControlWebService` has the following operations available:

➤ `BringAnalysisProcessingOnline`

➤ `BringWarehouseProcessingOnline`

➤ `ChangeSetting`

➤ `GetJobProperties`

➤ `GetProcessingStatus`

➤ `GetSettings`

➤ ProcessAnalysisDatabase

➤ ProcessWarehouse

➤ SetAnalysisJobEnabledState

➤ SetWarehouseJobEnabledState

➤ TakeAnalysisProcessingOffline

➤ TakeWarehouseProcessingOffline

In the ControllerService page, if you choose the operation GetSettings, it will show you the various processing jobs, its default value, and its current value. As you can see, the frequency with which the warehouse data refresh jobs are running is set to 120 seconds (or 2 minutes).

Team Foundation Server OLAP Cube

The star schema of the warehouse is suitable for analyzing the data. But as you get into reports that require aggregated values, the warehouse may not be the best choice. The aggregation of values can become slow, depending on the volume of the rows.

Enter the Team Foundation Server OLAP cube. This is a multi-dimensional database that aggregates data for better analysis. Hence, you can correlate data based on the different metrics (that is, work items, build, test, and so on). Team Foundation Server OLAP cube gets the data from warehouse on preset interval. By default, a scheduled job runs every two hours to refresh the data in the cube from the warehouse. Note that a full processing of the analysis database is scheduled to run on a daily basis, as indicated by the interval of 86400 seconds (or 24 hours) for the FullProcessIntervalSeconds setting.

The data in the cube can then be used by a variety of client tools, including Microsoft Excel and SQL Report Designer.

The cube consists of measures and dimensions. A *measure* is a numeric value that can be aggregated. *Dimensions* provide a way to summarize measures and categorize them based on additional metrics.

> **NOTE** *For a more complete list of the perspectives, measure groups, dimensions, and measures for the Team Foundation Server cube see MSDN at* http://aka.ms/CubeMetrics.

WORKING WITH TEAM FOUNDATION SERVER REPORTS

Team Foundation Server includes two sets of reports in most process templates: Microsoft Excel Reports and SQL Reporting Services Reports. There are about 40 reports in the two process templates that ship with Team Foundation Server. From a project management perspective, one of the great advantages of using Team Foundation Server is that you don't have to manually correlate data from a host of third-party sources. The available reports are readily available in a dashboard (or portal).

You learn more about the reports shipped with the three process templates later in this chapter. But first, let's start by looking at the tools you use to create Team Foundation Server reports.

Tools to Create Reports

You can use any tool that can connect to a data warehouse or an analysis database to create a report. Following are the two primary types of reports that you create from Team Foundation Server by connecting to either the Team Foundation Server data warehouse or the Team Foundation Server OLAP cube:

- ➤ Excel Reports
- ➤ RDL Reports

> **NOTE** *You can also use the work item queries to create a Microsoft Excel Report, which is discussed in more detail later in this chapter. The work item query data uses the Team Foundation Server Object Model to obtain the data just like Visual Studio would display work item query results, but you are in effect safely querying live data from the operational store.*

Figure 12-2 shows a map of these two report types and shows which is appropriate against which Team Foundation Server data store.

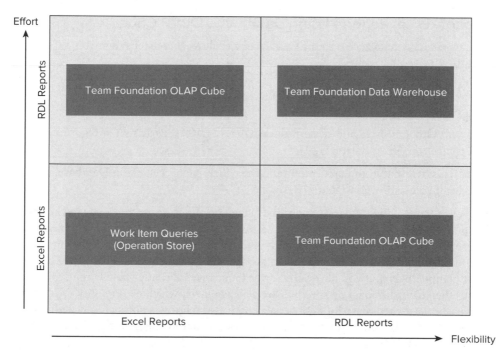

FIGURE 12-2

As you see, you can use the work item queries and the Team Foundation Server OLAP cube with Microsoft Excel or use Team Foundation Server OLAP Cube and the Data Warehouse with the RDL Reports.

To understand this better, let's dive in and create some reports.

> **NOTE** *To create reports, you need read access to the databases that make up the warehouse and the cube. You can get access to either the warehouse or the cube or both. Your access depends on the data store you are using and the type of reports you want to create. The administrator of the database can grant you read access. Refer to the MSDN documentation at* `http://aka.ms/reportPerms` *for information on permissions needed to access the warehouse and the analysis database.*

Working with Microsoft Excel Reports

As mentioned earlier, you can use Microsoft Excel to create reports from either the Team Foundation Server OLAP cube, or by using work item queries. Using Excel to create reports is a very approachable and rapid way to understand the data inside your Team Foundation Server databases, and so we focus the majority of the rest of this chapter on an explanation of the various ways of using it.

Let's first look at the steps to create a Microsoft Excel report from the cube. Whichever store you are querying data against, the key advantage with Microsoft Excel reports is the simplicity of using the tool—regardless of whether you are connecting to a pivot table and the cube or using work item queries.

Creating Microsoft Excel Reports Using Data in the OLAP Cube

First, ensure that you have read access to the OLAP cube. Follow these steps to create a quick pivot table report using Microsoft Excel:

1. Open Microsoft Office Excel.

2. Select the Data tab from the ribbon.

3. Click From Other Sources and select From Analysis Services, as shown in Figure 12-3. The Data Connection Wizard displays.

4. Provide the server name and credentials and then click Next. The Select Database and Table dialog displays, as shown in Figure 12-4.

5. In the Select the Database That Contains the Data You Want, select `Tfs_Analysis`. The interesting part is the list of perspectives and cube. As you see in Figure 12-4, the `Tfs_Analysis` database has a cube named Team System. It is essentially a representation of the entire warehouse, and contains about 15 measure groups and 23 dimensions. That is one powerful (but complex) cube. If you have SQL Server Enterprise Edition installed (and separately licensed) then five additional perspectives are also available, which can simplify the data access. However, because the license for SQL Server Enterprise Edition is not included with a standard installation of TFS we will show the standard case and continue by selecting the *Team System* cube then clicking Next.

6. In the next dialog, click Finish to see the Import Data dialog. Leave the selection as PivotTable Report and click OK.

7. You are now in the workbook with a list of fields from the Team System cube. You can now build a report using any of these fields.

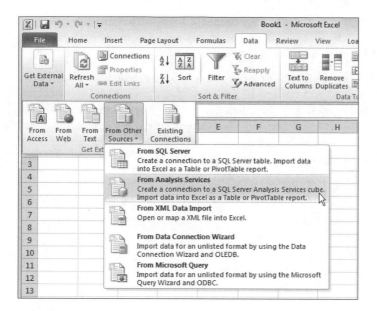

FIGURE 12-3

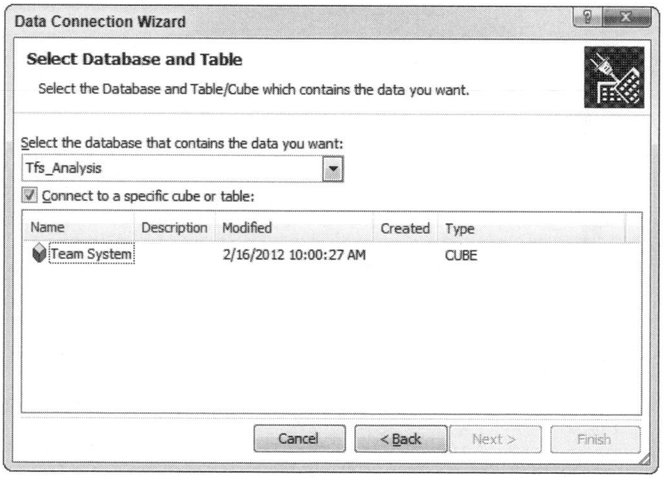

FIGURE 12-4

> **NOTE** Perspectives *are subsets of cubes that provide application- or business-specific views into the cubes. In other words, perspectives provide a simplified view of the cube for specific purposes. In* Tfs_Analysis *with SQL Server Enterprise Edition, there are perspectives specific to build, test results, work items, code churn, and code coverage.*

Next, we walk through an example that shows you how to create a report that answers the question, "How many active product backlog items or task work items are there in my project?" The example uses a project created using the Scrum process template.

To answer the question, you must know the count of work items of type Product Backlog Item or Task and with a state of New, To Do, Committed, or In Progress. You can list that by the team member the work items are assigned to by showing the fields related to Work Item. Then add Work Item Count to the Values area by dragging and dropping it. Add WorkItem.System_WorkItemType and WorkItem.System_State to the Report Filter area and WorkItem.System_AssignedTo to the Row Labels area. Figure 12-5 shows the selection in the PivotTable Field List.

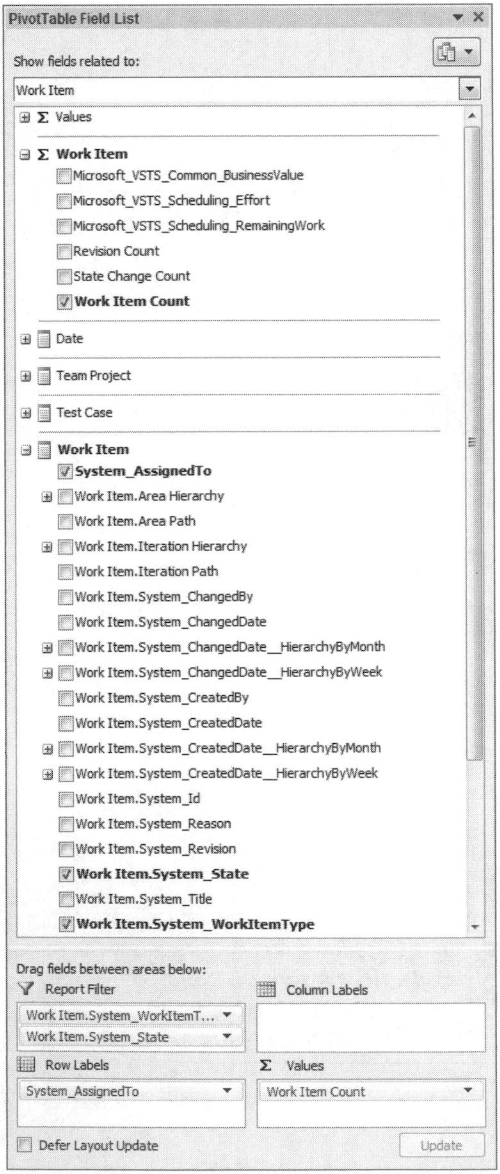

FIGURE 12-5

In the pivot table itself, select the dropdown for Work Item.System_WorkItemType, check the Select Multiple Items box and then select both Product Backlog Item and Task as shown in Figure 12-6. For the Work Item.System_State report field, perform the same procedure to select the desired work item states.

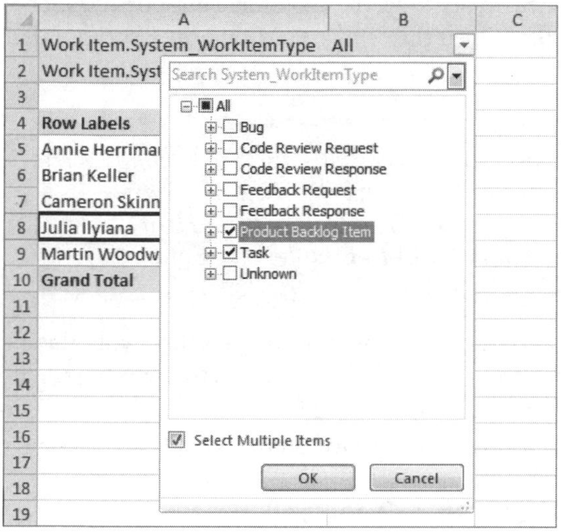

FIGURE 12-6

This results in a simple report that shows the active user story and task work items by team members, as shown in Figure 12-7.

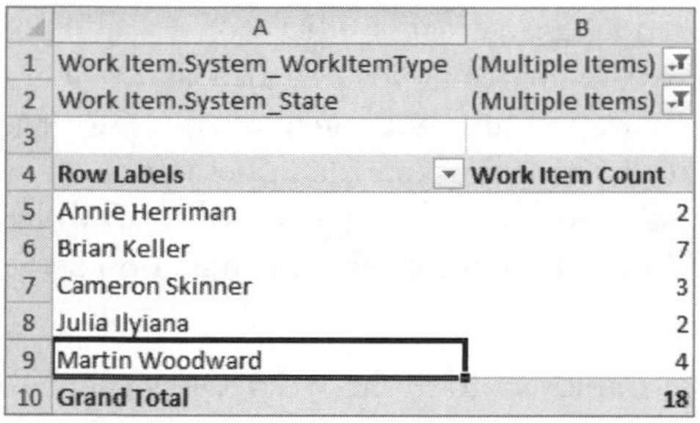

FIGURE 12-7

This is not a particularly impressive looking report, but it demonstrates the point. By choosing the appropriate fields that you need for the pivot table, you can create a report in a very quick and simple manner. The focus should be on choosing the right source and then drilling down on data that you find surprising so you can understand what issue you have uncovered.

> **NOTE** *To learn more information on the various perspectives and fact tables provided in the Team Foundation Server warehouse and the details on each one of them, refer to the Team Foundation Server help documentation at* http://aks.ms/tfsReports.

Customizing a Microsoft Excel Report

You don't necessarily start with a brand new report every time. In many cases, you may simply modify an existing report to get the data that you are looking for. In Team Explorer, you find existing Microsoft Excel reports in the team project under Documents ⇨ Excel Reports. The example reports you find in that directory vary by process template type. To customize a report, first choose the Microsoft Excel report that you want to modify. Open the report in Microsoft Excel by double-clicking the report filename in Team Explorer.

> **NOTE** *If you get a security warning in Microsoft Excel that says, "Data connections have been disabled," click the Options button to get the Microsoft Office Security Options window. You may have to change the selection from Help Protect Me from Unknown Content (Recommended) to Enable This Content.*

After you have the report open in Microsoft Excel, click the report cell to open the PivotTable Field List window and the toolbar. You use this field list to make necessary changes to the report. After you are finished with changes, you can either save them locally or publish them so others can see the updated report. You learn about the different publishing options later in this chapter.

Creating Microsoft Excel Reports Using Work Item Queries

Work item queries provide an easy way to retrieve information about work items in Team Foundation Server. The Shared Queries folder contains queries shared by everyone in your team project. The My Queries folder contains queries that only you can use. Chapter 10 provides more detail on work item queries.

In Team Foundation Server, you can use these work item queries to create a Microsoft Excel report, and do so quickly. Not only can you create Microsoft Excel reports, but you can also share them with the team by publishing them. It provides a quick-and-easy way to turn work item queries into reports. These report types are also available on a Team Foundation Server instance that does not have Reporting Services enabled—even the hosted Team Foundation Service (http://tfspreview.com) which lacks many of the other reporting features found in an on-premises Team Foundation Server instance.

Let's look at how to create a report in this way. In Team Explorer, go to the Work Items page. To create a report out of a team query, expand the Shared Queries node. Right-click on a work item query to view the menu shown in Figure 12-8.

Click the Create Report in Microsoft Excel option, which launches Microsoft Excel. The first thing that happens is that Microsoft Excel translates the work item query into data that Microsoft Excel can use to generate reports. After that, it presents a New Work Item Report window, as shown in Figure 12-9.

There are two buckets of reports—Current Reports and Trend Reports—in this example with six reports in each. However, the reports available depend on the type of work item query that you select. To understand where these reports come from, let's look at the query and the results shown in Figure 12-10.

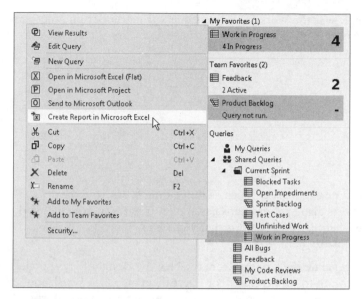

FIGURE 12-8

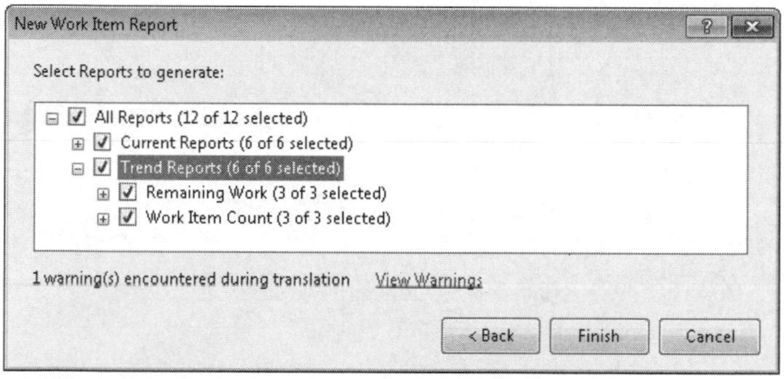

New Work Item Report ? ✕

Select Reports to generate:

☐ ☑ All Reports (12 of 12 selected)
   ⊞ ☑ Current Reports (6 of 6 selected)
   ☐ ☑ Trend Reports (6 of 6 selected)
      ⊞ ☑ Remaining Work (3 of 3 selected)
      ⊞ ☑ Work Item Count (3 of 3 selected)

1 warning(s) encountered during translation   View Warnings

    < Back   Finish   Cancel

FIGURE 12-9

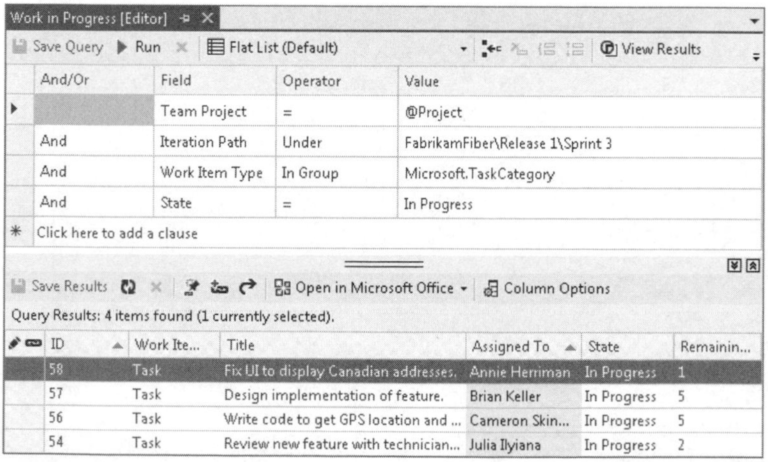

Work in Progress [Editor] 📌 ✕

💾 Save Query ▶ Run ✕ ⊞ Flat List (Default)   ⏺ View Results

	And/Or	Field	Operator	Value
▶		Team Project	=	@Project
	And	Iteration Path	Under	FabrikamFiber\Release 1\Sprint 3
	And	Work Item Type	In Group	Microsoft.TaskCategory
	And	State	=	In Progress
✱	Click here to add a clause			

💾 Save Results 🔄 ✕ ⬆ ⬇ ↪ ▣ Open in Microsoft Office ▾ ⊟ Column Options

Query Results: 4 items found (1 currently selected).

🔗 💬	ID ▲	Work Ite...	Title	Assigned To ▲	State	Remainin...
	58	Task	Fix UI to display Canadian addresses.	Annie Herriman	In Progress	1
	57	Task	Design implementation of feature.	Brian Keller	In Progress	5
	56	Task	Write code to get GPS location and ...	Cameron Skin...	In Progress	5
	54	Task	Review new feature with technician...	Julia Ilyiana	In Progress	2

FIGURE 12-10

The query we selected in the example was the Work In Progress query from the Scrum process template. The result of this query returns the following fields:

➤ ID

➤ Work Item Type

➤ Title

➤ Assigned To

➤ State

➤ Remaining Work

You get reports on the values that can be aggregated, such as Remaining Work, and the default Work Item count. Each of these reports also has variations based on attributes such as the Work Item Type, Assigned To, and State—hence, the six reports that you see in Figure 12-10. The trend reports are based on the work item history data.

Now, return to Microsoft Excel to generate the reports. From the New Work Item Report dialog (Figure 12-9), select the reports you want to see generated, or select them all. Click Finish and Microsoft Excel begins working on the reports. When the report generation is completed, you see a Microsoft Excel workbook with 13 worksheets—one worksheet with the table of contents (as shown in Figure 12-11) and 12 worksheets for each of the 12 reports.

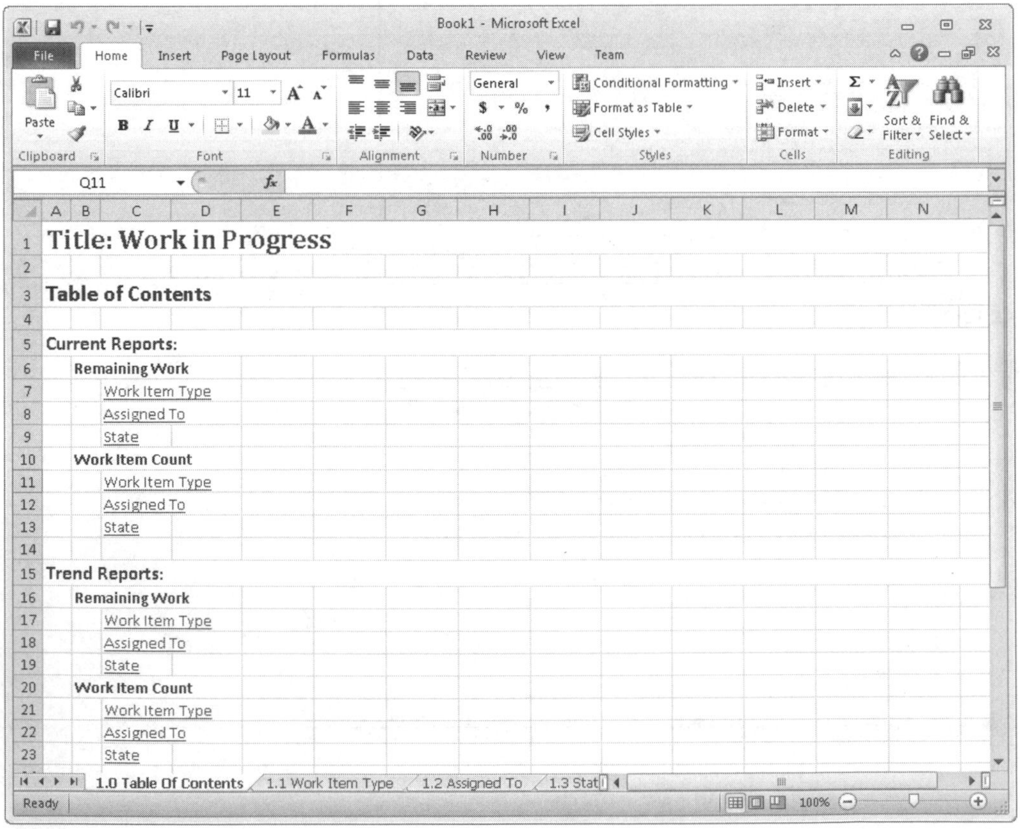

FIGURE 12-11

Each of these reports is a pivot table report. You can customize these reports by modifying the fields using the PivotTable Field List dialog, as shown in Figure 12-5.

Publishing Microsoft Excel Reports

Now that you understand the basics of creating and customizing Microsoft Excel reports that are based on the data from Team Foundation Server OLAP cube and the work item queries, let's look at the options you have to publish them. Obviously, you do not have to worry about publishing if you don't have to share the reports you create. In that case, you can simply save them locally. But it is highly likely that you will be sharing reports with the rest of the team.

The publishing options for Microsoft Excel reports depend on whether you have Microsoft Office SharePoint Server (MOSS) Enterprise running your dashboard/portals, or Windows SharePoint Services (WSS) for your portals. Table 12-1 summarizes the capabilities for MOSS Enterprise users versus WSS users.

TABLE 12-1: SharePoint Server Enterprise versus WSS/SharePoint

FEATURE	SHAREPOINT SERVER ENTERPRISE	WSS/SHAREPOINT
Team site	Portal with six dashboards.	Portal with two dashboards.
Reports	Dashboard uses Excel reports.	Dashboard uses Report Definition Language (RDL) Reports.
Viewing Microsoft Excel reports	Viewable as Web parts.	Open in Microsoft Excel from the document library.
Microsoft Excel reports are available in	Team Explorer under Documents ⇨ Excel Reports.	Team Explorer under Documents ⇨ Excel Reports.
Creating new Microsoft Excel reports	From Microsoft Excel, create a new report and publish it to Excel Services. Make it available on the dashboard using the New Excel Report button from the dashboard.	From Microsoft Excel, create a new report and save it to the document library.
Publishing Microsoft Excel reports	Publish to Excel Services and make the report available in the dashboard by using the Excel Web Access Web part.	Save the report to the document library and view it in Microsoft Excel.
Dashboards	A set of dashboards (for example, Work Progress, Product Quality, Test Progress, and so on) are created as part of the Team Project setup.	Excel reports are not available. RDL reports are presented in Web parts.

Publishing to a Document Library

You could publish a report to the shared documents from Team Explorer, or you could use the WSS portal site and upload the document.

To upload it from Team Explorer, get to the folder you want to upload the new report to. For this example, upload a new report, "Current Work Item count by state." To do that, first find the Excel Reports folder under Team Explorer ➪ Documents ➪ Excel Reports. Then, right-click the Excel Reports folder and select Upload Document from the menu.

You can then select the Microsoft Excel report that you have saved locally and upload it. After you have done so, refresh Team Explorer and the new report appears in the Documents page.

You could also upload the Microsoft Excel report from outside Team Explorer. To do that, open the Team Project portal. When you're in the project portal, click the Excel Reports link on the right navigation bar and upload the report to this folder.

Publishing to Excel Services

A project portal is a SharePoint site. If you are running SharePoint Server 2010 Enterprise, then you have access to Excel Services. You can publish Microsoft Excel reports to Excel Services. Doing so provides the option to display the Microsoft Excel report using the Excel Web Access Web part in the dashboard. This enables you to easily and quickly create Microsoft Excel reports and share them broadly with the team using dashboards.

First, start with a Microsoft Excel report. Create a Microsoft Excel report following the steps described earlier in this chapter, or open an already-created Microsoft Excel report.

Click File ➪ Save & Send ➪ Save to SharePoint to open the familiar dialog that enables you to Save As on the server. Verify that the path information is correctly set to the team's portal path. If not, change it to the correct path. Then, click the Publish Options button.

Now you are in the Publish Options dialog as shown in Figure 12-12.

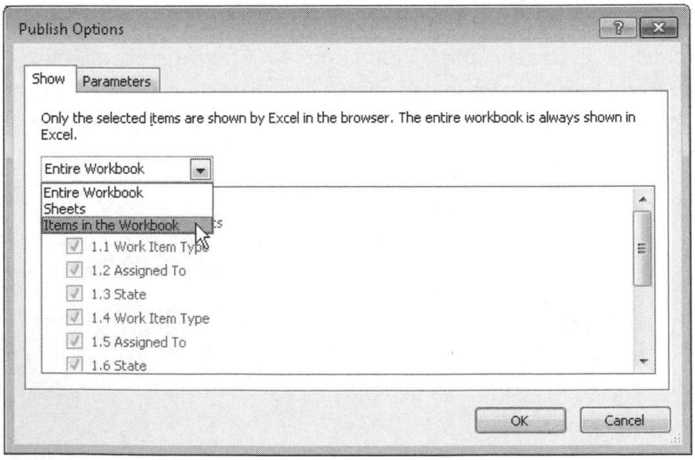

FIGURE 12-12

In this window, there are two tabs: Show and Parameters. You are only using the Show tab here. The Parameters tab is used to specify cells that you can provide value to while viewing the Microsoft Excel report.

In the dropdown, select Items in the Workbook because you want to publish the Microsoft Excel report to Excel Services and have the chart show up in the dashboard using the Excel Web Access part. You don't want the entire spreadsheet to show up in the dashboard; you just want the short version. Selecting "Items in the Workbook" in the dropdown changes the view in the box below the dropdown. Now you have the capability to select all charts or individual charts, as well as all pivot tables or individual pivot tables. In this example, you only have one chart and one pivot table. Select the 1.2 Assigned To chart as shown in Figure 12-12.

Click OK in this window and then click Save to publish the Microsoft Excel report. Now you are finished with the publishing.

The next step is to add the report to the dashboard. To launch the dashboard, in the Team Explorer Documents page, click the Show Project Portal link to open the project portal in the browser. Select Excel Reports from the left navigation to see the list of Microsoft Excel reports, including the new report you just published.

You now want to get this report onto the dashboard. From the Dashboards list, select the dashboard to which you want to add this report. You can choose between My Dashboard or the Project Dashboard. In this example, select the Project Dashboard.

To add the new report to this dashboard, click Site Actions on the top right-hand corner and select Edit Page.

If you have worked with SharePoint sites and Web parts, then the next few steps will be very familiar to you. You add a new Web part to this page by clicking the Add Web Part button in the Footer section.

The Add Web Parts to Footer window displays. Select the Excel Web Access Web part and click Add.

The Excel Web Access Web part is added to the dashboard page. Select a workbook that you want to display in this Web part. You do that by specifying the details in the tool pane. There is obviously lots of information that you can provide in this tool pane. The following are the two fields that you will update here:

➤ Workbook

➤ Title

Click OK on the tool pane window and exit the edit mode to see this report displayed in the dashboard.

Microsoft Excel reports make it truly easy for team members get the data and metrics that they want from Team Foundation Server, and for the team to keep their project portal up to date with the most useful information to them. The capability to create a report from a work item query is a great addition to the reporting capability in Team Foundation Server. Couple that with the Microsoft Excel services and dashboards, and no one will be able to complain about not having the right information at the right time.

Working with RDL Reports

This section briefly examines the tools available to create and customize Report Definition Language (RDL) reports. Team Foundation Server 2012 includes set of RDL reports out-of-the-box, and the reports vary by the type of process template you choose to use for your project.

There are two main tools available to work with RDL reports:

➤ SQL Server Report Builder

➤ SQL Server Business Intelligence Development Studio (BIDS)

SQL Server Report Builder

The Report Builder tool has full support for SQL Reporting Services and provides a Microsoft Office–like report authoring environment. Both SQL Server 2008 R2 and SQL Server 2012 include Report Builder 3.0. This version includes many improvements over previous versions that make it a compelling choice for report authors. It's designed for business analysts and developers who want to create custom reports quickly and easily. You can download the tool from `http://aka.ms/ sql2012rb`. With this tool, you can work with RDL files, make necessary changes, and save it as an RDL file. This file can then be used, for example, using the Report Designer.

After you have the tool installed, launch the report builder and start by connecting the report server. (For example, `http://<<Server instance name/reportserver>>`.) It is probably easier to start with an existing report and customize it than it is to create one from scratch.

To edit an existing report, select the reports folder in the report server, then the team project collection, followed by the actual team project. The folders with the reports display, and you can choose the report for customization from one of these folders.

The report data pane has the parameters, data set, and the built-in fields that you work with to modify the report.

> **NOTE** *SQL Server Developer Center on TechNet has several how-to topics on Report Builder. For more information, see "Getting Started with Report Builder" at* `http://aka.ms/sqlrbstart`.

SQL Server Business Intelligence Development Studio

Business Intelligence Development Studio (BIDS) is an integrated environment for developing cubes, data sources, and reports. It is a much more complex tool than Report Builder, but it gives you the ability to create highly complex and rich reports. To install BIDS, run the Setup program for SQL Server, and select the Client Components check box when you specify the components to install. BIDS actually is an add-on to Visual Studio 2008, therefore if you don't already have this older version of Visual Studio installed on your machine then BIDS installs a Visual Studio 2008 shell just for the BIDS tooling. This can live happily alongside your Visual Studio 2012 installation.

If you need to create complex and rich reports like the ones that are included with the process templates out the box, you should refer to the whitepaper by John Socha-Leialoha. The paper is called "Creating Reports for Team Foundation Server 2010," but it is still fully applicable to Team Foundation Server 2012. The whitepaper is available at `http://aka.ms/bidstfs`.

SUMMARY

In this chapter, you read about the various data stores in Team Foundation Server that provide the data for the various reports. You also learned about the tools that are available to create reports. This chapter examined how to create and customize Microsoft Excel reports, and the tools available to create and customize RDL reports (that is, Report Builder and BIDS), as well as the options available for publishing reports.

Reporting is a powerful feature in Team Foundation Server. It breaks down the usual barrier within teams caused by a lack of information. Team Foundation Server provides a powerful set of reports out-of-the-box and provides the capability to add additional reports based on your needs. And that is coupled with the capability to quickly share the information using dashboards and portals.

Chapter 13 looks at how to understand the architecture of the software that you are building, what Microsoft's approach is to software architecture's, and the tooling that's available in the Visual Studio 2012 release.

PART IV
Architecture

13

Introduction to Software Architecture

WHAT'S IN THIS CHAPTER?

➤ Why designing visually is important

➤ Microsoft's approach to a modeling strategy

➤ Modeling tools in Visual Studio 2012

In this introductory chapter, you learn about some main themes around software architecture and design — domain-specific languages (DSLs), model-driven development (MDD), and the Unified Modeling Language (UML) — and how they apply to Visual Studio Ultimate 2012.

This chapter then gives a brief overview of the architecture tools in Visual Studio 2012, including the support for the most common UML diagrams. Many of these tools are expounded on in later chapters of this part of the book.

Finally, this chapter wraps up with a brief glimpse at some of the changes and new features added to the architecture tools in Visual Studio 2012. New dependency graph features and better graph performance have been included to enhance your experience with the architecture tools.

Let's begin by first establishing the case for undertaking visual modeling — or visual design — in the first place.

DESIGNING VISUALLY

Two elementary questions immediately come to mind. Why design at all, rather than just code? Why design visually?

To answer the first question, consider the common analogy of building complex physical structures, such as bridges. Crossing a small stream requires only a plank of wood — no architect, no workers, and no plans. Building a bridge across a wide river requires a lot more — a set of plans drawn up by an architect so that you can order the right materials, planning the work, communicating the details of the complex structure to the builders, and getting a safety certificate from the local authority. It's the same with software. You can write a small program by diving straight into code, but building a complex software system requires some forethought. You must plan it, communicate it, and document it to gain approval.

Therefore, the four aims of visual design are as follows:

➤ To help you visualize a system you want

➤ To enable you to specify the structure or behavior of a system

➤ To provide you with a template that guides you in constructing a system

➤ To document the decisions you have made

Traditionally, design processes such as the *Rational Unified Process* have treated design and programming as separate disciplines, at least in terms of tools support. You use a visual modeling tool for design, and a separate integrated development environment (IDE) for coding. This makes sense if you treat software development like bridge building, and assume that the cost of fixing problems during implementation is much higher than the cost of fixing those problems during design.

For bridges, that is undoubtedly true. But in the realm of software development, is it really more costly to change a line of code than it is to change a design diagram? Moreover, just as bridge designers may want to prototype aspects of their design using real materials, so may software designers want to prototype certain aspects of their design in real code.

For these reasons, for several years now the trend has been toward tools that enable visual design and coding within the same environment, with easy switching between the two representations, thus treating design and coding as essentially two views of the same activity. The precedent was set originally in the Java space by tools such as Together-J and, more recently, in the .NET space by IBM-Rational XDE. Microsoft embraced this approach fully with Visual Studio 2010 Ultimate, and has continued to enhance the experience with Visual Studio Ultimate 2012.

Now, let's tackle the second question. If the pictorial design view and the code view are alternative, but equivalent, representations, then why design visually at all? The answer to that question is simple: A picture is worth a thousand words. To test that theory, just look at the figures in this chapter and imagine what the same information would look like in code. Then imagine trying to explain the information to someone else using nothing but a code listing.

Many people think modeling tools are only for use on large-scale projects that make use of the waterfall software development lifecycle. That is not the case at all. Agile development is very popular now, and several different agile methods, including Kanban and Scrum, are used for all sorts of development projects, small to large. The modeling tools in Visual Studio 2012, including the UML diagrams, dependency diagrams, and Architecture Explorer, can be used just as effectively by a team following an agile methodology. Remember, just because you are "agile" doesn't mean you don't need to understand your code base and what you are trying to build. "Agile" doesn't mean

"Undocumented." It just means that you only document enough so that everyone understands what they have to do. And the modeling tools and diagrams in Visual Studio 2012 help you do that.

MICROSOFT'S MODELING STRATEGY

Microsoft's Visual Studio 2012 modeling strategy is based on a three ideas:

➤ Model-driven development (MDD)

➤ Domain-specific languages (DSLs)

➤ The "Code Understanding" experience

Together these topics comprise Microsoft's vision for how to add value to the software development process through visual modeling.

Understanding Model-Driven Development

As a software designer, you may be familiar with the "code-generation" features provided by UML tools such as Rational Rose and IBM-Rational XDE. These tools typically do not generate "code" at all, but merely create "skeleton code" for the classes you devise. So, all you get is one or more source files containing classes populated with the attributes and operation signatures that you specified in the model.

> **NOTE** *The words "attribute" and "operation" are UML terminology. In the .NET world, these are often referred to as "field" and "method," respectively.*

The methods that are generated for each class by UML code-generation tools typically have complete signatures but empty bodies. This seems reasonable enough because, after all, the tool is not psychic. How would it know how you intend to implement those methods? Well, actually, it could know.

UML practitioners spend hours constructing dynamic models such as state charts and sequence diagrams that show how objects react (to method invocations) and interact (invoke methods on other objects). Yet, that information, which could be incorporated into the empty method bodies, is lost completely during code generation.

> **NOTE** *Note that not all tools lose this kind of information during code generation, but most of the popular ones do. In addition, in some cases, UML tools do generate code within method bodies — for example, when you apply patterns using IBM-Rational XDE — but, in general, the point is valid.*

Why do UML tools generally not take account of the full set of models during code generation? In part, it's because software designers do not provide information on the other models with sufficient precision to be as useful as auto-generated method bodies. The main reason for that is because the notation (UML) and tools simply do not allow for the required level of precision.

What does this have to do with MDD? Well, MDD is all about getting maximum value out of the modeling effort by taking as much information as possible from the various models right through to implementation.

Although the example of UML dynamic modeling information finding its way into implemented method bodies was useful in setting the scene, don't assume that MDD is only (or necessarily) about dynamic modeling. If you've ever constructed a UML deployment model and then tried to do something useful with it — such as generate a deployment script or evaluate your deployment against the proposed logical infrastructure — you will have seen how wasted that effort has been, other than to generate some documentation.

So, what's the bottom line? Because models are regarded as first-class development artifacts, developers write less conventional code, and development is, therefore, more productive and agile. In addition, it shows all the participants — developers, designers, analysts, architects, and operations staff — that modeling actually *adds value* to their efforts.

Understanding Domain-Specific Languages

UML fails to provide the kind of high-fidelity domain-specific modeling capabilities required by automated development. In other words, if you want to automate the mundane aspects of software development then a one-size-fits-all generic visual modeling notation will not suffice. What you need is one or more Domain-Specific Languages (DSLs) (or notations) highly tuned for the task at hand — whether that task is the definition of web services, the modeling of a hosting environment, or traditional object design.

> **WARNING** *A DSL is a modeling language that meets certain criteria. For example, a modeling language for developing web services should contain concepts such as web methods and protocols. The modeling language should also use meaningful names for concepts, such as fields and methods (for C#), rather than attributes and operations. The names should be drawn from the natural vocabulary of the domain.*

The DSL idea is not new, and you may already be using a DSL for database manipulation (it's called SQL) or XML schema definition (it's called XSD).

Visual Studio Ultimate 2012 embraces this idea by providing the capability to create DSLs for specific tasks. DSLs enable visual models to be used not only for creating design documentation, but also for capturing information in a precise form that can be processed easily, raising the prospect of compiling models into code.

> **NOTE** *The only DSL that Visual Studio Ultimate 2012 provides "out of the box" is the UML support. Users have the capability to create their own DSLs using the DSL toolkit.*

In that context, "your own problem domain" need not be technology-focused (such as how to model web services or deployment infrastructures) but may instead be business-focused. You could devise a DSL that is highly tuned for describing banking systems or industrial processes.

The "Code Understanding" Experience

Modeling is not just about building diagrams that help you understand requirements, architecture, and high-level design. It can also be about helping you gather a better understanding of the details of your code base. In Visual Studio Ultimate 2012, a majority of the work done on the architecture tools has been to enhance what is called the "Code Understanding" experience.

Think of the Code Understanding experience as the ability to understand both the new code you need to write, as well as the existing code you need to support. As a developer, you may need a better understanding of your code, how it fits into the wider system, and the frameworks that it is using, so that your team can more easily create tests, debug code, and add new features. The UML diagrams within Visual Studio 2012 can provide that information. Layer diagrams can show you the different layers of your application and help you to enforce code rules.

You may run into the situation where you need to understand why a certain module has a dependency on another module. Dependency graphs are a great way to see how the different assemblies and modules in your solution interact and depend on each other. Understanding these dependencies can make it easier to refactor code to remove dependencies on deprecated features.

> **NOTE** *The Visual Studio team used dependency graphs to do just that. While working on Visual Studio 2012, they found that DSLs had a dependency on a C++ assembly. This forced DSLs to run in x86 mode, even on 64-bit machines. The team used dependency graphs to understand where this dependency was, why it was occurring, and the effect of removing it. Armed with this knowledge, they were able to remove this dependency from Visual Studio 2012.*

So, when thinking about modeling and visualization, don't just assume those tools are for making pretty pictures of your requirements. You can also use these tools to drill down into your code base to help you solve problems.

THE ARCHITECTURE TOOLS IN VISUAL STUDIO ULTIMATE 2012

In Visual Studio 2010 Ultimate, the architecture tools underwent a huge transformation from Visual Studio 2008. Although there are some new tools in Visual Studio Ultimate 2012, by and large the modeling diagrams and tools that you used in Visual Studio 2010 work the same in 2012. All of these diagrams and tools can be used to help you more fully understand the software system being built. These tools enable you to create models at different levels of detail, depending on your need.

This section provides a very brief overview of each of the modeling diagrams. The chapters that follow in the book provide an in-depth look into each diagram type.

As mentioned previously, Visual Studio 2012 fully supports UML, specifically UML 2.1.2. Only five UML diagrams are supported out-of-the-box:

➤ Use case diagrams

➤ Activity diagrams

➤ Sequence diagrams

➤ Component diagrams

➤ Class diagrams

There are other tools and diagrams, not related to UML, included with Visual Studio Ultimate 2012. The Architecture Explorer can be used to understand the architecture of existing code, or of managed assemblies. Dependency graphs are used to provide a graphical view of the information from Architecture Explorer, as well as directly from your solution. Layer diagrams can be used to describe the logical architecture of your system and can even be used during the build process to enforce architecture considerations on the code base.

Use Case Diagrams

A *use case diagram* is a summary of who uses your application and what they can do with it. It describes the relationships among requirements, users, and the major components of the system.

Use case diagrams show the relationships between users (actors) and use cases within a system or application. They provide an overall view of how a system is used and the various roles and actions that take place within the system. Figure 13-1 shows an example of a use case diagram.

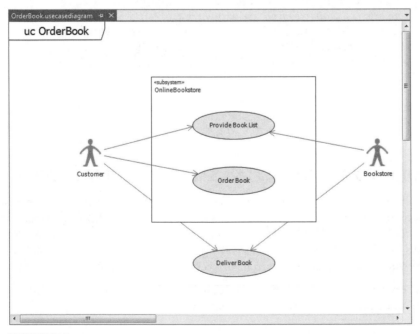

FIGURE 13-1

Activity Diagrams

Use case diagrams can be broken down into *activity diagrams*. An activity diagram shows the software process as the flow of work through a series of actions. It can be a useful exercise to draw an activity diagram showing the major tasks that a user will perform with the software application. Figure 13-2 shows an example of an activity diagram.

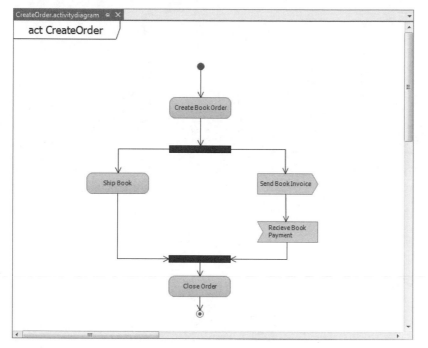

FIGURE 13-2

Sequence Diagrams

Sequence diagrams display interactions between different objects. This interaction usually takes place as a series of messages between the different objects. Sequence diagrams can be considered an alternate view to the activity diagram. A sequence diagram can show a clear view of the steps in a use case. Figure 13-3 shows an example of a sequence diagram.

Component Diagrams

Component diagrams help visualize the high-level structure of the software system. They show the major parts of a system and how those parts interact and depend on each other. One nice feature of component diagrams is that they show how the different parts of the design interact with each other, regardless of how those individual parts are actually implemented. Figure 13-4 shows an example of a component diagram.

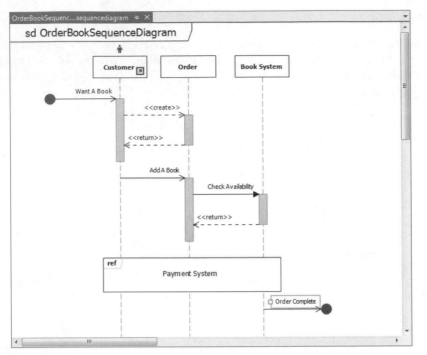

FIGURE 13-3

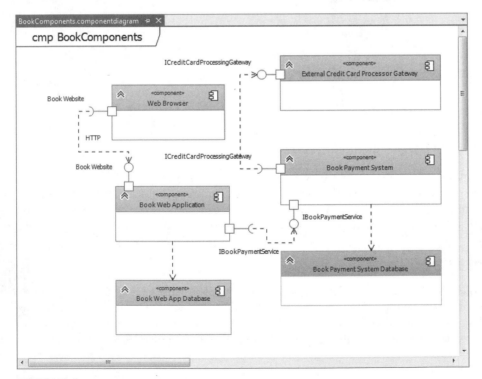

FIGURE 13-4

Class Diagrams

Class diagrams describe the objects in the application system. They do this without referencing any particular implementation of the system itself. This type of UML modeling diagram is also referred to as a conceptual class diagram. Figure 13-5 shows an example of a class diagram.

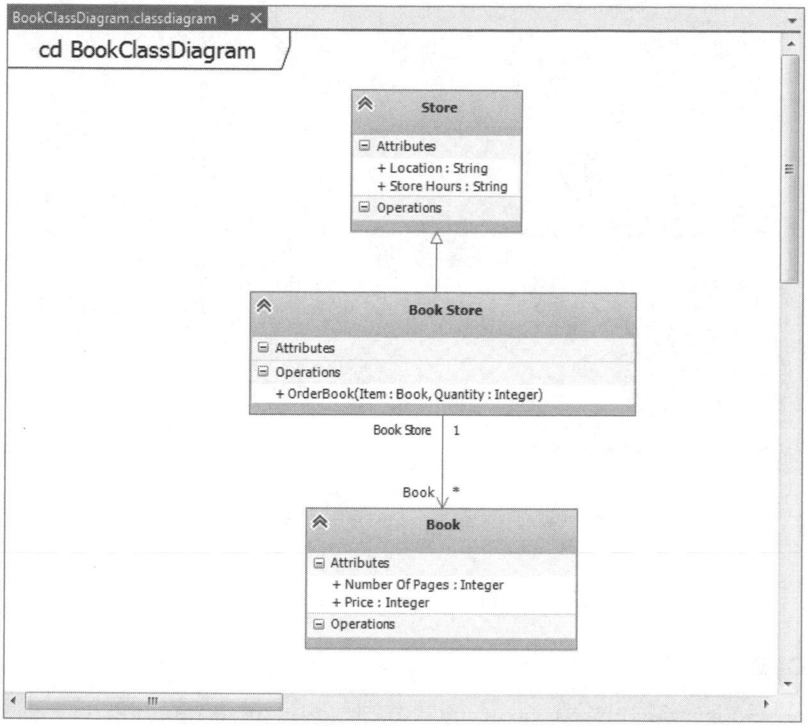

FIGURE 13-5

Layer Diagrams

Layer diagrams are used to describe the logical architecture of your system. A layer diagram organizes the objects in your code into different groups (or layers) that describe the different tasks those objects perform. Layers can also be composed of sublayers, which you can use to describe smaller, discrete tasks in the parent layer. In addition, you can use layer diagrams to show dependencies between different aspects of your code. Figure 13-6 shows an example of a layer diagram.

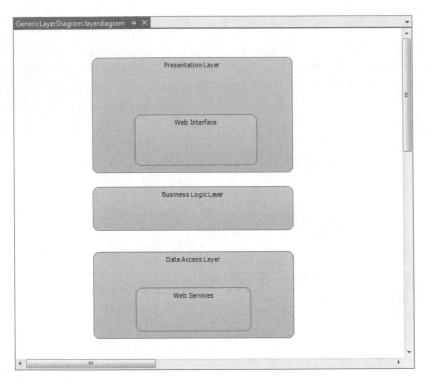

FIGURE 13-6

Architecture Explorer

The *Architecture Explorer* tool provided by Visual Studio 2012 helps in understanding the existing architecture of a code base. This tool enables you to drill down into an existing code base, or even into compiled managed code, to help you understand how the application works, without having to open a single code file.

The Architecture Explorer can also lead into the world of *dependency graphs*, which are a type of view in Visual Studio Ultimate 2012 that makes it easy to understand code that is new or unfamiliar. Dependency graphs make use of the Directed Graph Markup Language (DGML) to show the relationships between different areas of code in an easy-to-understand, graphical fashion.

> **NOTE** *The Architecture Explorer is not the only way to create dependency graphs. Chapter 15 also shows other ways you can create dependency graphs.*

WHAT'S NEW WITH ARCHITECTURE TOOLS IN VISUAL STUDIO ULTIMATE 2012

Although the previous section may make you think that there is nothing new about the architecture tools, that is not the case. In addition to the UML modeling diagrams and the Architecture Explorer that you had access to in Visual Studio 2010 Ultimate, Visual Studio 2012 provides new tools to help with your architecture needs. This section describes some of the new features available with regard to the architecture tools in Visual Studio 2012.

Architecture Menu Options

The architecture main menu option in Visual Studio 2012 has a couple of new features. The first is the ability to generate dependency graphs directly for a solution or an include file. The two menu options are Generate Dependency Graph ➢ For Solution and Generate Dependency Graph ➢ For Include File.

The For Solution option generates a dependency graph for the entire open solution and works for both managed and native code. The For Include File generates a dependency graph based on an include file, and, as you would expect, works only for native code.

Another new feature is the XMI Import feature. This feature was originally an add-on for Visual Studio 2010 from the Visual Studio Feature Packs, which has now been integrated directly into the product. XMI Import enables you to add UML elements from other tools to UML diagrams in Visual Studio Ultimate 2012 by importing them as XML Metadata Interchange (XMI) files. Using this feature, you can import UML sequence diagrams, class diagrams, and use case diagrams, and then view and use those diagrams.

XMI Export is not supported from Visual Studio Ultimate 2012 by default. However, there is an XMI Export source-code sample available with the VS VMSdk samples that can be used to create a custom XMI export option. More information on the SDK can be found at `http://aka.ms/VS12VMSDK`.

Dependency Graph Enhancements

There was a big investment in Visual Studio Ultimate 2012 to make dependency graphs better. One of the biggest gripes with dependency graphs in Visual Studio 2010 was they were very slow, and that graphing a large amount of information was painful and could lead to "out of memory" errors. This has been addressed in Visual Studio 2012 with the addition of the code index. The code index is a local database that contains information related to your dependency graphs. When you generate a dependency graph for the first time, Visual Studio creates a code index that contains all the dependencies that it finds. This helps improve the performance of future operations because when changes occur to the code base, only the affected code is reindexed. The code index also helps to fix the "out of memory" errors found in the previous version.

The addition of the code index means that dependency graphs are rendered faster and are easier to drill into and out of. Another new feature is the ability to do incremental layouts. In Visual Studio

2010, when you wanted to make a change to a dependency graph, you had to lay out the entire graph from scratch. With the new incremental layout feature, only the relevant portions of the graph are redrawn, making the graph visualization faster.

Visual Studio Visualization and Modeling SDK

You can use the Visual Studio Visualization and Modeling SDK (VsVmSDK) to create model-based development tools that can integrate into Visual Studio. You can use this toolset to create domain-specific languages as well as to extend the UML models and diagrams within Visual Studio 2012. The VsVmSDK was originally available with Visual Studio 2010 and has been enhanced for Visual Studio 2012.

One of the new features available in the toolset is a code index SDK, which enables you to create a tool that can bulk index assemblies into the code index, thereby speeding up dependency graph generation. The SDK also contains Team Build tasks that can index assemblies during the build process. More information on the SDK can be found at `http://aka.ms/VS12VMSDK`.

SUMMARY

This chapter began by establishing the case for doing design — specifically visual design — in the first place. The discussion highlighted the three pillars that support that vision — namely, MDD, DSLs, and the "Code Understanding" experience.

This chapter concluded with a brief look at some of the UML diagrams that are available in Visual Studio 2012, as well as some of the new architecture tool features, such as the enhancements to dependency graphs.

Chapter 14 looks at how these UML diagrams are used and implemented in Visual Studio Ultimate 2012. These diagrams are extremely useful from a modeling perspective, especially for communicating what the project is trying to accomplish, and how the different systems will interact.

14

Top-Down Design with Use Case, Activity, Sequence, Component, and Class Diagrams

WHAT'S IN THIS CHAPTER?

➤ Creating and using use case and activity diagrams

➤ Creating and using sequence and component diagrams

➤ Generating code from a class diagram

WROX.COM CODE DOWNLOAD FOR THIS CHAPTER

The wrox.com code downloads for this chapter are found at `www.wrox.com/remtitle .cgi?isbn=1118314081` on the Download Code tab. The files are in the Chapter 14 download folder and individually named as shown throughout this chapter.

Chapter 13 introduced you to architecture and modeling in the software space, and hinted at all the architectural goodness available in Visual Studio Ultimate 2012. This chapter dives deeper into several aspects of that, looking at use case, activity, sequence, component, and class diagrams.

One advantage of modeling tools is that they enable you to design the architecture of the application. Part of that design process is defining common terms around the problem domain, and then ensuring that everyone on the team understands those concepts. Using the use case, activity, and sequence diagrams, you can model your application, while ensuring that everyone on the team understands exactly what is being built.

This chapter is divided into five main sections:

➤ Use Case Diagrams

➤ Activity Diagrams

➤ Sequence Diagrams

➤ Component Diagrams

➤ Class Diagrams

Each section begins with a walkthrough of how to build a diagram, as well as a diagram explanation. After that, the discussion looks at all the objects available when building a particular diagram.

USE CASE DIAGRAMS

A *use case diagram* provides a graphical overview of the functionality of a system. It shows who is using the system and what they can do with it.

A use case diagram does not show details of use cases themselves; instead it provides a summary view of use cases, actors, and systems. Details (such as the order in which steps must be performed to accomplish the use case) can be described in other diagrams and documents, and then linked to the related use case. Use cases (and, by extension, use case diagrams) deal only with the functional requirements of a system. The architecture and any internal details are described elsewhere.

Creating a Use Case Diagram

The following steps walk you through the process of creating a use case diagram. You are going to create a use case diagram of a customer interacting with an online bookstore system. The customer should be able to view the books offered and order a book. The bookstore should be able to update the list of available books, as well as deliver ordered books to the customer.

1. Open Visual Studio by selecting Start ➪ All Programs ➪ Microsoft Visual Studio 2012 ➪ Visual Studio 2012, and create a new modeling project by selecting File ➪ New ➪ Project to open the New Project window. Select the Modeling Project template, give the project a name and location, and click OK. A new modeling project opens in Solution Explorer.

2. Right-click the project in Solution Explorer and select Add ➪ New Item from the context menu.

3. Select the UML Use Case Diagram template and name it `OrderBook.usecasediagram`. Click the Add button to create this diagram. A blank use case diagram named `OrderBook.usecasediagram` is created in the modeling project and opened as a tab in Visual Studio.

4. From the toolbox on the left side of Visual Studio, drag a subsystem boundary onto the use case diagram.

5. In the Properties window, change the `Name` property for the subsystem to be `OnlineBookstore.` This subsystem can be used to represent either an entire system or its major components. Any use cases that the subsystem supports are drawn inside the subsystem.

6.   Add the actors to the use case diagram. The actors represent classes of users, organizations, and external systems that interact with the system being built. By default, the `Actor` object is represented as a person icon. A different image can be used by modifying the `Image Path` property of the object.

Drop two `Actor` objects onto the use case diagram, one on either side of the `OnlineBookstore` subsystem.

7.   In the Properties window, name the left actor `Customer` and the right actor `Bookstore`. The use case diagram should appear similar to Figure 14-1.

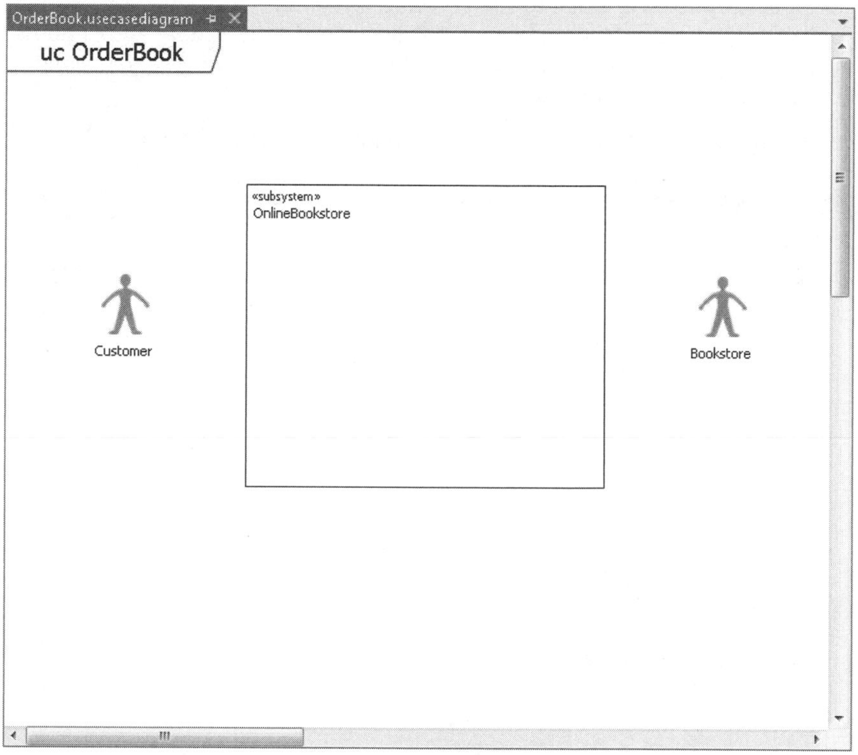

FIGURE 14-1

NOTE *To add multiple objects of the same type from the toolbox, double-click the toolbox object. Then, click multiple times on the diagram to add the objects. When finished, press the Esc key to return the cursor to its regular functionality.*

8.   When the actors are in place, drop the appropriate use cases onto the diagram. The use cases represent the activities that actors can perform, and appear as oval-shaped objects on the diagram.

Drop two use cases inside the `Online Bookstore` subsystem, and rename them **Provide Book List** and **Order Book.** Add one use case outside and below the subsystem and name it **Deliver Book.** The `Provide Book List` and `Order Book` use cases are part of the `OnlineBookstore` application, so they are drawn inside the subsystem. The `Deliver Book` use case is outside the scope of the application, so it is drawn external to the subsystem.

9. Finally, to finish this simple use case, use the `Association` object to show how each actor is related to each use case. An association indicates that an actor can take part in a particular use case. For example, the `Customer` actor can view a list of books at the online bookstore.

Double-click the `Association` object in the toolbox to select it. Click and hold the `Customer` actor and drag a line to the `Provide Book List` use case. An association is created between the actor and the use case. Do the same to the `Order Book` and `Deliver Book` use cases. Create associations the same way between the `Bookstore` actor and the `Provide Book List` and `Deliver Book` use cases.

When finished, the use case diagram should appear similar to Figure 14-2.

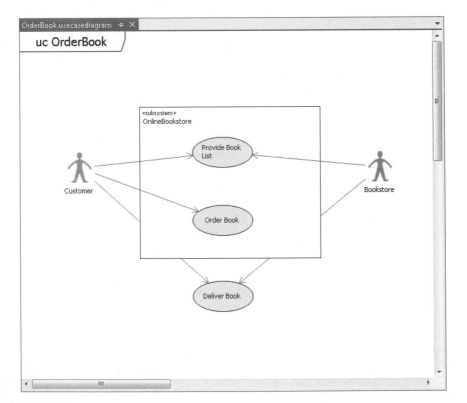

FIGURE 14-2

Although Figure 14-2 is a very simple use case diagram, it is still very informative. You can also have more-complex use case diagrams, with multiple subsystems, actors, and use cases. A best practice would be to start off describing the system with a few major use case diagrams. Each of those diagrams should define a major goal of the system. After those goals have been defined, use some of the other objects from the use case diagram toolbox to define the system in more detail.

Let's break the `Order Book` use case down in more detail. Figure 14-3 shows a use case diagram that does this by using the `Include` relationship.

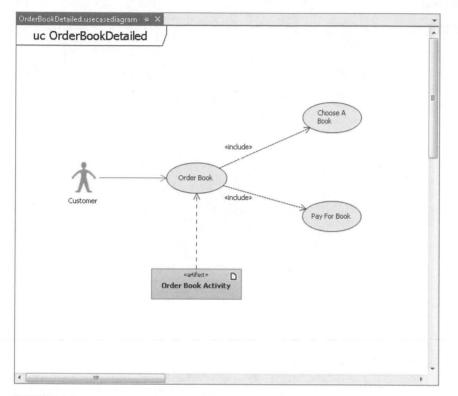

FIGURE 14-3

The `Include` relationship shows that a use case uses all the behavior of the included use case. To differentiate it from a regular association, the `Include` relationship is represented as a dotted line with an arrow on the end (per the UML 2.1.2 specification, available at `http://aka.ms/UML212`). The arrow should always point to the more detailed use case. The `Include` relationship is also labeled with the keyword `<<include>>`. Each of the included use cases is a step that the actor may have to take in order to complete the main use case. In this example, in order for the customer to order a book at the online bookstore, the customer must choose a book and then pay for the book.

A use case diagram does not specify in what order the particular use cases should happen, or when a particular use case is necessary. To make that information clear, attach an `Artifact` object to the general use case by dropping an `Artifact` object onto the use case diagram and then dragging a `Dependency` relationship between the `Artifact` element and the general use case. An `Artifact` element enables you to attach a separate document to the use case (for example, a text file that describes the steps to take) or reference another diagram.

Use Case Diagram Toolbox

Figure 14-4 shows the different elements and associations available for use case diagrams.

Table 14-1 describes the different elements and associations.

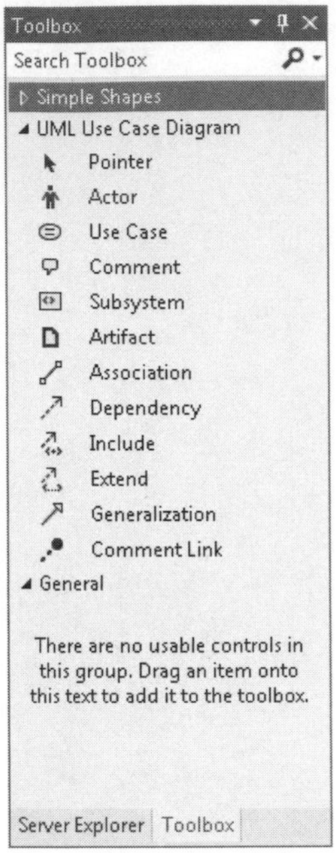

FIGURE 14-4

TABLE 14-1: Use Case Diagram Toolbox Objects

NAME	DESCRIPTION
Pointer	Turns the mouse back into a regular mouse pointer
Actor	Adds a user or external system that interacts with a system
Use Case	Adds a specification of actions that are performed in pursuit of a specific goal
Comment	Adds a comment for more details
Subsystem	Adds a system component. Place the use cases inside the subsystems that support it
Artifact	Adds a reference to a diagram or document
Association	Links an actor with a use case
Dependency	Specifies that the definition of one element depends on the definition of another
Include	Specifies that one use case invokes another use case
Extend	Specifies that one use case extends the definition of another in specific conditions

NAME	DESCRIPTION
Generalization	Specifies that one element is a specialized version of another, inheriting its features and constraints
Comment Link	Connects a comment to a diagram element

ACTIVITY DIAGRAMS

An *activity diagram* is used to show a business or software process as a workflow through a series of actions. These actions could be performed by any number of objects, including people, software, or computers. Activity diagrams can be used to model the logic captured in a particular use case or to model detailed business logic. One easy way to think of activity diagrams is to think of them as a flow chart.

An activity diagram always has a starting node, a series of activities, and a final node that indicates the end of the activity.

Creating an Activity Diagram

The following steps outline the process of creating an activity diagram that shows the sequence of activities for ordering a book from the online book store. A customer first chooses a book to order. After a book is chosen, the customer makes a decision whether to order more books or confirm the order. After the customer is finished selecting books, the customer confirms the book order and then pays for the order.

1. Using the same modeling project created earlier in the, "Creating a Use Case Diagram" section, right-click the project in Solution Explorer and select Add ➪ New Item from the context menu.

2. Select the UML Activity Diagram template and name it `OrderBook.activitydiagram`. Click the Add button to create this diagram. A blank activity diagram named `OrderBook. activitydiagram` is created in the modeling project and opened in a tab in Visual Studio.

3. From the toolbox, drag an `Initial Node` element onto the left of the diagram. This indicates the starting point for this activity. Every activity diagram requires this element.

4. Drag three `Action` elements onto the diagram to the right of the `Initial Node` element. Using the properties of the elements, name these items **Choose A Book, Confirm Order,** and **Pay For Book.** The action element represents a step in the activity that either the user or system performs.

5. From the toolbox, drag a `Merge Node` above the `Choose A Book` action. This node is used to merge multiple branches, usually split by a decision node (described shortly). A `Merge Node` requires two or more inputs and has a single output.

6. Drag and drop a `Decision Node` between the `Choose A Book` and `Confirm Order` actions. This node is used to create branching flows in the activity. For this activity diagram, after a book is chosen, the customer has a choice of confirming the order or selecting more books. A `Decision Node` has a single input and two or more outputs.

7. Drag an `Activity Final Node` to the right of the `Pay For Book` action. This indicates the end of the activity.

Next, you must add the connectors to show the flow of activity through this activity diagram. Double-click the `Connector` element to select it. On the activity diagram, drag a line between the `Initial Node` element and the `Merge Node`. Continue connecting the other elements on the diagram as follows:

1. Connect the `Merge Node` to the `Choose A Book` action.

2. Connect the `Choose A Book` action with the `Decision Node`.

3. Connect the `Decision Node` with the `Confirm Order` action.

4. Connect the `Decision Node` with the `Merge Node`.

5. Connect the `Confirm Order` action with the `Pay For Book` action.

6. Connect the `Pay For Book` action with the `Activity Final Node`.

7. Modify the `Guard` property of the `Connector` elements on the `Decision Node`, leaving the `Decision Node` to specify the reasons for the different pathways. On the `Connector` to the `Confirm Order` action, add the guard **Finished Ordering**. On the `Connector` to the `Merge Node`, add the guard **Wants To Order Multiple Books**.

When finished, the diagram should appear similar to Figure 14-5.

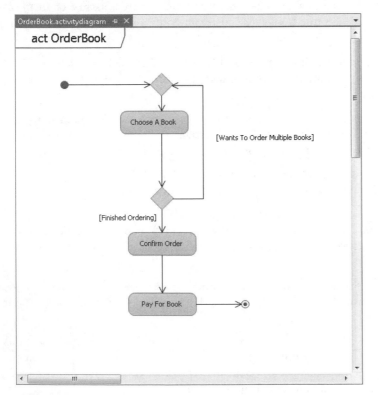

FIGURE 14-5

Concurrent Flow in an Activity Diagram

Activity diagrams can also be used to describe a sequence of actions that execute at the same time. This sequence of actions is known as a *concurrent flow*. Figure 14-6 shows an example of a concurrent flow activity diagram related to ordering a book online.

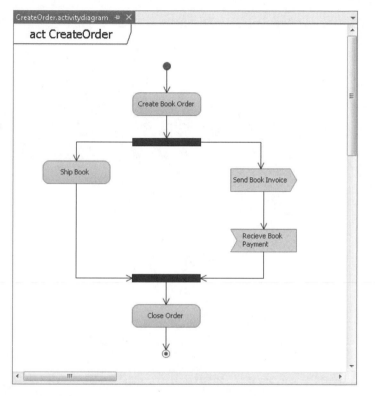

FIGURE 14-6

At the start of this activity diagram, an order is created. After an order is created, two different branch processes are started. The black bar that the `Create Book Order` action leads into is called a `Fork Node`, and is used to divide a single flow into concurrent flows. In this case, one flow leads to the `Ship Book` action. The other leads to the `Send Book Invoice` element.

The `Send Book Invoice` element is not a regular action element. It is a `Send Signal Action` element. This indicates an action that sends a message to another activity for something to happen. The `Receive Book Payment` is an `Accept Event Action` element. It is an action that waits for a message before the flow can continue. In the case of Figure 14-6, a book invoice will be sent, potentially to a payment system. The flow in the activity diagram waits until a response is received back, indicating that the book has been paid for. Both the `Ship Book` and the `Receive Book Payment` actions are then merged back into a single process using a `Join Node`. The activity ends with the closing of the order.

> **NOTE** *You can set the* Fork Node *and/or* Join Node *to a vertical orientation if you want.*

Activity Diagram Toolbox

Figure 14-7 shows the different elements and associations available for activity diagrams.

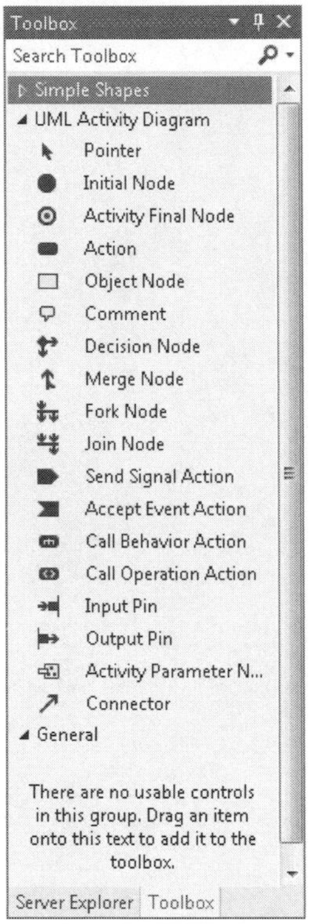

FIGURE 14-7

Table 14-2 describes the different elements and associations.

TABLE 14-2: Activity Diagram Toolbox Objects

NAME	DESCRIPTION
Pointer	Turns the mouse back into a regular mouse pointer
Initial Node	Adds the start of the activity
Activity Final Node	Adds an end to the activity
Action	Adds a single step that occurs in the activity

NAME	DESCRIPTION
Object Node	Adds a node that can transmit, buffer, filter, and transform objects
Comment	Adds a comment for more details
Decision Node	Divides a single incoming flow into a choice between alternate outgoing flows
Merge Node	Combines incoming alternate flows into a single outgoing flow
Fork Node	Divides a single incoming flow into concurrent outgoing flows
Join Node	Combines incoming concurrent flows into a single outgoing flow
Send Signal Action	Adds an action that sends a signal to another system or activity
Accept Event Action	Adds an action that waits for a signal or event
Call Behavior Action	An action that is defined in more detail on another activity diagram
Call Operation Action	An action that calls an operation on an instance of a class
Input Pin	Represents data that an action requires. It allows data to flow into an action
Output Pin	Represents data that an action produces. It allows data to flow out of an action
Activity Parameter Node	Creates a parameter that conveys data into or out of the activity
Connector	Adds a connection or flow between elements on the diagram

Adding an Activity Diagram to a Use Case Diagram

Earlier in this chapter when creating use case diagrams, you saw an Artifact element attached to a use case (see Figure 14-3). One available option with Artifact elements is the capability to associate them with an activity diagram (and, as an extension, any physical document).

To do this, drag an Artifact element onto the OrderBook.usecasediagram you created earlier in this chapter. In the properties window for the Artifact element, select the Hyperlink property. This will open the Open File dialog box, allowing you to select a diagram, document, or other file to associate with the Artifact element on the use case diagram.

> **NOTE** *To ensure that the file path remains valid on a team member's computer, only select files contained in the Visual Studio solution. Also, be aware that referencing Visual Studio UML diagrams outside the current project will not work properly.*

SEQUENCE DIAGRAMS

A *sequence diagram* is used to show the sequence of interactions between classes, components, subsystems, or actors. A sequence diagram is read from top to bottom, indicating the flow of time through the system. From left to right, the diagram itself shows the flow of control from one element to the next.

Creating a Sequence Diagram

The following steps walk you through creating a sequence diagram that shows the sequence of flow for ordering a book from the online bookstore. A customer first has the desire to purchase a book. At that point, the customer adds a book to a shopping cart. The order system checks the availability of the book and performs some internal processing. The availability of the book is returned to the ordering system. The payment system is represented by a separate sequence diagram, so a reference placeholder is inserted into this diagram. Finally, a message is sent to an unknown (or unspecified) system at the end of the process.

1. Using the same modeling project you have been using throughout this chapter, right-click the project in Solution Explorer, and, from the context menu, select Add ➪ New Item.

2. Select the UML Sequence Diagram template and name it **OrderBookSequenceDiagram .sequencediagram**. Click the Add button to create this diagram. A blank sequence diagram named `OrderBookSequenceDiagram.sequencediagram` is created in the modeling project and opened in a tab in Visual Studio.

3. From the toolbox, drag a `Lifeline` element onto the left of the diagram. This vertical line element represents participants in the described interaction. Time progresses down the lifeline, from top to bottom.

4. Using the Properties window, change the `Type` property to be **Customer** and set the `Actor` property equal to `True`. Notice the `Customer` lifeline has a symbol representing a person above it. This symbol is called an *actor* and indicates that this lifeline represents a participant external to the system being developed.

5. Drag two more `Lifeline` elements onto the diagram and set the `Type` properties to **Order** and **Book System,** respectively.

   The gray vertical shaded rectangles on each lifeline are called *execution occurrences*. These represent a period when the participant is executing an operation. Execution usually begins when the participant receives a message. From within an execution block, other messages can be sent to other participants, or even back to the execution block itself.

> **NOTE** *The box at the top of a lifeline has rounded corners to indicate that it has been generated from program code and is shown as a regular rectangle if it has been drawn by hand.*

This sequence diagram is started with a message from an unknown source. This is represented with an asynchronous message.

6. Select the `Asynchronous` element in the toolbox, select a blank space to the left of the `Customer` lifeline, and draw a line to the `Customer` lifeline. This creates the starting point into the sequence diagram, indicated by a black dot. This initial message is known as a *found message*. Change the `Name` property to **Want A Book.**

7. A create message must be sent to create a participant. If a participant receives a create message, it should be the first message it receives. Click the `Create` element in the toolbox. On the `Customer` lifeline, click the gray execution box area and drag a line to the `Order` lifeline. A dotted line is created between the two lifelines, and a gray execution box appears on the `Order` lifeline.

To start the ordering process, the customer must add an item that he or she wants to buy. This is represented using an `Asynchronous` message call. An `Asynchronous` element represents an interaction where the sender can continue immediately without waiting for the receiver.

8. In the toolbox, select the `Asynchronous` element. Click the `Customer` lifeline and drag a line to the `Order` lifeline. A solid line is created between the `Customer` and `Order` lifelines. Change the name of the element to **Add A Book.**

9. After a book is added, the book availability must be determined. This is done using a `Synchronous` message call. A `Synchronous` element represents an interaction where the sender waits for the receiver to return a response.

In the toolbox, select the `Synchronous` element. Click on the execution block on the `Order` lifeline and drag a line to the `Book System` lifeline. A solid arrow is created between the `Order` and `Book` lifelines. In addition, a dotted arrow is created from the `Book System` lifeline to the `Order` lifeline. This indicates control is to be returned to the sender—in this case, the `Order` lifeline.

10. Change the name of the element to **Check Book Availability.**

11. A participant can also send a message to itself—for example, if it were triggering internal methods for doing work. These messages are called *self messages*.

Select the `Asynchronous` element from the toolbox. On the `Book System` lifeline, click the `Check Book Availability` execution block. Drag a line farther down in the same block and release. This creates a solid arrow from the `Check Book Availability` execution block back onto the same execution block.

12. There is a complete payment system sequence that is not represented on this particular sequence diagram, but instead is shown on a separate diagram. To represent the contents of that separate diagram, use the `Interaction Use` element.

Click the `Interaction Use` element in the toolbox. Drag a box across all three lifelines, as all three are included in this reference. Change the name of the element to **Payment System.**

13. You can represent a message to an unknown or unspecified participant. This is known as a *lost message*.

Select the `Asynchronous` element from the toolbox. At the bottom of the `Book System` lifeline, drag a line from the lifeline to a blank area on the diagram. An arrow is created from the lifeline to a created black dot, indicating this message goes to an unknown participant.

When finished, the diagram should appear similar to Figure 14-8.

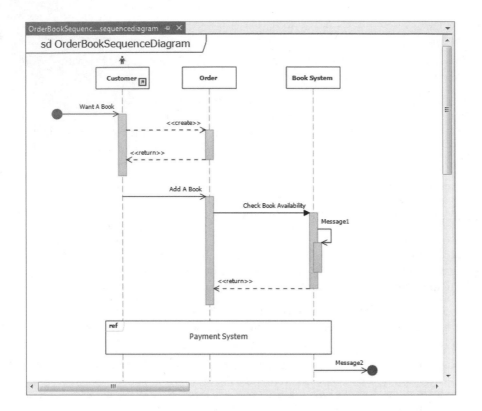

FIGURE 14-8

Sequence Diagram Toolbox

Figure 14-9 shows a screenshot of the different elements available for sequence diagrams.

Table 14-3 describes the different elements and associations.

TABLE 14-3: Sequence Diagram Toolbox Objects

NAME	DESCRIPTION
Pointer	Turns the mouse back into a regular mouse pointer
Lifeline	Adds a participant (such as a class or object) to an interaction sequence
Synchronous	Adds a message that calls an operation and expects a response
Asynchronous	Adds a message that calls an operation but does not expect a response
Create	Adds a message that calls an operation that creates an instance of the target
Comment	Adds a comment for more details

NAME	DESCRIPTION
Comment Link	Connects a comment to a diagram element
Interaction Use	Adds an interaction use to create a reusable sequence or to reference another sequence

FIGURE 14-9

COMPONENT DIAGRAMS

A sequence diagram enables you to model and visualize the messages of a system. With the *component diagram*, you can visualize the components of the system that implement the system functionality, as well as other puzzle pieces of the system (such as web services, user interfaces, COM components, and so on). A component diagram depicts the relationships between various components of your application or system.

A component diagram shows the parts of a design for a software system. These components could be executables, DLLs, or even entire systems. At this level, you aren't necessarily trying to decide exactly how things are being built. Rather, you are just trying to break down the architecture into something more manageable and understandable. You can use a component diagram to visualize the high-level structure of the system and the service behavior that the components both provide and consume.

Think of a *component* as a modular unit that is replaceable. You don't know how the internals of the component work. Instead, you know what interfaces a component provides or consumes.

Components on a component diagram have *interfaces*, either required interfaces or provided interfaces. An interface can be anything, from a website to a web service. A *required interface* indicates functionality that a component expects to consume. A *provided interface* indicates functionality that a component provides for other components to consume. Each required interface on a component diagram should be linked to a provided interface.

Creating component diagrams has a couple of nice benefits. It can help the development team understand an existing design and see potential ways to improve it. More importantly, thinking of the system as a collection of components with well-defined interfaces improves the separation between components, which can make the design easier to change as the requirements change.

Creating a Component Diagram

Use the following steps to create a component diagram that represents the different components of the online bookstore system. The different components include a web browser, the bookstore website (both the web application and the backend database), the bookstore payment system, and a way to process credit cards.

1. Using the same modeling project as used in previous sections, right-click the project in Solution Explorer and select Add ⇨ New Item from the context menu.

2. Select the UML Component Diagram template and name it `BookComponents .componentdiagram.` Click the Add button to create this diagram. A blank component diagram named `BookComponents.componentdiagram` is created in the modeling project and opened in a tab in Visual Studio.

3. There are two options for adding components to the diagram:

   ➤ Using the toolbox, click the `Component` element, then click a blank area of the diagram. An empty `Component` element appears on the diagram. This is useful for creating new components.

   ➤ Existing components from other diagrams in the same modeling project can also be added to the diagram. Either open the existing diagram or open the UML Model Explorer window (by selecting View ⇨ Other Windows ⇨ UML Model Explorer). Right-click the component to add to the component diagram and then select Copy. Right-click a blank area of the component diagram and select Paste Reference to create a copy of the component on the new diagram.

   > **NOTE** *You can also just drag the component from the Model Explorer onto the diagram.*

4. From the Toolbox window, click the `Component` element and click a blank area on the diagram to create a new `Component` element. Select the component and change its name to `Web Browser.` Following this same method, add the following components to the component diagram.

   ➤ `Book Web Application`

   ➤ `Book Web App Database`

➤ External Credit Card Processor Gateway

➤ Book Payment System

➤ Book Payment System Database

After you've added these components, the component diagram should resemble Figure 14-10.

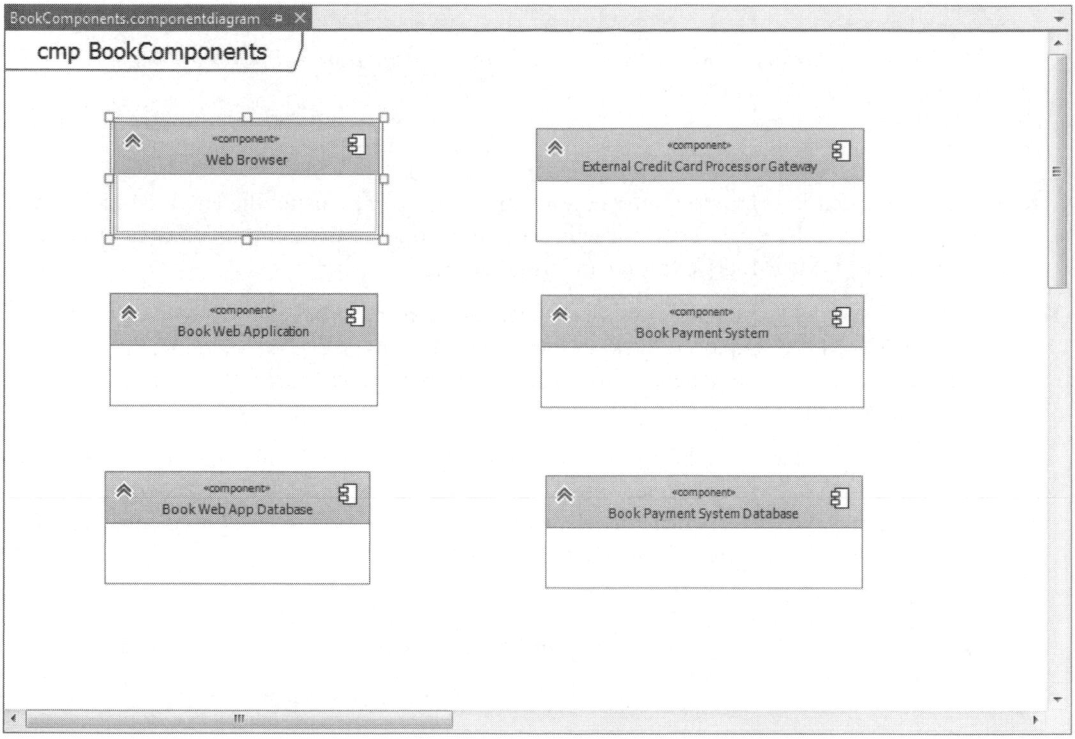

FIGURE 14-10

5. From the Toolbox window, click the `Provided Interface` element and then click on the `Book Web Application` component. The provided interface symbol (or lollipop) attaches itself to the `Book Web Application` component with a default name of `Interface1`. This component is going to represent the website used for ordering books. Select the `Provided Interface` element, and, in the Properties window, rename it to **Book Web Site.**

6. Add another `Provided Interface` element to the `Book Payment System` component, and name it **IBookPaymentService.** This element exposes a web service for interacting with the payment system. Finally, add a `Provided Interface` element to the `External Credit Card Processor Gateway` component and name it **ICreditCardProcessingGateway.** This element exposes a web service for interacting with the external credit card processor.

7. Add the required interfaces. A required interface represents behavior that a component consumes through an interface. As with adding components to the diagram, there are two options for adding interfaces (both required and provided interfaces) to the diagram. You can add a new interface from the Toolbox window, or, using the UML Model Explorer, you can drag an existing interface onto the diagram.

8. You must show that the `Web Browser` component utilizes the book website interface exposed by the `Book Web Application` component.

   From the toolbox, click the `Required Interface` element and then click the `Web Browser` component on the diagram. Rename the interface to **Book Web Site.**

> **NOTE** *The interface elements can be easily repositioned on a component by dragging them to the appropriate location.*

9. Add a required interface to the `Book Web Application` by using the UML Model Explorer. If the UML Model Explorer window is not visible, open it by going to View ➪ Other Windows ➪ UML Model Explorer in Visual Studio.

10. The UML Model Explorer shows all the elements that have been added to the central model. In the UML Model Explorer, click and drag the `IBookPaymentService` interface to the `Book Web Application` component. This creates another instance of the `IBookPaymentService` provided interface.

11. You need this interface to be a required interface. To change the interface type, select the `IBookPaymentService` provided interface on the `Book Web Application` component. Click the smart tag that appears near the element and select Convert to Required Interface. The interface type changes from provided to required.

> **NOTE** *You can also select the smart tag for a required interface and change it into a provided interface.*

12. Select the `Required Interface` element in the Toolbox window and click the `Book Payment System` component to create a required interface on that component. Rename the interface to be **ICreditCardProcessingGateway.** The component diagram should now resemble Figure 14-11.

13. Next you need to show which provided interfaces satisfy which required interfaces by using the `Dependency` element. A `Dependency` element always connects a required interface (or hook) to a provided interface (or lollipop).

   In the Toolbox window, select the `Dependency` element. On the component diagram, select the `Book Web Site` required interface on the `Web Browser` component and then select the `Book Web Site` provided interface on the `Book Web Application` component. A dotted arrow is created from the required interface to the provided interface, indicating that the provided interface satisfies the required interface. On the component diagram, select the dependency dotted arrow that was just created. In the Properties window, change the name to be **HTTP**. This provides a visual indicator on the component diagram that this is an HTTP connection between the two components.

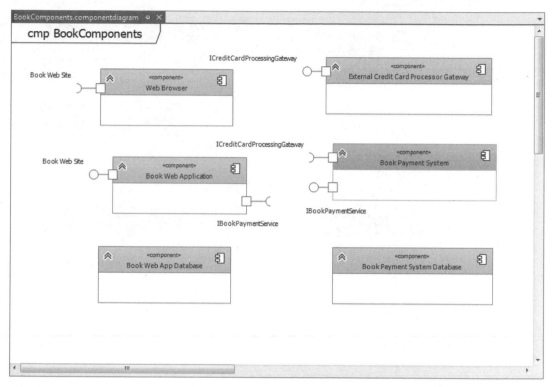

FIGURE 14-11

14. In the Toolbox window, select the Dependency element again. On the component diagram, select the IBookPaymentService required interface on the Book Web Application component. Then select the IBookPaymentService provided interface on the Book Payment System component. Finally, select the Dependency element from the toolbox and connect the ICreditCardProcessingGateway required interface on the Book Payment System component to the ICreditCardProcessingGateway provided interface on the External Credit Card Processor Gateway.

15. Create the dependency relationship between the Book Web Application and the Book Web App Database components by selecting the Dependency element from the Toolbox window, clicking the Book Web Application component, and then clicking the Book Web App Database component. A dotted arrow is drawn between the two, indicating the dependency of the web application on the database. Do the same thing between the Book Payment System component and the Book Payment System Database component. The component diagram is now complete, as shown in Figure 14-12.

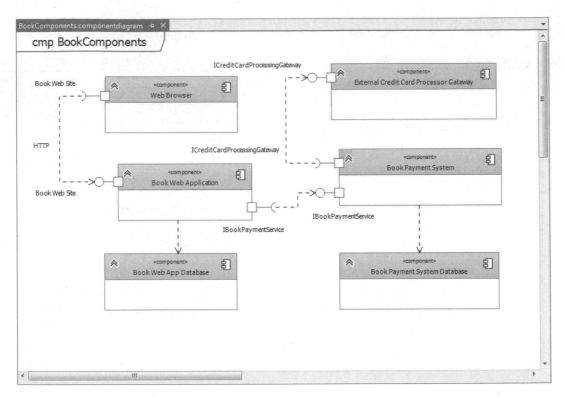

FIGURE 14-12

> **NOTE** *To show how a larger component is comprised of smaller components, a component can also be placed inside other components on a component diagram.*

Component Diagram Toolbox

Figure 14-13 shows the different elements and associations available for component diagrams.

Table 14-4 describes the different elements and associations.

TABLE 14-4: Component Diagram Toolbox Objects

NAME	DESCRIPTION
Pointer	Turns the mouse back into a regular mouse pointer
Component	Adds a component that defines a reusable unit of system functionality
Dependency	Defines how an element depends on another element. Begin the relationship from the dependent element

NAME	DESCRIPTION
Delegation	Designates behavior between a port on an outer component and an interface on an inner component
Provided Interface	Adds an interface that a component provides to other components
Required Interface	Adds an interface that a component requires from other components
Comment	Adds a comment for more details
Generalization	Defines how a component derives from another component. Begin the relationship from the derived component
Connector	Creates a default relationship between shapes based on the types of shapes being connected
Part Assembly	Specifies a connection between parts in a component. Connects a required interface on one part to a provided interface on another part

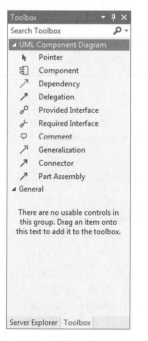

FIGURE 14-13

CLASS DIAGRAMS

Class diagrams depict the classes within an application or system and the relationship that exists between them. Different symbols represent the varying relationships that may exist (such as inheritance or association). This information is described independent of any reference to a particular implementation of the class. The purpose of the class diagram is to focus on the logical aspects of the classes instead of how they are implemented.

> **NOTE** *This chapter discusses UML class diagrams, or logical class diagrams. There is another type of class diagram, called a .NET class diagram, used to visualize program code. That is not discussed in this book. More information on this type of diagram can be found at* `http://aka.ms/vs12classdiagram.`

In a class diagram, a *type* is a class, interface, or enumeration. Class and interface objects can have attributes defined. An *attribute* is a value that can be attached to an instance of a class or an interface. Classes and interfaces can also have operations defined. An *operation* is a method or function that can be performed by an instance of a class or interface.

On a class diagram, you can draw associations between any pairs of types. An *association* indicates that the system being developed stores links between the instances of the associated types. An association is a diagrammatic method of showing an attribute or pair of attributes. For example, if you have a class `BookStore` that has an attribute of type `Book`, you can state that definition by drawing an association between `Bookstore` and `Book`.

Using the Model Explorer, you can locate interfaces you have defined on the component diagram and drag those directly onto the class diagram to create them.

Creating a Class Diagram

Use the following steps to create a class diagram that shows the relationship between a `Store` class, a `BookStore` class, and a `Books` class. A bookstore is a more specific version of a store, and a bookstore contains multiple books.

1. Using the same modeling project from before, right-click the project in Solution Explorer, and, from the context menu, select Add ➪ New Item.

2. Select the UML Class Diagram template and name it **BooksClassDiagram.classdiagram.** Click the Add button to create this diagram. A blank UML class diagram named BooksClassDiagram is created in the modeling project and opened in a tab Visual Studio.

3. In the Toolbox tab, click the `Class` element and then click a blank space on the UML class diagram. This creates a class object on the diagram. In the properties for the class, change the name to be **Store.** This is going to be a generic store class that the book store object inherits from. Set the `Is Abstract` property of the `Store` class to `True`, to indicate it is an abstract class.

> **NOTE** *Notice how, when setting the class to be abstract, the font of the title changes to italic.*

4. The `Store` class has a couple of generic attributes that apply to all stores, such as location and store hours.

Right-click the `Store` class and select Add ⇨ Attribute to create a new attribute. Name the attribute `Location`. Select the `Location` attribute, and, in the Properties window, set the `Type` property to be `String`. Add a second attribute named `StoreHours` and set its type to be `String` as well.

5. Create the book store class. The book store class inherits from the `Store` class created earlier, as it is a specialized type of store.

Using the Toolbox window, add another `Class` object to the diagram, under the `Store` object, and name it **BookStore**. Select the `Inheritance` element in the Toolbox window. Click the `BookStore` class and then click the `Store` class. A solid arrow appears that points from the `BookStore` class to the `Store` class, indicating that the `BookStore` inherits from the `Store`.

The inherited operations and attributes are not typically shown on specialized types, which is why the `Store` class attributes are not displayed on the `BookStore` class. However, you can use the smart tag on the inheritance arrow to add inherited operations to the specialized class. Simply click the smart tag and select Override Operations. Then select which operations to show on the specialized class.

6. Now create a class for the books. Add another class object to the class diagram, below the `BookStore` class, and rename it **Book**. Add two attributes to the `Book` class: `Price` of type `Integer`, and `NumberOfPages` of type `Integer`. Select the `Association` element from the Toolbox window, click the `BookStore` class, and then click on the `Book` class. An `Association` element is used to represent any kind of linkage between two elements, regardless of how the linkage is actually implemented in the code itself.

7. A `BookStore` can have multiple books in it, so you must modify the `Multiplicity` property for the `Book` class.

Select the `Association` linking the `BookStore` and `Book` classes. In the Properties window, click the arrow next to the `Second Role` property to expand it. Change the `Multiplicity` value to be `*`, indicating the `BookStore` can contain multiple books.

8. Add an operation for ordering books to the `BookStore` class. Right-click the class and select Add ⇨ Operation. Name the operation **OrderBook.**

9. You must set the parameters and the return type for this operation by selecting the `OrderBook` operation and going to the Properties window. In the Properties window, set the `Return Type` to be `Boolean`. Click the ellipsis in the `Parameters` field to open the Operation Parameter Collection Editor window.

In the Parameter Collection Editor window, click the Add button to create a new parameter. Set the name of the parameter to be `Item`, and the type to be `Book`. Click the Add button again to create a second parameter named `Quantity` with a type of `Integer`. Click the OK button to close the Operation Parameter Collection Editor window.

Figure 14-14 shows the final result of the class diagram.

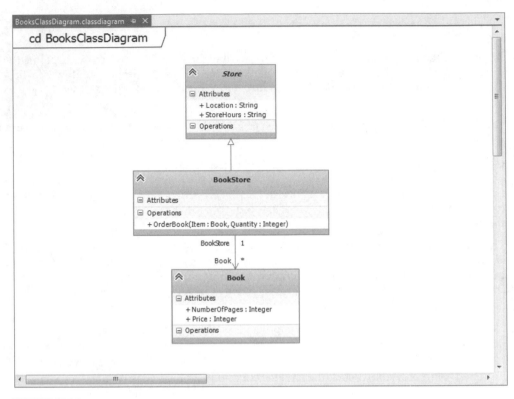

FIGURE 14-14

Class Diagram Toolbox

Figure 14-15 shows the different elements and associations available for class diagrams.

Table 14-5 describes the different elements and associations.

TABLE 14-5: Class Diagram Toolbox Objects

NAME	DESCRIPTION
Pointer	Turns the mouse back into a regular mouse pointer
Class	Adds a type that defines a class
Interface	Adds an interface to specify the attributes and operations that classes require to realize this interface
Enumeration	Adds a type that defines a list of specific values
Package	Adds a package to organize types according to their namespaces
Comment	Adds a comment for more details

NAME	DESCRIPTION
Association	Defines how an element interacts with another element. Begin the relationship from the referencing type
Aggregation	Specifies that the source type refers to parts of the target type. The parts can be shared with another owner
Composition	Specifies that the source type has parts of the target type. The parts cannot be shared with another owner
Dependency	Defines how a type depends on another type. Begin the relationship from the dependent type
Inheritance	Defines how a type inherits or realizes the members of another type
Package Import	Defines how a package imports types defined in another package. Begin the relationship from the package that uses another package
Connector	This connection tool creates a default relationship between shapes, based on the types of shape being connected

FIGURE 14-15

Generating Code from a UML Class Diagram

Visual Studio 2012 includes a new feature: the ability to generate code from a UML class diagram. Using the class diagram as a base, you can generate skeleton code from the class diagram elements.

In addition, you can also create UML class diagrams from your code base as well. This functionality wasn't available in Visual Studio 2010 unless you installed the Visual Studio 2010 Visualization and Modeling Feature Pack.

To generate code from a class diagram, right-click the class diagram and select `Generate Code` from the context menu. By default, executing this command generates a C# type for each type on the UML class diagram. The following are the default results for generating code:

➤ A C# type is produced for each type on the UML model. Each type is placed in a separate code file.

➤ A C# property is generated for each attribute of a UML class.

➤ A C# method is generated for each operation of a UML class.

➤ A C# field is generated for each navigable association in which the class participates.

➤ If the UML type is contained in a package, the generated C# type is placed inside a namespace, and the file is generated in a folder with the same name as the namespace.

However, you can customize this behavior — including the language generated as well as the different outputs — by modifying the text templates that are used for generating the code.

> **NOTE** *For more information on customizing the Generate Code command, see "Customizing the Generate Code Command" in the MSDN Library:* `http://msdn.microsoft.com/en-us/library/ff657795.aspx#custom.`

Figure 14-16 shows the `BookStore.cs` C# class that was generated by running the `Generate Code` command against the `BooksClassDiagram.classdiagram` class diagram created earlier in this section. A new class named `BookStore` that inherits from class `Store` was created. Also, a stub method for the operation `OrderBook` was created as well.

SUMMARY

This chapter examined the capabilities of use case, activity, sequence, component, and class diagrams. You looked at how to create a use case diagram, and learned about its different components. Next, you learned about activity diagrams, where, in addition to examining an example of how to build a diagram, you also learned how to link an activity diagram back to a use case diagram. You then examined sequence diagrams, their components, and how to create them.

You learned the purpose behind component diagrams, how to create them, and the different elements available to component diagrams. Finally, you learned about class diagrams and how they are used. You learned about the different elements that are available for class diagrams and concluded the chapter with a look at how to generate code from a class diagram.

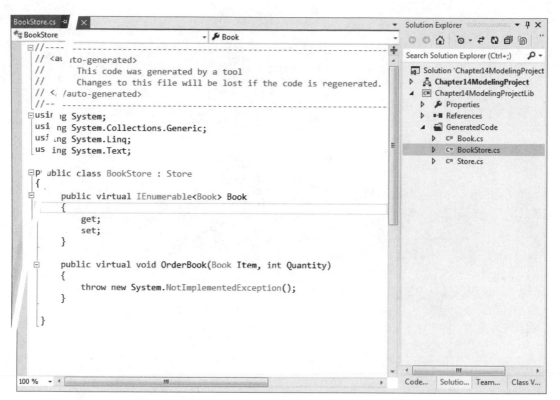

FIGURE 14-16

Chapter 15 discusses how you can use the Architecture Explorer to drill down into the existing project, which helps you to understand the different aspects of the project. The information in the Architecture Explorer can then be turned into a graphical view by creating a dependency graph.

15

Analyzing Applications Using Architecture Explorer and Dependency Graphs

WHAT'S IN THIS CHAPTER?

➤ Exploring the Architecture Explorer

➤ Using the Architecture Explorer to understand existing code

➤ Visualizing existing code using dependency graphs

WROX.COM CODE DOWNLOADS FOR THIS CHAPTER

The wrox.com code downloads for this chapter are found at www.wrox.com/remtitle
.cgi?isbn=1118314081 on the Download Code tab. The files are in the Chapter 15 download
folder and individually named as shown throughout this chapter.

Every software developer has been in the following situation at some point in time: You have
just started a new job with a new company, and you're expecting to go in and write some
brand-new, fancy application. You are up to speed on some of the latest coding technologies,
methodologies, and languages. You arrive for work ready to sit down and use everything you
know to crank out some code to help the company succeed.

And then it happens. There is a legacy system that was built several years ago that must be
updated. You are the lucky developer who has been assigned to make that update — never
mind that you have no idea or concept of how the application works, the inner workings of the
calls between different objects, or how it interacts with other third-party add-ins.

Before Visual Studio 2010 Ultimate, the only solution to this problem was to get your hands dirty in the code. You would have to open up the code files and start tracing (as best you could) how the logic flows between the different classes and components that make up the application. Maybe you would even try (as best you could) to diagram out the logic flow on a piece of scratch paper.

Visual Studio 2010 Ultimate changed all that with the introduction of the Architecture Explorer tool, and Visual Studio Ultimate 2012 has added even more functionality to make exploring your application easier. Using Architecture Explorer, you can quickly learn more about your current application by visualizing the organization and relationships among the various parts. By using Architecture Explorer in conjunction with dependency graphs, a developer is able to analyze an existing system and quickly understand it. These tools also enable the developer to find areas in the application that should be improved or modified.

This chapter examines both Architecture Explorer and dependency graphs. The chapter begins with a discussion about the Architecture Explorer tool, what it is, and how it was designed to be used. From there, you learn about using Architecture Explorer and how you can use it to drill down into your existing application.

After that, you learn how to take the information from Architecture Explorer and make it graphical by turning it into a dependency diagram. Dependency diagrams are a nice way to graphically view your code, as well as code contained in other managed DLLs (such as the .NET Framework). In Visual Studio Ultimate 2012, dependency graphs have received some nice enhancements, including the ability to visualize code without the use of Architecture Explorer. In this chapter you find out how to utilize those features and learn about the Code Index, a new back-end database for dependency graphs that helps speed the visualization process.

UNDERSTANDING THE CODE BASE

Though the example used through this chapter is rather simplistic, it works well to introduce the different capabilities of Architecture Explorer and dependency diagrams. So, let's take a look at the code base used throughout this chapter so that later sections will make more sense.

Figure 15-1 shows the projects and code files that make up the sample solution.

This solution is made up of two project files:

➤ `FirstProject` — This project contains two class files, `FirstClass.cs` and `SecondClass.cs`. The `FirstClass.cs` class file contains two methods, `Method1` and `Method2`. The `SecondClass.cs` class file contains one method, `Method3`.

➤ `SecondProject` — This project contains one class file, `ThirdClass.cs`. The `ThirdClass.cs` class file contains three methods: `Method4`, `Method5`, and `Method6`.

Getting confused yet? Let's add to it a little more:

➤ `Method1` calls `Method3` and `Method2`.

➤ `Method2` calls `Method1`.

➤ `Method3` doesn't call any other methods.

➤ `Method4` calls `Method1`.

> ➤ `Method5` calls `Method3`.

> ➤ `Method6` doesn't call any other methods.

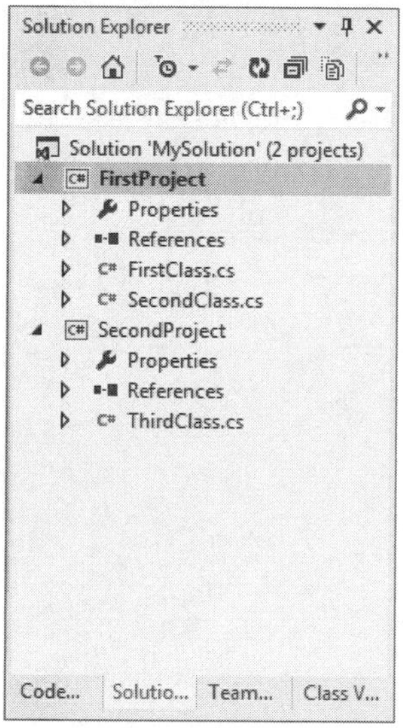

FIGURE 15-1

Whew! All of that sounds just a little bit confusing, and this is only a contrived solution with two projects and three classes. Imagine what it would seem like with a real software solution, with hundreds of projects, and thousands of classes and methods. As you are about to learn, though, Architecture Explorer and dependency graphs are going to help with the understanding of any project, both small and large.

ARCHITECTURE EXPLORER BASICS

In Visual Studio Ultimate 2012, you use Architecture Explorer to drill down into your existing code, which enables you to select the code you want to visualize using a dependency graph. You can use Architecture Explorer to browse existing source code open in Visual Studio Ultimate 2012, as well as browse compiled managed code located in `.dll` or `.exe` files. You can extend Architecture Explorer with third-party tools, providing the capability to browse other domains of code or other items. After you have drilled down into your code and selected the items you are interested in, you can turn that information into a dependency graph.

> **NOTE** *The Architecture Explorer is only available in Visual Studio Ultimate 2012, and will work on any managed code from .NET 2.0 onward.*

Understanding the Architecture Explorer Window

To open Architecture Explorer, open Visual Studio Ultimate 2012. From the main menu of Visual Studio, select View ⇨ Architecture Explorer. Alternatively, from the main menu of Visual Studio, you can select Architecture ⇨ Windows ⇨ Architecture Explorer.

> **NOTE** *The shortcut keys for opening Architecture Explorer are Ctrl+/ and Ctrl+R.*

Figure 15-2 shows an initial view of Architecture Explorer.

FIGURE 15-2

Architecture Explorer represents structures as *nodes* and relationships as *links*. As you browse through your code base using Architecture Explorer, nodes are displayed in successive columns to the right. The first column in Figure 15-2 shows the initial domains and views that are available for browsing. Selecting a domain or view causes a new node to appear to the right with the results of that selection.

> **NOTE** *You can browse all the way to the level of statements for Visual C# and Visual Basic projects. For other languages, you can browse to the procedure level.*

When you select a node in a column, the next column shows node information that is logically related to the selection made in the initial column. For example, selecting a class in a column shows the members of that class in the following column. You have the capability to select multiple nodes in multiple columns and then display that information as a dependency graph.

Architecture Explorer Options

As you can see in Figure 15-2, there are four options (represented as icons) available on the left side of the Architecture Explorer window.

The first option provides the capability to create a new dependency graph document from all the nodes currently selected in Architecture Explorer. To include only the nodes in the current column, you can press and hold the Ctrl key before clicking this option.

The second option enables you to add the selected nodes from Architecture Explorer to an existing dependency graph that is currently visible in Visual Studio. As with the first option, to include only the nodes that are in the current column, you can press and hold the Ctrl key before clicking this option.

The third option enables you to export the information from Architecture Explorer into a `.dgml` file. A Directed Graph Markup Language (DGML) file is the XML schema used to define a dependency graph. Selecting this option exports all the information open, in all of the columns, into a `.dgml` file that you can view at a later date.

The fourth option resets Architecture Explorer to its initial state, cleaning up the window and enabling you to start from the beginning.

Navigating through Architecture Explorer

To begin navigating through Architecture Explorer, select one of the rows in the first column. You have several options.

Under the Visual Studio column heading you can choose to view the information in your solution either by classes or through a solution view, which enables you to view the different files in your solution. If you don't want to drill down through all the files in a solution, you can click the Select Files option and open only the files you are interested in.

For this example, let's navigate through the code using the Class View options. In Architecture Explorer, select Class View under Visual Studio <My Solution>. This opens a new column to the right of the selected column, displaying a list of all the different namespaces in the solution, as shown in Figure 15-3.

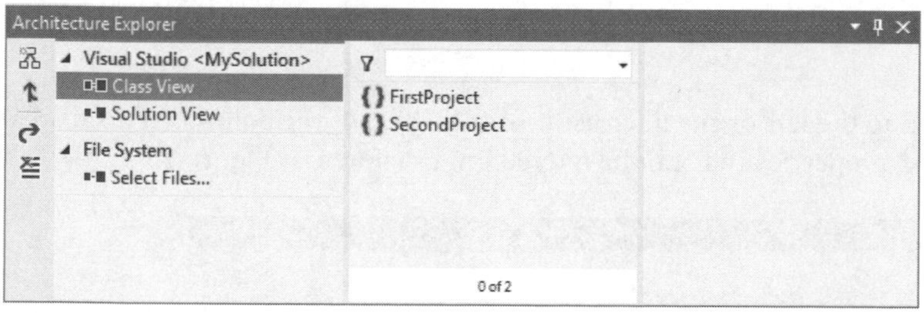

FIGURE 15-3

In Figure 15-3, you see that the two namespaces currently in the solution (`FirstProject` and `SecondProject`) are displayed on the right of the screen.

Obviously, for a large project, you could have many namespaces, which could result in a large scrolling list in this column. The list box at the top of the column enables you to filter the information in this column. For example, if you only wanted to see namespaces that began with "Second," you could type **Second** in the list box, press Enter, and the contents of the column would be filtered, as shown in Figure 15-4.

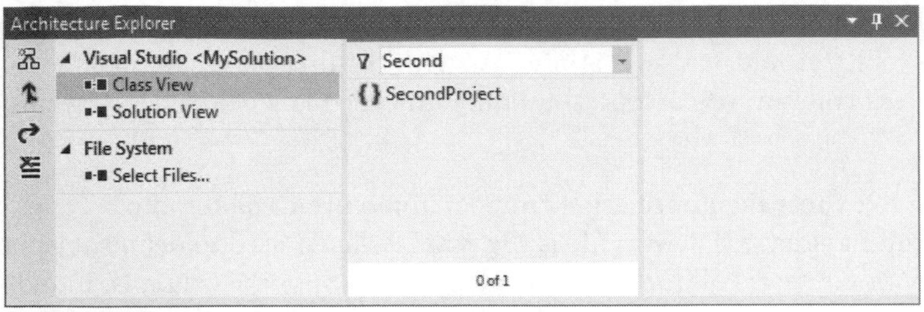

FIGURE 15-4

Notice the differences between Figure 15-3 and Figure 15-4. Figure 15-3 displays all the namespaces in the solution. Figure 15-4 displays only the namespaces that match the filter expression. Also, notice the filter icon that is added in the lower right of the column, giving a visual indication that the column is currently being filtered.

> **NOTE** *When you type in a filter, a substring search is performed. For example, if you enter* **c** *for the filter statement, it matches on both* `FirstProject` *and* `SecondProject`.

To clear the filtering on a column, simply delete the filter statement and press Enter. This removes the filter and displays the entire contents of the column.

From the namespace column, you can navigate into the different classes contained in a particular namespace. Selecting the `FirstProject` namespace opens a new column to the right, containing the classes contained in the `FirstProject` namespace — in this case, `FirstClass` and `SecondClass`. As mentioned previously, you have the capability to filter on this column by entering your filter criteria into the list box at the top of the column. You also have the capability to filter based on different categories and properties.

Click the filter button located to the left of the filter list box at the top of the column. This displays all the possible categories and properties that can be filtered on, as shown in Figure 15-5.

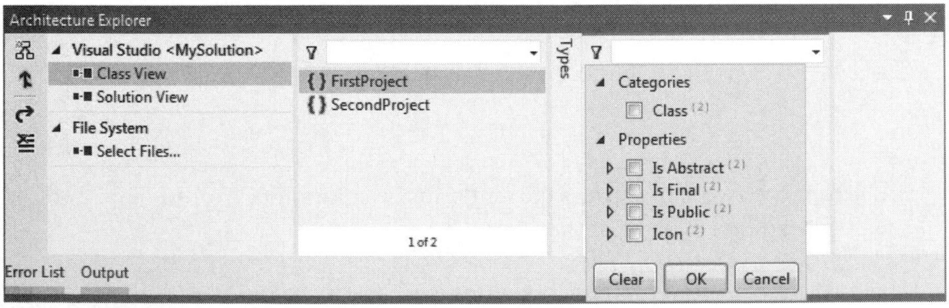

FIGURE 15-5

For this particular column on classes, you have the following filter options:

➤ Class

➤ Is Abstract

➤ Is Final

➤ Is Public

➤ Icon

You have the option of selecting one or multiple filter options, allowing you to drill down into the information contained in the column in a variety of ways.

Exploring Options for Namespaces

In addition to the filtering options mentioned previously, you have another option for controlling what is displayed in a column. In Figure 15-5, just to the left of the column containing the classes, there is a collapsed column labeled Types. Clicking that collapsed column expands it, as shown in Figure 15-6.

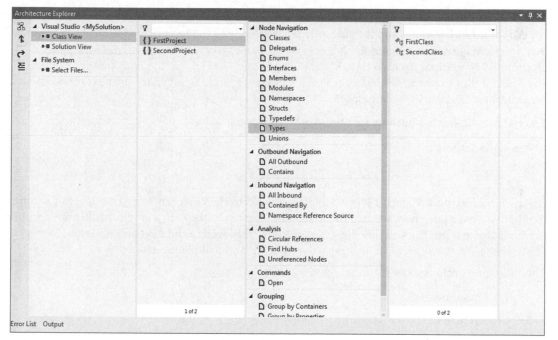

FIGURE 15-6

This column provides a variety of options for determining what is initially displayed in the column. The first section is the Node Navigation section. By default, the Types node is selected, which shows all the different available types — in this case, `FirstClass` and `SecondClass`. You have the capability to select the following nodes for display:

➤ Classes

➤ Delegates

➤ Enums

➤ Interfaces

➤ Members

➤ Modules

➤ Namespaces

➤ Structs

➤ Typedefs

➤ Types

➤ Unions

You can select multiple nodes by holding down the Ctrl key while you select the nodes. Each time you select a node, the column to the right recalculates with the new data to display.

You have the capability to organize the link types into two categories: outbound and inbound. These categories describe the direction of the link in relation to the currently selected node.

An *outbound link* points from the currently selected node to the next related node. For example, say that you have currently selected the `FirstProject` namespace. If you select All Outbound under Outbound Navigation, the two classes, `FirstClass` and `SecondClass`, are displayed. `FirstClass` and `SecondClass` exist in the `FirstProject` namespace, and, as such, are the next related nodes beneath the `FirstProject` namespace.

You have the following options for Outbound Navigation:

➤ All Outbound

➤ Contains

An *inbound link* points from a previously related node to the currently selected node. For example, say that you have currently selected the `FirstProject` namespace. If you select All InBound under Inbound Navigation, the solution file `MySolution` is displayed in the next column. `MySolution` exists above the `FirstProject` namespace from a hierarchical perspective.

The following options exist for Inbound Navigation:

➤ All Inbound

➤ Contained By

➤ Namespace Reference Source

You also have the capability to perform Analysis and Grouping options. Using the Analysis options, you can look for circular references or *hubs* (for example, classes) that are not being called or used. The Grouping options also enable you to group by container or properties.

The following options exist for Analysis:

➤ Circular References

➤ Find Hubs

➤ Unreferenced Nodes

The following options exist for Grouping:

➤ Group by Containers

➤ Group by Properties

Exploring Options for Classes

Previously, you learned about some of the Node Navigation options from a namespace perspective. Let's continue the example by selecting the `FirstClass` class in Architecture Explorer to see what Node Navigation options are from a class perspective. Figure 15-7 shows Architecture Explorer after the `FirstClass` class has been selected.

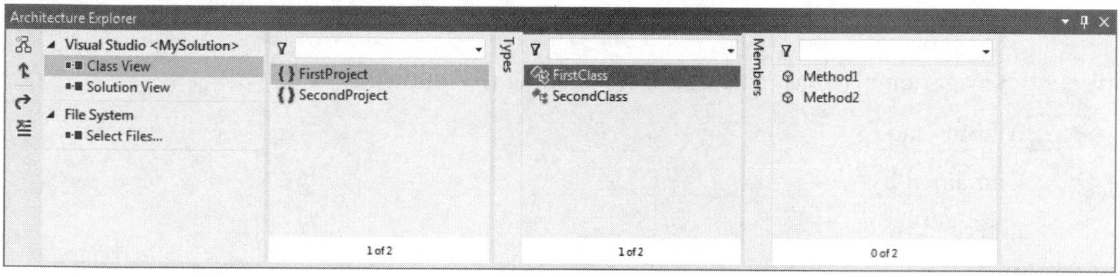

FIGURE 15-7

By default, Node Navigation defaults to Members. As you can see in Figure 15-7, `FirstClass` has only two members: two methods named `Method1` and `Method2`. As you might expect, the filtering options at the top of the column work the same as they have in previous columns. However, now that you are working on a class level as opposed to a namespace level, you have different navigation options.

From the Node Navigation options, you can view any of the following information about the selected class:

➤ Classes

➤ Delegates

➤ Enums

➤ Generic Arguments

➤ Generic Parameters

➤ Interfaces

➤ Members

➤ Structs

➤ Types

Outbound Navigation has several more options available to it, as you would expect. Classes can inherit from other classes, implement interfaces, and have attributes. The following are the Outbound Navigation options:

- ➤ All Outbound
- ➤ Contains
- ➤ Generic Arguments
- ➤ Generic Parameters
- ➤ Implements
- ➤ Inherits From
- ➤ Uses Attribute

Inbound Navigation also has more options, including the following:

- ➤ All Inbound
- ➤ Contained By
- ➤ Inherited By
- ➤ Used By

The Analysis patterns and Grouping options are the same as before.

Exploring Options for Members

For this example, drill down one more level to look at some of the Node Navigation options available at a member level. In Architecture Explorer, select the `Method1` method, as shown in Figure 15-8.

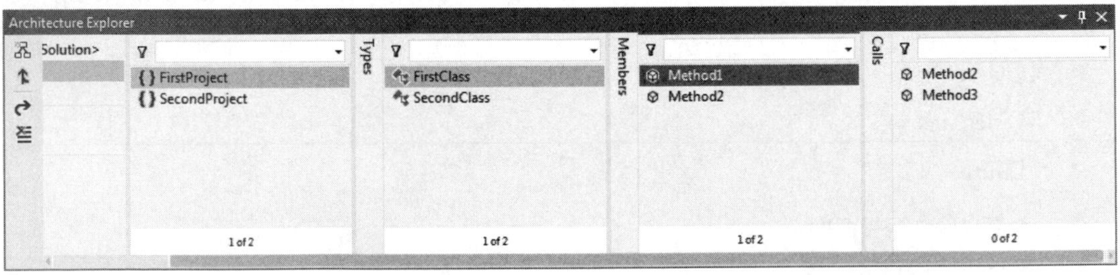

FIGURE 15-8

As you would expect, the Node Navigation options have changed again. By default, when you select a method, the resulting column in Architecture Explorer shows all the outbound calls that method makes (that is, all the methods that the selected method uses).

From a Node Navigation perspective, you can view any of the following information about the selected method:

➤ Classes

➤ Generic Arguments

➤ Generic Parameters

➤ Methods

➤ Parameters

➤ Types

Outbound Navigation has several more options available to it, as you would expect. The following are the Outbound Navigation options:

➤ All Outbound

➤ Calls

➤ Contains

➤ Function Pointers

➤ Generic Arguments

➤ Generic Parameters

➤ Parameters

➤ Return Types

➤ Uses Attribute

Inbound Navigation also has more options, including the following:

➤ All Inbound

➤ Called By

➤ Contained By

➤ Function Pointers

➤ Property Gets

➤ Property Sets

The Analysis patterns and Grouping options are the same as before.

DEPENDENCY GRAPHS

They say a picture is worth a thousand words, and *dependency graphs* prove that saying. Architecture Explorer is invaluable for its capability to drill down into the code base, but it can also present so much information that it can be a bit overwhelming as well. Given its capability to continuously scroll to the right, you could become confused after doing an intense, deep drill-down. Wouldn't it be nice to be able to visualize the information from Architecture Explorer? Dependency graphs enable you to do just that.

You can use a dependency graph to explore the relationships and organization of an existing code base. These graphs make it easy to understand code that is new or unfamiliar to you. The relationships on the graph make it readily apparent how different areas of code relate to one another and can show you how a change to one area of code could cause potential issues for other areas of the code. You have multiple ways to view your dependency graph information.

> **NOTE** *A dependency graph shows only those dependencies in code that have gone through a successful build. Any code that did not build successfully does not appear on the dependency graph.*

> **NOTE** *Dependency graphs are also referred to as directed graphs. The two terms are used interchangeably.*

Creating the First Dependency Graph

You actually have several different options for creating a dependency graph. Because the first half of this chapter has dealt with Architecture Explorer, let's continue that thread so you can see how you can create dependency graphs from Architecture Explorer. Later, you learn how you can create dependency graphs, without using Architecture Explorer, to get a quick overview of your source code or compiled code.

Previously, using Architecture Explorer, you learned how to drill down into your source code. You saw how to select the `FirstProject` namespace, the `FirstClass` class, and the `Method1` method. From here, let's select `Method2` and `Method3` in Architecture Explorer.

To display this information as a dependency graph, simply click the Create a New Graph Document button on the Architecture Explorer window. This takes all the information selected in Architecture Explorer and displays it as a dependency graph, as shown in Figure 15-9.

As you can see, this graph provides an easy-to-understand graphical overview of the information contained in Architecture Explorer. You can see that the `FirstProject` namespace contains the `FirstClass` class. The `FirstClass` class contains two methods: `Method1` and `Method2`. `Method1` makes references to both `Method2` and `Method3`. Also, you can see that `Method2` makes reference to `Method1`.

But the dependency graph can do much more than just show the layout of method calls. By hovering the mouse over a node in the graph, you can view detailed information about that node. Figure 15-10 shows the information that is displayed for `Method1` when you hover the mouse over the `Method1` node.

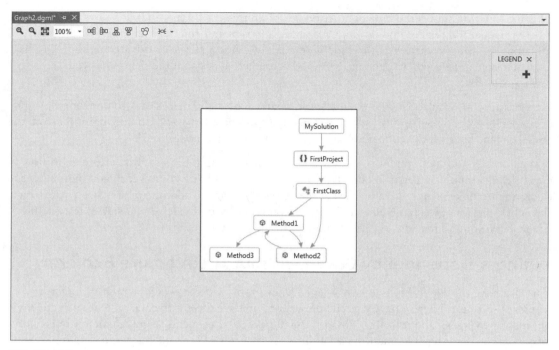

FIGURE 15-9

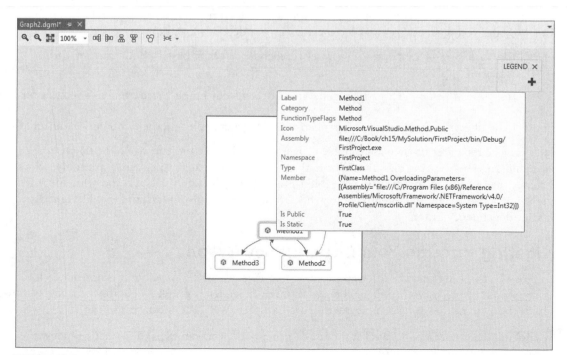

FIGURE 15-10

This information shows the type of function this is (in this case, a method). It shows the assembly where this method resides, along with namespace and type information. It also shows helpful information such as whether the method is static, and if it is a public or private method. All this information can help you understand your code base better, without requiring that you open a code file.

However, if you want to view the code file for a particular node, that is easy to do from the dependency graph. You simply right-click the node and select Go To ⇨ Go To Definition from the context menu to open the code file associated with the selected node.

You can easily add more nodes to an existing dependency graph. Let's say you create an initial dependency graph using Architecture Explorer. Now, let's say that you want to add more nodes to the graph to make it more detailed. Select the nodes you want to add in Architecture Explorer and then click the Add Selected Nodes to Existing Graph button on the left-hand side of the Architecture Explorer window. This adds the selected nodes to the existing graph.

Creating a Dependency Graph without Architecture Explorer

You also have the capability to create a dependency graph without even opening Architecture Explorer. This can be very handy when you want to analyze the entire code base of your code without having to worry about drilling down through particular elements using Architecture Explorer. For example, you can drag and drop a .NET assembly onto a blank diagram and it automatically decomposes the assembly for you.

From the main menu of Visual Studio 2010, select Architecture ⇨ Generate Dependency Graph. This provides you with two options for generating your dependency graph:

➤ *For Solution* — This option generates a dependency graph based off the current open solution.

➤ *For Include File* — This option generates a dependency graph based off a C++ include file.

Figure 15-11 shows an example of a dependency graph generated using the For Solution option.

Each project generates its own assemblies, which, in the example project, would be `FirstProject` `.exe` and `SecondProject.exe`. In addition, there is a reference to an `Externals` assembly, which includes the references and calls into the .NET Framework. Though the black-and-white picture might not show it well, the legend is color-coded to help you easily understand the different aspects of your dependency graph.

Navigating through Your Dependency Graph

You may be thinking that the information shown in Figure 15-11 is nice, but it is not that helpful. It sure would be nice if you could drill down into the dependency graph in a manner similar to how you drill down into information in Architecture Explorer. Well, guess what? You can!

By clicking the arrow icon located at the top-left of a node, you can expand the node to view the detailed information in that node, as shown in Figure 15-12. The arrow icon will become visible when you mouse-over the node.

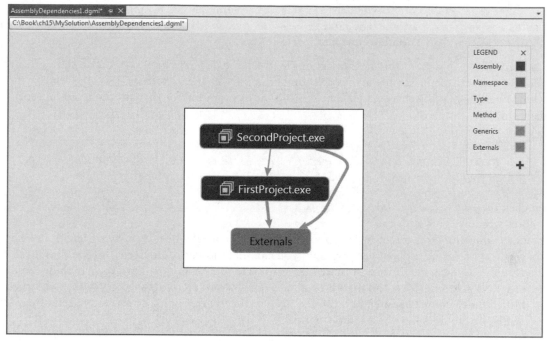

FIGURE 15-11

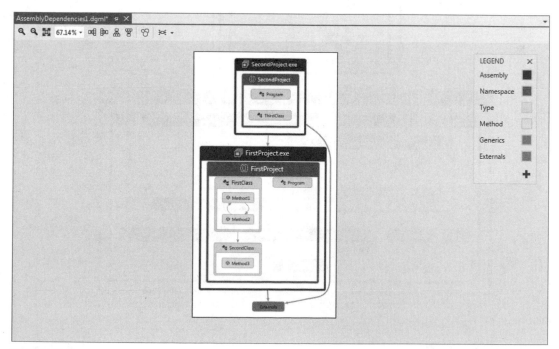

FIGURE 15-12

`FirstProject.exe` is comprised of the `FirstProject` namespace. The namespace contains three classes: `FirstClass`, `SecondClass`, and `Program`. `FirstClass` contains two methods: `Method1` and `Method2`. `SecondClass` contains one method: `Method3`.

The dependency graph shows the interactions between the different methods. It also shows that the `SecondProject.exe` assembly makes calls to `Method3` in the `SecondClass` class. To view exactly which object is making this call, you can expand the information for that assembly on the dependency graph.

> **NOTE** *The information displayed in Figure 15-12 is the same information displayed in Figure 15-9, just in a different format. You can format a dependency graph using a variety of different options.*

The next question you might have is whether you can drill down into that external node. The answer is, yes! Using a dependency graph, you can drill down into external assemblies (such as the .NET Framework). This is an incredibly powerful tool. You now have the capability to delve into the .NET Framework and map how all the objects and methods interact with each other, enabling you to come to a much better and deeper understanding of how the .NET Framework works. Figure 15-13 shows an example of this.

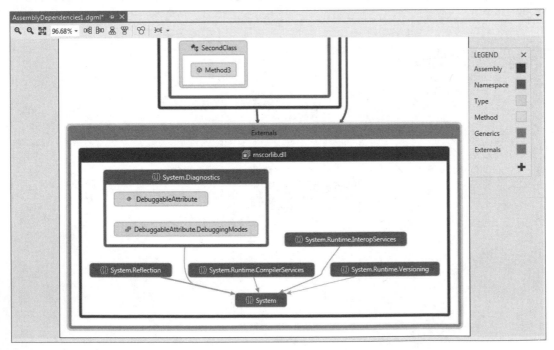

FIGURE 15-13

You also have the capability to interact with your dependency graph by right-clicking the graph and selecting from a variety of context menu options. You will recognize many of the options from Architecture Explorer. The exact options depend on what is selected on the dependency graph.

You can select a specific node on a graph and then choose the Select menu option from the context menu. This enables you to do the following:

➤ Select all incoming links to the selected node

➤ Select all outgoing links from the selected node

➤ Select both incoming and outgoing links from the selected node

➤ Select all connected nodes to the selected node

➤ Select all children of the selected node

You have the capability to add groups and categories to the graph, enabling you to organize the graph in a more readable fashion.

Refer to Figure 15-12 to see another nice feature of dependency graphs, which is the capability to apply different analyzers to the information on the graph. You saw these analyzers before when you worked with Architecture Explorer, but they make even more sense when you see them in conjunction with the dependency graph.

From the Legend, click the Add button, select Analyzer, and then select Circular References. This analyzer looks for circular references, or infinite loops, in your graph. When those references are found, it highlights them (in red) on the dependency graph, instantly bringing them to your attention, as shown in Figure 15-14.

A second analyzer that is available is the Find Hubs analyzer. This analyzer shows which hubs are Node Property in the top 25 percent of high-connected nodes. This is a quick-and-easy way to see which hubs are involved with a majority of the work in the application.

A third analyzer that is available is the Unreferenced Nodes analyzer. This analyzer highlights any nodes that are not referenced by any other nodes. They are orphans. This is a good way to find areas of the code that are not being used either because of oversight or because they are no longer needed.

Dependency Graph Legend

In the upper-right corner of each dependency graph is the *legend* (see Figure 15-11). You can use the legend to help you understand all the different components that make up the dependency graph. One nice feature of the legend is that it is completely customizable, which means you can control the shapes and colors that are used on the graph, thus enabling you to customize the graph to your needs.

For the dependency graph shown in Figure 15-11, if you were to click the Add button on the legend, you would have the following four options that could be added to the graph:

➤ Node Property

➤ Node Category

➤ Link Property

➤ Link Category

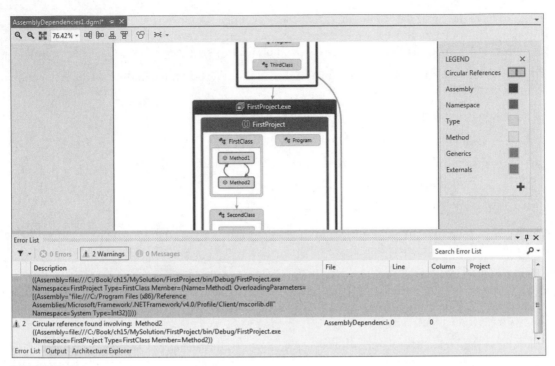

FIGURE 15-14

Each of these options has sub-options underneath it that you can add to the legend. To see these suboptions, you will need to expand the nodes in the diagram, where they look similar to Figure 15-12. For Node Property, the options are the following:

➤   Is Abstract

➤   Is Final

➤   Is Private

➤   Is Public

➤   Is Static

➤   StrongName

➤   Error

➤   File Path

➤   Group

➤   Circular References

For Node Category, the options are the following:

➤   Assembly

➤   Class

- ➤ Method
- ➤ Namespace
- ➤ Externals
- ➤ `FileSystem.Category.FileOfType.exe`

For Link Property, the options are the following:

- ➤ Circular Link
- ➤ Weight

And, finally, for Link Category, the option is the following:

- ➤ Calls

When you have added a new item to the legend, you can customize its appearance. You can click the icon in the legend and select from the following four customization options:

- ➤ *Background* — This lets you select a color for the background of the node.
- ➤ *Stroke* — This selects the color that outlines the node.
- ➤ *Foreground* — This sets the text color in the node.
- ➤ *Icons* — This enables you to select from a variety of icons to add into the node itself.

Dependency Graph Toolbar

You can use the dependency graph toolbar to modify the look and feel of a dependency graph. At the far left of the toolbar are the zoom controls. As you can imagine, a dependency graph can grow to be quite large. These tools enable you to zoom into and out of areas of the graph that you are interested in. You can use the drop-down list box to fit the graph to the page or to select pre-specified zoom options. You can also use the scroll wheel on the mouse to zoom in and out of the graph, and there is a scale located at the top left of the graph that you can use for zooming, as well as a button to fit to diagram to the screen. Figure 15-15 shows the dependency graph toolbar.

FIGURE 15-15

You use the next five toolbar icons to specify the directional flow of the dependency graph. These options include (reading from left to right) Left-to-Right, Right-to-Left, Top-to-Bottom, and Bottom-to-Top. The third option (a Top-to-Bottom flow) is the default. Simply click the appropriate button on the toolbar and the dependency graph re-orients itself. The fifth option is the Quick Clusters view. This view shows the nodes as clusters or hubs. In this view, the graph is arranged with the most-dependent nodes near the center, and the least-dependent nodes at the outer edges of the clusters of hubs.

The final button on the toolbar provides the capability to control when cross-group links are shown. A cross-group link represents a relationship between two nodes, located in different groups. By default, cross-group links are shown only on selected nodes. Using this button, you can make a change to show all cross-group links on the graph or to hide all cross-group links on the graph.

Dependency Graph Enhancements in Visual Studio 2012

One of the mandates with visualization in Visual Studio 2012 was to make visualization easier to use, as well as improve responsiveness. Earlier in this chapter you saw how visualization has been made easier to use. Now it's time to see how dependency graphs have been made better and faster.

You might have noticed while working through the examples earlier in this chapter that the graphs were much more responsive than in Visual Studio 2010.

When you generated a dependency graph for the entire solution, you probably saw the window in Figure 15-16 open.

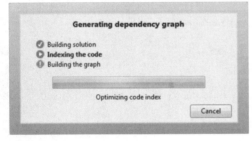

FIGURE 15-16

When you generate a dependency graph, the first thing that happens is the solution is built. Next, the assemblies are indexed and stored in a SQL Server localdb database. This database is referred to as the *Code Index*. Then, the graph is built using the indexed information from the Code Index. Although this means the initial visualization of the graph takes longer to generate, after you start working with the graph you can very quickly drill down into elements or add new elements to the graph.

Zooming in and out of a dependency graph is much faster now as well. In Visual Studio 2010, the entire graph was stored in memory, which meant that a large graph could take up a lot of memory, causing the entire computer to slow down. In Visual Studio 2012, that is no longer the case. Through the use of the Code Index, only the portion of the graph that is being utilized at the time is brought into memory, making it much more responsive.

As just mentioned, the Code Index is created when the dependency graph is initially generated. It is possible to prepopulate the index during the automated build process, using build tasks. To do this, you need to make use of the Visual Studio Visualization and Modeling SDK, which is freely available from Microsoft.

> **NOTE** *For more information on the Visual Studio Visualization and Modeling SDK, see the MSDN information available at* `http://archive.msdn.microsoft.com/vsvmsdk.`

You can view the contents of the Code Index using Server Explorer in Visual Studio 2012. Open the Server Explorer window in Visual Studio 2012. Right-click the Data Connections icon and select Add Connection from the context menu. This opens the Choose Data Source window. Select Microsoft SQL Server, then click the Continue button. This opens the Add Connection window, shown in Figure 15-17.

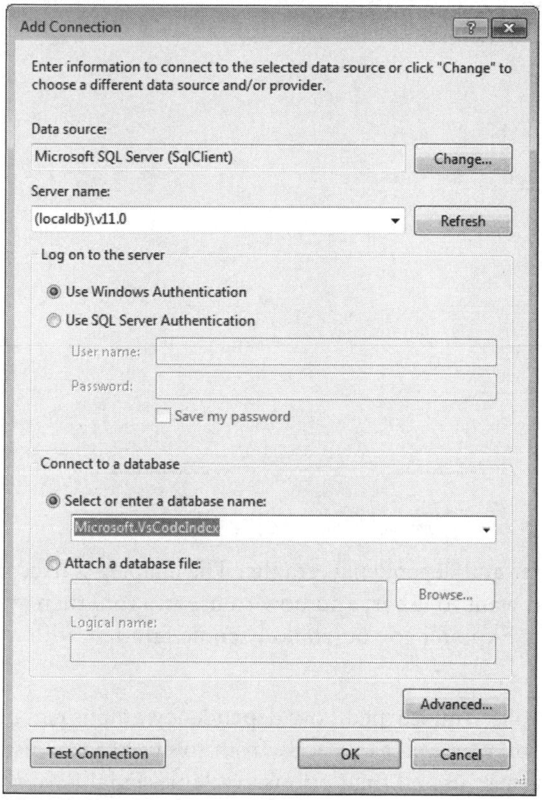

FIGURE 15-17

In the Server Name field, enter `(localdb)\v11.0`. Select the database named Repository. This is the Code Index database. Click OK to close the window and connect to the Code Index. Figure 15-18 shows a list of tables from the Code Index. At this point, you can open the tables to view the data collected by the indexing.

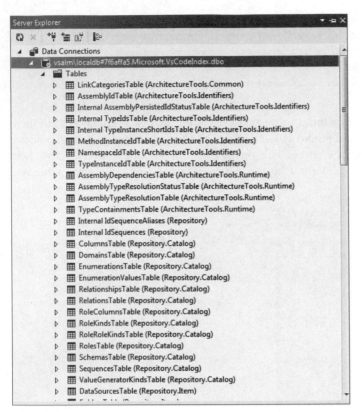

FIGURE 15-18

SUMMARY

This chapter examined both Architecture Explorer and dependency graphs. The chapter started off discussing Architecture Explorer, why you would want to use it, and how to use it. From there, you walked through an example of using Architecture Explorer so you could become familiar with many of its features.

The discussion then moved on to dependency graphs. You learned how dependency graphs can be created with information from Architecture Explorer, as well as directly from solutions. You also learned about dependency graphs in depth and how to use all the options available. Finally, you looked at some of the enhancements to dependency graphs in Visual Studio 2012, including the use of the Code Index to speed performance.

Chapter 16 is the final chapter on the architecture tools available in Visual Studio Ultimate 2012. Chapter 16 looks at layer diagrams, how they are built, and how they are useful in dividing your code base into understandable sections, as well as how they can be used as a validation tool during the build process.

16

Using Layer Diagrams to Model and Enforce Application Architecture

WHAT'S IN THIS CHAPTER?

➤ Understanding a layer diagram

➤ Creating layer diagrams

➤ Defining dependencies on a layer diagram

In the other chapters in this section of the book, you have learned about some of the different modeling diagrams available in Visual Studio Ultimate 2012. This chapter examines the final diagram — the layer diagram.

Layer diagrams are used to describe the structure of an application at a high level. You can also use these diagrams to verify that the developed code conforms to the high-level design laid out in the layer diagram. One nice feature about layer diagrams is the capability to validate application design architecture against the code base, ensuring that the code and architecture continue to match during the development process.

In a way similar to a traditional architecture diagram, a layer diagram shows the major components of the architecture design. Dependencies between the components are also laid out on the diagram. A diagram consists of one or more nodes, referred to as *layers*. A layer can represent any sort of logical group — for example, a namespace or a class file. Dependencies on a layer diagram can be defined explicitly based on your proposed architecture, or you can have the tool discover them from the existing relationships in the code. You can also incorporate layer diagrams into the automated build process, which enables you to verify that code changes adhere to the architectural design.

This chapter examines layer diagrams in detail. You first learn how a layer diagram is created. Next, you find out how to add layers to a diagram, both by using the toolbox and by building layers from an existing code base. You see how you can use the Layer Explorer to provide a detailed look at what artifacts are contained within a layer. The chapter wraps up by looking a layer validation, and how to include layer validation in the build process.

CREATING A LAYER DIAGRAM

To use a layer diagram, you must add a new one to the solution with which you are currently working. Creating a new blank layer diagram requires the use of either an existing modeling project, or the creation of a new modeling project in the current solution. Because layer diagrams are simply another type of diagram in Visual Studio, they must have a modeling project to be stored in.

> **NOTE** *For this chapter, you use the sample solution from Chapter 15, which is available from this book's web page on* `www.wrox.com`.

To create a new blank layer diagram in the solution, select Architecture from the Visual Studio main menu, and then select New Diagram. This opens the Add New Diagram window, as shown in Figure 16-1.

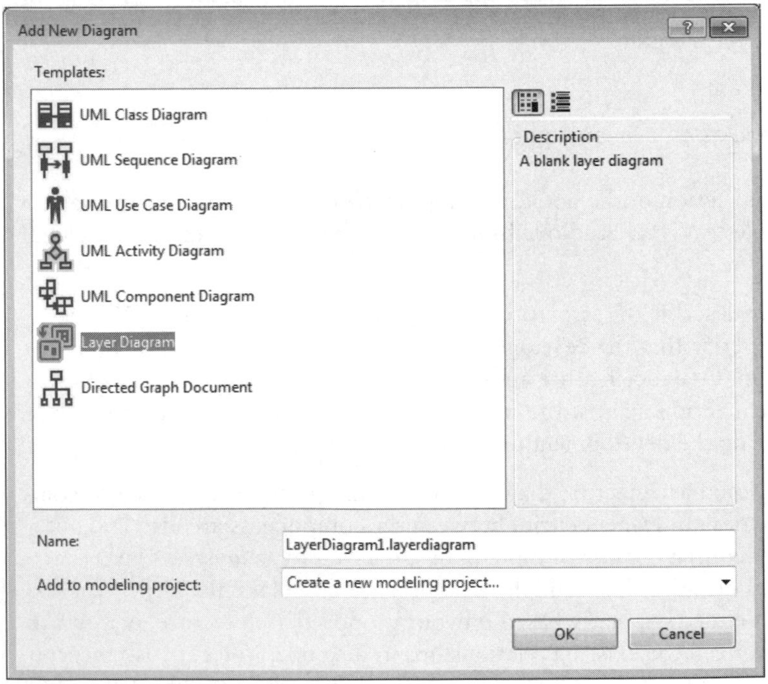

FIGURE 16-1

In the Add New Diagram window, select the Layer Diagram. In the Name field, enter the name of your layer diagram. All layer diagrams end in `.layerdiagram`.

If the solution contains an existing modeling project, you can select it in the Add to Modeling Project dropdown box. If the current solution does not contain a modeling project, then select Create a New Modeling Project in the dropdown box, and the Add New Diagram window prompts you to create a new modeling project.

After you have selected the layer diagram model type, given a name to the model, and selected the appropriate option from the Modeling Project dropdown box, click the OK button. If a new modeling project is being created, the Create New Modeling Project window opens.

Modeling Project is the only option available for creating a new modeling project, though you can control the .NET Framework support for the modeling project by selecting the appropriate version for the framework at the top of the window. Enter a name for the modeling project and the location to store the project and then click OK. The modeling project is created; a new blank layer diagram is created inside the modeling project; and the new blank layer diagram opens in a tab in Visual Studio.

> **NOTE** *Although a layer diagram is located in a modeling project, it can link to any artifact in the current Visual Studio solution.*

DEFINING LAYERS ON A LAYER DIAGRAM

The next step is to define the different layers on the layer diagram. Each layer on a layer diagram appears as a rectangle. Different layers can be nested inside each other, which is called *grouping*. The different layers in a layer diagram are used to define logical groups of artifacts, including methods, classes, and namespaces.

You can define layers on the layer diagram by dragging objects from the layer diagram toolbox, dragging objects from Solution Explorer, or dragging objects from the Architecture Explorer. The easiest way is to use the layer diagram toolbox. Use the objects in the layer diagram toolbox to define a layer diagram with three sections.

1. Drag a layer object from the toolbox onto the blank diagram. A rectangle appears on the diagram with the default name Layer 1. Double-click the layer and change the name to **UI Layer**.

2. Drag another layer object from the toolbox and place it directly below the UI Layer object. Double-click this object and rename it **Business Logic Layer**.

3. Drag a third layer object onto the diagram below the other two and rename it **Data Access Layer**. Figure 16-2 shows what the layer diagram should look like at this point.

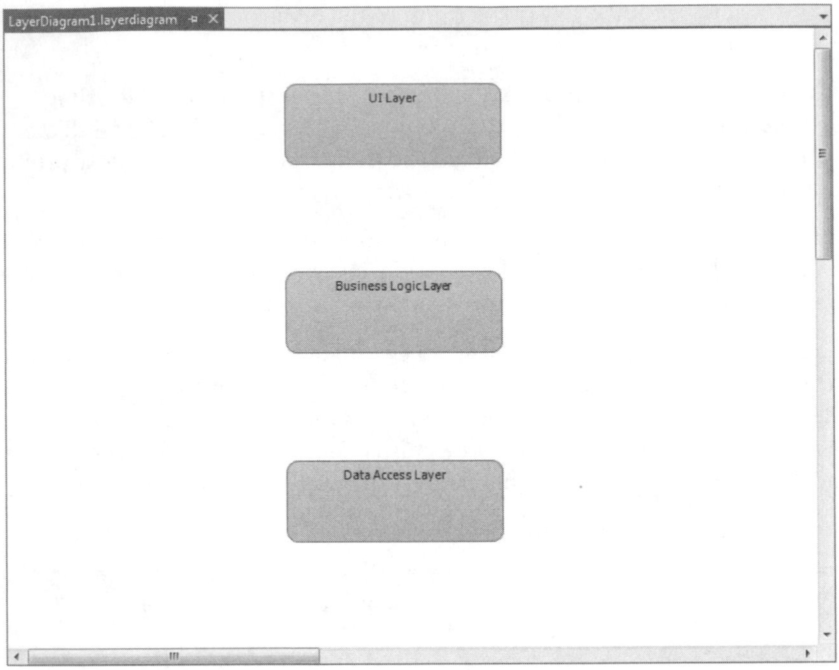

FIGURE 16-2

For each layer, you can specify certain properties by selecting the layer object, and referring to the Properties window in Visual Studio:

➤ *Forbidden Namespaces* — Use this property to specify that artifacts associated with a layer must not belong to the specified namespaces. Separate each namespace with a semicolon (;).

➤ *Forbidden Namespace Dependencies* — Use this property to specify that artifacts associated with a layer cannot depend on the specified namespaces. Separate each namespace with a semicolon (;).

➤ *Required Namespaces* — Use this property to specify that artifacts associated with a layer must belong to one of the specified namespaces. Separate each namespace with a semicolon (;).

At this point, you have created three "unlinked" layers. The layers are referred to as "unlinked" because currently no code files are associated with these layers. This is useful to help represent different parts of an application that have not yet been developed. You continue to build off this layer diagram later in this chapter. But, for now, let's continue to look at the different ways layers can be added to a layer diagram.

Creating a Layer for a Single Artifact

As mentioned previously, a layer represents a logical grouping of artifacts. There may be times when a single artifact (such as a project, or even a single code file) must be represented as its own layer.

This is easy to do with a layer diagram. In fact, you can use any of the following sources to add layers to a layer diagram:

➤ *Solution Explorer* — From within Solution Explorer, you can drag and drop any file or project contained in the Solution Explorer onto the layer diagram surface. A new layer is created with the name of that file or project, and it contains a link to the file or project.

➤ *Architecture Explorer* — Using the Architecture Explorer, you can drill down to the information you are interested in (such as namespaces) and drag and drop those namespaces onto the surface. Those namespaces appear as a layer on the diagram, again with that layer linked to the information that was dropped onto the diagram.

➤ *Dependency Graphs* — You also have the capability to drop dependency graph information directly onto a layer diagram to create layers.

Adding Multiple Objects to a Layer Diagram

When you drag and drop multiple items to a layer diagram at the same time, the default action is to create a single layer on the diagram, with all the objects contained within that layer. To create a separate layer for each artifact dropped as a group, simply hold down the Shift key while dropping the artifacts onto the layer diagram. A layer for each artifact appears on the diagram, and each layer is linked to its appropriate artifact.

To add an artifact to an existing layer, simply drop the artifact onto an existing layer on the layer diagram. A link is established between the layer and the artifact.

> **NOTE** *As a general rule, you should always place artifacts in the same layer if they have some sort of close interdependence. Artifacts that can be easily updated separately (or, for example, are used in separate applications) should be in different layers*

The Layer Explorer

To understand how links are added to a layer diagram and how to view the linked information between a particular layer on a layer diagram and its linked artifacts, let's continue to build off the layer diagram from Figure 16-2.

From Solution Explorer, click `FirstClass.cs` and drag and drop it onto the UI Layer of the layer diagram. Visually, the only thing that changes on the diagram is that the number 1 appears in the top-right corner of the UI Layer. This number indicates the number of artifacts that have been linked to this particular layer. Now, drag the `SecondClass.cs` object from the Solution Explorer onto the Business Logic layer. You should see the number 1 appear on that layer. Finally, drag the `ThirdClass.cs` object from the Solution Explorer to the Data Access Layer. The layer diagram should now resemble Figure 16-3.

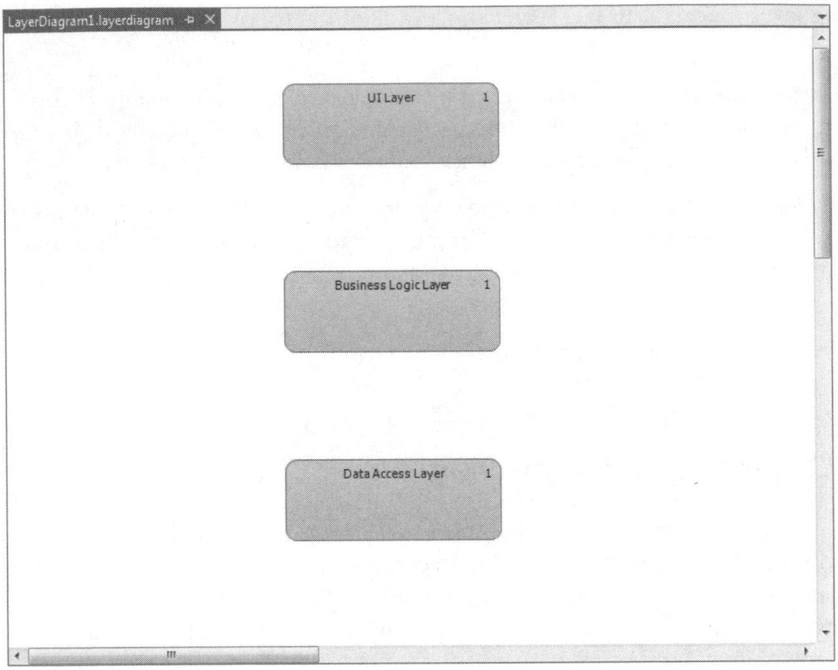

FIGURE 16-3

In Figure 16-3, you see three layers, with each layer containing one artifact. But how do you go about viewing which artifacts are contained within which layers? That is where the Layer Explorer comes in.

You use the Layer Explorer to view artifacts that are linked to a particular layer and to move artifacts between layers. To open the Layer Explorer, right-click a layer in the layer diagram and select View Links. By default, the Layer Explorer opens on the right-hand side of Visual Studio, usually as a tab in the same window as the Solution Explorer, as shown in Figure 16-4.

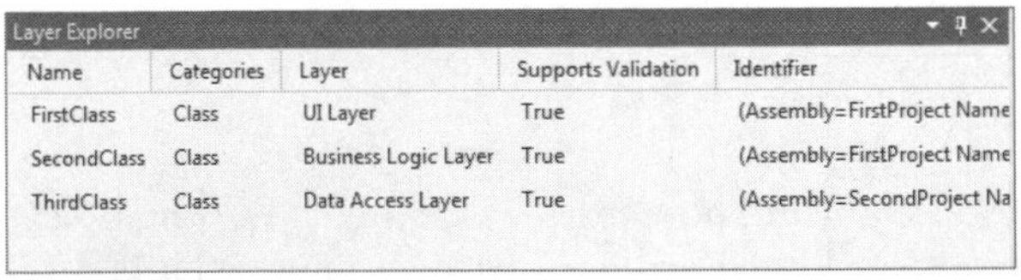

Name	Categories	Layer	Supports Validation	Identifier
FirstClass	Class	UI Layer	True	(Assembly=FirstProject Name
SecondClass	Class	Business Logic Layer	True	(Assembly=FirstProject Name
ThirdClass	Class	Data Access Layer	True	(Assembly=SecondProject Na

FIGURE 16-4

The Layer Explorer displays all the artifacts that are linked to a particular layer. As shown in Figure 16-4, the Layer Explorer contains a series of columns that display different properties about the linked artifacts:

- ➤ The Name column displays the name of the linked artifact.

- ➤ The Categories column displays information about the type of artifact. This could be class, namespace, or project file, just to name a few.

- ➤ The Layer column displays the layer that the artifact belongs to.

- ➤ The Supports Validation column indicates whether the linked artifact participates in the layer-validation process. If this column is set to `False`, the linked artifact does not participate. If this column is set to `True`, the linked artifact does participate, and the layer-validation process can verify that the project conforms to dependencies to or from this element.

- ➤ The Identifier column is used to provide a reference to the linked column.

To display all the artifacts on a layer diagram, click anywhere on the layer diagram. This deselects any layers that have been selected, which, in turn, displays all the artifacts linked to different layers in the Layer Explorer.

To delete an artifact from the layer diagram, select the artifact in the Layer Explorer, right-click the artifact, and select Delete. This deletes the artifact from both the Layer Explorer and the layer diagram.

To move an artifact from one layer to another, you have a couple of options. In the Layer Explorer, you can right-click the artifact in question and select Cut. Then, in the layer diagram, right-click the appropriate layer and select Paste. Also, you can simply drag the artifact from the Layer Explorer onto a layer on the layer diagram. The artifact is removed from its initial layer and added to the new layer.

An artifact can be a member of multiple layers. One way to add an artifact to multiple layers is to drag the object onto the multiple layers from Solution Explorer. A second option is to right-click the artifact in the Layer Explorer, select Copy, and then right-click the layer in the layer diagram and select Paste. In either event, a second instance of the artifact appears in the Layer Explorer, but it's linked to a different layer.

DEFINING DEPENDENCIES

After you have defined the layers in the layer diagram, the next step is to identify the dependencies between the different layers. A dependency between two layers exists whenever an artifact that exists in one layer references or uses an artifact that exists in another layer. For example, a dependency exists between the Business Logic Layer and the Data Access Layer when a class in the Business Logic Layer calls or makes reference to a class in the Data Access Layer.

Depending on how the layer diagram was built, you may want to have the dependencies discovered for you automatically, or you may want to define them by hand. More than likely, you will use a combination of the two options.

If the layer diagram was created by dragging existing code artifacts onto the diagram (such as files from a project in Solution Explorer or Architecture Explorer), then the dependencies between the different layers in which those objects exist can be found automatically. If you right-click the layer diagram surface and select Generate Dependencies, Visual Studio analyzes the artifacts that exist in each layer, identifies all the dependencies between the different artifacts, and then represents those dependencies on the layer diagram as a series of arrows connecting one layer to another.

A dependency can be a *uni-directional* dependency, meaning that Layer1 is dependent on objects in Layer2, but Layer2 is not dependent on any objects in Layer1. Dependencies can also be *bi-directional*, meaning that, just as there are objects in Layer1 that depend on Layer2, there are objects in Layer2 that depend on Layer1.

Dependencies on a layer diagram can also be defined by hand. This is helpful especially when you are creating the layer diagram as part of the design phase. In that phase, you don't know the specific code artifacts that you will be creating. But you do know the different high-level areas of your application, and you want to define how they will interact or depend on each other.

Let's use the layer diagram from Figure 16-3 and add some dependencies between the different layers. In the layer diagram, you have three different layers: the UI Layer, the Business Logic Layer, and the Data Access Layer.

The UI Layer is dependent on artifacts in the Business Logic Layer. Without the Business Logic Layer, there is no information for the UI Layer to display. This dependency is represented by using a Dependency object from the layer diagram area of the Visual Studio toolbox. Click the Dependency object in the layer diagram area of the Visual Studio toolbox. Then, on the layer diagram, click the UI Layer followed by the Business Logic Layer. A dependency arrow connects the two layers, stretching from the UI Layer to the Business Logic Layer, as shown in Figure 16-5.

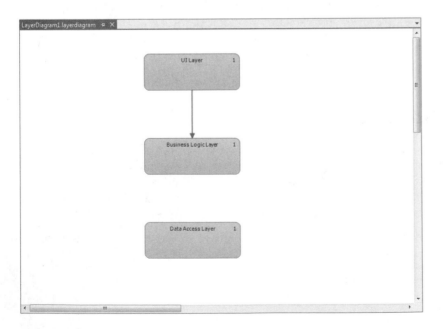

FIGURE 16-5

A dependency object has properties, just like any other object in Visual Studio. The property window in Visual Studio displays the properties available. You can define a name and description of the dependency. You can also control the direction of the dependency arrow here. If you need to reverse the direction, select Backward in the Direction property. You can also turn the dependency into a bi-directional dependency by selecting Bi-directional in the Direction property.

You also have a dependency between the Business Logic Layer and the Data Access Layer. The Business Logic Layer cannot perform its functions, or provide information to the UI Layer, without information from the Data Access Layer. Using the same method described previously, you can create a dependency between the two layers by selecting the Dependency object and connecting the Business Logic Layer and the Data Access Layer.

Dependencies cannot be generated for certain types of artifacts in a layer diagram. For example, if you add a text file to a layer in a layer diagram, there are no dependencies generated either to or from that particular layer around that text file. To determine if an artifact is going to generate dependencies, select the layer that contains the artifact and open the Layer Explorer by right-clicking the layer and selecting View Links. In the Layer Explorer, if the value in the Supports Validation column is set to `False`, then the artifact does not generate any dependencies for that layer.

VALIDATING THE LAYER DIAGRAM

At this point, you may be saying to yourself, "Okay, layer diagrams are great and all, but what is the actual benefit to me? Why do I want to go to all this effort of creating different layers and linking my code artifacts to these different layers?" The answers to these questions lie in the capability to validate the architecture.

Validation enables you to confirm that all the dependencies defined between all the different layers are being respected. This provides the capability to enforce rules and dependencies between different layers. For example, you may have segregated your code base where different namespaces are not supposed to interact. You can define that segregation using a layer diagram and dependencies, and then add your code artifacts to their appropriate layers. If a developer miscodes something (such as accessing a namespace he or she is not supposed to access), it may not be readily apparent by just looking at the code. However, by using the validation features of a layer diagram, an error is immediately thrown, pinpointing the problem area, so that you can quickly and easily resolve it.

To validate a layer diagram, right-click anywhere on the layer diagram and select Validate Architecture from the context menu. Visual Studio analyzes the layer diagram, as well as all the artifacts associated with the layer diagram. It follows all the dependencies to ensure that there are no violations.

If no problems are found, a message is displayed in the output window that the architecture validation has succeeded. If problems are discovered in the layer diagram validation, they are displayed in the Error List window in Visual Studio.

Using the layer diagram from Figure 16-5, let's look at an example of validating the diagram. To validate the layer diagram as it exists in Figure 16-5, right-click the layer diagram and select Validate Architecture. Visual Studio goes through the validation process, including compiling the code, and then verifies any dependencies that exist on the diagram. Figure 16-6 shows the results from the Output window in Visual Studio.

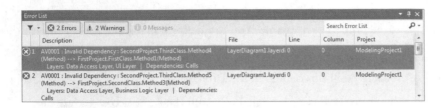

FIGURE 16-6

There are two validation errors in the layer diagram. The errors indicate that a dependency on the layer diagram has not been satisfied. In the layer diagram shown in Figure 16-6, the UI Layer contains the class named `FirstClass`, the Business Logic Layer contains the class named `SecondClass`, and the Data Access Layer contains the class named `ThirdClass`. `ThirdClass` has a dependency on both `FirstClass` and `SecondClass`, so, therefore, the Data Access Layer has a dependency on the Business Logic Layer and the UI Layer. However, as can be seen from the diagram in Figure 5-8, that is not what is defined. Instead, the only dependency defined is between the Business Logic Layer and the UI Layer.

Because the dependencies listed in the diagram do not match the actual dependencies in the code, an error is thrown when the diagram is validated. At this point, the error needs to be resolved before you move forward. There are several different options for resolving the error.

The first option is to change the dependency information on the layer diagram — in this case, adding dependency links between the Data Access layer and the other two layers. A second option is to modify the links of the different layer diagrams. For example, move all the classes into the same layer. A third option is to modify the code base to remove the dependency in the code and satisfy the dependency defined in the layer diagram.

If for some reason you don't want to change the code base or modify the dependency information in the layer diagram, you can suppress the validation error. Right-click the error message in the Error List window, select Manage Validation Errors, and then select Suppress Errors. This suppresses this error message and prevents this specific error from being thrown again the next time the layer diagram is validated.

> **NOTE** *If you right-click the error message and select Go To, you can easily navigate to the code that is causing the dependency violation.*

More than likely, the first time validation is run against a layer diagram there will be conflicts. At that point, you need to update the code base until the conflicts no longer exist. As new code is developed and existing code is refactored, there may be the occasion to add new artifacts to the layer diagram. This may or may not be necessary, depending on how the initial layer diagram was created. Regardless, this is an iterative process, so be patient, and be sure to make the correct design decisions as related to what you want to build.

LAYER DIAGRAMS AND THE BUILD PROCESS

You can use layer diagrams (and, in fact, almost any diagram contained within a modeling project) to help validate your project or solution during the build process. In this context, "build process" means pressing F5 in Visual Studio to compile and run your code locally, as well as to incorporate your modeling diagrams as part of an automated build using Team Foundation Build.

To ensure that an individual diagram is included in the build process, the Build Action property of the diagram must be set to `Validate`. To do this, select the appropriate diagram in the modeling project in Solution Explorer. In the Properties window for that diagram you see the Build Action property. In the dropdown box for this property, select `Validate` to ensure that this diagram is validated as part of the build process.

To ensure that the architecture of all diagrams included in the modeling project is validated during the build process, the Validate Architecture property of the modeling project must be set to `True`. To do this, select the modeling project in Solution Explorer. In the Properties window for the modeling project, you see a property named Validate Architecture. Set this property equal to `True` to enforce (during a build) validation of all the diagrams contained within the modeling project.

Finally, to ensure that any code changes made by anyone on the team conform to the architecture defined on the layer diagram, layer validation can be added to the automated build process. This way, any time a build is run on the solution, all team member contributions are taken into consideration, and any differences or exceptions to the architecture are reported as a build error on the build report.

To automate layer diagram validation during the build process, double-click the build definition in Team Explorer and then click Process. Under Build Process Parameters, expand Compilation and then enter the following MSBuild Argument parameter:

```
/p:ValidateArchitecture=true
```

SUMMARY

Layer diagrams provide a nice architectural way of structuring the design of the application and confirming that the code being developed matches the original architectural design.

This chapter looked at how to create layer diagrams and how to add layers to the diagram. You saw how to create blank layers, how to create layers on the diagram, and how those layers can be validated against the code base to ensure no design or architecture decisions have been violated.

This ends this section of the book on the architecture tools in Visual Studio Ultimate 2012. Chapter 17 starts the next section of the book, which focuses on the different tools available to developers to help write better code. In Chapter 17, you learn about some of the features in Visual Studio 2012 that are of most interest to developers.

PART V
Software Development

17

Introduction to Software Development

WHAT'S IN THIS CHAPTER?

➤ Application lifecycle management features of most interest to developers in Visual Studio 2012

➤ Learning how My Work surfaces the items you care most about

➤ Managing interruptions using suspend and resume

➤ Seeking peer feedback on your code using the new code review capabilities

Visual Studio originally came into popularity in the 1990s by providing individual developers with the tools they needed to build great software. Most applications in that timeframe were created by individuals or relatively small teams working at a common location. However, over the course of many years, organizations developed increasingly larger and more complex code bases. The code is typically edited by a number of developers from all over the world, and teams must embrace rapidly changing requirements in order to keep up with the pace of business opportunities.

Simply having the tools at your disposal to create applications as an individual developer is no longer enough. You need tools to help you to analyze large code bases, and to help you to identify hot spots that might be causing you problems. You need tools that will provide you with the confidence that not only does the application still work after making your changes, but that it is more efficient, and the quality of the code is improving as your team matures. This is where Visual Studio 2012 comes in.

Visual Studio 2012 is also very useful for new "green field" development, on the rare occasions that you are starting a project from scratch. From day one you can use the same tools that help you work with large code bases to ensure that all newly created code maintains the same standards you envisioned during the project kick-off meeting. As the code base grows, and more developers come onto the project, you can ensure that you are not spending time prematurely optimizing code, but rather easily identifying new performance bottlenecks as they occur.

Visual Studio 2012 provides developers of both managed and unmanaged code with an enhanced set of advanced tools for identifying inefficient, insecure, or poorly written code. You can specify coding best practices, and ensure that those are checked with every build, as well as ensuring that the code is fully unit tested every time.

With Visual Studio 2012, Microsoft also recognizes as the transition of teams transition to become more agile to support evolving requirements and business opportunities comes at a price with regard to helping developers stay "in the zone" writing code. A developer who's agile might be frequently changing context from one priority to the next. In this chapter you learn about the new suspend and resume capability that can help developers more efficiently manage their development workspaces during the transitions.

You also learn about how Visual Studio 2012 and Team Foundation Server 2012 introduce new code review tooling that facilitates peer review of source code in a transparent, traceable manner.

The chapters in this part of the book dive deeper into the additional functionality provided by Visual Studio 2012 for the developer.

WHAT'S NEW FOR DEVELOPERS IN VISUAL STUDIO 2012

Visual Studio 2012 introduces hundreds of new and improved features for developers. Across Visual Studio you will find improvements to languages, frameworks, project types, usability, performance, extensibility, documentation — the list goes on and on. This book is by no means comprehensive across all of these categories. However, there are several categories of new and improved application lifecycle management capabilities that relate directly to developing complex software in team environments, which are covered in this section, including the following:

➤ Overhauled unit testing experience

➤ Code analysis, code metrics, and code clone analysis

➤ Profiling and performance

➤ Advanced debugging with IntelliTrace

➤ The new My Work view, which includes suspending and resuming work and facilitating code reviews

Unit Testing

Unit testing is a popular approach for improving code quality by writing small tests that validate small blocks of code. Unit tests are especially important in complex or evolving code bases, where one small change may have cascading consequences on functionality elsewhere in the code base. By writing and maintaining a suite of unit tests, developers can quickly be alerted that a change they just made affected a piece of functionality that was previously working correctly.

Visual Studio has supported built-in unit testing capabilities since Visual Studio 2005. Visual Studio 2005 introduced a new proprietary unit testing framework known as the Visual Studio Unit Testing Framework. Developers welcomed the addition of unit testing to Visual Studio, but this integration didn't support the more popular unit testing frameworks such as NUnit or xUnit.net.

With Visual Studio 2012, Microsoft has completely overhauled its support for unit tests. The entire unit testing framework is extensible now, which means that third parties such as NUnit and xUnit.net can publish adapters that enable their respective testing types to run within Visual Studio. The makers of NUnit and xUnit.net have already announced plans to provide these adapters. At the time of writing, several other unit testing adapters were being planned as well, including unit testing adapters for JavaScript.

Visual Studio 2012 continues to provide support for tests built with the traditional Visual Studio Unit Testing Framework, and it adds support for unit tests written in C++. You can even run tests from a variety of these frameworks across the same solution.

Visual Studio Ultimate 2012 has also introduced a capability known as Microsoft Fakes, which is similar to mocking frameworks. Microsoft Fakes allows you to test "untestable" code by creating stubs and shims which effectively simulate environments or other artifacts which may not, in fact, be available from within your development or test environment. This allows you to write unit tests which test parts of your application which interact with, for example, a SharePoint farm, without actually having a SharePoint farm present, since the SharePoint farm in this case can be faked. Or you can test code which relies on the system date, but you can override the actual system date that your application code is aware of by faking it to be any time in the past or future.

The overall experience for viewing, running, and debugging tests has also been improved. You learn all about the improvements to unit testing with Visual Studio 2012 in Chapter 18.

Improved Code Analysis

Earlier versions of Visual Studio shipped with *code analysis* rules to enable developers to analyze .NET source code to check for common issues and security flaws. In Visual Studio 2012, support for analyzing C++ source code has been added, as well as some overall tooling improvements to make code analysis easier to configure and view the results from. Chapter 19 focuses on code analysis.

Code Metrics

Code metrics can be calculated by Visual Studio 2012 to provide you with detailed quantitative measurements of your source code. This ranges from basic calculations — such as number of lines of code — to more advanced metrics, such as depth of class inheritance or cyclomatic complexity (which is essentially the number of possible paths through your code's logic). These and other metrics can make it possible for you to better understand the overall maintainability of your code, and they can offer clues about where you might benefit from refactoring or other architecture changes to improve the maintainability of your code over time. Code metrics are especially helpful when maintaining large or complex code bases. Code metrics are covered in Chapter 19.

Code Clone Analysis

A new capability from Microsoft Research known as *code clone analysis* has been introduced in Visual Studio 2012 to help developers discover semantically similar blocks of code. As developers, we are often guilty of copying blocks of code from one class or project into another class or project if it provides all or most of the same functionality we need. Unfortunately, this usually creates a problem where we find ourselves independently maintaining two pieces of code that were designed to do the same thing. Most of the time, these blocks of code would benefit from being refactored into a single location. For older code bases, how do you find such refactoring opportunities?

Code clone analysis is the answer to this question. With code clone analysis you can look across your entire solution for blocks of code which are similar in structure and composition. They don't even need to be identical; code clone analysis is adept at finding blocks of code that might have started out the same and evolved over time to become slightly different. You can learn all about code clone analysis in Chapter 19.

Profiler

The Visual Studio 2012 *profiler* enables you to pinpoint possible performance bottlenecks within your application. You can use the profiler while running your application or while running tests. You can even capture performance baselines to help you easily determine if performance is getting better or worse as you check in new code. Chapter 20 covers use of the Visual Studio 2012 profiler.

Advanced Debugging with IntelliTrace

IntelliTrace is an advanced debugging capability introduced in Visual Studio 2010 that enables you to capture a full historical stack trace of an application's execution. It's very helpful to "rewind" the debugger and understand the historical state of your application. Developers could use IntelliTrace whenever they debugged a local application, or testers could enable IntelliTrace in test environments so that an IntelliTrace file could be attached to a bug — which further aided the developer understand exactly what took place when diagnosing the issue.

With Visual Studio 2012, Microsoft has further extended the usefulness of IntelliTrace by enabling organizations to capture traces from applications running in production environments. This provides developers with greater insights into bugs coming from production environments and enables teams to again improve the overall health and quality of their code.

IntelliTrace is covered in depth in Chapter 21.

MY WORK

In previous chapters you worked with Team Explorer, which is the interface within Visual Studio that provides developers with access to Team Foundation Server (source control, work items, builds, reports, and so on). You may have noticed a new area of Team Explorer titled *My Work*. My Work is new in Visual Studio 2012 and provides developers with a personalized view into the work that matters most to them.

To open My Work, open Visual Studio ⇨ Team Explorer. If Team Explorer is not visible, click View ⇨ Team Explorer. Click the Home icon if you are not already at the Team Explorer home page. Click My Work to see a view similar to that shown in Figure 17-1.

My Work is a personalized view for each developer. Using My Work, a developer can:

➤ See work in progress, including pending changes

➤ Suspend and resume work (more on this later in this chapter)

➤ View any work items that are currently assigned to him

➤ Request code reviews and respond to code review requests from others (more on this later in this chapter)

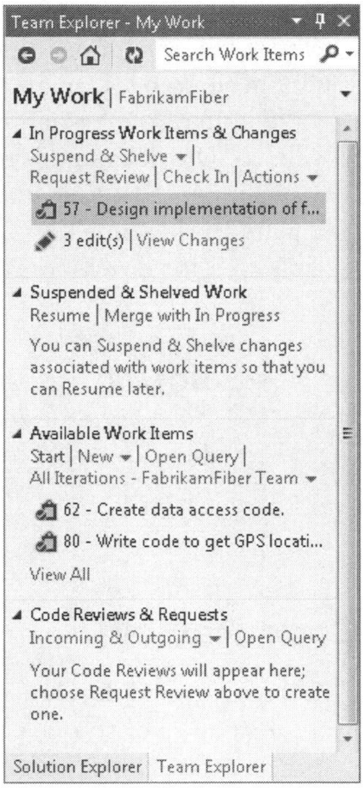

FIGURE 17-1

> **NOTE** *You can add your own queries to the My Queries category and display them in the My Work pane by clicking the drop-down arrow next to the currently selected query under the Available Work Items category, then selecting your personal query.*

Suspend and Resume

With Visual Studio 2012, Microsoft provides an easy way for developers to suspend their in-progress work if they get interrupted. An interruption might be an important bug fix that a developer needs to make, or it could simply be that the developer is shutting down her machine for the evening.

Interruptions have historically been very costly for developers. Team Foundation Server has always made it easy to quickly shelve file edits for later, but for a developer to be productive it often means setting breakpoints, declaring watch variables, and opening several specialized tool windows from within Visual Studio. Thankfully, the new suspend and resume capabilities are designed to help developers preserve all of this state information and then quickly get back *in the zone* when they are ready to resume this work.

Refer to the top of the My Work pane in Figure 17-1; note that there are three pending file edits and work item 57 is in-progress. If this developer gets interrupted, he can quickly press Suspend & Shelve to back up all the pending changes as a shelveset on Team Foundation Server 2012 and take note of the Visual Studio 2012 environment. The suspended work appears in the Suspended & Shelved Work category of the My Work pane. When the developer is ready to work on this again, he can simply click Resume. Visual Studio unshelves the pending file edits, resets any breakpoints, and opens all the same files and tool windows (even across multiple monitors). This can be a very valuable tool for developers to quickly switch contexts with minimal overhead.

> **NOTE** *If a developer moves to a different machine, her suspended environment does not follow her. She is still able to resume work and unshelve any pending file edits from Team Foundation Server, but the overall state of her environment (breakpoints, tool windows, and so on) is not restored onto the other machine.*

Code Review

Most seasoned developers have grown to appreciate the value of peer reviews of source code. *Code reviews* are quite simply a process whereby developers inspect each other's changes to look for possible bugs or missed optimizations prior to committing those changes to the repository. Code reviews are also a great way to teach junior developers, and it provides a way to educate more people on your team about sections of your code base that they may not otherwise be exposed to.

Code reviews have now been built into Visual Studio 2012 and Team Foundation Server 2012 to facilitate this process. One advantage of using these tools to facilitate code reviews is that they become traceable and reportable — a team can audit a code change later on to discover whether it was properly reviewed before being committed. By managing code reviews with Team Foundation Server, it also means that team members who are geographically distributed can easily participate in code reviews without the need to meet in person or on a teleconference.

To initiate a code review, click on Request Review within the My Work pane of Team Explorer. You are presented with a dialog similar to what's shown in Figure 17-2. You can specify one or more team members who should be asked to review this code, along with a title and description for the code review. Any related work items that were In Progress from your My Work view are automatically associated with this code review request as well, which can provide additional context for the reviewers into the intended edits. Click Submit Request when you are finished. You return to the My Work view, and a new Code Review Request

FIGURE 17-2

work item appears in your Code Review & Requests category of this view. You can monitor this Code Review Request work item to see its status.

Likewise, your team members see your Code Review Request work item in their My Work view. When they open this Code Review Request they see a dialog similar to Figure 11-3.

This dialog includes several pieces of functionality:

➤ *Send Comments* enables you to save your in-progress comments for this code review. This is primarily intended to be used when you want to have a dialog with the person who submitted the code review request, such as to ask clarifying questions before you continue your review.

➤ *The Accept and Decline* links enable you to indicate to others whether or not you will work on this request. For quick code reviews, there is no need to formally click Accept for a code review, but doing so is helpful to signal to others that you are working on a longer code review or you plan to work on it later.

➤ *Send & Finish* submits your code review and removes it from your list of pending code reviews. Use this when you are finished with your code review.

➤ *Add Reviewer* enables you to add other people from the team to this request. Use this when you are unable to complete a code review request or when you know that another team member has expertise for a specific type of code change.

➤ There are three levels of comments that you can leave as part of a code review. Overall comments are meant to capture impressions of the overall set of changes being reviewed. You can leave file-level comments by right-clicking any given file and clicking Add File Comments. You can also open

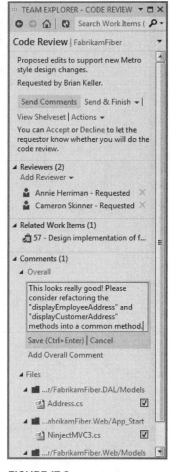

FIGURE 17-3

any file, select some text, right-click the text, and select Add Comment to leave line-level comments. These three levels of comments enable you as a reviewer to be very specific with the type of feedback you are giving to the originator. The checkboxes next to each file also provide you with an easy way to ensure that you have reviewed each file in the Code Review Request.

After you have submitted your response, the originator sees the response in his My Work pane. Figure 17-4 shows the result of this response. The originator can choose to reply to any specific comments, which is useful if this code review is audited later on. He can also continue to add or remove reviewers until he is satisfied that the code has received an adequate level of review. Finally, clicking Close Review closes the Code Review Request work item. When these changes are checked in, the Code Review Request work item is automatically included in the changeset, along with any linked Code Review Responses.

FIGURE 17-4

> **NOTE** *If developers want to be notified via e-mail about any new or updated code reviews they can subscribe to alerts using Team ⇨ Project Alerts. This is sometimes helpful because updates to the My Work view must be refreshed manually. Your Team Foundation Server 2012 instance needs to be configured to support alerts. Contact your Team Foundation Server administrator if this option is unavailable.*

SUMMARY

This chapter provided a quick look at the areas of Visual Studio 2012 that will be of most interest to developers and provided a preview of what to look forward to in this next section of the book.

Chapter 18 focuses in detail on the unit testing, why you should care about it as a developer, and what tools Visual Studio provides to help you create and run unit tests.

18

Unit Testing

WROX.COM CODE DOWNLOADS FOR THIS CHAPTER

The wrox.com code downloads for this chapter are found at www.wrox.com/remtitle .cgi?isbn=1118314081 on the Download Code tab. The files are in the Chapter 18 download folder and individually named as shown throughout this chapter.

Programmatic unit testing involves writing code to verify a system at a lower and more granular level than with other types of testing. It is used *by* programmers *for* programmers, and is quickly becoming standard practice at many organizations. All editions of Visual Studio include unit testing features that are fully integrated with the IDE and with other features (such as reporting and source control). Developers no longer need to rely on third-party utilities (such as NUnit) to perform their unit testing, although they still have the option to use them and in fact, can integrate them into Visual Studio using the test adapter framework.

This chapter describes the concepts behind unit testing, why it is important, and how to create effective unit test suites. You learn about the syntax of writing unit tests, and you see how to work with Visual Studio's integrated features for executing and analyzing those tests. The discussion then goes into more detail about the classes available to you when writing your unit tests, including the core `Assert` class and many important attributes.

You find out how Visual Studio enables the generation of unit tests from existing code, as well as the generation of member structures when writing unit tests. And you delve into Microsoft Fakes, a new technology in Visual Studio 2012 that enables you to shim and stub your code for easier testing. Finally, you take a brief look at the new test adapter framework in Visual Studio 2012 and how you can use that framework to utilize third-party testing frameworks in your testing process.

UNIT TESTING CONCEPTS

You've likely encountered a number of traditional forms of testing. Your quality assurance staff may run automated or manual tests to validate behavior and appearance. Load tests may be run to establish that performance metrics are acceptable. Your product group might run user acceptance tests to validate that systems do what the customers expect. Unit testing takes another view. Unit tests are written to ensure that code performs as the *programmer* expects.

Unit tests are generally focused at a lower level than other testing, establishing that underlying features work as expected. For example, an acceptance test might walk a user through an entire purchase. A unit test might verify that a ShoppingCart class correctly defends against adding an item with a negative quantity.

Unit testing is an example of *white box testing*, where knowledge of internal structures is used to identify the best ways to test the system. This is a complementary approach to *black box testing*, where the focus is not on implementation details but rather on overall functionality compared to specifications. You should leverage both approaches to effectively test your applications.

Unit testing as a concept has been around for decades. However, in recent times, the process of performing unit tests by writing code to execute those tests has become popular. This form of programmatic unit testing is now what many people refer to as a "unit test" — and sometimes people use the term "unit test" to cover all forms of testing conducted using the programmatic unit testing frameworks, even if those tests are actually not tests of the unit of code, but are actually full integration tests.

Benefits of Unit Testing

A common reaction to unit testing is to resist the approach because the tests seemingly make more work for a developer. However, unit testing offers many benefits that may not be obvious at first.

The act of writing tests often uncovers design or implementation problems. The unit tests serve as the first users of your system, and they frequently identify design issues or functionality that is lacking. The act of thinking about tests causes the developer to question the requirements of the application, and, therefore, seek clarification from the business very early in the lifecycle of the software development project. This makes things easy and inexpensive to rectify as the clarification is received.

After a unit test is written, it serves as a form of living documentation for the use of the target system. Other developers can look to an assembly's unit tests to see example calls into various classes and members. An important benefit of unit tests for framework APIs is that the tests introduce a dependency at compile time, making it trivial to determine if any code changes have affected the contract represented by the API.

Perhaps one of the most important benefits is that a well-written test suite provides the original developer with the freedom to pass the system off to other developers for maintenance and further enhancement, knowing that their intentions of how the code would be used are fully covered by tests. Should those developers introduce a bug in the original functionality, there is a strong likelihood that those unit tests can detect that failure and help diagnose the issue. In addition, because there is a full set of unit tests making up the regression tests, it is a simple task for the maintenance team to introduce a new test that demonstrates the bug first, and then confirm that it is correctly fixed by the code modification. Meanwhile, the original developer can focus on current tasks.

It takes the typical developer time and practice to become comfortable with unit testing. After a developer has saved enough time by using unit tests, he or she latches on to them as an indispensable part of the development process.

Unit testing does require more explicit coding, but this cost will be recovered, and typically exceeded, when you spend much less time debugging your application. In addition, some of this cost is typically already hidden in the form of test console-or Windows-based applications that a developer might have previously used as a test harness. Unlike these informal testing applications, which are frequently discarded after initial verification, unit tests become a permanent part of the project, and run each time a change is made to help ensure that the system still functions as expected. Tests are stored in source control as part of the same solution with the code they verify and are maintained along with the code under test, making it easier to keep them synchronized.

> **NOTE** *Unit tests are an essential element of regression testing.* Regression testing *involves retesting a piece of software after new features have been added to make sure errors or bugs are not introduced. Regression testing also provides an essential quality check when you introduce bug fixes in your product.*

It is difficult to overstate the importance of comprehensive unit test suites. They enable a developer to hand off a system to other developers with confidence that any changes they make should not introduce undetected side effects. However, because unit testing only provides one view of a system's behavior, no amount of unit testing should ever replace integration, acceptance, and load testing.

Writing Effective Unit Tests

Because unit tests are themselves code, you are generally unlimited in the approaches you can take when writing them. However, you should follow some general guidelines:

➤ Always separate your unit test assemblies from the code you are testing. This separation enables you to deploy your application code without unit tests, which serve no purpose in a production environment.

➤ Avoid altering the code you are testing solely to allow easier unit testing. A common mistake is to open accessibility to class members to allow unit tests direct access. This compromises design, reduces encapsulation, and broadens interaction surfaces. You will see later in this chapter that Visual Studio offers features to help address this issue. However, be open minded to the idea that often what makes code easy to test in isolation makes that code more maintainable.

➤ Each test should verify a small slice of functionality. Do not write long sequential unit tests that verify a large number of items. Although creating focused tests results in more tests, the overall suite of tests is easier to maintain. In addition, identifying the cause of a problem is much easier when you can quickly look at a small failed unit test, immediately understand what it was testing, and know where to search for the bug.

➤ All tests should be autonomous and isolated. Avoid creating tests that rely on other tests to be run beforehand. Tests should be executable in any combination and in any order. To verify that your tests are correct, try changing their execution order and running them in isolation.

➤ Test both expected behavior (normal workflows) and error conditions (exceptions and invalid operations). This often means that you have multiple unit tests for the same method, but remember that developers always find ways to call your objects that you did not intend. Expect the unexpected, code defensively, and test to ensure that your code reacts appropriately.

The final proof of your unit testing's effectiveness is when it saves you more time during development and maintenance than you spent creating the tests. Experience has shown that you will realize this savings many times over.

Third-Party Tools

Unit testing is not a new concept. Before Visual Studio introduced integrated unit testing, developers needed to rely on third-party frameworks. The de facto standard for .NET unit testing has been an Open Source package called *NUnit*. NUnit has its original roots as a .NET port of the Java-based JUnit unit testing framework. JUnit is itself a member of the extended xUnit family.

There are many similarities between NUnit and the unit testing framework in Visual Studio. The structure and syntax of tests and the execution architecture are conveniently similar. If you have existing suites of NUnit-based tests, it is generally easy to convert them for use with Visual Studio.

Visual Studio's implementation of unit testing is not merely a port of NUnit. Microsoft has added a number of features including IDE integration, code generation, new attributes, and enhancements to the `Assert` class. The implementation is part of a broader testing platform across both Visual Studio and Team Foundation Server. For example, these tests can be run through the test controller/ agent system, associated with test case work items, and queued with automated tests to run from Microsoft Test Manager.

VISUAL STUDIO UNIT TESTING

Unit testing is a feature available in all editions of Visual Studio. This section describes how to create, execute, and manage unit tests.

Unit tests are themselves normal code, identified as unit tests through the use of attributes. Like NUnit 2.0 and later, Visual Studio uses .NET reflection to inspect assemblies to find unit tests.

> **NOTE** *Reflection is a mechanism by which details about .NET objects can be discovered at execution time. The* System.Reflection *assembly contains members that help you identify classes, properties, and methods of any .NET assembly. Reflection even enables you to call methods and access properties of classes.*

You also use attributes to identify other structures used in your tests and to indicate desired behaviors.

Creating Your First Unit Test

This section takes a slower approach to creating a unit test than you will in your normal work. This gives you a chance to examine details you could miss using only the built-in features that make unit testing easier. Later in this chapter, you look at the faster approaches.

In order to have something to test, create a new C# Class Library project named ExtendedMath. Rename the default Class1.cs to Functions.cs. You add code to compute the Fibonacci for a given number. The Fibonacci Sequence, as you may recall, is a series of numbers where each term is the sum of the prior two terms. The first six terms, starting with an input factor of 1, are 1, 1, 2, 3, 5, 8.

Open Functions.cs and insert the following code:

```
namespace ExtendedMath
{
    public static class Functions
    {
        public static int Fibonacci(int factor)
        {
            if (factor < 2)
                return (factor);
            int x = Fibonacci(--factor);
            int y = Fibonacci(--factor);

            return x + y;
        }
    }
}
```

You are now ready to create unit tests to verify the Fibonacci implementation. Unit tests are recognized as tests only if they are contained in separate projects called *test projects*. Test projects can contain any of the test types supported in Visual Studio. Add a test project named ExtendedMathTesting to your solution by adding a new project and selecting the Test Project template. If the test project includes any sample tests for you (such as UnitTest1.cs) then you can safely delete them. Because you will be calling objects in your ExtendedMath project, make a reference to that class library project from the test project. You may notice that a reference to the Microsoft.VisualStudio.QualityTools.UnitTestFramework.dll assembly has already been made for you. This assembly contains many helpful classes for creating units tests. You'll use many of these throughout this chapter.

After you have created a new test project, add a new class file (not a unit test; that file type is covered later) called FunctionsTest.cs. You use this class to contain the unit tests for the Functions class. You use unit testing objects from the `ExtendedMath` project and the `UnitTestFramework` assembly mentioned earlier, so add `using` statements at the top so that the class members do not need to be fully qualified:

```
using ExtendedMath;
using Microsoft.VisualStudio.TestTools.UnitTesting;
```

Identifying Unit Test Classes

To enable Visual Studio to identify a class as potentially containing unit tests, you must assign the `TestClass` attribute. If you forget to add the `TestClass` attribute, the unit tests methods in your class are not recognized.

To indicate that the `FunctionsTest` class contains unit tests, add the `TestClass` attribute to its declaration:

```
namespace ExtendedMath
{

  [TestClass]
    public class FunctionsTest
    {
    }
}
```

Unit tests are required to be hosted within public classes, so don't forget to include the `public` descriptor for the class. Note also that parentheses after an attribute are optional if you are not passing parameters to the attribute. For example, `[TestClass()]` and `[TestClass]` are equivalent.

Identifying Unit Tests

Having identified the class as a container of unit tests, you're ready to add your first unit test. A unit test method must be public, nonstatic, accept no parameters, and have no return value. To differentiate unit test methods from ordinary methods, they must be decorated with the `TestMethod` attribute.

Add the following code inside the `FunctionsTest` class:

```
[TestMethod]
public void FibonacciTest()
{
}
```

Unit Test Success and Failure

You have the shell of a unit test, but how do you test? A unit test indicates failure to Visual Studio by throwing an exception. Any test that does not throw an exception is considered to have passed, except in the case of `ExpectedException` attribute, which is described later.

The unit testing framework defines the `Assert` object. This object exposes many members, which are central to creating unit tests. You learn more about `Assert` later in the chapter.

Add the following code to the `FibonacciTest`:

```
[TestMethod]
public void FibonacciTest()
{

  const int FACTOR = 8;
  const int EXPECTED = 21;

  int actual = ExtendedMath.Functions.Fibonacci(FACTOR);

  Assert.AreEqual(EXPECTED, actual);
}
```

This uses the `Assert.AreEqual` method to compare two values, the value you expect and the value generated by calling the `Fibonacci` method. If they do not match, an exception is thrown, causing the test to fail.

When you run tests, you see the Test Results window. Success is indicated with a green checkmark and failure with a red X. A special result, inconclusive (described later in this chapter in the section "Using the Assert Methods"), is represented by a question mark.

To see a failing test, change the `EXPECTED` constant from 21 to 22 and rerun the test. The Test Results window shows the test as failed. The Error Message column provides details about the failure reason. In this case, the Error Message shows the following:

```
Assert.AreEqual failed. Expected:<22>, Actual:<21>
```

This indicates that either the expected value is wrong, or the implementation of the Fibonacci algorithm is wrong. Fortunately, because unit tests verify a small amount of code, the job of finding the source of bugs is made easier.

REMEMBER THE THREE A'S

When writing a unit test method, it is useful to remember the "Three-A's" pattern for your method — Arrange, Act, Assert. First, you arrange your test by setting up the variables, and then you invoke the code under test, and finally assert that the invoked code has passed the expectations. Use paragraphs of code (with empty lines between) for each of the A's.

Using this pattern makes is easy to look at test code written by others, and to determine exactly what is being done. In addition, it encourages you to only test one thing per test method.

Managing and Running Unit Tests

After you have created a unit test and rebuilt your project, Visual Studio automatically inspects your projects for unit tests. All unit tests that are found are displayed in the unit Test Explorer window, shown in Figure 18-1. This is a new window in Visual Studio 2012 for managing and running tests.

From this window you have multiple options, such as running all your unit tests, running only tests that have not been run yet, and viewing unit test run results.

FIGURE 18-1

> **NOTE** *For more detailed information on the Unit Test Explorer window, refer to Chapter 22.*

Running Tests Directly from Code

You also have the capability to run a unit test directly from code. To do that, open the unit test and navigate to the method. Right-click the unit test method in the code and, from the context menu, select Run Tests. The selected test method runs.

Debugging Unit Tests

Because unit tests are simply methods with special attributes applied to them, they can be debugged just like other code.

You can set breakpoints anywhere in your code, not just in your unit tests. For example, the `FibonacciTest` calls into the `ExtendedMath.Fibonacci` method. You could set a breakpoint in either method and have execution paused when that line of code is reached.

However, setting program execution does not pause at your breakpoints unless you run your unit test in debugging mode. The Test Explorer window enables you to right-click a test and select Debug Selected Tests. The selected unit test are run in debug mode, pausing execution at any enabled breakpoints and giving you a chance to evaluate and debug your unit test or implementation code as necessary.

> **NOTE** *If you have enabled code coverage for your application, you see a message indicating that you cannot debug while code coverage is enabled. Click OK and you continue debugging as normal, but code coverage results are not available. Code coverage is examined in detail in Chapter 22.*

PROGRAMMING WITH THE UNIT TEST FRAMEWORK

This section describes in detail the attributes and methods available to you for creating unit tests. You can find all the classes and attributes mentioned in this section in the `Microsoft.VisualStudio.TestTools.UnitTesting` namespace.

Initialization and Cleanup of Unit Tests

Often, you need to configure a resource that is shared among your tests. Examples might be a database connection, a log file, or a shared object in a known default state. You might also need ways to clean up from the actions of your tests, such as closing a shared stream or rolling back a transaction.

The unit test framework offers attributes to identify such methods. They are grouped into three levels: Test, Class, and Assembly. The levels determine the scope and timing of execution for the methods they decorate. Table 18-1 describes these attributes.

TABLE 18-1: Unit Test Framework Attributes

ATTRIBUTES	FREQUENCY AND SCOPE
`TestInitialize`, `TestCleanup`	Executed before (`Initialize`) or after (`Cleanup`) any of the class's unit tests are run
`ClassInitialize`, `ClassCleanup`	Executed a single time before or after any of the tests in the current class are run
`AssemblyInitialize`, `AssemblyCleanup`	Executed a single time before or after any number of tests in any of the assembly's classes are run

Having methods with these attributes is optional, but do not define more than one of each attribute in the same context. Also, keep in mind that you cannot guarantee the order in which your unit tests will be run, and that should govern what functionality you place in each of these methods.

TestInitialize and TestCleanup Attributes

Use the TestInitialize attribute to create a method that is executed one time before every unit test method in the current class. Similarly, TestCleanup marks a method that is always run immediately after each test. Like unit tests, methods with these attributes must be public, nonstatic, accept no parameters, and have no return values.

Following is an example test for a simplistic shopping cart class. It contains two tests and defines the TestInitialize and TestCleanup methods.

```
using Microsoft.VisualStudio.TestTools.UnitTesting;

[TestClass]
public class ShoppingCartTest
{
    private ShoppingCart cart;


  [TestInitialize]
    public void TestInitialize()
    {
        cart = new SomeClass();
        cart.Add(new Item("Test");)
    }


  [TestCleanup]
    public void TestCleanup()
    {
        // Not required - here for illustration
        cart.Dispose();
    }

    [TestMethod]
    public void TestCountAfterAdd()
    {
        int expected = cart.Count + 1;
        cart.Add(new Item("New Item");)
        Assert.AreEqual(expected, cart.Count);
    }

    [TestMethod]
    public void TestCountAfterRemove()
    {
        int expected = cart.Count - 1;
        cart.Remove(0);
        Assert.AreEqual(expected, cart.Count);
    }
}
```

When you run both tests, TestInitialize and TestCleanup are both executed twice. TestInitialize is run immediately before each unit test and TestCleanup immediately after.

ClassInitialize and ClassCleanup Attributes

The ClassInitialize and ClassCleanup attributes are used very similarly to TestInitialize and TestCleanup. The difference is that these methods are guaranteed to run once and only once no matter how many unit tests are executed from the current class. Unlike TestInitialize and TestCleanup, these methods are marked static and accept a TestContext instance as a parameter.

The importance of the TestContext instance is described later in this chapter.

The following code demonstrates how you might manage a shared logging target using class-level initialization and cleanup with a logging file:

```
private System.IO.File logFile;


[ClassInitialize]
    public static void ClassInitialize(TestContext context)
    {        // Code to open the logFile object     }


[ClassCleanup]
    public static void ClassCleanup(TestContext context)
    {        // Code to close the logFile object     }
```

You could now reference the logFile object from any of your unit tests in this class, knowing that it will automatically be opened before any unit test is executed and closed after the final test in the class has completed.

> **NOTE** *This approach to logging is simply for illustration. You see later how the* TestContext *object passed into these methods enables you to more effectively log details from your unit tests.*

The following code shows the flow of execution if you run both tests again:

```
ClassInitialize
    TestInitialize
        TestCountAfterAdd
    TestCleanup
    TestInitialize
        TestCountAfterRemove
    TestCleanup
ClassCleanup
```

AssemblyInitialize and AssemblyCleanup Attributes

Where you might use ClassInitialize and ClassCleanup to control operations at a class level, use the AssemblyInitialize and AssemblyCleanup attributes for an entire assembly. For example, a method decorated with AssemblyInitialize is executed once before any test in that current assembly, not just those in the current class. As with the class-level initialize and cleanup methods, these must be static and accept a `TestContext` parameter:

```
[AssemblyInitialize]
    public static void AssemblyInitialize(TestContext context)
    {        // Assembly-wide initialization code       }
```

```
[AssemblyCleanup]
    public static void AssemblyCleanup(TestContext context)
    {          // Assembly-wide cleanup code       }
```

Consider using `AssemblyInitialize` and `AssemblyCleanup` in cases where you have common operations spanning multiple classes. Instead of having many per-class initialize and cleanup methods, you can refactor these to single assembly-level methods.

Using the Assert Methods

The most common way to determine success in unit tests is to compare an expected result against an actual result. The `Assert` class features many methods that enable you to make these comparisons quickly.

Assert.AreEqual and Assert.AreNotEqual

Of the various `Assert` methods, you will likely find the most use for `AreEqual` and `AreNotEqual`. As their names imply, you are comparing an expected value to a supplied value. If the operands are not value-equivalent (or are equivalent for `AreNotEqual`) then the current test fails.

A third, optional argument can be supplied: a string that will be displayed along with your unit test results, which you can use to describe the failure. Additionally, you can supply parameters to be replaced in the string, just as the `String.Format` method supports. The string message should be used to explain why failing that `Assert` is an error. If you have multiple `Assert`s in a single test method, then it is very useful to provide a failure message string on every `Assert` so that you can very quickly identify which `Assert` failed.

```
[TestMethod]
public void IsPrimeTest()
{
    const int FACTOR = 5;
    const bool EXPECTED = true;

    bool actual = CustomMath.IsPrime(FACTOR);


    Assert.AreEqual(EXPECTED, actual, "The number {0} should have been computed as
              prime, but was not.", FACTOR);
}
```

`Assert.AreEqual` and `AreNotEqual` have many parameter overloads, accepting types such as `string`, `double`, `int`, `float`, `object`, and `generic` types. Take the time to review the overloads in the Object Browser.

When using these methods with two string arguments, one of the overrides allows you to optionally supply a third argument. This is a Boolean, called `ignoreCase`, that indicates whether the comparison should be case-insensitive. The default comparison is case-sensitive.

Working with floating-point numbers involves a degree of imprecision. You can supply an argument that defines a delta by which two numbers can differ yet still pass a test — for example, if you're computing square roots and decide that a "drift" of plus or minus 0.0001 is acceptable:

```
[TestMethod]
public void SquareRootTeset()
{
    const double EXPECTED = 3.1622;

  const double DELTA = 0.0001;
    double actual = CustomMath.SquareRoot(10);


  Assert.AreEqual(EXPECTED, actual, DELTA, "Root not within acceptable range");
}
```

> **NOTE** *When asserting that two instances of a complex type are equal, you are actually testing the behavior of the* `Equals()` *operator on that class. This is important to bear in mind if you are ever overriding the* `Equals` *operator in your own classes.*

Assert.AreSame and Assert.AreNotSame

`AreSame` and `AreNotSame` function in much the same manner as `AreEqual` and `AreNotEqual`. The important difference is that these methods compare the *references* of the supplied arguments. For example, if two arguments point to the same object instance, then `AreSame` passes. Even when the arguments are exactly equivalent in terms of their state, `AreSame` fails if they are not, in fact, the same object. This is the same concept that differentiates `object.Equals` from `object .ReferenceEquals`.

A common use for these methods is to ensure that properties return expected instances, or that collections handle references correctly. The following example adds an item to a collection and ensures that what you get back from the collection's indexer is a reference to the same item instance:

```
[TestMethod]
public void CollectionTest()
{
    CustomCollection cc = new CustomCollection();
    Item original = new Item("Expected");
    cc.Add(original);
    Item actual = cc[0];


  Assert.AreSame(original, actual);
}
```

Assert.IsTrue and Assert.IsFalse

As you can probably guess, `IsTrue` and `IsFalse` are used simply to ensure that the supplied expression is true or false as expected. Returning to the `IsPrimeNumberTest` example, you can restate it as follows:

```
[TestMethod]
public void IsPrimeTest()
{
    const int FACTOR = 5;


    Assert.IsTrue(CustomMath.IsPrime(FACTOR), "The number {0} should have been
                computed as prime, but was not.", FACTOR);
}
```

Assert.IsNull and Assert.IsNotNull

Similar to `IsTrue` and `IsFalse`, these methods verify that a given object type is either `null` or not `null`. Revising the collection example, this ensures that the item returned by the indexer is not `null`:

```
[TestMethod]
public void CollectionTest()
{
    CustomCollection cc = new CustomCollection();
    cc.Add(new Item("Added"));
    Item item = cc[0];


    Assert.IsNotNull(item);
}
```

Assert.IsInstanceOfType and Assert.IsNotInstanceOfType

`IsInstanceOfType` simply ensures that a given object is an instance of an expected type. For example, suppose you have a collection that accepts entries of any type. You'd like to ensure that an entry you're retrieving is of the expected type, as shown here:

```
[TestMethod]
public void CollectionTest()
{
    UntypedCollection untyped = new UntypedCollection();
    untyped.Add(new Item("Added"));
    untyped.Add(new Person("Rachel"));
    untyped.Add(new Item("Another"));

    object entry = untyped[1];


    Assert.IsInstanceOfType(entry, typeof(Person));
}
```

As you can no doubt guess, `IsNotInstanceOfType` tests to ensure that an object is not the specified type.

Assert.Fail and Assert.Inconclusive

Use `Assert.Fail` to immediately fail a test. For example, you may have a conditional case that should never occur. If it does, call `Assert.Fail` and an `AssertFailedException` is thrown, causing the test to abort with failure. You may find `Assert.Fail` useful when defining your own custom `Assert` methods.

`Assert.Inconclusive` enables you to indicate that the test result cannot be verified as a pass or fail. This is typically a temporary measure until a unit test (or the related implementation) has been completed. Assert.Inconclusive can also be used to indicate that more work is needed to complete a unit test.

> **NOTE** *There is no* `Assert.Succeed` *because success is indicated by completion of a unit test method without a thrown exception. Use a* `return` *statement if you want to cause this result from some point in your test.* `Assert.Fail` *and* `Assert.Inconclusive` *both support a string argument and optional arguments, which are inserted into the string in the same manner as* `String.Format`. *Use this string to supply a detailed message back to the Test Results window, describing the reasons for the nonpassing result.*

Using the CollectionAssert class

The `Microsoft.VisualStudio.TestTools.UnitTesting` namespace includes a class, `CollectionAssert`, that contains useful methods for testing the contents and behavior of collection types.

Table 18-2 describes the methods supported by `CollectionAssert`.

TABLE 18-2: CollectionAssert Methods

METHOD	DESCRIPTION
AllItemsAreInstancesOfType	Ensures that all elements are of an expected type
AllItemsAreNotNull	Ensures that no items in the collection are `null`
AllItemsAreUnique	Searches a collection, failing if a duplicate member is found
AreEqual	Ensures that two collections have reference-equivalent members
AreNotEqual	Ensures that two collections do not have reference-equivalent members
AreEquivalent	Ensures that two collections have value-equivalent members

continues

TABLE 18-2: *(continued)*

METHOD	DESCRIPTION
AreNotEquivalent	Ensures that two collections do not have value-equivalent members
Contains	Searches a collection, failing if the given object is not found
DoesNotContain	Searches a collection, failing if a given object is found
IsNotSubsetOf	Ensures that the first collection has members not found in the second
IsSubsetOf	Ensures that all elements in the first collection are found in the second

The following example uses some of these methods to verify various behaviors of a collection type, `CustomCollection`. When this example is run, none of the assertions fail, and the test results in success. Note that proper unit testing would spread these checks across multiple smaller tests.

```
[TestMethod]
public void CollectionTests()
{
    CustomCollection list1 = new CustomCollection();
    list1.Add("alpha");
    list1.Add("beta");
    list1.Add("delta");
    list1.Add("delta");


    CollectionAssert.AllItemsAreInstancesOfType(list1, typeof(string));
    CollectionAssert.AllItemsAreNotNull(list1);

    CustomCollection list2 = (CustomCollection)list1.Clone();


    CollectionAssert.AreEqual(list1, list2);
    CollectionAssert.AreEquivalent(list1, list2);

    CustomCollection list3 = new CustomCollection();
    list3.Add("beta");
    list3.Add("delta");


    CollectionAssert.AreNotEquivalent(list3, list1);
    CollectionAssert.IsSubsetOf(list3, list1);
    CollectionAssert.DoesNotContain(list3, "alpha");
    CollectionAssert.AllItemsAreUnique(list3);
}
```

The final assertion, `AllItemsAreUnique(list3)`, would have failed if tested against `list1` because that collection has two entries of the string `"delta"`.

Using the StringAssert class

Similar to `CollectionAssert`, the `StringAssert` class contains methods that enable you to easily make assertions based on common text operations. Table 18-3 describes the methods supported by `StringAssert`.

TABLE 18-3: StringAssert Methods

METHOD	DESCRIPTION
Contains	Searches a string for a substring and fails if not found
DoesNotMatch	Applies a regular expression to a string and fails if any matches are found
EndsWith	Fails if the string does not end with a given substring
Matches	Applies a regular expression to a string and fails if no matches are found
StartsWith	Fails if the string does not begin with a given substring

Following are some simple examples of these methods. Each of these assertions will pass:

```
[TestMethod]
public void TextTests()
{
    StringAssert.Contains("This is the searched text", "searched");

    StringAssert.EndsWith("String which ends with searched", "ends with searched");

    StringAssert.Matches("Search this string for whitespace",
                new System.Text.RegularExpressions.Regex(@"\s+"));

    StringAssert.DoesNotMatch("Doesnotcontainwhitespace",
                new System.Text.RegularExpressions.Regex(@"\s+"));

    StringAssert.StartsWith("Starts with correct text", "Starts with");
}
```

`Matches` and `DoesNotMatch` accept a string and an instance of `System.Text` `.RegularExpressions.Regex`. In the preceding example, a simple regular expression that looks for at least one whitespace character was used. `Matches` finds whitespace and `DoesNotMatch` does not find whitespace, so both pass.

Expecting Exceptions

Normally, a unit test that throws an exception is considered to have failed. However, you'll often want to verify that a class behaves correctly by throwing an exception. For example, you might provide invalid arguments to a method to verify that it properly throws an exception.

The `ExpectedException` attribute indicates that a test succeeds only if the indicated exception is thrown. Not throwing an exception or throwing an exception of a different type results in test failure.

The following unit test expects that an ObjectDisposedException will be thrown:

```
[TestMethod]

[ExpectedException(typeof(ObjectDisposedException))]
public void ReadAfterDispose()
{
    CustomFileReader cfr = new CustomFileReader("target.txt");
    cfr.Dispose();
    string contents = cfr.Read();   // Should throw ObjectDisposedException
}
```

The ExpectedException attribute supports a second, optional string argument. The Message property of the thrown exception must match this string or the test fails. This enables you to differentiate between two different instances of the same exception type.

For example, suppose you are calling a method that throws a FileNotFoundException for several different files. To ensure that it cannot find one specific file in your testing scenario, supply the message you expect as the second argument to ExpectedException. If the exception thrown is not FileNotFoundException and its Message property does not match that text, the test fails.

Defining Custom Unit Test Properties

You may define custom properties for your unit tests. For example, you may want to specify the author of each test and be able to view that property from the Test List Editor.

Use the TestProperty attribute to decorate a unit test, supplying the name of the property and a value:

```
[TestMethod]

[TestProperty("Author", "Deborah")]
public void ExampleTest()
{
    // Test logic
}
```

Now, when you view the properties of that test, you see a new entry, Author, with the value Deborah. If you change that value from the Properties window, the attribute in your code is automatically updated.

TestContext Class

Unit tests normally have a reference to a TestContext instance. This object provides runtime features that might be useful to tests, such as details of the test itself, the various directories in use, and several methods to supplement the details stored with the test's results. TestContext is also very important for data-driven unit tests, as you see later.

Several methods are especially useful to all unit tests. The first, WriteLine, enables you to insert text into the results of your unit test. This can be useful for supplying additional information about the test, such as parameters, environment details, and other debugging data that would normally be excluded from test results.

Here is a simple example of a unit test that accesses the `TestContext` to send a string containing the test's name to the results:

```
[TestClass]
public class TestClass
{
    private TestContext testContextInstance;

    public TestContext TestContext
    {
        get { return testContextInstance; }
        set { testContextInstance = value; }
    }

    [TestMethod]
    public void TestMethod1()
    {
        TestContext.WriteLine("This is test {0}", TestContext.TestName);
    }
}
```

The `AddResultFile` method enables you to add a file, at runtime, to the results of the test run. The file you specify is copied to the results directory alongside other results content. For example, this may be useful if your unit test is validating an object that creates or alters a file, and you would like that file to be included with the results for analysis.

Finally, the `BeginTimer` and `EndTimer` methods enable you to create one or more named timers within your unit tests. The results of these timers are stored in the test run's results.

INTRODUCTION TO MICROSOFT FAKES

One of the many features people have asked for from Visual Studio is for it to ship with a *mocking framework*. A mocking framework enables you to provide a fake implementation of a type or object, along with logic that verifies how calls were made to the mocked object. There are several good mock frameworks currently available in the community, including Moq, Rhino, and NMock. Although these tools have strong followings and a good reputation, there was still a need to provide a mocking framework to customers who may be unable to utilize open-source or third-party tools. Hence the introduction of the Microsoft Fakes framework in Visual Studio 2012.

Developers often need to test individual components of their code in isolation from other components. Commonly, this is performed using dummy implementations of code that are not currently being tested. In reality, it can be very difficult to implement this dummy code because the actual code being tested is expecting real code on the other end. The Fakes framework helps developers create, maintain, and inject dummy implementation of components into the developer's unit test, making it quick and easy to isolate specific unit tests from the actual environment.

> **NOTE** *The Fakes Framework is derived from the Moles project by Microsoft Research. The Fakes framework is not backward compatible with Moles, but the migration is straightforward.*

Currently, the Fakes framework focuses on two kinds of test fakes for .NET programming: stubs and shims.

Stubs are concrete implementations of interfaces and abstract classes that can be passed into the system being tested. A developer provides method implementations via .NET delegates or lambdas. A stub is realized by a distinct type that is generated by the Fakes framework. As such, all stubs are strongly typed. You cannot use stubs for static or non-overridable methods. Instead, you should use shims in those instances.

Shims are runtime method interceptors. They enable you to provide your own implementation for almost any method available to your code in .NET, including types and methods from the .NET base class libraries.

Choosing between Stubs and Shims

Stub types and shim types are built on different underlying technologies. As such, they have different requirements, properties, and use cases. Table 18-3 provides a list of the different aspects to consider when choosing between a stub and a shim.

TABLE 18-3: Stubs versus Shims

ASPECT	STUB/SHIM	REASON
Performance	Stub	The runtime code rewriting used by shims introduces some performance issues at runtime. Stubs do not do this.
Static Methods	Shim	Stub can only influence overridable methods. They cannot be used for static, non-virtual, and sealed virtual methods.
Internal Types	Stub/Shim	Both Stubs and Shims can be used with internal types made accessible through the `InternalsVisibleToAttribute` attribute.
Private Methods	Shim	Shim types can replace private methods if all the types on the method signature are visible.
Interfaces/Abstract Methods	Stub	Stubs implement interfaces and abstract methods that can be used for testing. Shims can't do this because they don't have method bodies.

The general recommendation is to use stubs to isolate dependencies within your codebase by hiding components behind interfaces. You should use shims to isolate third-party components that don't provide a testing API.

Using Stubs

Stubs are a part of the Fakes framework that enables you to easily isolate unit tests from the environment. You do this by generating a Fakes assembly, based off an actual target assembly. When the

Fakes assembly is generated, a stub type is created for each non-sealed class and interface in the target assembly that contains virtual or abstract methods, properties, or events. The stub type provides a default implementation of each virtual member and adds a delegate property that you can customize to provide specific behavior.

For this example, you are going to make a list of books. To get started, create a new C# class library project named FakesUsingStubs. Rename the Class1.cs file to be Book.cs. Add the following code to the Book.cs file to create a Book class:

```csharp
public class Book
{
    public int Isbn {get;set;}
    public int ListItemId {get;set;}

    public Book (int isbn, int listItemId)
    {
        Isbn = isbn;
        ListItemId = listItemId;
    }
}
```

Now add the following class, BookListToStub. This class contains a list of books and has a method, AddBookToList, for adding a new book to the list.

```csharp
public class BookListToStub
{
    public int ListId {get;set}
    public int CustomerId {get;set;}
    private List<Book> _books = new List<Book>();
    public ReadOnlyCollection<Book> Books {get; set;}
    private IListSave _listSave;

    public BookListToStub(int listId, int customerId, IListSave listSave)
    {
        ListId = listId;
        CustomerId = customerId;
        _listSave = listSave;
        Books = new ReadOnlyCollection<Book>(_books);
    }

    public void AddBookToList(int isbn)
    {
        Var bookItemId = _listSave.SaveListItem(ListId, isbn);
        _books.Add(new Book(isbn, bookItemId));
    }
}
```

The saving functionality is implemented using a class called ListSave that implements the interface IListSave.

```csharp
public interface IListSave
{
    int SaveListItem(int listId, int isbn);
}

public class ListSave : IListSave
```

```
    {
        public int SaveListItem(int listId, int isbn)
        {
            throw new NotImplementedException("Forgot to add SQL Code");
        }
    }
}
```

As you can see from the preceding snippet of code, the actual code to perform the save has not been implemented yet. Normally, that would make testing the save functionality difficult. Microsoft Fakes enables you to stub out the saving functionality so that you can test the rest of the code even though the saving functionality does not currently exist.

Right-click your solution and add a new C# Test Project to the solution, named `FakesUsingStubs` `.Tests`. Rename the default unit test file to `BookListToStubTests.cs`. Add a reference to the `FakesUsingStubs` project by right-clicking the References folder, selecting Add Reference from the context menu, and then selecting the `FakesUsingStubs` assembly. To create your shims and stubs, right-click the `FakesUsingStubs` assembly, and select `Add Fakes Assembly`. When you do this, several things happen behind the scenes:

➤   A file named `.fakes` is created in the Fakes folder within your project. This file controls how your fakes are generated.

➤   The target assembly is scanned, and fakes types (both Stubs and Shims) are created for the types found. These types are named `StubX` and `ShimX` based on the type they target.

➤   These fake types are added to a new assembly created in a sub-folder called FakeAssemblies.

To complete your testing, you need to mock out the database call to isolate the logic in the `AddBookToList` method. Open the `BookListToStubTests.cs` file, and add the following test method:

```
[TestMethod]
public void AddBook_BookShouldBeAddedToList()
{
    int bookItemId = 77;
    int listId = 1;
    int customerId = 25;
    int isbn = 12345;

    //Stub IListSave
    var listSave = new Fakes.StubIListSave();
    listSave.SaveListItemInt32Int32 = (1,i) => bookItemId;

    var list = new BookListToStub(listId, customerId, listSave);
    list.AddBookToList(isbn);

    var book = list.Books[0];
    Assert.AreEqual(isbn, book.Isbn);
}
```

When you created the Fakes assembly, you created a stub method for the `IListSave` interface that can be overridden using a delegate. In this case, you have create a delegate that returns the `bookItemId`, which is what you would expect from the save functionality that is not implemented. If you execute the unit test, it executes with no errors.

Using Shims

Shims are runtime method interceptors. They enable you to provide your own implementation for almost any method available to your code in .NET, including types and methods from the .NET base class libraries.

For this example, you are again going to make a list of books, but with some changes to the code. Instead of implementing an interface you are going to implement a static class for the data access layer. To get started, created a new C# class library project named `FakesUsingShims`. Rename the `Class1.cs` file to be `Book.cs`. Add the following code to `Book.cs` file, to create a Book class:

```
public class Book
{
    public int Isbn {get;set;}
    public int ListItemId {get;set;}

    public Book (int isbn, int listItemId)
    {
        Isbn = isbn;
        ListItemId = listItemId;
    }
}
```

Now add the following class, `BookListToShim`. This class contains a list of books and has a method, `AddBookToList`, for adding a new book to the list. Notice this method now makes use of a new class, `DAL`, that contains the saving functionality:

```
public class BookListToShim
{
    public int ListId {get;set}
    public int CustomerId {get;set;}
    private List<Book> _books = new List<Book>();
    public ReadOnlyCollection<Book> Books {get; set;}

    public BookListToStub(int listId, int customerId)
    {
        ListId = listId;
        CustomerId = customerId;
        Books = new ReadOnlyCollection<Book>(_books);
    }

    public void AddBookToList(int isbn)
    {
        var bookItemId = DAL.SaveListItem(ListId, isbn);
        _books.Add(new Book(isbn, bookItemId));
    }
}
```

Create a new C# class file named `DAL.cs`. Add the following code to implement the saving functionality.

```
public static class DAL
{
    public static int SaveListItem(int listId, int isbn)
    {
        throw new NotImplementedException("Forgot to add SQL Code");
    }
}
```

As before, the actual code to perform the save has not been implemented yet. Microsoft Fakes allows you to shim out the saving functionality, enabling you to test the rest of the code even though the saving functionality does not currently exist.

Right-click your solution and add a new C# Test Project to the solution, named FakesUsingShims .Tests. Rename the default unit test file to BookListToShimTests.cs. Add a reference to the FakesUsingShims project by right-clicking the References folder, selecting Add Reference from the context menu, and then selecting the FakesUsingShims assembly. Right-click the FakesUsingShims assembly and select Add Fakes Assembly to generate the shim and stub code.

To complete your testing, you need to mock out the database call to isolate the logic in the AddBookToList method. Open the BookListToShimTests.cs file, and add the following test method:

```
[TestMethod]
public void AddBook_BookShouldBeAddedToList()
{
    int bookItemId = 77;
    int listId = 1;
    int customerId = 25;
    int isbn = 12345;

    using (ShimsContext.Create())
    {

        Fakes.ShimDAL.SaveListItemInt32Int32 = (l,i) => bookItemId;

        var list = new BookListToStub(listId, customerId);
        list.AddBookToList(isbn);

        var book = list.Books[0];
        Assert.AreEqual(isbn, book.Isbn);
    }
}
```

In the test method, you create a ShimsContext, which enables you to scope the amount of shimming you are implementing. The rest of the code is very similar to the stubs example, and works in the same way, with a delegate being used to override the SaveListItem method.

TEST ADAPTERS

The unit testing framework in Visual Studio 2012 has been completely revamped so the unit testing engine is extensible. This allows third-party unit testing frameworks, such as NUnit or XUnit, to create test adapters for Visual Studio unit testing. Now a developer can use any testing framework that provides an adapter, for unit test creation.

You can download most third-party unit test frameworks using the Visual Studio Extension Manager inside of Visual Studio, or you can get them directly from the Visual Studio Gallery on the MSDN website.

To download a third-party test framework adapter using the Visual Studio Extension Manager, open Visual Studio and select Tools ➪ Extensions and Updates from the main menu. The Extension and Updates dialog box opens. In the dialog box, select Online ➪ Visual Studio Gallery ➪ Tools ➪ Testing, as shown in Figure 18-2.

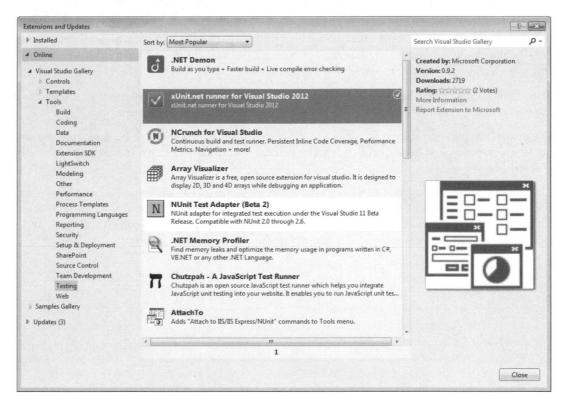

FIGURE 18-2

Select the Unit Test framework to install, and click the Download button. If you already have a testing framework installed, you see a green checkmark instead of a download button. Clicking the Download button automatically downloads and installs the testing framework. You need to restart Visual Studio 2012 before you can start using the testing framework.

After you have restarted Visual Studio, you can start creating unit tests using the new test framework, and you can execute those unit tests inside of Visual Studio 2012.

There are a couple of limitations with using test adapters. For example, even though you can run them using the Agile Test Runner as part of the Team Foundation Build process, you are not able to associate the automation with a test case. This means that you can't use them as part of your test controller/agent infrastructure.

SUMMARY

Microsoft has brought the advantages of unit testing to the developer by fully integrating features with the Visual Studio development environment. If you're new to unit testing, this chapter has provided an overview of what unit testing is, and how you can create effective unit tests. This chapter examined the creation and management of unit tests and detailed the methods and attributes available in the unit test framework. You should be familiar with attributes for identifying your tests, as well as many of the options that the `Assert` class offers for testing behavior of code.

You also learned about the Microsoft Fakes framework, and how you can use shims and stubs to help you test your code more effectively while isolating different systems in your environment. Finally, the chapter covered test adapters, how test adapters enable you to utilize third-party testing frameworks, and how you can install test adapters.

You should become familiar with the benefits of unit testing, keeping in mind that unit tests are not a replacement for other forms of testing, but they are a very strong supplement.

Obviously, testing is an important aspect to prove that your code is ready to be deployed into production. However, just because the code passes all the unit tests doesn't mean that it is necessarily ready to ship.

Chapter 19 examines the code analysis tools in Visual Studio 2012 that help you quickly look for common mistakes, security issues, or even violations of standards. You also find out how to use Code Metrics to help you identify parts of the systems that may prove difficult to maintain, and how code cloning can help you find duplicate code to refactor in your solution.

19

Code Analysis, Code Metrics, and Code Clone Analysis

WHAT'S IN THIS CHAPTER?

➤ Enabling and running code analysis in Visual Studio 2012

➤ Correcting code analysis rule violations

➤ Understanding code metrics and how to use them

➤ Using Code Clone Analysis to find similar code fragments in your code base

WROX.COM CODE DOWNLOADS FOR THIS CHAPTER

The wrox.com code downloads for this chapter are found at www.wrox.com/remtitle .cgi?isbn=1118314081 on the Download Code tab. The files are in the Chapter 19 download folder and individually named as shown throughout this chapter.

This chapter describes the code analysis, code metric, and code clone analysis features included with the Visual Studio 2012 Premium and Ultimate editions. These tools can quickly and easily inspect your code to find common mistakes, make suggestions for improvements, and even indicate violations of standards.

The discussion begins by examining the origins of the Static Code Analysis tool. You find out about Microsoft's .NET "Design Guidelines for Class Library Developers" and how it is related to the tools. You also take a brief look at what is new with these tools in Visual Studio 2012.

Then you do a bit of exploration into the code analysis itself and how to take advantage of its full integration with Visual Studio 2012. This includes enabling static code analysis review for your projects, selecting rules to apply, and working with the results of the analysis.

However, using the IDE is not always an option, and sometimes you need additional flexibility. The Static Code Analysis tool is available to you from the command line. You find out how to use the command line for code analysis and how to include code analysis with your automated builds.

Next, you look at Code Metrics, a tool in Visual Studio that can provide insight into how maintainable your code is. Each code metric is examined in detail, and you learn how to understand what code metrics are trying to tell you.

The chapter wraps up with a look at a new feature in Visual Studio 2012: Code Clone Analysis. Fragments of code, called code clones, happen throughout all projects as code is copied and pasted into different areas. Code clone analysis enables you to find these similar fragments of code, which makes it easier to apply changes or refactor your code base.

THE NEED FOR ANALYSIS TOOLS

Ensuring that developers follow best practices and write consistent code is a major challenge in today's software development projects. The act of documenting standards and practices is often skipped or overlooked. However, even in projects for which standards have been established, getting developers to read and follow those practices is another major challenge.

One of the best resources available for .NET developers is Microsoft's .NET Framework "Design Guidelines for Class Library Developers" (Design Guidelines). These guidelines document Microsoft's (formerly) internal practices for developing class libraries, and are freely available at `http://msdn.microsoft.com/en-us/library/ms229042.aspx`.

The guidelines cover a range of subjects, including naming conventions, usage guidelines, and performance and security considerations. When you put them into practice, they help ensure that your approach is consistent with that of other developers. In addition, they have evolved over a number of years to reflect a considerable amount of knowledge, best practices, and lessons learned.

As useful as the design guidelines are, the reality of software creation is that many developers are not familiar with their contents. Most times, this is not a fault of the developer, but rather the process that the developer must follow. For some companies, design guidelines are not as important as simply getting the project finished, regardless of the long-term benefit that following those guidelines will have. The desire to automate the process of evaluating code for compliance with these guidelines led to the creation of *FxCop*, a tool that was used internally at Microsoft and later evolved into the Code Analysis tool in Visual Studio.

What's New for Code Analysis in Visual Studio 2012

One of the most important updates is that code analysis is now available in all editions of Visual Studio 2012, including a subset of the most critical warnings in the Express editions of Visual Studio. All the code analysis rules are available in the Professional, Premium, and Ultimate editions.

Support has also been provided for 64-bit C++ projects, as well as the ability to create custom rule sets for C++ projects.

One of the most difficult areas around code analysis has been managing the large result sets it can return. Visual Studio 2012 addresses this through the use of a new Code Analysis results window, which includes filtering to quickly and easily narrow result information.

Finally, code editor highlighting has been added for code analysis results. Selecting a message in the Code Analysis results window highlights the line of code in the source code editor that triggered the message. This makes it easy to correlate the message to the offending line of code.

USING CODE ANALYSIS

An example project that demonstrates the use of managed code analysis is presented throughout this chapter. To begin the project, create a new C# Class Library project and name it SampleLibrary. Rename the Class1.cs file to **PayCalculator.cs** and insert the following code, which fails to meet several code analysis guidelines:

```csharp
using System;
using System.Collections.Generic;
using System.Linq;
using System.Text;
using System.Threading.Tasks;

namespace SampleLibrary
{
    public class PayCalculator
    {
        public enum Pay_Level
        {
            EntryLevel = 20,
            Normal = 35,
            Senior = 50
        }

        public static int MaximumHours;
        public const double BONUS = 0.10;

        static PayCalculator()
        {
            MaximumHours = 100;
        }

        public static double ComputePayment(int hours, Pay_Level level)
        {
            if (hours > MaximumHours)
            {
                throw new ArgumentOutOfRangeException("Employee works too much");
            }

            return ((int)level * hours);
        }
    }
}
```

While this code compiles and runs as expected, you can make several improvements to it, and the Code Analysis tool helps you find them. These improvements help make your code easier to understand, and possibly catch potential run-time errors (such as buffer overflows).

Built-in Code Analysis Rules

As mentioned earlier, Visual Studio ships with nearly 200 rules for managed Code Analysis, as well as more than 300 rules for native code, each of which helps to enforce the practices documented in the .NET Framework Design Guidelines, as well as other practices recommended by Microsoft. This section briefly describes each of the 12 rule groups to help you understand when you might apply them to your projects.

Table 19-1 describes the groups of rules included with Visual Studio 2012.

TABLE 19-1: Groups of Rules

RULE GROUP (NUMBER OF RULES)	DESCRIPTION
Design (67)	Typically focused on the interfaces and structure of code, this group enforces proper implementation of common concepts such as classes, events, collections, namespaces, and parameters. These rules revolve around the Microsoft .NET Framework Design Guidelines.
Globalization (11)	This group includes practices to support the internationalization of code. This can include avoiding strings of literal text, correct use of `CultureInfo`, and formatting.
Interoperability (16)	This group is focused on the correct use of COM Interop. Included are rules for proper use of `PInvoke`, the `ComVisible` attribute, and marshalling.
Maintainability (6)	These are rules to help make your code easier to maintain. This group identifies potential problems such as complexity and overuse of inheritance.
Mobility (2)	These are rules to help detect code that will not run effectively in mobile or disconnected environments.
Naming (24)	This group enforces naming standards as described in the Design Guidelines. Using these rules verifies that names of items such as assemblies, classes, members, and variables conform to standards. Some rules even help to detect misspellings in your assigned names.
Performance (16)	These rules help to detect places in your code that may be optimized for performance. They detect a variety of wasteful or extraneous code.
Portability (3)	These are rules to find code that might not be easily portable between operating environments.

RULE GROUP (NUMBER OF RULES)	DESCRIPTION
Reliability (6)	The rules in this group help detect problems with your code that may lead to intermittent failures, including failure to dispose of objects, improper use of the garbage collector, bad threading use, and more. These rules can be extremely useful because intermittent errors are frequently the most difficult to identify and correct.
Security (44)	These rules help to identify insufficient or incorrect security practices. Rules exist to find missing attributes, improper use of permissions, and opportunities for SQL injection attacks.
Usage (42)	These rules cover a broad spectrum of recommended practices. Whereas the design group rules typically involve API structure, these rules govern the methodologies of code. Practices include proper exception management, handling of arithmetic overflow, serialization, and inheritance.
Native (362)	These rules cover information related to C/C++ source code, including buffer overruns, uninitialized memory, null pointer dereferences, and memory and resource leaks.

Of course, the rules that ship with Visual Studio are only a starting point. Microsoft and others will certainly make additional rules available, and you can add your own custom rules and rule groups as well.

Code Analysis Rule Sets

With Visual Studio 2012, you can group code analysis rules into rule sets, making it easy for everyone to get started using code analysis. The code analysis rules that ship by default are already grouped into specified rule sets, but you have the capability to create your own custom rule sets as needed.

Table 19-2 shows the rule sets included with Visual Studio 2012.

TABLE 19-2: Rule Sets

RULE SET	DESCRIPTION
Microsoft All Rules	This rule set contains all code analysis rules.
Microsoft Basic Correctness Rules	This rule set focuses on logic errors and common mistakes made when using the .NET framework APIs.
Microsoft Basic Design Guideline Rules	This rule set focuses on enforcing best practices to make code easy to understand and use.
Microsoft Extended Correctness Rules	This rule set expands on the basic correctness rules to maximize the reported logic and framework usage errors.

continues

TABLE 19-2 *(continued)*

RULE SET	DESCRIPTION
Microsoft Extended Design Guideline Rules	This rule set expands on the basic design guideline rules to maximize the number of reported usability and maintainability issues.
Microsoft Globalization Rules	This rule set focuses on problems that may occur if your application has not been properly localized.
Microsoft Managed Minimum Rules	This rule set focuses on the most critical problems in your code for which Code Analysis is most accurate. It contains a small number of rules and is intended for use in Visual Studio Express editions.
Microsoft Managed Recommended Rules	This rule set focuses on the most critical problems in your code, including security holes and application crashes. This is the default rule set applied to newly created projects and is recommended for inclusion in any custom rule set you create.
Microsoft Security Rules	This rule set contains all Microsoft security rules.
Microsoft Mixed (C++/CLR) Minimum Rules	This rule set focuses on the most critical problems in C++ projects, including security holes and application crashes.
Microsoft Mixed (C++/CLR) Recommended Rules	This rule set focuses on the most common and critical problems in C++ projects, including security holes, application crashes, and important logic and design errors. It is designed for use in Visual Studio Professional and higher.

To create a new rule set, in Visual Studio, select File ⇨ New ⇨ File…, and then select Code Analysis Rule Set under the General tab. Using this new rule set, you can use the Add or Remove child rule set buttons to add existing rule sets to your custom rule set.

Enabling Code Analysis

By default, code analysis is disabled for projects in Visual Studio. To enable analysis, open your project's Properties window and select Code Analysis from the left-hand side tabs. You see a drop-down of the different rule sets available for use with code analysis. You no longer see a collapsed list of rules as with previous versions, but instead you see the new menu showing the selected rule set, as shown in Figure 19-1.

> **WARNING** *To enable and configure Code Analysis for ASP.NET applications, from the main menu in Visual Studio, select Website ⇨ Code Analysis Configuration. You can also enable (but not configure) Code Analysis from the Build page of the ASP.NET project's Property Pages.*

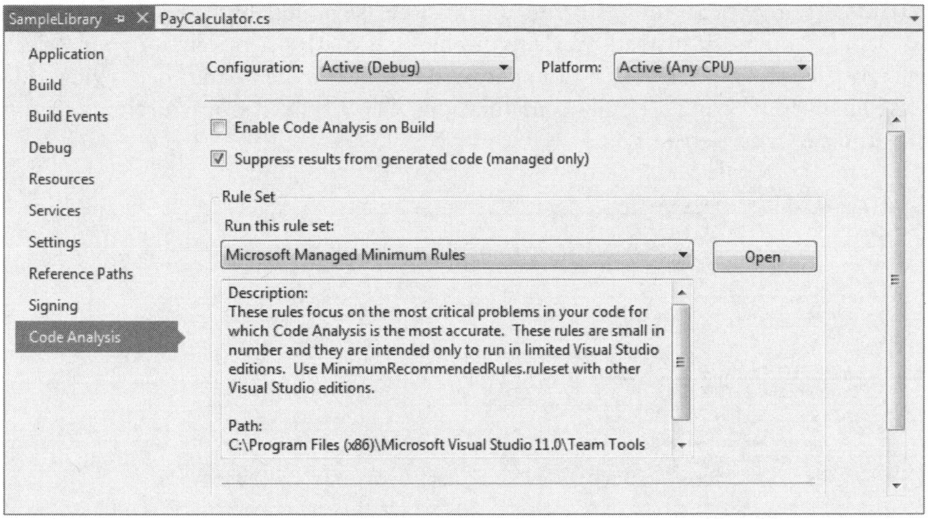

FIGURE 19-1

To enable code analysis upon build, select the Enable Code Analysis on Build checkbox. Select the desired rule set in the dropdown list box, or choose multiple rule sets. Save your settings via Save Selected Items on the File menu, or by pressing Ctrl+S.

To view the rules contained in an individual rule set, select the rule set in the dropdown list box and then click the Open button. The individual rules that comprise that rule set open. You can disable rules or entire groups of rules by deselecting their checkboxes.

In addition, you can set each rule in a rule set to one of the following:

➤ *Warning* (the default) — Warnings serve as an advisory that something may need to be corrected, but they do not prevent the project's build from succeeding.

➤ *Error* — Errors prevent a build when those rules are violated, so you may want to set certain rules or groups of rules to Error if they are critically important.

➤ *Inherit* — Inherit means this rule uses the same indicator that the group it is contained in uses.

➤ *None* — This means no setting.

Use the dropdown list in the Action column to choose among Warning, Error, None, or Inherit. As with enabling rules, you can set these actions for specific rules or for entire groups of rules.

Figure 19-2 illustrates how to enable and disable specific rules and how each can be set to Warning or Error as necessary.

Finally, you can specify different sets of code analysis properties for each configuration. By default, settings apply to the Active build configuration, but you can be more specific. For example, you might want to treat certain critical rules as Errors in your Release builds, but treat those same rules as Warnings in Debug. You might instead decide to disable code analysis entirely for your Release builds. Simply choose a build type from the Configuration dropdown menu and then review your settings. To make changes affecting all build configurations, select the All Configurations option and then modify and save your settings.

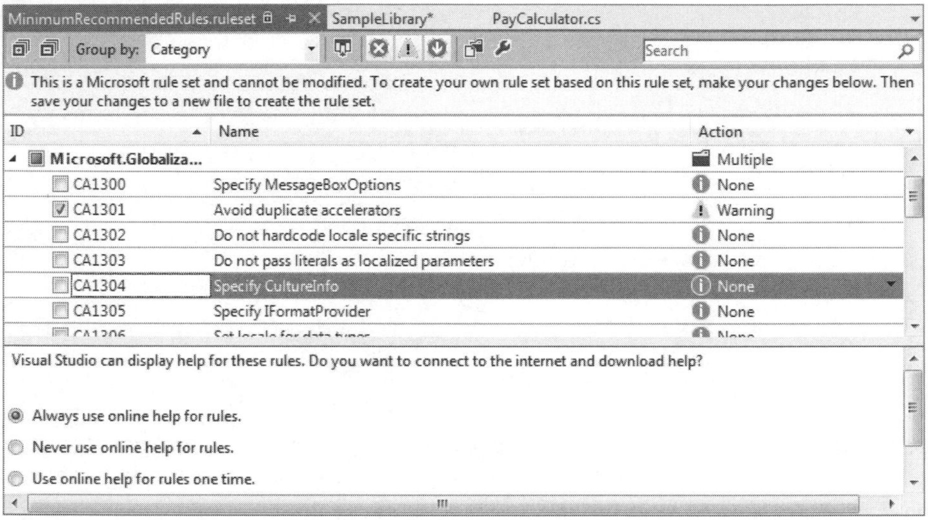

FIGURE 19-2

Executing Code Analysis

After you have enabled code analysis and configured the rules to reflect your development standards, code analysis is performed each time you build your project. Go ahead and build your sample project now.

> **NOTE** *You can also execute code analysis on your project by choosing Build ⇨ Run Code Analysis on [Project Name] or by right-clicking the desired project within Solution Explorer and selecting Run Code Analysis.*

The output window includes details about your build, including results from calling code analysis. After the build, the Code Analysis window (a new window in Visual Studio 2012) may appear, displaying a number of warnings and possibly some errors. If you do not see the Code Analysis window, choose Analyze ⇨ Windows ⇨ Code Analysis. By default this window appears as a tab in the same well as Solution Explorer.

By default, the Microsoft Minimum Recommended Rules rule set is selected, and thus, no warnings are generated. For the purpose of this example, return to the rule set selection and choose the Microsoft All Rules rule set.

Figure 19-3 shows the Code Analysis window displaying code analysis results for the `SampleLibrary` assembly.

The new Code Analysis window provides some nice features for working with code analysis results. There is a search box at the top of the window that enables you to search for specific results. The Analyze dropdown box enables you to rerun code analysis for the entire solution or for specific files in the solution. The Settings button enables you to change the rule set used by a particular project in the solution.

Directly below the search box are two dropdown filter boxes. The first enables you to filter the results based off the project name. The second enables you to filter based off the result type, such as error or warning.

Analysis of the `SampleLibrary` code indicates ten potential rule violations. Selecting an item in the list displays the full description of the violation indicating how your code is in violation of a rule. It also displays the file and line number indicating (when appropriate) specific source files and code related to each warning.

Code Analysis	▾ ♯ ×
Analyze ▾ ⚙ Search	🔍 ▾
All Projects (10) ▾ All Results (10) ▾

CA1014 **Mark assemblies with CLSCompliantAttribute** (Global)

CA2210 **Assemblies should have valid strong names** (Global)

CA1053 **Static holder types should not have constructors** PayCalculator.cs (Line 9)

CA1707 **Identifiers should not contain underscores** PayCalculator.cs (Line 11)

CA1034 **Nested types should not be visible** PayCalculator.cs (Line 11)

CA1008 **Enums should have zero value** PayCalculator.cs (Line 11)

CA2211 **Non-constant fields should not be visible** PayCalculator.cs (Line 18)

CA1709 **Identifiers should be cased correctly** PayCalculator.cs (Line 19)

CA1810 **Initialize reference type static fields inline** PayCalculator.cs (Line 22)

CA2208 **Instantiate argument exceptions correctly** PayCalculator.cs (Line 30)

FIGURE 19-3

Some warnings do not relate to specific code, but perhaps to a lack of an attribute or security setting. Other warnings may refer directly to problem code, perhaps naming violations or performance issues. You can double-click the warning, and the code editor switches to the related code.

Each time you run code analysis, the results are stored in an XML file. This file is named `<Project Name>.CodeAnalysisLog.xml`, and is located in your project's build output directory (that is, `\bin\Debug` or `\bin\Release`). For the `SampleLibrary` project, the file is `SampleLibrary.dll .CodeAnalysisLog.xml`.

If you open the file from within the IDE, you see the raw, unformatted XML. However, the XML has an associated XSL template that formats the data into HTML, similar to what is shown in Figure 19-4.

To see this view, open the XML file with Internet Explorer. To customize rendering, you can supply your own XSL templates. If you choose to do this, you should make a copy of the included template and modify the copy to suit your needs. The base template is in your Visual Studio installation directory as `\Team Tools\Static Analysis Tools\FxCop\Xml\CodeAnalysisReport.xsl`.

Working with Rule Violations

Several issues should be addressed in the sample `PayCalculator` class. For each warning or error, you must determine whether the rule actually applies to your project or a specific section of code.

If it does, you must modify the project to address the issue; otherwise, you may choose to ignore the rule. This section describes how to act on identified issues and how to ignore, or suppress, a given rule.

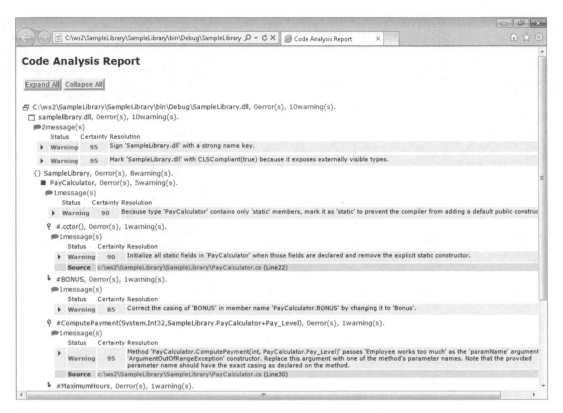

FIGURE 19-4

As part of this discussion, you immediately go into the code and make corrections as necessary, but your organization or project may require the use of work items to track any changes. Or perhaps you don't have time to immediately address an identified problem but would like to use a work item as a reminder. Fortunately, you can easily create work items directly from Code Analysis rule violations. Simply right-click the warning or error and choose Create Work Item from the menu. Choose the type of work item you want to create, and the New Work Item dialog displays. Make any necessary changes and save your new work item.

Correcting Problems

Looking through the Error List shown in Figure 19-3, you should see item CA1810, with a description of "Initialize Reference Type Static Fields Inline PayCalculator.cs (Line 22)".

Click the error number (CA1810) to display the documentation for the rule that triggered this warning, including suggestions for resolving the issue. You are currently assigning the value of `100` to `MaximumHours` inside the static constructor of `PayCalculator`. The rule's Help text states that your code may perform more efficiently if you make that assignment when the variable is defined.

To address this issue, double-click this warning to see the static constructor of the `PayCalculator` class. Change the code to assign the value in the declaration as follows:

```
public static int MaximumHours = 100;
```

Next, delete the static `PayCalculator` constructor entirely. Build the project and look at the Code Analysis window. The specific warning should no longer be in the list.

There is another easy problem to correct. Many of the code analysis rules relate to standard naming conventions. Find the warning CA1707 "Identifiers Should Not Contain Underscores PayCalculator .cs (Line 9)" and double-click. The rule helps to enforce the naming convention that underscores should not be used in type names. Use the built-in refactoring support to rename it. Right-click the `Pay_Level` enumeration and choose Refactor ⇨ Rename. Change the name to **PayLevel**, click OK, and then Apply.

Mark the `PayCaclulator` class definition static as follows:

```
public static class PayCalculator
```

Rules can also help ensure that you're using the Framework correctly. You can see from the following warning that the rule has detected that you might not be creating the `ArgumentOutOfRangeException` correctly; CA 2208 "Instantiate Argument Exceptions Correctly PayCalculator.cs (Line 30)". Replace this argument with one of the method's parameter names. Note that the provided parameter name should have the exact casing as declared on the method. To fix this, change the line that throws the exception to the following:

```
if (hours > MaximumHours)
{

    throw new ArgumentOutOfRangeException("hours", "Employee works too much");
}
```

One of the remaining warnings, CA1014 "Mark Assemblies with CLSCompliantAttribute (Global)" is a fairly common suggestion. Consider addressing this when creating a reusable library assembly that might be consumed by code of more than one .NET language. Common Language Specification (CLS) compliance specifies that your assembly must meet the common structure and syntax supported by all .NET languages as defined in the CLS. Keep in mind that there may be times when CLS compliance is not possible, such as when exposing unsigned types.

To address this warning, open `AssemblyInfo.cs` and add the following line:

```
[assembly: System.CLSCompliant(true)]
```

The `assembly:` notation is used because the attribute applies to the entire assembly, and not to a specific class or member. You can find other assembly-level attributes in the `AssemblyInfo.cs` file.

Now, build the project. The violations you corrected should no longer generate messages in the Error List. The remaining six warnings are addressed shortly.

Suppressing Messages

Visual Studio 2012 ships with many rules, and not all of them are appropriate for every project. There is a chance that some rules trigger warnings that simply don't apply to certain parts of your project. To prevent these irrelevant messages from recurring, right-click the rule violation and choose Suppress Message ⇨ In Source.

When you suppress a message, Visual Studio automatically adds an attribute to your code to indicate that a rule should not apply. You can apply the `SuppressMessage` attribute to a code construct, such as a field, method, or class, and to an entire assembly.

> **WARNING** *Suppressing a message is not the same as disabling a rule. Suppression prevents the specific violation of a rule from recurring, but other violations of the same rule are still identified. You should disable a rule only if you're certain it could never be meaningfully applied to any part of your project.*

Let's continue with the `SampleLibrary` example and use message suppression to clean up more of the code analysis violation messages.

The warnings for CA1709 states, "Identifiers Should Be Cased Correctly PayCalculator.cs (Line 19)" Assume that your organization has different naming conventions for constants, and you know that this rule does not apply to this `BONUS` constant. Right-click the message and choose Suppress Message ⇨ In Source. The message is crossed out in the Code Analysis window, and the `PayCalculator` class is modified to include the following attribute immediately before the declaration of `BONUS`:

```
[System.Diagnostics.CodeAnalysis.SuppressMessage(
    "Microsoft.Naming",
    "CA1709: IdentifiersShouldBeCasedCorrectly",    MessageId = "BONUS")]
```

The next time Code Analysis is run, the engine recognizes this attribute. Moreover, even when the CA1709 rule is violated at this point, no message is created. Messages for any other violations of this rule elsewhere in the code are still reported as normal.

"Two more messages don't apply to the project. CA2211 "Non-constant Fields Should Not Be Visible PayCalculator.cs (Line 18)" reminds you that external users of the class could change the value of `PaymentCalculator.MaximumHours`. This is the behavior you want, so right-click the message and choose Suppress Message ⇨ In Source. The message CA1008 "Enums Should Have Zero Value PayCalculator.cs (Line 11)" also does not apply, as all employees are required to have an employee level, so there is no reason to set a zero value for `PaymentCalculator.PayLevel`. Suppress this message in source as well.

As you can see, suppressing messages can quickly add a number of attributes to your code. If you find that you always suppress a given message, it is probably better to exclude the rule altogether; then your code does not require the additional `SuppressMessage` attributes. However, as noted previously, use caution when doing this, because you could unintentionally be missing valid violations that should be addressed.

The warning CA2210 "Assemblies Should Have Valid Strong Names (Global)" applies to the overall assembly. If you know that you'll never use this assembly in the Global Assembly Cache (GAC), and will have no other need for strong names, you can suppress this message. Right-click the warning and select Suppress Message ⇨ In Suppression File. Do this for all the remaining warnings. However, because there is no specific code to which the `SuppressMessage` attribute can be applied, a new file, `GlobalSuppressions.cs`, is added to the project with the following code:

```
[assembly: System.Diagnostics.CodeAnalysis.SuppressMessage(
    "Microsoft.Design",
    "CA2210:AssembliesShouldHaveValidStrongNames")]
```

There are two warnings left: CA 1034 "Nested Types Should Not Be Visible" and CA1053 "Static Holder Types Should Not Have Constructors PayCalculator.cs (Line 9)". Suppress both warning messages, build the project, and you should now see an empty Code Analysis. This indicates all enabled Code Analysis rules have either been passed or suppressed.

> **NOTE** *The effect of assembly-level suppression is basically the same as if you had excluded the rule altogether. The advantage of the attribute-based approach is that it is easy to see which rules have been suppressed project-wide by viewing the* GlobalSuppressions.cs *file. In addition, you could add comments to that file to indicate the reason for suppressing the rule to other developers. Excluding a rule by not selecting it in the Code Analysis section of the project's properties has the same effect but does not offer a way to document why certain exclusions were made.*

USING THE COMMAND-LINE ANALYSIS TOOL

A command-line interface is available for code analysis. You can find this tool, called FxCopCmd .exe, in your Visual Studio 2012 installation directory under Team Tools\Static Analysis Tools\FxCop.

FxCopCmd can perform any of the code analysis functions that are available to you in the Visual Studio IDE. In fact, the IDE uses FxCopCmd under the covers to execute analysis and generate reports.

FxCopCmd Options

Table 19-3 shows some of the options that FxCopCmd.exe supports.

TABLE 19-3: FxCopCmd Options

OPTION	DESCRIPTION
/f[ile]: *<directory/file>*	Assembly file(s) or directory(ies) to analyze. If a directory is used without a filename, Code Analysis tries to analyze all files in that directory with .dll or .exe extensions. You can specify this option more than once. It is required, unless you specify a project file with the /project option.
/r[ule]: *<directory/file>*	A rule assembly file or a directory to browse for rule assemblies. If a directory without a filename is supplied, Code Analysis looks for rules in any files with a .dll extension. You can specify this option more than once.
/r[ule]id:<[+|-]	Enables or disables a specific rule, supplying its Category and Category#CheckId> values — for example, /rid: +!Microsoft.Usage#CA2225.

continues

TABLE 19-3 *(continued)*

OPTION	DESCRIPTION
`/ruleset:<<+|-|=>file>`	Specifies the rule set to be used for the analysis.
`/rulesetdirectory:<directory>`	Specifies a directory to search for rule set files specified by the `/ruleset` switch.
`/o[ut]:<file>`	Names a file in which the results of the analysis are stored in XML form. Required, unless the `/console` option is used.
`/p[roject]:<file>`	Loads a project file that contains the settings for FxCopCmd to use (discussed shortly). Required if you do not use both the `/file` and `/rules` options.
`/t[ypes]:<type list>`	Used to constrain analysis to only the specified type(s). Supply a list of comma-delimited type names. Wildcards can be used to specify multiple types. (Optional)
`/i[mport]:<directory/file>`	Loads analysis reports or project files to exclude items from the current test that appear as excluded in the imported file. You may specify a file or a directory. If a directory is specified, Code Analysis attempts to load all files with an .xml extension. (Optional)
`/s[ummary]`	Displays a summary after analysis. (Optional)
`/v[erbose]`	Gives more detailed status output. (Optional)
`/q[uiet]`	Suppresses output of status details. (Optional)
`/u[pdate]`	Saves the results of the current analysis to the specified project file. Ignored if you do not supply the `/project` option. (Optional)
`/c[onsole]`	Uses the console to display the analysis results. This is required unless you have specified the `/out` option.
`/c[onsole]xsl:<file>`	Applies an XSL file to transform XML output before displaying.
`/plat[form]:<directory>`	Location of platform assemblies. (Optional)
`/d[irectory]: <directory>`	Location to search for assembly dependencies. (Optional)
`/help (or) /?`	Help about command-line options.
`/fo[rceoutput]`	Write output XML and project files, even in the case where no violations occurred.

OPTION	DESCRIPTION
/dic[tionary]:<file>	Use a custom dictionary file.
/ignoreinvalidtargets [Short form: /iit]	Silently ignore invalid target files.
/asp[net]	Analyze only ASP.NET generated binaries, and honor global suppressions in App_Code.dll for all assemblies under analysis.
/searchgac [Short form: /gac]	Search Global Assembly Cache for missing references.
/successfile [Short form: /sf]	Create .lastcodeanalysissucceeded file in output report directory if no build-breaking messages occur during analysis.
/timeout:<seconds> [Short form: /to:<seconds>]	Overrride timeout for analysis deadlock detection. Analysis is aborted when analysis of a single item by a single rule exceeds the specified amount of time. Specify a value of 0 to disable deadlock detection.
/savemessagestoreport: <Active|Excluded|Absent (default: Active)> [Short form: / smr:<Active|Excluded|Absent (default: Active)>]	Save messages of specified kind to output report.
/ignoregeneratedcode [Short form: /igc]	Suppress analysis results against generated code.
/overriderulevisibilities [Short form: /orv]	Run all overridable rules against all targets.
/failonmissingrules [Short form: /fmr]	Treat missing rules or rule sets as an error, and halt execution.
/cul[ture]	Culture for spelling rules.
/outxsl:<file> [Short form: /oxsl:<file>]	Reference the specified XSL in the XML report file; use /outxsl:none to generate an XML report with no XSL style sheet.
/applyoutxsl [Short form: /axsl]	Apply the XSL style sheet to the output.

Notice that most of the commands have long and short forms available. For example, /summary and /s are equivalent. Arguments support the use of wildcards (*) to specify multiple items. Arguments with spaces in them must be surrounded with double quotes.

For example, to conduct analysis of a single assembly `CustomLibrary.dll`, use the following command:

```
FxCopCmd /f:SampleLibrary.dll /o:"FxCop Results.xml" /s
```

The `/f` (or `/file`) argument indicates which assembly to analyze, and the `/o` (or `/output`) option indicates that analysis output should be stored as XML in `FxCop Results.xml`. Finally, the `/s` (or `/summary`) option displays a short summary of the results of the analysis.

FxCopCmd Project Files

FxCopCmd's command-line options offer a good deal of flexibility, but to fine-tune your analysis you should consider using a *project file*. A project file enables you to set options such as targets and rule assemblies, exclusions, and output preferences. You can then simply use the `/project` option to tell FxCopCmd to use those settings, instead of supplying a detailed list of arguments.

You should create a default FxCopCmd project file that you can copy and customize for each project. Create a new file named `EmptyCodeAnalysisProject.fxcop` and enter the following:

```
<?xml version="1.0" encoding="UTF-8"?>
<FxCopProject Version="1.36" Name="Temporary FxCop Project">
        <ProjectOptions>
        </ProjectOptions>
        <Targets>
        <Target Name="$(TargetFile)" Analyze="True" AnalyzeAllChildren="True" />
        </Targets>
        <RuleFiles>
        </RuleFiles>
        <FxCopReport Version="1.36" LastAnalysis="2004-04-20 22:08:53Z">
        </FxCopReport>
</FxCopProject>
```

Copy this to a new file and add your project's settings. The rules and files specified in your project file serve as the basis for FxCopCmd execution. You can specify additional rules and target files on the command line with the `/rules` and `/file` options.

For example, here is a simple project file that specifies a target assembly, `SampleLibrary.dll`, and includes one rule assembly, the default Code Analysis naming conventions assembly:

```
<?xml version="1.0" encoding="UTF-8"?>
<FxCopProject Version="1.36" Name="Sample Library Code Analysis Project">
        <ProjectOptions>
        </ProjectOptions>
        <Targets>

            <Target Name="C:\SampleLibrary\bin\Debug\SampleLibrary.dll"
                Analyze="True"
                AnalyzeAllChildren="True" />
        </Targets>
        <RuleFiles>
            <RuleFile Name="$(FxCopDir)\Rules\NamingRules.dll" Enabled="True"
                AllRulesEnabled="True" />
        </RuleFiles>
        <FxCopReport Version="1.36" LastAnalysis="2004-04-20 22:08:53Z">
        </FxCopReport>
</FxCopProject>
```

Save this to a file named `SampleLibrary.fxcop`. To execute Code Analysis for `SampleLibrary` using this project file, use the following command:

```
FxCopCmd /p:SampleLibrary.fxcop /o:"FxCop Results.xml" /s
```

Build Process Code Analysis Integration

You have now seen how to use FxCopCmd from the command line to analyze your code and report potential defects. However, with the full integration of code analysis with the Visual Studio IDE, why would you need to use FxCopCmd?

A common use of FxCopCmd is to enable automated code analysis from a build process. You can do this with Team Build, Visual Studio 2012's MSBuild, or one of many other build automation packages available (such as NAnt).

By integrating Code Analysis with your builds, you can ensure that your entire team's work is being evaluated against a consistent set of rules. You quickly discover when a developer has added non-standard code. Developers quickly learn those rules and practices, because they don't want to be the person responsible for "breaking the build."

CREATING CODE ANALYSIS RULES

Visual Studio 2012 includes many code analysis rules, but no matter how comprehensive the rules from Microsoft are, they can never fully cover the specific requirements of your own projects. Perhaps you have specific naming conventions, or a standard way to load database connection strings. In many cases, you can create a custom code analysis rule to help diagnose the issue and help developers take corrective action.

> **NOTE** *Creating custom code analysis rules is not for the faint of heart and is beyond the scope of this book. For more information on creating custom code analysis rules, including a step-by-step example, refer to the Microsoft Code Analysis Team Blog at* `http://blogs.msdn.com/b/codeanalysis/archive/2010/03/26/how-to-write-custom-static-code-analysis-rules-and-integrate-them-into-visual-studio-2010.aspx.`

CODE METRICS

The Code Metrics tool is a set of software metrics that provide insight into the code that is being developed. Code Metrics provides a quick-and-easy way to determine the complexity of the code and to isolate code areas that may be difficult to maintain in the future. This can be especially helpful when maintaining a large or complex code base. Code metric information is calculated at the method level, and then rolled up all the way to the assembly level. Visual Studio 2012 calculates five different code metrics:

> ➤ *Cyclomatic Complexity* — This measures the structural complexity of the code. It is created by calculating the number of different code paths through the code, including `if` statements,

switch statements, and so on. A high number for Cyclomatic Complexity indicates that the code may be too complex and should be refactored.

➤ *Depth of Inheritance* — This indicates the number of class definitions that extend to the root of the class hierarchy. Although inheritance in itself is not bad, having a lengthy inheritance level can make the code difficult to understand and troubleshoot. As with Cyclomatic Complexity, you want to have a low number for Depth of Inheritance.

➤ *Class Coupling* — This indicates the total number of dependencies that a class has on other classes, based on parameters, local variables, return types, and method calls, base classes, interface implementations, fields defined on external types, and attribute decoration. This calculation does not include primitive or built-in types. A high level of Class Coupling indicates that changes in other classes could affect a specific class. You want a low number for Class Coupling.

➤ *Lines of Code* — This indicates the number of executable lines of code in a method. This is an approximate count, based off the IL code, and only includes executable lines of code. Comments, braces, and white space are excluded. For Lines of Code, a low value is good, and a high value is bad.

➤ *The Maintainability Index* — This is a combination of several metrics, including Cyclomatic Complexity, average Lines of Code, as well as computational complexity. This metric is calculated using the following formula:

```
MAX(0,(171-5.2*ln(Halstead Volume)-0.23*(Cyclomatic Complexity)-16.2*ln(Lines
                         of Code))*100/171)
```

The Maintainability Index is a value between 1 and 100. Unlike the previous four metrics, for Maintainability Index, the higher the value, the easier the code is to maintain. Table 19-4 shows the Maintainability Index ranges and what they indicate.

TABLE 19-4: Maintainability Index Ranges

COLOR	LEVEL	RANGE
Green	High Maintainability	Between 20 and 100
Yellow	Moderate Maintainability	Between 10 and 20
Red	Low Maintainability	Between 0 and 9

Some tools and compilers generate code that is automatically added to a project. Many times the developer is not aware of this code or shouldn't make changes to the generated code. For the most part, Code Metrics ignore generated code when it calculates values. This is important, because it enables the results to reflect only the code the developer can see and change.

> **NOTE** *Code generated by Windows forms is not ignored, because that is code a developer can see and change.*

You have the ability to generate code metrics for your entire solution, or for a selected project. To generate code metrics against the entire solution, do one of the following:

➤ Click the Analyze menu option and then select Calculate Code Metrics For Solution.

➤ Right-click the solution in Solution Explorer and select `Calculate Code Metrics`.

To generate code metrics for one or more projects in a solution, first select all the projects to be involved and then do one of the following:

➤ Click the Analyze menu option and then select Calculate Code Metrics For Selected Project(s).

➤ Right click the solution in Solution Explorer and select Calculate Code Metrics.

The Code Metrics Results window displays with the results, as shown in Figure 19-5.

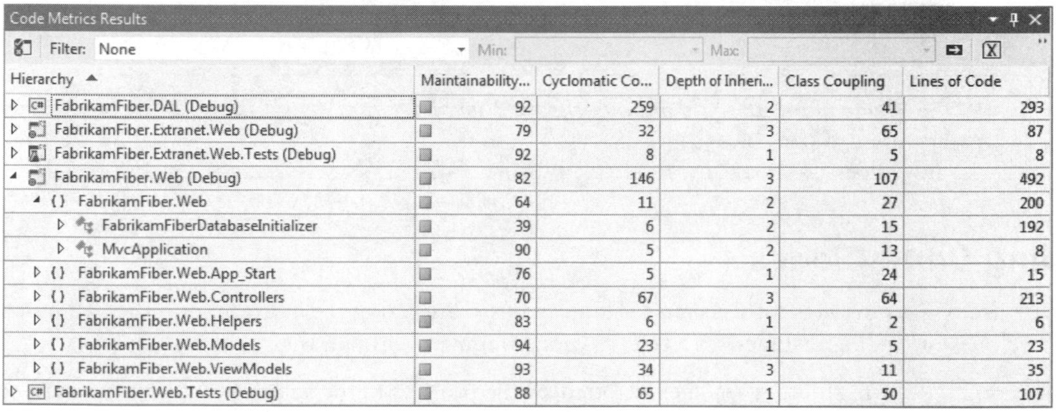

Hierarchy ▲	Maintainability...	Cyclomatic Co...	Depth of Inheri...	Class Coupling	Lines of Code
▷ FabrikamFiber.DAL (Debug)		92	259	2	41	293
▷ FabrikamFiber.Extranet.Web (Debug)		79	32	3	65	87
▷ FabrikamFiber.Extranet.Web.Tests (Debug)		92	8	1	5	8
▲ FabrikamFiber.Web (Debug)		82	146	3	107	492
▲ {} FabrikamFiber.Web		64	11	2	27	200
▷ FabrikamFiberDatabaseInitializer		39	6	2	15	192
▷ MvcApplication		90	5	2	13	8
▷ {} FabrikamFiber.Web.App_Start		76	5	1	24	15
▷ {} FabrikamFiber.Web.Controllers		70	67	3	64	213
▷ {} FabrikamFiber.Web.Helpers		83	6	1	2	6
▷ {} FabrikamFiber.Web.Models		94	23	1	5	23
▷ {} FabrikamFiber.Web.ViewModels		93	34	3	11	35
▷ FabrikamFiber.Web.Tests (Debug)		88	65	1	50	107

FIGURE 19-5

You can drill down into the results using the triangle controls located to left of the Hierarchy column. You can filter the results using the toolbar at the top of the window. The Filter dropdown box contains the names of all the results columns. Select a column in the dropdown box and then enter a minimum number value. The results are then filtered accordingly. The dropdown box keeps track of the last ten filters that you defined.

You can copy a row of results to the clipboard as a text string by right-clicking a row in the results window and selecting Copy. This copies both the name and value of each column on the selected row. You can also right-click a row and select Open Selection in Microsoft Excel. This takes all the information from that row, and all rows nested underneath that row, and opens them in a workbook in Microsoft Excel.

Finally, you can create a Team Foundation work item based off a row of results in the Code Metric Results window. Right-click a row of results, select Create Work Item, and then select the appropriate work item type, such as Task. This creates a new work item, with the title set to the hierarchy name of the row selected, and copies the code metric data for that line into the history tab.

CODE CLONE ANALYSIS

As developers, we are often guilty of copying blocks of code from a class or project to another class or project if it provides all or most of the functionality that we need. When these separate fragments of code are very similar, they're referred to as *code clones*. Code clones can make it difficult to make application updates because you have to find and make the same or similar changes in multiple areas of your code base. Many times it makes sense to refactor the code clones into a single location. However, it can be very difficult to isolate all the areas where code clones exist, especially in older code bases.

This is where *code clone analysis* (also referred to as *code clone detection*) comes into play. Code clone analysis enables you to look across your entire solution for blocks of code that are similar in structure and composition. One nice feature is that the blocks of code do not have to be identical. Code clone analysis is adept at finding blocks of code that are similar but not necessarily exact. For example, blocks of code that are similar but have different variable names or parameters — or have statements in a different order — can be detected through analysis.

> **NOTE** *Code clone analysis only works for Visual C# and Visual Basic projects in Visual Studio 2012.*

Finding Code Clones

There are two main ways for using code clone analysis: analyzing the entire solution for all potential code clones or finding instances of a selected code fragment through the solution.

Analyzing the entire solution searches through all the projects in the solution, looking for instances of code clones. This can be particularly useful during code reviews. It is important to note that code clones of fewer than ten statements are not discovered when the entire solution is being analyzed. To analyze the entire solution, select Analyze ➪ Analyze Solution for Code Clones from the main menu in Visual Studio 2012. Figure 19-6 shows the results of the analysis, shown in the Code Clone Analysis Results window.

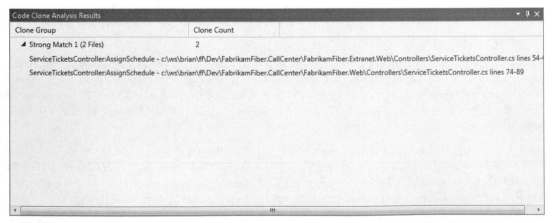

FIGURE 19-6

By default the results are grouped and sorted based on the strength of the match. Exact matches are shown first, followed by matches that are close (i.e. strong) but not necessarily exact. In Figure 19-6, you have one strong match. There are two other match terms for describing matches — Medium and Weak — each denoting a code clone that is less exact.

You can also use code clone analysis to find a particular code fragment in a solution. Unlike an analysis of the entire solution that was shown earlier, this type of search can find cone clones less than ten lines in length. To search for a specific fragment of code, highlight the code fragment, right-click it, and select Find Matching Clones in Solution from the context menu. The solution searches for a match to the code fragment and displays the results in the Code Clone Analysis Results window.

Reviewing the Code Clone Analysis Results

You have a couple of different options for analyzing the results provide by code clone analysis. In the Code Clone Analysis Results window, you can hover your mouse over a specific line to show the matching code in a pop-up window. This provides you a way to quickly see the code for that particular match. You can also double-click a line in the results window to automatically open the file containing the code clone; then you can navigate to its location within the file. Opening the file in this way automatically color codes the code clone, to make it easy to find.

You also have the ability to compare two files using the same tool that is used to compare versions in source control in Team Foundation Server. To do this, select two files listed in the Code Clone Analysis Results window, right-click the selection, and choose Compare from the context menu. This opens the new comparison tool in Visual Studio 2012 so you can view the two code clones side by side.

How Code Clone Analysis Works

Code clone analysis finds both exact copies of code and similar code that is not exact. Code clones usually result from developers copying a chunk of code and then making modifications to the code based off its new requirements. You can make the following modifications, and the clone will still be recognized:

➤   Rename identifiers

➤   Add new statements

➤   Delete statements

➤   Rearrange statements

Even if you can make any of these modifications to a code clone, the clone is still flagged during analysis. There are rules for what is not found as well, including the following:

➤   Two classes with similar sets of field declarations (type declarations are not compared; only statements in methods and property definitions are compared)

➤   Fragments with more than 40 percent changed tokens

➤   Code elements that have been specifically excluded from code clone analysis via a `.codeclonesettings` file

➤   Certain generated code, including `.designer.cs` files, `.designer.vb` files, and `InitializeComponent` methods

Excluding Items from Code Clone Analysis

At the project level you can exclude items from code clone analysis by using a `.codeclonesettings` file. This is an XML file that must exist in the top-level directory of the project. You can use this file to exclude specific files or specific methods from analysis.

The base elements of the exclusion file consists of a `CodeCloneSetting` element with an `Exclusions` child.

```
<CodeCloneSettings>
    <Exclusions>
    .
    .
    .
    </Exclusions>
</CodeCloneSettings>
```

Within the `Exclusions` element, you list the different exclusions, including `File`, `Namespace`, `Type`, and `FunctionName`.

```
<CodeCloneSettings>
    <Exclusions>

        <File>MyFile.cs</File>
        <File>MyTemplates\*.cs</File>

        <Namespace>MyCompany.MyProject</Namespace>
        <Namespace>*.AProject</Namespace>

        <Type>MyCompany.MyProject.MyClass</Type>
        <Type>*.AClass*</Type>

        <FunctionName>MyCompany.MyProject.MyClass.MyMethod</FunctionName>
        <FunctionName>MyProject.*.AMethod</FunctionName>

    </Exclusions>
</CodeCloneSettings>
```

As you can see, you can either use absolute names or names containing wildcards.

SUMMARY

This chapter demonstrated the need for static analysis tools and introduced you to the .NET Framework "Design Guidelines for Class Library Developers." These guidelines are a very important resource that Microsoft has made freely available, and they're the basis for Visual Studio 2012's included Code Analysis rules.

In this chapter, you learned about the Code Analysis tool, including how it now integrates with Visual Studio 2012 and enables rule analysis to be performed with a simple build. You learned how to configure and execute analysis, and how to work with the resulting rule violation messages.

To support projects using a repeatable build process, or those that need additional flexibility, you learned how to use the command-line Managed Code Analysis tool, and how to create FxCopCmd project files to store settings.

Next, you were introduced to Code Metrics. The five different code metric values were explained, and you saw how easy it was to run and view the results of the code metrics calculation.

Finally, you learned about Code Clone Analysis, and how you can use this tool to find code clones, or similar fragments of code, throughout your solution.

Chapter 20 looks at the code profiling capabilities of Visual Studio 2012, and how you can use them to find and fix performance problems in your code.

20

Profiling and Performance

WHAT'S IN THIS CHAPTER?

➤ Understanding the profiling features in Visual Studio 2012

➤ Understanding available profiling types

➤ Using Performance Explorer to configure profiling sessions

➤ Profiling reports and available views

➤ Profiling JavaScript

WROX.COM CODE DOWNLOADS FOR THIS CHAPTER

The wrox.com code downloads for this chapter are found at `www.wrox.com/remtitle .cgi?isbn=1118314081` on the Download Code tab. The files are in the Chapter 20 download folder and individually named as shown throughout this chapter.

One of the more difficult tasks in software development is determining why an application performs slowly or inefficiently. Before Visual Studio 2005, developers were forced to turn to external tools to effectively analyze performance. Now, however, Visual Studio includes profiling tools that are fully integrated with both the IDE and other Visual Studio features.

This chapter introduces Visual Studio 2012's profiling tools. Note that the profiling features discussed in this chapter are available in Visual Studio Premium 2012 or higher.

You find out how to use the profiler to identify problems such as inefficient code, overallocation of memory, and bottlenecks. You learn about the two main profiling options — sampling and instrumentation — including how to use each, and when each should be applied. In Visual Studio 2012, there are two sampling options: one for CPU sampling and the other for memory allocation sampling. This chapter examines both options. This chapter also briefly reviews the profiling method, introduced in Visual Studio 2010, to see thread contentions using concurrency profiling.

After learning how to run profiling analyzers, you find out how to use the detailed reporting features that enable you to view performance metrics in a number of ways, including results by function, caller/callee inspection, call tree details, and other views.

Not all scenarios can be supported when using the Visual Studio 2012 IDE. For times when you need additional flexibility, you can use the command-line options for profiling applications, which are covered in this chapter. This enables you to integrate profiling with your build process and to use some advanced profiling options.

INTRODUCTION TO PERFORMANCE ANALYSIS

Profiling is the process of observing and recording metrics about the behavior of an application. Profilers are tools used to help identify application performance issues. Issues typically stem from code that performs slowly or inefficiently, or code that causes excessive use of system memory. A profiler helps you to more easily identify these issues so that they can be corrected.

Sometimes, an application may be functionally correct and seem complete, but users quickly begin to complain that it seems "slow." Or, perhaps you're only receiving complaints from one customer who finds a particular feature takes "forever" to complete. Fortunately, Visual Studio 2012 profiling tools can help in these situations.

A common use of profiling is to identify *hotspots*, sections of code that execute frequently, or for a long duration, as an application runs. Identifying hotspots enables you to turn your attention to the code that provides the largest benefit from optimization. For example, halving the execution time of a critical method that runs 20 percent of the time can improve your application's overall performance by 10 percent.

Types of Profilers

Most profiling tools fall into one (or both) of two types: *sampling* and *instrumentation*.

A *sampling profiler* takes periodic snapshots (called *samples*) of a running application, recording the status of the application at each interval, including which line of code is executing. Sampling profilers typically do not modify the code of the system under test, favoring an outside-in perspective.

Think of a sampling profiler as being like a sonar system. It periodically sends out sound waves to detect information, collecting data about how the sound refracts. From that data, the system displays the locations of detected objects.

The other type, an *instrumentation profiler*, takes a more invasive approach. Before running analysis, the profiler adds *tracing markers* (sometimes called *probes*) at the start and end of each function. This process is called *instrumenting* an application. Instrumentation can be performed in source code or, in the case of Visual Studio, by directly modifying an existing assembly. When the profiler is run, those probes are activated as the program execution flows in and out of instrumented functions. The profiler records data about the application and which probes were hit during execution, generating a comprehensive summary of what the program did.

Think of an instrumentation profiler as the traffic data recorders you sometimes see while driving. The tubes lie across the road and record whenever a vehicle passes over. By collecting the results from a variety of locations over time, an approximation of traffic flow can be inferred.

A key difference between sampling and instrumentation is that sampling profilers observe your applications while running any code, including calls to external libraries (such as the .NET Framework). Instrumentation profilers gather data only for the code that you have specifically instrumented.

Visual Studio Profiling

Visual Studio 2012 offers powerful profiling tools that you can use to analyze and improve your applications. The profiling tools offer both sampling and instrumented approaches. Like many Visual Studio features, profiling is fully integrated with the Visual Studio IDE and other Visual Studio features, such as work item tracking, the build system, version control check-in policies, and more.

> **NOTE** *The profiling tools in Visual Studio can be used with both managed and unmanaged applications, but the object allocation tracking features only work when profiling managed code.*

The profiling tools in Visual Studio are based upon two tools that have been used for years internally at Microsoft. The sampling system is based on the Call Attributed Provider (CAP) tool, and the instrumentation system is based on the Low-Overhead Profiler (LOP) tool. Microsoft did not simply repackage existing internal tools and call it a day. They invested considerable development effort to add new capabilities and to fully integrate them with other Visual Studio features.

USING THE PROFILER

The Visual Studio developers have done a good job making the profiler easy to use. You follow four basic steps to profile your application:

1. Create a performance session, selecting a profiling method (CPU sampling, instrumentation, memory sampling, or concurrency) and its target(s).

2. Use the Performance Explorer to view and set the session's properties.

3. Launch the session, executing the application and profiler.

4. Review the collected data as presented in performance reports.

Each step is described in the following sections.

Creating a Sample Application

Before describing how to profile an application, create a sample application that you can use to work through the content of this chapter. Of course, this is only for demonstration, and you can certainly use your own existing applications instead.

Create a new C# Console Application and name it `DemoConsole`. This application demonstrates some differences between using a simple class and a structure.

First, add a new class file called `WidgetClass.cs` with the following class definition:

```
namespace DemoConsole
{
    public class WidgetClass
    {
        private string _name;
        private int _id;

        public int ID
        {
            get { return _id; }
            set { _id = value; }
        }

        public string Name
        {
            get { return _name; }
            set { _name = value; }
        }

        public WidgetClass(int id, string name)
        {
            _id = id;
            _name = name;
        }
    }
}
```

Also, add the `System.Collections` namespace to the file. Now, slightly modify that class to make it a value type. Make a copy of the `WidgetClass.cs` file named `WidgetValueType.cs` and open it. To make `WidgetClass` into a structure, change the word `class` to `struct`. Now, rename the two places you see `WidgetClass` to `WidgetValueType` and save the file.

You should have a `Program.cs` already created for you by Visual Studio. Open that file and add the following two lines in the `Main` method:

```
ProcessClasses(2000000);
ProcessValueTypes(2000000);
```

Add the following code to this file as well:

```
public static void ProcessClasses(int count)
{
    ArrayList widgets = new ArrayList();
    for (int i = 0; i < count; i++)
        widgets.Add(new WidgetClass(i, "Test"));
    string[] names = new string[count];
    for (int i = 0; i < count; i++)
        names[i] = ((WidgetClass)widgets[i]).Name;
}
public static void ProcessValueTypes(int count)
{
    ArrayList widgets = new ArrayList();
    for (int i = 0; i < count; i++)
        widgets.Add(new WidgetValueType(i, "Test"));
    string[] names = new string[count];
    for (int i = 0; i < count; i++)
```

```
                names[i] = ((WidgetValueType)widgets[i]).Name;
        }
    }
}
```

You now have a simple application that performs many identical operations on a class and a similar structure. First, it creates an `ArrayList` and adds two million copies of both `WidgetClass` and `WidgetValueType`. It then reads through the `ArrayList`, reading the `Name` property of each copy and storing that name in a string array. You'll see how the seemingly minor differences between the class and structure affect the speed of the application, the amount of memory used, and its effect on the .NET garbage collection process.

Creating a Performance Session

To begin profiling an application, you must first create a performance session. This is normally done using the Performance Wizard, which walks you through the most common settings. You may also create a blank performance session or base a new performance session on a unit test result. Each of these methods is described in the following sections.

Using the Performance Wizard

The easiest way to create a new performance session is to use the Performance Wizard. In Visual Studio 2012, there is a menu item called Analyze, which is where the Performance Wizard and other profiler menu items are located. Select Analyze ⇨ Launch Performance Wizard. A three-step wizard guides you through the creation of your session.

The first step, shown in Figure 20-1, is to select the profiling method.

As mentioned earlier, Visual Studio 2012 has the following four profiling options:

- ➤ CPU Sampling
- ➤ Instrumentation
- ➤ .NET Memory Allocation (sampling)
- ➤ Resource contention data (concurrency)

CPU Sampling is the recommended method to get started, and is chosen by default, as you see in Figure 20-1.

The second step, shown in Figure 20-2, is to select the application you are profiling. In this case, you are profiling the recently created `DemoConsole` application. You should see the `DemoConsole` application listed under One or More Available Projects. If there are multiple applications listed there, you can select more than one to profile.

As you see in Figure 20-2, with Visual Studio 2012 you can also profile an executable (or `.exe` file) or an ASP.NET/JavaScript application. If you choose to profile an executable then you must provide the path for the executable with any command-line arguments and the start-up directory. If you choose to profile an ASP.NET application then you must supply the URL for the web application. Select the `DemoConsole` application as the target for profiling.

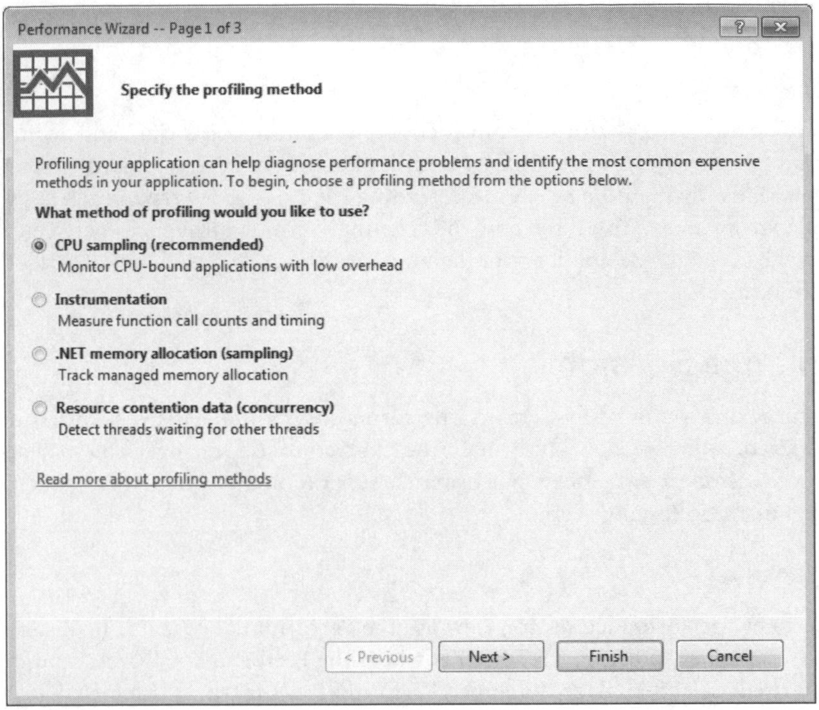

FIGURE 20-1

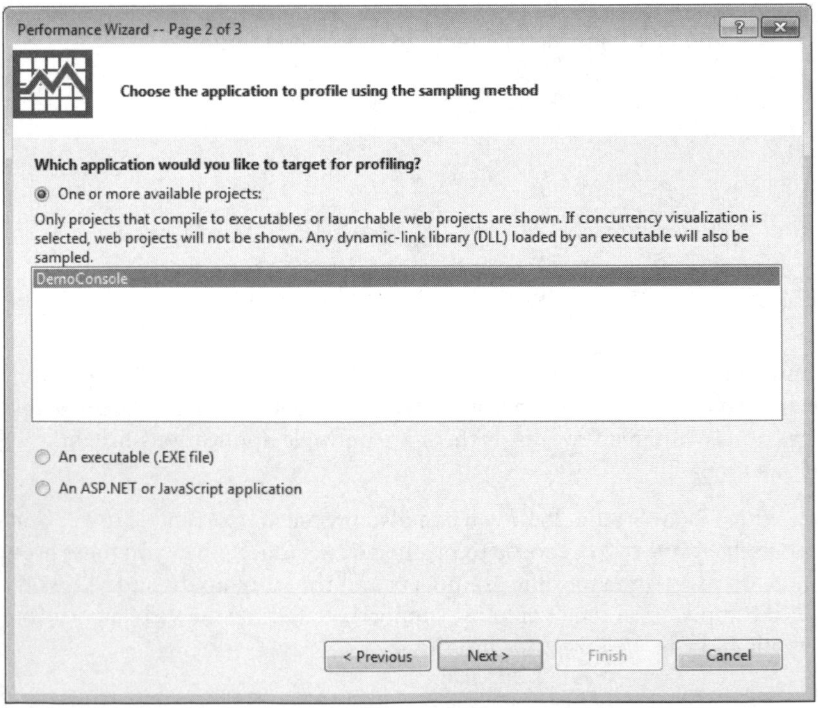

FIGURE 20-2

The final step in the wizard summarizes the selections in Step 1 and Step 2. Note that, in Visual Studio 2012, the profiling session is set to start after the wizard is finished. This is because the Launch Profiling After the Wizard Finishes checkbox is enabled by default, as shown in Figure 20-3. To just save the settings and start a profiling session at a later time, disable this checkbox and click Finish.

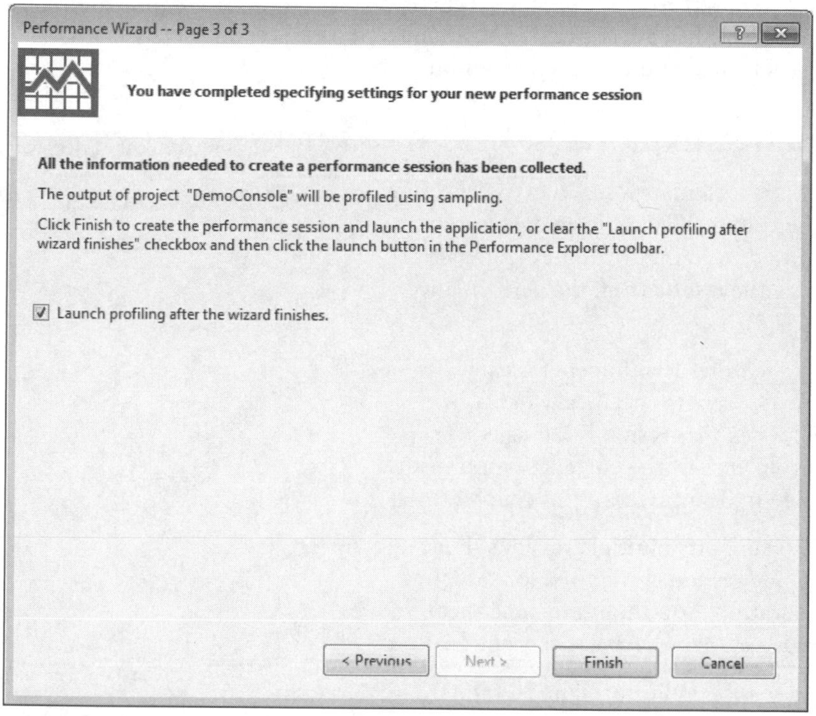

FIGURE 20-3

Although you can now run your performance session, you may want to change some settings. These settings are described later in this chapter in the "Setting General Session Properties" section. Adding a Blank Performance Session

There may be times (for example, when you're profiling a Windows Service) when manually specifying all of the properties of your session would be useful or necessary. In those cases, you can skip the Performance Wizard and manually create a performance session.

Create a blank performance session by selecting Analyze ⇨ Profiler ⇨ New Performance Session. You see a new performance session, named `Performance1`, in the Performance Explorer window. This window is described in detail later in this chapter in the section "Using the Performance Explorer."

After creating the blank performance session, you must manually specify the profiling mode, target(s), and settings for the session. As mentioned previously, performance session settings are described later in this chapter in the section "Setting General Session Properties."

Creating a Performance Session from a Unit Test

The third option for creating a new performance session is from a unit test. Refer to Chapter 18 for a full description of the unit testing features in Visual Studio 2012.

There may be times when you have a test that verifies the processing speed (perhaps relative to another method or a timer) of a target method. Perhaps a test is failing because of system memory issues. In such cases, you might want to use the profiler to determine what code is causing problems.

To create a profiling session from a unit test, first run the unit test. Then, in the Test Results window, right-click the test and choose Create Performance Session from the context menu. Visual Studio 2012 then creates a new performance session with the selected unit test automatically assigned as the session's target. When you run this performance session, the unit test is executed as normal, but the profiler is activated and collects metrics on its performance.

Using the Performance Explorer

After you have created your performance session, you can view it using the Performance Explorer. The Performance Explorer, shown in Figure 20-4, is used to configure and execute performance sessions and to view the results from the performance sessions.

The Performance Explorer features two folders for each session: Targets and Reports. Targets specifies which application(s) are profiled when the session is launched. Reports lists the results from each of the current session's runs. These reports are described in detail later in this chapter.

Performance Explorer also supports multiple sessions. For example, you might have one session configured for sampling and another for instrumentation. You should rename them from the default PerformanceX names for easier identification.

If you accidentally close a session in Performance Explorer, you can reopen it by using the Open option of the File menu. You are likely to find the session file (ending with .psess) in your solution's folder.

Setting General Session Properties

Whether you used the Performance Wizard to create your session or added a blank one, you might want to review and modify the session's settings. Right-click the session name (for example, DemoConsole) and choose Properties. You see the Property Pages dialog for the session. It features several sections, described next.

FIGURE 20-4

> **NOTE** *This discussion focuses on the property pages that are applicable to all types of profiling sessions. These include the General, Launch, Tier Interactions, CPU Counters, Windows Events, and Windows Counters pages. The other pages each apply only to a particular type of profiling. The Sampling page is described later in this chapter in the section "Configuring a Sampling Session," and the Binaries, Instrumentation, and Advanced pages are described in the "Configuring an Instrumentation Session" section later in this chapter.*

General Property Page

Figure 20-5 shows the General page of the Property Pages dialog.

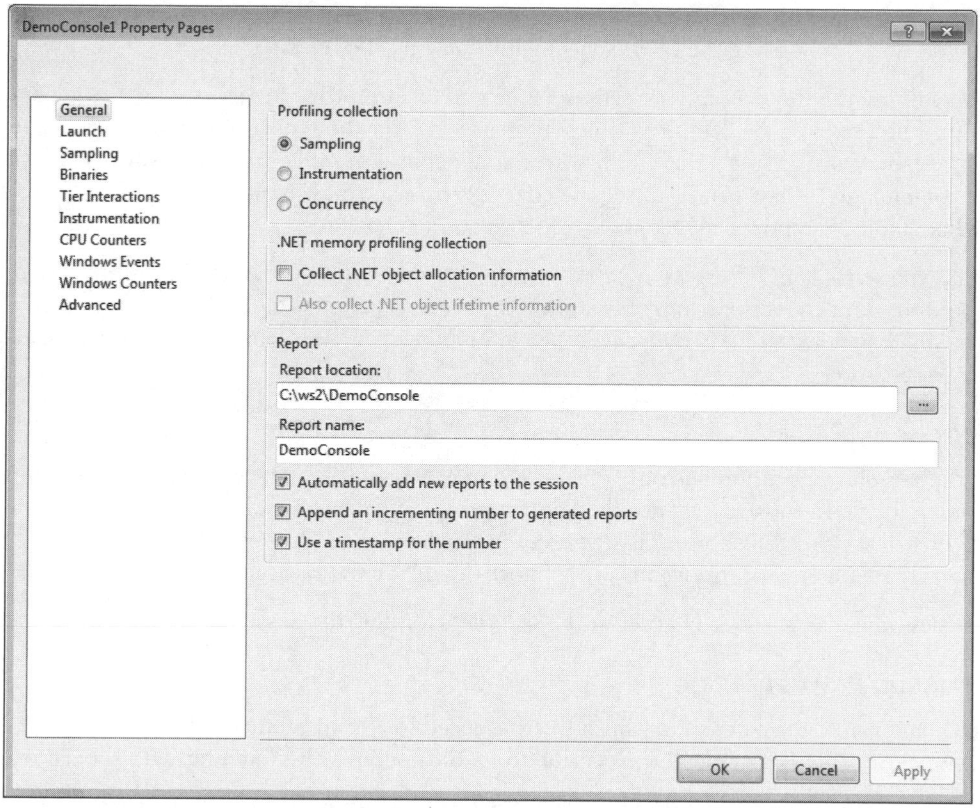

FIGURE 20-5

The Profiling Collection panel of this dialog reflects your chosen profiling type (that is, Sampling, Instrumentation, or Concurrency).

The .NET Memory Profiling Collection panel enables the tracking of managed types. When the first option, Collect .NET Object Allocation Information, is enabled, the profiling system collects details about the managed types that are created during the application's execution. The profiler tracks the number of instances, the amount of memory used by those instances, and which members created the instances. If the first option is selected, then you can choose to include the second option, Also Collect .NET Object Lifetime Information. If selected, additional details about the amount of time each managed type instance remains in memory is collected. This enables you to view further effects of your application, such as its effect on the .NET garbage collector.

The options in the .NET Memory Profiling Collection panel are off by default. Turning them on adds substantial overhead and causes both the profiling and report-generation processes to take additional time to complete. When the first option is selected, the Allocation view of the session's report is available for review. The second option enables display of the Objects Lifetime view. These reports are described later in this chapter in the section "Reading and Interpreting Session Reports."

In the Data Collection Control panel, you can toggle the launch of data collection control while the profiling is launched. If you have checked the Launch Data Control Collection checkbox, then, during the profiling session, you see the Data Collection Control window. Using this window, you can specify marks that could become handy while analyzing the report after the profiling session is completed. You do that by choosing the Marks view while viewing the report.

Finally, you can use the Report panel to set the name and location for the reports that are generated after each profiling session. By default, a timestamp is used after the report name so that you can easily see the date of the session run. Another default appends a number after each subsequent run of that session on a given day. (You can see the effect of these settings in Figure 20-15 later in this chapter, where multiple report sessions were run on the same day.)

For example, the settings in Figure 20-5 run a sampling profile without managed type allocation profiling, and the data collection control is launched. If run on January 1, 2012, it produces a report named `DemoConsole120101.vsp`. Another run on the same day produces a report named `DemoConsole120101(1).vsp`.

Launch Property Page

Although the sample application has only one binary to execute and analyze, your projects might have multiple targets. In those cases, use the Launch property page to specify which targets should be executed when the profiling session is started or "launched." You can set the order in which targets will be executed using the "move up" and "move down" arrow buttons.

Targets are described later in this chapter in the section "Configuring Session Targets."

Tier Interaction Proprety Page

Tier Interaction profiling is a capability initially introduced in Visual Studio 2010. This method captures additional information about the execution times of functions that interact with the database.

Multi-tier architecture is commonly used in many applications, with tiers for presentation, business, and database. With Tier Interaction profiling, you can now get a sense of the interaction between the application tier and the data tier, including how many calls were made and the time of execution.

As of this writing, Tier Interaction profiling only supports the capturing of execution times for synchronous calls using ADO.NET. It does not support native or asynchronous calls.

To start collecting tier interaction data, select the Enable Tier Interaction Profiling checkbox, as shown in Figure 20-6.

After you run the profiling with this selection turned on, you are presented with the profiling report. Select the Tier Interactions view from the Current View dropdown list, shown in Figure 20-7. This example shows the results of running the profiling on the "Fabrikam Fiber" sample application. This application is available in the demo virtual machine for Visual Studio 2012 available for download from Microsoft.

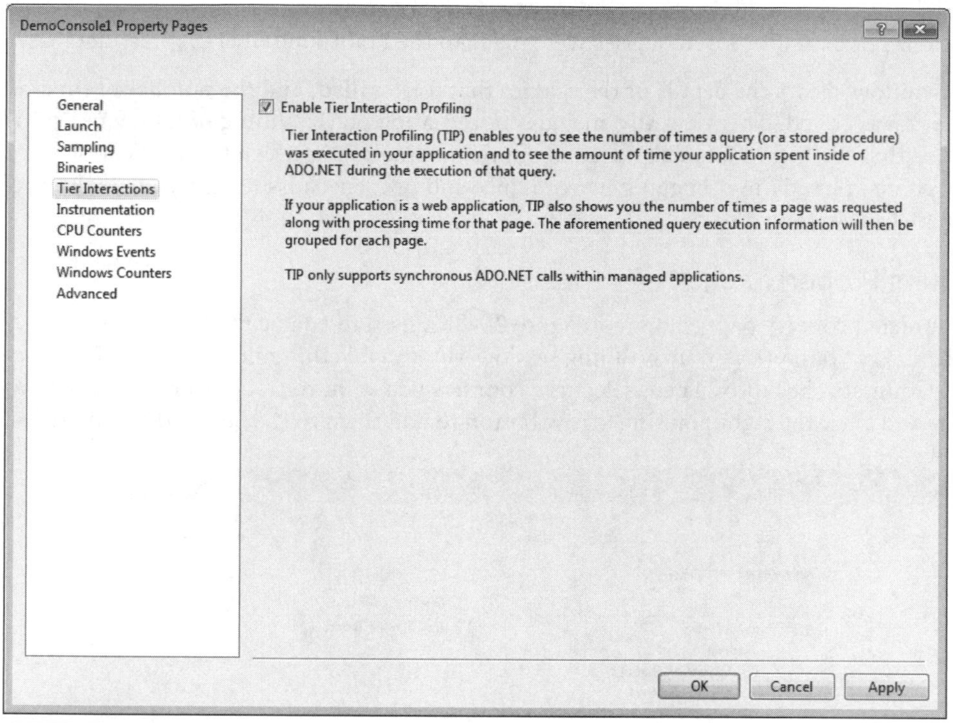
DemoConsole1 Property Pages
General
Launch
Sampling
Binaries
Tier Interactions
Instrumentation
CPU Counters
Windows Events
Windows Counters
Advanced
Enable Tier Interaction Profiling
Tier Interaction Profiling (TIP) enables you to see the number of times a query (or a stored procedure) was executed in your application and to see the amount of time your application spent inside of ADO.NET during the execution of that query.
If your application is a web application, TIP also shows you the number of times a page was requested along with processing time for that page. The aforementioned query execution information will then be grouped for each page.
TIP only supports synchronous ADO.NET calls within managed applications.
OK
Cancel
Apply

FIGURE 20-6

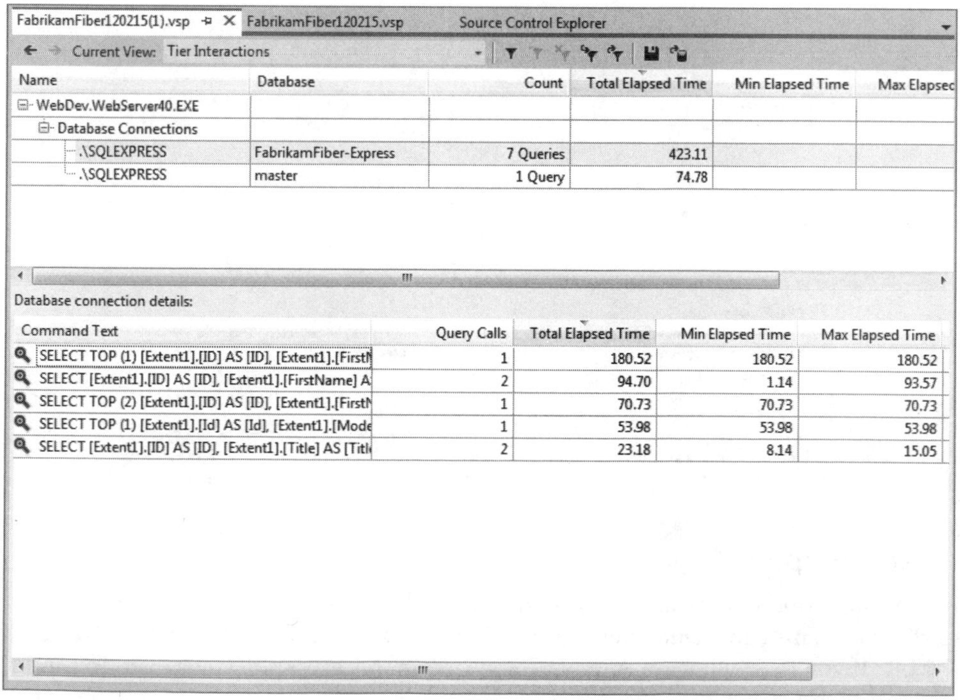
FabrikamFiber120215(1).vsp
FabrikamFiber120215.vsp
Source Control Explorer
Current View: Tier Interactions
Name
Database
Count
Total Elapsed Time
Min Elapsed Time
Max Elapsed
WebDev.WebServer40.EXE
Database Connections
.\SQLEXPRESS
FabrikamFiber-Express
7 Queries
423.11
.\SQLEXPRESS
master
1 Query
74.78
Database connection details:
Command Text
Query Calls
Total Elapsed Time
Min Elapsed Time
Max Elapsed Time
SELECT TOP (1) [Extent1].[ID] AS [ID], [Extent1].[First
1
180.52
180.52
180.52
SELECT [Extent1].[ID] AS [ID], [Extent1].[FirstName] A
2
94.70
1.14
93.57
SELECT TOP (2) [Extent1].[ID] AS [ID], [Extent1].[First
1
70.73
70.73
70.73
SELECT TOP (1) [Extent1].[Id] AS [Id], [Extent1].[Mode
1
53.98
53.98
53.98
SELECT [Extent1].[ID] AS [ID], [Extent1].[Title] AS [Titl
2
23.18
8.14
15.05

FIGURE 20-7

This view shows the associated database connections, and how many queries were called from the web application. For example, seven queries were made to the FrabrikamFiber-Express database

The bottom window shows the details of the queries that were called, and the number of times each of these queries was called. This view also includes information on the timing of these queries. You can quickly see that the information captured about the interaction between the application tier and data tier can come in handy in debugging performance and bottleneck issues associated with the interaction between these two tiers.

CPU Counters Property Page

The CPU Counters property page (shown in Figure 20-8) is used to enable the collecting of CPU-related performance counters as your profiling sessions run. Enable the counters by checking the Collect CPU Counters checkbox. Then, select the counters you want to track from the Available Counters list, and click the right-pointing arrow button to add them to the Selected Counters list.

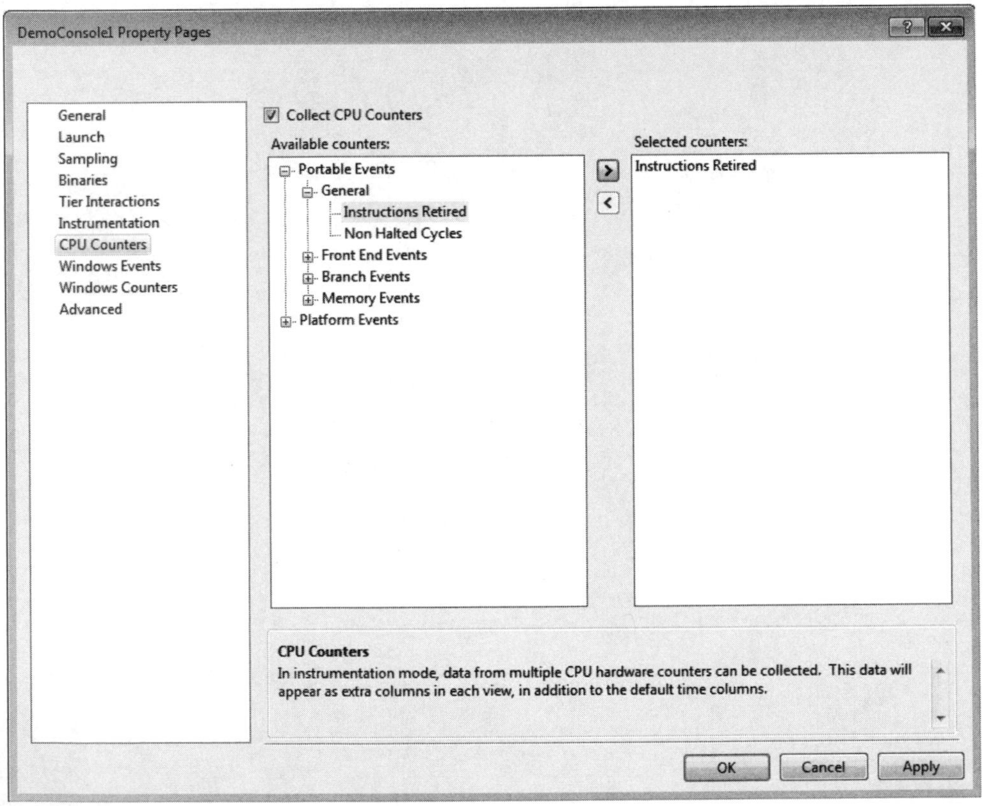

FIGURE 20-8

Windows Events Property Page

The Windows Events property page enables you to collect additional trace information from a variety of event providers. This can include items from Windows itself, such as disk and file I/O, as well as the .NET CLR. If you're profiling an ASP.NET application, for example, you can collect information from IIS and ASP.NET.

Windows Counters Property Page

The Windows Counters property page (shown in Figure 20-9) is used to enable the collection of Windows counters. These are performance counters that can be collected at regular intervals. Enable the counters by checking the Collect Windows Counters box. Then, select the Counter Category you want to choose from. Select the counters from the list, and click the right-pointing arrow button to add them to the list on the right.

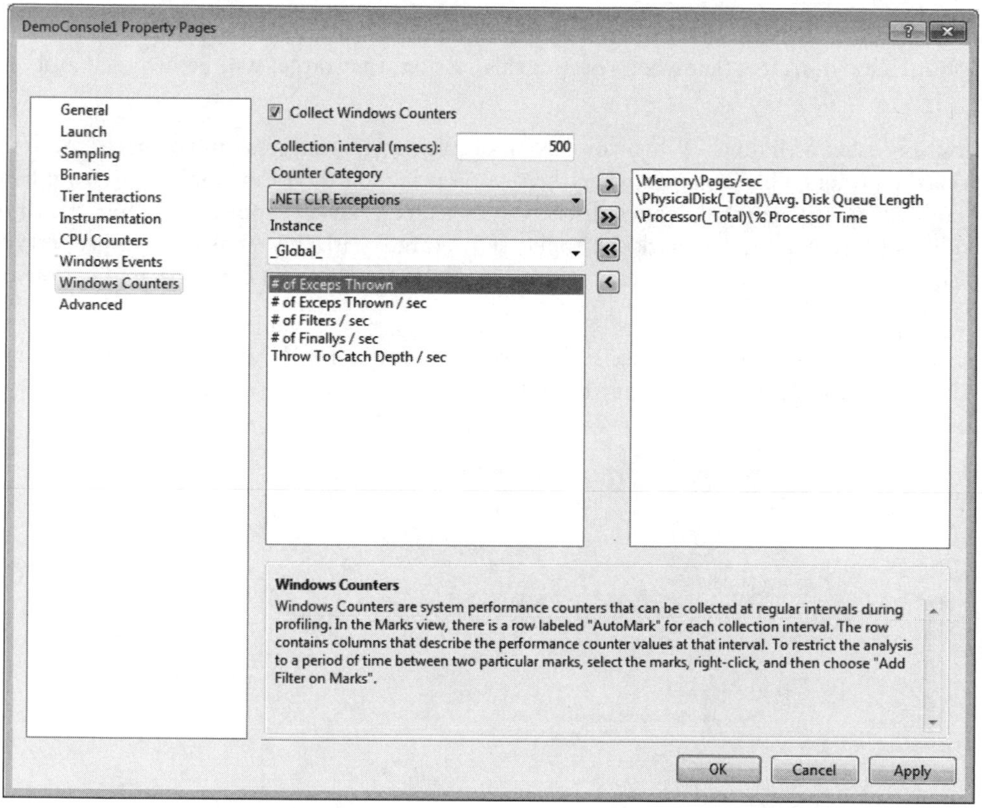

FIGURE 20-9

Configuring Session Targets

If you used the Performance Wizard to create your session, you already have a target specified. You can modify your session's targets with the Performance Explorer. Simply right-click the Targets folder and choose Add Target Binary. Or, if you have a valid candidate project in your current solution, choose Add Target Project. You can also add an ASP.NET website target by selecting Add Existing Web Site.

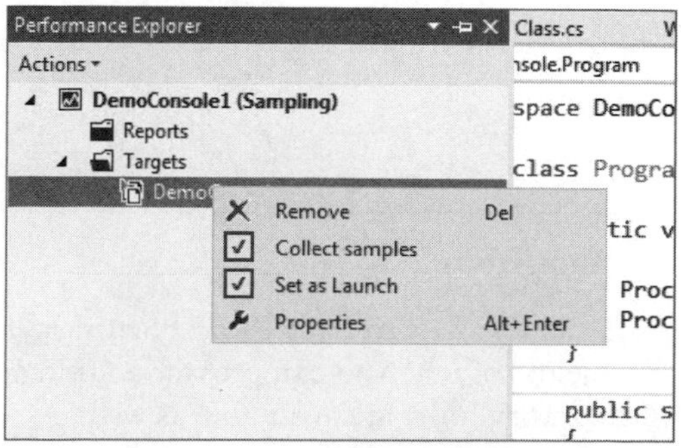

FIGURE 20-10

Each session target can be configured independently. Right-click any target and you see a context menu like the one shown in Figure 20-10.

> **NOTE** *The properties of a target are different from those of the overall session, so be careful to right-click a target, not the performance session's root node.*

If the session's mode is instrumentation, an Instrument option is also available instead of the Collect Samples option. This indicates that when you run this session, that target will be included and observed.

The other option is Set as Launch. When you have multiple targets in a session, you should indicate which of the targets will be started when the session is launched. For example, you could have several assembly targets, each with launch disabled (deselected), but one application .exe that uses those assemblies. In that case, you mark the application's target with the Set as Launch property. When this session is launched, the application is run, and data is collected from the application and the other target assemblies.

If you select the Properties option, you see a Property Pages dialog for the selected target (shown in Figure 20-11). Remember that these properties only affect the currently selected target, not the overall session.

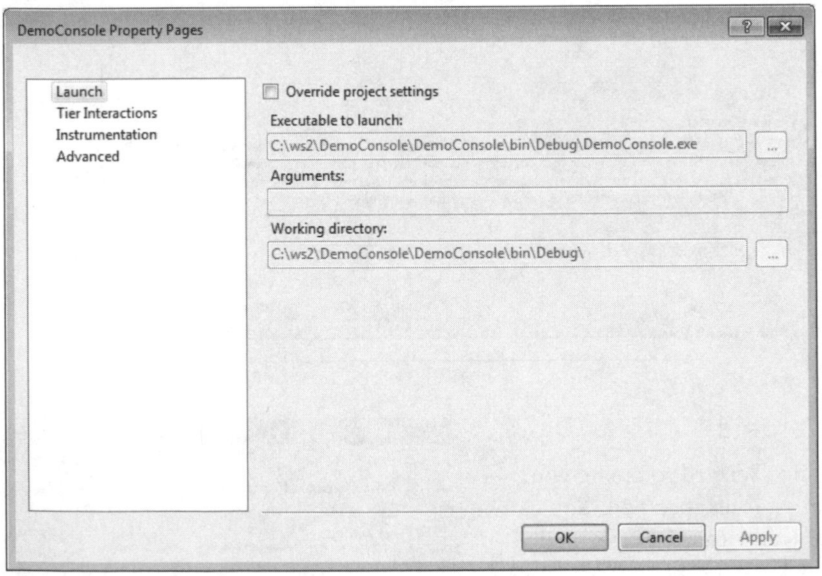

FIGURE 20-11

If you choose Override Project Settings, you can manually specify the path and name of an executable to launch. You can provide additional arguments to the executable and specify the working directory for that executable as well.

> **NOTE** *If the selected target is an ASP.NET application, this page instead contains a URL to Launch field.*

The Tier Interactions property page shows up here if you have chosen the tier interaction for the performance session.

The Instrumentation property page (shown in Figure 20-12) has options to run executables or scripts before and/or after the instrumentation process occurs for the current target. You may exclude the specified executable from instrumentation as well.

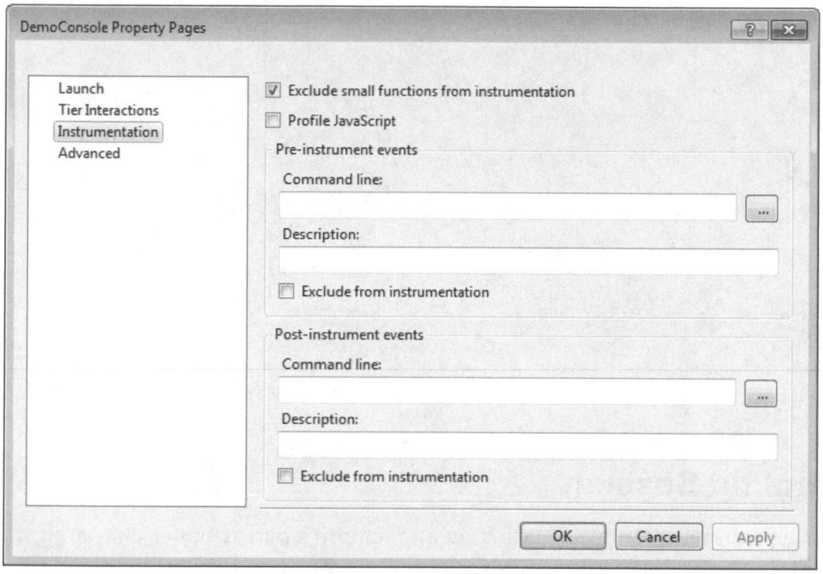

FIGURE 20-12

> **NOTE** *Because the instrumentation of an assembly changes it, when you instrument signed assemblies it breaks them because the assembly no longer matches the signature originally generated. To work with signed assemblies, you must add a post-instrument event, which calls to the strong-naming tool,* sn.exe. *In the command-line field, call* sn.exe, *supplying the assembly to sign and the key file to use for signing. You must also check the Exclude from Instrumentation option. Adding this step signs those assemblies again, allowing them to be used as expected.*

The Advanced property page is identical to the one under the General project settings. It is used to supply further command-line options to VSInstr.exe, the utility used by Visual Studio to instrument assemblies when running an instrumentation profiling session.

The Advanced property page is where you specify the .NET Framework run-time to profile, as shown in Figure 20-13. As you see in the figure, the machine being used for demonstration purposes here has .NET 2.0 and .NET 4.0 Beta installed; hence, those two options can be seen in the dropdown list.

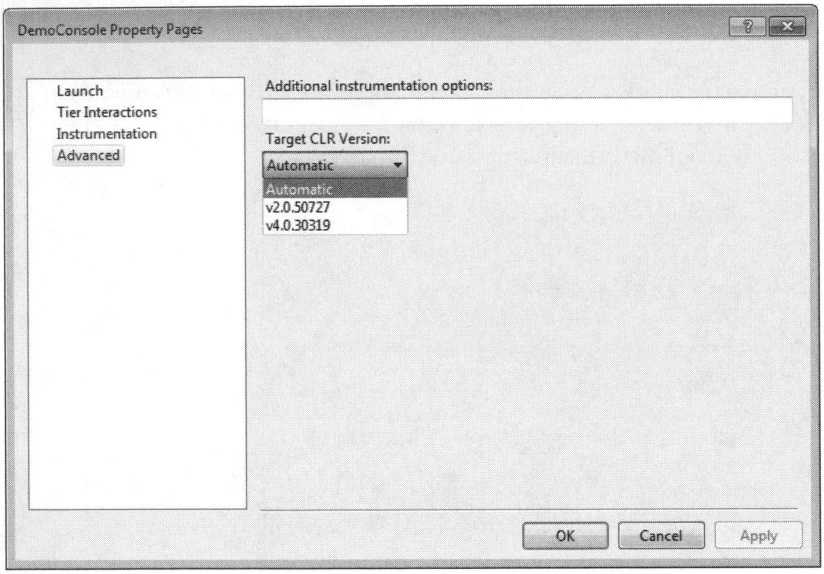

FIGURE 20-13

Configuring a Sampling Session

Sampling is a very lightweight method of investigating an application's performance characteristics. Sampling causes the profiler to periodically interrupt the execution of the target application, noting which code is executing and taking a snapshot of the call stack. When sampling completes, the report includes data such as function call counts. You can use this information to determine which functions might be bottlenecks or critical paths for your application, and then create an instrumentation session targeting those areas.

Because you are taking periodic snapshots of your application, the resulting view might be inaccurate if the duration of your sampling session is too short. For development purposes, you could set the sampling frequency very high, enabling you to obtain an acceptable view in a shorter time. However, if you are sampling against an application running in a production environment, you might want to minimize the sampling frequency to reduce the effect of profiling on the performance of your system. Of course, doing so requires a longer profiling session run to obtain accurate results.

By default, a sampling session interrupts the target application every 10 million clock cycles. If you open the session property pages and click the Sampling page, as shown in Figure 20-14, you may select other options as well.

You can use the Sampling Interval field to adjust the number of clock cycles between snapshots. Again, you might want a higher value (resulting in less frequent sampling) when profiling an application running in production, or a lower value for more frequent snapshots in a development environment. The exact value you should use will vary depending on your specific hardware and the performance of the application you are profiling.

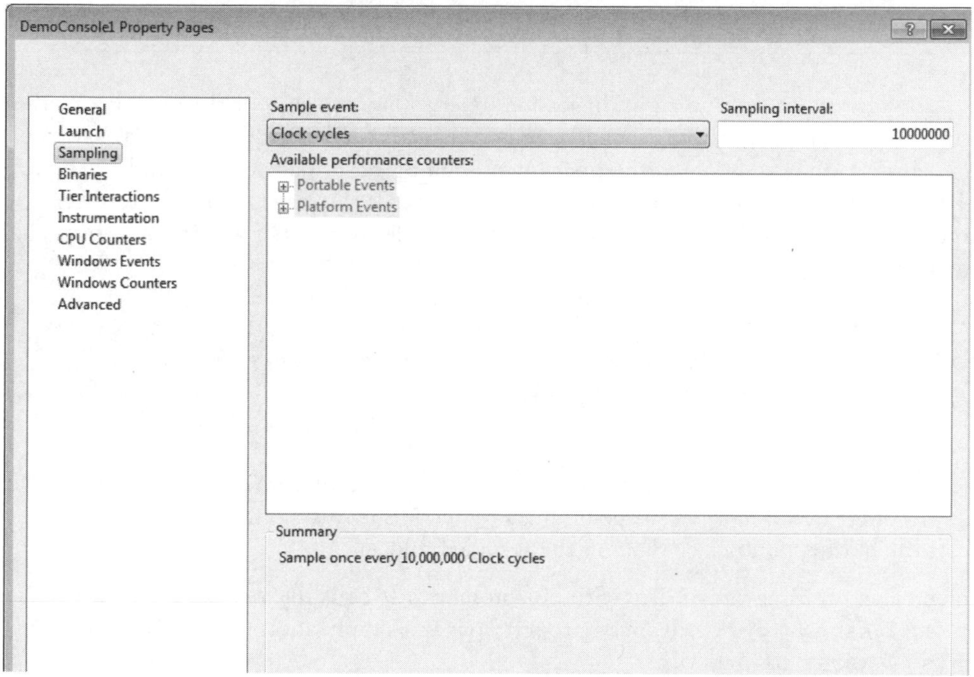

FIGURE 20-14

If you have an application that is memory-intensive, you may try a session based on page faults. This causes sampling to occur when memory pressure triggers a page fault. From this, you are able to get a good idea of what code is causing those memory allocations.

You can also sample based on system calls. In these cases, samples are taken after the specified number of system calls (as opposed to normal user-mode calls) has been made. You may also sample based on a specific CPU performance counter (such as misdirected branches or cache misses).

> **NOTE** *These alternative sampling methods are used to identify very specific conditions; sampling based on clock cycles is what you need most of the time.*

Configuring an Instrumentation Session

Instrumentation is the act of inserting probes or markers in a target binary, which, when hit during normal program flow, cause the logging of data about the application at that point. This is a more invasive way of profiling an application, but because you are not relying on periodic snapshots, it is also more accurate.

> **NOTE** *Instrumentation can quickly generate a large amount of data, so you should begin by sampling an application to find potential problem areas, or hotspots. Then, based on those results, instrument specific areas of code that require further analysis.*

When you're configuring an instrumentation session (refer to Figure 20-1 for the profiling method options), three additional property pages can be of use: Instrumentation, Binaries, and Advanced. The Instrumentation tab is identical to the Instrumentation property page that is available on a per-target basis, as shown in Figure 20-12. The difference is that the target settings are specific to a single target, whereas the session's settings specify executables to run before/after *all* targets have been instrumented.

> **NOTE** *You probably notice the Profile JavaScript option in Figure 20-12. That option is examined a little later in this chapter.*

The Binaries property page is used to manage the location of your instrumented binaries. By checking Relocate Instrumented Binaries and specifying a folder, Visual Studio takes the original target binaries, instrument them, and place them in the specified folder.

For instrumentation profiling runs, Visual Studio automatically calls the `VSInstr.exe` utility to instrument your binaries. Use the Advanced property page to supply additional options and arguments (such as `/VERBOSE`) to that utility.

Configuring a .NET Memory Allocation Session

The .NET memory allocation profiling method interrupts the processor for every allocation of managed objects. The profiler collects details about the managed types that are created during the application's execution. (See Figure 20-1 for the profiling method options.) The profiler tracks the number of instances, the amount of memory used by those instances, and which members created the instances.

When you check the Also Collect .NET Object Lifetime Information option in the General properties page (Figure 20-5), additional details about the amount of time each managed type instance remains in memory is collected. This enables you to view further effects of your application, such as its effect on the .NET garbage collector.

Configuring a Concurrency Profiling Session

Concurrency profiling is a method that was introduced in Visual Studio 2010. Using this method, you can collect the following two types of concurrency data:

➤ *Resource contention* — This captures information every time a function in the application is waiting for a resource because of a synchronous event.

➤ *Thread execution* — This captures information on thread contention, processor utilization, execution delays, and other system events.

Executing a Performance Session

After you have configured your performance session and assigned targets, you can execute (or launch) that session. In the Performance Explorer window (Figure 20-4), right-click a specific session, and choose Start Profiling.

> **NOTE** *Before you launch your performance session, ensure that your project and any dependent assemblies have been generated in Release Configuration mode. Profiling a Debug build is not as accurate because such builds are not optimized for performance and have additional overhead.*

Because Performance Explorer can hold more than one session, you designate one of those sessions as the current session. By default, the first session is marked as current. You can invoke the current session by selecting the Actions ➪ Start Profiling menu command.

You may also run a performance session from the command line. For details, see the section "Command-Line Profiling Utilities," later in this chapter.

When a session is launched, you can monitor its status via the output window. You see the output from each of the utilities invoked for you. If the target application is interactive, you can use the application as normal. When the application completes, the profiler shuts down and generates a report.

When profiling an ASP.NET application, an instance of Internet Explorer is launched, with a target URL as specified in the target's URL to Launch setting. Use the application as normal through this browser instance, and Visual Studio monitors the application's performance. After the Internet Explorer window is closed, Visual Studio stops collecting data and generates the profiling report.

> **NOTE** *You are not required to use the browser for interaction with the ASP.NET application. If you have other forms of testing for that application (such as the Web and load tests described in Chapter 25), simply minimize the Internet Explorer window and execute those tests. When you're finished, return to the browser window and close it. The profiling report is then generated and includes usage data resulting from those Web and load tests.*

Managing Session Reports

When a session run is complete, a new session report is added to the Reports folder for the executed session. The "Setting General Session Properties" section earlier in this chapter (as well as Figure 20-5) provides more details about how to modify the report name, location, and other additional properties in the General property page description.

As shown in Figure 20-15, the Reports folder holds all of the reports for the executions of that session.

Double-click a report file to generate and view the report. Or, you can right-click a report and select Open to view the report within Visual Studio (as shown in Figure 20-15).

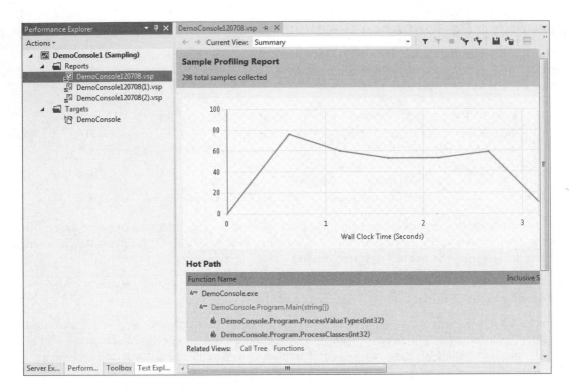

FIGURE 20-15

In Visual Studio 2012, you can also compare two performance reports. With this capability, you can compare the results from a profiling session against a baseline. This will help, for example, in tracking the results from profiling sessions from one build to the next. To compare reports, right-click a report name and select Compare Performance Reports.

This opens a dialog in which you can select the baseline report and the comparison report, as shown in Figure 20-16.

Choose the Baseline File and the Comparison File and then click OK. This generates an analysis that shows the delta between the two reports, and an indicator showing the directional move of the data between these two reports (Figure 20-17). This gives you a clear sense of how the application profile is changing between two runs.

FIGURE 20-16

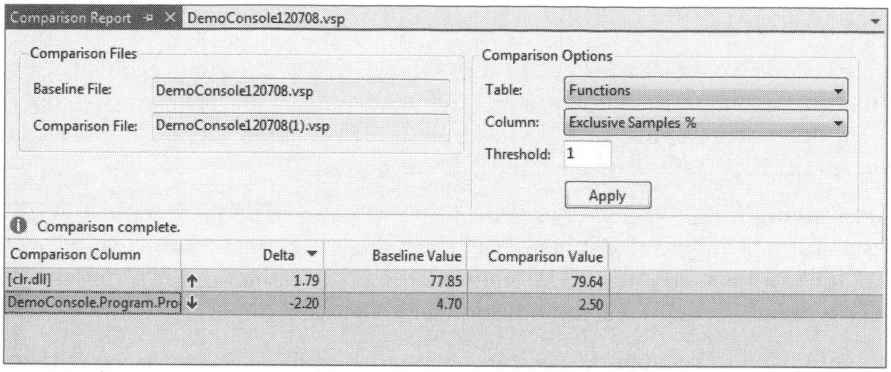

FIGURE 20-17

Another useful option to consider when you right-click a report is Export Report Data. When you select this option, it displays the Export Report dialog box shown in Figure 20-18. You can then select one or more sections of the report to send a target file in XML or comma-delimited format. This can be useful if you have another tool that parses this data, or for transforming via XSL into a custom report view.

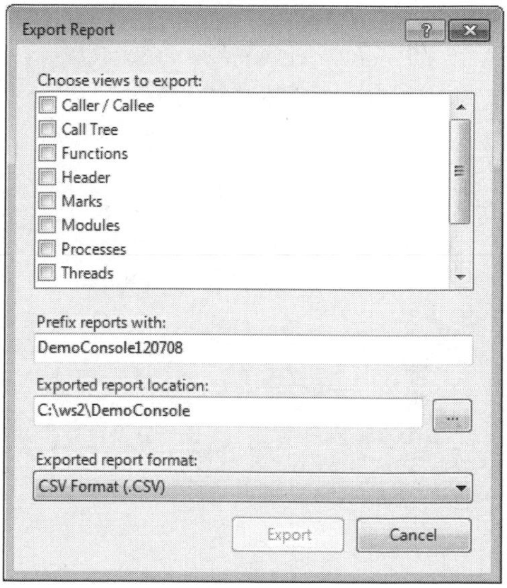

Reading and Interpreting Session Reports

A performance session report is composed of a number of different views. These views offer different ways to inspect the large amount of data collected during the profiling process. The data in many views are interrelated, and you see that entries in one view can lead to further detail in another view. Note that some views have content only if you have enabled optional settings before running the session.

FIGURE 20-18

The amount and kinds of data collected and displayed by a performance session report can be difficult to understand and interpret at first. The following sections examine each section of a report, describing its meaning and how to interpret the results.

In any of the tabular report views, you can select which columns appear (and their order) by right-clicking in the report and selecting Choose Columns. Select the columns you want to see, and how you want to order them, by using the move buttons.

Report Information and Views

The specific information displayed by each view depends on the settings used to generate the performance session. Sampling and instrumentation produce different contents for most views, and including .NET memory profiling options affects the display as well. Before exploring the individual views that make up a report, it is important to understand some key terms.

Elapsed time includes all of the time spent between the beginning and end of a given function. *Application time* is an estimate of the actual time spent executing your code, subtracting system events. Should your application be interrupted by another during a profiling session, elapsed time includes the time spent executing that other application, but application time excludes it.

Inclusive time combines the time spent in the current function with time spent in any other functions that it may call. *Exclusive time* removes the time spent in other functions called from the current function.

> **NOTE** *If you forget these definitions, hover your mouse pointer over the column headers and a tool tip gives you a brief description of the column.*

Summary View

When you view a report, Summary view is displayed by default. There are two types of summary reports, depending on whether you ran a sampling or instrumented profile. Figure 20-19 shows a Summary view from a sampling profile of the DemoConsole application.

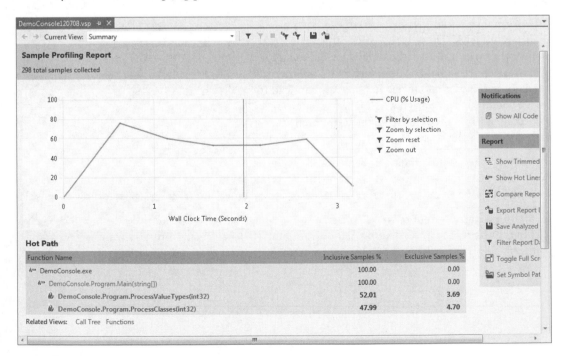

FIGURE 20-19

The Summary view in Visual Studio 2012 has three data sections (on the left of the screen), one Notifications section (in the top right of the screen), and a Report section (in the lower-right portion of the screen), as shown in Figure 20-19.

The first data section you see in the Summary view is the chart at the top showing the percentage of CPU usage. This chart provides a quick visual cue into any spikes you have in CPU usage. You can select a section of the chart (for example, a spike in the chart), and then you can either zoom in by selecting the Zoom by Selection link to the right of the chart, or you can filter the data by selecting the Filter by Selection link, also to the right of the chart.

The second section in the Summary view is the Hot Path. This shows the most expensive call paths. (They are highlighted with a flame icon next to the function name.) It's not a surprise that the call to `ProcessClasses` and to `ProcessValueTypes` were the expensive calls in this trivial example.

The third data section shows a list of Functions Doing Most Individual Work. A large number of exclusive samples here indicate that a large amount of time was spent on that particular function.

> **NOTE** *Notice that several of the functions aren't function names, but names of DLLs — for example,* `[clr.dll]`. *This occurs when debugging samples are not available for a function sampled. This frequently happens when running sampling profiles, and occasionally with instrumented profiles. The "Common Profiling Issues" section later in the chapter describes this issue and how to correct it.*

For the DemoConsole application, this view isn't showing a lot of interesting data. At this point, you would normally investigate the other views. For example, you can click one of the methods in the Hot Path to take you to the function details page, but because the DemoConsole application is trivial, sampling to find hotspots is not as useful as the information you can gather using instrumentation. Let's change the profiling type to instrumentation and see what information is revealed.

In Performance Explorer, right-click the DemoConsole profile and select Properties. Change the Profiling Collection option to Instrumentation, and click OK to close the properties window. Right-click the DemoConsole profile and select Start Profiling to start profiling, this time using instrumentation. Note that instrumentation profiling takes longer to run. When profiling and report generation are complete, you see a Summary view similar to that shown in Figure 20-20.

The Summary view of an instrumented session has three sections similar to the Summary view of a sampling session.

You can also get to the Call Tree view (which is examined shortly) or Functions view using the shortcut link provided below the Hot Path information.

The Summary view has an alternate layout that is used when the .NET Memory Profiling Collection options are enabled on the General page of the session properties. Figure 20-21 shows this view.

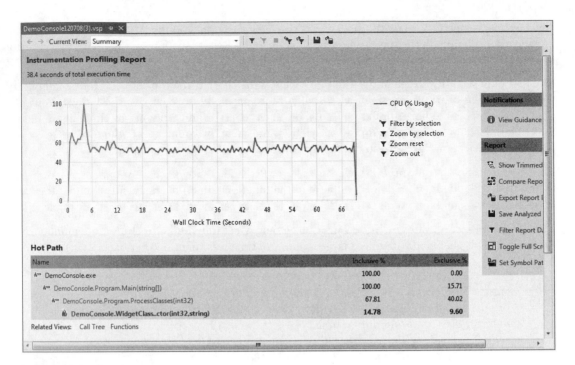

FIGURE 20-20

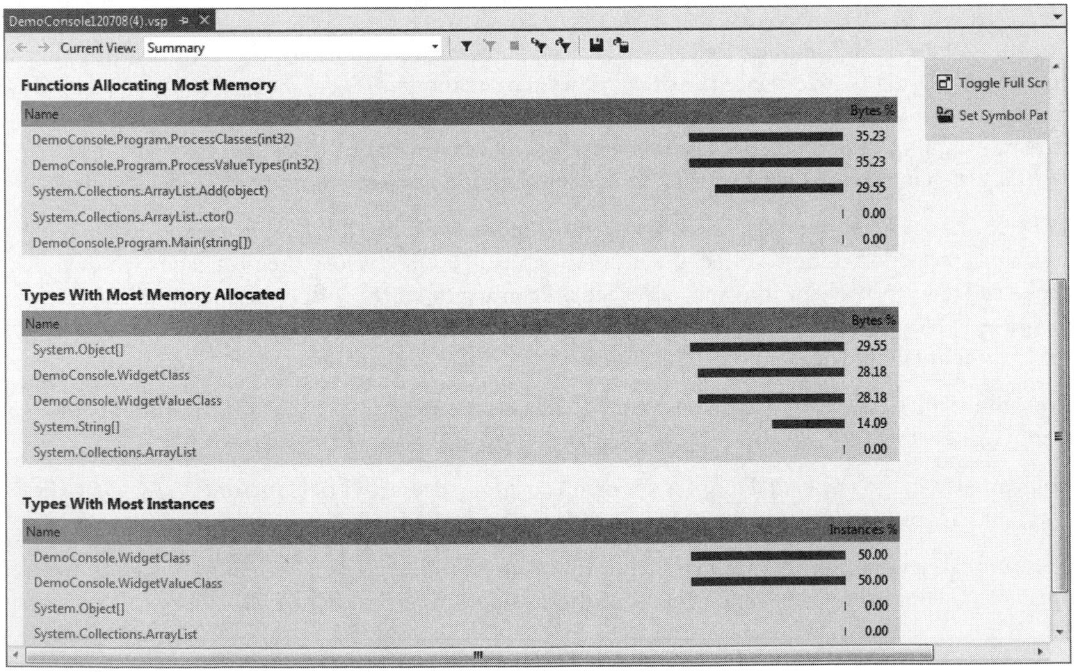

FIGURE 20-21

Notice that the three main sections in this view are different. The first section, Functions Allocating Most Memory, shows the functions in terms of bytes allocated. The second section, Types with Most Memory Allocated, shows the types by bytes allocated, without regard to the functions involved. Finally, Types with Most Instances shows the types in terms of number of instances, without regard to the size of those instances.

Also note the Notifications section and the Report section to the right of the CPU usage chart. If you click the View Guidance link in the Notifications section, you are shown any available errors, warnings, or informational messages. In this case, as shown in Figure 20-22, there are several information messages. You learn what these mean later in this chapter in the "Objects Lifetime View" section.

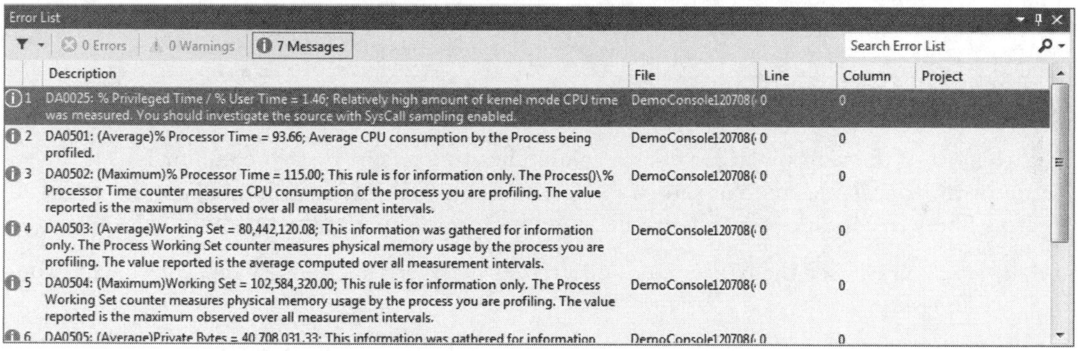

FIGURE 20-22

Using the Summary view, you can quickly get a sense of the most highly used functions and types within your application. In the following discussions, you see how to use the other views to dive into further detail.

Functions View and Functions Details View

Let's switch to the Functions view. You do that by selecting Functions from the Current View drop-down at the top of the report. In this view, you can begin to see some interesting results.

The Functions view shown in Figure 20-23 lists all functions sampled or instrumented during the session. For instrumentation, this is functions in targets that were instrumented and called during the session. For sampling, this includes any other members/assemblies accessed by the application.

Note that `ArrayList.Add` and `ArrayList.get_Item` were each called four million times. This makes sense, because `ProcessValueTypes` and `ProcessClasses` (which use that method) were each called two million times. However, if you look at the Hot Path information in the Summary views, there is a noticeable difference in the amount of time spent in `ProcessingValueTypes` over `ProcessClasses`. Remember that the code for each is basically the same — the only difference is that one works with structures, and the other with classes. You can use the other views to investigate further.

From the Functions view, right-click any function, and you can go to that function's source, see it in module view, see the function details, or see the function in Caller/Callee view (discussed in detail shortly). You can double-click any function to switch to the Functions Details view. You can also select one or more functions, right-click, and choose Copy to add the function name and associated data to the clipboard for use in other documents.

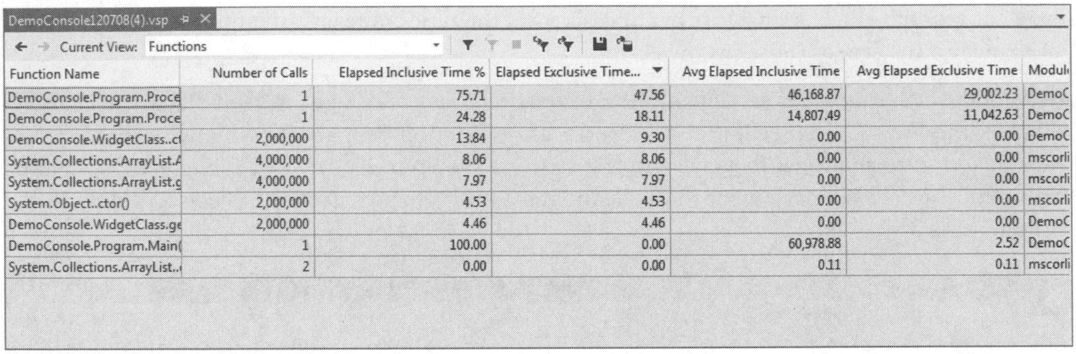

Function Name	Number of Calls	Elapsed Inclusive Time %	Elapsed Exclusive Time... ▼	Avg Elapsed Inclusive Time	Avg Elapsed Exclusive Time	Modul
DemoConsole.Program.Proce	1	75.71	47.56	46,168.87	29,002.23	DemoC
DemoConsole.Program.Proce	1	24.28	18.11	14,807.49	11,042.63	DemoC
DemoConsole.WidgetClass..ct	2,000,000	13.84	9.30	0.00	0.00	DemoC
System.Collections.ArrayList.A	4,000,000	8.06	8.06	0.00	0.00	mscorli
System.Collections.ArrayList.g	4,000,000	7.97	7.97	0.00	0.00	mscorli
System.Object..ctor()	2,000,000	4.53	4.53	0.00	0.00	mscorli
DemoConsole.WidgetClass.ge	2,000,000	4.46	4.46	0.00	0.00	DemoC
DemoConsole.Program.Main(	1	100.00	0.00	60,978.88	2.52	DemoC
System.Collections.ArrayList..	2	0.00	0.00	0.11	0.11	mscorli

FIGURE 20-23

As with most of the views, you can click a column heading to sort by that column. This is especially useful for the four Time columns shown in Figure 20-23. Right-clicking in the Functions view and selecting Show in Modules view shows the functions grouped under their containing binary.

In this view, you can see the performance differences between functions, which could help you to focus on an issue.

Double-clicking a function from the Functions view loads up the Function Details view. Figure 20-24 shows the section of this view that is a clickable map with the calling function, the called functions, and the associated values.

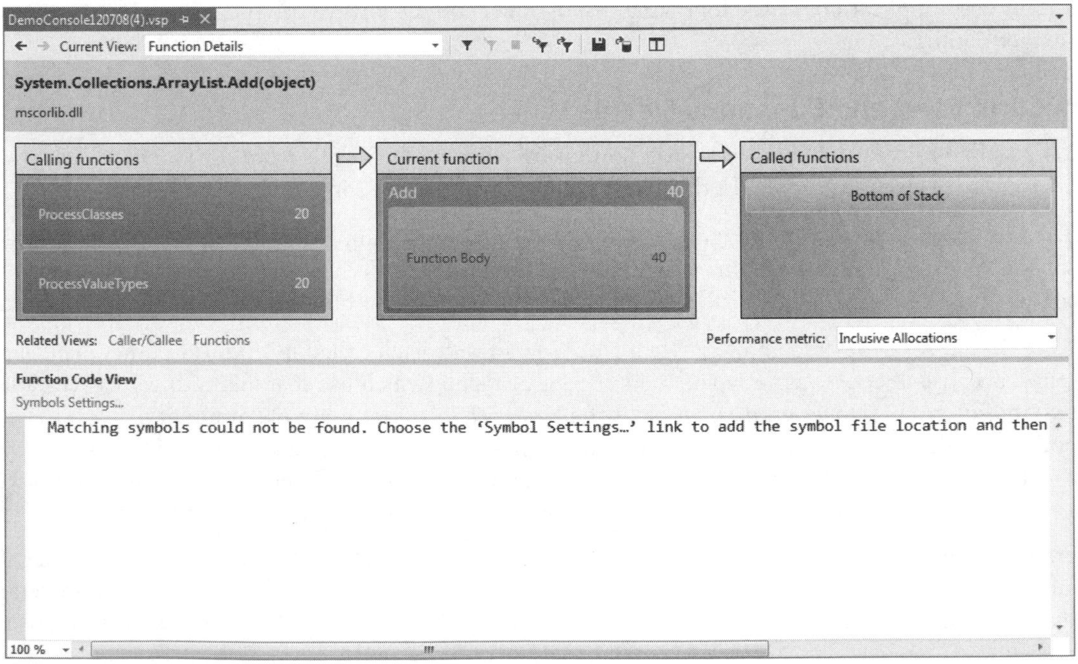

FIGURE 20-24

The Caller/Callee view presents this data in a tabular fashion.

Caller/Callee View

As shown in Figure 20-25, the Caller/Callee view displays a particular function in the middle, with the function(s) that call into it in the section above it, and any functions that it calls in the bottom section.

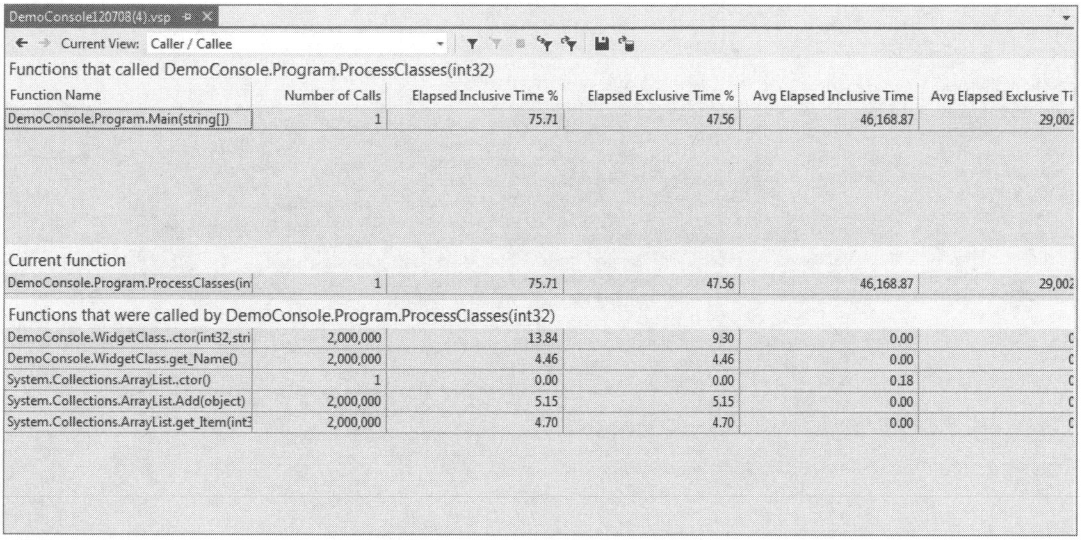

Function Name	Number of Calls	Elapsed Inclusive Time %	Elapsed Exclusive Time %	Avg Elapsed Inclusive Time	Avg Elapsed Exclusive Ti
Functions that called DemoConsole.Program.ProcessClasses(int32)					
DemoConsole.Program.Main(string[])	1	75.71	47.56	46,168.87	29,002
Current function					
DemoConsole.Program.ProcessClasses(in	1	75.71	47.56	46,168.87	29,002
Functions that were called by DemoConsole.Program.ProcessClasses(int32)					
DemoConsole.WidgetClass..ctor(int32,stri	2,000,000	13.84	9.30	0.00	C
DemoConsole.WidgetClass.get_Name()	2,000,000	4.46	4.46	0.00	C
System.Collections.ArrayList..ctor()	1	0.00	0.00	0.18	C
System.Collections.ArrayList.Add(object)	2,000,000	5.15	5.15	0.00	C
System.Collections.ArrayList.get_Item(int3	2,000,000	4.70	4.70	0.00	C

FIGURE 20-25

This is particularly useful for pinpointing the execution flow of your application, helping to identify hotspots. In Figure 20-25, the ProcessClasses method is in focus and shows that the only caller is the Main method. You can also see that ProcessClasses directly calls four functions. The sum of times in the caller list matches the time shown for the set function. For example, select the ArrayList.get_Item accessor by double-clicking or right-clicking it and then choose Set Function. The resulting window then displays a table similar to what is shown in Figure 20-26.

You saw ArrayList.get_Item in the main Functions view, but couldn't tell how much of that time resulted from calls by ProcessValueTypes or ProcessClasses. Caller/Callee view enables you to see this detail.

Notice that there are two callers for this function, and that the sum of their time equals the time of the function itself. In this table, you can see how much time that the ArrayList.get_Item method actually took to process the two million requests from ProcessValueTypes versus those from ProcessClasses. This enables you to analyze the processing time differences, and, if it is substantially different, to drill down on the differences to find out what could be causing the performance difference.

Call Tree View

The Call Tree view shows a hierarchical view of the calls executed by your application. The concept is somewhat similar to the Caller/Callee view, but in this view, a given function may appear twice if it is called by independent functions. If that same method were viewed in Caller/Callee view, it would appear once, with both parent functions listed at the top.

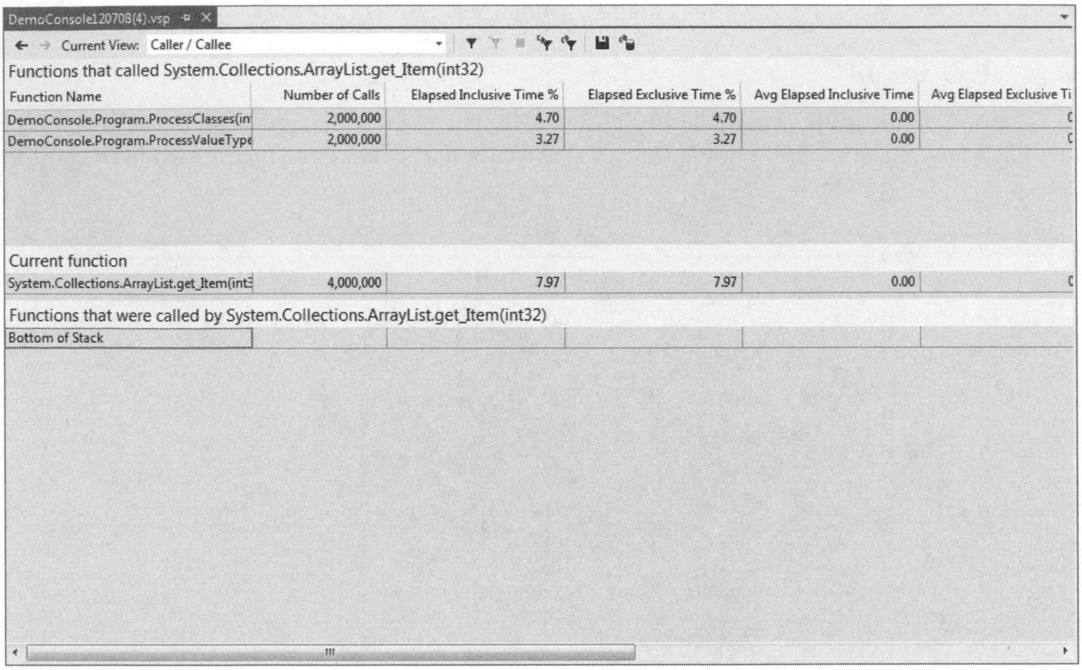

FIGURE 20-26

By default, the view has a root (the function at the top of the list) of the entry point of the instrumented application. To quickly expand the details for any node, right-click and choose Expand All. Any function with dependent calls can be set as the new root for the view by right-clicking and choosing Set Root. This modifies the view to show that function at the top, followed by any functions that were called directly or indirectly by that function. To revert the view to the default, right-click and choose Reset Root.

Another handy option in the context menu is Expand Hot Path. This expands the tree to show the Hot Paths with the flame icon. This is a very helpful shortcut to jump right into the functions that are potential bottlenecks.

Allocation View

If you configured your session for managed allocation profiling by choosing Collect .NET Object Allocation Information on the General property page for your session (Figure 20-5), you have access to the Allocation view. This view displays the managed types that were created during the execution of the profiled application.

You can quickly see how many instances, the total bytes of memory used by those instances, and the percentage of overall bytes consumed by the instances of each managed type.

Expand any type to see the functions that caused the instantiations of that type. You see the breakdown of instances by function as well, so, if more than one function created instances of that type, you can determine which created the most. This view is most useful when sorted by Total Bytes

Allocated or Percent of Total Bytes. This tells you which types are consuming the most memory when your application runs.

> **NOTE** *An instrumented profiling session tracks and reports only the types allocated directly by the instrumented code. A sampling session may show other types of objects. This is because samples can be taken at any time, even while processing system functions (such as security). Try comparing the allocations from sampling and instrumentation sessions for the same project. You will likely notice more object types in the sampling session.*

As with the other report views, you can also right-click any function to switch to an alternative view, such as source code, Functions view, or Caller/Callee view.

Objects Lifetime View

The Objects Lifetime view is available only if you have selected the Also Collect .NET Object Lifetime Information option of the General properties for your session (refer to Figure 20-5). This option is only available if you have also selected the Collect .NET Object Allocation Information option.

> **NOTE** *The information in this view becomes more accurate the longer the application is run. If you are concerned about the results you see, increase the duration of your session run to help ensure that the trend is accurate.*

Several of the columns are identical to those in the Allocation view table, including Instances, Total Bytes Allocated, and Percent of Total Bytes. However, in this view, you can't break down the types to show which functions created them. The value in this view lies in the details about how long the managed type instances existed and their effect on garbage collection.

The columns in this view include the number of instances of each type that were collected during specific generations of the garbage collector. With COM, objects were immediately destroyed, and memory freed, when the count of references to that instance became zero. However, .NET relies on a process called *garbage collection* to periodically inspect all object instances to determine whether the memory they consume can be released.

Objects are placed into groups, called *generations*, according to how long each instance has remained referenced. Generation zero contains new instances, generation one instances are older, and generation two contains the oldest instances. New objects are more likely to be temporary or shorter in scope than objects that have survived previous collections. So, having objects organized into generations enables .NET to more efficiently find objects to release when additional memory is needed.

The view includes Instances Alive at End and Instances. The latter is the total count of instances of that type over the life of the profiling session. The former indicates how many instances of that type were still in memory when the profiling session terminated. This might be because the references to those instances were held by other objects. It might also occur if the instances were released right before the session ended, before the garbage collector acted to remove them. Having values in this column does not necessarily indicate a problem; it is simply another data item to consider as you evaluate your system.

Having a large number of generation-zero instances collected is normal, fewer in generation one, and the fewest in generation two. Anything else indicates there might be an opportunity to optimize the scope of some variables. For example, a class field that is only used from one of that class's methods could be changed to a variable inside that method. This would reduce the scope of that variable to live only while that method is executing.

Like the data shown in the other report views, you should use the data in this view not as definitive indicators of problems, but as pointers to places where improvements might be realized. Also, keep in mind that, with small or quickly executing programs, allocation tracking might not have enough data to provide truly meaningful results.

COMMAND-LINE PROFILING UTILITIES

Visual Studio abstracts the process of calling several utilities to conduct profiling. You can use these utilities directly if you need more control, or if you need to integrate your profiling with an automated batch process (such as your nightly build). The general flow is as follows:

1. Configure the target (if necessary) and environment.
2. Start the data logging engine.
3. Run the target application.
4. When the application has completed, stop the data logging engine.
5. Generate the session report.

These utilities can be found in your Visual Studio installation directory under `\Team Tools\ Performance Tools`. For help with any of the utilities, supply a `/?` argument after the utility name.

Table 20-1 lists the performance utilities that are available as of this writing:

TABLE 20-1: Performance Tools

UTILITY NAME	DESCRIPTION
Vsinstr.exe	Used to instrument a binary
Vsperfcmd.exe	Used to launch a profiling session
Vsperfmon.exe	Starts the monitor for the profiling sessions
Vsperfreport.exe	Used to generate a report after a profiling session is completed
VsperfCLREnv.exe	Used to set environment variables required to profile a .NET application

> **NOTE** *Refer to MSDN documentation at* `http://msdn.microsoft.com/en-us/` `library/bb385768(VS.100).aspx` *for more information on the command-line profiling tools.*

Profiling JavaScript

In Visual Studio 2012, you can profile JavaScript. With this option, you can collect performance data for JavaScript code. To do that, you start by setting up an instrumentation session. Then, in the Instrumentation property page, select the Profile JavaScript option, as shown in Figure 20-27.

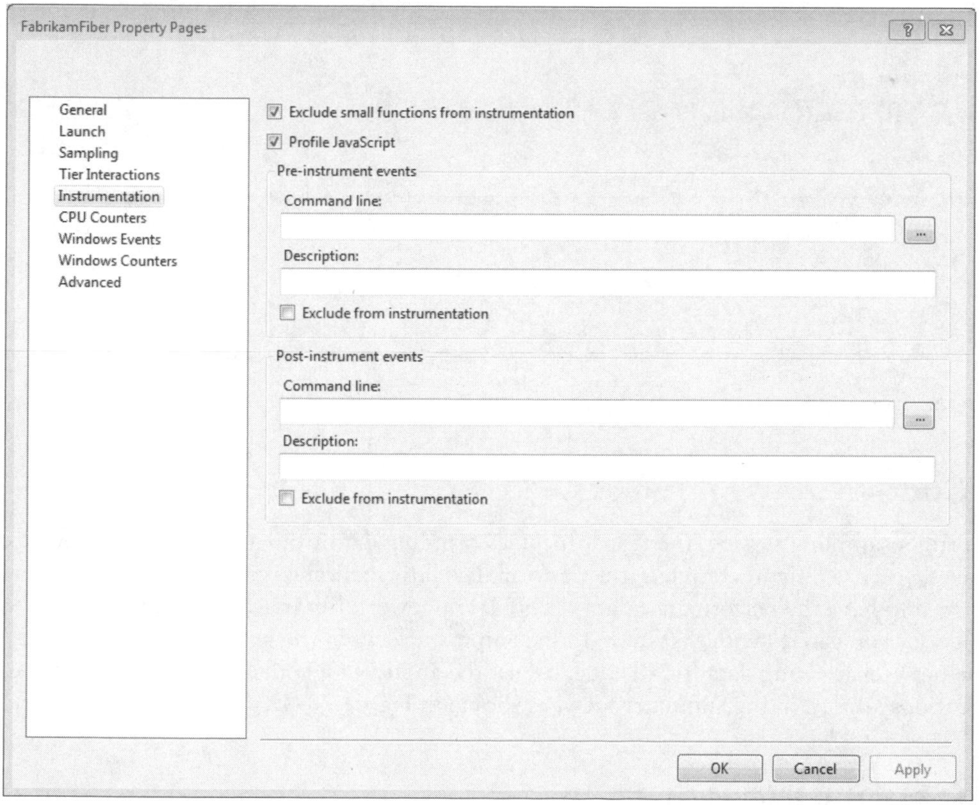

FIGURE 20-27

When you run this profiling session, the profiler includes performance information on JavaScript functions, along with function calls in the application. This example again uses the "Fabrikam Fiber" application. Figure 20-28 shows the Function Details view with the called functions and the elapsed times. It also shows the associated JavaScript code in the bottom pane, and that helps in identifying any potential issues with the script. This feature is very helpful to assess the performance of JavaScript functions and identifies any issues with the scripts.

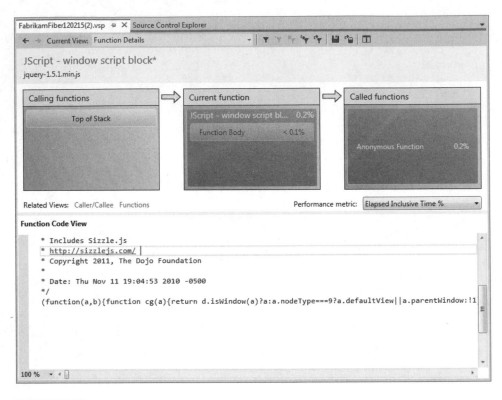

FIGURE 20-28

Just My Code

When you run a sampling session, the report includes profiling data from all the code in the project. In most cases, you are only interested in the performance information of your code. For example, you don't need to have the performance data of .NET Framework libraries, and, even if you have it, there is not a lot you can do with that data. In the Summary view of the profiling report, you can now toggle between viewing data for all code, or just the application code. The setting for that is in the Notifications section in the Summary view, as shown in Figure 20-29.

COMMON PROFILING ISSUES

Profiling is a complex topic, and it's not without a few pitfalls to catch the unwary. This section documents a number of common issues you might encounter as you profile your applications.

Debugging Symbols

When you review your profiling reports, you might notice that some function calls resolve to unhelpful entries such as [ntdll.dll]. This occurs because the application has used code for which it cannot find debugging symbols. So, instead of the function name, you get the name of the containing binary.

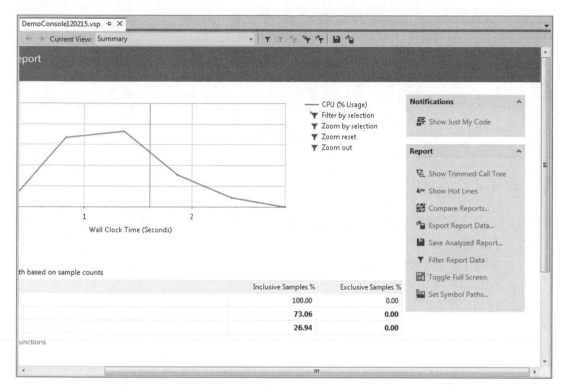

FIGURE 20-29

Debugging symbols, files with the `.pdb` extension (for "program database"), include the details that debuggers and profilers use to discover information about executing code. Microsoft Symbol Server enables you to use a web connection to dynamically obtain symbol files for binaries as needed.

You can direct Visual Studio to use this server by choosing Tools ➪ Options. Expand the Debugging section and choose Symbols. Check the box next to the Microsoft Symbol Servers location. Now, close and reopen a report; the new symbols are used to resolve function names.

> **NOTE** *The first time you render a report with symbols set to download from Microsoft Symbol Server, it takes significantly longer to complete than it will on subsequent times.*

If your profiling system does not have Internet access — perhaps because of security restrictions — you can download and install the symbol packages for Windows from the Windows Hardware Developer Center. As of this writing, this is http:// msdn.microsoft.com/en-us/windows/hardware/gg463028. Select the package appropriate for your processor and operating system and install the symbols.

Instrumentation and Code Coverage

When running an instrumentation profile, be certain that you are not profiling a target for which you have previously enabled *code coverage*. Code coverage, described in Chapter 7, uses another form of instrumentation that observes which lines of code are accessed as tests are executed. Unfortunately, this instrumentation can interfere with the instrumentation required by the profiler.

If your solution has a test project and you have previously used code coverage, open your Test Run Configuration under Test ⇨ Edit Test Run Configurations, and select the Code Coverage page. Ensure that the binaries you are profiling do not have code coverage enabled. If they do, uncheck them and rebuild your solution. You should then be able to use instrumentation profiling without conflict.

SUMMARY

In this chapter, you learned about the value of using profiling to identify problem areas in your code. This chapter examined the differences between sampling and instrumentation, when each should be applied, and how to configure the profiler to execute each type. You learned about the different profiling methods. You saw the Performance Explorer in action, and learned how to create and configure performance sessions and their targets.

You then learned how to invoke a profiling session, and how to work with the reports that are generated after each run. You looked at each of the available report types, including Summary, Function, Call Tree, and Caller/Callee.

Although Visual Studio 2012 offers a great deal of flexibility in your profiling, you might find you must specify further options or profile applications from a batch application or build system. You learned about the available command-line tools. Profiling is a great tool that you can use to ensure the quality of your application.

In Chapter 21, you learn about a great feature in Visual Studio 2012 called IntelliTrace, as well as some other nifty debugging capabilities (including data tips and breakpoints).

Debugging with IntelliTrace

Many developers resent the fact that debugging has become one of the key components in
software development. Many developers have been known to spend a considerable amount
of time simply on debugging. Adding salt to the wound are programming bugs for which the
behavior is not reproducible. In many instances, developers may wish there was a way to travel
back in time to capture what happened and then be able to wave a magic wand to debug the
issue. That wish has now come true in Visual Studio Ultimate 2012. (Not the magic wand
part — that feature did not make the cut.)

This chapter examines the IntelliTrace feature, which debuted in Visual Studio 2010 Ultimate
and has been enhanced in Visual Studio Ultimate 2012. In this chapter, you find out how to
use this feature to aid in your debugging effort, and how you can use it in a production environment to help debug production applications.

INTELLITRACE BASICS

In many cases, as a developer, you have discovered that debugging is a regular activity. It is also a task that can become monotonous. For example, at some point a tester might have passed on a bug to you that you could not reproduce. You may also have experienced the agony of stepping through one step past the point where the issue occurs, only to discover that it is time to start all over again. These are just a couple of common occurrences, and there are no doubt plenty more.

Visual Studio Ultimate 2012 includes capabilities to address issues such as the famous "no repro" bug status. A key feature in this capability is the IntelliTrace feature. The key tactics used to address the nonreproducible bug are to capture as much information as possible when the bug is encountered, and to use the capability to leverage this information while debugging. The one feature that could top this would be for the bug to automatically resolve itself.

Now it's time to take a deeper look at this debugging feature through an example.

IntelliTrace — An Example

The following steps walk you through an example of using IntelliTrace to debug an application:

1. To get started, open the `Chapter21SampleApp` in Visual Studio 2012. Press F5 to compile and run the application.

   The application runs, and a window with three buttons opens, as shown Figure 21-1. By pressing F5 to run the application, you are running it in Debug mode. Notice the IntelliTrace window on the right side of Visual Studio. Currently nothing is shown in the window. IntelliTrace gathers data behind the scenes while the application is executing, but you must break the execution of the application before the IntelliTrace information can be viewed. Let's walk the application through its paces and look at the IntelliTrace results.

2. Click the Ex1: Generate Random Number button on the application form to generate a random number and display it in a message box. Click the OK button to close the message box.

3. Click the Ex2: File Access button. The application attempts to read from a text file and displays the results in the text box. You should see results displayed there.

4. Click the Ex3: File Access button. The application attempts to read and display the contents of a different text file. Notice, however, that the application did not display anything. Something must be wrong with the application. However, the application did not throw an error or display any other signs that something is wrong.

At this point, before IntelliTrace, you would have had to go back into the code and look at the functionality around the application to try to determine where something might be wrong. Maybe you would have gone back in to add a lot of breakpoints, and then started stepping slowly through your code. Regardless, you had to go back and run the same tests again. With IntelliTrace, you don't have to do that.

The application did not perform as expected when you clicked the Ex3: File Access button. Use IntelliTrace to figure out why. In the IntelliTrace window in Visual Studio, click the Break All link. This breaks into the debugging session and displays the IntelliTrace information collected so far, as shown in Figure 21-2.

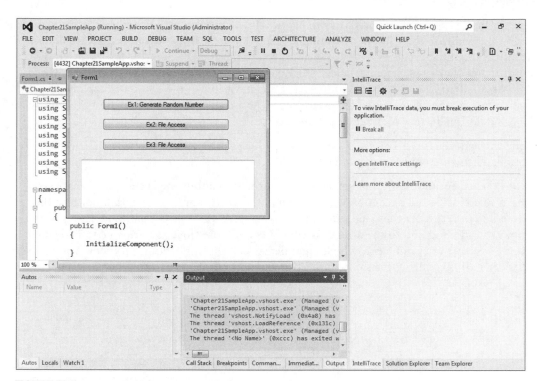

FIGURE 21-1

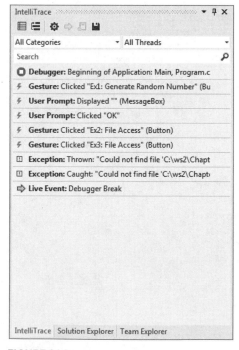

FIGURE 21-2

By default, IntelliTrace is configured only to capture IntelliTrace event information, so that is what is displayed initially in the window. Selecting a particular event in the window displays detailed information about the event, as well as navigates you to the code responsible for the event. For example, if you click the Gesture: Clicked "Ex1: Generate Random Number" event, the window displays detailed information related to the event and navigates to the Form1.cs tab and to the btnEx1_Click method that caused the event to fire. As a result, you can easily find the code related to the different IntelliTrace messages you may receive.

Looking through the IntelliTrace captured events, you can see two exception events. Select the Exception: Thrown event as shown in Figure 21-3.

Selecting the exception event displays detailed information about the event, in this case, you see that a File Not Found exception was thrown and that the application could not find the file named test2.txt. At the same time, in the Form1.cs tab, Visual Studio navigates to the AccessFile2 method and to the offending line of code. From this, you are able to determine that the test2.txt file does not exist, which must be causing the application problem. You are able to determine all this during the same initial test run without having to restart the application or rerun any tests.

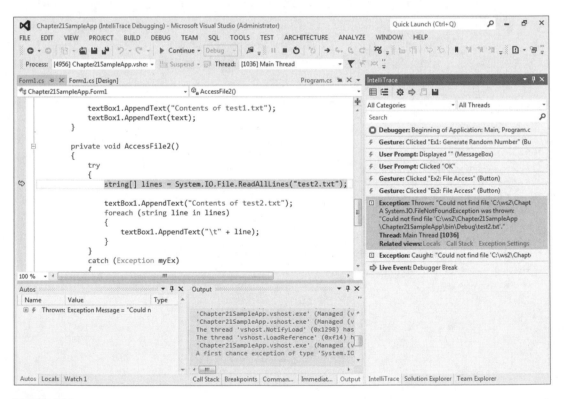

FIGURE 21-3

Navigating the IntelliTrace Events View

As you can imagine, for a long-running test or debugging session, the IntelliTrace events view could contain a large number of events. The IntelliTrace window has several options to make it easier to navigate the event information.

There are two dropdown boxes at the top of the IntelliTrace window. The one on the right is the Threads dropdown box. This enables you to view all the application threads for which the IntelliTrace event information was captured, and you can select only the specific threads you want to view in the window. The second dropdown box (on the left), displays all the different event categories for which IntelliTrace was configured to monitor for the particular test run. You can uncheck specific categories to remove those events from the window.

Finally, there is a search box underneath the two dropdown boxes, which you can use to search for particular words or phrases for the displayed events. For example, if you only want to display the Exception events, you can enter the word **Exception** in the search box and click the magnifying glass search icon. The contents of the window are filtered to only show events that contain the word Exception.

Collecting Method Call Information

As mentioned earlier, by default, IntelliTrace only collects specified event information. You can also configure IntelliTrace to collect method call information. Think of this as another way to navigate through the call stack, but you can see details around the call information. To set this, in Visual Studio, select Debug ⇨ IntelliTrace ⇨ Open IntelliTrace Settings. The Visual Studio Options window displays with the IntelliTrace settings General tab active, shown in Figure 21-4.

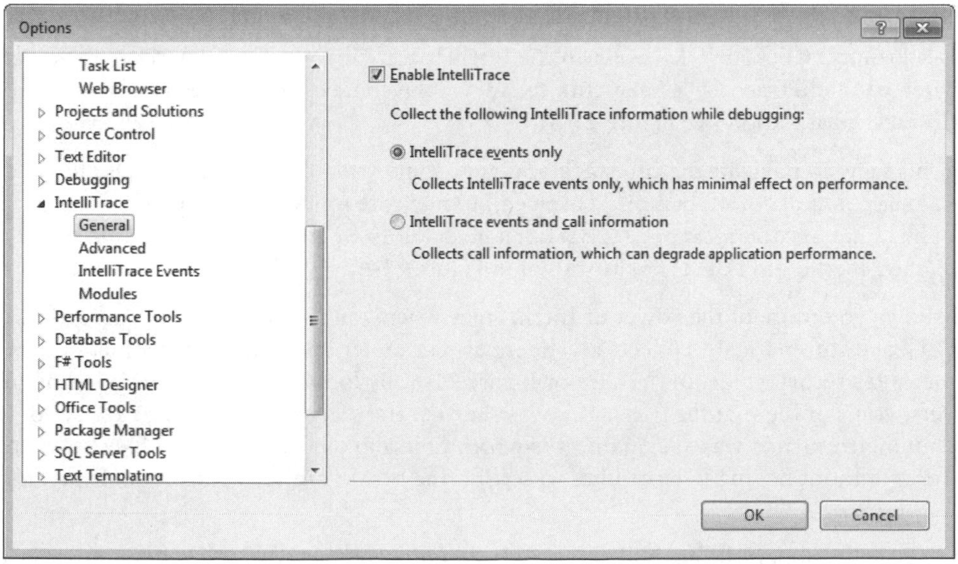

FIGURE 21-4

On this tab, you can turn IntelliTrace on or off for debugging sessions by selecting or deselecting the Enable IntelliTrace checkbox. You can also control what information IntelliTrace collects. As mentioned earlier, by default IntelliTrace only collects event information, which has a minimal effect on application performance. However, you can configure IntelliTrace to gather both event and method call information by selecting the IntelliTrace Events and Call Information radio button.

You should consider some things before selecting this option, though. This option collects detailed method call information, which leads to some application performance degradation. Also, the Edit and Continue features of the debugger are disabled as call information is collected. Finally, this change does not take effect until the next debugging session, so if you have made this change while in the middle of debugging, call information is not collected unless you restart your session.

To continue the example, select the IntelliTrace events and call information radio button and then click OK to close the options window. If you are currently in a debugging session in Visual Studio, stop the debugging session. Press F5 to compile and run the same application again.

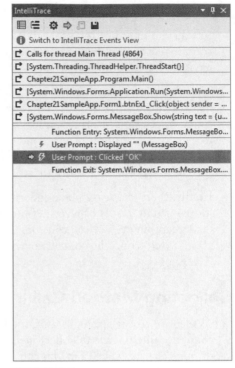

FIGURE 21-5

Click through all three buttons, as before, and then click the Break All link in the IntelliTrace window to break into the debugging session.

Select the User Prompt: Clicked "OK" event in the IntelliTrace window to display the event details. Click the Switch to IntelliTrace Calls View link to, switch the context of the IntelliTrace view from events to call stack information (see Figure 21-5).

You can use this view to navigate the call stack and view some variable information. Double-click the `Chapter21SampleApp.Form1.btnEx1_Click` call to navigate to its call information. Then double-click the `Chapter21SampleApp.Form1.GetRandomNumber` call. You are navigated to the `GetRandomNumber` method in `Form1.cs`, as shown in Figure 21-6.

Figure 21-6 shows you more of the power of IntelliTrace when you're collecting method call information. IntelliTrace automatically collects all the input-parameter information for a method, as well as the method's return value. In the case of Figure 21-6, by looking in the locals window in the bottom left, you can see that the `minValue` was set to 0, the `maxValue` was set to 100, and the random number returned was 35. Again, it is worth pointing out that you are able to view all this information without having to remember to set specific breakpoints, or rerun the debugging process.

Having this data collection at the method entry and exit points enables you to treat the method as a black box, and can make it easier for you to determine why the method is providing the incorrect information or causing some other error.

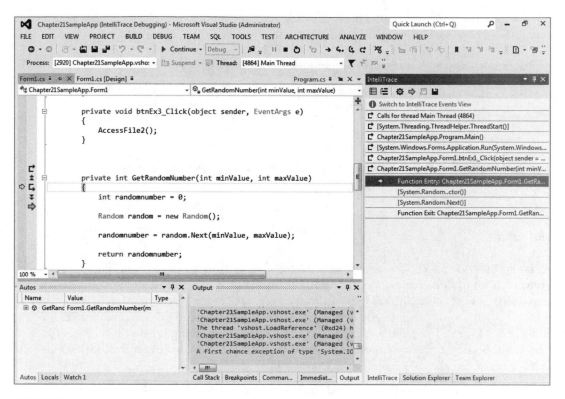

FIGURE 21-6

When you are viewing IntelliTrace information in the call view, a navigation bar appears in the code window. You can see this navigation bar in Figure 21-6. You can use the navigation bar to walk through the call stack instead of clicking on call information in the IntelliTrace window. The navigation bar contains five icons that have the following associated actions. (This list is ordered to match the order of the icons in the navigation bar.)

➤ Return to the caller

➤ Go to the prior call or the event

➤ Step in

➤ Go to the next call or the event

➤ Return to live debugging

Collecting Detailed Information

Try this. Assuming you are still in Visual Studio — in debugging mode and in the GetRandomNumber method from the last section — right-click the randomnumber variable in that method and select Add Watch from the context menu. This adds the variable randomnumber to the watch window. You might expect its value to be the same as the return value from the method (in this example, 35). However, as Figure 21-7 shows, the variable displays the message [IntelliTrace data has not been collected]. Wait, what? This is the variable that contains the value being returned by the function, so how could the value not be collected?

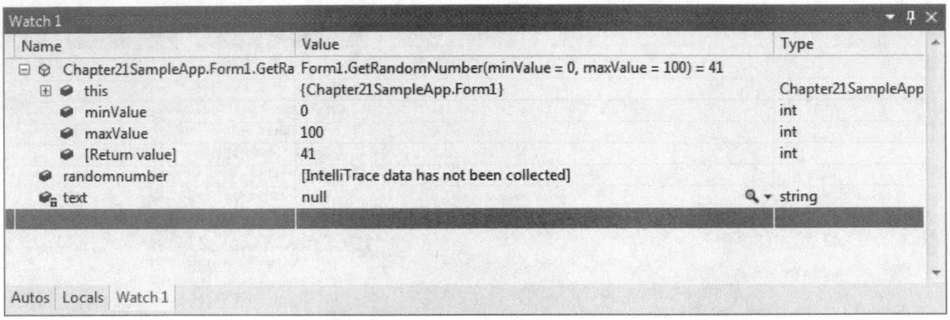

FIGURE 21-7

Although IntelliTrace collects a lot of valuable debugging information for you, it doesn't collect *every* little bit of information. Collecting all the information would lead to an extremely large collection file, which could ultimately be difficult to use. One of the places that IntelliTrace makes a tradeoff is with local variables. By default, local variable information is not captured via IntelliTrace collection. However, you can work around this by setting debugging breakpoints or tracepoints in your code. Setting a breakpoint or a tracepoint forces IntelliTrace to collect the local variable information at that break. Take a look at an example of this:

1. If you are still in debugging mode in Visual Studio, select Debug ⇨ Stop Debugging to halt the debugging process. Double-click Form1.cs to open the file in Visual Studio. Navigate to the GetRandomNumber method and add a breakpoint on each of the following three lines:

    ```
    Random random = new Random();
    randomnumber = random.Next(minValue, maxValue);
    return randomnumber;
    ```

2. Press F5 to run the application. Click the Ex1: Generate Random Number button. Visual Studio breaks into the application at the first breakpoint. Notice that you can make full use of IntelliTrace to move backward through the call stack, as well as view IntelliTrace event information. Click the Continue button on the Visual Studio toolbar to continue debugging.

    Visual Studio now breaks at the second statement. Hover the mouse over the randomnumber variable, and a data tip displays to show the current value of randomnumber. You can also see the value of randomnumber by looking in the Locals tab in Visual Studio. You see that the randomnumber value is currently equal to zero. This is because the debugger stopped the application before the line of code has executed.

3. Click the Continue button on the Visual Studio toolbar to move to the return statement.

    At this point, the random number has been generated and stored in the randomnumber variable. You can see this by either viewing the variable in the Locals window or by hovering your mouse over the variable name in the method.

Saving Your IntelliTrace Session

By default, when you exit your debugging session in Visual Studio, your IntelliTrace information is automatically deleted. It is not saved. If you want to save your IntelliTrace information to later review and use, you need to explicitly save the results to a file. Saving the results to a file enables you to pass them on to another developer, who could then review your debugging session to try to resolve any exceptions that occurred.

To do so, in Visual Studio, select Debug ⇨ IntelliTrace ⇨ Save IntelliTrace Session. This opens a Save As window, where you can choose to save your IntelliTrace session as a .iTrace file. By default, the file includes a timestamp.

Now generate a new IntelliTrace session, save the IntelliTrace session to a file, and then view the file:

1.   If you are still in debugging mode in Visual Studio, select Debug ⇨ Stop Debugging to halt the debugging process. Make sure you have added the three breakpoints specified in the previous session and then press F5 to start debugging the application. Click through each of the buttons in the application to execute its functionality. When the breakpoints are triggered, simply click Continue on the Visual Studio toolbar to continue executing the application logic.

2.   After you have clicked all three buttons on the app, click the Break All link in the IntelliTrace window to break into the debugging session. From within the IntelliTrace window, you can click the Save icon to save the session information, or select Debug ⇨ IntelliTrace ⇨ Save IntelliTrace Session.

3.   Save the session to your Documents folder, and take the default name. This saves the IntelliTrace session information to the .iTrace file.

4.   Select Debug ⇨ Stop Debugging to stop the debugging process, and close Visual Studio.

5.   Open Windows Explorer and navigate to your Documents folder. You see a file similar to Figure 21-8. The important take-away from this is how big the IntelliTrace session file is, even for the small amount of debugging that you performed. In this example, it is almost 14 MB. Depending on the length of your debugging session, how much event information you are collecting, and how many breakpoints you have set to capture local variable information, this file can grow quite large.

You might expect the IntelliTrace file to be a simple XML file that you can open and view in a text editor, but that is not the case. Because of the amount of information gathered by IntelliTrace, the data is stored in a proprietary format to make it easier for Visual Studio to work with.

To open the IntelliTrace session file, simply double-click the session file, and it opens in Visual Studio (see Figure 21-9).

When you open a IntelliTrace session file, it initially displays the IntelliTrace summary screen. This summary screen can contain a good bit of initial information to help you understand the debugging session. In the following sections, you examine these sections out of order.

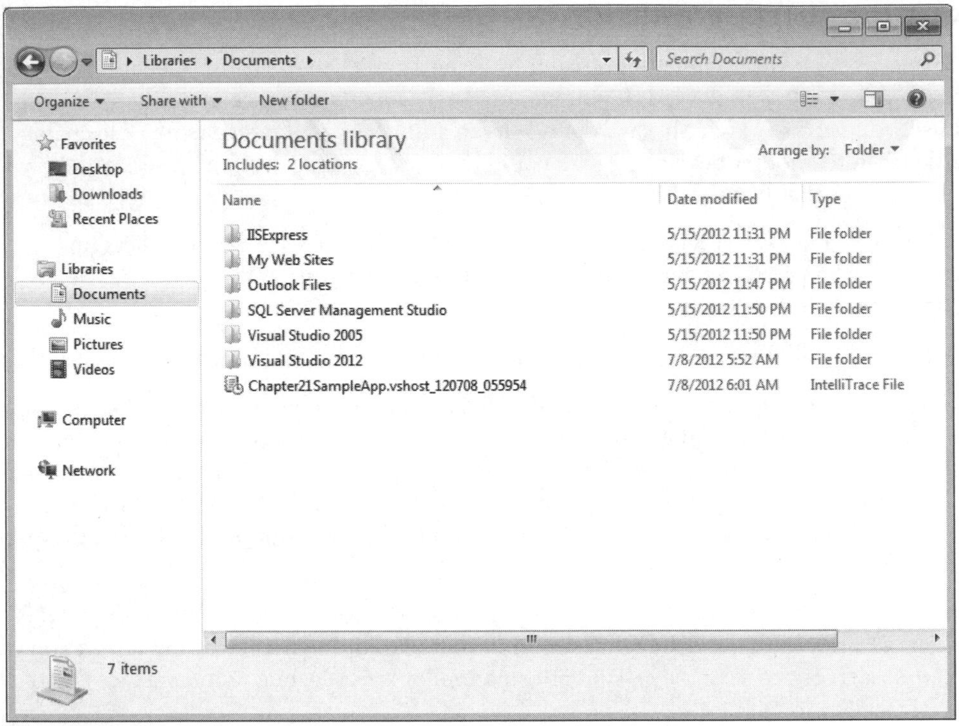

FIGURE 21-8

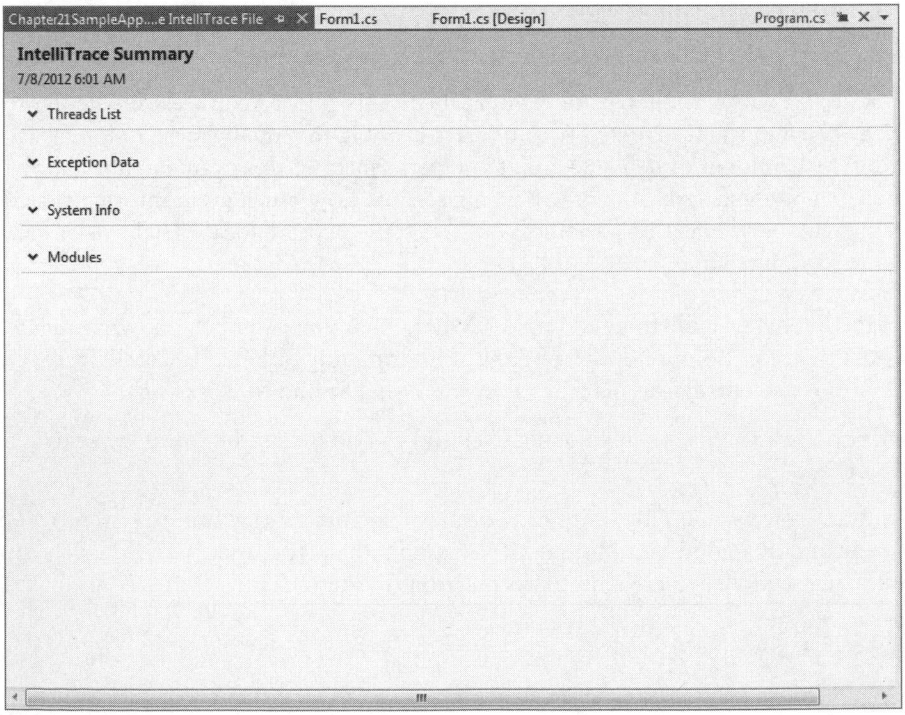

FIGURE 21-9

Threads List

The Threads List section displays detailed information about the threads, including their thread IDs, thread names, and the start and end time of each thread.

Modules

The Modules section shows you all the different modules (DLLs, executables, and so on) for which data was collected during the IntelliTrace collection process. Information displayed here includes the module name, the module path, and the module ID.

> **NOTE** *Later in this chapter, in the "IntelliTrace Options" section, you learn how to include or exclude specific modules during the IntelliTrace collection process by modifying the IntelliTrace Collection settings.*

System Info

The System Info section contains detailed system information about the machine on which the IntelliTrace information was collected, as shown in Figure 21-10.

Information collected includes total system memory, type of operating system, and processor information, just to name a few values. Having this machine information at your fingertips can make it easier to understand why the application might be having issues on a particular type of machine.

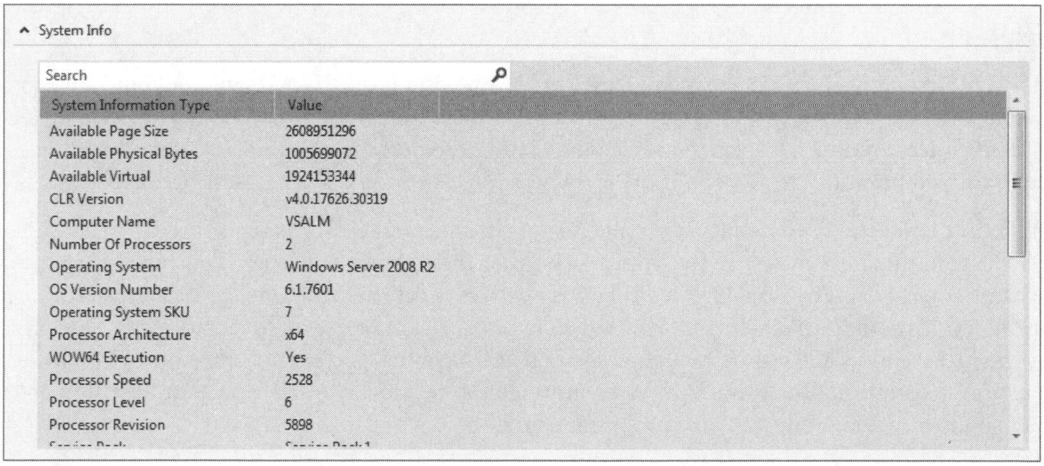

FIGURE 21-10

Exception Data

If any exceptions were triggered during the IntelliTrace collection process, that information is displayed here, as shown in Figure 21-11.

Select the `System.IO.FileNotFoundException`. The call stack for the exception is displayed, which shows you, in this case, that the `Chapter21SampleApp.Form1.AccessFile2` method was triggered, and then several `System.IO.File` methods were triggered.

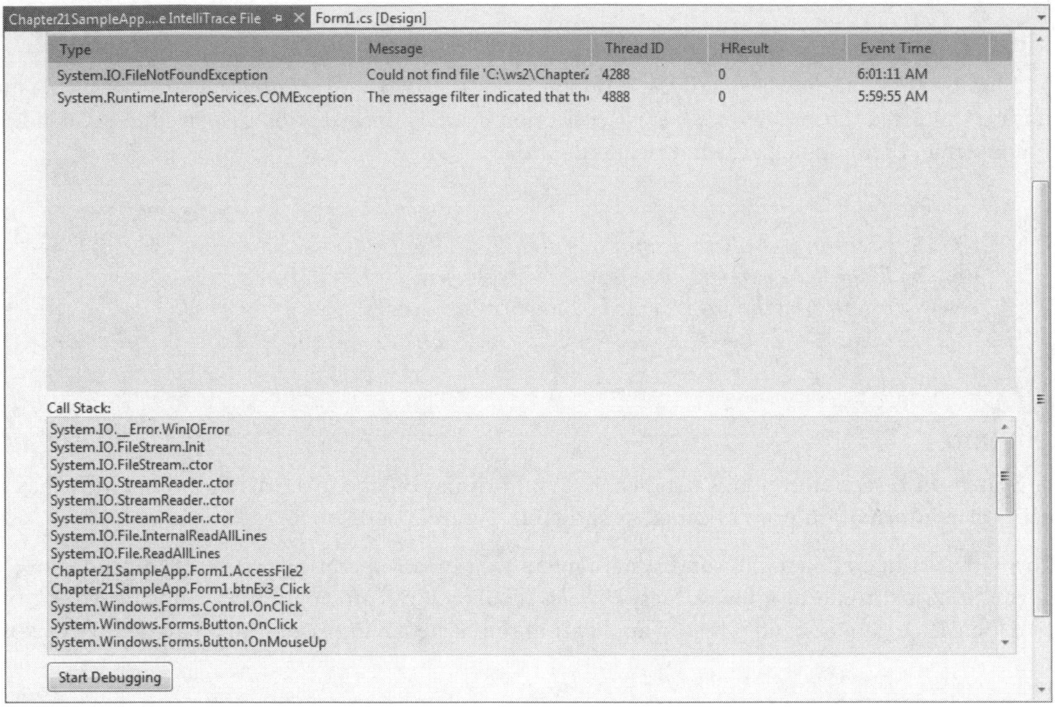

FIGURE 21-11

What is really interesting is that, when you select the exception, the Start Debugging button becomes enabled. Clicking the Start Debugging button actually puts Visual Studio into debug mode, navigates the IntelliTrace window to where the exception occurred, opens the code file associated with the exception, and navigates to the line of the file where the exception occurred (see Figure 21-12).

Notice that you are in full debugging mode, using the IntelliTrace file as the source information. As such, you only have access to the information that IntelliTrace collected. You can do anything that you would normally do when working with collected information, including view event information, navigate the call stack, and view variable information that was collected. Also, remember that the full solution has not been opened for you at this point, just the specific code file. This is to aid you in determining the root cause of the problem. After this is found, you should still open the entire solution before making the appropriate changes.

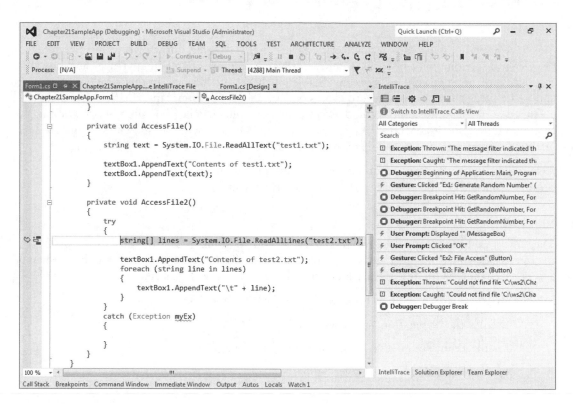

FIGURE 21-12

IntelliTrace Options

There are multiple options you can configure around IntelliTrace. Open the IntelliTrace settings window by clicking Debug ➪ IntelliTrace ➪ Open IntelliTrace Settings. The Visual Studio Options window displays, as shown in Figure 21-4.

You should notice the following four configuration sections within the IntelliTrace option node:

➤   General

➤   Advanced

➤   IntelliTrace Events

➤   Modules

Let's look at the configurations available in each of these sections.

General

You have already learned about this section earlier in this chapter, but it's worth reviewing here. In the General section, you can enable IntelliTrace by clicking the Enable IntelliTrace checkbox. With this checkbox you can enable (check) or disable (uncheck) IntelliTrace. In this window, you can also choose between the options to record events only or collect additional information that includes events, diagnostics, calls, and method level tracing. Of course, collecting more information means that a larger log file is generated. As you can see in the Options window shown in Figure 21-4, collecting more information has more of an impact on performance than merely collecting events.

Also, note that the Edit and Continue option is disabled with the latter option. The Options dialog prompts you with this warning when you change the setting.

Advanced

The Advanced option provides several settings. As shown in Figure 21-13, you can set the location to store the generated log file, and specify the maximum size that the log file should be. Remember, this is important, as the IntelliTrace log files can grow to a very large size.

In addition, there are three checkboxes at the bottom of the screen:

➤ Display the Navigation Gutter while in Debug Mode

➤ Enable Team Foundation Server Symbol Path Lookup

➤ Prompt to Enable Source Server Support

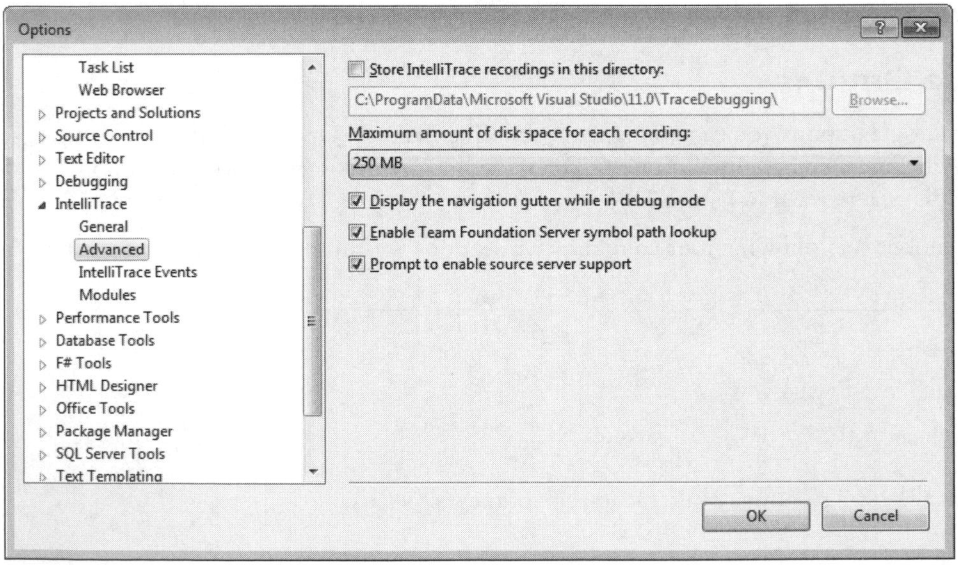

FIGURE 21-13

IntelliTrace Events

As shown in Figure 21-14, the IntelliTrace Events section lists all the diagnostic events that are collected while debugging an application. The list of events is broken down by framework categories. Here, you can select (that is, choose to collect) or deselect (choose not to collect) the diagnostic events shown on this list. This enables you to target your event collection to only the specific technologies you care about. By default, only a certain subset of events are collected.

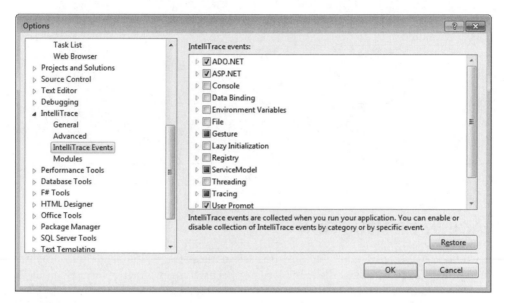

FIGURE 21-14

> **NOTE** *The more event information you collect, the larger the IntelliTrace collection file is, so take this into consideration if you decide to collect a large number of events.*

Modules

As shown in Figure 21-15, this section enables you to manage the list of modules for which data is collected during debugging.

Here you can add new assemblies to collect debugging information, as well as exclude and remove assemblies for which you don't want to collect debugging information.

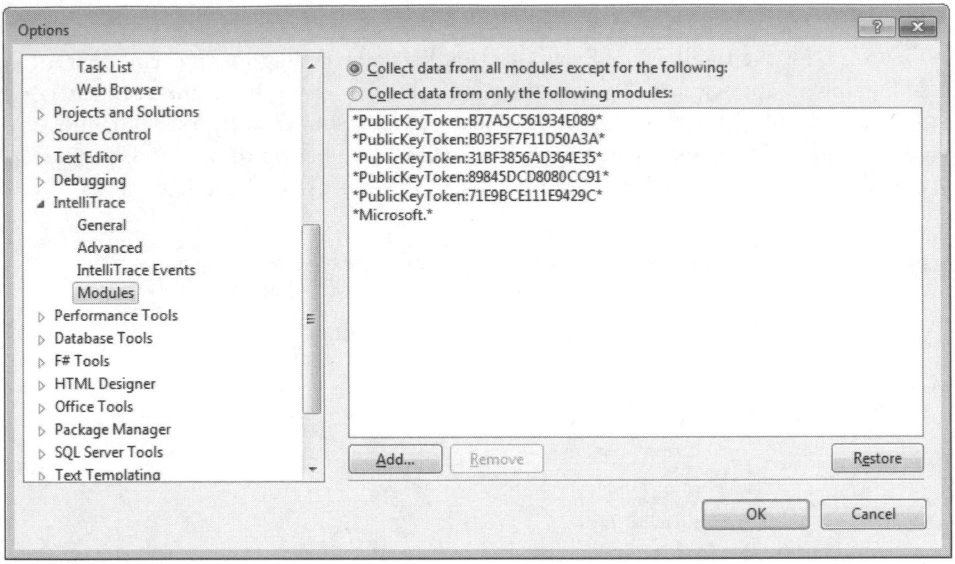

FIGURE 21-15

INTELLITRACE IN PRODUCTION

With Visual Studio 2010, IntelliTrace could only be used in a test or development environment, required Visual Studio 2010 to be installed, and was not licensed for production use. Wouldn't it be nice, though, to be able to gather IntelliTrace information on an application when you're having troubles with it in a production environment? Think about it. Being able to generate an IntelliTrace file that you could then open in Visual Studio Ultimate 2012 and walk through the results as a standard debug scenario would be really powerful.

Microsoft thought so, too, because with Visual Studio 2012, Microsoft released a set of IntelliTrace standalone collection utilities that you can use to create IntelliTrace logs and gather other debugging information about production applications. You don't have to have Visual Studio 2012 installed on the machine being tested. The utilities themselves don't alter the computer they are put on, and removing the utilities is as simple as deleting a folder. This makes it easy to install and use these utilities on production web servers, as well as other computers.

> **NOTE** *Although Visual Studio 2012 does not have to be installed to collect the information, the IntelliTrace log file can only be read using Visual Studio Ultimate 2012.*

Installing the IntelliTrace Stand-Alone Collector

To get started collecting IntelliTrace information in a production environment, you first need to install the IntelliTrace collector files on the machine in question. To do so, first create a folder on the machine, such as `c:\IntelliTrace`. This folder is where you copy and run all the IntelliTrace collection files.

Next, you need to copy the `IntelliTraceCollection.cab` file to the `c:\IntelliTrace` folder. You can find the `IntelliTraceCollection.cab` file in either of the following two places:

➤ Download it from the MSDN Download Center at `http://aka.ms/IntelliTraceCab`.

➤ Copy it from a machine that has Visual Studio Ultimate 2012. You can find the file at `VSInstallDirectory\Common7\IDE\CommonExtensions\Microsoft\IntelliTrace\11.0.0`.

After you have copied the file to `c:\IntelliTrace`, open a command prompt and navigate to that directory. You are going to use the Windows command `expand.exe` to extract the contents of the `.cab` file using the following syntax:

```
expand.exe IntelliTraceCollection.cab -F:*.* c:\IntelliTrace
```

> **NOTE** *If you don't expand the* `.cab` *file in this manner, the needed folder structure is not maintained.*

Figure 21-16 shows the `c:\IntelliTrace` folder after the file has been expanded.

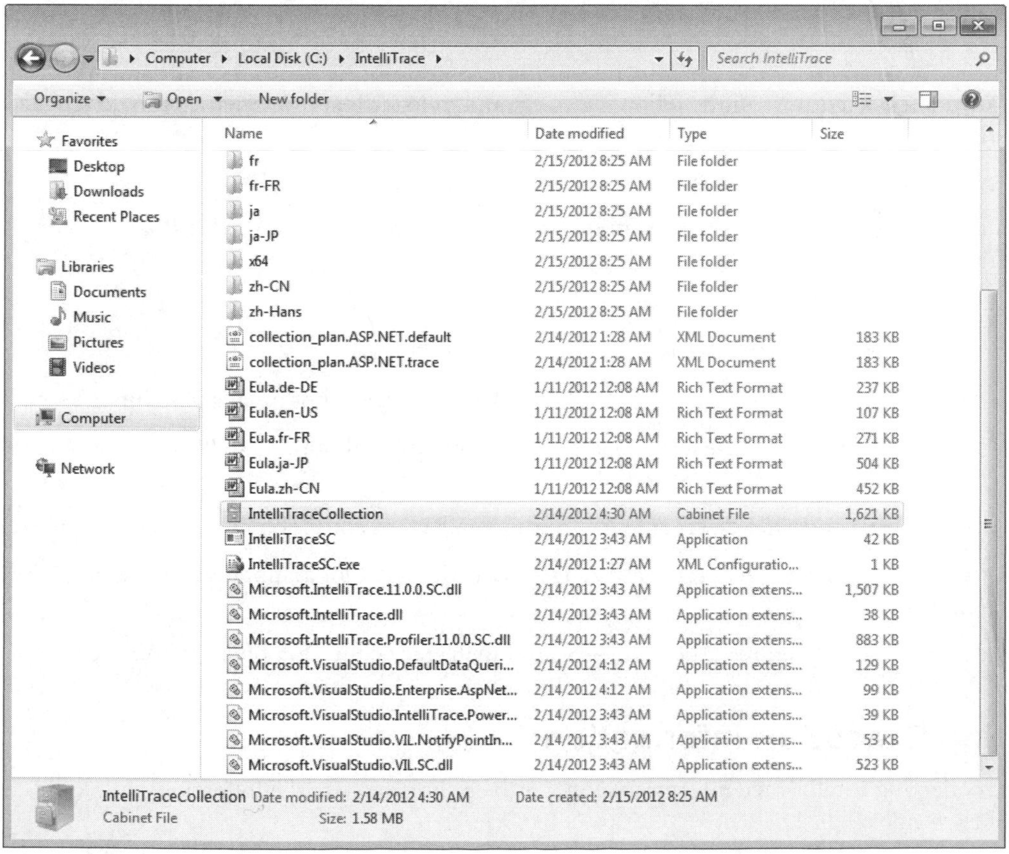

FIGURE 21-16

You can choose to collect the IntelliTrace logs in the same folder where you unpacked the `.cab` file, for example `C:\IntelliTrace`, or you can store the log results to a different location when you run the collection. Wherever you decide to store the log files, though, if you are collecting data from a web application, you need to grant the application pool identities full access to the folder. This can be done using the following command:

```
icacls.exe c:\IntelliTraceLogs /grant "IIS APPPOOL\MyDefaultAppPool":(F)
```

The preceding line of code says to grant full rights to the folder `c:\IntelliTraceLogs` for the application pool `MyDefaultAppPool`.

Configuring IntelliTrace PowerShell Commandlets

To collect IntelliTrace data in a production environment, PowerShell must be enabled on the machine doing the collecting. You need to open a PowerShell window as administrator (hold down the Shift key, right-click the PowerShell icon, and select Run As Administrator from the context menu).

> **NOTE** *On 64-bit operating systems, make sure you are using the 64-bit Powershell command prompt.*

In the PowerShell window, run the following command to load the PowerShell commandlets needed for IntelliTrace:

```
Import-Module c:\IntelliTrace\Microsoft.VisualStudio.IntelliTrace.Powershell.dll
```

After running this command, you can run the following command to see the list of available IntelliTrace commands:

```
Get-Help *IntelliTrace*
```

There are five commandlets available:

➤ `Checkpoint-IntelliTraceCollection` — Creates a snapshot of an active IntelliTrace log

➤ `Get-IntelliTraceFileInfo` — Gets basic information about an IntelliTrace (`.iTrace`) log file

➤ `Start-IntelliTraceCollection` — Starts IntelliTrace collection on an IIS application pool

➤ `Get-IntelliTraceCollectionStatus` — Gets the status of all application pools on the current server

➤ `Stop-IntelliTraceCollection` — Stops IntelliTrace collection on an IIS Application pool

Collecting Execution Information

To start collecting IntelliTrace information on a web application, use the following syntax in the PowerShell window:

```
Start-IntelliTraceCollection AppPool CollectionPlan OutputPath
```
Where:

➤ *AppPool* — The name of the application pool for the web application

➤ *CollectionPlan* — The `.xml` file defines what information IntelliTrace collects

➤ *OutputPath* — The folder to which the IntelliTrace log file is written

The IntelliTrace collector contains two collection plan files:

➤ `collection_plan.ASP.NET.default.xml` — Collects IntelliTrace event information only

➤ `collection_plan.ASP.NET.trace.xml` — collects method calls and IntelliTrace events

> **NOTE** *To modify what information is collected, you must modify these XML files by hand. Be very careful! Typing something incorrectly breaks the IntelliTrace collection.*

After executing the preceding command, IntelliTrace is now running, gathering information about the web application and application pool. To find the current collection status, you can run the `Get-IntelliTraceCollectionStatus` Powershell commandlet.

As a best practice, you shouldn't leave IntelliTrace running any longer than is necessary. There is an overhead cost on the system being collected against, depending on the detail of information collected. However, if you want to examine the data that has been captured so far, without stopping the collection process, run the `Checkpoint-IntelliTraceCollection` commandlet. This makes a copy of the `.iTrace` file at that particular point in time. You can then open this file and analyze it in Visual Studio while IntelliTrace continues to gather information. When you are ready to stop gathering data, simply run the `Stop-IntelliTraceCollection` commandlet.

> **NOTE** *For detailed information on how to optimize IntelliTrace collection on production servers, go to* `http://blogs.msdn.com/b/visualstudioalm/archive/2012/05/18/optimizing-intellitrace-collection-on-production-server.aspx`*.*

When you have the IntelliTrace `.iTrace` log file from the production system, you can open it in Visual Studio Ultimate 2012 and begin your analysis, as described earlier in this chapter.

SUMMARY

This chapter introduced you to IntelliTrace and shows you how its debugging features can be used to "step back in time" while you're debugging an application. You learned how to utilize IntelliTrace at a basic level to examine events that are thrown during the debugging process. You saw how

IntelliTrace lets you step forward and backward through the debugging process — with the ability to view variable and parameter information — without having to rerun your tests.

You found out how to configure IntelliTrace, to capture just event information or both event and method call information. You walked through the different configuration options, such as where to store IntelliTrace log files, and how to exclude certain assemblies from collection.

Finally, you read about a new feature of IntelliTrace in Visual Studio 2012: the ability to collect IntelliTrace data in a production environment. Using PowerShell commandlets, you can collect IntelliTrace log files against production web applications, making it much easier to debug production errors.

In Chapter 22, you are introduced to the testing capabilities in Visual Studio 2012. You find out about the various test types, diagnostic test adapters, and tools for working with tests. You also learn about working with test results, ordered tests, and the test settings.

PART VI
Testing

Introduction to Software Testing

WHAT'S IN THIS CHAPTER?

➤ Understanding the different types of tests supported by Visual Studio 2012

➤ Learning how to create and run tests within Visual Studio 2012

The next several chapters introduce the testing functionality supported by Visual Studio 2012. Visual Studio provides support for authoring a range of tests, all designed to help you identify bugs in your software before your users do.

One of the most substantial investments Microsoft made in Visual Studio 2010 was improved support for software testing, and they have continued to enhance that functionality with Visual Studio 2012. Microsoft has also focused considerably on *better integration* of those testing activities into the rest of the software development lifecycle, such as the handoff of detailed bug reports from a tester to a developer.

Perhaps the most notable addition to Visual Studio 2010 was the completely revamped support for authoring, executing, and managing *manual tests*. Manual testing — essentially just a form of testing that requires human input and validation — is usually performed by *generalist testers*, and is by far the most common type of testing conducted in the software development industry. Hence it became a natural extension of the Visual Studio family of products to support the generalist tester with better tools and testing frameworks. Manual testing is covered in detail in Chapter 23.

Visual Studio 2010 also introduced support for managing virtualized testing environments. This functionality — known as *lab management* — makes it possible to automatically spin up virtual machines for testing your software under a variety of configurations, known as a *build-deploy-test* workflow. With Visual Studio 2012, Microsoft has focused on making it easier to set up and configure these test lab environments and has also extended the out-of-the-box support to provide these workflows for physical (non-virtual) machines and third-party virtualization stacks. Lab Management is covered in greater detail in Chapter 26.

There are a host of other fit-and-finish improvements Microsoft has made to the software testing capabilities of Visual Studio 2012, many of which are covered in this section. The overhauled unit testing experience of Visual Studio 2012 is covered in-depth in Chapter 18, and is excluded from this section only because unit testing (despite the name) is not traditionally thought of as a software testing function.

ROLE-BASED TESTING TOOLS

The testing tools in Visual Studio 2012 are tailored for different testing-oriented roles generally found within software development and testing teams. Some individuals may perform more than one role, in which case a team member may use multiple tools.

➤ *Visual Studio Test Professional 2012* — The Test Professional product is primarily targeted at generalist testers who will be authoring, executing, and managing manual tests. It includes the Microsoft Test Manager and Test Runner tools. These tools are introduced in more detail later in this chapter, and covered extensively in Chapter 23.

➤ *Visual Studio Premium 2012* and *Visual Studio Ultimate 2012* — The Premium and Ultimate editions of Visual Studio 2012 include functionality that is designed for specialist testers. A *specialist tester* is usually a software developer who focuses on writing software that is responsible for testing other software. Examples of duties that this role might perform include authoring tests that simulate large-scale load against a Web application, or converting manual test cases into automated tests that can be run without requiring human intervention. Visual Studio Premium 2012 includes the capabilities to write coded user interface (UI) tests. Visual Studio Ultimate 2012 includes all of the functionality from Premium, in addition to the capability to author web performance tests and load tests. Both Premium and Ultimate also include the functionality found in Visual Studio Test Professional 2012.

You learn about the aforementioned test types next. For now, it is just important to know that testers who focus on manual testing can likely purchase the less-expensive Test Professional product, whereas testers responsible for developing automated tests should look into either Premium or Ultimate. Team members responsible for managing and monitoring test plans (for example, test leads) may also use the Test Professional product to do so.

Note that Visual Studio Professional, Premium, and Ultimate include the capability to author unit tests (see Chapter 18), as well as generic tests and ordered tests (covered later in this chapter). For more information on the overall Visual Studio 2012 family of products, see Chapter 1.

TYPES OF TESTS

Visual Studio 2012 provides support for authoring and executing a variety of test types, each with its own purpose for testing your applications. A successful test plan likely includes a mix of multiple types of tests from the following list:

➤ *Manual test* — A manual test simply requires a human to interact with an application, verify some expected result, and report on whether or not a test was successful. As you see in Chapter 23, a manual test is the only type of test that is represented as a Visual Studio Team Foundation Server 2012 work item (a test case), instead of as a source code file. Manual tests are covered in detail in Chapter 23.

➤ *Coded UI test* — A coded UI test provides the capability to author tests that automatically interact with the user interface of an application, verify some expected result, and file bugs if an error is encountered. Because this whole process is automatic, it can be run very frequently, and without human interaction, but it is typically more expensive to author and maintain than a manual test would be. Coded UI tests are detailed in Chapter 24.

➤ *Unit tests* — These are low-level tests verifying that target application code functions as the developer expects. Unit tests are essentially code that tests other code. Unit testing is described in detail in Chapter 18.

➤ *Web performance test* — A web performance test is used to verify functionality or performance of a web application. For example, you may create a web performance test to verify that a user can create a new account on your site. This web performance test could be one of a suite of web performance tests that you run periodically to verify that your website is working as you expect. For more information on web performance tests, see Chapter 25.

➤ *Load tests* — These tests verify that a target application performs and scales as necessary. A target system is stressed by repeatedly executing a variety of tests. Visual Studio records details of the target system's performance and automatically generates reports from the data. Load tests are frequently based on sets of web performance tests. However, even non-web applications can be tested by selecting a number of unit tests to execute. For more information, see Chapter 25.

➤ *Generic tests* — These tests enable calling of alternative external testing systems, such as an existing suite of tests leveraging a third-party testing package. Results of those tests can be automatically parsed to determine success. This could range from something as simple as the result code from a console application to parsing the XML document exported from an external testing package. You can find more information on working with generic tests in the product documentation at `http://aka.ms/GenericTests`.

➤ *Ordered tests* — Essentially containers of other tests, these tests establish a specific order in which tests are executed, and enable the same test to be included more than once. For details, see the section "Using Ordered Tests," later in this chapter.

Sometimes, you can use more than one test to verify that a given piece of an application is behaving correctly. For example, both coded UI tests and web performance tests can be used to verify the functionality of a web application. But, as you become more familiar with coded UI tests versus web performance tests, you will see that the former is better suited for validating functionality and UI layout, whereas the latter is better suited for checking performance and scalability (when used within a load test). You get a better sense of which test to use in different situations in the detailed chapters for each test type.

DIAGNOSTIC DATA ADAPTERS

A key challenge with software testing is that of providing developers with enough information about a failing test so that the developer can adequately debug and fix the problem. How often have you seen bugs get resolved as No Repro because a developer wasn't able to reproduce a bug discovered by a tester? Unfortunately, the phrase "It works on my machine" has become an all-too-common part of the software development pop culture.

One of the major ways in which Microsoft is attempting to eliminate the No Repro problem in this release of Visual Studio is with *diagnostic data adapters*. A diagnostic data adapter is responsible for collecting information about one or more machines under test. You can attach the information collected from these diagnostic data adapters to a bug, providing the developer with a rich amount of information with which to diagnose a problem.

Visual Studio 2012 ships with several diagnostic data adapters that can be enabled during test runs, including the following:

➤ *Action log* — This adapter is useful for manual tests. It can capture a log of exactly what steps testers took when they encountered a bug. For example, a developer studying the action log can determine that a tester clicked the Username textbox, typed "Brian," and then pressed the Enter key. A developer no longer has to guess about what testers were doing when they encountered a bug. Action logs can also be used as action recordings, which testers can use to fast-forward pieces of a manual test during subsequent test runs (see Chapter 23). The action recordings can even be used to automate a manual test by turning it into a coded UI test (see Chapter 24).

➤ *ASP.NET Profiler* — This data adapter can be used on remote machines when conducting a load test. It provides granular profiling information about an ASP.NET application, which can be used to more accurately diagnose performance bottlenecks. This data diagnostic adapter is available for use only with ASP.NET load tests.

➤ *Code coverage* — Code-coverage information can be used to determine which code paths are executed during an automated test. This can be analyzed later to determine if there are sections of code that are not being touched by your test plan, possibly indicating that additional test coverage is necessary. Code coverage is only available for automated tests, not for manual tests.

➤ *IntelliTrace* — IntelliTrace is a powerful way of capturing granular debugging information about a .NET application being tested. This information can then be loaded into Visual Studio Ultimate 2012 by a developer to analyze exactly what was happening when a bug was encountered. For more information about working with IntelliTrace, see Chapter 21.

➤ *Event log* — This adapter can capture events that were written to the Windows event log while a test was executing.

➤ *System information* — This adapter gathers system information and attaches it to a bug. Now a developer no longer has to guess about the operating system version, 32- versus 64-bit, how much RAM, what version of browser, or other such critical information about the machines involved in a test run.

➤ *Test impact* — Test impact analysis analyzes which blocks of code are exercised by your tests. You can later use this data can to help determine which tests need to be rerun based on which blocks of code were changed in your application since the last time those tests were run. Test impact analysis can, therefore, help your generalist testers focus on running the most important tests, based on which pieces of your application are churning. You explore the benefits of test impact analysis with manual testing in Chapter 23.

➤ *Video recorder* — The video recorder data adapter captures a recording of an application under test. This recording can help a developer diagnose problems with an application's UI and can be used with both manual and automated tests (such as a coded UI test). Starting with Visual Studio 2012, audio can also be enabled with video recordings. Audio can be enabled for automated tests, but it is most useful for manual tests so that testers can dictate comments while they are testing applications.

> **NOTE** *Visual Studio 2010 provided developers with the ability to use test impact analysis data from within the development environment to choose to run only automated tests that were affected by recent code changes. However, this feature was seldom used by developers, and Microsoft removed it from the development environment in Visual Studio 2012. It is still available, however, for generalist testers to use when determining which manual and automated tests to rerun based on code changes. This is detailed in Chapter 23.*

You can also use a diagnostic data adapter to impact a machine during a test. Visual Studio 2012 ships with one such adapter:

➤ *Network emulation* — The network emulation data adapter doesn't collect any data. Instead you can use it to force a machine into behaving as if it had a slower network connection. For example, you may want to simulate the experience that users in remote locations have when connecting to your corporate network over a 56 K modem link.

You can also create your own custom diagnostic data adapters. For example, you might be interested in capturing inbound network traffic on a given port that may be relevant to the behavior of your application. Or, you might want to author a custom adapter that impacts a machine, such as by rapidly reading from and writing to the hard disk in order to simulate heavy hard disk activity during a test. For information on creating a custom diagnostic data adapter, see the product documentation topic "Creating a Diagnostic Data Adapter to Collect Custom Data or Impact a Test System" at `http://aka.ms/CustomDDA`.

Using the right set of adapters can dramatically reduce the amount of time required to diagnose and solve a failing test and can also reduce the back-and-forth communication required between a developer and a tester. You discover how to configure diagnostic data adapters for manual tests in Chapter 23. Configuring diagnostic data adapters for automated tests within Visual Studio is covered later in this chapter, in the section titled "Test Settings."

MICROSOFT TEST MANAGER

Microsoft Test Manager provides a single environment from which to author and manage test cases, manage test plans, and define and manage your physical and virtual test environments (if using Lab Management). Figure 22-1 shows a typical view within Microsoft Test Manager.

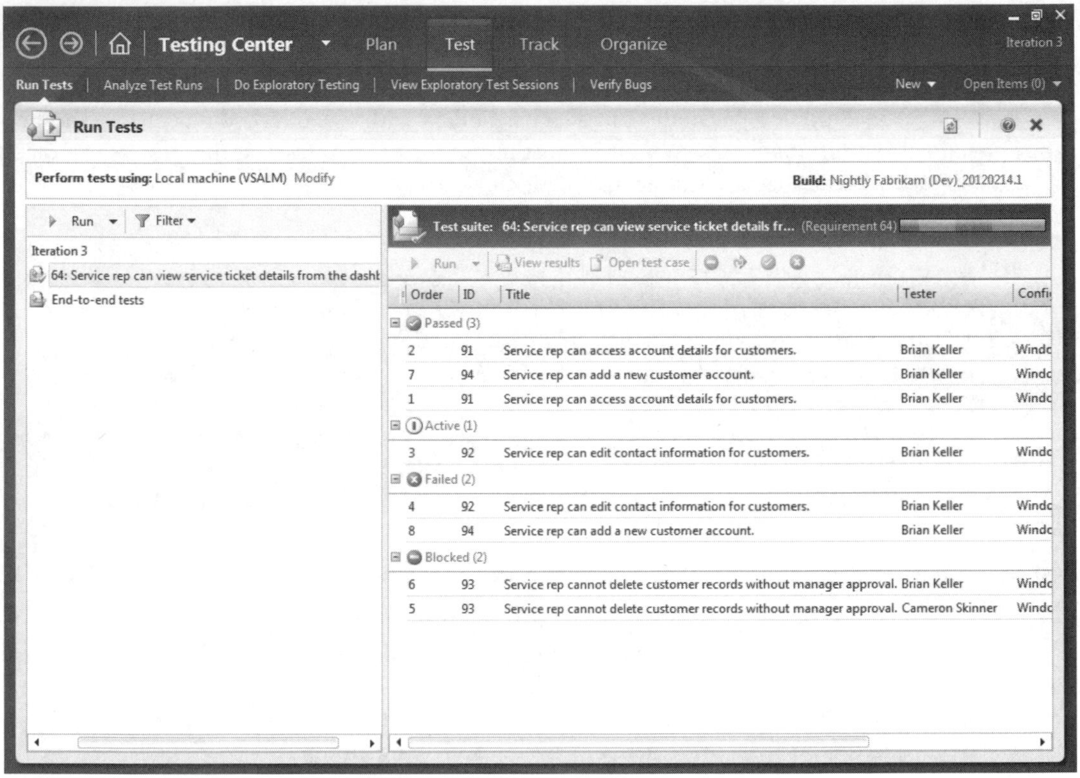

FIGURE 22-1

You become familiar with using Microsoft Test Manager in Chapters 23 and 26.

> **NOTE** *Even if you aren't making use of the manual testing or lab-management capabilities of Visual Studio 2012, you might want to use Microsoft Test Manager to create and manage your test plans. As you see in Chapter 23, test plans can include automated tests (for example, unit tests, coded UI tests, and so on), in addition to manual tests. Organizing automated tests into test plans is an effective way of tracking the overall status of your testing efforts.*

MANAGING AUTOMATED TESTS WITH VISUAL STUDIO

With the exception of manual tests (which are represented as work items within Team Foundation Server), all other test types within Visual Studio are stored as source code files. These tests are usually authored with Visual Studio, stored within source control (such as Team Foundation Server, although this is not a requirement), and are tracked as essential artifacts of your development project. As your project grows, so should the suite of tests you write, which can help you verify the expanded functionality of your software.

Because these tests are so critical to project success, it is not uncommon for projects to have dozens, sometimes even hundreds or thousands, of tests.

In the rest of this chapter, you begin by learning about *test projects*, a special project type that you can use to contain your automated tests. You learn about the creation of test projects and test settings files.

Then, you discover the Test Explorer window, how to organize and run your tests, and how to view the results. Finally, you're introduced to an additional test type called an *ordered test*. Ordered tests are essentially containers of other tests, offering a convenient way to group and execute tests in a specified order.

> **NOTE** *If you are upgrading from earlier versions of Visual Studio to Visual Studio 2012 you will notice that several testing windows are gone in this release. The Test View, Test Runs, and Test Results windows are gone, having been replaced with a unified Test Explorer window. Test categories and test lists have also been removed from Visual Studio. Instead, the focus for this release is on a cleaner, more simplified view of testing. Additionally, significant work has gone into performance to make tests run faster — even if you have hundreds or thousands of tests in your solution.*
>
> *If you are accustomed to accessing properties for tests to configure settings such as individual test timeout values, test owners, and data bindings, you now need to hand-edit the source code for your tests to make these changes. These attributes are documented at* `http://aka.ms/UTNamespace`*.*

Test Project Types

Visual Studio 2012 provides test project templates for the type of test you want to work with. This is slightly different from the one-size-fits-all Test Project template provided with earlier versions of Visual Studio.

However, even if you select one type of test project you can add other types of tests to this project later on. You can even delete the original tests provided with each template to create, in essence, an empty test project.

Creating a Test Project

To create a new test project within Visual Studio you can right-click an existing solution and choose Add ⇨ New Project. You may also use the File menu by selecting Add ⇨ New Project. You see the Add New Project dialog, as shown in Figure 22-2.

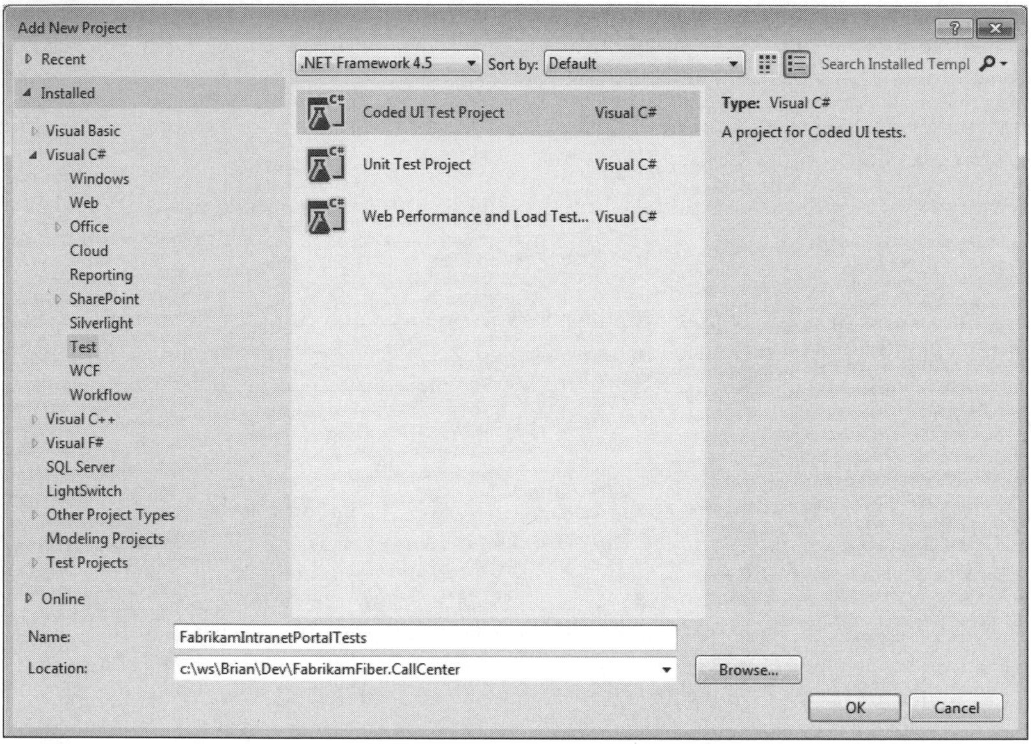

FIGURE 22-2

Under Installed Templates, choose the Test category under the language you want to use for your tests (either Visual Basic, Visual C#, or C++). Select the type of test project you want to create. Your list of available test project types will vary based on the edition of Visual Studio 2012 you have, as discussed earlier in this chapter. If you do not already have a solution, you can create one here.

When your test project is created, Visual Studio creates a default test within the project folder. You can add new tests to this project by right-clicking your project, selecting Add, and then selecting the type of test you want to add.

Test Explorer

Test Explorer is the primary window in Visual Studio 2012 for viewing tests, running tests, and analyzing test results. Open Test Explorer in Visual Studio by clicking Test ⇨ Windows ⇨ Test Explorer. Tests are only displayed here after you have built your solution for the first time after opening Visual Studio.

If you have tests within your solution, click Build ⇨ Build Solution. Visual Studio builds your solution and looks for any tests that it understands how to run. If you have third-party test types within your solution (such as nUnit or xUnit.net) you need to have the appropriate test adapter installed in order for those tests to show up in this list.

> **NOTE** *You can download additional unit testing adapters in the Visual Studio gallery at* `http://visualstudiogallery.msdn.microsoft.com`.

Figure 22-3 shows a list of tests in Test Explorer. The ! icon indicates that these tests have not yet been run. There are a few ways to run tests:

➤ You can click the Run All button to run all of the tests in this list.

➤ You can select individual tests (Ctrl+click, or select a range of tests by holding Shift and clicking the beginning and ends of the range of tests). After you have selected the tests you want to run, right-click a test within this range and select Run Selected Tests.

➤ You can run tests with the debugger enabled by right-clicking a test (or a range of tests) and selecting Debug Selected Tests. This runs your tests in a debugging mode, which enables you to set breakpoints in your tests or break execution if there is a problem with your test code.

➤ Click the Run button to select additional options, such as running only the tests that failed the last time they were run.

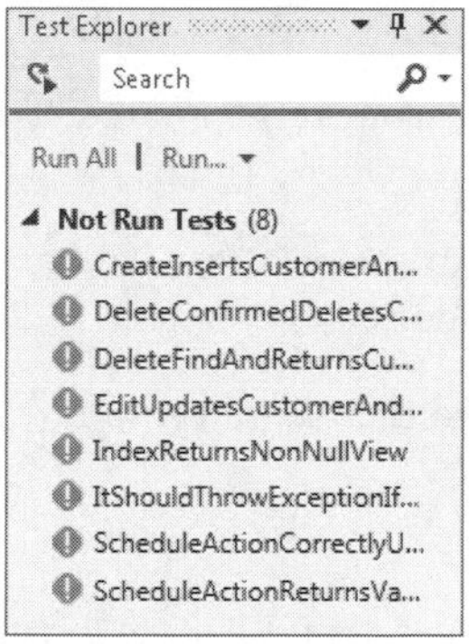

FIGURE 22-3

You can also configure your tests to run automatically after most builds by enabling the upper-left button in Test Explorer (the play icon with a curved arrow pointing at it). This runs your tests after almost every build of your solution. Certain cases, like starting your project with or without debugging, do not trigger your tests to run automatically.

After you run your tests you see your test results in the same window, as shown in Figure 22-4. If any tests have failed, you can get additional details about the failure in the lower portion of this window. This enables you to click into the code for your test and for the application being tested.

You can right-click a failing test from within Test Explorer and select Copy to copy the results for this test to your clipboard. This can be helpful if you want to create a bug from this information. If you are filing a bug, you may also want to attach the results of any Diagnostic Data Adapters you have enabled within your test settings. You can find these by right-clicking your solution within Solution Explorer and clicking Open Folder in Windows Explorer. The output of your test settings are in the `TestResults` folder.

You can also use the Search box within Test Explorer to narrow down the list of tests you want to run. This is especially helpful if you have a lot of tests in your solution.

You can search by test name, or use special search operators:

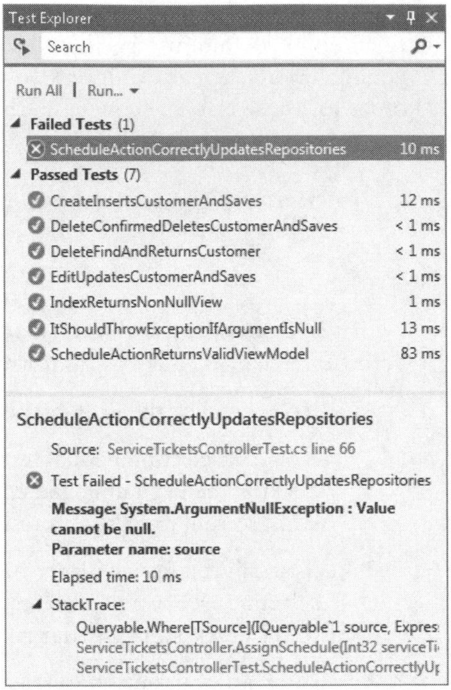

➤ *FilePath* — Enables you to search for tests based on a specific file path. For example, `FilePath:FabrikamFiber.Extranet.Web` returns tests in the `\FabrikamFiber.Extranet.Web` folder within your solution.

FIGURE 22-4

➤ *FullName* — Enables you to scope based on the fully qualified name of a test. For example, `FullName:FabrikamFiber.Extranet.Web.Controllers` returns just test methods in that class.

➤ *Result* — Enables you to scope your results by the status of your tests. For example, `Result:Failed` returns only tests that failed the last time they were run.

➤ You can also use multiple operators, such as `FilePath:FabirkamFiber.Extranet.Web Result:Failed`, which returns only failing tests in this folder.

After you run a search you can click Run All to run just the tests in that search result.

Code Coverage

Code coverage is a technique that enables a developer to see exactly which lines are run when automated tests are run. This can be a helpful technique when determining whether or not your suite of automated tests is fully exercising your code.

To view code coverage data, click Test ⇨ Analyze Code Coverage ⇨ All Tests. The Code Coverage Results view shown in Figure 22-5 enables you to view your solution's binaries based on the percentage of code that was covered by your tests. You can expand a binary (such as a DLL) to view namespaces, classes, and function calls. Double-click a function to view the relevant code in the editor. You can click Show Code Coverage Coloring within the toolbar of the Code Coverage Results view to colorize the code within your solution. Red coloring indicates code that was not exercised by your tests and that you might want to consider writing additional tests for.

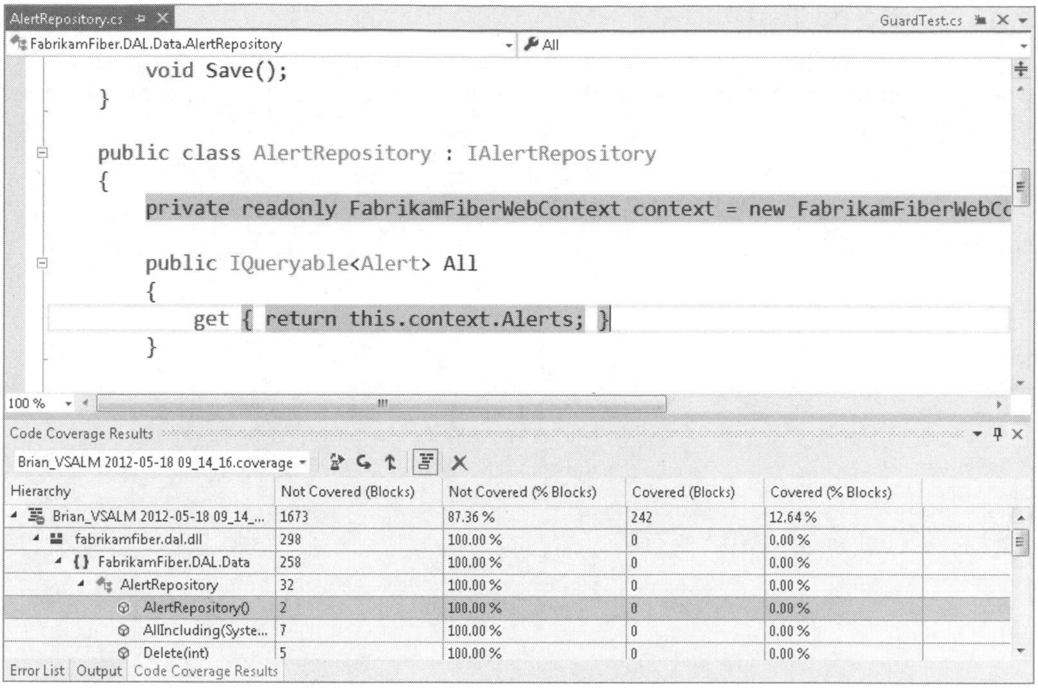

FIGURE 22-5

Using Ordered Tests

Sometimes you need to control the order in which tests run. Another type of test that Visual Studio supports is the *ordered test.* An ordered test is simply composed of other logically related tests. You can add one or more tests as members of an ordered test. You can also arrange those tests to execute in a specific sequence. In addition, you can add the same test to an ordered test multiple times.

> **NOTE** *Don't feel constrained by the term "test" when creating your test suites. There may be perfectly valid cases when a "test" doesn't actually test anything. Perhaps you've created a utility method that erases your customer table. Create a unit test to call this method and add it to your ordered test wherever you need that table reset.*

Being able to specify the order of test execution (as well as including a test more than once) has a variety of applications. For example, you may have a Create User test that, after execution, adds a new user to your database. Your next test, Log User In, may rely on the existence of that new user. By ordering your tests, you ensure that the first test successfully creates the user before the second test attempts to log in that user.

Creating an Ordered Test

An ordered test is simply another type of test, so you create ordered tests much the same way as other tests. Right-click your test project and select Add ⇨ Ordered Test. You see the Ordered Test Editor, as shown in Figure 22-6.

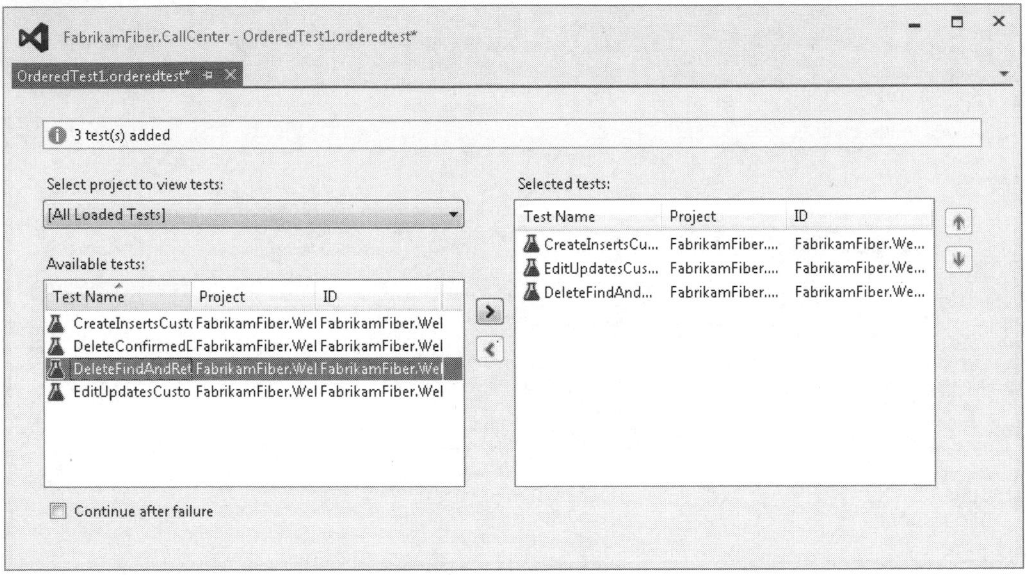

FIGURE 22-6

Using the right and left arrow buttons, add one or more of the tests to the ordered test. The list of tests includes the tests from all projects in the current solution. You can add multiple tests at the same time by holding the Ctrl key while clicking each test. As mentioned before, the same test can be added more than once.

> **NOTE** *You are only able to add tests that are created with a Microsoft test type to an ordered test. Third-party test types, such as nUnit or xUnit.net, do not show up in the list of available tests.*

You may order the execution of the contained tests by adjusting their positions with the up and down arrow buttons. The test at the top of the list is executed first, proceeding sequentially down the list.

One of the key features of an ordered test is that tests run one at a time in a specified sequence. Using the Continue After Failure checkbox, you can indicate whether the ordered test continues to process remaining tests if a test fails. By default, this is unchecked, indicating that the ordered test aborts when any test fails. Check the box to cause the ordered test to always execute all contained tests, regardless of success.

An ordered test is executed just like other tests. You can run an ordered test from the Test Explorer window.

When you execute an ordered test, the Test Explorer window activates, displaying progress as the test is executing and results when the test is complete.

Test Settings

Test settings provide a way of defining how tests are executed within Visual Studio. Such settings include timeout values, remote execution settings, and the diagnostic data adapters you want to enable (see "Diagnostic Data Adapters," earlier in this chapter).

Depending on the type of test project you created, you may also have a default *test settings file* added to your solution under the Solution Items folder. Test settings files have an extension of .testsettings. You can double-click these files to display those settings.

By default, most test projects do not have a test settings file. Only the web performance and load test project templates include test settings files by default. If you created another test type that did not include a test settings file, you can choose to add one by right-clicking the solution and selecting Add ➪ New Item ➪ Test Settings.

You can maintain multiple test settings files and switch among them based on the type of testing you want to conduct. Click Test ➪ Test Settings to set the test setting that you want to use. The first time you add a test settings file to your solution you need to click Test ➪ Test Settings ➪ Select Test Settings File to add it to this list.

The default test setting is designed to run with minimal overhead, but it does not collect any diagnostic data. The Trace and Test Impact test setting enables the System information, Trace Impact, and IntelliTrace data adapters. Consider using the Local test setting for everyday testing, and switch to the Trace and Test Impact test setting if you need to file a bug from test results. This way, additional diagnostic data is available, along with the bug you are filing.

You can edit test settings files by double-clicking them in Solution Explorer. This opens the Test Settings editor shown in Figure 22-7. The Data and Diagnostics tab enables you to declare which diagnostics data adapters should be enabled. You can use the Configure button to set advanced properties for some of the adapters.

You can also configure test settings to collect data from remote machines that are part of your test environment. For example, you might be running a test locally that makes a call to an application running on a remote web server. You can configure Visual Studio to collect data from both the local and remote machines by installing a Test Agent on the remote machine(s), and connecting these to a Test Controller. Then, use the Roles tab within the test settings editor. You learn more about configuring Test Controllers and Test Agents in Chapter 25.

Take some time to explore the rest of the tabs within the Test Settings editor. There are several settings in here that can affect the ways in which your tests run, such as setup and clean up scripts (which can run before and after your test runs) and timeout values, which can be used to control what happens if your tests are taking too long to run.

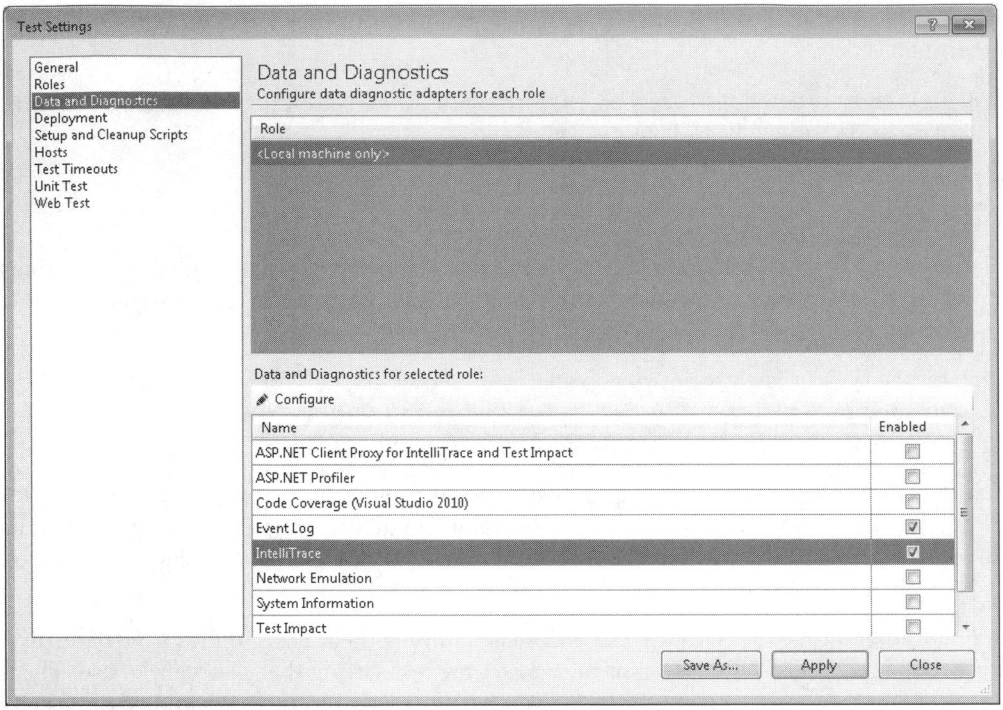

FIGURE 22-7

SUMMARY

This chapter covered details about testing in Visual Studio 2012. You learned about the various types of tests, diagnostic data adapters, and tools for working with tests. You learned about test projects and how to add other tests and test settings files to test projects.

You then learned about the Test Explorer window and how to organize, run, and troubleshoot tests using this view. You discovered how code coverage data can be used to analyze which lines of code were exercised by your automated tests.

You learned about how to use ordered tests to group other tests together to be run as a unit. Contained tests are executed in a specified order, and you can optionally indicate that you want the test to abort when any test fails.

You found out about the important role that test settings play in determining how tests are run, and which data gets collected during test runs.

The details covered in this chapter should prepare you to effectively manage and orchestrate the testing of your Visual Studio projects. Whether your project has just a few or many hundreds of tests, using the tools and techniques described in this chapter will help you to achieve success.

In Chapter 23, you learn how generalist testers can benefit by using Microsoft Test Manager to work with test plans; to author, organize, and run test cases; and to file rich, actionable bugs that developers can use to quickly understand the root cause of issues.

Manual Testing

➤ Using Microsoft Test Manager to create and manage test plans

➤ Running test cases and publishing the results

➤ Conducting exploratory testing

➤ Taking advantage of fast-forward for manual testing to speed up test runs

Across the software development industry, manual testing still makes up about 70 percent of the testing efforts as compared to creating automated tests, or specialized testing efforts such as performance and scale testing. Yet, manual testing has historically been overlooked by most software development tool vendors. With Visual Studio 2010, Microsoft set about to fix that disparity by building an entirely new set of tools targeted specifically at the generalist tester. *A generalist tester* is a person who tests software manually by directly interacting with the software in the way a user might, and filing bugs when the tester encounters broken functionality or unexpected behavior. Microsoft has continued to improve that experience with Visual Studio 2012.

In this chapter, you learn how Visual Studio 2012 can make generalist testers more efficient at authoring, managing, and executing manual test cases. You begin to understand how the testing framework in Visual Studio 2012 bridges the gap between testers and developers by capturing rich diagnostics during test runs, which can then be analyzed by developers to help them diagnose and resolve bugs. You find out about the new exploratory testing approach enabled in this release, which works in tandem with the formal testing approach introduced in 2010. You also learn about some of the fit-and-finish work that has gone into this release since this functionality was first introduced in 2010.

MICROSOFT TEST MANAGER

Microsoft Test Manager is a tool designed specifically for generalist testing teams. With Test Manager, you can create and manage test plans and test cases, author and execute manual tests, and file rich bugs. In Chapter 26, you also see how you can use Test Manager to create and manage physical and virtual test environments.

> **NOTE** *Microsoft Test Manager is available to customers who purchase Visual Studio 2012 Premium, Ultimate, or Test Professional. Most generalist testers purchase Visual Studio 2012 Test Professional unless they also have a need to write code. It is sometimes confusing to think of Visual Studio as providing functionality for manual testers because Visual Studio has historically been focused on software programmers, but this is all part of Microsoft's vision to create application lifecycle management tools for the entire team—not just for programmers.*

Test Manager requires a connection to Team Foundation Server. Team Foundation Server stores all testing artifacts used by Test Manager, such as test plans, test cases, bugs, and the results of test runs. Test Manager also encourages the use of Team Foundation Build for building the software that you are testing and reporting on the results of each build, although it is possible to use Test Manager even if you don't use Team Foundation Build.

The first time you start Microsoft Test Manager, you are prompted to connect to Team Foundation Server, as shown in Figure 23-1. Type in the name of your server as provided by your Team Foundation Server administrator and click Add. If your Team Foundation Server is configured for a nonstandard port, type the server name as

FIGURE 23-1

`servername:portnumber`. If your Team Foundation Server instance has been configured for a non-standard virtual application directory, you may need to supply the full URI path. Consult with your Team Foundation Server administrator for assistance. Click Add when you are finished.

Next, you are prompted to connect to a team project, as shown in Figure 23-2. Select your team project and click Connect Now.

USING TEST PLANS

A *test plan* is used within Test Manager to manage your entire testing effort for a given iteration. This includes your test cases, test results, the configurations you plan to test (for example, different operating systems and web browsers), and several other settings that are covered in this chapter.

You will usually have different test plans for different iterations of your application's development lifecycle. For example, early test plans may focus on testing core functionality, whereas future test plans may be targeted at fit-and-finish work (such as layout, rendering, spelling, and so on).

If your team project doesn't already include a test plan, you need to create one, as shown in Figure 23-3. Click Add to create a new plan. After the plan has been created, select the plan and click Select Plan.

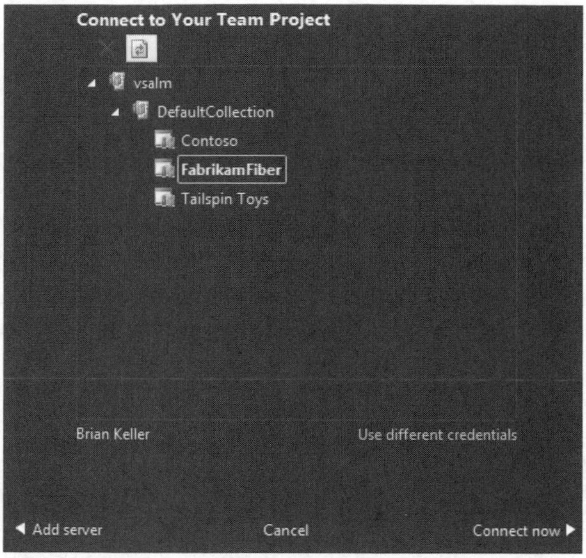

FIGURE 23-2

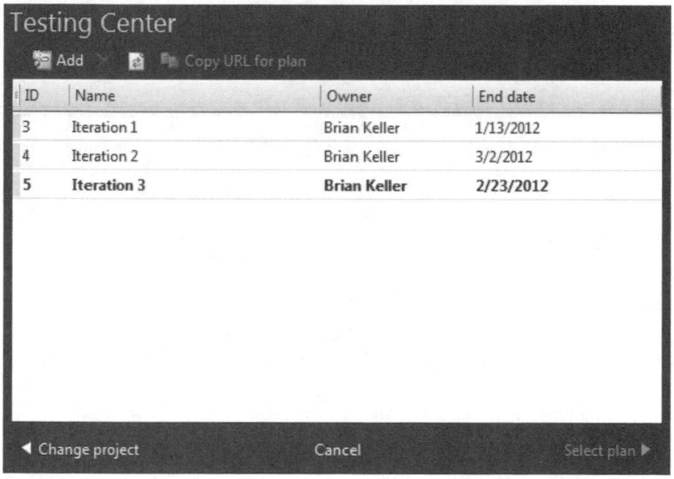

FIGURE 23-3

You are now ready to begin working with your test plan. If at any time you want to switch to a different test plan or Team Foundation Server instance, you can click on the name of your test plan in the upper-right hand corner of Test Manager.

You should spend a few minutes familiarizing yourself with the navigation menu at the top of Test Manager. Test Manager is divided into two *activity centers*, the Testing Center and the Lab Center, which can be toggled by clicking the text for Testing Center. This chapter focuses on the Testing Center. (You learn more about the Lab Center in Chapter 26.)

Each activity center consists of several *activities*. You can access activities by clicking the headings for each activity center and then clicking the subheadings underneath those headings. The Testing Center is divided into the following four main areas of activities:

➤ *Plan*—The Plan area is used to manage your overall test plan. This includes the plan's properties, as well as the individual test suites and test cases that make up your plan. Your plan's results are also available here, which shows several graphs related to the progress of your testing efforts.

➤ *Test*—The Test area is used to view the list of test cases that are ready to be run. From here, you can launch test runs to execute test cases and save the results, file bugs, and so on. You can also start conducting exploratory testing from here, which is discussed later in this chapter.

➤ *Track*—The Track area enables you to change the build that you are currently testing. This tab also helps testers discover which tests might be most important to run based on the build in use.

➤ *Organize*—The Organize area provides an easy way of accessing and modifying all your test cases, test configurations, and other test plans.

You read more about these areas in the remainder of this chapter.

For now, focus on configuring the properties of your test plan. Click Plan and then click Properties. Test Manager displays the test plan properties activity for your test plan, as shown in Figure 23-4.

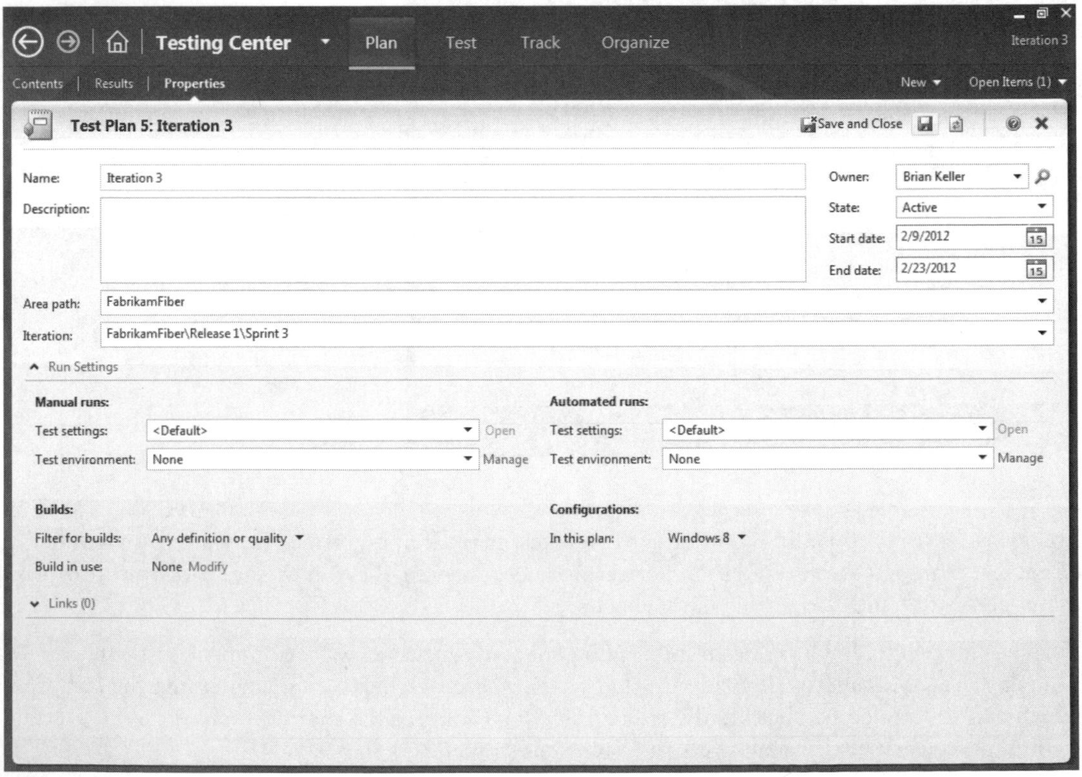

FIGURE 23-4

The upper portion of your test plan's properties includes metadata that you can use to describe the plan (such as name, description, and owner). This metadata can be useful for planning purposes, but it doesn't actually affect the functionality of your test plan. For example, setting your plan's State to Inactive or the Iteration Start Date to occur in the future doesn't prevent this plan from being used by testers. It's only useful for describing your plan.

Now take a look at the rest of the properties you can set for your test plan.

Configuring Test Settings

Test settings define which data diagnostic adapters will be used when conducting your test runs. Data diagnostic adapters were introduced in Chapter 22. Data diagnostic adapters can collect data from the machines being tested or affect the machines being tested (such as by emulating a slower network connection). This data can be very useful for developers when they receive a bug by providing rich data about how the bug was encountered and even the state of the application at various points in time leading up to the bug discovery.

From within your plan properties, you can select the default test settings, which should be used for both manual and automated test runs. You can also create a new test setting entry, or modify existing test settings. You learn more about test settings for automated runs in Chapter 26 when you learn about configuring test environments.

Figure 23-5 shows an example of test settings for manual runs. The Data and Diagnostics tab enables you to configure which data diagnostic adapters should be enabled when this test setting is used. Note that some data diagnostic adapters have additional options that can be configured (such as the frame rate and bit rate to use when capturing video recordings).

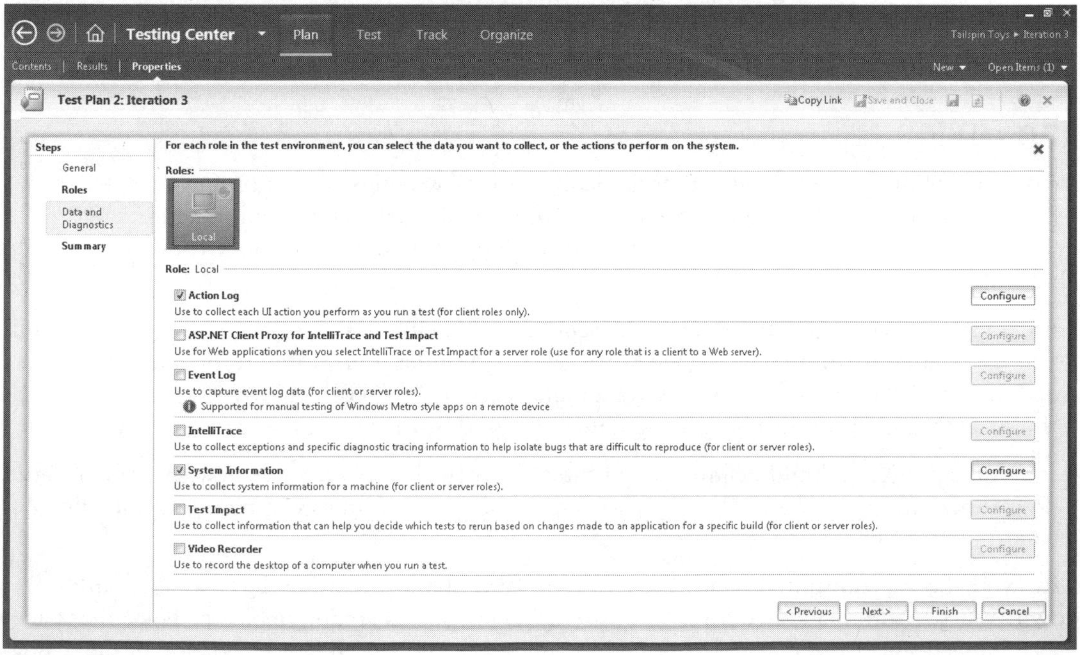

FIGURE 23-5

> **NOTE** *You can configure test settings for multiple machines within a test environment. For example, you can collect an event log from a database server, IntelliTrace from a web server, and a video recording of the tester's actions on a web client machine. To configure data collection from multiple machines within an environment you need to configure test agents and a test controller. Consult the product information for details on configuring such an environment:* http://aka.ms/TestEnvironments. *Note that data diagnostic adapters have varying amounts of overhead, including start-up time, CPU usage, and storage space for the various artifacts that will be included with test results. The product documentation includes a matrix that explains this in greater detail.*

It is a good practice for the testing team to work with the development team in defining which data diagnostic adapters should be enabled for each machine within the environment. This helps ensure that developers have everything they need to diagnose a problem when they receive a bug, along with attachments from the test run.

> **NOTE** *The data you capture based on your test settings is added as attachments to your test runs, as well as to any bugs you file. All of this information is stored in Team Foundation Server. Because this information can require a very large amount of storage space, Microsoft released the Test Attachments Cleaner as part of the Team Foundation Server Power Tools. The Test Attachments Cleaner enables you to easily clean up attachments from old test runs and bugs. You can download the Team Foundation Server Power Tools from* http://aka.ms /TFPowerTools.

Using Builds

As your testing progresses, you will periodically select new builds to test. From your test plan's properties, you can first configure the filter for your builds to match the build definition (as defined in Team Foundation Build) and, optionally, the build quality to use as a filter from among all available builds.

For example, it is common to have a tester scout a build before the rest of the team tries the build. *Scouting* usually involves installing the software and running some initial tests to ensure that it's worth using by the rest of the team. After a build is scouted, you can change the status of that build to indicate that it's a suitable build candidate to be used by the rest of the team.

After you configure a build definition and filter, you can click Modify to view the Assign Build dialog shown in Figure 23-6. Start by choosing with which build to begin testing and click Assign to Plan.

After you choose your initial build, you can view newer builds by using the Available Builds dropdown. When examining a newer build, any work items (such as requirements or bugs) that have been changed since your currently selected build are displayed in the lower portion of the dialog.

This is determined by compiling a list of work items that are linked to changesets from all builds between the current build and the build you are considering.

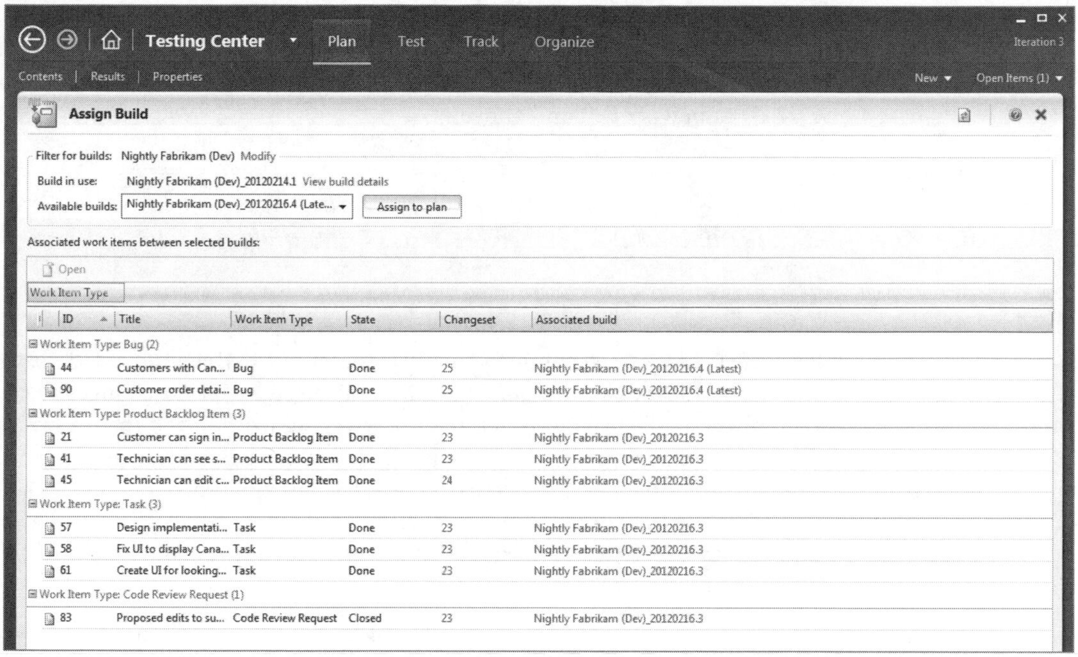

FIGURE 23-6

> **NOTE** *Part I provides more information on changesets.*

This information can help you decide whether to continue testing with your existing build or to switch to a newer build (by clicking Assign to Plan). For example, maybe your testing efforts for a given feature are blocked until a requirement is implemented or a bug is fixed. In Figure 23-6, you can see that three product backlog items and two bugs have been changed since the currently assigned build. Clicking Assign to Plan updates the test plan to use that newer build. Afterward, results from test runs are recorded against this newer build by default, although it is possible for testers to override this value by clicking Run with Options when starting their test runs.

> **NOTE** *Assigning a new build to a test plan affects the entire team working on that test plan. Also note that you can't assign builds older than the one you have already selected. For these reasons, carefully consider which newer builds to assign to your test plan.*

You can also access the Assign Build activity by clicking Track ➪ Assign Build.

Analyzing Impacted Tests

Test impact analysis is a powerful feature that can help improve the productivity of testers by enabling them to quickly identify tests to rerun based on changes to code. You can enable test impact analysis to run in the background while tests are being executed. This feature records which sections of code are executed while each test runs. Test impact analysis works with managed code (that is, code based on .NET Framework 2.0 and above).

> **NOTE** *To utilize test impact analysis, you should ensure that Test Impact is enabled in your test settings while running your tests. Test settings were discussed earlier in this chapter.*

To use test impact analysis, click Track ⇨ Recommended Tests to get to the Recommended Tests activity. Here, you can see a list of test cases that may have been affected by recent changes to source code. Test impact analysis works by comparing your newly assigned build to the previously assigned build. Test impact analysis compiles a list of the test cases which passed the last time they were run. It then analyzes the blocks of code that were executed the last time those tests were run and compares that result with the list of code changes in the new build you are selecting. Using this technique, test impact analysis provides a recommended list of tests that appear to have the highest risk of failing based on those code changes.

Use the Recommended Tests activity to quickly compile a list of tests that might be useful to rerun. To mark a test to be rerun, click that test (or select a range of tests) and then click the Reset to Active button. This causes that test case to appear as Active from the Run Tests activity (which you learn about later in this chapter, see "Running Tests and Tracking Results").

> **NOTE** *You should be careful not to rely too heavily on test impact analysis because there are certain factors that may affect the tests not captured by test impact analysis. This includes changes to test data (which may result in different paths through a code base), and changes to other libraries or applications with which your test application interacts, but which aren't being analyzed by test impact analysis. For this reason, you should examine your test plan from multiple angles (including test impact analysis, changes to work items, and so on) and routinely consider rerunning all your tests, regardless of whether they are known to have been affected.*

Defining Test Configurations

Often, your software must be supported on a variety of hardware and software configurations. Correspondingly, your test plan should account for these configurations if they have the potential to affect the functionality or behavior of the application you are testing. Test Manager enables you to define *test configurations* to represent the matrix of environments that you want to test and tracks the pass/fail status separately for each assigned configuration.

The test plan properties page enables you to select the default test configurations that should be applied to tests in your plan. You can override these defaults for an individual test case or test suite, but, by default, if you want all your tests to be run on Windows 7 with Internet Explorer 9 and Windows 8 with Internet Explorer 10, you must specify that in your test plan properties.

Figure 23-7 shows the Test Configuration Manager that is used to build the matrix of test configurations you might want to include in your test plan. Creating a new test configuration enables you to select one or more configuration variables (such as operating system and browser) and their assigned values.

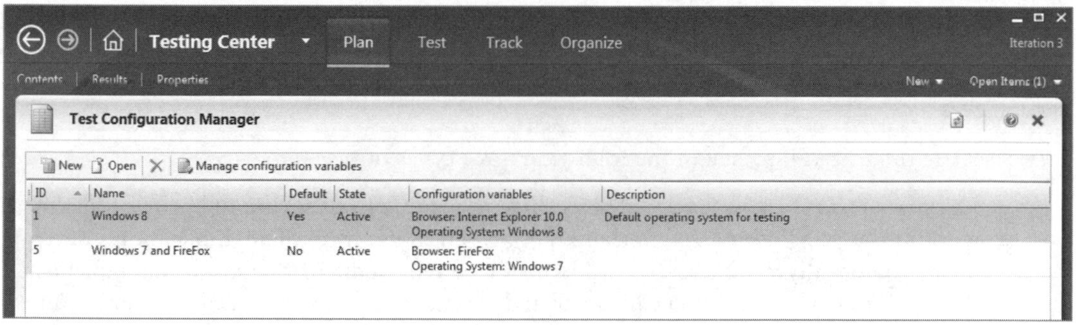

FIGURE 23-7

Configuration variables for operating system and browser are provided to you by default. But you might want to create your own configuration variables, or modify the existing variables to include additional browser and operating system choices. You can do this by clicking Manage Configuration Variables. You can create configuration variables for anything that you want to track for your testing efforts. For example, maybe it's important to test with different operating system languages, service pack levels, database versions, or even keyboard layouts. All these changes in the environment can be represented using configuration variables.

After you have created your configuration variables in Test Configuration Manager, click New to assign variables and their values to a test configuration. You can then add these test configurations to your test plan from within the Test Plan Properties activity.

In Chapter 26, you learn how you can use the new Lab Management feature of Visual Studio 2012 to help you run tests in a variety of environments to quickly address a wide range of test configurations. For now, you will be running all of your tests locally.

Plan Contents

If you click Plan ⇨ Contents, you can use the Contents planning activity to create and organize the *test cases* that make up your test plan. A test case is simply a set of interactions with a software application that are designed to validate application functionality or behavior. For example, you might have a test case that confirms that a new user can create an account within your application. Test cases are represented as work items in Team Foundation Server, and, correspondingly, in Test Manager. In this chapter, you will learn how to author test cases and manage them within your test plan. Figure 23-8 shows the Contents planning activity.

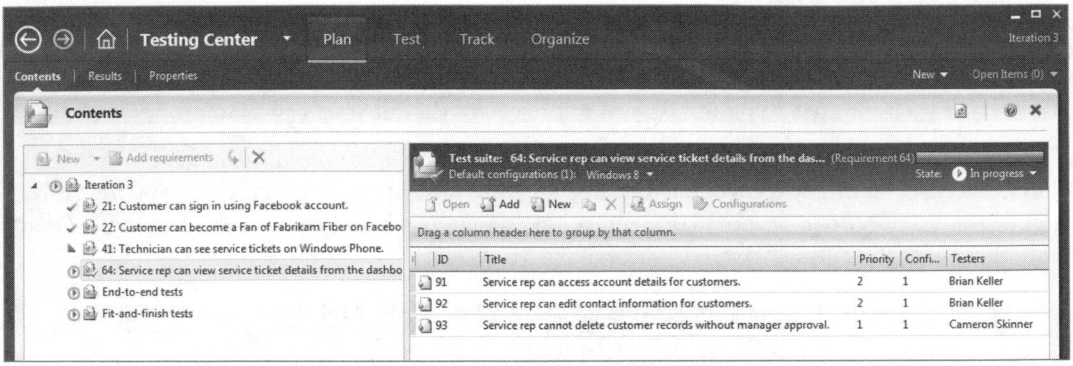

FIGURE 23-8

Test cases are organized into one of the following three types of *test suites*:

➤ *Requirements-based test suite*—This includes any test cases that are linked to requirement work items via a "Tests" relationship. For any given iteration of an application's development, you usually want to start by adding all the requirements that are being implemented in that iteration. This way, you can create and execute test cases that verify an application is on track to deliver the promised functionality. Click Add Requirements to add a requirements-based test suite to your plan. You are prompted to select the requirement work items for which you want to create test suites.

The work item types used here vary based on the process template you're using for your team project. For example, for a team project created with the MSF for Agile process template, the default requirement work item type is a User Story; for a team project created with the Visual Studio Scrum process template, the default work item type is a Product Backlog Item.

➤ *Query-based test suite*—This enables you to specify a dynamic work item query for selecting test cases. For example, you might want to include all test cases with a priority of 1, even if they are for requirements that were finished in earlier iterations. This can help ensure that critical functionality that used to work doesn't break (or *regress*) as the application progresses. Click New ➪ *Query-based suite* to add this to your plan. You will be prompted to create the work item query to which to bind this suite. The sort order of the query will define the test order of the suite.

➤ *Static test suite*—This is simply a list of test cases that can be added manually to the suite. A static test suite can also be used as a container for other test suites, giving you a hierarchical option for organizing your tests. Click New ➪ Suite to add a static test suite to your plan.

You can also copy suites from other plans by clicking the blue arrow. For example, when you create your Beta 2 test plan, you might want to carry forward some of the Beta 1 test suites.

If you highlight a test suite, you see all of that test suite's test cases to the right. You learn how to work with test cases next. For now, note that you can change the State of a test suite by clicking the State dropdown. Test suites can have one of the following three valid states:

➤ *In planning*—This state indicates that you are still authoring your test cases and that they aren't yet ready to run.

➤ *In progress*—This state means that test cases in this suite should be run by the testing team. Only test suites that are "In progress" show up in the Test activity for testers to run. This is the default state for new test suites.

➤ *Completed*—This state should be used when you no longer want to run the test cases that make up this suite. For example, if all of the test cases that make up this suite are passing for current builds, then you may deem it unnecessary to continue to run those tests.

Authoring Test Cases

You can add a test case to a requirements-based test suite or a static test suite by first highlighting that suite, and then clicking New or Add on the right side of the activity window. Click New to create a brand new test case, or Add to browse for an existing test case. When you are adding test cases to a requirements-based test case, a "Tests/Tested By" link is made between your test case work item and the requirement work item.

Clicking New displays a new test case form. Figure 23-9 shows a test case that has already been authored.

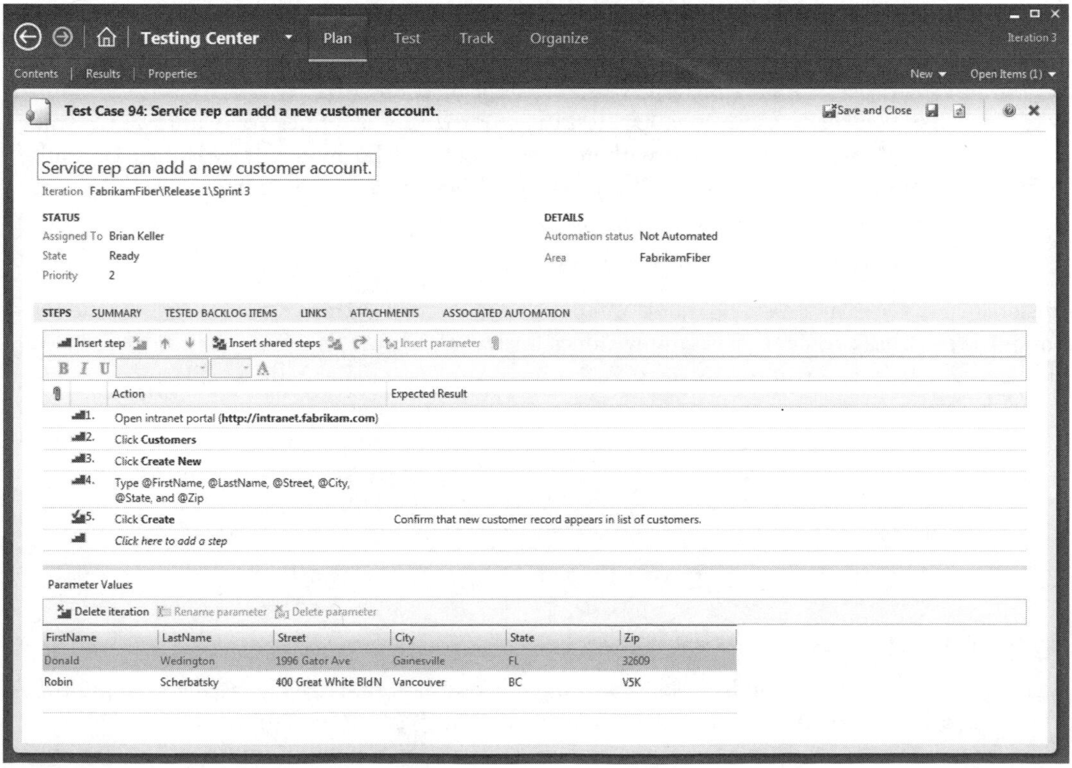

FIGURE 23-9

The top portion of this form should look familiar if you've worked with any other work items in Team Foundation Server. But the Steps tab is where the test case form gets interesting because this is where you can author the steps that a generalist tester should take when running this test case.

You can start by simply typing the actions that you want the tester to perform during the test case. Each step should go on a new row. Starting with Visual Studio 2012, you can add rich text within test steps to help improve readability for your testers. For example, you might choose to make any text that a tester needs to type bold to make it easier to read.

You can place your cursor on a new row and begin typing, or press Enter when you are ready to type a new row. You can also use the toolbar to manage the insertion/deletion of steps or to move steps up or down in the list of test steps.

The Expected Result column is used to tell the tester what he or she should be verifying as the tester runs the test case. For example, after creating a new account, the tester should see a message indicating that the account creation was successful. Specifying an expected result changes the test step to be a *validation step*. The tester is expected to report on the status of each validation step to indicate whether that test step was successful.

You can also add attachments (such as an image) to a test step to provide further instructions to a tester about what to do or what the tester should be verifying. To add an attachment, right-click a test step and click Manage Test Step Attachments. You are prompted to upload the files that you want to attach to this test step.

Finally, you can use parameters to provide different values for a test step. For example, you might want to test the process of creating a new user account by trying different values for username, password, and so on. Instead of writing a new test case for each set of values you want to test, you can simply parameterize a single test case with multiple values. Each row of data you specify results in a separate iteration of the test case during a test run. To create a new parameter, use the @ symbol within a test step preceding a variable name, as shown here:

```
Type @username and @password and click OK
```

This creates two parameters, `username` and `password`, in the Parameter Values table at the bottom of the test case. You can then supply values for these parameters within the table. These values will be used later when you run the test. Each row of your Parameter Values table corresponds to a unique iteration when running this test case.

> **NOTE** *Parameter Values can also be used by coded UI tests, as you see in Chapter 24.*

Using Shared Steps

There may be times when you have steps within your test plan that are repeated across multiple test cases. A good example of this is the process of creating an account, or signing into a website, before completing other steps within a test case. Instead of authoring (and maintaining) these common steps within each test case, you can utilize *shared steps*.

Shared steps enable you to author and maintain common test steps within a unique container. Like test cases, shared steps are also persisted as work items within Team Foundation Server. Shared steps are most valuable for protecting your test cases in the event that these common test steps change, such as if you modify the process of creating an account or signing into the application. Instead of needing to change these steps within multiple test cases, you can simply update the shared steps work item. Test cases that include those shared steps are updated automatically. Action recordings, which you learn about later, are also stored within shared steps. This means that you can update the action recordings for a set of shared steps in a single location, instead of needing to re-create the action recording for each test case that includes those shared steps.

To create shared test steps from within a test case, highlight the first step in the series of common steps that you want to convert into shared steps. While pressing the Shift key, click the last step in the list of steps that you want to convert into shared steps and then right-click this range of steps and select Create Shared Steps, as shown in Figure 23-10.

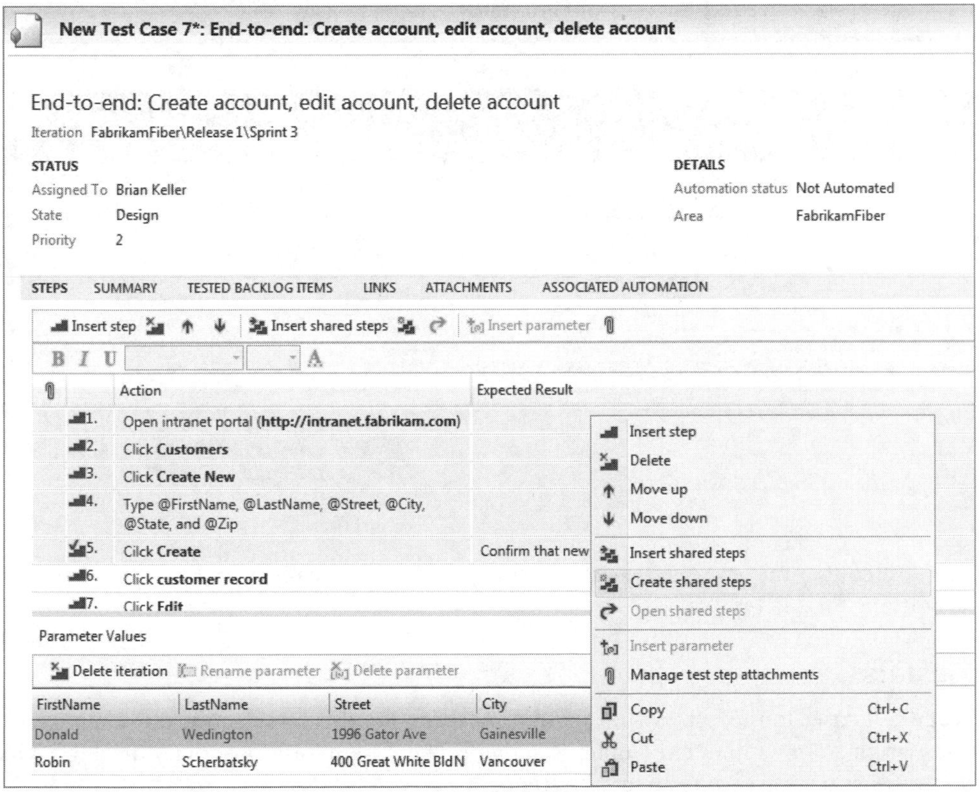

FIGURE 23-10

You are prompted to give your shared steps a name. Afterward, the common steps in your test case are collapsed into a single, bolded test step, as shown in Figure 23-11. You can open and edit shared steps by right-clicking them and selecting Open Shared Steps. You can also re-use other shared steps by right-clicking and choosing Insert Shared Steps.

Assigning Configurations

In the "Defining Test Configurations" section of this chapter, you learned how you can assign test configurations to a test plan. This defines the default test configurations that all test cases in this test plan should utilize. However, you can also override your test plan's test configurations setting for individual test cases, or for an individual test suite.

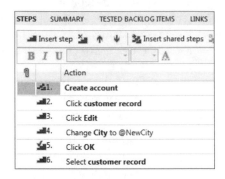

To override the test configuration for an individual test case, first select a test suite from within the Contents planning activity. Then select one or more test cases from the right-hand pane of the activity. Click Configurations to display the Select Test Configurations activity shown in Figure 23-12. Click All Configurations to display the full list of configurations available. From here, you can select the test configurations that should be assigned to this test case.

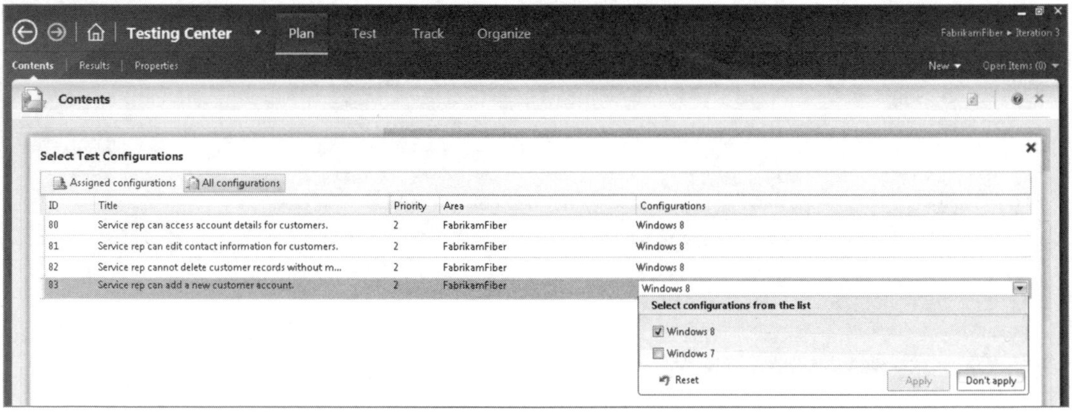

FIGURE 23-11

FIGURE 23-12

To apply new test configurations to an entire test suite, right-click the test suite and choose Select Test Configurations for All Tests.

Assigning Testers

You can assign test cases to the testers who should run them. Do this by selecting a test suite and then clicking Assign from within Plan Contents activity. The Assign Testers activity displays, which enables you to assign test cases to individual testers.

> **NOTE** *Assigning testers to test cases is only used as a guide to help the test team divide work. Test Manager doesn't prevent a tester from running test cases that are assigned to another tester. Also note that the Testers value is different from the Assigned To field in the test case work items. The Testers value is used to indicate which tester(s) will execute the test case, whereas the Assigned To field is usually meant to indicate who is responsible for authoring and maintaining the test case.*

Now that you know how to work with test plans, it's time to learn how to run test cases and track their results using Test Manager.

RUNNING TESTS AND TRACKING RESULTS

Open the Run Tests activity (click Test ⇨ Run Tests) to see a view of your test suites and test cases like the one shown in Figure 23-13. The Run Tests activity helps you select which tests to run and track the status of previous test runs.

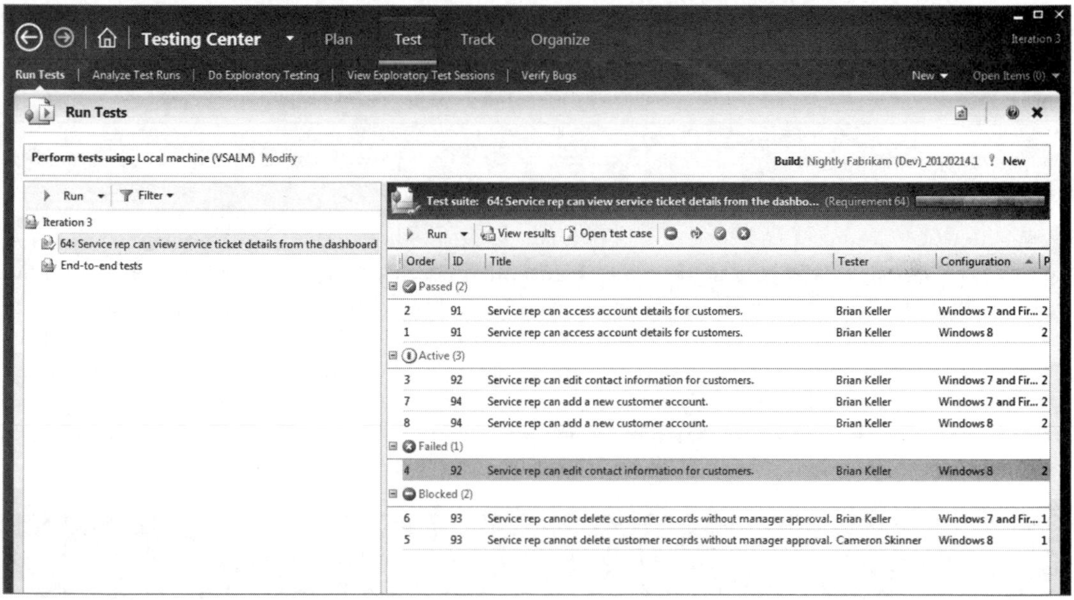

FIGURE 23-13

Any test suites that are set to a status of "In progress" are shown along the left side of the activity pane. Along the right side of the activity pane you see the test cases within the currently selected test suite.

Note that each test case may be listed multiple times if there are multiple test configurations assigned to that test case. You can use the Filter button to choose which test configurations you are ready to test. This way, you can show just the test configurations that you can support on the machine configuration you are currently testing with.

This view also shows you the status of each test case from the last time it was run (passed, failed, or active for tests that have not yet been run). Tests that are not ready to be run are marked with a blocked icon. You might want to block certain test cases if they are not yet implemented in the current build you are using, or if you know that they will fail because they depend on other test cases that are failing. For example, a test case that relies on logging in as a new user account could fail if the test case for creating a new account is failing. You can toggle which test cases are blocked by using the Block Test and Reset Test to Active buttons on the right side of the activity pane.

You can learn more about previous runs for a test case by selecting that test case and clicking View Results. You can also use the Analyze Test Runs activity (click Test ⇨ Analyze Test Runs) to view a list of *test runs*, as shown in Figure 23-14. A test run is a continuous testing session during which one or more test cases are executed, or can represent an exploratory testing session as well (which you learn about later).

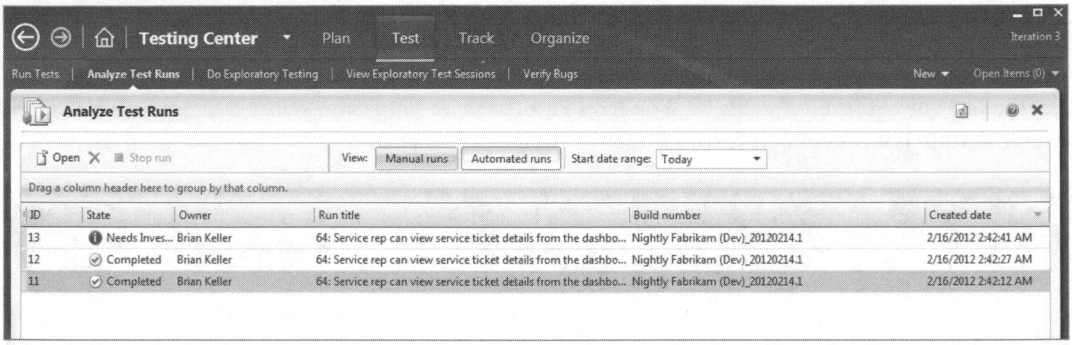

FIGURE 23-14

The Verify Bugs activity (click Test ➪ Verify Bugs) can provide a list of bugs that were either created by you or assigned to you, as shown in Figure 23-15. Click Assigned to Me or Created by Me to toggle between these views. If a developer has fixed a bug, he or she usually assigns it back to the tester to confirm that the bug can be closed. You can use this activity to determine if any bugs are ready to be verified before being closed. The Integration Build column shows you which build the bug fix has been checked in to so that you can ensure that you are testing with that build (or newer) before attempting to verify a fix. Selecting a bug and clicking Verify launches a new test run for the test case that was originally used to discover that bug.

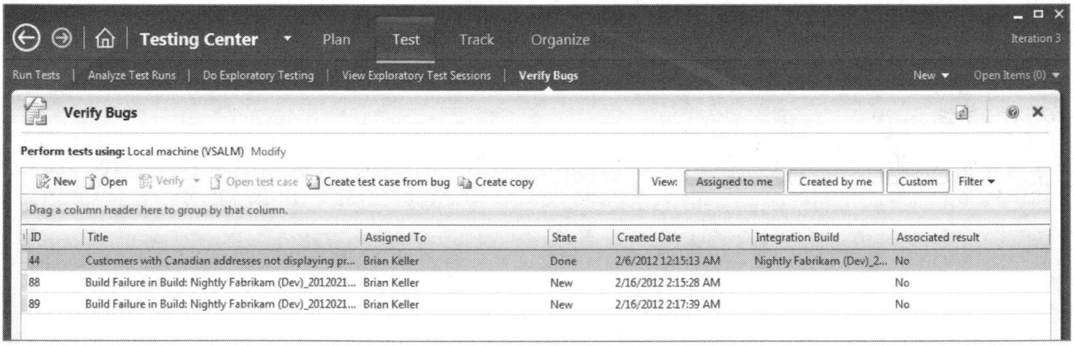

FIGURE 23-15

You can also click Custom to construct a custom query from this view, such as to build a query composed of the bugs belonging to all of the members of your team.

Using Test Runner

Test Runner is used to exercise test runs. To start a test run, return to the Run Tests activity (Test ➪ Run Tests) and select a test case that you want to run. You can also select a range of test cases to run by pressing Shift-click or Ctrl-click. Click Run above the list of test cases to begin a test run.

> **NOTE** *You can also run all the active tests within a test suite by clicking the Run icon located above the list of test suites. Click the down arrow next to the Run icon and choose Run with Options if you want to override the test plan's default test settings, build, or test environment for your test run. For example, you may decide to perform most of your testing with a test setting that has a minimum number of data diagnostic adapters enabled. This can minimize system overhead and speed your test runs. Then, if you find a bug, you can rerun the test with a test setting that is configured to capture more information (for example, a video recording or IntelliTrace file), which can help the developer diagnose and fix the bug.*

Test Runner launches as shown in Figure 23-16. Test Runner is now ready to help you run the test cases that you selected for this run.

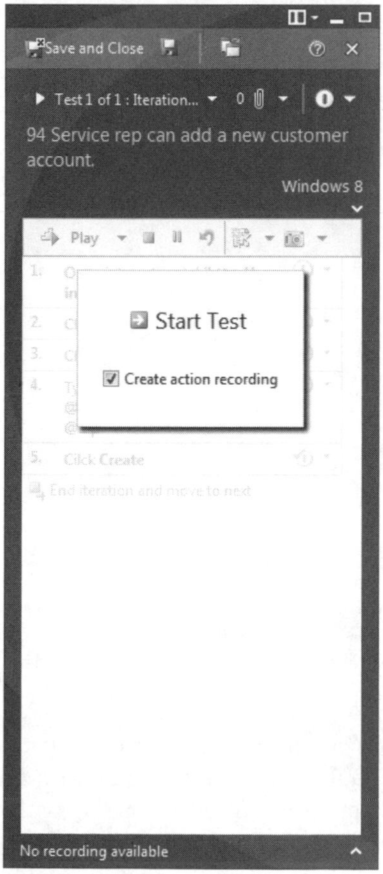

FIGURE 23-16

Test Runner enables you to record an *action recording* that you can use to "fast-forward" through test steps during future test runs. This feature is known as *fast-forward for manual testing.* Playing back an action recording can dramatically speed a manual test run by performing actions far faster than a human can perform them. Action recordings also make a generalist tester's job less mundane by enabling the tester to focus on examining an application for bugs instead of following a mindless script of clicking and typing repeatedly. You can even use action recordings as the basis for creating fully automated coded UI tests, as you see in Chapter 24.

To create an action recording, select Create Action Recording and click Start Test.

Test Runner opens a list of test steps for the test case you are currently running, as shown in Figure 23-17. If a step has an Expected Result value, it is shown here as well to help guide the tester about what he or she should be validating.

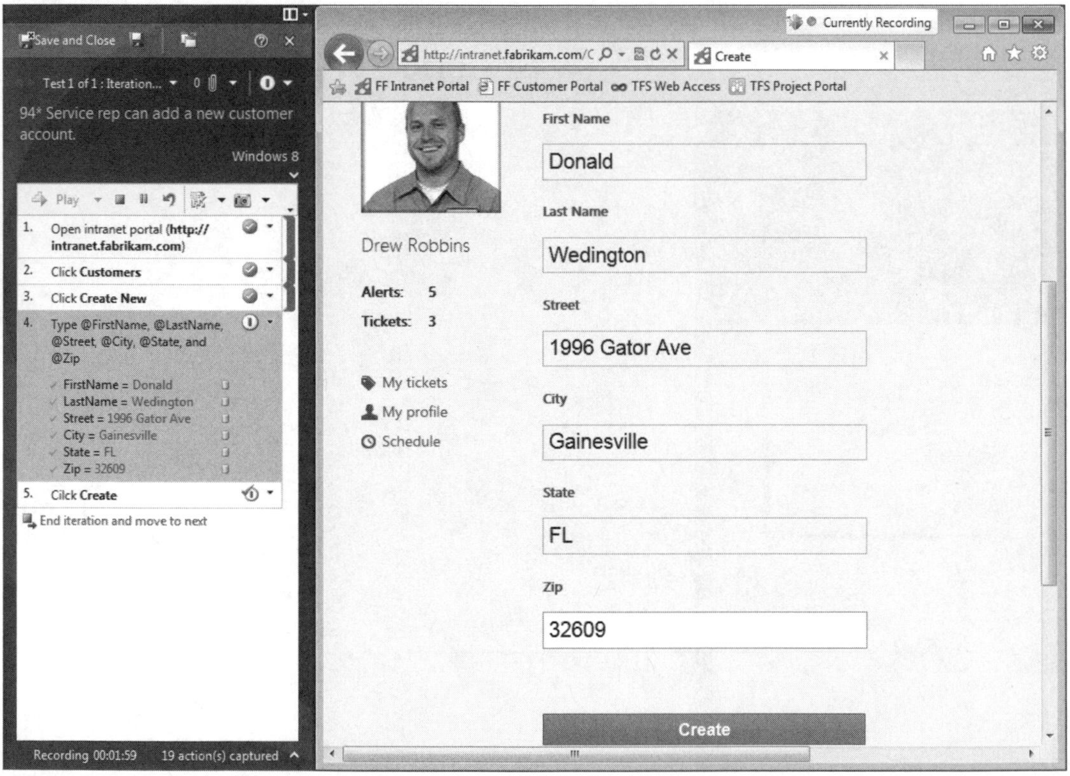

FIGURE 23-17

If you choose to create an action recording then every interaction you have with the applications you are testing are captured. To gather a clean recording, you should be careful not to perform steps that are not part of your test case. This includes launching other applications or interacting with the desktop. Interactions with the Test Runner user interface are excluded from your action recording by default, so you don't have to worry about these polluting your recording. You can exclude other applications (such as an instant messaging application) by configuring the test settings for the Action Log, as shown in Figure 23-5. You can also use the Pause button on the Test Runner toolbar to pause the action recording, which enables you to interact with other applications before returning to your test run.

> **NOTE** *The capability for Test Runner to capture action recordings is limited to the type of application being tested. See the "Supported Technology" section later in this chapter for more information.*

As you are running a test case, you can report on whether each test step passes or fails. Do this by clicking the dropdown to the right of each test step or by using the keyboard shortcuts. By default, Windows key + Shift + P passes a test step, and Windows key + Shift + F fails a test step.

You are only required to report on the status of validation steps, those that are marked with a check mark icon. Failing to indicate whether or not a validation step has passed causes the test case to default to a failed state.

If you are capturing an action recording, you should report on the status of each test step as you perform it. This makes it possible for the action recording log to correlate individual test steps with the actions that they are composed of. This is important for playing back individual test steps later on, and produces more maintainable code when using the action recording to create coded UI tests.

If your test has parameter values, they are automatically copied to your clipboard as they are encountered in your test case. This way, you can simply place your cursor where these values should be entered and press Ctrl + V to paste them. If you are capturing an action recording, Test Runner remembers the field that you pasted those values into and binds that field to the parameter. The binding is used later during playback. Figure 23-17 shows a test step with parameter values being bound to fields on a web application.

After you have finished running your test case iteration, click End Iteration. If your test run includes multiple test cases, or multiple iterations for a given test case, then you can select the next test case or iteration to run from the dropdown menu, as shown in Figure 23-18. A test case can consist of multiple iterations if you are using parameter values. Each row of your parameter values generates a unique iteration.

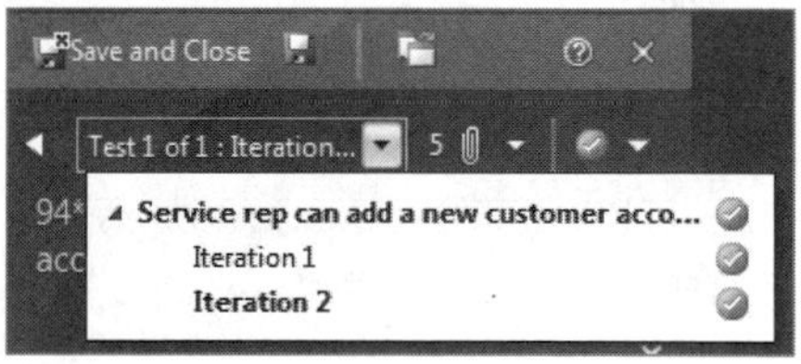

FIGURE 23-18

If an action recording is available for the test case you are running, you see the text Action Recording Available at the bottom of Test Runner. This means that you can use this action recording to play back one or more test steps.

To play back an action recording, select the first step that you want to play back and then press Shift and click the last step that you want to play back. Now, click Play, as shown in Figure 23-19.

Test Runner begins playing back the actions that you recorded earlier. This includes launching applications, clicking windows and controls, and entering values. It is important that you don't use your mouse or keyboard while this is being played back, or else you might interfere with the playback.

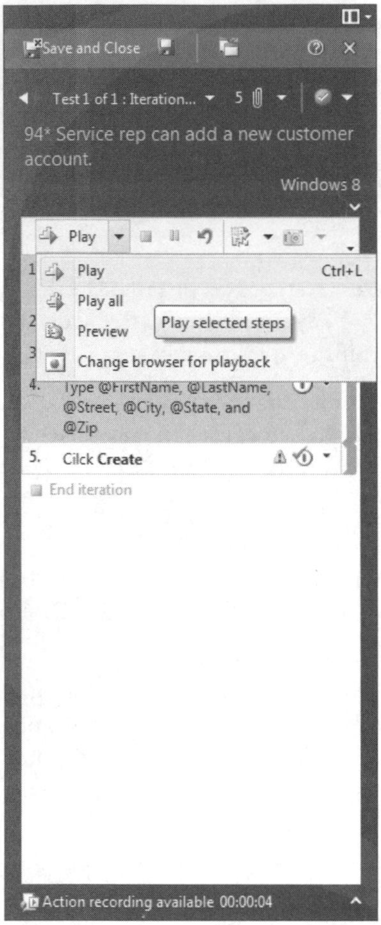

FIGURE 23-19

You can use action recordings to play back an entire test case or just sections of a test case. You can also launch playback multiple times within a test case, selecting a new range of test steps each time. Launching multiple times is helpful to give you a chance to inspect the application and verify that it's behaving properly. You may also choose to play back steps of the recording that you know work, and manually perform actions that may not match the last recording (such as if the user interface for the application you are testing changed for a given set of steps). Depending on the type of user interface change, it may eventually become necessary to rerecord the action recording for a test case.

Supported Technologies for Action Recordings

Fast-forward for manual testing requires that your application be built using one of several supported technologies. The testing framework requires that it understands the underlying technology so that it can interact with the application being tested. The list of supported technologies is expected to grow over time, and Visual Studio 2012 offers an extensibility framework to allow third parties to build their own testing providers. However, if your application uses a technology for which there is not a testing provider available, you are unable to benefit from fast-forward for manual testing. You can still benefit from the other capabilities of Microsoft Test Manager.

> **NOTE** *For a complete list of supported technologies and caveats, consult the Visual Studio 2012 product documentation at* `http://aka.ms/TestAutomation`.

Filing Bugs and Saving Test Results

You can use Test Runner at any time during a test run to file bugs by clicking the Create Bug icon. If you are adding new information to an existing bug, click the down arrow next to the Create Bug icon and choose Update an Existing Bug to add your new test attachments and test run information to the existing bugs. When you file a bug with Test Runner, all of the attachments from your active test run iteration are included with the bug, making it easier for the developers to understand how your bug was discovered, and providing them with richer information that may be helpful for resolving the bug later on. For example, if you opted to capture an IntelliTrace file it is included here. When the developer opens this bug, he or she can use this data to help diagnose and fix the bug more quickly.

When you are finished with a test run, you should publish the results to Team Foundation Server by clicking Save and Close to save your test run results. You can alternatively abandon a test run by clicking on the X to close Test Runner. These test results can be viewed later from within Test Manager, as shown in Figure 23-20.

Depending on the test settings you are using, and whether you are capturing an action recording, you may have a variety of attachments included with your test runs. This might include a video recording, action recordings, system information, or any other artifacts that are captured by the data diagnostic adapters you have configured in your test settings. You can also capture additional information (such as screenshots or comments) by using the toolbar above the list of test steps within Test Runner. Some test settings, such as IntelliTrace, only include attachments if a test fails. This is helpful in reducing the amount of storage space required for your test runs.

> **NOTE** *Saving the results of a failed test run does not automatically file a bug. If you don't file a bug for a failed test then the developer may never learn that there is a problem. However, you can file a bug later from a test run by clicking Test ⇨ Analyze Test Runs, opening a test run, selecting a test, and clicking Create bug.*

EXPLORATORY TESTING

The process outlined earlier is sometimes referred to as *formal test case management*. With formal test case management, a test team starts with a list of requirements that a development team is planning and they write a series of test cases designed to validate that the requirements are implemented correctly.

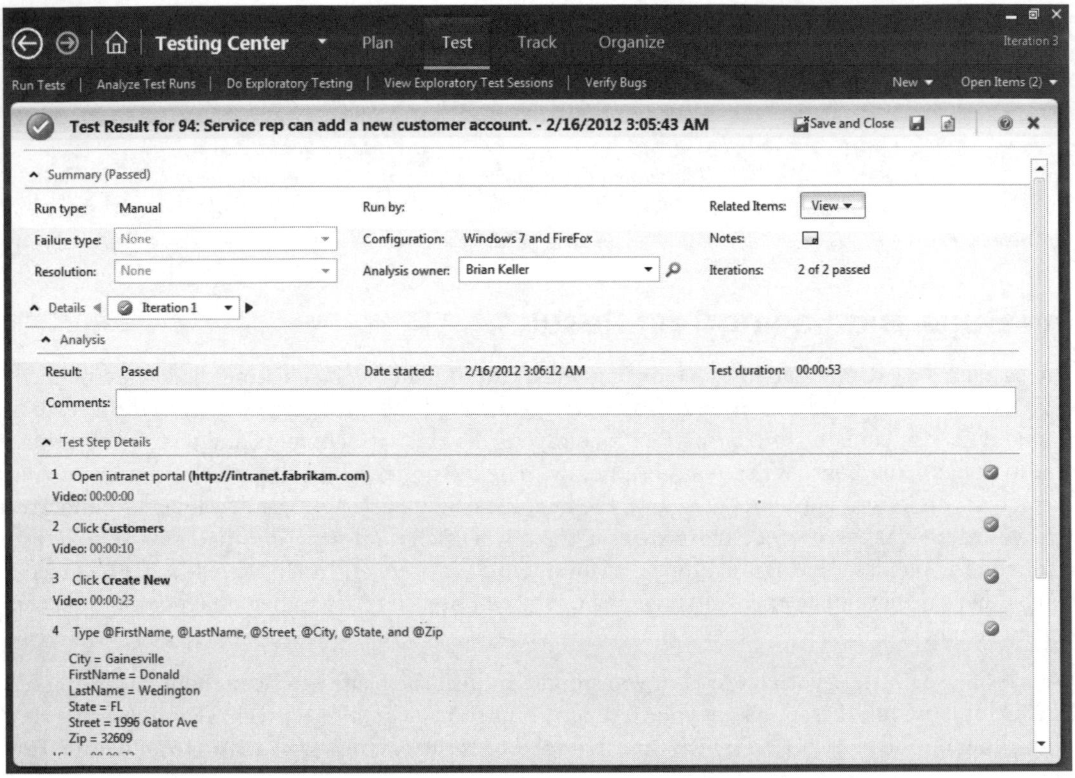

FIGURE 23-20

Consider a requirement that a customer can pay for an order with a credit card, which might result in several test cases. One of those test cases should validate that an order is successful when a customer enters a valid credit card number. Another one of those test cases should validate that an error message is displayed if the user attempts to provide an invalid credit card number. Any good test plan captures those test cases and runs tests to validate that each case is successful.

Oftentimes, though, a seasoned tester has other ideas for finding bugs based on applying creative reasoning and experience from finding other software bugs in the past. What happens if the billing address is too big for the textbox provided on the payment page? What if a user presses the web browser's Back key after submitting a payment and then submits it again—is the customer charged twice for the same order? What if a user is very sensitive about privacy when paying for an order online—is it clear from every page in the process where to find a link to the privacy policy?

One could argue that all of the example cases are legitimate test conditions and that an organization should author and run test cases for each of them. And some organizations take this approach. But taking this approach for every single requirement in the system could result in test plans that become cumbersome to author and maintain.

With *exploratory testing*, also referred to as *agile testing*, an organization puts their trust in testers to spend time applying their experience and creativity to trying to find these types of bugs. Oftentimes a tester who is unhindered by a scripted test case can find a multitude of bugs very quickly by attempting to break the application from a variety of angles. The tester might spend an hour or two at a time just trying to break the application in different ways and could file several bugs along the way; oftentimes these bugs are ones for which nobody thought to write a formal test case. This is the promise of exploratory testing and why it has grown in popularity in recent years.

However, exploratory testing has its critics. The following reasons are often used to argue against an exploratory testing approach:

➤ Exploratory testing can generate poor bugs because a tester doesn't always remember exactly what they were doing in the moments leading up to filing a bug.

➤ Management has poor visibility into what testers are doing during exploratory testing sessions. How do you know when you are "done" with exploratory testing unless you have a good record of what you tested?

➤ If a bug is discovered during an exploratory testing approach, how can you ensure that after the bug is fixed it won't be regressed in the future? This assumes that a subsequent testing session also happens to take this same approach, and the very nature of exploratory testing means that this isn't guaranteed.

These are all valid criticisms of traditional exploratory testing approaches. However with Visual Studio 2012, Microsoft has addressed these criticisms by building first-class support for exploratory testing directly into Microsoft Test Manager:

➤ Testers can capture rich data, based on their test settings (discussed earlier in this chapter), which can provide contextual, actionable information about test runs if bugs are encountered.

➤ Exploratory testing session results can be stored in Team Foundation Server and analyzed to determine who conducted exploratory testing, what approaches they used, how many bugs they uncovered, and so on. This can give management the metrics they need to understand the effect of exploratory testing and to help understand when you are "done" testing an application.

➤ If a bug is encountered, a test case can be created at the same time to help determine if bugs are regressed in the future.

To understand this approach it may be useful to take a look at an exploratory testing session being run with Microsoft Test Manager. To get started with an exploratory testing session, click Test ➪ Do Exploratory Testing. You see a screen similar to that of Figure 23-21.

From this screen you can either click Explore to start an ad hoc exploratory testing session, or you can click on one or more work items in the list below then click Explore Work Item. By default this list of work items includes the requirements for your test plan iteration, but you can click Unfiltered to edit this query.

If you selected a work item for your exploratory testing session, your test results are automatically linked to that work item. This enables you to report on a given work item later to see if a tester has spent time testing it with an exploratory testing approach. It also means that any bugs you file during this exploratory testing session by default are linked to that work item, although you can modify this before filing the bug if desired.

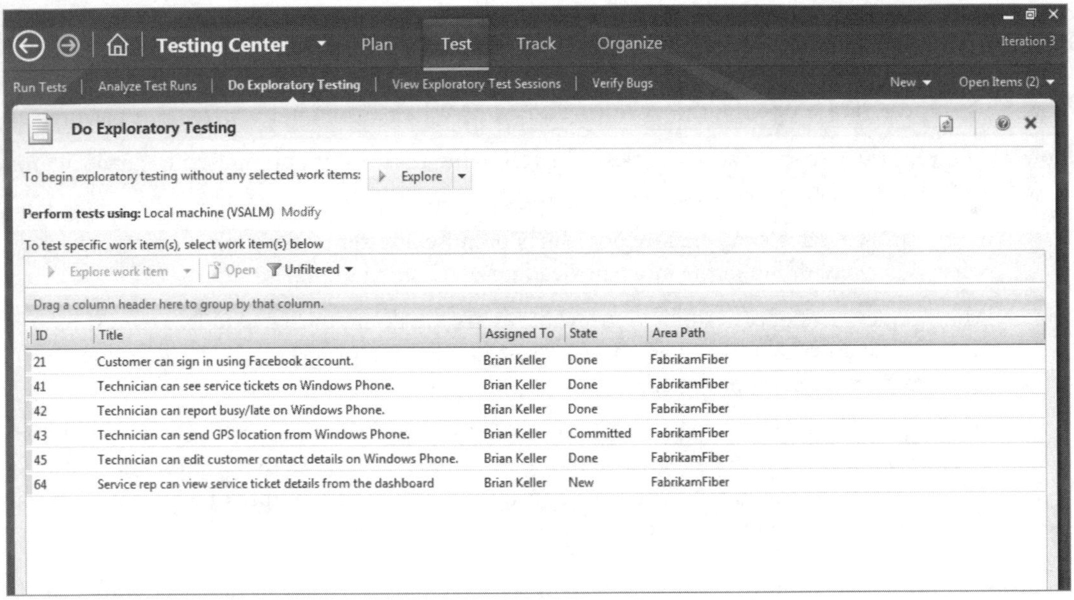

FIGURE 23-21

> **NOTE** *James Whittaker, who has led software testing teams at both Microsoft and Google, has written multiple books on the topic of exploratory testing. In his books he discusses the ideas of exploratory testing tours. A tour helps to guide a tester along a specific theme during an exploratory testing session. One tour might ask the tester to assume the role of a malicious user trying to hack an application, or another tour might ask the tester to assume the role of a new user who might be looking for documentation on unfamiliar features. You might choose to create a standard list of tours as work items in Team Foundation Server and use them when launching your exploratory testing sessions. In this way you can report later to see which tours have received testing coverage and which ones still need to be run, or which tours have historically resulted in the most bugs.*

After you have started your exploratory testing session, Test Runner launches and you can begin testing your application. Test Runner begins collecting data based on your test settings. The main difference is that Test Runner does not provide a list of test steps because you are not running a specific test case. At this point you can begin testing your application in an exploratory fashion using whatever approach you want to look for bugs.

If and when you find a bug, you can use Test Runner to capture notes, screenshots, and file a bug as you normally would. When filing a bug from an exploratory testing session, however, the bug looks slightly different from a bug created with a test case. Figure 23-22 shows a bug that was created from an exploratory testing session.

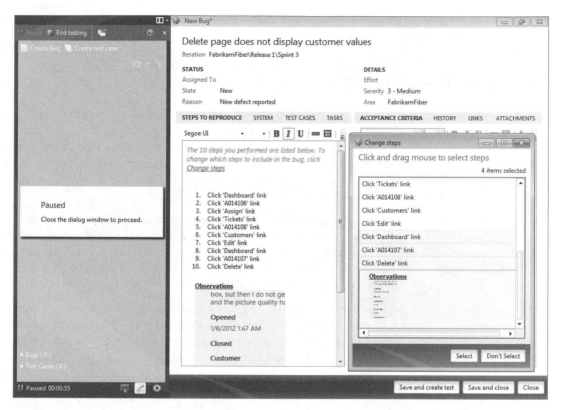

FIGURE 23-22

Notice that all of the steps you took since starting the exploratory testing session are listed in the bug by default, assuming that the application you are testing is supported for action recordings as discussed earlier in this chapter. But with an exploratory testing session, you might be testing multiple aspects of the application before you run across a valid bug. Including all of these actions might cause confusion for a developer who is looking at this bug trying to understand what the root cause was.

You can click Change Steps if you want to scope your actions down to the steps you believe are most relevant for the bug you have found. Use the Change Steps dialog (also shown in Figure 23-22) to select the range of test steps you believe are relevant to the bug. When in doubt, you should err on the side of including additional steps. The root cause of the bug might be because of some action you performed during a preceding action. When you change the steps for your bug, the action log is scoped accordingly.

You can choose to save this bug at this point, but you can also create a test case from this bug as well by clicking Save and Create Test. Creating a test case based on this bug helps to ensure that it becomes a part of your formal test plan in the future. That way after the bug is fixed, you ensure that your team tests this functionality in future builds to verify that it doesn't regress.

Your test case is prepopulated with all the steps you selected earlier. You can modify this list of test steps before saving it. For example, if the bug you discovered was on a customer details page several levels deep in your application you might need to add some preliminary steps that instruct the tester on how to get to that particular page.

RUNNING AUTOMATED TESTS

Over time, you may decide to add automated tests to your test plan. Automated tests are more expensive to author and maintain, but they have the benefit of being capable of running without manual interaction, making them suitable for quickly catching bugs caused by changes to source code. In Chapter 22 you learned how you can use Visual Studio to manage automated tests (such as unit tests, coded UI tests, and web performance tests). But you can also manage automated tests as part of the same test plans that you use within Test Manager.

Automated tests can be run as part of your automated builds, and the status of those tests can be published along with the rest of the tests within your test plan. The main advantage of managing your automated tests along with your manual tests is that you can gain a consolidated view across your entire test plan of how your application's quality is trending. Automated tests can also be triggered automatically as part of a build-deploy-test workflow, which you will learn about in Chapter 26.

To utilize automated tests within Test Manager, you must first create an automated test in Visual Studio and check it in as part of your Team Foundation Server source control. Next, from within Visual Studio, open the work item corresponding to the test case that you want to automate. Click the Associated Automation tab, as shown in Figure 23-23.

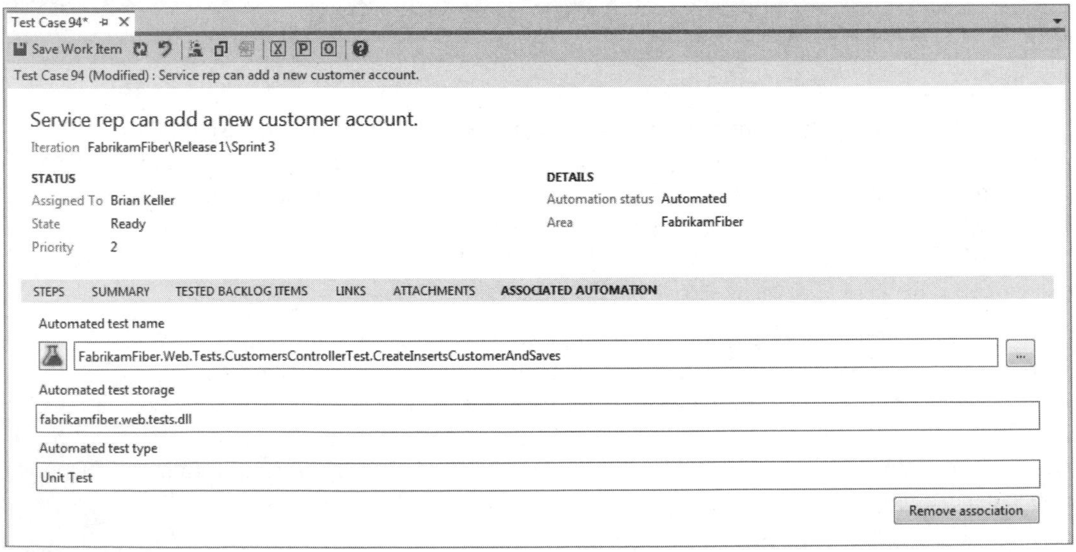

FIGURE 23-23

Use the ellipsis (. . .) to the right of the Automated Test Name field to browse for the automated test you want to use when running this test case. After you've selected it, the rest of the fields on this form are populated for you. Save the work item.

Now, when you run this test from within Test Manager, it runs automatically without requiring user intervention. Additionally, if you configure Team Foundation Build to run this test as part of an automated build (see Chapter 5), then the status of this test is automatically reported back to your test plan, so there is no need to run this test from within Test Manager unless you want to reproduce a test run.

You learn how to create a coded UI test in Chapter 24. After creating a coded UI test, you may want to revisit this topic to wire up your coded UI test as associated automation for an existing test case.

> **NOTE** *Before you can run automated tests within Test Manager for the first time, you must first define an automated test environment and automated test settings for your test plan. Test settings within Test Manager were first introduced in this chapter; automated test settings and test environments are covered in greater detail in Chapter 26.*

SUMMARY

This chapter provided you with a basic understanding of how Microsoft Test Manager can help testers author, manage, and execute manual test plans. You learned how features such as test impact analysis can help you determine which test cases to run next.

You learned how Test Runner guides a generalist tester through the steps that make up a test case, and how it allows for granular reporting of whether each test step passed or failed. You saw how action recordings can make generalist testers more efficient by helping them "fast forward" through ranges of test steps. You also learned how you can run tests in an exploratory fashion, and how you can discover and create new test cases as required during this approach.

You also learned how Microsoft Test Manager combined with Team Foundation Server 2012 can improve communications between testers and developers by automatically capturing rich information about test runs. This information can help developers understand how bugs were encountered, and can even provide them with information to help them more quickly resolve those bugs.

In Chapter 24, you discover how you can convert manual test cases into fully automated UI tests by starting with the action recordings you captured using Test Runner. In Chapter 26, you learn how Microsoft Test Manager can be used to create virtual environments for running your tests.

24

Coded User Interface Testing

WHAT'S IN THIS CHAPTER?

➤ Understanding how you can use coded UI tests to create automated functional tests

➤ Learning how to create a coded UI test from scratch, or from existing action recordings

➤ Learning techniques for making coded UI tests more robust

WROX.COM CODE DOWNLOADS FOR THIS CHAPTER

The wrox.com code downloads for this chapter are found at `www.wrox.com/remtitle .cgi?isbn=1118314081` on the Download Code tab. The files are in the Chapter 24 download folder and individually named as shown throughout this chapter.

In Chapter 23, you learned about the support that Visual Studio 2012 has for manual testing. Manual tests are relatively cheap to author, which makes them well-suited for testing your application while it's undergoing regular changes. As the user interface (UI) undergoes churn (perhaps because of usability feedback, or additional features being implemented), it's easy to update manual test cases to reflect those changes. After all, a manual test is essentially just a textual list of steps.

The downside of manual tests is that, by definition, they require human intervention to execute and validate. As an application grows, it may become cost-prohibitive to run every manual test for every build you're testing. The desire is to use automated tests that can be run routinely to help ensure application integrity, without requiring ongoing human testing resources. Visual Studio 2012 enables you to create *coded UI tests*, which are designed for functional UI testing.

A coded UI test provides a mechanism to automatically execute and validate a test case. Unlike most other automated tests (such as unit tests), a coded UI test operates at the user-interface layer and "drives" the application in much the same manner as a human sitting in front of a mouse and keyboard would. You can program a coded UI test to validate elements of the UI at various points during the test to confirm that the application is behaving properly. For example, is the checkout total accurately reflected in the correct location on a form after adding a given number of items to the shopping cart?

You can author coded UI tests in C# or Visual Basic, and Visual Studio provides tools to help auto-generate much of this required code. Note that coded UI tests require that the application being tested was built using one of the supported technologies—for example, Windows Presentation Foundation (WPF), Windows Forms, HTML/AJAX, and so on. See the "Supported Technologies" section later in this chapter for more information.

In this chapter, you learn how to work with coded UI tests. You start by creating a simple coded UI test using the Coded UI Test Builder and adding some validation logic. Next, you parameterize this test to run multiple times using different sets of input data. Lastly, you discover how you can create coded UI tests using action recordings, which can be generated while running manual tests.

CREATING CODED UI TESTS USING THE CODED UI TEST BUILDER

One way of recording a coded UI test is to use the Coded UI Test Builder. By using the Test Builder, you can record a given path through an application, usually by emulating a scenario that you expect a user to perform. Along the way, you can add validation logic to ensure that the application is behaving correctly. The Test Builder is responsible for generating source code (in C# or Visual Basic) that represents the coded UI test. You can then customize this source code, such as to parameterize inputs and expected outputs for creating a data-driven test.

Setting up the Sample Application

The tutorial presented here utilizes a very simple WPF-based calculator. You can download this sample from this book's website at www.wrox.com. A version of the calculator written using Windows Forms is also available for you to try, although the source code and screenshots in this chapter match that of the WPF version.

Begin by opening the solution for the SimpleWPFCalculator application. Press F5 to launch the application. This is a very primitive application, but it serves as a good example for learning how to work with coded UI tests. To use the application, simply enter an integer into each textbox and click the buttons corresponding to each math operation to generate the respective results, as shown in Figure 24-1. (In this example, the Subtract button was clicked.)

Create a desktop shortcut for your application to make it easier to launch when you are creating your tests. From within Windows Explorer, browse to the project directory where you unzipped the sample application. Open the SimpleWPFCalculator\bin\Debug folder and right-click the SimpleWPFCalculator.exe file. Choose Create Shortcut and then drag the shortcut that is generated onto your computer's desktop. Confirm that double-clicking this shortcut launches the WPF calculator application.

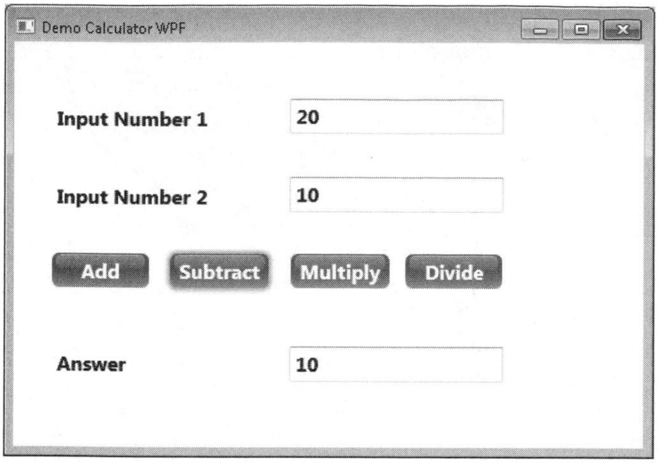

FIGURE 24-1

Create a Test Project

Next, you need a test project in which to house your coded UI tests. Click File ⇨ New ⇨ Project, which displays the New Project dialog shown in Figure 24-2. Select Visual C# ⇨ Test ⇨ Coded UI Test Project. Name your project `CodedUITestProject` and click OK when finished.

> **NOTE** *You may also choose Visual Basic as the language for your test project, but the sample code in this chapter shows a C# test project.*

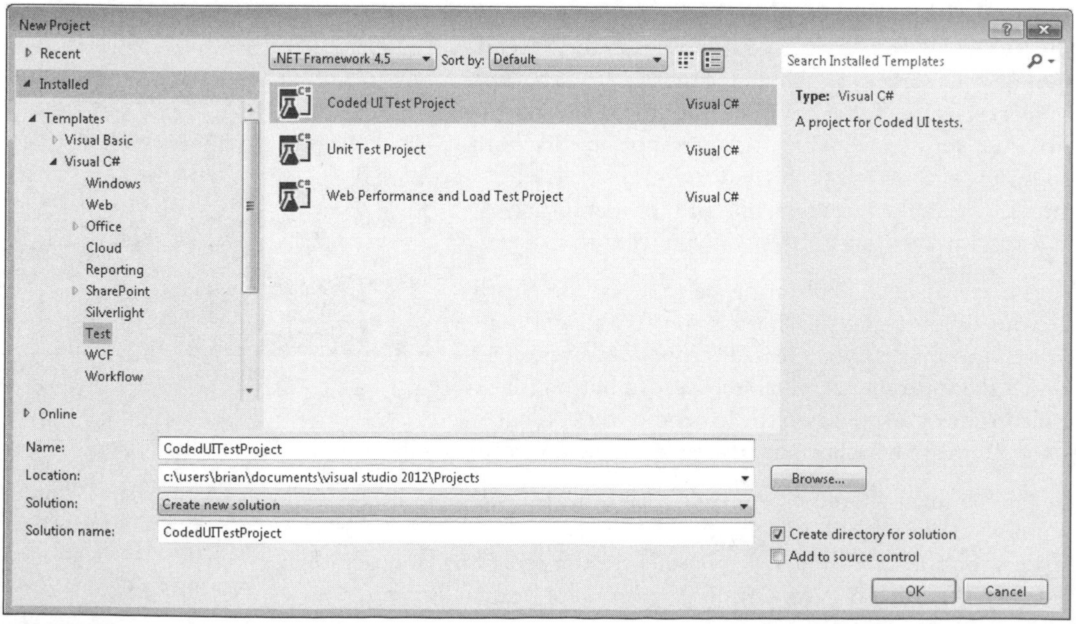

FIGURE 24-2

Your first coded UI test, `CodedUITest1.cs`, is created as part of your new project. The dialog shown in Figure 24-3 displays, providing you with options for generating your test.

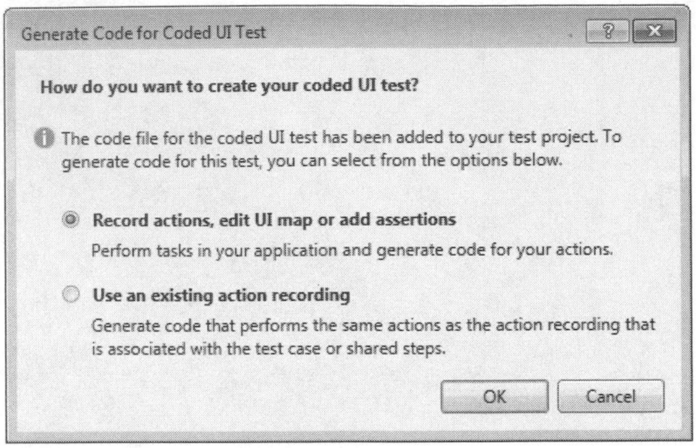

FIGURE 24-3

This first option, Record Actions, Edit UI Map or Add Assertions, launches the Coded UI Test Builder. This enables you to record a coded UI test from scratch by navigating through the application in the same manner that a user might. In the "Creating Coded UI Tests Using Action Recordings" section, later this chapter, you find out how to convert existing manual test cases into coded UI tests by selecting the second option in this dialog.

For now, choose the first option and click OK. Visual Studio now minimizes to make room for you to begin recording your test.

Coded UI Test Builder

The Coded UI Test Builder now appears in the lower right of your screen, as shown in Figure 24-4. The Test Builder is, as the name implies, a tool that can help you construct your coded UI tests. It is responsible for both recording actions you perform (for example, clicking buttons, typing text, and so on), and for identifying controls and their properties that you want to validate.

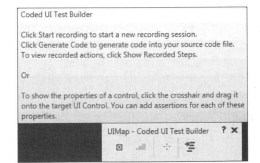

FIGURE 24-4

Minimize any open applications so that you can clearly see your desktop and the shortcut to the WPF calculator application that you created earlier. However, don't launch the shortcut yet. Click the Record button (the circle inside of a square on the left end of the toolbar) of the Test Builder when you are ready to begin recording your test.

The Test Builder should now resemble Figure 24-5, which indicates that it is recording your actions. At any time, you can click Pause (the leftmost button) to instruct Test Builder to stop recording your actions, and click the Record button again when you are ready to resume.

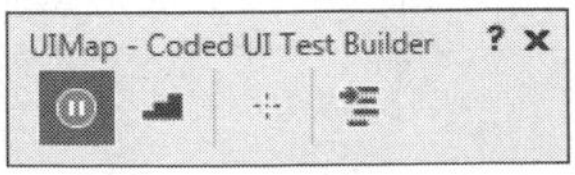

FIGURE 24-5

NOTE *When you begin recording, Test Builder captures any and all actions you perform, even if they aren't part of the application you are trying to test. For example, if you are recording a test and you respond to an instant message, or click the Start menu to launch an unrelated application, these actions are captured. This might result in unnecessary playback steps when executing your coded UI tests and could even cause your tests to fail unexpectedly. For this reason, you should take care to close unrelated applications prior to recording your tests so you can make clean recordings. You can also pause the Test Builder if you must perform unrelated actions during a test. Just be sure you do not interact with the application being tested while the Test Builder is paused. Doing so could cause the application you are testing to get into a state other than what it was in when you paused the Test Builder, and, hence, subsequent steps you record might fail on playback.*

You are now ready to begin recording the coded UI test by using the application in the same manner you would expect a user to. Launch the WPF calculator application by double-clicking the desktop shortcut you created earlier. Type **20** in the first textbox, then type **10** in the second textbox, and click the Add button.

You can visually inspect the actions that the Test Builder has captured by clicking Show Recorded Steps (the second button from the left) of the Test Builder. The window shown in Figure 24-6 appears, showing you an easy-to-read list of the steps you have performed while recording your test. Note that you can pin this window if you'd like to have it remain visible while you are recording. You can also right-click and delete any unwanted actions that you may have recorded accidentally.

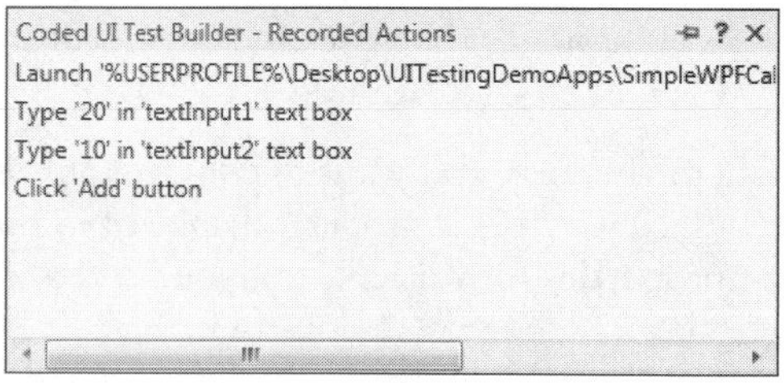

FIGURE 24-6

At this point in your test, you are ready to add some validation logic to confirm that the result of your addition operation is correct. But, before you add an assertion, you should convert the steps you have performed so far into source code. Do so by clicking Generate Code (the rightmost button) within the Test Builder.

The dialog shown in Figure 24-7 prompts you for the name of the method you want to create within your coded UI test. You should use descriptive method names to make it easier to understand your generated code. Type **EnterDataAndClickAdd**; optionally you can provide a description which will be added as a comment to the source code that you generate. Click Add and Generate when you are ready to resume building your coded UI test. The Test Builder converts your recorded steps into source code, which is added to your Visual Studio project files. You will inspect this code later.

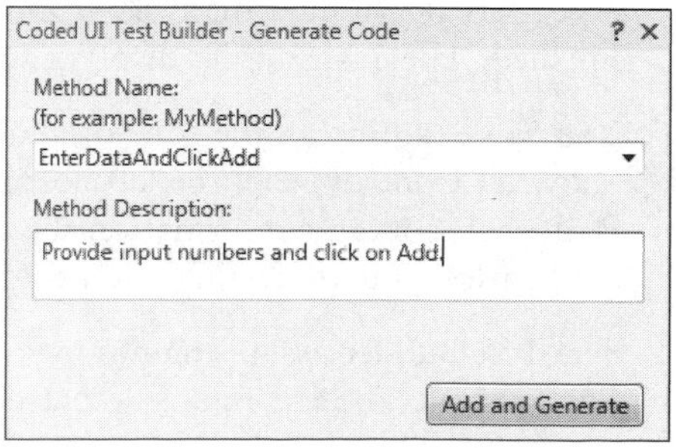

FIGURE 24-7

FIGURE 24-6 (window content)
Coded UI Test Builder - Recorded Actions
Launch '%USERPROFILE%\Desktop\UITestingDemoApps\SimpleWPFCal
Type '20' in 'textInput1' text box
Type '10' in 'textInput2' text box
Click 'Add' button

FIGURE 24-7 (window content)
Coded UI Test Builder - Generate Code
Method Name:
(for example: MyMethod)
EnterDataAndClickAdd
Method Description:
Provide input numbers and click on Add.
Add and Generate

You can now add assertion logic to validate the properties of one or more controls. The Test Builder enables you to easily select the control you want to validate. Do so by clicking and dragging the crosshair icon from the Test Builder onto the bottommost textbox of the calculator. As you hover over controls and windows of your desktop and applications, notice that they become highlighted to indicate which control you are selecting. After you have selected the bottommost textbox of the calculator, release your mouse button.

The properties for the `textAnswer` textbox you have selected are displayed as shown in Figure 24-8.

You can use the up/down/left/right arrows of this dialog to navigate through the control hierarchy. You don't need to do so for this test, but this is helpful for controls that are difficult to select using the crosshairs, or invisible controls (such as a panel that may be used a container for other controls).

For some controls, such as context menus, you may notice that they are difficult to select. For example, a context menu might disappear once you drag it over the control. In these cases, you can simply hover your mouse pointer over the control you are trying to capture, then press Ctrl+I. This will highlight the selected control and show its properties in the Coded UI Test Builder.

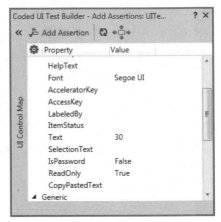

FIGURE 24-8

For this test, you want to confirm that the number 30 (the sum of 20 plus 10) is properly displayed in the textbox. In the list of properties for this control, you see that the `Text` property of the `UITextAnswerEdit` control in your UI Map currently has a value of 30. Highlight this row, then click Add an Assertion (the second button from the left on the toolbar). The dialog box in Figure 24-9 displays, enabling you to define the behavior of your assertion. Click the Comparator dropdown to examine your assertion choices. Accept the default value (AreEqual) for Comparator and the current value (30) for Comparison Value. You should also add a value for the message that is displayed if the assertion fails. This is very helpful when you are diagnosing failed tests later on, especially if you have many assertions in your tests. Click OK when finished. The Test Builder displays a message indicating that your assertion has been added.

FIGURE 24-9

You can examine all the controls that have been captured as part of your coded UI test by clicking Show UI Control Map (the leftmost button on the toolbar). The *UI Control Map* is built by the Test Builder. It contains information about all of the controls necessary to interact with and validate the application you are testing. Figure 24-10 shows the controls that you have added so far.

The Test Builder assigns names to your controls based on the type of control and its control name. For example, the `textAnswer` control is be named `UITextAnswerEdit`.

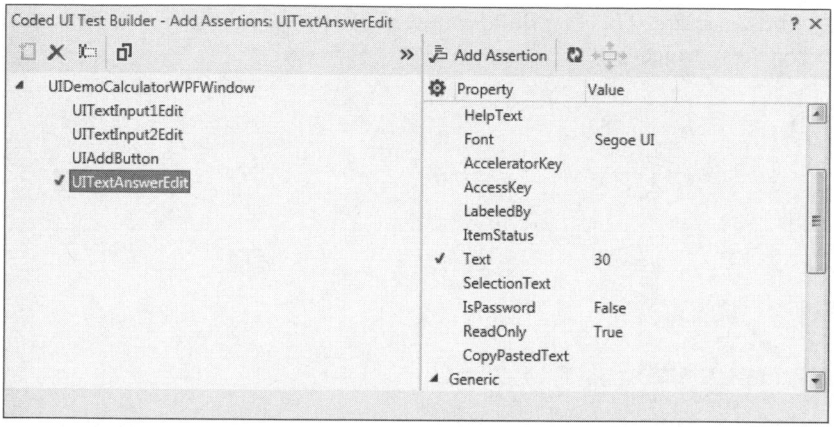

FIGURE 24-10

> **NOTE** *If you don't see meaningful names for your controls, or you can't locate the controls at all, it might be due to one or more of the following factors. The first might be because the application you are testing was built using an unsupported technology, or a mixture of technologies (some of which are unsupported). For example, if you are testing a web application which has an embedded Flash object, you will be able to identify controls on the web page but not within the Flash object. See "Supported Technologies" later in this chapter for more information. If you are finding unique controls but the names are not meaningful (e.g., textbox1, button1, etc.) then this likely indicates that the developers building the application you are testing haven't taken the time to provide meaningful names to the controls. You should consider having a discussion with them to explain to them why it might be helpful to have consistent naming conventions for the controls within the application, which can in turn improve the readability and maintainability of the tests you are writing. Finally, if you are testing a web application, some controls might simply not have any names at all since you are not always required to name a control using HTML. This is another reason for your application developers to start assigning unique, meaningful names to the controls within your application.*

The controls in the UI Control Map are organized hierarchically; for this application, notice that `UIDemoCalculatorWPFWindow` is a parent control of the rest of the controls in this application. You can click on any control in this tree to examine its properties. These properties, along with the relative location of a control within the control hierarchy, are used by your coded UI test to find the correct control to use during test playback.

Click Generate Code from within the Test Builder (the rightmost button) to codify the assertion you just added. The dialog shown in Figure 24-11 displays, prompting you to name the method that corresponds to your assertion. Name the method `AssertAdd`, optionally provide a meaningful comment, and click Add and Generate. The Test Builder now converts the assertion you defined into C# and inserts this into your test project.

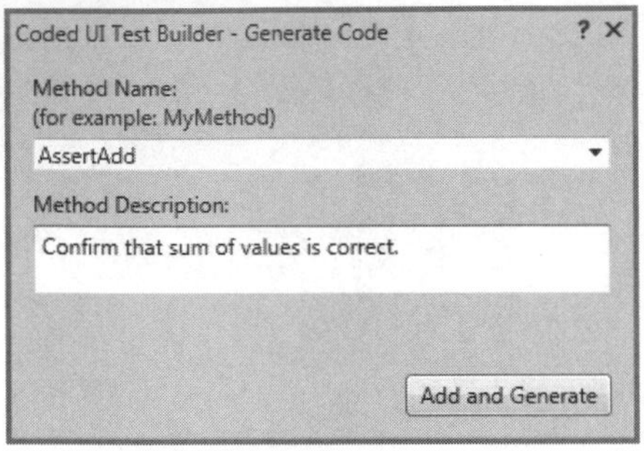

FIGURE 24-11

> **NOTE** *The dialog you encountered in Figure 24-9 may at first appear to be duplicative of the dialog you encountered in Figure 24-11. The difference is subtle, and one which will become clearer as you work with more coded UI tests. Essentially, Figure 24-11 asks you to define a method in your code which is responsible for validating all of the assertions you added earlier. In this example, you are only adding one assertion (to confirm that the* textAnswer *control has a text value equal to 30). But you could have added additional control properties to validate by repeating the process you went through with Figure 24-9. For example, you might have wanted to also validate that the* textAnswer *control has its* ReadOnly *value set to* True.*

Now, click the Record button (leftmost button) in the Test Builder again to resume recording your test case. Click the Subtract button in the calculator, and then click Generate Code (the rightmost button) in the Test Builder. Name this method **ClickSubtract** and click Add and Generate.

Now, add another assertion by following the same steps you followed earlier. After dragging the crosshair onto the bottommost textbox in the calculator, you see the expanded UI Control Map. The UITextAnswerEdit control should be highlighted. Select the Text property and add an assertion stating that this property should now be equal to 10. Click Generate Code and name the assertion **AssertSubtract**.

Repeat these steps for the multiplication and division functions. Name the methods for clicking those buttons **ClickMultiply** and **ClickDivide**, respectively. Name the corresponding assertions **AssertMultiply** and **AssertDivide**. When you are finished, close the Test Builder, which returns you to Visual Studio. You can always return to the Test Builder in the future by clicking Test Generate Code for Coded UI Test.

Generated Code

From within Visual Studio, you can now examine the code that was generated by the Test Builder while you were recording your test actions and assertions. The CodedUITestMethod1() method within the CodedUITest1.cs file is the main execution harness for your test, and calls all of the action and assertion methods you defined earlier, as shown here:

```
[TestMethod]
public void CodedUITestMethod1()
{
 this.UIMap.EnterDataAndClickAdd();
 this.UIMap.AssertAdd();
 this.UIMap.ClickSubtract();
 this.UIMap.AssertSubtract();
 this.UIMap.ClickMultiply();
 this.UIMap.AssertMultiply();
 this.UIMap.ClickDivide();
 this.UIMap.AssertDivide();
}
```

To better understand what each underlying method is actually doing, you can examine the partial class file named UIMap.Designer.cs. Right-click the EnterDataAndClickAdd method call and select Go to Definition. This method is defined as follows (some comments have been removed in the following text):

```
public void EnterDataAndClickAdd()
{
 WpfEdit uITextInput1Edit = this.UIDemoCalculatorWPFWindow.UITextInput1Edit;
 WpfEdit uITextInput2Edit = this.UIDemoCalculatorWPFWindow.UITextInput2Edit;
 WpfButton uIAddButton = this.UIDemoCalculatorWPFWindow.UIAddButton;

 ApplicationUnderTest uIDemoCalculatorWPFWindow = ApplicationUnderTest.Launch(
this.EnterDataAndClickAddParams.UIDemoCalculatorWPFWindowExePath,
this.EnterDataAndClickAddParams.UIDemoCalculatorWPFWindowAlternateExePath);

    uITextInput1Edit.Text = this.EnterDataAndClickAddParams.UITextInput1EditText;

    uITextInput2Edit.Text = this.EnterDataAndClickAddParams.UITextInput2EditText;

    Mouse.Click(uIAddButton, new Point(50, 16));
}
```

This method is responsible for performing four distinct actions, as defined by the actions you recorded earlier. This method will first launch the application, then enter values into two textboxes, then click on the Add button. Notice, however, that the parameters for this method are defined elsewhere in this file. Scroll down to the class named EnterDataAndClickAddParams (not the virtual class of the same name):

```
public class EnterDataAndClickAddParams
{
  public string UIDemoCalculatorWPFWindowExePath =
  "C:\\Users\\Brian\\Desktop\\ UITestingDemoApps\\
SimpleWPFCalculator\\bin\\Debug\\SimpleWPFCalculator.exe";

  public string UIDemoCalculatorWPFWindowAlternateExePath = "%USERPROFILE%\\
DesktopUITestingDemoApps\\SimpleWPFCalculator\\bin\\Debug\\
SimpleWPFCalculator.exe";

  public string UITextInput1EditText = "20";

  public string UITextInput2EditText = "10";
}
```

The reason that the parameters are separated from the actual method doing the work is that this makes it easier to override the parameters with new values. This is very important when creating data-driven tests that will run multiple times, using different values each time. You do this later in this chapter.

Notice that there are two slightly different values defined to describe from where the application under test will be launched, `UIDemoCalculatorWPFWindowExePath` and `UIDemoCalculatorWPFWindowAlternateExePath`. Whenever possible, Visual Studio looks for ways to make your tests more robust so that they are less prone to accidental failure resulting from changes to your application or test environment. The actual values you have for your test vary, based on where you stored your application. But, for this example, notice that Visual Studio stored both the absolute path to the executable and the relative path based on the `%USERPROFILE%` environment variable. This makes your tests more fault-tolerant in the event that your executable changes locations later on.

Also, notice that the Test Builder interpreted your test actions as launching an application executable, instead of double-clicking that application's shortcut on your desktop. This is also a way of making your test more fault-tolerant. In the future, you might decide to delete or move the shortcut to the executable, but you are less likely to move the actual executable itself. Recording tests can be a relatively expensive investment, so Visual Studio uses tricks like this to make it less likely that you must re-record your tests later on.

> **NOTE** *You should refrain from making changes directly to the* `UIMap.Designer` `.cs` *file. Because this is a designer-generated file, any changes you make here might be overwritten later on as you refine your test. Instead, Visual Studio provides a UI Map Editor that you learn about later in this chapter.*

Notice also that in the `EnterDataAndClickAdd()` method there is a `Mouse.Click` call which passes a `Point(X,Y)` value as an argument. This sometimes confuses people who are new to coded UI tests because they assume that coded UI tests are driven by fixed X and Y coordinates. They further wonder whether or not resizing a form or moving controls later on will cause their tests to break. But in fact, coded UI tests use the properties of controls from your UI map to locate controls, not their X and Y coordinates.

The `Point(X,Y)` value is used by the `Mouse.Click` method to control the position *within* a control that a mouse click is made. For most controls (such as the WPF Button being used in this application) it doesn't matter where a click is registered—the end result is the same. There are only a few controls where the position of a click makes a difference. One such example is a `SplitButton` control, such as the one you click when you are going to shut down or sleep your Windows PC. But for most controls, this value does not affect your test. In most cases you can feel free to resize or move controls around your forms or web pages without worrying about breaking your tests.

> **NOTE** *For a deeper explanation of how coded UI tests use search and filter properties to locate controls, see* `http://tinyurl.com/SearchAndFilter`.

Running Your Test

You are now ready to run your test and confirm that everything was properly recorded. Do so by returning to the `CodedUITest1.cs` file and right-clicking anywhere within the `CodedUITestMethod1()` code block. Select Run Tests. Avoid using your mouse or keyboard while the test runs. If you have recorded your test properly, the calculator will launch, the values 20 and 10 are inserted into the text-boxes, and each of the four operation buttons are exercised. When finished, the test results are displayed in the Test Explorer window (Test ⇨ Windows ⇨ Test Explorer) as shown in Figure 24-12.

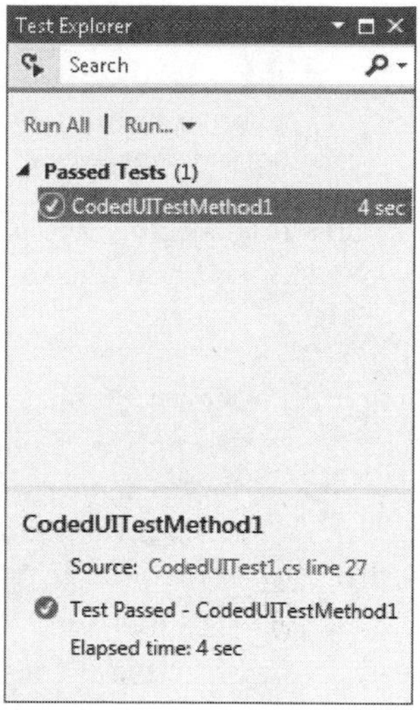

Congratulations! You have now authored your first coded UI test. But what if you want to test values other than 20 and 10? One approach would be to author new tests, each with their own values. But this would be very time-consuming. A better solution is to create a data-driven test by binding the values for this test case to a database, or a CSV or XML file.

FIGURE 24-12

Creating a Data-Driven Test

The process of creating a data-driven coded UI test is very similar to that of creating a data-driven unit test. You can use a database, CSV file, or XML file to drive your coded UI tests with different values. For each row of data, your coded UI test are run once.

The sample application for this chapter includes an XML dataset named `CalcData.xml`. The contents of this file are as follows:

```xml
<?xml version="1.0" encoding="utf-8"?>
<DataContextData>
  <DataContextRow InputValue1 ="10"
                  InputValue2 ="2"
                  ExpectedAddAnswer ="12"
                  ExpectedSubtractAnswer="8"
                  ExpectedMultiplyAnswer="20"
                  ExpectedDivideAnswer="5"/>
  <DataContextRow InputValue1 ="20"
                  InputValue2 ="10"
                  ExpectedAddAnswer ="30"
                  ExpectedSubtractAnswer="10"
                  ExpectedMultiplyAnswer="200"
                  ExpectedDivideAnswer="2"/>
</DataContextData>
```

Start by adding the `CalcData.xml` file to your project. Right-click your CodedUITestProject from within Solution Explorer and select Add ⇨ Existing Item. You may need to change the file filter to show `All Files (*.*)`. Browse to the `CalcData.xml` file and click Add to add it to your project.

Next, you need to make this file a deployment item. Change the properties for this file in Solution Explorer. Set `Build Action` to `Content`, and set `Copy to Output Directory` to `Copy if Newer`. This ensures that the XML file is available alongside the DLL for your test.

Next you need to add `DataSource` and `DeploymentItem` attributes to your coded UI test method. Change the `[TestMethod]` attribute preceding the `CodedUITestMethod1()` method to the following:

```
[DataSource("Microsoft.VisualStudio.TestTools.DataSource.XML", "|DataDirectory|\\
CalcData.xml", "DataContextRow", DataAccessMethod.Sequential),
DeploymentItem("CalcData.xml"), TestMethod]
```

This line specifies the name and relative path of the file, the type of data source (such as CSV or XML), and how the rows of data should be accessed (`Sequential` or `Random`).

> **NOTE** *Previous releases of Visual Studio featured a Data Source Wizard that simplified the process of creating the* `DataSource` *and* `DeploymentItem` *attributes. Unfortunately, this functionality was removed in Visual Studio 2012 when Microsoft overhauled the testing framework. Microsoft has indicated that it would like to re-implement this functionality in a future version of Visual Studio, or possibly as an update to Visual Studio 2012, but at the time of writing there are no specific roadmap details available for this functionality.*
>
> *If you have access to an older version of Visual Studio, you might want to use it to generate* `DataSource` *and* `DeploymentItem` *definitions that you can learn from and apply to your testing projects in Visual Studio 2012. For more information on these and other attributes that you can use to configure and extend your tests, see* http://aka.ms/UTNamespace.

You can now begin overriding the parameters that you recorded earlier by data-binding them to your XML data source. The architecture of coded UI tests makes it easy to do this from within one central location—the `CodedUITest1.cs` file. Modify the `CodedUITest1` method by inserting the following highlighted lines.

```
this.UIMap.EnterDataAndClickAddParams.UITextInput1EditText =
TestContext.DataRow["InputValue1"].ToString();
this.UIMap.EnterDataAndClickAddParams.UITextInput2EditText =
TestContext.DataRow["InputValue2"].ToString();

this.UIMap.EnterDataAndClickAdd();
this.UIMap.AssertAddExpectedValues.UITextAnswerEditText =
TestContext.DataRow["ExpectedAddAnswer"].ToString();
this.UIMap.AssertAdd();

this.UIMap.ClickSubtract();
this.UIMap.AssertSubtractExpectedValues.UITextAnswerEditText =
TestContext.DataRow["ExpectedSubtractAnswer"].ToString();
this.UIMap.AssertSubtract();

this.UIMap.ClickMultiply();
this.UIMap.AssertMultiplyExpectedValues.UITextAnswerEditText =
TestContext.DataRow["ExpectedMultiplyAnswer"].ToString();
```

```
this.UIMap.AssertMultiply();

this.UIMap.ClickDivide();
this.UIMap.AssertDivideExpectedValues.UITextAnswerEditText =
TestContext.DataRow["ExpectedDivideAnswer"].ToString();
this.UIMap.AssertDivide();
```

The code you added now overrides the values from each of the respective `ExpectedValues` methods within the `UIMap` `.Designer.cs` file by data binding the values to the corresponding columns within your XML data source.

Run your test again by right-clicking within your test method and selecting Run Tests. Your coded UI test now executes twice—once for each row of the XML data source. When finished, the test results panel of the Test Explorer window should indicate that 3/3 tests have passed successfully. This includes each data row, as well as the overall test, as shown in Figure 24-13.

FIGURE 24-13

You can now maintain the `CalcData.xml` file within your test project to add new rows of data. These rows will be used during future test runs, thus providing you with an easy way to grow your test coverage. Any time you make changes to `CalcData.xml`, you need to rebuild your solution (Build ⇨ Build Solution) in order to deploy the updated file.

Failing Tests

You can force your test to fail by changing the values in the `CalcData.xml` file. Try changing the value for the first instance of `ExpectedAddAnswer` from 12 to 14. Click Build ⇨ Build Solution and then run your test again. The test fails as shown in Figure 24-14.

For coded UI tests with multiple assertions, it can be useful to know more about exactly which assertion caused the test to fail. If you entered a message as shown in Figure 24-9 when you defined your assertion then it displays here, providing you with more information about why the test failed. If you didn't provide additional details in Figure 24-9 then you would only know that the expected value of 14 does not match the actual value of 12, and you might need to spend time investigating what those values are meant to represent in the UI of your application.

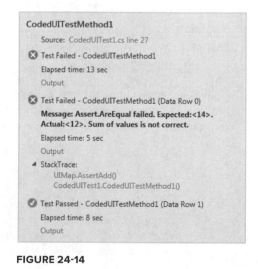

FIGURE 24-14

Because your test ran with multiple iterations of data (from your XML file) only the first iteration failed. The second iteration passed as expected.

> **NOTE** *Note that a test iteration fails and aborts immediately after the first assertion within a given test iteration has failed. For example, if you see a message that the* `AssertAdd()` *assertion failed, you still won't know whether or not the subtraction/multiplication/division operations are working properly. If you require more granular reporting of your test runs, it is advisable to create multiple coded UI tests, each verifying one unit of functionality.*

Finally, if you click the Output link for a test result you see any test attachments that were added during the test run. By default, the coded UI test runner automatically takes a screenshot of your running application and attaches that to your test results if a test fails. This can be helpful for reviewing failed tests later on to inspect the state of the application at the time of the test failure.

Taking Screenshots

You can also programmatically capture screenshots that can be saved to your test results. This can be useful even if a coded UI test passes because you can examine it later to see if there was anything that appeared incorrectly in the user interface for which you didn't explicitly code assertions.

The following code takes a screenshot of your WPF calculator application. It saves it to your test result as a file named `AddResult.bmp`. Add this immediately before the call to `AssertAdd()` in your test method:

```
Image pic = this.UIMap.UIDemoCalculatorWPFWindow.CaptureImage();
pic.Save(@"c:\AddResult.bmp");
TestContext.AddResultFile(@"c:\AddResult.bmp");
```

Alternatively, you can capture a screenshot of the entire desktop by replacing the first line in the preceding code with the following line:

```
Image pic = UITestControl.Desktop.CaptureImage();
```

Taking a screenshot of the entire desktop can be helpful if you are testing applications that utilize multiple windows at once. These screenshots are accessible by clicking the Output link from within the test results view of Test Explorer.

> **NOTE** *You can conduct image comparisons within coded UI tests by following the steps outlined at* `http://tinyurl.com/ImageCompare`. *These steps utilize a free set of testing libraries known as TestApi, available at* `http://testapi .codeplex.com`. *TestApi provides several helpful libraries and tools, many of which you can access directly from your coded UI tests.*

UI Map Editor

Earlier in this chapter you read about the UI Map, which is generated by the Test Builder, and you looked at the `UIMap.Designer.cs` partial class file where most of the logic for your coded UI test is written. But you also discovered that you should not make changes directly to that file because it is meant to be maintained by the Visual Studio designers, including the Test Builder, and any changes you make by hand might be overwritten later by the designer.

Visual Studio 2012 includes a built-in UI Map Editor that you can run by simply double-clicking the `UIMap.uitest` file from within Solution Explorer. The UI Map Editor opens as shown in Figure 24-15.

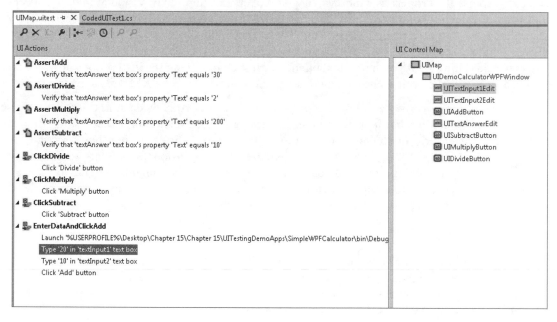

FIGURE 24-15

The panel on the left is the UI Actions panel and contains all the methods you created when you clicked Generate Code from within the Test Builder. These are listed in alphabetical order only and do not necessarily reflect the order in which they will be executed (if at all). The order in which these might be called is defined by your `CodedUITestMethod1()` method.

The UI Actions panel provides you with a few useful capabilities for maintaining your coded UI tests. You can delete entire methods or individual actions by selecting them and pressing delete. For example, maybe when you were recording your test you accidentally clicked a control or typed some text that you didn't mean to type. You can come back to this view to clean up your extra actions.

Another common use of the UI Actions panel is to split methods into smaller methods. For example, you might want to split the `EnterDataAndClickAdd()` method into three different methods—one to launch the application, another to enter some data, and a third to click the Add button. This gives you more flexibility when programming your test methods. To do this, you need to place your cursor on a row within the `EnterDataAndClickAdd()` method and then click Split into a New Method in the toolbar. Visual Studio alerts you that if you split this method, you need to manually update your test code within the `CodedUITestMethod1()` to call the new methods. You can also use the UI Actions panel to rename the new split methods to reflect what they do (such as `LaunchApp()`, `EnterData()`, and `ClickAdd()`).

You can insert delays between steps from here as well. By default, the coded UI test playback engine attempts to run tests as quickly as possible by examining the UI thread to determine if controls are ready to be interacted with. However, you may know that your application automatically refreshes some number of seconds after a form is initially loaded. To test the post-refresh status of the page you might want to use the Insert Delay Before button on the toolbar.

You can also use the Properties window (View ⇨ Properties Window) in Visual Studio to inspect additional parameters for any of the actions in the UI Actions panel. The available properties vary based on the type of action you have selected. For example, the action `Type '20' in 'testIn-put1' text box` enables you to override the value 20 with a different value by entering it into the property grid. However if you have databound your test by following the instructions provided earlier in this chapter then this value is overridden by the values from your XML file.

Another useful property available on all actions is Continue on Error. By default, this is set to False for all actions—meaning that if an action fails, the test fails and execution for that test iteration is stopped. But sometimes you might want a test to try to keep executing even if a specific action fails. A good example of this is when the application you are testing occasionally presents additional dialogs that do not affect the end result of your test run. Your application might randomly present a dialog asking if you want to complete a customer satisfaction survey. In this case, you probably want an action in your test logic that clicks No and continues, but unless you enable Continue on Error for that action then your test might fail if it doesn't find the relevant No button to click in subsequent test runs.

The UI Control Map on the right side of the UI Map Editor is the same one you saw earlier in Figure 24-10. As you highlight various actions within the UI Actions pane notice that the relevant controls within the UI Control Map hierarchy are highlighted. You can also edit properties for these controls by accessing the Properties window within Visual Studio.

The actual properties available to you for a given control vary based on the type of control, and the type of application. For example, web applications use both search and filter properties to locate controls, whereas rich client applications such as WPF or Windows Forms only use search properties. Most of the time you probably don't need to change the properties for controls in your UI Map, although occasionally if the names of controls or their positions within your control hierarchy changes you may need to examine these properties.

Now that you know how to create a coded UI test from scratch by using the Test Builder, it's time to examine an approach of creating a coded UI test from an existing manual test.

CREATING CODED UI TESTS USING ACTION RECORDINGS

Creating a coded UI test from an existing manual test can be less time-consuming than recording a coded UI test from scratch. If your team is already creating manual test cases and associated action recordings, you can benefit from these artifacts when creating your coded UI tests.

For this section, it is assumed that you know how to create manual tests and their associated action recordings. For more information about manual testing, see Chapter 23.

Start by creating a test like the one shown in Figure 24-16. For simplicity, this test only validates that the addition and subtraction functions of the calculator work properly. You can easily extend this test to support multiplication and division if you want. Also note that this test uses parameterized values for the inputs and expected results.

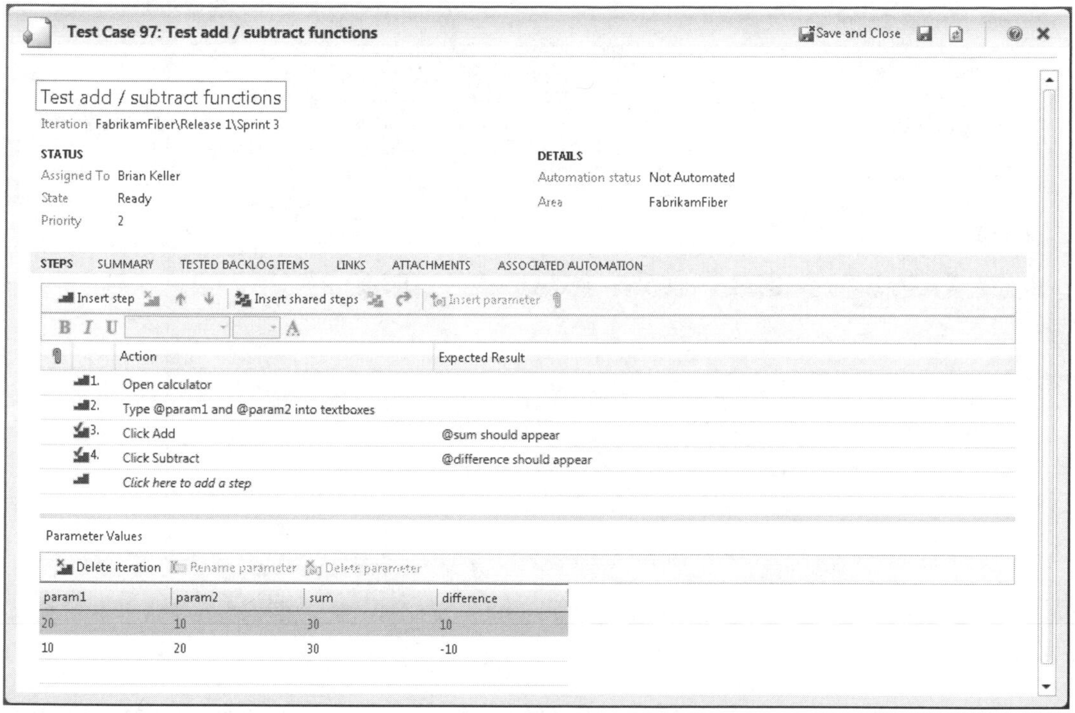

FIGURE 24-16

Now, run this manual test and create an action recording for it. Be sure to mark each test step as Pass while you are recording so that your actions are properly associated with each test step.

Now that the manual test has been created, along with an associated action recording, you are ready to convert this into a coded UI test. Create a new test project (or you can use the one you created earlier in this chapter). Right-click the project and add a coded UI test. The dialog shown in Figure 24-3 displays again. This time, select Use an Existing Action Recording.

The Work Items Picker shown in Figure 24-17 enables you to select the test case work item from which you want to create a coded UI test. Find and select the work item you created earlier for your manual test case and then click OK.

> **NOTE** *The test case work item has a field called Automation Status. You might want to instruct your test team to set this value to Planned when manual test cases are ready for a developer to convert into a coded UI test. You can then create a query to use from the Work Items Picker to find test cases whose Automation Status is equal to Planned.*

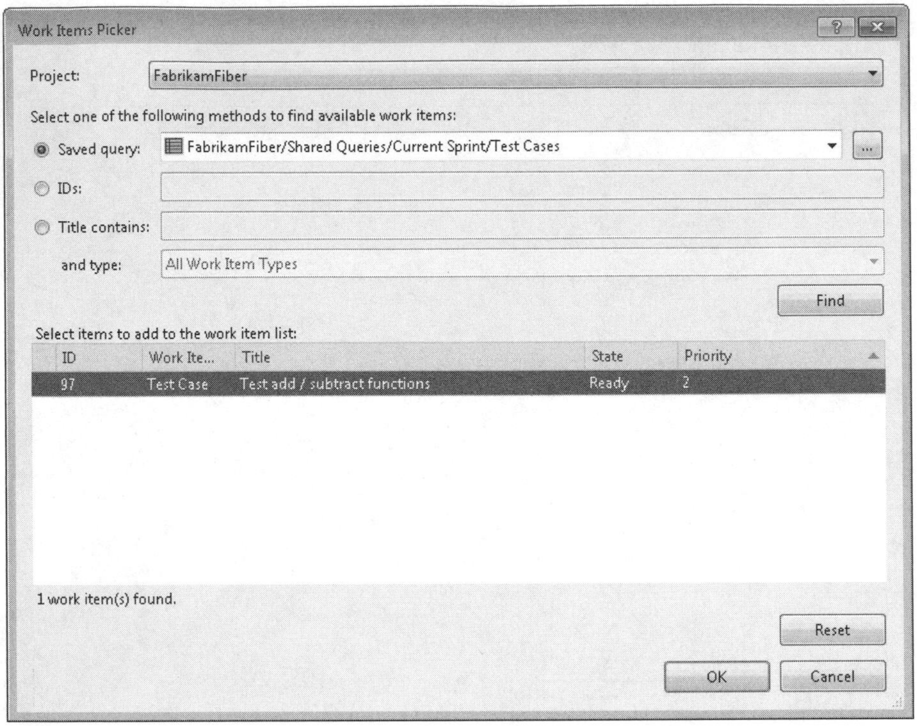

FIGURE 24-17

Visual Studio converts the action recording from your manual test into a coded UI test. The structure of this coded UI test resembles that of the one you created from scratch earlier, but there are a few key differences. Here is the code for CodedUITestMethod1:

```
[DataSource("Microsoft.VisualStudio.TestTools.DataSource.TestCase",
"http://vsalm:8080/tfs/defaultcollection;FabrikamFiber", "97",
DataAccessMethod.Sequential), TestMethod]
public void CodedUITestMethod1()
{
  this.UIMap.Opencalculator();
  this.UIMap.Typeparam1andparam2intotextboxesParams.UITextInput1EditText =
TestContext.DataRow["param1"].ToString();
  this.UIMap.Typeparam1andparam2intotextboxesParams.UITextInput2EditText =
TestContext.DataRow["param2"].ToString();
  this.UIMap.Typeparam1andparam2intotextboxes();
  this.UIMap.ClickAdd();
  this.UIMap.ClickSubtract1();
}
```

> **NOTE** *The path to your Team Foundation Server instance in the* [DataSource]
> *attribute varies from that listed here. Additionally, the* ClickSubtract1 *method*
> *above is named simply* ClickSubtract *if you are using a new test project instead*
> *of adding this coded UI test to the existing project you created earlier in this*
> *chapter (which already contains a* ClickSubtract *method).*

First, notice the attribute on this test method that is data-binding it to the parameter values stored in the test case work item you created. This means that you can update the test parameters centrally from within the work item without needing to maintain a separate database or XML file as you did earlier. This makes it easy for generalist testers (who may not work with source control within Visual Studio) to update test case data.

Next, notice that the names of the method calls in this test method match the text that was used for each test step in the manual test. This can make for cumbersome method names if you have verbose test steps, but it also makes it possible to see exactly which method call corresponds to each part of the test execution.

Finally, you may notice that this coded UI test doesn't contain any assertions yet. Manual tests rely on human beings to perform validation of the intended UI behavior, so, in order to automate validation steps, you must program the appropriate test logic.

Add a new line after the `ClickAdd()` method call. Right-click this empty line and select Generate Code for Coded UI Test ⇨ Use Coded UI Test Builder. Alternatively, you can access this menu via the Test menu.

The Coded UI Test Builder displays again as shown earlier in Figure 24-4. Open the calculator application and use the crosshair to select the bottommost textbox, as you did earlier. Add an assertion on the `Text` property of the `UITextAnswerEdit` textbox. The assertion should be Are Equal and the comparison value is empty (you override this value programmatically). Optionally, you can provide a meaningful value for Message on Assertion Failure if you want. After you have added this, click Generate Code and name your assertion method `AssertAdd2`. Click Add and Generate.

> **NOTE** *The reason you are naming this method* `AssertAdd2` *(as opposed to simply* `AssertAdd`*) is to avoid naming conflicts with the assertion method you created earlier in this chapter. If you are using a new test project, then this naming distinction is not necessary.*

Add another assertion on the same control/property, but this time, name it `AssertSubtract2`. Close the Coded UI Test Builder when you are finished. Visual Studio opens again, and you will notice that two assert method calls have been added to your coded UI test method. Rearrange the method calls so that the assertions appear after their respective action method calls. When finished, your test method should contain the following lines:

```
this.UIMap.ClickAdd();
this.UIMap.AssertAdd2();
this.UIMap.ClickSubtract1();
this.UIMap.AssertSubtract2();
```

You now need to data-bind the parameters used by the assertions to the parameters stored within your test case. Add the following highlighted lines to your test method:

```
this.UIMap.ClickAdd();
this.UIMap.AssertAdd2ExpectedValues.UITextAnswerEditText =
TestContext.DataRow["sum"].ToString();
this.UIMap.AssertAdd2();

this.UIMap.AssertSubtract2ExpectedValues.UITextAnswerEditText =
```

```
TestContext.DataRow["difference"].ToString();
this.UIMap.ClickSubtract1();
this.UIMap.AssertSubtract2();
```

You can run your test by right-clicking within the test method and clicking Run Tests. Your test should run once for each data row within your test case's parameter value table. Try manipulating the parameters in your test case and run your coded UI test again to see the data-binding relationship.

If this were a real testing project, you might also want to spend some time refactoring the code in the duplicative Add and Subtract method calls into common methods for easier long-term maintenance. You can use the UI Map Editor to delete duplicate methods and then hand-edit the appropriate code UI test methods to call the correct methods. Many of the same best practices you know from maintaining complex applications apply when maintaining complex test projects.

You can also add your coded UI test as associated automation for the original manual test case. By associating the test case with the automated test, the automated test can be run as part of your test plan, and tracked along with the rest of your test cases. Chapter 23 provides more details on how to create this association.

SUPPORTED TECHNOLOGIES

Coded UI tests require that your application be built using one of several supported technologies. The coded UI testing framework requires that it understands the underlying technology so that it can interact with the application being tested. The list of supported technologies is expected to grow over time, and Visual Studio 2012 offers an extensibility framework to allow third parties to build their own testing providers. However, if your application uses a technology for which there is not a testing provider available, you are unable to author coded UI tests for it.

> **NOTE** *For a complete list of supported technologies and caveats, consult the Visual Studio 2012 product documentation at* `http://aka.ms/TestAutomation`*.*

SUMMARY

Coded UI tests provided a powerful way of crafting automated tests for functional UI testing of your applications. In this chapter, you saw how you can either create a coded UI test from scratch, by interacting with an application the way you expect a user would, or from an existing action recording from a manual test, thus leveraging some of the work already done by your testing team.

You also found out how you can enhance your coded UI tests by data-binding them to create multiple test runs out of the same set of test steps.

In Chapter 25, you see how you can use web performance tests to help speed up your web applications. You also find out how to simulate the results of hundreds (or even thousands) of users interacting with your web application by using Visual Studio's load-testing capabilities.

Web Performance and Load Testing

WROX.COM CODE DOWNLOADS FOR THIS CHAPTER

The wrox.com code downloads for this chapter are found at `www.wrox.com/remtitle .cgi?isbn=1118314081` on the Download Code tab. The files are in the Chapter 25 download folder and individually named as shown throughout this chapter.

This chapter continues coverage of the testing features of Visual Studio 2012 by describing web performance and load tests.

With web performance testing, you can easily build a suite of repeatable tests that can help you analyze the performance of your web applications and identify potential bottlenecks. Visual Studio enables you to easily create a web performance test by recording your actions as you use your web application. In this chapter, you find out how to create, edit, and run web performance tests, and how to execute and analyze the results.

Sometimes you need more flexibility than a recorded web performance test can offer. In this chapter, you see how to use coded web performance tests to create flexible and powerful web performance tests using Visual Basic or C# and how to leverage the web performance testing framework.

Verifying that an application is ready for production involves additional analysis. How will your application behave when many people begin using it concurrently? The load-testing features of Visual Studio enable you to execute one or more tests repeatedly, tracking the performance of the target system. The second half of this chapter examines how to load test with the Load Test Wizard, and how to use the information Visual Studio collects to identify problems before users do.

Finally, because a single machine may not be able to generate enough load to simulate the number of users an application will have in production, you find out how to configure your environment to run *distributed load tests*. A distributed load test enables you to spread the work of creating user load across multiple machines, called *agents*. Details from each agent are collected by a controller machine, enabling you to see the overall performance of your application under stress.

WEB PERFORMANCE TESTS

Web performance tests enable verification that a web application's behavior is correct. They issue an ordered series of HTTP/HTTPS requests against a target web application, and analyze each response for expected behaviors. You can use the integrated Web Test Recorder to create a test by observing your interaction with a target website through a browser window. After the test is recorded, you can use that web performance test to consistently repeat those recorded actions against the target web application.

Web performance tests offer automatic processing of redirects, dependent requests, and hidden fields, including ViewState. In addition, coded web performance tests can be written in Visual Basic or C#, enabling you to take full advantage of the power and flexibility of these languages.

> **WARNING** *Although you can use web performance tests with ASP.NET web applications, you are not required to do so. In fact, although some features are specific to testing ASP.NET applications, any web application can be tested via a web performance test, including applications based on classic ASP, services built with WCF, or even non-Microsoft technologies.*

Later in this chapter, you see how to add your web performance tests to load tests to ensure that a web application behaves as expected when many users access it concurrently.

Web Performance Tests versus Coded UI Tests

At first glance, the capabilities of web performance tests may appear similar to those of coded user interface (UI) tests (see Chapter 24). But although some capabilities do overlap (such as record and playback, and response validation), the two types of tests are designed to achieve different testing goals and should be applied appropriately. Web performance tests should be used primarily for performance testing, and you can use them as the basis for generating load tests. You should use coded

UI tests for ensuring proper UI behavior and layout, but they cannot be easily used to conduct load testing. Conversely, whereas web performance tests can be programmed to perform simple validation of responses, coded UI tests are much better suited for this task.

Creating a Sample Web Application

Before creating a web performance test, you need a web application to test. Although you could create a web performance test by interacting with any live website such as Microsoft.com, Facebook, or YouTube, those sites will change and will likely not be the same by the time you read this chapter. Therefore, the remainder of this chapter is based on a website created with the Personal Web Site Starter Kit.

The Personal Web Site Starter Kit is a sample ASP.NET application provided by Microsoft. The Personal Web Site Starter Kit first shipped with Visual Studio 2005 and ASP.NET 2.0, but there is a version that is compatible with Visual Studio 2012 at the website for this title. If you intend to follow along with the sample provided in this chapter, first visit this book's page at www.wrox.com to download and open the Personal Web Site Starter Kit project template, following the instructions contained in the Readme.txt file.

This site will become the basis of some recorded web performance tests. Later, you will assemble these web performance tests into a load test in order to put stress on this site to determine how well it will perform when hundreds of friends and family members converge simultaneously to view your photos.

Creating Users for the Site

Before you create tests for your website, you must create a few users for the site. You do this using the Web Site Administration Tool that is included with ASP.NET applications created with Visual Studio.

From within Visual Studio, select Website ➪ ASP.NET Configuration. On the resulting page, select Security, and then select Create or Manage Roles. Enter **Administrators** as the role name and then click Add Role. Repeat this process to add a role named **Friends**.

You now have two roles into which users can be placed. Click the Security tab again, and then click Create user. You see the window shown in Figure 25-1.

Your tests assume the following users have been created:

➤ *Admin* — In the Administrator role

➤ *Sue* — In the Friends role

➤ *Daniel* — In the Friends role

➤ *Andrew* — In the Friends role

For purposes of this example, enter **@qwerty@** for the Password of each user, and any values you want for the E-mail and Security Question fields.

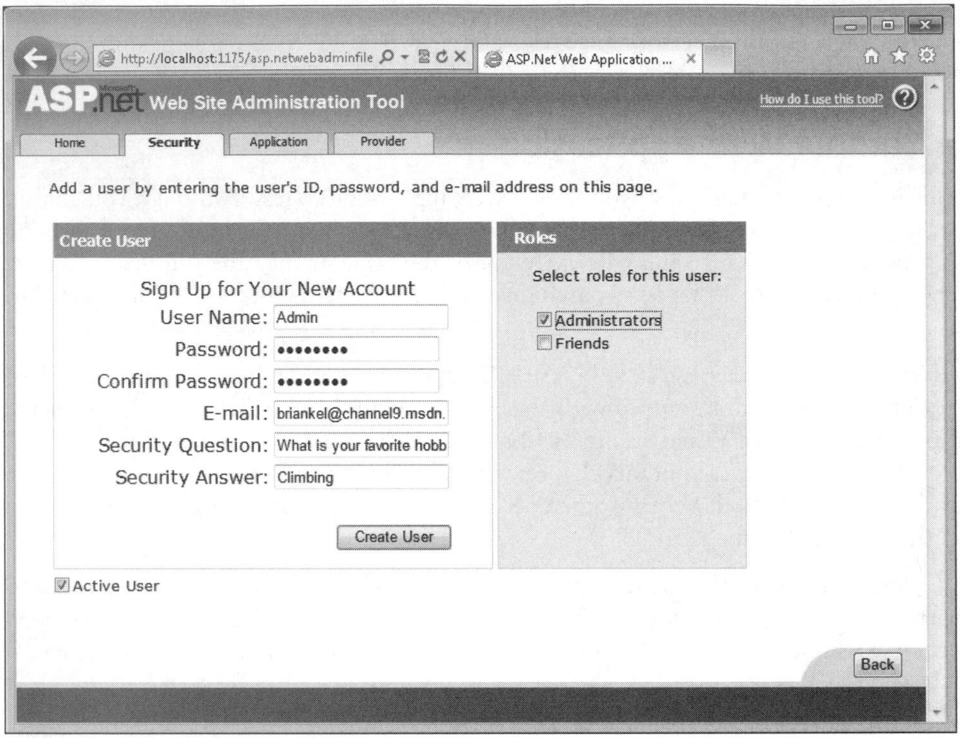

FIGURE 25-1

Configuring the Sample Application for Testing

Most of the time, when you are performance testing a web application, you generate load against a remote server or a farm of remote servers. But for purposes of this chapter, both the web application and the load you generate take place on the same machine.

Visual Studio includes a feature called the ASP.NET Development Server. This is a lightweight web server, similar to (but not the same as) IIS (Internet Information Services), that chooses a port and temporarily hosts a local ASP.NET application. The hosted application accepts only local requests and is torn down when Visual Studio exits.

The Development Server defaults to selecting a random port each time the application is started. To execute web performance tests, you'd have to manually adjust the port each time it was assigned. To address this, you have two options.

The first option is to select your ASP.NET project and choose the Properties window. Change the Use Dynamic Ports property to `false`, and then select a port number, such as 5000. You can then hard-code this port number into your local web performance tests.

The second (and more flexible) option is to use a special value, called a *context parameter*, which automatically adjusts itself to match the server, port, and directory of the target web application. You find out how to do this shortly.

Creating and Configuring Web Tests

There are three main methods for creating web performance tests. The first (and, by far, the most common) is to use the Web Test Recorder. This is the recommended way of getting started with web performance testing and is the approach discussed in this chapter. The second method is to create a test manually, using the Web Test Editor to add each step. Using this approach is time-consuming and error-prone, but may be desired for fine-tuning web performance tests. Finally, you can create a coded web performance test that specifies each action via code and offers a great deal of customization. You can also generate a coded web performance test from an existing web performance test. Coded web performance tests are described in the "Coded Web Performance Tests" section later in this chapter.

To create a new web performance test, you should create a new test project and add it to your solution. Right-click your solution and select Add ⇨ New Project. You see the Add New Project dialog, as shown in Figure 25-2. Expand either Visual C# or Visual Basic and then highlight the Test node. Choose a Web Performance and Load Test Project and name your project **SampleWebTestProject**. Click OK.

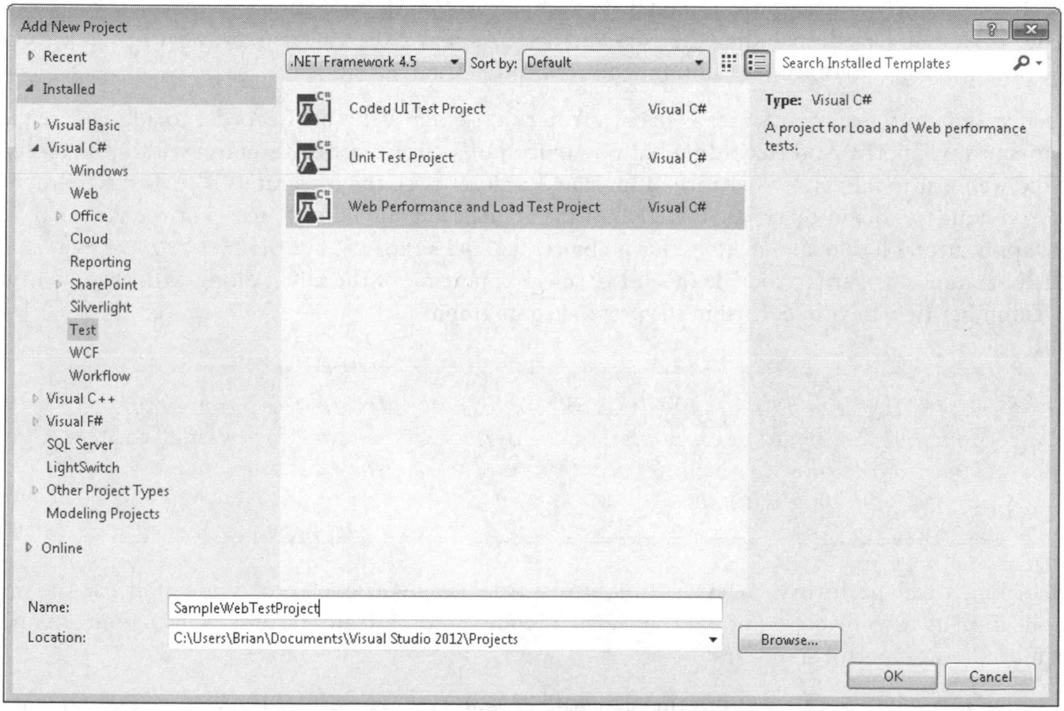

FIGURE 25-2

> **NOTE** *You can create your test project using either Visual Basic or Visual C#, but the examples in this chapter use Visual C#.*

After clicking OK, your test project is created along with your first test, named `WebTest1.webtest`. A `Local.testsettings` file is also created in your Solution Items folder, which you take a closer look at later.

> **NOTE** *After you have a test project, you can quickly create other web performance tests by right-clicking your test project and selecting Add ⇨ Web Performance Test. This automatically creates a new web performance test with default settings, named* `WebTest2.webtest` *(incrementing the number if that name already exists), and launches the Web Test Recorder within your browser.*

Recording a Web Performance Test

The ASP.NET Development Server must also be running before you can navigate to your site and record your test. If it isn't already running (as indicated by an icon in the taskbar notification area), you can start it by selecting your Personal Web Site project in Visual Studio and pressing Ctrl+F5, which builds and launches your Personal Web Site project in a new browser instance. Take note of the URL being used, including the port number. You may close this new browser instance (the Development Server continues running) and return to Visual Studio.

Open your empty test, `WebTest1.webtest`. You can use the Web Test Recorder to add web requests to this test. Click the Add Recording button (an icon of a circle within a square) within the toolbar of the web test to launch an instance of Internet Explorer with the integrated Web Test Recorder docked window. Begin by typing the URL of the application you want to test. For the Personal Web Site application on a local machine, this is something like `http://localhost:5000/SampleWeb/default.aspx`. Be sure to include the `default.aspx` portion of the URL, along with the dynamic port number (which you learned in the previous paragraph).

> **NOTE** *If you don't see the Web Test Recorder within Internet Explorer at this time then you might be encountering one of the known issues documented at Mike Taute's blog. See* `http://tinyurl.com/9okwqp` *for a list of troubleshooting steps and possible fixes.*

Recording a web performance test is straightforward. Using your web browser, simply use the web application as if you were a normal user. Visual Studio automatically records your actions, saving them to the web performance test.

First, log in as the `Admin` user with the password of `@qwerty@` you created earlier (but do not check the Remember Me Next Time option). The browser should refresh, showing a "Welcome Admin!" greeting. This is only a short test, so click Logout at the upper-right corner.

Your browser should now appear as shown in Figure 25-3. The steps have been expanded so you can see the details of the Form Post Parameters that were recorded automatically for you. You find out more about these later in this chapter, but for now, notice that the second request automatically includes `ViewState`, as well as the Username and Password form fields you used to log in.

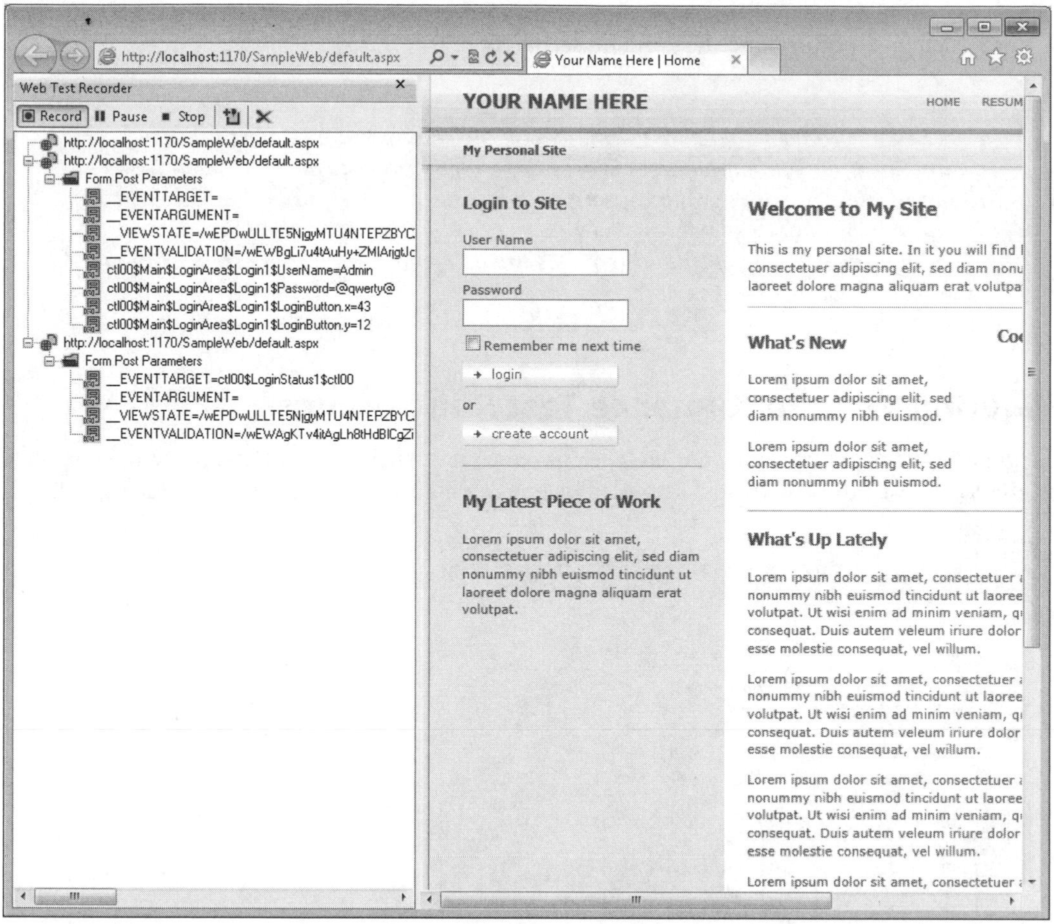

FIGURE 25-3

> **NOTE** *The Web Test Recorder captures any HTTP/HTTPS traffic sent or received by your instance of Internet Explorer as soon as it is launched. This includes your browser's home page and might include certain browser add-ins and toolbars that send data. For pristine recordings, you should set your Internet Explorer home page to be blank and disable any add-ins or toolbars that could generate excess noise.*

The Web Test Recorder provides several options that may be useful while recording. The Pause button in the upper-left corner temporarily suspends recording and timing of your interaction with the browser, enabling you to use the application or get a cup of coffee without affecting your web performance test. You read more about the importance of timing of your web performance test later, as this can affect playback conditions. Click the X button if you want to clear your recorded list. The other button, Add a Comment, enables you to add documentation to your web performance test, perhaps at a complex step. These comments are very useful when you convert a web performance test to a coded web performance test, as you see later.

> **NOTE** *Calls to web pages are normally composed of a main request followed by a number of dependent requests. These dependent requests are sent separately to obtain items such as graphics, script sources, and stylesheets. The Web Test Recorder does not display these dependent requests explicitly while recording. You see later that all dependent requests are determined and processed automatically when the Web test is run.*

Configuring Web Performance Test Run Settings

When you're finished recording your web performance test, click Stop and the browser closes to display the Web Test Editor with your recorded web performance test, as shown in Figure 25-4.

FIGURE 25-4

The Web Test Editor displays your test as a series of requests to be sent to the web application. The first request is the initial page being loaded. The second request is the login request being sent. And the third request is the logout request.

Frequently, you'll need to use the Web Test Editor to change settings or add features to the tests you record. This may include adding validation, extracting data from web responses, and reading data from a source. These topics are covered later in this chapter, but for now, you use this test as recorded.

Parameterizing the Web Server

You may recall from the earlier section "Configuring the Sample Application for Testing," that using the ASP.NET Development Server, is convenient, but it poses a slight challenge because the port it uses is selected randomly with each run. Although you could set your website to use a static port, there is a better solution.

Using the Web Test Editor, click the Parameterize Web Servers toolbar button. (You can hover your mouse cursor over each icon to see the name of each command.) You could also right-click the web test name and choose Parameterize Web Servers. In the resulting dialog, click the Change button. You see the Change Web Server dialog, shown in Figure 25-5.

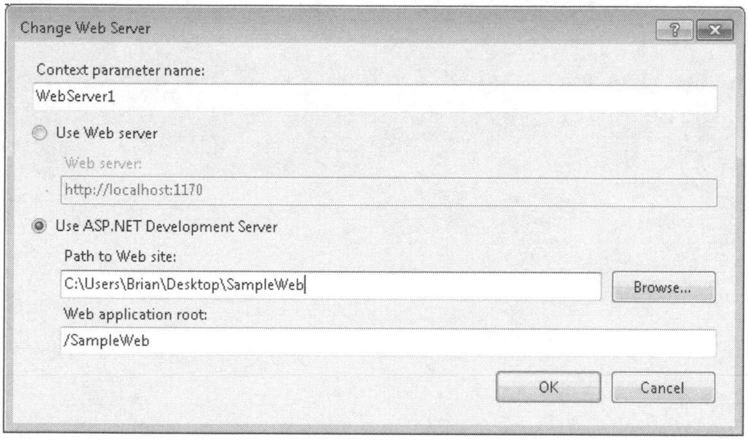

FIGURE 25-5

Use this dialog to configure your web performance test to target a standard web application service (such as IIS), or to use the ASP.NET Development Server. In this example, you are using the Development Server, so choose that option and browse to the path where you extracted the Personal Web Site project at the beginning of this chapter. For "Web application root" type **/SampleWeb**. Click OK twice.

Notice the Web Test Editor has automatically updated all request entries, replacing the static Web address with a reference to this context parameter, using the syntax {{WebServer1}}. In addition, the context parameter WebServer1 has been added at the bottom of the web performance test under Context Parameters. (You see later in this chapter the effect of this on the sample Web performance test in Figure 25-10.)

> **NOTE** *Context parameters (which are named variables that are available to each step in a web performance test) are described in the section "Extraction Rules and Context Parameters," later in this chapter.*

Now, when you run the web performance test, Visual Studio automatically finds and connects to the address and dynamic port being used by the ASP.NET Development Server. If the ASP.NET Development Server is not started, it launches automatically. If you have more than one target server or application, you can repeat this process as many times as necessary, creating additional context parameters.

Test Settings

Before you run a web performance test, you may want to review the settings that will be used for the test's runs. First select an active test settings file by clicking on Test ⇨ Test Settings ⇨ Select Test Settings File. Browse to the `local.testsettings` file that was created when you added your test project to this solution. Now double-click this file within Solution Explorer to open it in the editor. Select the Web Test entry from the list on the left side and you see the options shown in Figure 25-6.

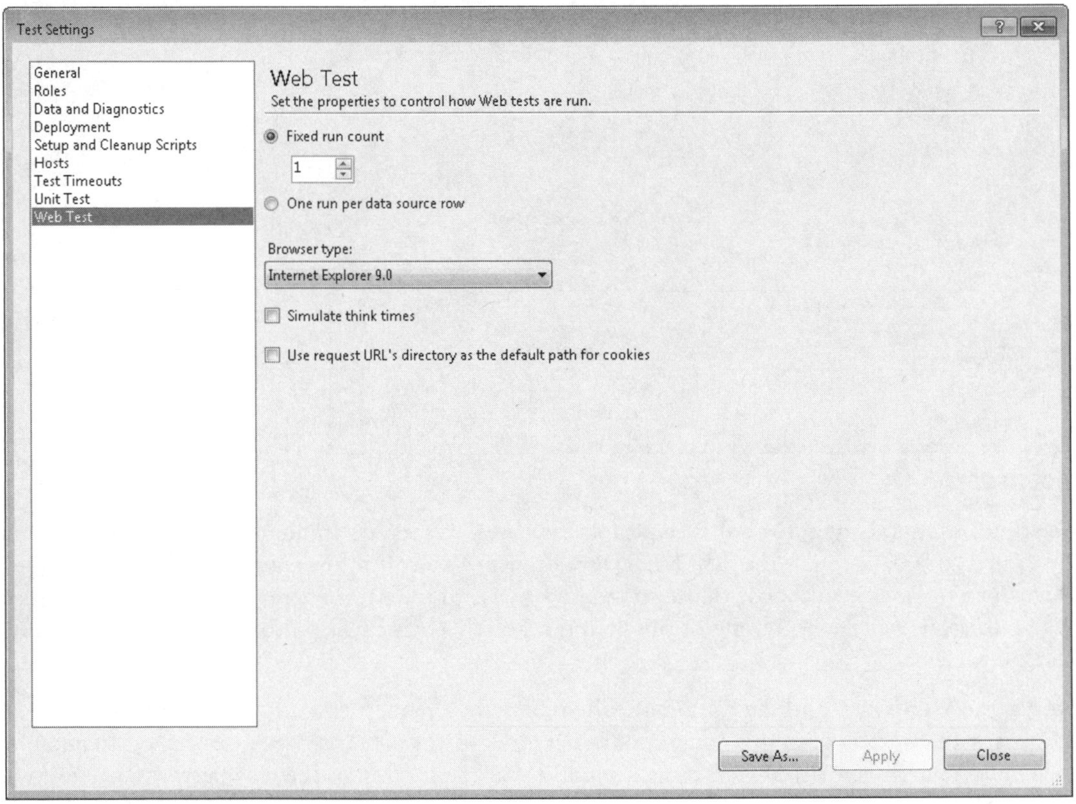

FIGURE 25-6

The Fixed Run Count option enables you to specify the specific number of times your web performance tests will be executed when included in a test run. Running your test a few times (for example, three to ten times) can help eliminate errant performance timings caused by system issues on the client or server and can help you derive a better estimate for how your website is actually performing. Note that you should not enter a large number here to simulate load through your web performance test. Instead, you should create a load test (discussed later in this chapter) referencing your web performance test. Also, if you assign a data source to your web performance test, you may instead choose to run the web performance test one time per entry in the selected data source. Data-driven web performance tests are examined in detail later in this chapter.

The Browser Type setting enables you to simulate using one of a number of browsers as your web performance test's client. This automatically sets the user agent field for requests sent to the web performance test to simulate the selected browser. By default, this is Internet Explorer, but you may select other browsers (such as Chrome or a smartphone).

> **NOTE** *Changing the browser type does not help you determine if your web application will render as desired in a given browser type because web performance tests only examine HTTP/HTTPS responses and not the actual rendering of pages. Changing the browser type is only important if the web application being tested is configured to respond differently based on the user agent sent by the requesting client. For example, a web application may send a more lightweight user interface to a mobile device than it would to a desktop computer.*

> **NOTE** *If you want to test more than one browser type, you need to run your web performance test multiple times, selecting a different browser each time. However, you can also add your web performance test to a load test and choose your desired browser distributions. This causes each selected type to be simulated automatically. You see how to do this later in this chapter in the section "Load Tests."*

The Simulate Think Times option enables the use of delays in your web performance test to simulate the normal time taken by users to read content, modify values, and decide on actions. When you recorded your web performance test, the time it took for you to submit each request was recorded as the "think time" property of each step. If you turn this option on, that same delay occurs between the requests sent by the web performance test to the web application. Think times are disabled by default, causing all requests to be sent as quickly as possible to the web server, resulting in a faster test. Later in this chapter, you see that think times serve an important role in load tests.

The final option in this dialog determines how cookies sent as part of a request should be retained and used for subsequent requests. Visual Studio also enables you to emulate different network speeds for your tests. From within Test Settings, select Data and Diagnostics on the left. Enable the Network Emulation adapter and click Configure. From here you can select a variety of network speeds (such as a dial-up 56K connection) to examine the effect that slower connection speeds have on your web application.

> **NOTE** *Note that these settings affect every run of this web performance test, but are ignored when performing a load test. Later in this chapter, you discover that load tests have their own mechanism for configuring settings such as browser type, network speed, and the number of times a test should be run.*

> **NOTE** *For more information on how test settings affect your web performance tests, see* `http://aka.ms/AutomatedTestSettings.`

Running a Web Performance Test

To run a web performance test, click the Run button (the leftmost button on the Web Test Editor toolbar, as shown in Figure 25-4). The Test Results window (View ➪ Other Windows ➪ Test Results) displays the result of your test run.

Observing Test Execution and Results

When the test run is started, a window specific to that web performance test execution displays. If you are executing your web performance test from the Web Test Editor window, you must click the Run button in this window to launch the test. The results are automatically displayed, as shown in Figure 25-7. You can also open the test results for a specific test by double-clicking the web performance test from within the Test Results window.

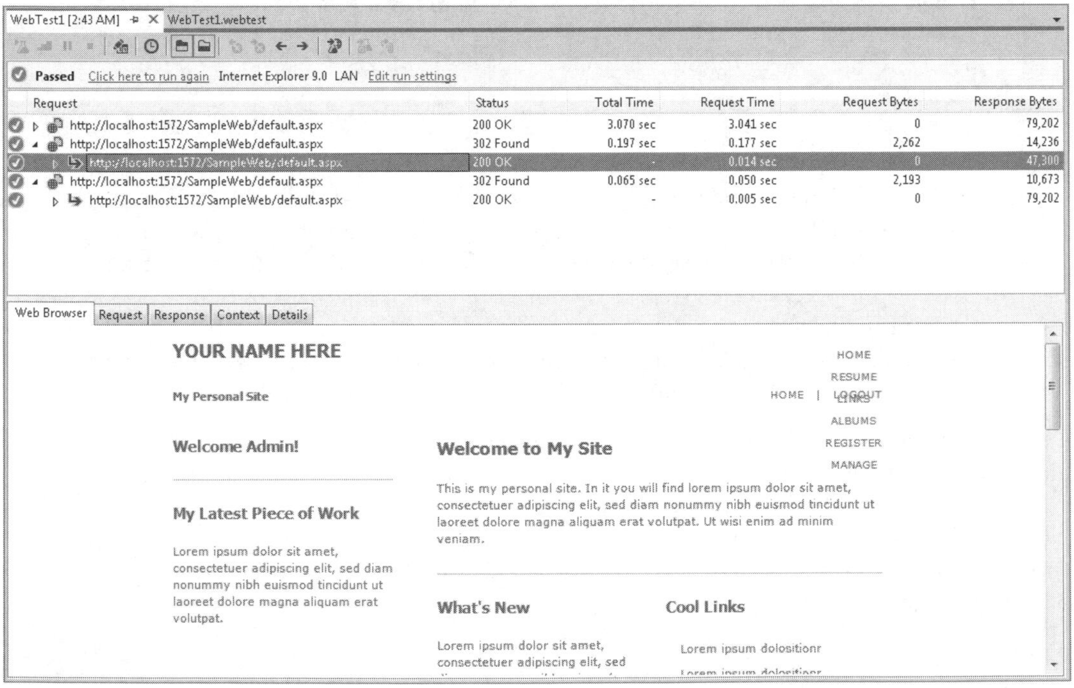

FIGURE 25-7

You may also choose to step through the web performance test, one request at a time, by choosing Run Test (Pause Before Starting), which is available via the dropdown arrow attached to the Run button.

This window displays the results of all interactions with the web application. A toolbar, the overall test status, and two hyperlinked options are shown at the top. The first option reruns the web performance test and the second option enables you to change the browser type via the Web Test Run Settings dialog.

> **NOTE** *Changes made in this dialog only affect the next run of the web performance test and are not saved for later runs. To make permanent changes, modify the test settings by double-clicking your* `.testsettings` *file from within Solution Explorer.*

Below that, each of the requests sent to the application are shown. You can expand each top-level request to see its dependent requests. These are automatically handled by the web performance test system and can include calls to retrieve graphics, script sources, cascading stylesheets, and more.

Each item in this list shows the request target, as well as the response's status, time, and size. A green checkmark indicates a successful request and response, whereas a red icon indicates failure.

If your test encountered any errors, you can click the Find Previous Error and Find Next Error icons in the toolbar to navigate through the errors in your test run.

The lower half of the window enables you to see full details for each request. The first tab, Web Browser, shows you the rendered version of the response. As you can see in Figure 25-7, the response includes "Welcome Admin!" text, indicating that you successfully logged in as the Admin account.

The Request tab shows the details of what was supplied to the web application, including all headers and any request body, such as might be present when an HTTP POST is made.

Similarly, the Response tab shows all headers and the body of the response sent back from the web application. Unlike the Web Browser tab, this detail is shown textually, even when binary data (such as an image) is returned.

The Context tab lists all of the context parameters and their values at the time of the selected request. Finally, the Details tab shows the status of any assigned validation and extraction rules. This tab also shows details about any exception thrown during that request. Context parameters and rules are described later in this chapter.

Editing a Web Performance Test

You'll often find that a recorded web performance test is not sufficient to fully test your application's functionality. You can use the Web Test Editor, as shown in Figure 25-4, to further customize a web performance test, adding comments, extraction rules, data sources, and other properties.

> **WARNING** *It is recommended that you run a recorded web performance test once before attempting to edit it. This verifies that the test was recorded correctly. If you don't do this, you might not know whether a test is failing because it wasn't recorded correctly or because you introduced a bug through changes in the Web Test Editor.*

Setting Request Properties

From within the Web Test Editor, right-click a request and choose Properties. If the Properties window is already displayed, simply selecting a request shows its properties. You can modify settings such as cache control, target URL, and whether the request automatically follows redirects.

The Properties window also offers a chance to modify the think time of each request. For example, perhaps a co-worker dropped by with a question while you were recording your web performance test and you forgot to pause the recording. Use the Think Time property to adjust the delay to a more realistic value.

Adding Comments

Comments are useful for identifying the actions of a particular section of a web performance test. In addition, when converting your web performance test to a coded web performance test, your comments are preserved in code.

Because the requests in this example refer to the same page, it is helpful to add comments to help distinguish them. Add a comment by right-clicking the first request and choosing Insert Comment. Enter **Initial site request**. Insert a comment for the second request as **Login** and for the third request as **Logout**.

Adding Transactions

A *transaction* is used to monitor a group of logically connected steps in your web performance test. A transaction can be tracked as a unit, giving details such as number of times invoked, request time, and total elapsed time.

> **NOTE** *Don't confuse web performance test transactions with database transactions. Although both are used for grouping actions, database transactions offer additional features beyond those of web performance test transactions.*

To create a transaction, right-click a request and select Insert Transaction. You are prompted to name the transaction and to select the start and end request from dropdown lists.

Transactions are primarily used when running web performance tests under load with a load test. Read more about viewing transaction details in the section "Viewing and Interpreting Load Test Results," later in this chapter.

Extraction Rules and Context Parameters

Extraction rules are used to retrieve specific data from a web response. This data is stored in *context parameters*, which live for the duration of the web performance test. Context parameters can be read from and written to by any request in a web performance test. For example, you could use an extraction rule to retrieve an order confirmation number, storing that in a context parameter. Then, subsequent steps in the test could access that order number, using it for verification or supplying it with later web requests.

> **NOTE** *Context parameters are similar in concept to the* `HttpContext.Items` *collection from ASP.NET. In both cases, you can add names and values that can be accessed by any subsequent step. Whereas* `HttpContext.Items` *entries are valid for the duration of a single page request, web performance test context parameters are accessible through a single web performance test run.*

Referring to Figure 25-4, notice that the first request has an Extract Hidden Fields entry under Extraction Rules. This was added automatically when you recorded the web performance test because the system recognized hidden fields in the first form you accessed. Those hidden fields are now available to subsequent requests via context parameters.

A number of context parameters are set automatically when you run a web performance test, including the following:

➤ $TestDir — The working directory of the web performance test.

➤ $WebTestIteration — The current run number. For example, this would be useful if you selected more than one run in the Test Settings and needed to differentiate the test runs.

➤ $ControllerName *and* $AgentName — Machine identifiers used when remotely executing web performance tests. You read more about this topic later in this chapter.

To add an extraction rule to a web performance test, right-click any request and select Add Extraction Rule. The dialog shown in Figure 25-8 displays.

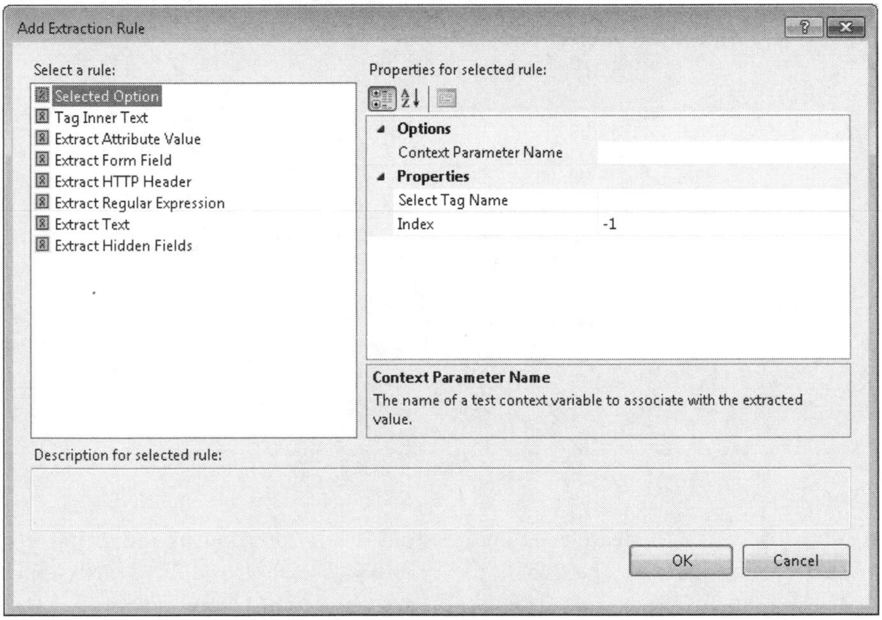

FIGURE 25-8

The built-in extraction rules can be used to extract any attribute, HTTP header, or response text. Use Extract Regular Expression to retrieve data that matches the supplied expression. Use Extract Hidden Fields to easily find and return a value contained in a hidden form field of a response. Extracted values are stored in context parameters whose names you define in the properties of each rule.

You can add your own custom extraction rules by creating classes that derive from the ExtractionRule class found in the Microsoft.VisualStudio.TestTools.WebTesting namespace.

Validation Rules

Generally, checking for valid web application behavior involves more than just getting a response from the server. You must ensure that the content and behavior of that response is correct. Validation rules offer a way to verify that those requirements are met. For example, you may want to verify that specific text appears on a page after an action, such as adding an item to a shopping cart. Validation rules are attached to a specific request, and cause that request to show as failed if the requirement is not satisfied.

Add a validation rule to the test to ensure that the welcome message is displayed after you log in. Right-click the second request and choose Add Validation Rule. You see the dialog shown in Figure 25-9.

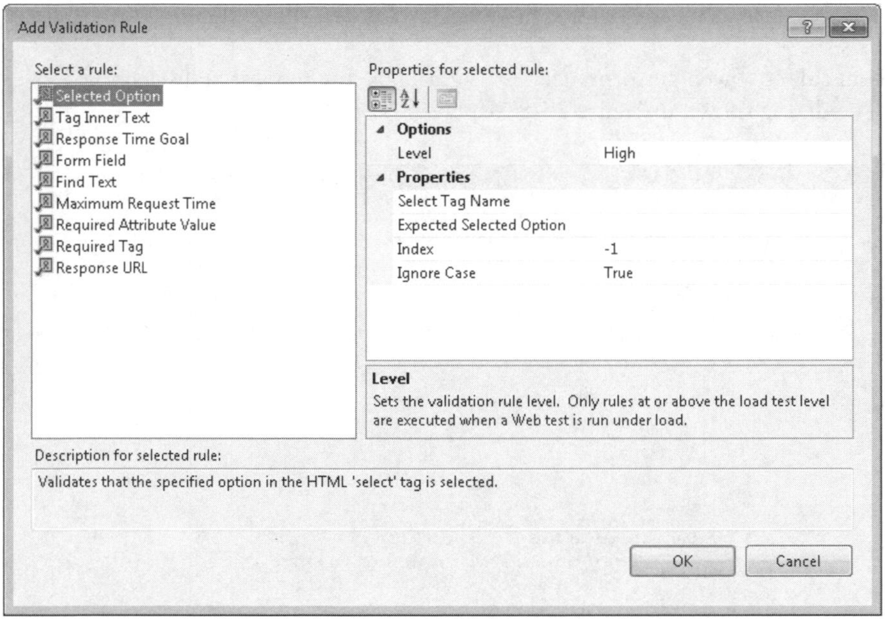

FIGURE 25-9

As with extraction rules, you can also create your own custom validation rules by inheriting from the base `ValidationRule` class, found in the `WebTestFramework` assembly, and have them appear in this dialog. Choose the Find Text rule and set the Find Text value to **Welcome Admin.** Set Ignore Case to **false**, and Pass If Text Found to **true**. This rule searches the web application's response for a case-sensitive match on that text and passes if found. Click OK and the web performance test should appear as shown in Figure 25-10.

Verify that this works by running or stepping through the web performance test. You should see that this test actually does not work as expected. You can use the details from the web performance test's results to find out why.

View the Details tab for the second request. You'll see that the Find Text validation rule failed to find a match. Notice that the text of the response on the Response tab shows that instead of "Welcome Admin" being returned, there is a tab instead of a space between the words. You need to modify the validation rule to match this text.

FIGURE 25-10

To fix this, you could simply replace the space in the Find Text parameter with a tab. However, you could use a regular expression as well. First, change the Find Text parameter to `Welcome\s+Admin`. This indicates you expect any whitespace characters between the words, not just a space character. To enable that property to behave as a regular expression, set the Use Regular Expression parameter to `true`.

Save your web performance test and rerun it. The web performance test should now pass.

> **NOTE** *Bear in mind that the validation logic available within web performance tests is not as sophisticated as that of coded UI tests (see Chapter 24). With coded UI tests, it is easier to confirm that a given string appears in the right location of a web page, whereas with web performance test validation rules, you are generally just checking to confirm that the string appears somewhere in the response.*

The functionality that extraction and validation rules provide comes at the expense of performance. If you want to call your web performance test from a load test, you might want to simulate more load at the expense of ignoring a number of extraction or validation rules.

Each rule has an associated property called Level. This can be set to Low, Medium, or High. When you create a load test, you can similarly specify a validation level of Low, Medium, or High. This setting specifies the maximum level of rule that is executed when the load test runs. For example, a validation level of Medium runs rules with a level of Low or Medium, but excludes rules marked as High.

Data-Driven Web Performance Tests

You can satisfy many testing scenarios using the techniques described so far, but you can go beyond those techniques to easily create data-driven web performance tests. A *data-driven web performance test* connects to a data source and retrieves a set of data. Pieces of that data can be used in place of static settings for each request.

For example, in your web performance test, you may want to ensure that the login and logout processes work equally well for all of the configured users. You find out how to do this next.

Configuring a Data Source

You can configure your web performance test to connect to a database (for example, SQL Server or Oracle), a comma-separated value (CSV) file, or an XML file. For this example, a CSV file will suffice. Using Notepad, create a new file and insert the following data:

```
Username,Password
Admin,@qwerty@
Sue,@qwerty@
Daniel,@qwerty@
Andrew,@qwerty@
```

Save this file as `Credentials.csv`.

The next step in creating a data-driven web performance test is to specify your data source. Using the Web Test Editor, you can either right-click the top node of your web performance test and select Add Data Source, or click the Add Data Source button on the toolbar.

In the New Test Data Source Wizard, select CSV File and click Next. Browse to the `Credentials .csv` file you just created and click Next. You see a preview of the data contained in this file. Note that the first row of your file was converted to the appropriate column headers for your data table. Click Finish. You are prompted to make the CSV file a part of your test project. Click Yes to continue. When the data source is added, you see it at the bottom of your web performance test in the Web Test Editor, and the `Credentials.csv` file is added to the Solution Explorer.

Expand the data source to see that there is a new table named `Credentials` in your Web Test Editor. Click this table and view the Properties window. Notice that one of the settings is Access Method. This has three valid settings:

➤ *Sequential* — Reads each record in first-to-last order from the source. This loops back to the first record and continues reading if the test uses more iterations than the source has records.

➤ *Random* — Reads each record randomly from the source and, like sequential access, continues reading as long as necessary.

➤ *Unique* — Reads each record in first-to-last order, but does so only once.

Use this setting to determine how the data source feeds rows to the web performance test. For this test, choose Sequential.

Binding to a Source

Several types of values can be bound to a data source, including form post and URL query parameters' names and values, HTTP headers, and file upload field names. Expand the second request in the Web Test Editor (which you earlier labeled as `Login`), expand Form Post Parameters, click the parameter for UserName, and view the Properties window. Click the down arrow that appears in the Value box.

You see the data-binding selector, as shown in Figure 25-11.

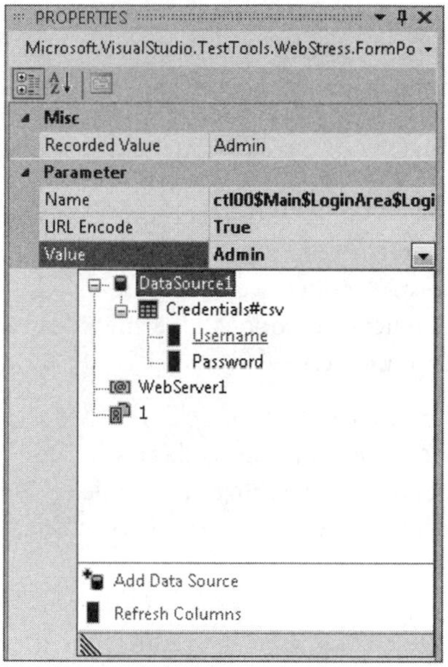

FIGURE 25-11

Expand your data source, choose the `Credentials` table, and then click the `Username` column to bind to the value of this parameter. A database icon appears in that property, indicating that it is a bound value. You can select the Unbind entry to remove any established data binding. Repeat this process for the `Password` parameter.

> **NOTE** *When binding to a database you may choose to bind to values from either a table or a view. Binding to the results of stored procedures is not supported for web performance tests.*

Before you run your web performance test, you must indicate that you want to run the test one time per row of data in the data source. Refer to the earlier section "Test Settings" and Figure 25-6. In the Web Tests section of your test settings, choose the One Run per Data Source Row option.

The next time you run your web performance test, it automatically reads from the target data source, supplying the bound fields with data. The test repeats one time for each row of data in the source. Your test should now fail, however, because you are still looking for the text "Welcome Admin" to appear after the login request is sent.

To fix this, you must modify your validation rule to look for welcome text corresponding to the user being authenticated. Select the Find Text validation rule and view the Properties window. Change the Find Text value to `Welcome\s+{{DataSource1.Credentials#csv.Username}}` and rerun your test. Your test should now pass again.

Coded Web Performance Tests

As flexible as web performance tests are, there may be times when you need more control over the actions that are taken. Web performance tests are stored as XML files with `.webtest` extensions. Visual Studio uses this XML to generate the code that is executed when the web performance test is run. You can tap into this process by creating a coded web performance test, enabling you to execute a test from code instead of from XML.

Coded web performance tests enable you to perform actions not possible with a standard web performance test. For example, you can perform branching based on the responses received during a web performance test or based on the values of a data-bound test. A coded web performance test is limited only by your ability to write code. The language of the generated code is determined by the language of the test project that contains the source web performance test.

A coded web performance test is a class that inherits from either a base `WebTest` class for C# tests, or from a `ThreadedWebTest` base for Visual Basic tests. You can find these classes in the `Microsoft.VisualStudio.TestTools.WebTesting` namespace. All the features available to Web performance tests that you create via the IDE are implemented in classes and methods contained in that namespace.

> **NOTE** *Although you always have the option to create a coded web performance test by hand, the most common (and the recommended) method is to generate a coded web performance test from a web performance test that was recorded with the Web Test Recorder and then customize the code as needed.*

You should familiarize yourself with coded web performance tests by creating a number of different sample web performance tests through the IDE and generating coded web performance tests from them to learn how various web performance test actions are accomplished with code.

Using the example web performance test, click the Generate Code button on the Web Test Editor toolbar. You are prompted to name the generated file. Open the generated file and review the generated code.

Here is a segment of the C# code that was generated from the example web performance test (some calls have been removed for simplicity):

```csharp
public override IEnumerator<WebTestRequest> GetRequestEnumerator()
{
    ...
    // Initial site request
    ...

    yield return request1;
    ...

    // Login
    ...
    WebTestRequest request2 = new
      WebTestRequest((this.Context["WebServer1"].ToString() +
```

```
        "/SampleWeb/default.aspx"));
    ...

    Request2.ThinkTime = 14;
    Request2.Method = "POST";
    FormPostHttpBody request2Body = new FormPostHttpBody();
    ...
    Request2Body.FormPostParameters.Add(
      "ctl00$Main$LoginArea$Login1$UserName",
      this.Context["DataSource1.Credentials#csv.Username"].ToString());

    request2Body.FormPostParameters.Add(
      "ctl00$Main$LoginArea$Login1$Password",
      this.Context["DataSource1.Credentials#csv.Password"].ToString());
    ...

    if ((this.Context.ValidationLevel >=
      Microsoft.VisualStudio.TestTools.WebTesting.ValidationLevel.High))
    {
     ValidationRuleFindText validationRule3 = new ValidationRuleFindText();
     validationRule3.FindText = ("Welcome\\s+" +
       this.Context["DataSource1.Credentials#csv.Username"].ToString());
       validationRule3.IgnoreCase = false;
       validationRule3.UseRegularExpression = true;
       validationRule3.PassIfTextFound = true;
    }
    ...
    yield return request2;
    ...


    // Logout
    ...
    WebTestRequest request3 = new
      WebTestRequest((this.Context["WebServer1"].ToString() +
    "/SampleWeb/default.aspx"));
    Request3.Method = "POST";
    ...
    yield return request3;
    ...
  }
```

This GetRequestEnumerator method uses the yield statement to provide WebTestRequest instances, one per HTTP request, back to the web test system.

Notice that the methods and properties are very similar to what you have already seen when creating and editing web performance tests in the Web Test Editor. Also notice that the comments you added in the Web Test Editor appear as comments in the code, making it easy to identify where each request begins.

Taking a closer look, you see that the Find Text validation rule you added earlier is now specified with code. First, the code checks the ValidationLevel context parameter to verify that you're including rules marked with a level of High. If so, the ValidationRuleFindText class is instantiated and the parameters you specified in the IDE are now set as properties of that instance. Finally, the instance's `Validate` method is registered with the request's `ValidateResponse` event, ensuring that the validator executes at the appropriate time.

You can make any changes you want and simply save the code file and rebuild. Your coded web performance test automatically appears alongside your other tests in Test Manager and Test View.

> **NOTE** *Another advantage of coded web performance tests is protocol support. Although normal web performance tests can support both HTTP and HTTPS, they cannot use alternative protocols. A coded web performance test can be used for other protocols, such as FTP.*

> **NOTE** *For detailed descriptions of the classes and members available to you in the WebTesting namespace, see* `http://aka.ms/WTNamespace`.

LOAD TESTS

Load tests are used to verify that your application performs as expected while under the stress of multiple concurrent users. You configure the levels and types of load you want to simulate and then execute the load test. A series of requests is generated against the target application, and Visual Studio monitors the system under test to determine how well it performs.

Load testing is most commonly used with web performance tests to conduct smoke, load, and stress testing of web applications. However, you are certainly not limited to this. Load tests are essentially lists of pointers to other tests, and they can include any other test type except for manual tests.

> **NOTE** *You can use load tests with coded UI tests, but doing so requires that you configure a physical or virtual machine with a test agent for each concurrent user you want to simulate. This is because a coded UI test assumes that it has exclusive "virtual" control over the mouse and keyboard for a machine. You can find details on using coded UI tests with load tests at* `http://aka.ms/CUITLoad`.

> **NOTE** *You cannot use load tests with third-party test adapters, such as NUnit or xUnit.net.*

For example, you could create a load test that includes a suite of unit tests. You could stress-test layers of business logic and database access code to determine how that code will behave when many users are accessing it concurrently, regardless of which application uses those layers.

As another example, you can use ordered tests to group a number of tests and define a specific order in which they will run. Because tests added to a load test are executed in a randomly selected order, you may find it useful to first group them with an ordered test, and then include that ordered test in the load test. You can find more information on ordered tests in Chapter 22.

Creating and Configuring Load Tests

This section describes how to create a load test using the New Load Test Wizard. You examine many options that you can use to customize the behavior of your load tests.

As described earlier in this chapter in the section "Web Performance Tests," you use a test project to contain your tests, and, like Web performance tests, load tests are placed in test projects. Right-click your existing test project and choose Add ➪ Load Test.

When you add a new load test, the New Load Test Wizard starts. This wizard guides you through the many configuration options available for a load test.

Scenarios and Think Times

A load test is composed of one or more *scenarios*. A scenario is a grouping of web performance and/or unit tests, along with a variety of preferences for user, browser, network, and other settings. Scenarios are used to group similar tests or usage environments. For example, you might want to create a scenario for simulating the creation and submission of an expense report by your employees, whereby your users have LAN connectivity and all use Internet Explorer 9.

When the New Load Test Wizard is launched, the first screen describes the load test creation process. Click Next and you are prompted to assign a name to your load test's first scenario, as shown in Figure 25-12.

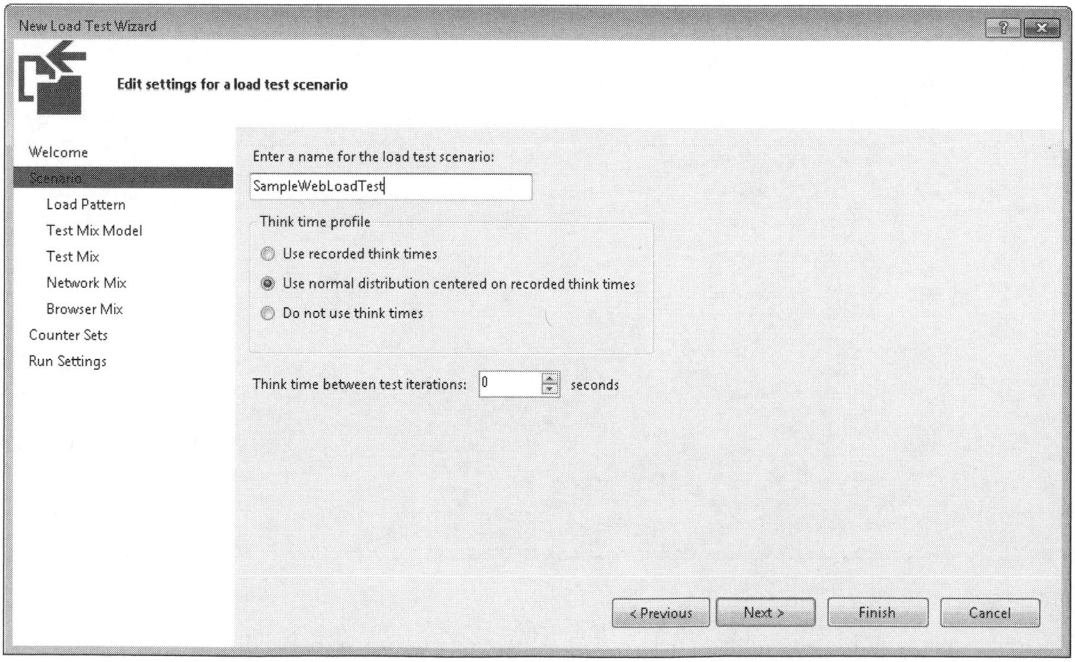

FIGURE 25-12

Note that the New Load Test Wizard only supports the creation of a single scenario in your load test, but you can easily add more scenarios with the Load Test Editor after you complete the wizard.

The second option on this page is to configure think times. You may recall from the earlier section "Web Performance Tests" that think time is a delay between each request, which can be used to approximate how long a user will pause to read, consider options, and enter data on a particular page. These times are stored with each of a web performance test's requests and can be hand-edited by examining the properties for each web request. The think time profile panel enables you to turn these off or on.

If you enable think times, you can either use them as is, or apply a normal distribution that is centered around your recorded think times as a mean. The normal distribution is generally recommended if you want to simulate the most realistic user load, based on what you expect the average user to do. You can also configure the think time between test iterations to model a user who pauses after completing a task before moving to the next task.

You can click on any step on the left side to jump to that page of the wizard or click Next to navigate through sequential pages.

Load Patterns

The next step is to define the load pattern for the scenario. The Load Pattern, shown in Figure 25-13, enables simulation of different types of user load.

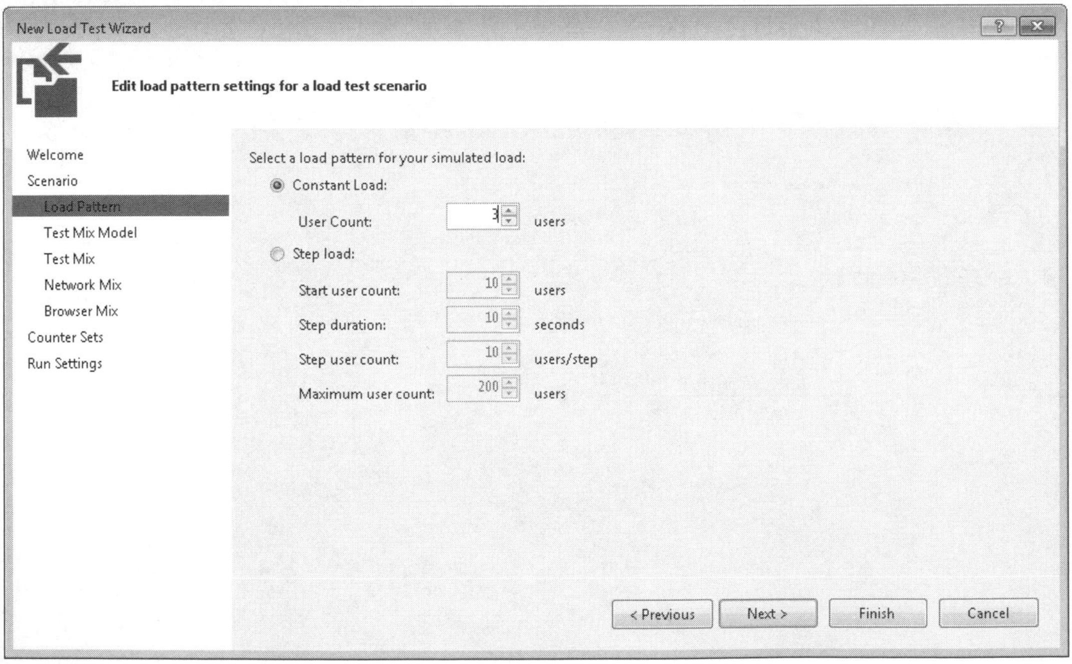

FIGURE 25-13

In the wizard, you have two load pattern options: Constant and Step. A *constant load* enables you to define a number of users that will remain unchanged throughout the duration of the test. Use a constant load to analyze the performance of your application under a steady load of users. For example, you may specify a baseline test with 100 users. This load test could be executed prior to release to ensure that your established performance criteria remain satisfied.

A *step load* defines a starting and maximum user count. You also assign a step duration and a step user count. Every time the number of seconds specified in your step duration elapses, the number of users is incremented by the step count, unless the maximum number of users has been reached. Step loads are very useful for stress-testing your application, finding the maximum number of users your application will support before serious issues arise.

> **NOTE** *A third type of load profile pattern, called "Goal Based," is available only through the Load Test Editor. See the section "Editing Load Tests," later in this chapter, for more details.*

You should begin with a load test that has a small, constant user load and a relatively short execution time. After you have verified that the load test is configured and working correctly, increase the load and duration as you require.

Test Mix Model

The Test Mix Model (shown in Figure 25-14) determines the frequency at which tests within your load test are selected from among other tests within your load test. The test mix model provides several options for realistically modeling user load. The options for test mix model are as follows:

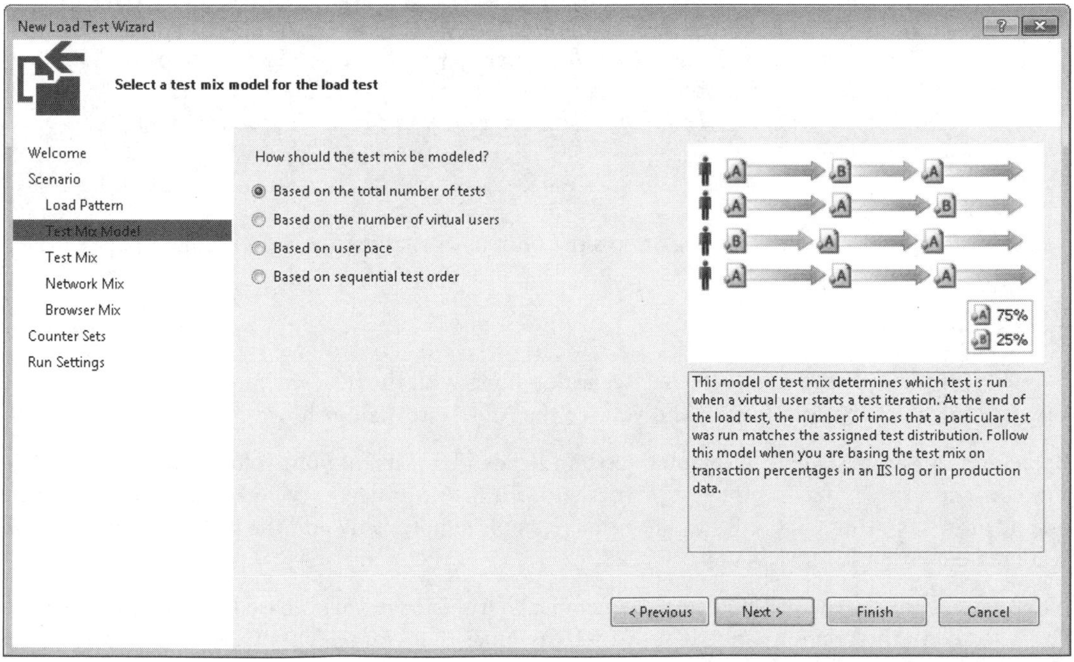

FIGURE 25-14

➤ *Based on the total number of tests* — This model enables you to assign a percentage to each test that dictates how many times it should be run. Each virtual user runs each test corresponding to the percentage assigned to that test. An example of where this might be useful is if you know that the average visitor views three photos on your website for every one comment that they leave on a photo. To model that scenario, you would create a test for viewing photos and a test for leaving comments, and assign them percentages of 75 percent and 25 percent, respectively.

➤ *Based on the number of virtual users* — This model enables you to assign a percentage of virtual users who should run each test. This model might be useful if you know that, at any given time, 80 percent of your visitors are browsing the catalog of your e-commerce website, 5 percent are registering for new accounts, and 15 percent are checking out.

➤ *Based on user pace* — This model executes each test a specified number of times per virtual-user per hour. An example of a scenario where this might be useful is if you know that the average user checks e-mail five times per hour, and looks at a stock portfolio once an hour. When using this test mix model, the think time between iterations value from the Scenario page of the wizard is ignored.

➤ *Based on sequential test order* — If you know that your users generally perform steps in a specific order (for example, logging in, then finding an item to purchase, then checking out) you can use this test mix model to simulate a sequential test behavior for all virtual users. This option is functionally equivalent to structuring your tests as ordered tests.

> **NOTE** *Don't worry if you are having a difficult time choosing a test mix model right now. You can always experiment with different test mix models later as you learn more about the expected behavior of your application's users. You may also discover that your application exhibits different usage patterns at different times of the day, during marketing promotions, or during some other seasonality.*

The option you select on this dialog affects the options available to you on the next page of the wizard.

Test Mix

Now, select the tests to include in your scenario, along with the relative frequency with which they should run. Click the Add button and you see the Add Tests dialog shown in Figure 25-15.

By default, all the tests (except manual tests and coded UI tests) in your solution are displayed. You can constrain these to a specific test project with the Select project to view tests" dropdown. Select one or more tests and click OK. To keep this example simple, only add the web performance test you created earlier in this chapter.

Next, you return to the test mix step. Remember that this page varies based on the test mix model you selected in the previous step. Figure 25-16 assumes that you selected Based on the Total Number of Tests as your test mix model.

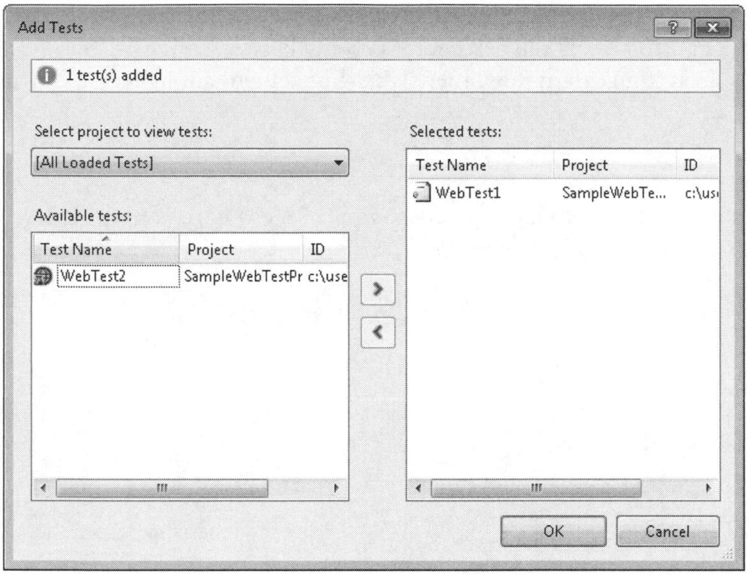

FIGURE 25-15

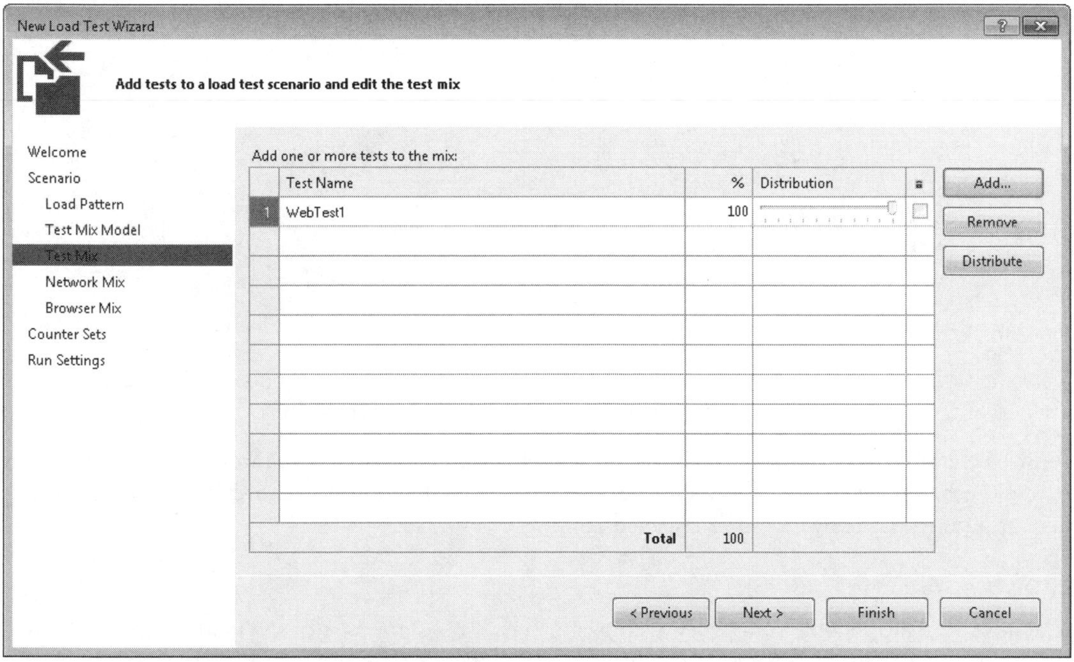

FIGURE 25-16

Use the sliders to assign the chance (in percentage) that a virtual user will select that test to execute. You may also type a number directly into the numeric fields. Use the lock checkbox in the far-right column to freeze tests at a certain number, and use the sliders to adjust the remaining "unlocked" test distributions. The Distribute button resets the percentages evenly between all tests. But, because you only have a single test in your test mix right now, there is nothing else to configure on this page, and the slider is disabled.

Network Mix

You can specify the kinds of network connectivity you expect your users to have (such as LAN, Cable-DSL, and Dial-up). This step is shown in Figure 25-17.

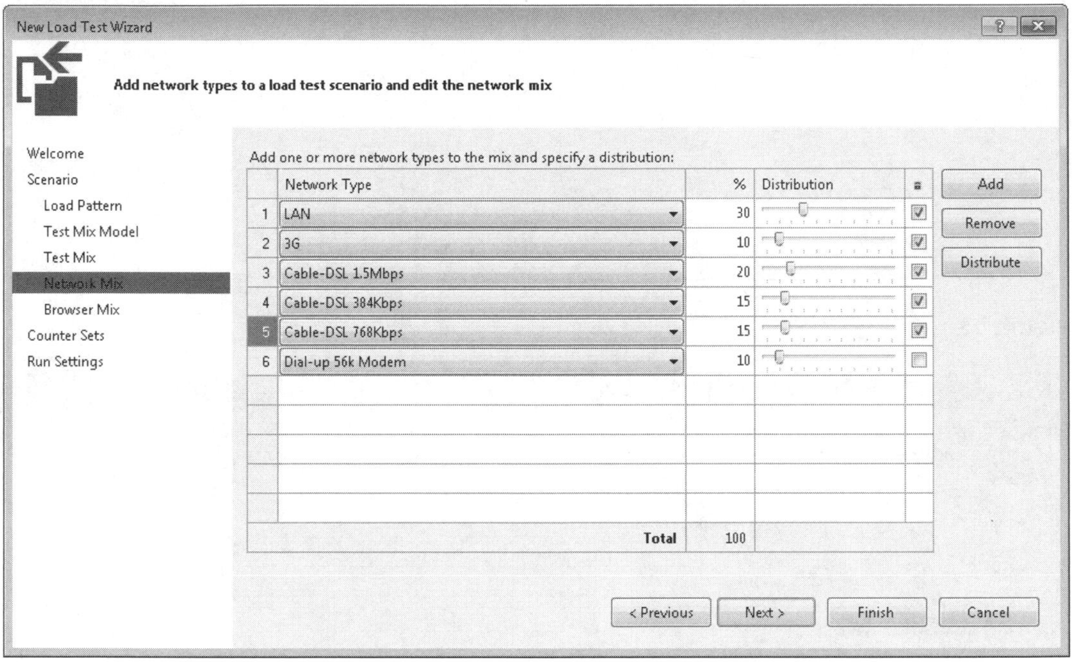

FIGURE 25-17

Like the test mix step described earlier, you can use sliders to adjust the percentages, lock a particular percent, or click the Distribute button to reset to an even distribution.

As with the test mix settings, each virtual user selects a browser type at random according to the percentages you set. A new browser type is selected each time a test is chosen for execution. This also applies to the browser mix described next.

Browser Mix

The next step (applicable only when web performance tests are part of the load test) is to define the distribution of browser types that you want to simulate. Visual Studio then adjusts the headers sent to the target application according to the selected browser for that user.

As shown in Figure 25-18, you may add one or more browser types, and then assign a percent distribution for their use.

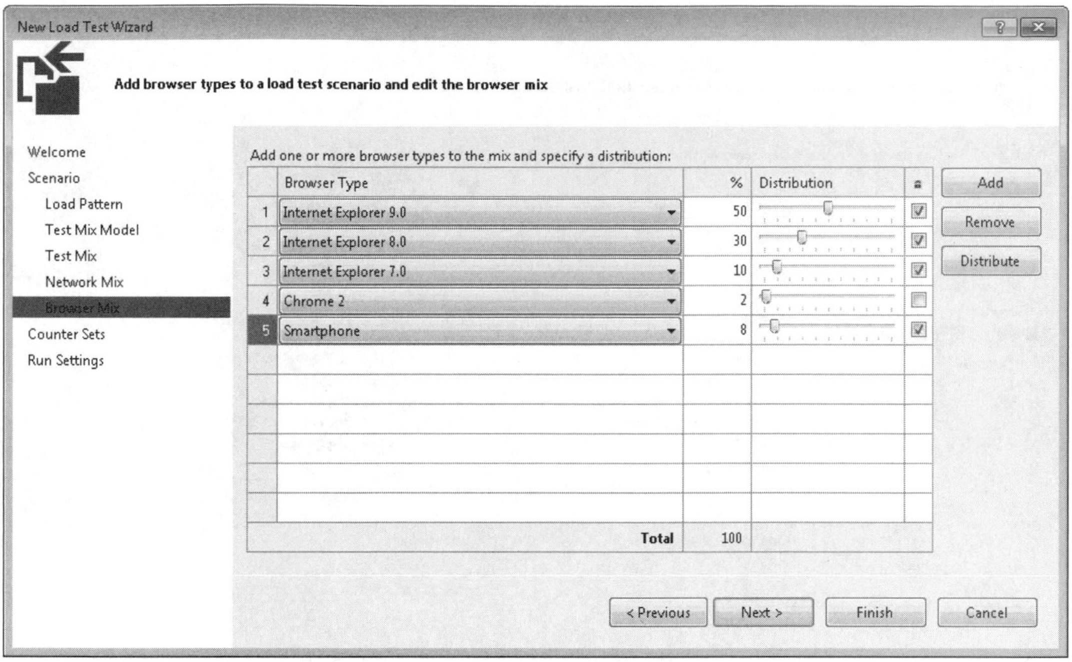

FIGURE 25-18

Performance Counter Sets

A vital part of load testing is the tracking of performance counters. You can configure your load test to observe and record the values of performance counters, even on remote machines. For example, your target application is probably hosted on a different machine from the one on which you're running the test. In addition, that machine may be calling to other machines for required services (such as databases or web services). Counters from all of these machines can be collected and stored by Visual Studio.

A *counter set* is a group of related performance counters. All of the contained performance counters are collected and recorded on the target machine when the load test is executed.

Select machines and counter sets using the wizard step shown in Figure 25-19. Note that this step is optional. By default, performance counters are automatically collected and recorded for the machine running the load test. If no other machines are involved, simply click Next.

> **NOTE** *After the wizard is complete, you can use the editor to create your own counter sets by right-clicking Counter Sets and selecting Add Custom Counter Set. Right-click the new counter set and choose Add Counters. Use the resulting dialog box to select the counters and instances you want to include.*

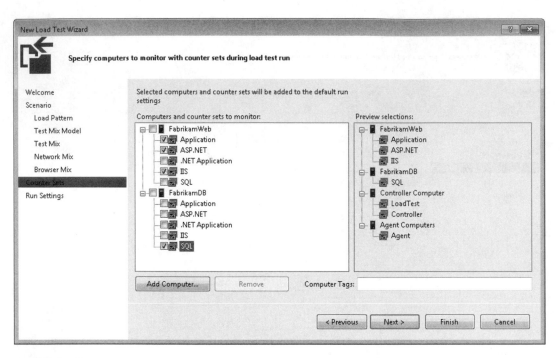

FIGURE 25-19

To add a machine to the list, click Add Computer and enter the name of the target machine. Then, check any counter sets you want to track to enable collection of the associated performance counters from the target machine.

> **NOTE** *If you encounter errors when trying to collect performance counters from remote machines, be sure to visit Ed Glas's blog post on troubleshooting these problems at* http://tinyurl.com/bp39hj.

Run Settings

The final step in the New Load Test Wizard is to specify the test's run settings, as shown in Figure 25-20. A load test may have more than one run setting, but the New Load Test Wizard only creates one. In addition, run settings include more details than are visible through the wizard. These aspects of run settings are covered later in the section "Editing Load Tests."

First, select the timing details for the test. Warm-up Duration specifies a window of time during which (although the test is running) no information from the test is tracked. This gives the target application a chance to complete actions such as just-in-time (JIT) compilation or caching of resources. After the warm-up period ends, data collection begins and continues until the Run Duration value has been reached.

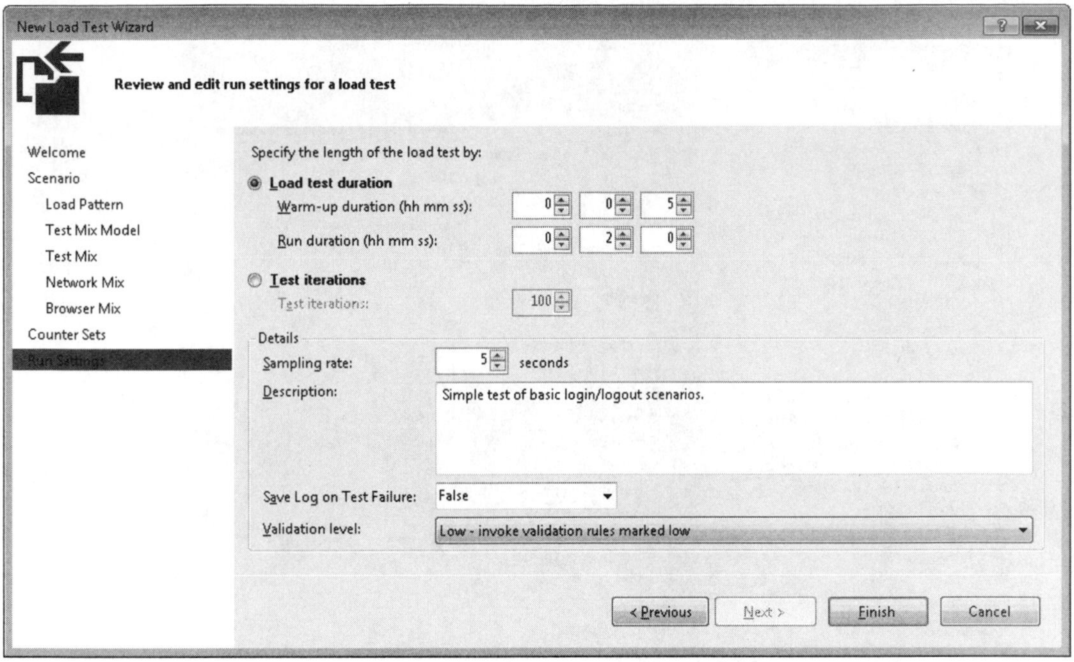

FIGURE 25-20

The Sampling Rate determines how often performance counters are collected and recorded. A higher frequency (lower number) produces more detail, but at the cost of a larger test result set and slightly higher strain on the target machines.

Any description you enter is stored for the current run setting. Save Log on Test Failure specifies whether or not a load test log should be saved in the event that tests fail. Often, you do not want to save a log on test failure because broken tests skew the results for actual test performance.

Finally, the Validation Level setting indicates which web performance test validation rules should be executed. This is important, because the execution of validation rules is achieved at the expense of performance. In a stress test, you may be more interested in raw performance than you are that a set of validation rules pass. There are three options for validation level:

➤   *Low* — Only validation rules marked with Low level are executed.

➤   *Medium* — Validation rules marked Low or Medium level are executed.

➤   *High* — All validation rules are executed.

Click Finish to complete the wizard and create the load test.

Editing Load Tests

After completing the New Load Test Wizard (or whenever you open an existing load test), you see the Load Test Editor shown in Figure 25-21.

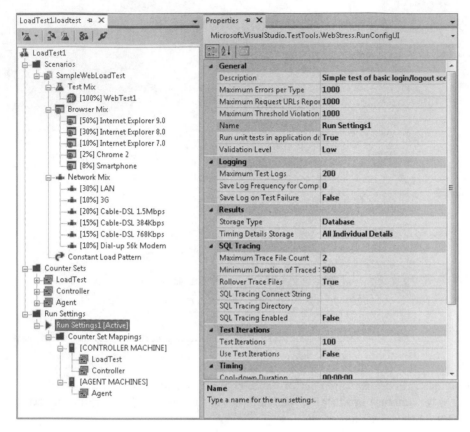

FIGURE 25-21

The Load Test Editor displays all of the settings you specified in the New Load Test Wizard. It provides access to more properties and options than the wizard, including the capability to add scenarios, create new run settings, configure SQL tracing, and much more.

Adding Scenarios

As you've already seen, scenarios are groups of tests and user profiles. They are a good way to define a large load test composed of smaller, more specific testing objectives.

For example, you might create a load test with two scenarios. The first might include tests of the administrative functions of your site, including ten users with the corporate-mandated Internet Explorer 9.0 on a LAN. The other scenario might test the core features of your site, running with 90 users who have a variety of other browsers and who are connecting from their phones or home VPN network connections. Running these scenarios together under one load test enables you to more effectively gauge the overall behavior of your site under realistic usage.

The New Load Test Wizard generates load tests with a single scenario, but you can easily add more using the Load Test Editor. Right-click the Scenarios node and choose Add Scenario. You are then prompted to walk through the Add Scenario Wizard, which is simply a subset of the New Load Test Wizard that you've already seen.

Run Settings

Run settings, as shown on the right-hand side of Figure 25-21, specify such things as duration of the test run, where and if results data is stored, SQL tracing, and performance counter mappings.

A load test can have more than one run setting, but as with scenarios, the New Load Test Wizard only supports the creation of one. You might want multiple run settings to enable you to easily switch between different types of runs. For example, you could switch between a long-running test that runs all validation rules, and another shorter test that runs only those marked as Low level.

To add a new run setting, right-click the Run Settings node (or the load test's root node) and choose Add Run Setting. You can then modify any property or add counter set mappings to this new run setting node.

SQL Tracing

You can gather tracing information from a target SQL Server instance through SQL Tracing. Enable SQL Tracing through the run settings of your load test. As shown in Figure 25-21, the SQL Tracing group has several settings.

First, set the SQL Tracing Enabled setting to True. Then click the SQL Tracking Connect String setting to make the ellipsis button appear. Click that button and configure the connection to the database you want to trace.

Use the SQL Tracing Directory setting to specify the path or Universal Naming Convention (UNC) to the directory in which you want the SQL Trace details stored.

Finally, you can specify a minimum threshold for logging of SQL operations. The Minimum Duration of Traced SQL Operations setting specifies the minimum time (in milliseconds) that an operation must take in order for it to be recorded in the tracing file.

Goal-Based Load Profiles

As you saw in the New Load Test Wizard, you had two options for load profile patterns: Constant and Step. A third option, Goal Based, is only available through the Load Test Editor.

The goal-based pattern is used to raise or lower the user load over time until a specific performance counter range has been reached. This is an invaluable option when you want to determine the peak loads your application can withstand.

To access the load profile options, open your load test in the Load Test Editor and click your current load profile, which is either Constant Load Profile or Step Load Profile. In the Properties window, change the Pattern value to Goal Based. You should now see a window similar to Figure 25-22.

First, notice the User Count Limits section. This is similar to the step pattern in that you specify an initial and maximum user count, but you also specify a maximum user count increment and decrement and minimum user count. The load test dynamically adjusts the current user count according to these settings in order to reach the goal performance counter threshold.

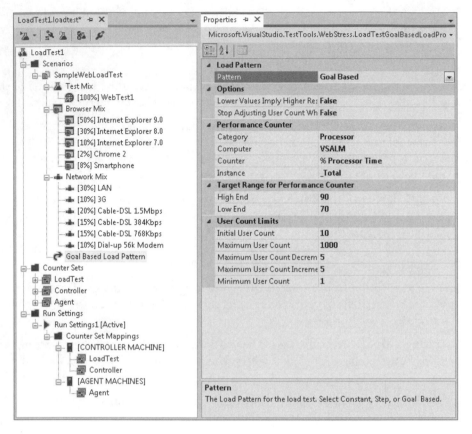

FIGURE 25-22

By default, the pattern is configured against the % Processor Time performance counter. To change this, enter the category (for example, Memory, System, and so on), the computer from which it is collected (leave this blank for the current machine), and the counter name and instance — which is applicable if you have multiple processors.

You must then tell the test about the performance counter you selected. First, identify the range you're trying to reach using the High-End and Low-End properties. Set the Lower Values Imply Higher Resource Utilization option if a lower counter value indicates system stress. For example, you would set this to True when using the system group's Available MBytes counter. Finally, you can tell the load test to remain at the current user load level when the goal is reached with the Stop Adjusting User Count When Goal Achieved option.

Storing Load Test Run Data

A load test run can collect a large amount of data. This includes performance counter information from one or more machines, details about which test passed, and durations of various actions. You may choose to store this information in a SQL Server database.

To select a results store, you must modify the load test's run settings. Refer to Figure 25-21. The local run settings have been selected in the Load Test Editor. In the Results section of the Properties window is a setting called Storage Type, which you can either set to None or Database.

You can use your database to store data from load tests running on the local machine or even remote machines. Running remote load tests is described later in this chapter in the "Distributed Load Tests" section.

Executing Load Tests

In the Load Test Editor, click the Run button at the upper-left corner, or right-click any load test setting node and select Run Load Test. You see the status of your test in the Test Results window, as shown in Figure 25-23.

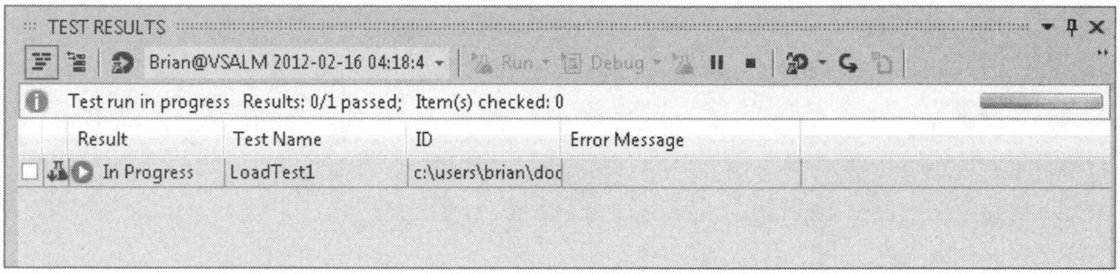

FIGURE 25-23

Viewing and Interpreting Load Test Results

After the status of your test is In Progress or Complete, you can double-click to see the Load Test Monitor window, shown in Figure 25-24. You may also right-click and choose View Test Results Details. When a load test is run from the Load Test Editor, the Test Results window is bypassed, immediately displaying the Load Test Monitor.

You can observe the progress of your test and then continue to use the same window to review results after the test has completed.

At the top of the screen, just under the file tabs, is a toolbar with several view options. First, if you are viewing detailed information from a results store, you have a Summary view that displays key information about your load test. The next two buttons enable you to select between Graphs and Tables view. The Details (available if you are viewing detailed information from a results store) provides a graphical view of virtual users over time. The Show Counters Panel and graph options buttons are used to change the way these components are displayed.

Graphs View

The most obvious feature of the Load Test Monitor is the set of four graphs, which is selected by default. These graphs plot a number of selected performance counters over the duration of the test.

The tree in the left-hand (Counter) pane shows a list of all available performance counters, grouped into a variety of sets — for example, by machine. Expand the nodes to reveal the tracked performance counters. Hover over a counter to see a plot of its values in the graph. Double-click the counter to add it to the graph and legend.

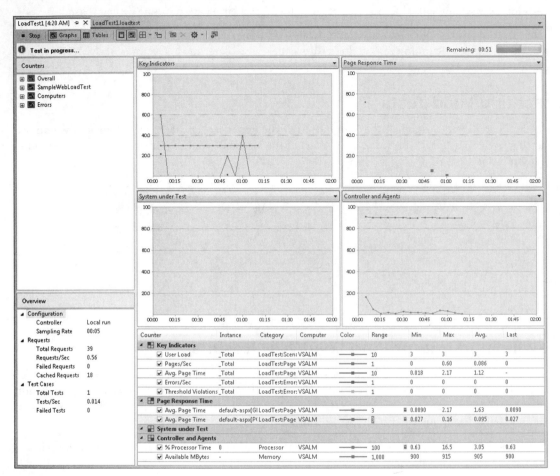

FIGURE 25-24

> **NOTE** *Selecting performance counters and knowing what they represent can require experience. With so many available counters, it can be a daunting task to know when your application isn't performing at its best. Fortunately, Microsoft has applied its practices and recommendations to predefine threshold values for each performance counter to help indicate that something might be wrong.*

As the load test runs, the graph is updated at each snapshot interval. In addition, you may notice that some of the nodes in the Counters pane are marked with a red error or yellow warning icon. This indicates that the value of a performance counter has exceeded a predefined threshold and should be reviewed. You also see small warning icons in the graph itself at the points where the violations occurred. You use the Thresholds view to review these in a moment.

The list at the bottom of the screen is a legend that shows details of the selected counters. Those that are checked appear in the graph with the indicated color. If you select a counter, it is displayed with a bold line.

Tables View

When you click the Tables button, the main panel of the load test results window changes to show a dropdown list with a table. Use the dropdown list to view each of the available tables for the load test run. Each of these tables is described in the following sections.

Tests Table

This table goes beyond the detail of the Summary pane, listing all tests in your load test and providing summary statistics for each. Tests are listed by name and containing scenario for easy identification. You see the total count of runs, pass/fail details, as well as tests per second and seconds per test metrics.

Pages Table

The Pages table shows all of the pages accessed during the load test. Included with each page are details of the containing scenario and web performance test, along with performance metrics. The Total column shows the number of times that page was rendered during the test. The Page Time column reflects the average response time for each page. Page Time Goal and % Meeting Goal are used when a target response time was specified for that page. Finally, the Last Page Time shows the response time from the most recent request to that page.

Transactions Table

A *transaction* is a defined subset of steps tracked together in a web performance test. For example, you can wrap the requests from the start to the end of your checkout process in a transaction named Checkout for easy tracking. For more details, see the section "Adding Transactions," earlier in this chapter.

In this table, you see any defined transactions listed, along with the names of the containing scenario and web performance test. Details include the count, response time, and elapsed time for each transaction.

SQL Trace Table

The SQL Trace table is only enabled if you previously configured SQL Tracing for your load test. You can find details for doing that in the "SQL Tracing" section earlier in this chapter

This table shows the slowest SQL operations that occurred on the machine specified in your SQL Tracing settings. Note that only those operations that take longer than the Minimum Duration of Traced SQL Operations appear.

By default, the operations are sorted with the slowest at the top of the list. You can view many details for each operation, including duration, start and end time, CPU, login name, and others.

Thresholds Table

If there were any threshold violations during your test run they will be listed here. Each violation is listed according to the sampling time at which it occurred. You can see details about which counter on which machine failed, as well as a description of what the violating and threshold values were.

Errors Table

As with threshold violations, if your test encountered any errors, you will see a message such as "4 errors." Click this text or the Errors table button to see a summary list of the errors, which includes the error type (such as Total or Exception) and the error's subtype. SubType contains the specific Exception type encountered — for example, `FileNotFoundException`. Also shown are the count of each particular error and the message returned from the last occurrence of that error.

If you configured a database to store the load test results data, you can right-click any entry and choose Errors to display the Load Test Errors window. This table displays each instance of the error, including stack and details (if available), according to the time at which they occurred. Other information (such as the containing test, scenario, and web request) is displayed when available.

Excel Reports

If you have Excel (2007 or newer) installed, you can create a detailed Excel report from a load test run by clicking the Create Excel Report button from the toolbar. This launches a wizard in Excel that enables you to choose from a variety of reports, including reports that compare multiple load test runs against one another. This can be useful when you're examining, for example, performance regressions between one build of your application and another.

DISTRIBUTED LOAD TESTS

In larger-scale efforts, a single machine may not have enough power to simulate the number of users you need to generate the required stress on your application. Visual Studio 2012 also has a licensing restriction that limits you to simulating at most 250 users from your development environment. Fortunately, Visual Studio enables you to scale load generation across a distributed collection of machines.

There are a number of roles that the machines play in this scenario. *Client* machines are typically developer machines on which the load tests are created and selected for execution. The *controller* is the "headquarters" of the distributed load test, coordinating the actions of one or more *agent* machines. The controller also collects the test results from each associated agent machine. The agent machines actually execute the load tests and provide details to the controller. The controller and agents are collectively referred to as a *test rig*.

There are no requirements for the location of the application under test. Generally, the application is installed either on one or more machines either outside the rig or locally on the agent machines, but the architecture of distributed testing is flexible.

Installing Controllers and Agents

Before using controllers and agents, you must install the required Windows services on each machine. The Visual Studio 2012 Agents package includes setup utilities for these services. This setup utility enables you to install the test controller and test agent.

Installing the test controller installs a Windows service for the controller, and prompts you to assign a Windows account under which that service runs. Refrain from registering your test controller with a team project collection if you want to run load tests from Visual Studio. Enable the Configure for Load Testing option and select a SQL Server or SQL Server Express instance where you want to store your load test results.

> **NOTE** *Install your controller and verify that the Visual Studio Test Controller Windows service is running before configuring your agent machines.*

After the controller service has been installed, run the Test Agent setup on each agent machine, specifying a user under whom the service should run and the name of the controller machine.

You can later configure your test controller and test agents using the respective entries on the Start Menu under Programs ➪ Microsoft Visual Studio 2012. For additional instructions on configuring test controllers or test agents, consult the product documentation at `http://aka.ms/LoadTestRig`.

Configuring Controllers

After you have run the installation packages on the controller and agent machine(s), configure the controller by first opening your `.testsettings` file from within Solution Explorer. Switch to the Roles tab, then change the Test execution method to Remote execution. Now select Controllers ➪ Manage Test Controllers to open the dialog shown in Figure 25-25.

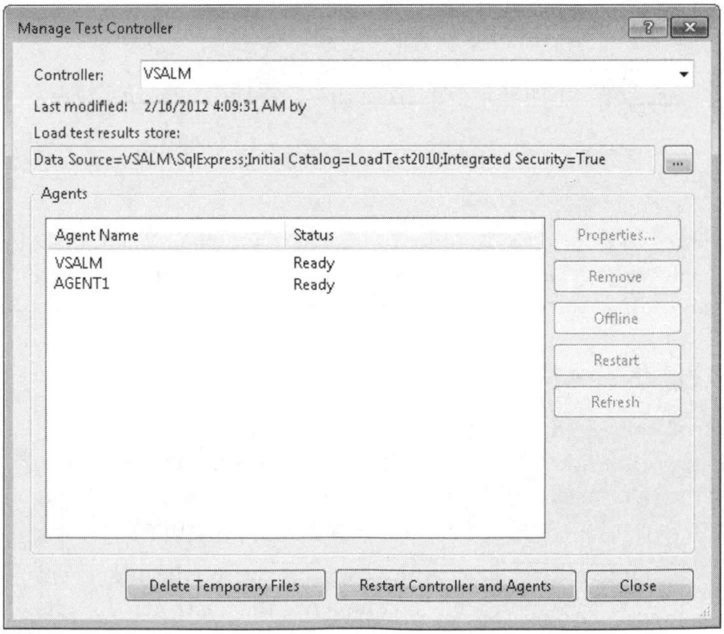

FIGURE 25-25

Type the name of a machine in the Controller field and press Enter. Ensure that the machine you specify has had the required controller services installed. The Agents panel then lists any currently configured agents for that controller, along with each agent's status.

Load Test Results Store points to the repository you are using to store load test data. Click the ellipsis (...) button to select and test a connection to your repository.

The Agents panel shows any test agents that have been registered with your test controller. You can temporarily suspend an agent from the rig by clicking the Offline button. Restart the agent services on a target machine with the Restart button.

You also have options for clearing temporary log data and directories, as well as restarting the entire rig.

Configuring Agents

Using the Manage Test Controller dialog just described, select an agent and click the Properties button. You are able to modify several settings, described in the following sections.

Weighting

When running a distributed load test, the load test being executed by the controller has a specific user load profile. This user load is then distributed to the agent machines according to their individual weightings.

For example, suppose two agents are running under a controller that is executing a load test with ten users. If the agents' weights are each 50, then five users are sent to each agent.

IP Switching

This indicates the range of IP addresses to be used for calls from this agent to the target web application.

Attributes

You may assign name-value attributes to each agent in order to later restrict which agent machines are selected to run tests. There are no restrictions on the names and values you can set. You can then use the Roles tab of the Test Settings editor to configure your test runs to use specific agents.

Running a Distributed Load Test

Now that you have installed and configured your rig (a controller and at least one agent machine) and modified your test run configuration to target the controller, you may execute the load test. Execute the test using any one of the options described in the earlier section "Executing Load Tests," ensuring that the correct test settings have been selected (Test ➪ Test Settings).

The controller is then signaled to begin the test. The controller contacts the (qualifying) agent machines and distributes tests and load to each. As each test completes, the controller collects test run details from each agent. When all agents have completed, the controller finalizes the test and the test run ends, displaying your test results.

SUMMARY

This chapter described web performance and load tests in detail. You first learned how to use the Web Test Recorder to easily record a new web performance test. You then learned how to use the Web Test Editor to finely tune the web performance test, adding features such as validation and extraction rules. You also looked at coded web performance tests, which enable you to create very flexible tests.

The next section introduced load tests, which can be composed of any automated testing type, such as web performance and unit tests. You learned how to use the Load Test Wizard to create an initial load test. You then used the Load Test Editor to add scenarios, SQL tracing, and other options not available through the wizard.

You then saw the power of the Load Test Monitor, used to graphically view performance counter details as well as errors, transactions, SQL operations, and more.

Finally, you learned how to run load tests in a distributed environment. You now know how to install and configure the controller and agent machines, and how to use the controller to parcel out load to the agent machines, collecting results in the test repository.

In Chapter 26, you find out how you can use the lab management capabilities of Visual Studio 2012 to help you establish physical and virtual test labs. Test labs are a powerful way of managing multiple environments with which to stage builds of your software, run automated and manual tests, and help developers reproduce and diagnose bugs.

Lab Management

WHAT'S IN THIS CHAPTER?

➤ Understanding the lab management capabilities of Visual Studio 2012

➤ Using lab management to run tests, capture bugs, and share snapshots

➤ Configuring end-to-end build-deploy-test workflows

As software development projects become more complex, so do the environments in which that software will run. Such an environment could consist of multiple machines, specific fire-wall (and other security) settings, databases, and a variety of other configurations that could affect the way in which your software behaves.

To effectively test software, testers must create a test environment that simulates the pro-duction environment. Traditionally, this could require securing several dedicated physical machines and developing a potentially labor-intensive process for staging those machines on a regular basis with new builds of your software. And, given the variety of possible configura-tions, it's usually necessary to have multiple test environments in order to find problems that may arise when you ship your software to customers running different environments, each with their own unique configurations.

With the rising popularity and availability of virtualization technology, many testing teams have begun to turn to virtualization to make better use of hardware and to more efficiently stage testing environments. But, despite the advances in virtualization, there are still several challenges related to the process of managing a virtual test lab, which can make this a costly and time-consuming endeavor.

The lab management capabilities of Visual Studio 2012 address the challenge of working with such virtual test lab environments. Lab management capabilities are built into Team Foundation Server 2012 and provide the following capabilities:

➤ Creation, management, and teardown of environments consisting of one or more virtual machines (VMs) from templates or stored virtual machines.

➤ Automated deployment of builds into virtual environments.

➤ Execution of manual and automated tests across virtual environments.

➤ Automated collection of rich diagnostics across virtual environments during test runs, allowing for more actionable bugs to be filed as an outcome of failed tests.

➤ Use of snapshots to enable environments to be quickly restored to a given state (such as immediately after a new build of software is deployed or when a new bug is discovered). Testers and developers can share snapshots to help diagnose and fix bugs.

➤ Network isolation of virtualized environments, allowing clones of environments without fear of IP address collisions or naming conflicts with other machines on your network.

To achieve all of these capabilities, you need to be using virtual environments that are running Hyper-V on host machines managed by System Center Virtual Machine Manager (2008 R2 or 2012). These environments are known as *SCVMM environments*.

Team Foundation Server 2012 also introduces improved support for achieving some of these capabilities when using physical (non-virtual) environments, or third-party virtualization technologies other than Hyper-V. These environments are known as *standard environments*. Standard environments do not have the same dependency on System Center Virtual Machine Manager that SCVMM environments have, so they are quite a bit easier to get started with if you don't already have System Center deployed. But there are a few limitations of standard environments as compared with SCVMM environments that are discussed in the "Standard Environments" section later in this chapter.

LAB MANAGEMENT INFRASTRUCTURE

Lab management is a core capability of Team Foundation Server 2012. In order to work with SCVMM environments, your Team Foundation Server needs to be configured to integrate with an SCVMM server. Configuration and administration of lab management is covered extensively in the product documentation and isn't covered in detail in this book, but a few key concepts are introduced here.

> **NOTE** *Team Foundation Server 2012 includes a license for SCVMM which you may use for development and testing purposes. For more information on licensing, see the Visual Studio Licensing Whitepaper at* `http://www.microsoft.com/visualstudio/licensing`*.*

SCVMM uses a *library server* to store saved copies of VMs, which can then later be deployed to a *VM host group* (made up of one or more *VM hosts*). A library server is essentially a file server that SCVMM is aware of and has read/write access to. Each library server can contain one or more *library shares*, which is basically a shared folder.

A library server can contain *VM templates* that enable you to customize a VM at the time of deployment. This enables you to specify such settings as machine name, domain or workgroup membership, and product key. VM templates are a powerful tool for building out your test lab because they provide the most control over how VMs are deployed.

In order to configure and test with lab management environments, users need to be licensed for Microsoft Test Manager (included with Visual Studio Test Professional, Premium, and Ultimate).

Golden Images

While setting up your test lab, you need to consider the VM configurations on which you need to test your software. For example, maybe your software needs to be tested to run in environments containing machines running Windows 7, Windows Server 2008, and Windows Server 2008 R2. You should also consider which other prerequisite software must be installed, such as Internet Information Server (IIS) or database engines such as SQL Server.

The product documentation for lab management refers to the concept of using *golden images* for populating your library server. A golden image is a VM or VM template that contains all of the prerequisites necessary for testing your software. In the previous example, you might configure a golden image for each operating system version that will eventually be involved in your test environments.

Agents

You can install *test agents* into environments to provide additional capabilities that are helpful in deployment, testing, and network isolation with your virtual environments. The test agent is responsible for the following functions:

➤ Allowing an environment to participate in Team Foundation Build workflows. This includes the capability to deploy new builds and other deployment artifacts to your environments.

➤ Enabling manual or automated tests (such as unit tests, coded UI tests, or web performance tests) to be executed in your environments, including the collection of test run information from diagnostic data adapters.

➤ Network isolation capabilities for an SCVMM environment. With network isolation enabled, you don't have to worry about VMs in your test lab conflicting (computer name or IP address) with other machines on your network. This makes it possible to have multiple virtual environments with the same IP address and/or machine name without needing to set up dedicated networks for each one.

> **NOTE** *The previous version of lab management included with Team Foundation Server 2010 included three different agents: a build agent, a test agent, and a lab agent. All these capabilities are now included in a single test agent with Team Foundation Server 2012. Team Foundation Server 2012 also automatically installs and configures test agents into your environments as required, which can save you a lot of preparation time as compared with the 2010 version of lab management.*

The preceding descriptions should provide you with a basic understanding of what is necessary to configure the infrastructure required for taking advantage of lab management. But it is by no means a substitute for the detailed product documentation. Your test lab administrator should carefully consult the product documentation for instructions on configuring and optimizing your lab management infrastructure. Once configured, you can benefit by using lab management as detailed in the remainder of this chapter.

> **NOTE** *You can find the product documentation for lab management at* `http://aka.ms/LabManagement2012`.

SCVMM ENVIRONMENTS

An SCVMM environment consists of one or more VMs that can be deployed and managed together. An environment usually contains all the VMs necessary to run a set of test cases. For example, an environment could consist of a database server and a web server, each running Windows Server 2012. A separate virtual environment might also contain similarly configured database and web servers, but use Windows Server 2008 to offer expanded test coverage.

The first step in creating an SCVMM environment is to define the VMs or VM templates that will make up your environment. You use Microsoft Test Manager, introduced in Chapter 23, to do this. Before completing this step, you must have one or more golden images (VMs or templates) stored in your SCVMM library.

Click Start ➪ All Programs ➪ Microsoft Visual Studio 2012 ➪ Microsoft Test Manager. If this is your first time launching Microsoft Test Manager, you may need to define which Team Foundation Server instance and team project you are connecting to. When connected, open the Lab Center and click Library ➪ Virtual Machines and Templates. The Virtual Machines and Templates activity appears, as shown in Figure 26-1.

From here, you can manage all the VMs and templates that are available to the team project you are connected to. To add a new VM or template, click the Import button in the upper-left area of the screen.

Begin by defining the path to your new VM or VM template. This path defines the location within the SCVMM library server where your VM or template is stored. Use the Browse button to explore the library server path(s) defined in SCVMM.

Next, provide a name for your VM or template. You can optionally provide a description (useful for describing what's installed on this VM or VM template), along with a default role (discussed later in this chapter).

The Machine Properties tab enables you to specify default parameters that will be used when your VM is deployed (such as the amount of RAM that should be assigned to your VM when deployed). If you are using a VM template, then the OS Profile tab is available, enabling you to define additional parameters (such as the machine name, domain or workgroup membership, and product key). You can use the Machine Tags tab to construct advanced deployment workflows.

Clicking Next displays a summary of your actions. Click Finish and your VM or template is listed in the Virtual Machines and Templates activity within Test Manager.

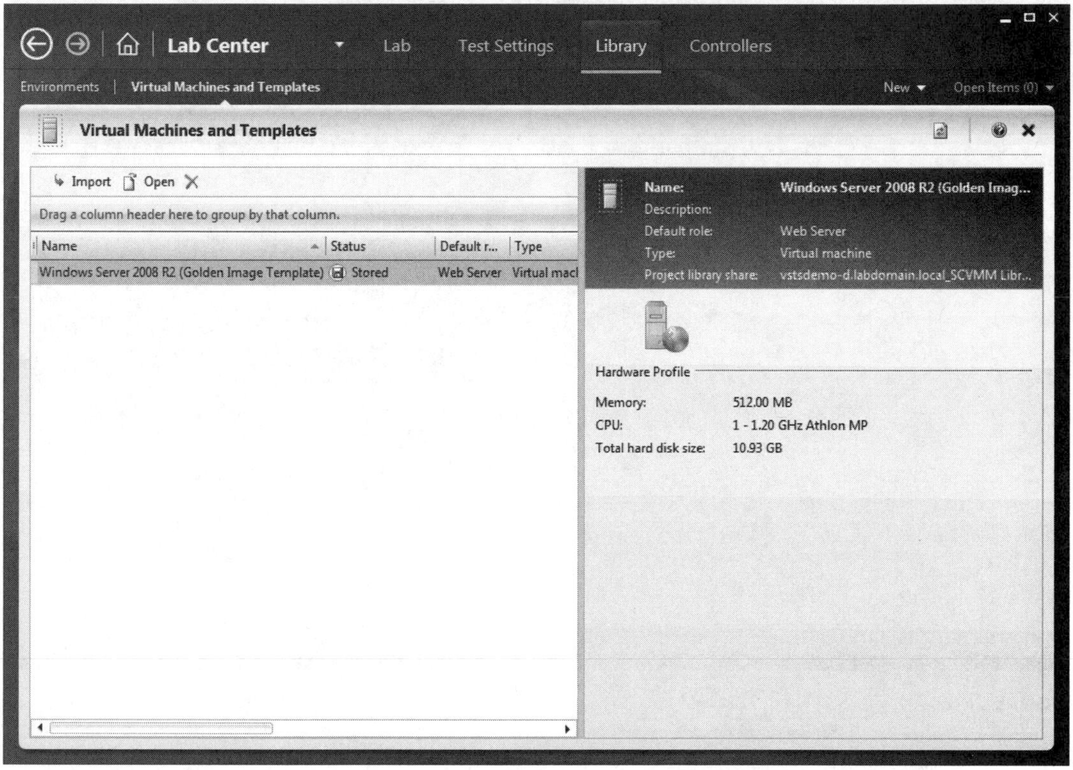

FIGURE 26-1

> **NOTE** *You can repeat this process for defining as many VMs and VM templates as you want. You can even use the same VM template from your SCVMM library as the basis for multiple VMs or templates within Test Manager (such as to specify various default parameters).*

After you have configured one or more VMs or templates, you are ready to define an environment. Click Library ➪ Environments. From the Environments activity shown in Figure 26-2, you can assemble one or more VMs or templates into an environment that you can later deploy to a VM host group.

Click New to create a new virtual environment. Start by indicating whether you are configuring an SCVMM environment or a standard environment (described later in this chapter). You can provide a name and description for your environment. You can also specify the location on the SCVMM library server where the environment definition should be stored, along with environment tags that you can use for defining advanced build workflows.

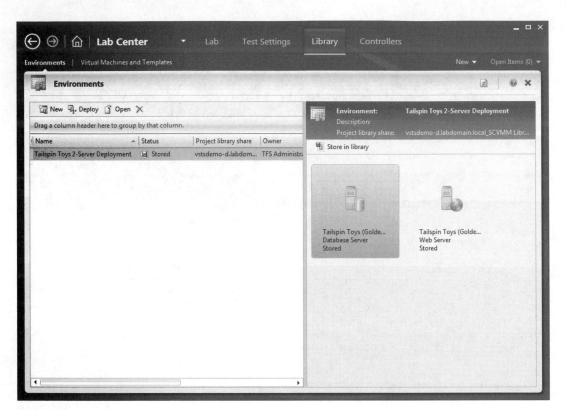

FIGURE 26-2

The Machines tab shown in Figure 26-3 is where you can begin constructing your virtual environment based on the VMs or templates you defined earlier. To do this, first select a VM or template from the list of VMs and templates on the right side of the screen. Next, select Add to Environment. This adds the VM to the environment on the left side of the screen. You can add the same VM template multiple times, if desired.

After adding one or more VMs or templates to your environment, you can specify which role these machines play in your environment (such as a web server or database server). Roles are used by test settings and build workflows as you see later on. You can also specify the name that lab management uses to refer to the VM within the environment. Note that this name does not need to be the same as the computer name. If you plan to define several environments, you might want to put some time into a useful naming convention to make it easier for testers and developers to differentiate environments from one another.

The Machine Properties tab shown in Figure 26-4 enables you to define the parameters that should be assigned to each of the VMs within your environment. This screen should look similar to the Machine Properties tab you encountered when defining a VM or template, except that it also includes the capability for you to select different VMs in your environment by clicking on the role icons across the top of the screen. Any machine properties you defined earlier are shown here as default values and you can override them in this step.

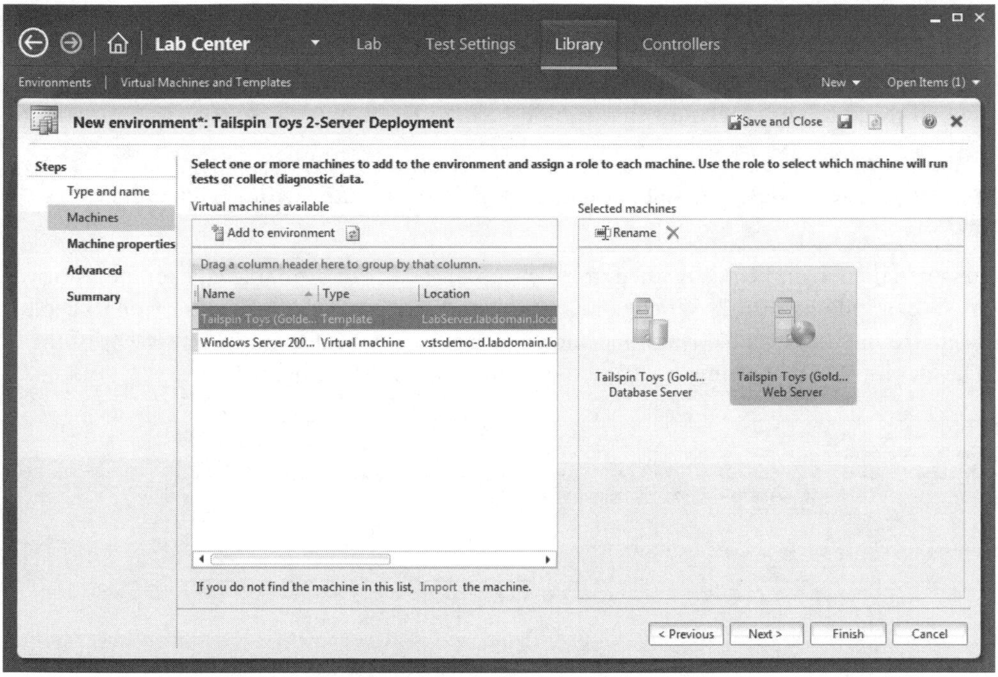

FIGURE 26-3

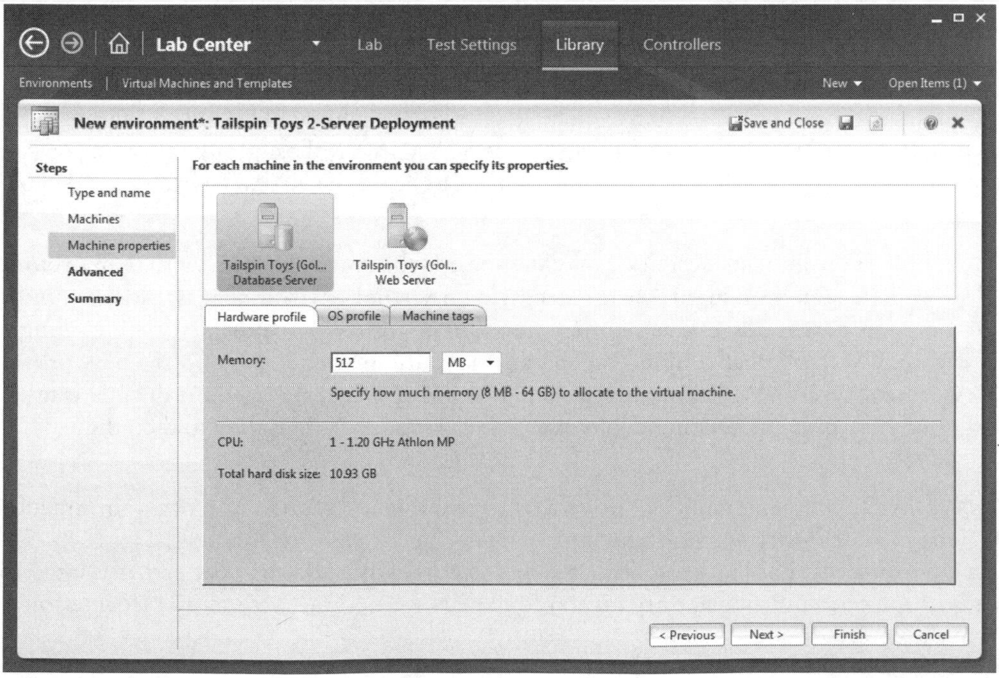

FIGURE 26-4

The Advanced tab enables you to define how test agents should be configured on the VMs within your environment. This includes the test controller that is used to orchestrate tests and collect diagnostics data; whether or not you want to utilize network isolation; and, if you plan on running coded UI tests, the user account that should be used to execute those tests as an interactive process.

The Summary tab describes your selections. Click Finish to finalize your environment definition.

After your virtual environment is defined, it shows up in the list of available environments in your library, as shown in Figure 26-2. When your virtual environment is defined, it is ready to deploy. Select the environment within your library and click the Deploy button in the upper-left of the screen. The Deploy the Environment dialog shown in Figure 26-5 displays.

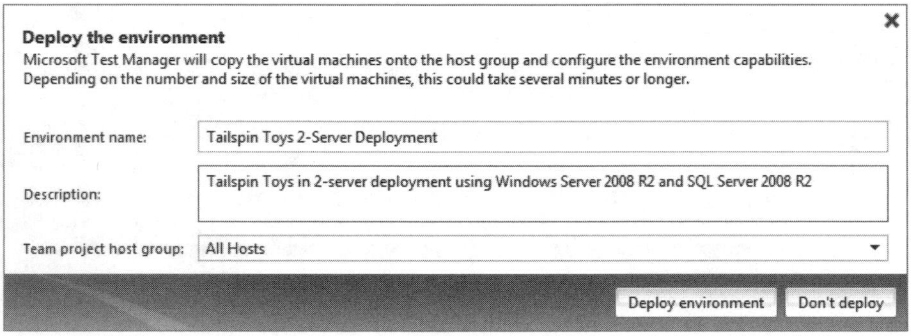

Deploy the environment
Microsoft Test Manager will copy the virtual machines onto the host group and configure the environment capabilities. Depending on the number and size of the virtual machines, this could take several minutes or longer.

Environment name: Tailspin Toys 2-Server Deployment

Description: Tailspin Toys in 2-server deployment using Windows Server 2008 R2 and SQL Server 2008 R2

Team project host group: All Hosts

[Deploy environment] [Don't deploy]

FIGURE 26-5

From this dialog, you can provide a name and a description for what will become a running instance of your virtual environment. You can also specify the SCVMM VM host group to where you want to deploy your environment. Click Deploy Environment to begin the virtual environment deployment process.

From the Lab ➪ Environments activity, you can monitor the status of your virtual environment as it is deployed, as shown in Figure 26-6. Deploying a virtual environment is a long-running operation that can potentially take an hour or more to complete. Various factors (including the size of your VMs, whether or not template customization is required, and the network speed between your SCVMM library server and VM hosts) affect the amount of time it takes to deploy your environment. During deployment, the test agent is installed and configured automatically.

After it's deployed, you can manage your virtual environment from the Lab ➪ Environments activity. This includes starting, stopping, and pausing the virtual environment. Figure 26-7 shows an environment that has been deployed and is currently running. Any errors related to the VMs within your environment are displayed here as well, along with more information describing the error.

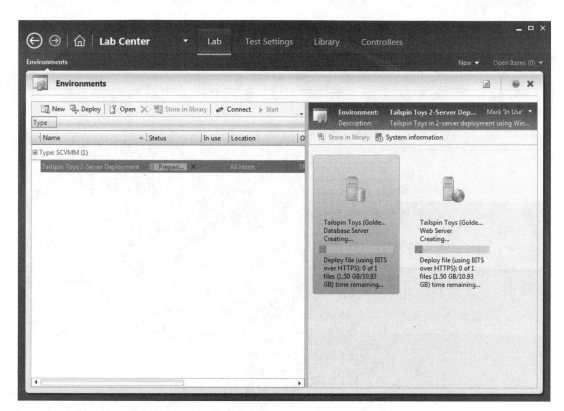

FIGURE 26-6

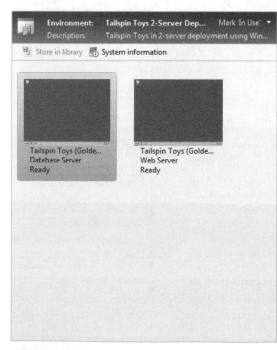

FIGURE 26-7

You can select a running virtual environment and click Connect to open the Environment Viewer shown in Figure 26-8. The Environment Viewer enables you to interact with the VMs running within your environment.

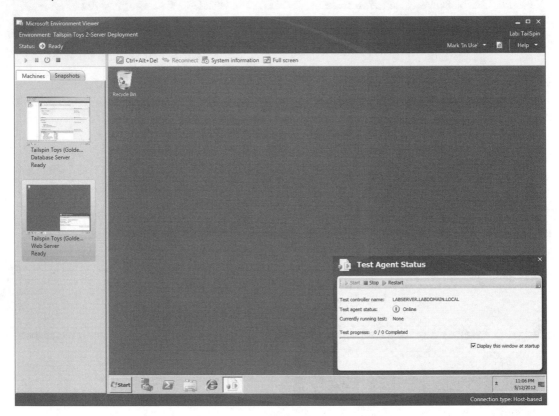

FIGURE 26-8

From the Environment Viewer you can also stop, start, and pause the running environment, and mark an environment as In Use (upper-right corner). This signals to other members of your team that you are using the environment and they should not attempt to connect to it.

The System Information button enables you to view properties of the running VMs (such as the fully qualified machine name). This information can be useful for connecting to the VM from outside of the environment (such as when using a web browser on a client machine to connect to a website running within your virtual environment).

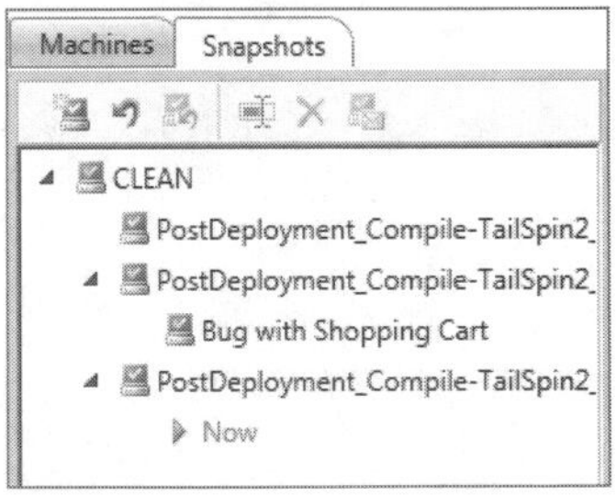

You can also manage *snapshots* for your environment from here by clicking on the Snapshots tab on the left side of the screen, as shown in Figure 26-9. Snapshots enable you to save the state of the entire environment at any point in time, and likewise to restore the

FIGURE 26-9

state of an environment by restoring a snapshot. If you have multiple machines in your environment, all of the machines in this environment will be snapshotted and restored together as a cohesive unit.

Snapshots have the following useful applications:

➤ A snapshot can provide a clean "baseline" state that you can use prior to installing or deploying each new build.

➤ You can create snapshots after installing a new build, providing a way to always restore to a known state prior to any tests being executed that may potentially "dirty" an environment. This includes rolling back to a known good baseline data set used for testing as well.

➤ Snapshots can be created by testers when they find a bug. These snapshots can then be shared with the development team to help them diagnose the bug and deliver a fix.

From the Snapshots tab you can create new snapshots, rename them, delete them, or restore your environment to an existing snapshot.

Now that you understand the basics of creating, deploying, and working with running environments, it's time to explore software testing with environments.

TESTING WITH ENVIRONMENTS

When you have a running environment, you can use it to run your tests.

Create New Test Settings

In Chapter 23, you configured test settings to define which diagnostics data to collect as you run your tests (such as video, IntelliTrace files, and action logs). But now that you are going to run tests with an environment, you may want to create a new test setting that specifies how the tests should collect data from each machine within your environment. This step is optional, but it can provide valuable diagnostics data to your developers when bugs are discovered.

From within Test Manager, click Testing Center ➪ Plan ➪ Properties. Your test plan properties display, as shown in Figure 26-10.

> **NOTE** *The discussion in this section assumes that you have already configured your first test plan as described in Chapter 23.*

From within your test plan properties, create a new test settings definition (Manual Runs ➪ Test Settings ➪ New). Provide a name and (optionally) a description for your new test settings. Click Next.

The Roles tab shown in Figure 26-11 enables you to select the environment for which you want to define test settings. When defining test settings for automated tests, you can also select the role from where automated tests are run. When configuring manual tests, the tests are always run from the local machine where Test Manager is running. After selecting your environment, click Next.

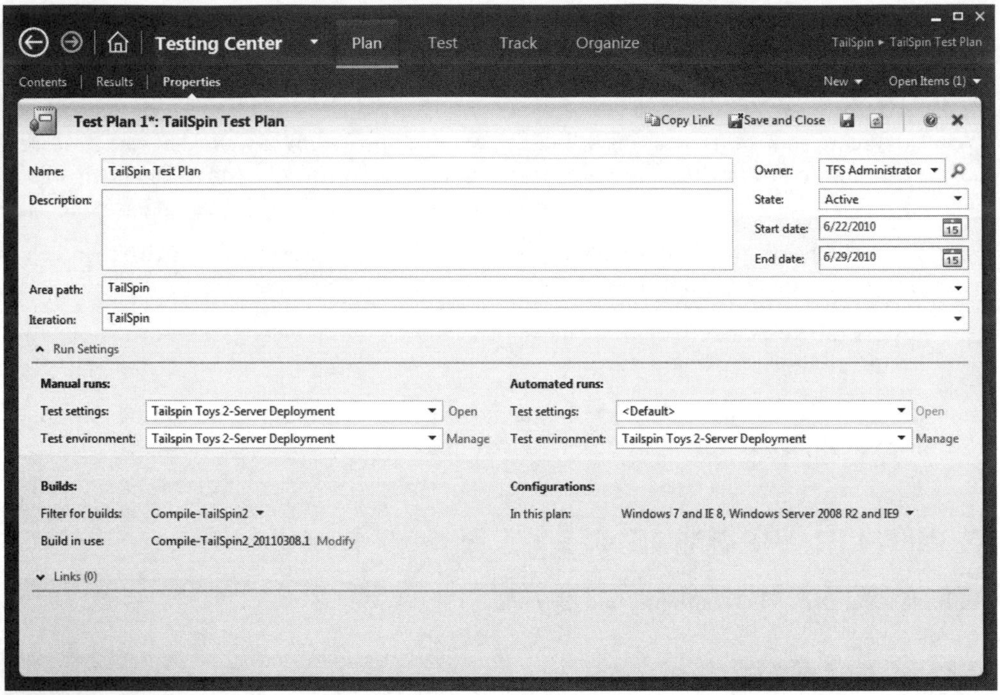

FIGURE 26-10

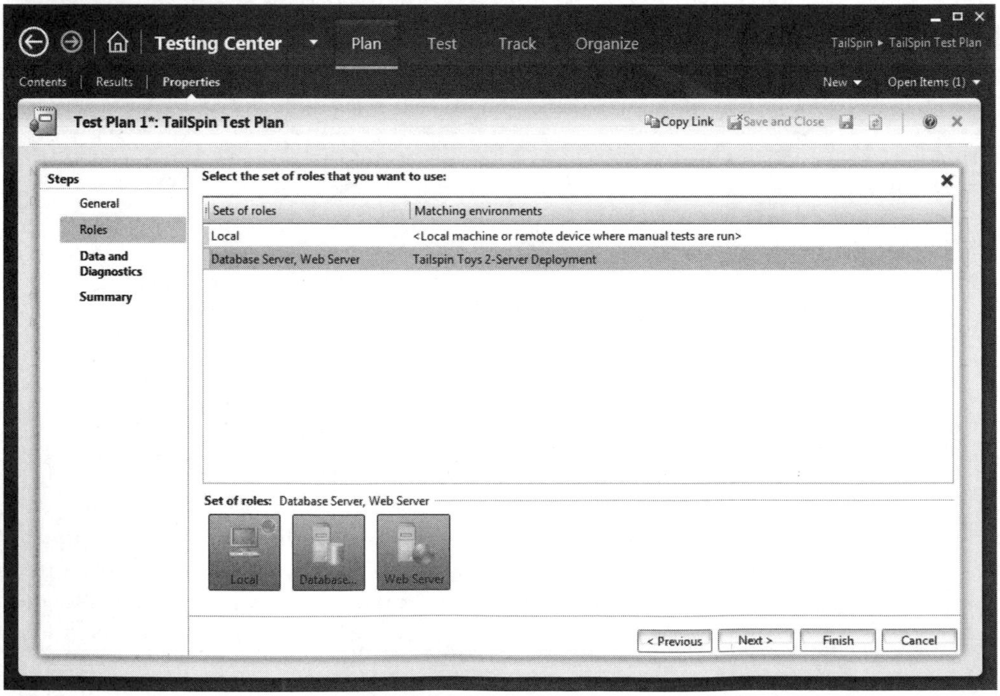

FIGURE 26-11

The Data and Diagnostics tab shown in Figure 26-12 enables you to define the individual diagnostics data adapters that are used for each machine within your virtual environment. Data diagnostics adapters were covered in detail in Chapter 23. From here, you can configure the adapters for each machine within your environment. For example, you might want to capture an event log from a database server, IntelliTrace from a web server, and a video recording from a machine which is running coded UI tests.

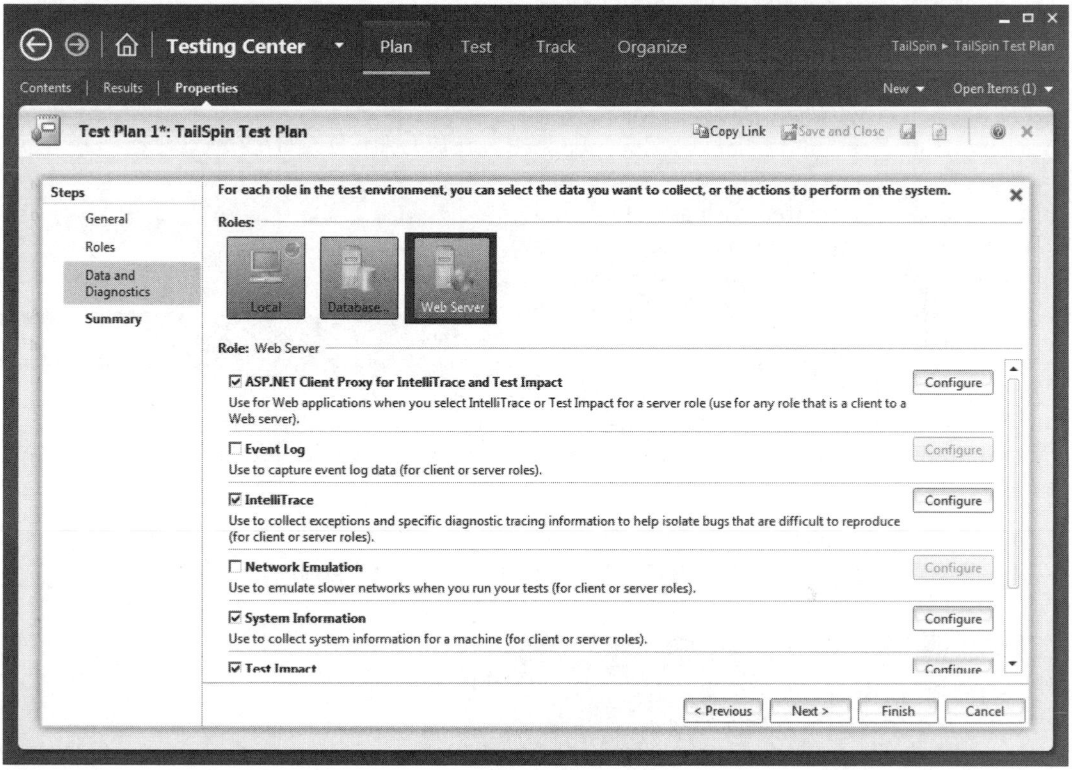

FIGURE 26-12

Run Manual Tests with an Environment

Run a test case as you normally would by clicking on the Test ⇨ Run Tests activity.

> **NOTE** *You can enable action logs and recordings only on the local machine where Test Manager is running. Therefore, if you are testing a web-based application, it may helpful to use your local browser to perform the tests and use the fully qualified DNS URL for the web role machine in your lab management environment. You can find that URL by clicking the System Information button as previously discussed in this chapter.*

> **NOTE** *The discussion in this section assumes that you have already created one or more test cases as defined in Chapter 23.*

Select a test case that you want to run with your environment and click Run ⇨ Run with Options.

The Run Options dialog shown in Figure 26-13 appears, enabling you to select the test settings and environment with which you want to run your test. If your manual test has associated automated tests (such as a coded UI test) and your test plan is associated with a build definition, then you can also opt to run this test as an automated test. For now, if your test has associated automated tests, just select the Run All the Tests Manually checkbox.

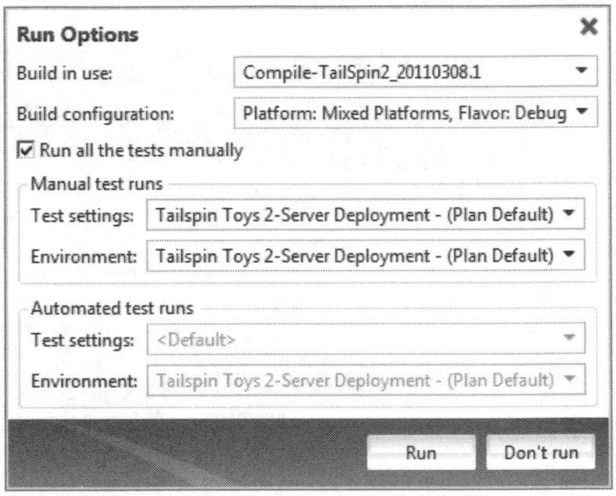

If you defined new test settings for collecting data from your environment, select it here. Also, select

FIGURE 26-13

your running environment from the Environment dropdown. Click Run to launch your test run and Microsoft Test Runner.

When Microsoft Test Runner is open, you can click the Connect to Environment button (shown in Figure 26-14) to open the Environment Viewer for your environment.

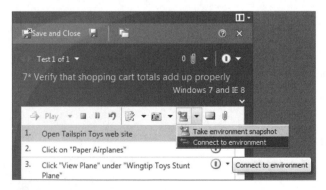

FIGURE 26-14

When the Environment Viewer is open, you can then begin running your test just like you would run any other manual test. You might want to use the Snapshots tab to restore the environment to a known state (such as immediately after a given build was deployed). You can even switch among multiple machines within your environment if your test case requires it. Figure 26-15 shows a test case being run with an environment.

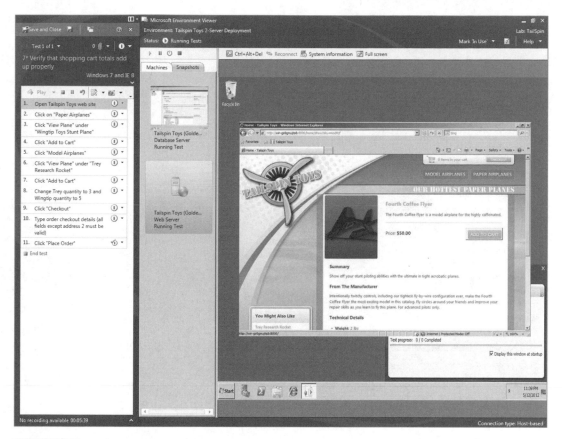

FIGURE 26-15

If you discover a bug while you are testing, you might want to create an environment snapshot that you can share with the development team to help them diagnose the problem. Even though you could do this directly from within the Environment Viewer, a better way is to do it from within Microsoft Test Runner. This automatically attaches a pointer to the environment snapshot to the test results and any bug reports that are created.

To create an environment snapshot with Microsoft Test Runner, click the rightmost icon along the Microsoft Test Runner toolbar (shown in the upper-right corner of Figure 26-16). This creates a new snapshot of the environment and saves an .lvr file to your test results. The .lvr file is a pointer to the environment snapshot that you can open later to restore your environment to this snapshot.

Click the Create Bug icon within Microsoft Test Runner to create a new bug along with your test results (hover your mouse over the toolbar icons to discover the Create Bug icon). Figure 26-17 shows the new bug creation form, along with a reference to the .lvr file created earlier.

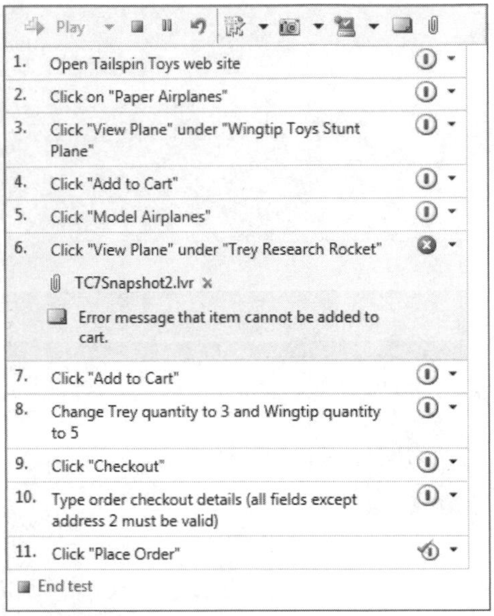

FIGURE 26-16

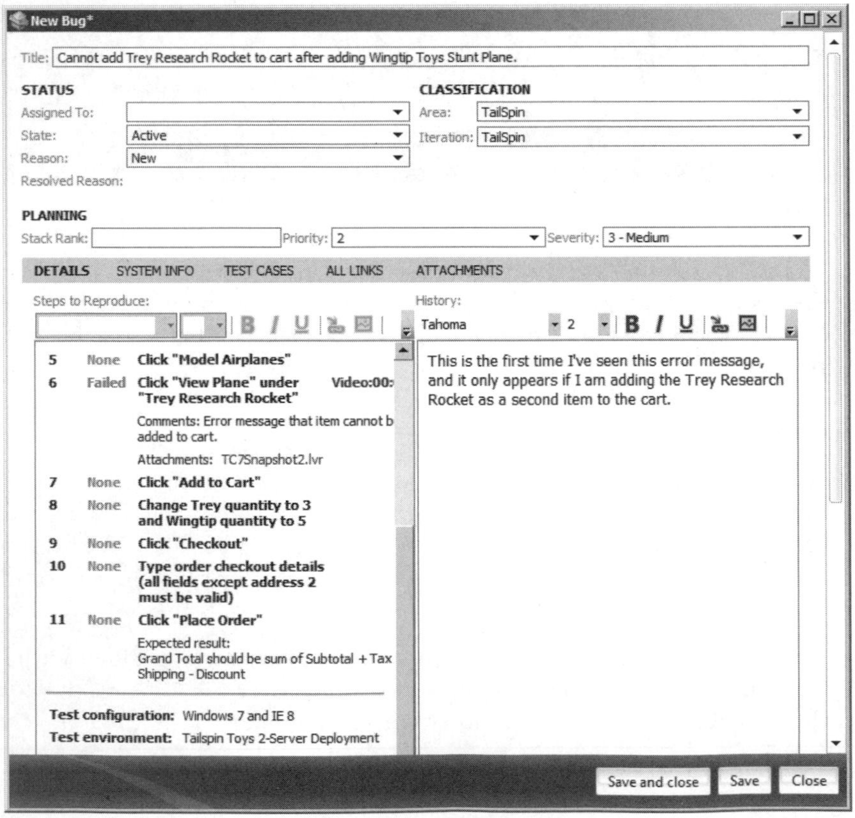

FIGURE 26-17

When reviewing this bug later, a developer who has Test Manager installed can open the `.lvr` file simply by clicking it from within the bug work item. The dialog shown in Figure 26-18 displays when an `.lvr` file is opened. This dialog gives you the option of connecting to the running environment as-is, or restoring the environment to the state it was in when the snapshot was created.

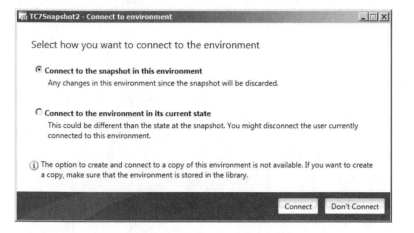

FIGURE 26-18

> **NOTE** *You may want to create copies of your running environment so that multiple people can be working with their own copies of a virtual environment. This is especially helpful when a tester finds a bug and wants to create a snapshot for the development team to use in diagnosing the problem.*
>
> *To do this, the tester should shut down the environment after creating a bug with a snapshot. From the Lab Center ⇨ Lab ⇨ Environments activity, right-click the virtual environment and select Store in Library. Depending on the performance of your SCVMM hosts and the size of your environment, this may be a long-running operation.*
>
> *When a copy of the environment has been stored in the SCVMM library, Figure 26-18 includes an option for the developer to connect to a copy of the environment from where the `.lvr` file was created.*

You have now seen how you can take advantage of an environment when running manual tests. You can use a similar process for running manual tests that have associated automation (such as coded UI tests and unit tests). You can also run such tests as part of an automated end-to-end build-deploy-test workflow. You find out how to configure this next.

AUTOMATED BUILD-DEPLOY-TEST WITH ENVIRONMENTS

The true power of lab management comes to life when combined with the automated build, deployment, and testing capabilities of Team Foundation Server. As the development team produces new builds, they can be automatically deployed into one or more environments. You can create a snapshot from an SCVMM environment, thus providing the testing team with a baseline for running any manual tests against an environment with that build. Then, you can automatically run any automated tests, thus providing valuable data about any possible regressions in your test plan. This entire workflow can take place without any manual intervention.

Team Foundation Build is covered in detail in Chapter 5, but this discussion provides an overview of the settings used when configuring Team Foundation Build for use with lab management. Certain steps within the Team Foundation Build configuration are omitted because they are covered in Chapter 5. This example assumes that you have an environment preconfigured.

The first step in creating a build definition for use with lab management is to select `LabDefaultTemplate.11.xaml` as the build process template. You configure this on the Process tab of your build definition. Selecting this template changes the build process parameters to those shown in Figure 26-19. Next, you define the Lab Process Settings parameters by clicking the ellipsis on the right-hand side of that row.

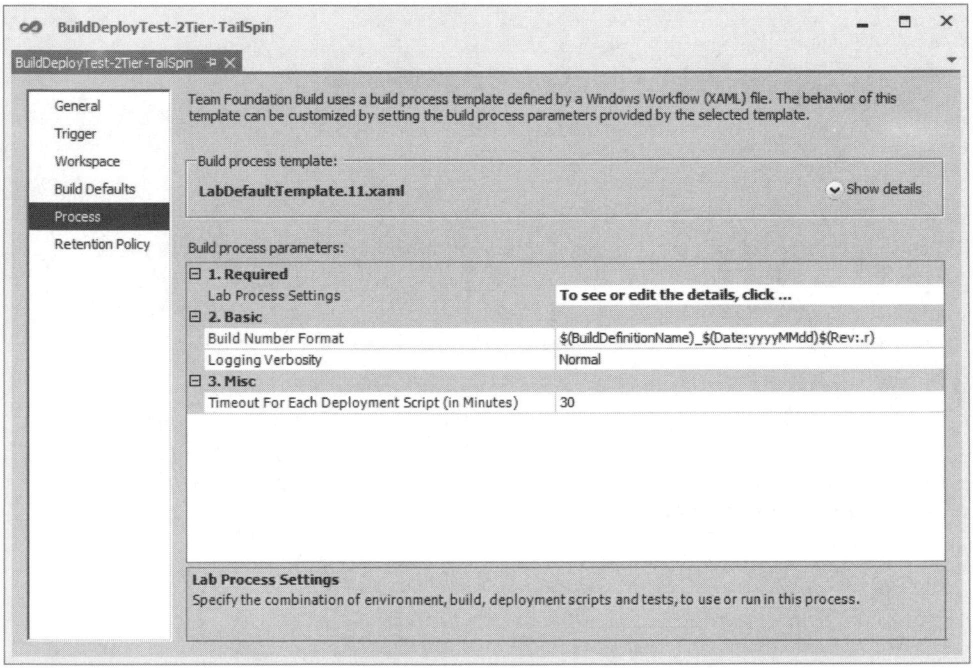

FIGURE 26-19

As shown in Figure 26-20, the first page of the Lab Workflow Parameters wizard enables you to define which environment should be used as part of your build workflow.

If this is an SCVMM environment, you can also choose to restore the environment to an environment snapshot prior to proceeding with the workflow. This is useful for establishing a clean baseline for your lab environment before attempting to install a new build or running any tests.

The Build page of the Lab Workflow Parameters wizard defines which build of your software should be used. You can rely on another build definition to create a new build, or you can select an existing build that was generated by another build definition. You can also point to a specific location where your software build resides, even if it wasn't created using Team Foundation Build.

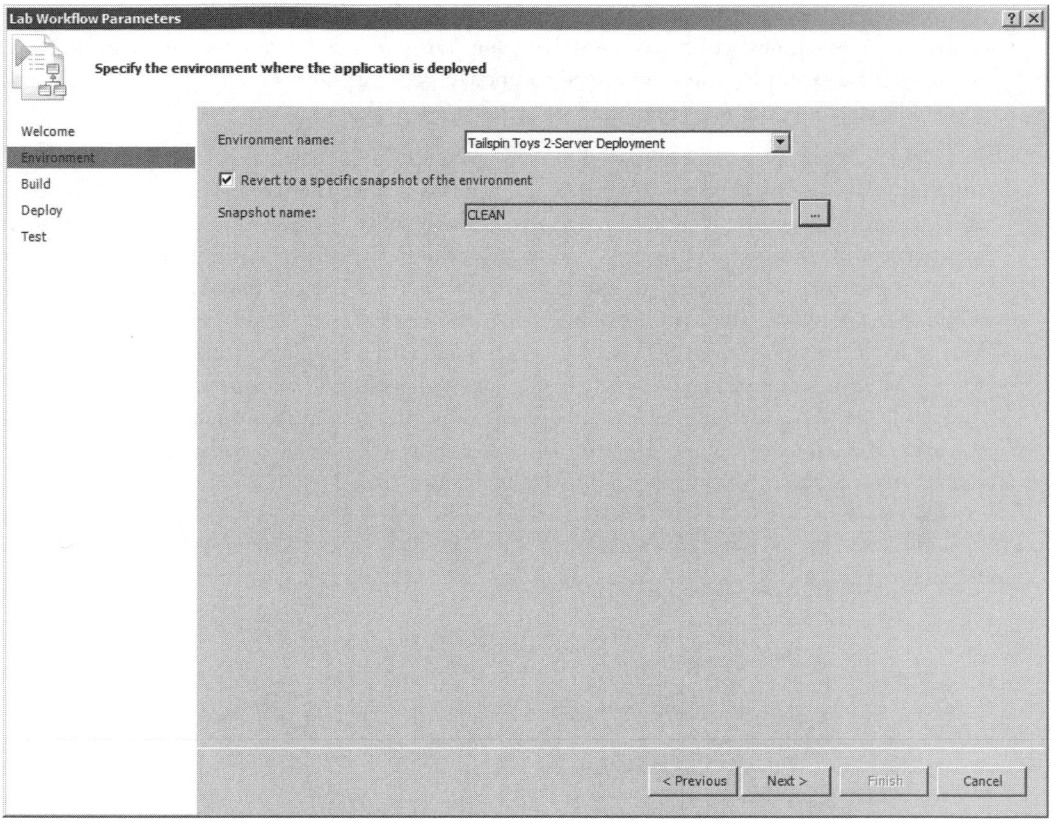

FIGURE 26-20

As shown in Figure 26-21, the Deploy page of the Lab Workflow Parameters wizard enables you to specify how a build should be deployed within one or more machines running in a an environment.

The grid enables you to define a sequence of workflow steps that should be executed in order during the build deployment phase. The first column specifies the name of the machine within the environment that defines where the given deployment step should be run. Note that this is not the computer name; it's the name of the machine that was provided when you configured the environment.

The second column specifies the command that should be run as part of that workflow step. This might include copying files to a web server directory, running an `.msi` file, or even running a batch file. You can use the following variable names here to parameterize your commands.

➤ `$(BuildLocation)`—This resolves to the location that your build is initially copied to by Team Foundation Build.

➤ `$(InternalComputerName_MachineName)`—This resolves to the hostname of the machine within the environment. For example, this macro would return `mywebserver` for a machine with a fully qualified domain name (FQDN) of `mywebserver.contoso.com`. To use this command, replace `MachineName` with the name of the machine as defined within your environment. This variable is especially useful when you don't always know the machine name of the machines within your environment, but your deployment scripts rely on those names. As an example, you might need to update a configuration file in your web application to use the machine name of the database server in your environment.

➤ $(ComputerName_MachineName)—This returns the FQDN of the machine within the environment. To use this command, replace MachineName with the name of the machine, as defined within your environment. Typically, the FQDN of a machine is a concatenation of its hostname and its domain suffix. As an example, the FQDN for a machine with a hostname of mywebserver in the contoso.com domain is mywebserver.contoso.com. Note that when using network isolation, $(InternalComputerName_MachineName) is the same for a VM in each copy of a given SCVMM environment but its FQDN is different. As an example, for a VM with hostname mywebserver in a network isolated environment, this macro returns VSLM_<uid>.contoso.com where <uid> is a unique alphanumeric identifier. This value can be important when using network isolation, where the InternalComputerName is the same on each copy of a given SCVMM environment.

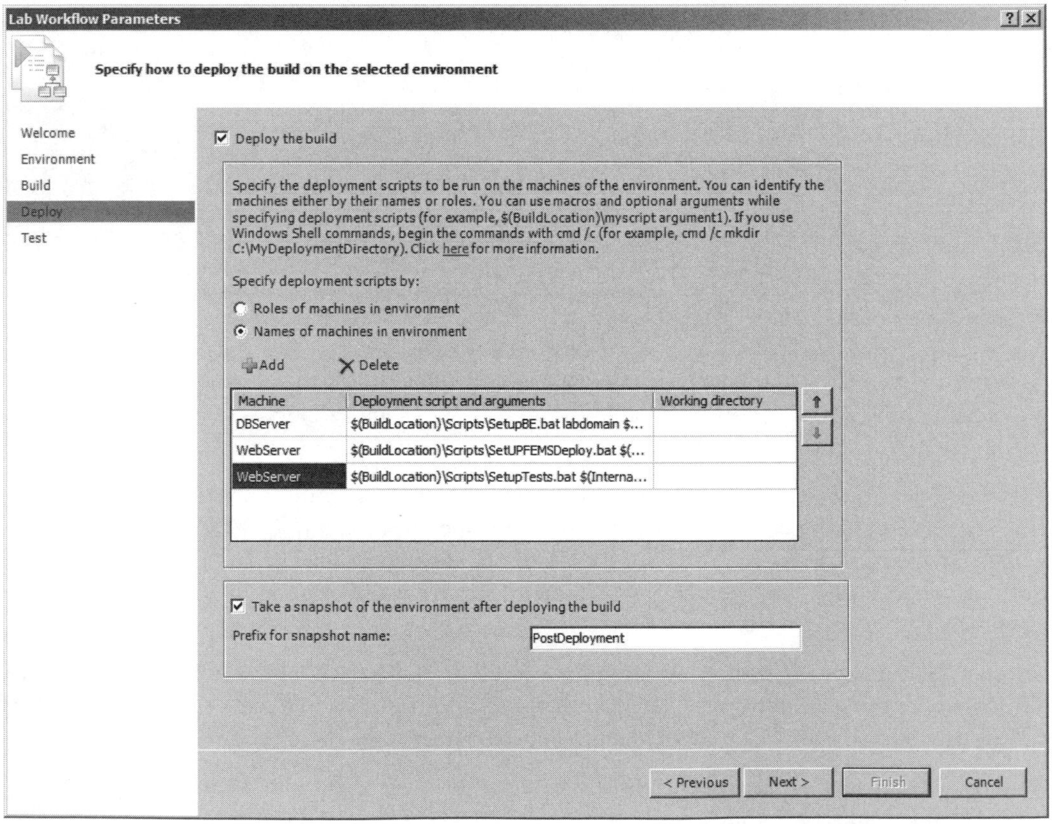

FIGURE 26-21

Finally, after deploying a build, you can create a new snapshot of an SCVMM environment by enabling the bottom checkbox and providing a name with which to preface such snapshot names. This then creates new snapshots with names based on the build name and build number such as those in Figure 26-9.

The Tests page of the Lab Workflow Parameters wizard enables you to run any automated tests that you may have in your test plan. Your test cases need to have associated automation (such as coded UI tests or unit tests). After builds are deployed, these tests are run automatically, and the test results are published to your test plan. You also need to specify automated test settings as defined earlier.

STANDARD ENVIRONMENTS

As mentioned earlier, a standard environment is a new type of environment within Team Foundation Server 2012 that enables you to take advantage of lab management capabilities without a dependency on Hyper-V or System Center Virtual Machine Manager. With a standard environment, your machines can be physical machines or virtual machines. The virtualization technology you use is also irrelevant, so although you can use Hyper-V, you can also use any other third-party virtualization technology as well.

The two primary limitations of standard environments are that you are unable to utilize network isolation, and you are unable to access virtualized snapshots (either automatically from build-deploy-test workflows, or manually from within Microsoft Test Manager). If you are using a virtualization technology that supports snapshotting (or an equivalent technique) you can manually work with snapshots using the traditional management interface for that virtualization stack.

The implication of not being able to use snapshots within your build-deploy-test workflows means that, if you utilize a standard environment, you need to design your deployment scripts in such a way that you address situations where you might need to uninstall previous builds in order to install a new one. It may also possible for you to extend the build-deploy-test workflow to programmatically restore your environment to a baseline snapshot prior to deployment, but this approach varies based on the virtualization technology you are utilizing and may require extensive customizations to the build process template.

Then, run tests by specifying an environment like you did earlier in this chapter with an SCVMM environment. You can connect to your physical environments by using the Environment Viewer like you did with tests running in an SCVMM environment, but you can't see icons for functions such as snapshotting and powering the environment on and off.

Standard environments are a great way to get started with the lab management capabilities without the upfront time and effort required to install and configure System Center Virtual Machine Manager. But you can always choose to upgrade to System Center Virtual Machine Manager later if you want to take advantage of the additional capabilities offered by SCVMM environments. Standard environments are also ideal if the software you are testing needs to run in physical (non-virtual) environments, such as when special hardware—which might not be accessible when using virtualization—is required.

SUMMARY

In this chapter, you have seen how you can use lab management to help create and manage environments that you can use to test builds of your software in a variety of configurations. You learned how to create new environments and define which diagnostic data should be collected on various machines as tests are run on those environments. You learned the benefits of snapshots and how to work with them and share them among team members.

You also found out how you can establish an end-to-end workflow to automatically build and deploy your software, then you can run automated tests within those environments. You also learned how standard environments, introduced in this release, provide an easy alternative to SCVMM environments.

Finally, you learned how you can use standard environments as an alternative to SCVMM environments.

INDEX

A comprehensive guide to Team Foundation Server 2012

Professional Team Foundation Server 2012

Ed Blankenship, Martin Woodward, Grant Holliday, Brian Keller

Written by Microsoft employees, this detailed guide covers what developers and administrators need to know to use Team Foundation Server 2012 to effectively manage and deliver software products. Whether you are in an enterprise or a smaller development shop, this fully revised edition has what you need. It goes into detail on the new features of TFS 2012, it offers step-by-step instructions, and it even assists those who are studying for the TFS Administration exam. You'll find a broad overview of TFS, thorough coverage of core functions, a look at extensibility options, and more.

- An update of the leading Wrox book on Team Foundation Server, written by an expert team of Microsoft employees

- Provides a broad overview of Team Foundation Server for developers, software project managers, testers, business analysts, and others wanting to learn how to use TFS

- Offers administrators the necessary knowledge to efficiently monitor and manage the TFS environment

- Covers core TFS functions including project management, work item tracking, version control, test case management, build automation, reporting, and how to write extensions for TFS 2012